Physics Galaxy

Lecture Notes on
MECHANICS

JEE (Mains + Advance) | BITSAT | NEET

Vol. I

All Notes with Video Explanations!

Ashish Arora

Title : Lecture Notes on Mechanics Vol. I

Language : English

Author's Name : Ashish Arora

Typeset & Published by :

Career Launcher Infrastructure (P) Ltd.

A-45, Mohan Cooperative Industrial Area, Near Mohan Estate Metro Station, New Delhi - 110044

Marketed by :

G.K. Publications (P) Ltd.

Plot No. 63, Sector-27A, Near Sector - 28 Metro Station, Faridabad, Haryana-121003

ISBN : **978-93-90187-42-3**

Printer's Details: Printed in India, New Delhi.

For product information :

Visit ***www.gkpublications.com*** or email to ***gkp@gkpublications.com***

Dedicated
to
My Parents, Son, Daughter
and
My beloved wife

In his teaching career since 1992 Ashish Arora personally mentored more than 10000 IITians and students who reached global heights in various career and profession chosen. It is his helping attitude toward students with which all his students remember him in life for his contribution in their success and keep connections with him live. Below is the list of some of the successful students in International Olympiad personally taught by him.

NAVNEET LOIWAL	*International GOLD Medal in IPhO-2000 at LONDON*, Also secured **AIR-4** in **IIT JEE 2000** PROUD FOR INDIA : Navneet Loiwal was the first Indian Student who won first International GOLD Medal for our country in International Physics Olympiad.
DUNGRA RAM CHOUDHARY	**AIR-1** in **IIT JEE 2002**
HARSHIT CHOPRA	*National Gold Medal in INPhO-2002* and got **AIR-2** in **IIT JEE-2002**
KUNTAL LOYA	A Girl Student got position **AIR-8** in **IIT JEE 2002**
LUV KUMAR	*National Gold Medal in INPhO-2003* and got **AIR-3** in **IIT JEE-2003**
RAJHANS SAMDANI	*National Gold Medal in INPhO-2003* and got **AIR-5** in **IIT JEE-2003**
SHANTANU BHARDWAJ	*International SILVER Medal in IPhO-2002 at INDONESIA*
SHALEEN HARLALKA	*International GOLD Medal in IPhO-2003 at CHINA* and got **AIR-46** in **IIT JEE-2003**
TARUN GUPTA	*National GOLD Medal in INPhO-2005*
APEKSHA KHANDELWAL	*National GOLD Medal in INPhO-2005*
ABHINAV SINHA	*Hon'ble Mension Award in APhO-2006* at *KAZAKHSTAN*
RAMAN SHARMA	*International GOLD Medal in IPhO-2007* at *IRAN* and got **AIR-20** in **IIT JEE-2007**
PRATYUSH PANDEY	*International SILVER Medal in IPhO-2007* at *IRAN* and got **AIR-85 in IIT JEE-2007**
GARVIT JUNIWAL	*International GOLD Medal in IPhO-2008* at *VIETNAM* and got **AIR-10** in **IIT JEE-2008**
ANKIT PARASHAR	*National GOLD Medal in INPhO-2008*
HEMANT NOVAL	*National GOLD Medal in INPhO-2008* and got **AIR-25** in **IIT JEE-2008**
ABHISHEK MITRUKA	*National GOLD Medal in INPhO-2009*
SARTHAK KALANI	*National GOLD Medal in INPhO-2009*
ASTHA AGARWAL	*International SILVER Medal in IJSO-2009* at *AZERBAIJAN*
RAHUL GURNANI	*International SILVER Medal in IJSO-2009* at *AZERBAIJAN*
AYUSH SINGHAL	*International SILVER Medal in IJSO-2009* at *AZERBAIJAN*
MEHUL KUMAR	*International SILVER Medal in IPhO-2010* at *CROATIA* and got **AIR-19** in **IIT JEE-2010**
ABHIROOP BHATNAGAR	*National GOLD Medal in INPhO-2010*
AYUSH SHARMA	*International Double GOLD Medal in IJSO-2010* at *NIGERIA*
AASTHA AGRAWAL	*Hon'ble Mension Award in APhO-2011* at *ISRAEL* and got **AIR-93** in **IIT JEE 2011**
ABHISHEK BANSAL	*National GOLD Medal in INPhO-2011*
SAMYAK DAGA	*National GOLD Medal in INPhO-2011*
SHREY GOYAL	*National GOLD Medal in INPhO-2012* and secured **AIR-24** in **IIT JEE 2012**
RAHUL GURNANI	*National GOLD Medal in INPhO-2012*
JASPREET SINGH JHEETA	*National GOLD Medal in INPhO-2012*
DIVYANSHU MUND	*National GOLD Medal in INPhO-2012*
SHESHANSH AGARWAL	*International SILVER Medal in IAO-2012 at KOREA*
SWATI GUPTA	*International SILVER Medal in IJSO-2012 at IRAN*
PRATYUSH RAJPUT	*International SILVER Medal in IJSO-2012 at IRAN*
SHESHANSH AGARWAL	*International BRONZE Medal in IOAA-2013 at GREECE*
SHESHANSH AGARWAL	*International GOLD Medal in IOAA-2014 at ROMANIA*
SHESHANSH AGARWAL	*International SILVER Medal in IPhO-2015 at INDIA* and secured **AIR-58** in **JEE(Advanced)-2015**
VIDUSHI VARSHNEY	*International SILVER Medal in IJSO-2015 to be held at SOUTH KOREA*
AMAN BANSAL	**AIR-1 in JEE Advanced 2016**
KUNAL GOYAL	**AIR-3 in JEE Advanced 2016**
GOURAV DIDWANIA	**AIR-9 in JEE Advanced 2016**
DIVYANSH GARG	*International SILVER Medal in IPhO-2016 at SWITZERLAND*

ABOUT THE AUTHOR

The complexities of Physics have given nightmares to many, but the homegrown genius of Jaipur-Ashish Arora has helped several students to live their dreams by decoding it.

Newton Law of Gravitation and Faraday's Magnetic force of attraction apply perfectly well with this unassuming genius. A Pied Piper of students, his webportal https://www.physicsgalaxy.com, The world's largest encyclopedia of video lectures on high school Physics possesses strong gravitational pull and magnetic attraction for students who want to make it big in life.

Ashish Arora, gifted with rare ability to train masterminds, has mentored over 10,000 IITians in his past 24 years of teaching sojourn including lots of students made it to Top 100 in IITJEE/JEE(Advance) including AIR-1 and many in Top-10. Apart from that, he has also groomed hundreds of students for cracking International Physics Olympiad. No wonder his student Navneet Loiwal brought laurel to the country by becoming the first Indian to win a Gold medal at the 2000 - International Physics Olympiad in London (UK).

His special ability to simplify the toughest of the Physics theorems and applications rates him as one among the best Physics teachers in the world. With this, Arora simply defies the logic that perfection comes with age. Even at 18 when he started teaching Physics while pursuing engineering, he was as engaging as he is now. Experience, besides graying his hair, has just widened his horizon.

Now after encountering all tribes of students - some brilliant and some not-so-intelligent - this celebrated teacher has embarked upon a noble mission to make the entire galaxy of Physics inform of his webportal PHYSICSGALAXY.COM to serve and help global students in the subject. Today students from more than 180 countries are connected with this webportal and his youtube channel 'Physics Galaxy'. Daily about more than 35000 video lectures are being watched and his pool of video lectures has cross and sutdents post their queries in INTERACT tab under different sections and topics of physics.

Physics Galaxy video lectures have already crossed 27 million views till now and growing further to set new benchmarks and all the video lectures of Physics Galaxy can be accessed through Physics Galaxy mobile application available on iOS and Android platform.

Dedicated to global students of middle and high school level, his website also www.physicsgalaxy.com has teaching sessions dubbed in American accent and subtitles in 87 languages.

PREFACE

Physics is one of the most difficult subjects, for students of Science, because it requires good visualization power and high cognitive ability. To extend, it is very difficult to sail through in the present age of competition without mastering the concepts of Physics in depth. Scoring in Physics does not require hard work or rote learning but a simple understanding of physical situations which exist in the surroundings of our everyday life. Thus, in order to command the concepts of Physics, you should try to understand its core concepts in practical approach instead of merely depending on the theory.

It is against this backdrop that we have come up with ***Physics Galaxy*** series which include ***Lecture Notes*** which are designed for quick reference of video lectures available on the *YouTube channel of Physics Galaxy;* it can be easily accessed through ***www.physicsgalaxy.com*** or by the *mobile app of Physics Galaxy*.

The purpose of these *Lecture Notes* is to help students quickly revise the concepts in a systematic and coherent way after watching Video Lecture on any particular topic. In case of any confusion while understanding the solutions, students can simply scan the QR codes printed on each page of the book via 'Android' or 'iOS' device to quickly open the respective video lecture and understand the concept in a better way.

Furthermore, the handwritten format of the screenshots gives a better understanding of the concepts explained in the video lectures and helps in easily memorizing the concepts.

To sum up, by compiling screenshots of the video explanations, I have tried my best to make the entire content error free. However, owing to the nature of work, there is a slight possibility of inadvertent errors left untouched.

Therefore, I shall be grateful to the readers if they can point out errors and help me rectifying them for future editions. Feel free to give your valuable feedbacks at ***ashisharora@physicsgalaxy.com***.

Date : August, 2018

Ashish Arora

PHYSICSGALAXY.COM
B-80, Model Town, Malviya Nagar, Jaipur-302017
e-mails: ashisharora@physicsgalaxy.com
ashash12345@gmail.com

CONTENTS

Chapter 1
Motion in One Dimensions

Lecture Notes Modules

Module-1: Introduction

Rectilinear Motion:

Motion of a body along a St. line

↓

Motion in One Dimension (1D)

Refrence frame:

It is a region/zone from where observations are taken for motion parameters of a body.

[displacement, velocity, accn, time]

* It can be at rest or may be moving.

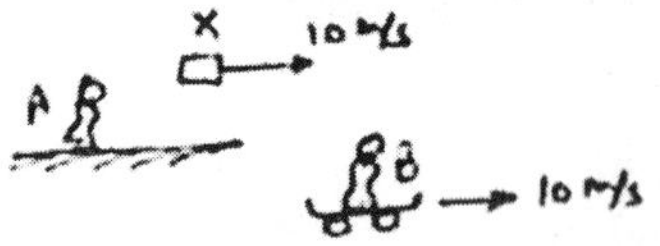

x 10 m/s

A

B 10 m/s

Scan for Video Explanation

Web Reference at www.physicsgalaxy.com

Module-1: Introduction

Ex:

A 3 m/s

Ref frame → ground

Speed of Car w.r.to ground frame is $v_{cA} = 3$ m/s

B 1 m/s

ref. frame → trolley.

Speed of car w.r.to ref frame of trolley $v_{cB} = 2$ m/s

"A ref frame is a co-ordinate system with a clock for measurement of time. It may be at rest on ground or may be attached to a moving body/observer."

Scan for Video Explanation

Web Reference at www.physicsgalaxy.com

Module-1: Introduction

Motion Parameters:

Distance & Displacement:

distance covered
↳ path length

Displacement
↳ $\overrightarrow{AB}$

Rectilinear motion

$\overrightarrow{OB}$ distance → OAB
displacement → $\overrightarrow{OB}$

Speed & Velocity:

Speed → rate of change of position (magnitude)

Velocity → Rate of change of position (mag & dir)

Scan for Video Explanation

Module-1: Introduction

Average Speed & Average Velocity:

$$\text{Average Speed} = \frac{\text{Total distance travelled}}{\text{Time taken}}$$

$$\text{Average Velocity} = \frac{\text{Total displacement}}{\text{time taken}}$$

$$\text{Avg speed} = \frac{l}{t_2 - t_1} \leftarrow \text{Avg vel.}$$

$$\text{Avg Speed} = \frac{l_1 + l_2}{t_2 - t_1}$$

$$\text{Avg vel} = \frac{l_1 - l_2}{t_2 - t_1} = \left(\frac{\Delta l}{\Delta t}\right) \text{ cast}$$

Scan for Video Explanation

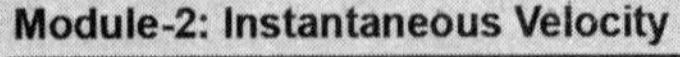

Module-2: Instantaneous Velocity

Instantaneous Velocity:

It is the velocity of a particle at an instant.

t t+dt
x x+dx +x

at the instant t instantaneous vel can be given

$$\boxed{\vec{v} = \frac{d\vec{x}}{dt}}$$ ← rate of change of position w.r.to time.

$y = f(x)$, $\left(\frac{dy}{dx}\right)$

Inst vel → differentiation of position w.r.to time

for a given motion of position $x = f(t)$ then inst vel is the slope of x vs t curve.

Scan for Video Explanation

Web Reference at www.physicsgalaxy.com

Module-2: Instantaneous Velocity

Ex : If a particle moves such that its displacement is given as

$$x = 4t^4 - 3t^2 + 7t + 6$$

Find its velocity at t = 2 sec.

Soln:

$$v = \frac{dx}{dt} = 16t^3 - 6t + 7$$

$$= 16 \times 8 - 6 \times 2 + 7$$

$$= 128 - 12 + 7 = 123 \text{ m/s}$$

NOTE: As differentiation of displacement is velocity, on integrating velocity we get displacement.

Scan for Video Explanation

Web Reference at www.physicsgalaxy.com

Module-3: Solved Example-1

Ex : **If velocity of a particle is given as**

$$v = (3t^2 + 2) \text{ m/s}$$

Find the displacement covered by the particle from t = 1 to t = 2 sec.

Sol:

$$v = 3t^2 + 2$$

$$\frac{dx}{dt} = 3t^2 + 2$$

integrating both sides

$$\int_{x_1}^{x_2} dx = \int_{t=1}^{t=2} (3t^2 + 2)\, dt$$

$$x_2 - x_1 = \left[t^3 + 2t\right]_1^2$$

$$x_2 - x_1 = (8 + 4) - (1 + 2)$$

$$= 12 - 3 = 9\text{m Ans.}$$

Web Reference at www.physicsgalaxy.com

Scan for Video Explanation

Module-4: Solved Example-2

Ex : **A body moves at velocity v = 2t + 4 m/s. Find the average velocity of body from t = 1s to t = 2s. Initially at t = 0 body starts from origin.**

↑ x = 0.

Sol^n: let at $t_1 = 1$ sec $x = x_1$

& at $t_2 = 2$ sec $x = x_2$

avg vel $v = \frac{x_2 - x_1}{t_2 - t_1} = \frac{x_2 - x_1}{1} = x_2 - x_1$

$v_{avg} = 7$ m/s Ans.

$$\frac{dx}{dt} = 2t + 4$$

$$\int_{x_1}^{x_2} dx = \int_1^2 (2t + 4)\, dt$$

$$x_2 - x_1 = \left[t^2 + 4t\right]_1^2 = (4 + 8) - (1 + 4)$$

$$= 12 - 5 = 7$$

Web Reference at www.physicsgalaxy.com

Scan for Video Explanation

Module-5: Acceleration

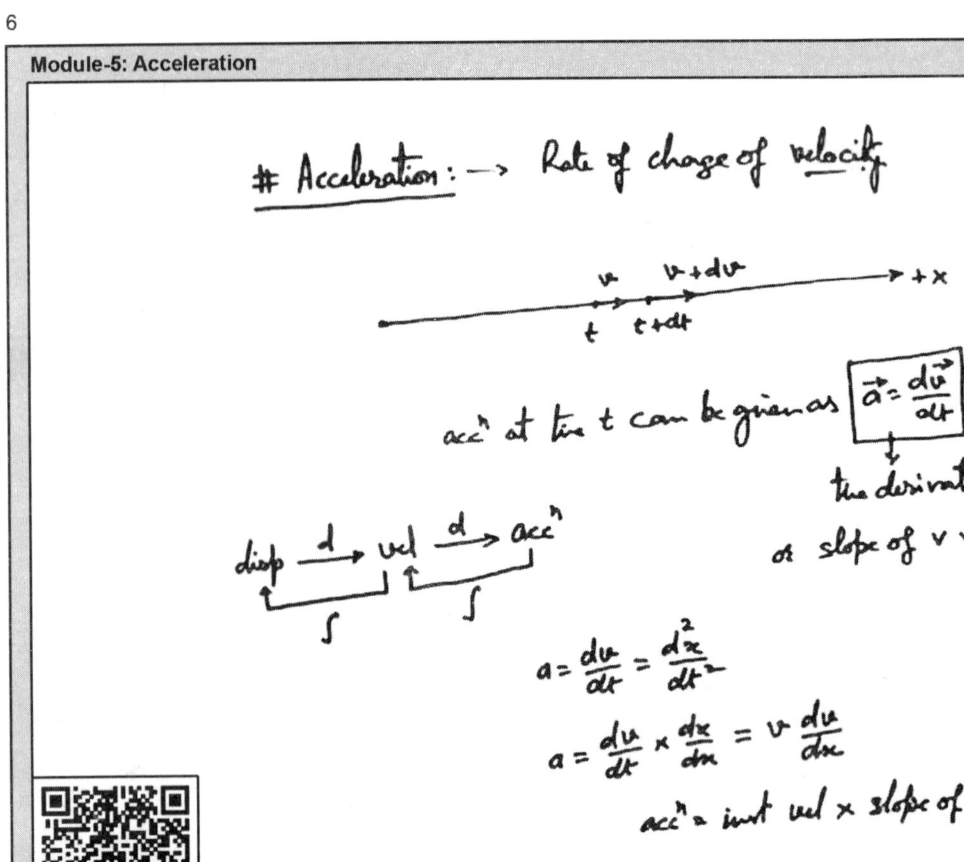

Scan for Video Explanation

Web Reference at www.physicsgalaxy.com

Module-5: Acceleration

$$a = \frac{dv}{dt} \quad \text{—(1)} \qquad \text{OR} \qquad a = v\frac{dv}{dx} \quad \text{—(2)}$$

If a is given as a f^n of time → we use eq^n (1)

If a is given as a f^n of disp → we use eq^n (2)

If a is given in terms of v → either eq^n (1) or eq^n (2)

Ex: If for a part its disp is $x = 3t^3 + 2t^2 + 5t + 6$ m find acc^n of part at t = 1 sec

Sol^n: Inst vel $v = \frac{dx}{dt} = 9t^2 + 4t + 5$ m/s

acc^n $a = \frac{dv}{dt} = 18t + 4$ m/s²

at t = 1 sec $a = 18 + 4 = 22$ m/s² Ans.

Scan for Video Explanation

Web Reference at www.physicsgalaxy.com

Module-5: Acceleration

Average Acceleration:

For a motion of particle between two instants its avg acc^n can be given as-

$$\langle \vec{a}_{avg} \rangle = \frac{\text{Total change in vel}}{\text{Time Taken}} = \frac{\Delta \vec{V}}{\Delta t} = \frac{\vec{v}_2 - \vec{v}_1}{t_2 - t_1}$$

Ex. If a truck moving at 4m/s toward south takes a turn toward east & its vel changes to 3m/s. If turing time is 10sec, find the avg acc^n of truck.

Sol^n: $\vec{v}_1 = 4$ m/s $\downarrow$

$\vec{v}_2 = 3$m/s $\rightarrow$

(Triangle sides: 5, 3, 4; labels $-\vec{v}_1$, $\vec{v}_2$, θ)

$$|\vec{a}_{avg}| = \frac{|\vec{v}_2 - \vec{v}_1|}{10} = \frac{5}{10} = 0.5 \text{ m/s}^2$$

in dir 53° N of E.

$\tan\theta = 4/3$

$\theta = 53°$

Web Reference at www.physicsgalaxy.com

Scan for Video Explanation

Module-6: Solved Example-3

Ex : If a car accelerats with acceleration depends on displacement as

$$a = 6x^2 + 2x + 5$$

Find velocity of particles when it is at x = 3m. Given that initially it starts from x = 1 with velocity 2 m/s.

Sol^n: $t=0$ $\rightarrow a$, $x=1$m, $u=2$m/s

we use $a = v\frac{dv}{dx} = 6x^2 + 2x + 5$

$$\int_2^v v\,dv = \int_1^3 (6x^2 + 2x + 5)\,dx$$

$$\left[\frac{v^2}{2}\right]_2^v = \left[2x^3 + x^2 + 5x\right]_1^3$$

$$\frac{v^2}{2} - 2 = (2\times 27 + 9 + 15) - (2 + 1 + 5)$$

$$v^2 = (78 - 8 + 2)\times 2$$

$v^2 = (72)\times 2$

$= 144$

$v = \sqrt{144} = 12$ m/s.

Web Reference at www.physicsgalaxy.com

Scan for Video Explanation

Module-7: Solved Example-4

Ex : A particle moves with acceleration given as

$$a = 8t + 6 \text{ m/s}^2$$

Find displacement of particles at t = 3 sec if at t = 0 it starts from origin with initial speed 1 m/s.

Sol:

$u = 1$ m/s → a

$t = 0$ ---------- $t = 3$

We use $\frac{dv}{dt} = 8t + 6$

$$\int_1^v dv = \int_0^t (8t+6)\,dt$$

$$v - 1 = \frac{8t^2}{2} + 6t \Rightarrow v = 4t^2 + 6t + 1 \text{ m/s}$$

$$\frac{dx}{dt} = 4t^2 + 6t + 1$$

$$\int_0^x dx = \int_0^t (4t^2 + 6t + 1)\,dt$$

$$x = \frac{4t^3}{3} + 3t^2 + t$$

at $t = 3$ sec

$$x = \frac{4(3)^3}{3} + 3(3)^2 + 3$$

$$= 36 + 27 + 3 = 66 \text{ m. Ans.}$$

Scan for Video Explanation

Web Reference at www.physicsgalaxy.com

Module-8: Solved Example-5

Ex : Instantaneous velocity of a particle is given as

$$v = 5e^t \text{ m/s}$$

Find the average acceleration and average velocity of particle between instants t_1 = 2 sec and t_2 = 4 sec.

(Given at t = 0, x = 0)

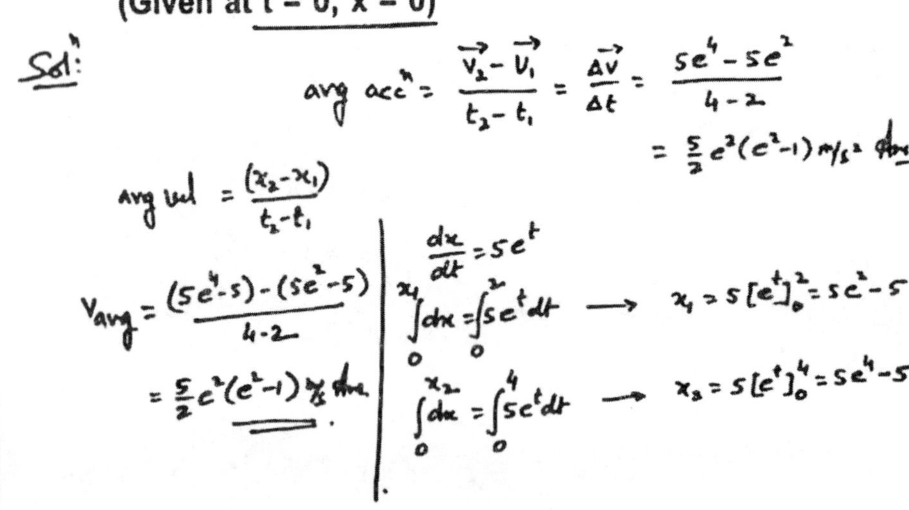

Scan for Video Explanation

Web Reference at www.physicsgalaxy.com

Module-9: Cases of Uniform Acceleration

Analysis of Motion with Uniform Acceleration:

When a particle moves at constant accⁿ a &
starts with initial velocity u, the vel of particle
after time t can be obtained as-

$$a = \frac{dv}{dt}$$

$$\int_u^v dv = \int_{t=0}^{t} a\,dt$$

$$v - u = at$$

$$\boxed{v = u + at} \quad \text{—(1)}$$

First Speed Equation for constantly accelerated motion.

Web Reference at www.physicsgalaxy.com

Scan for Video Explanation

Module-9: Cases of Uniform Acceleration

further we use

$$v = u + at$$

$$\frac{dx}{dt} = u + at$$

$$\int_0^s dx = \int_0^t (u + at)\,dt$$

$$s = ut + \frac{at^2}{2}$$

$$\boxed{s = ut + \tfrac{1}{2}at^2} \quad \text{—(2)}$$

Second Speed eqⁿ for uniformly accelerated motion.

Web Reference at www.physicsgalaxy.com

Scan for Video Explanation

Module-9: Cases of Uniform Acceleration

Similarly if we use $a = v\frac{dv}{dx}$

$$\int_u^v v\,dv = \int_0^s a\,dx$$

$$\left[\frac{v^2}{2}\right]_u^v = as$$

$$\frac{v^2 - u^2}{2} = as$$

$$\boxed{v^2 = u^2 + 2as} \quad \text{—(3)}$$

Third Speed Eqn for Uniformly accelerated motion.

Scan for Video Explanation

Web Reference at www.physicsgalaxy.com

Module-9: Cases of Uniform Acceleration

Displacement of a particle during nth second for uniformly accelerated motion:

1st Sec 2nd Sec 3rd Sec

$t=0$ u $t=1$ $t=2$ $t=3$

$\vec{a}$

disp. covered in nth second of motion

nth Second ↓ $t=n-1$ to $t=n$

$$\overrightarrow{\Delta S_n} = \vec{S}_n - \vec{S}_{n-1}$$

$$= \left[un + \tfrac{1}{2}an^2\right] - \left[u(n-1) + \tfrac{1}{2}a(n-1)^2\right]$$

$$= un + \tfrac{1}{2}an^2 - un + u - \tfrac{1}{2}an^2 - \tfrac{1}{2}a + an$$

$$\boxed{\Delta S_n = u + \tfrac{1}{2}a(2n-1)}$$

Scan for Video Explanation

Web Reference at www.physicsgalaxy.com

Module-9: Cases of Uniform Acceleration

NOTE: All the speed Equations are Vector Equations & the motion parameters $\vec{s}, \vec{v}, \vec{u}, \vec{a}$ are taken with appropriate signs acc to the ref frame chosen.

(1) $\vec{v} = \vec{u} + \vec{a}t$

(2) $\vec{s} = \vec{u}t + \frac{1}{2}\vec{a}t^2$

(3) $v^2 = u^2 + 2\vec{a}.\vec{s}$

(4) $\vec{\Delta s_n} = \vec{u} + \frac{\vec{a}}{2}(2n-1)$

Web Reference at www.physicsgalaxy.com

Scan for Video Explanation

Module-10: Solved Example-6

Ex : **A car is moving at 20 m/s. The driver applies the brakes which causes a retardation of 4 m/s². Find the distance travelled by car before it stops, if reaction time of driver is 0.4 sec.**

Sol: Reaction time : The time taken by a human to execute the action after one sees a need of it.

→ 20 m/s ← 4 m/s² $v_f = 0$

Car rest.

t=0 t=0.4 sec

$S_1 = 20 \times 0.4 = 8m.$

$S_2 = 50m$

$v_f^2 = u^2 + 2aS$

$0 = (20)^2 - 8S_2$

$S_2 = \frac{400}{8} = 50m$

$S_1 + S_2 = 8 + 50 = 58m$ Ans.

Web Reference at www.physicsgalaxy.com

Scan for Video Explanation

Module-11: Solved Example-7

Ex : A particle starts at initial speed 17 m/s and retards at 2 m/s^2. Find the distance covered by the particle in 9th second of motion.

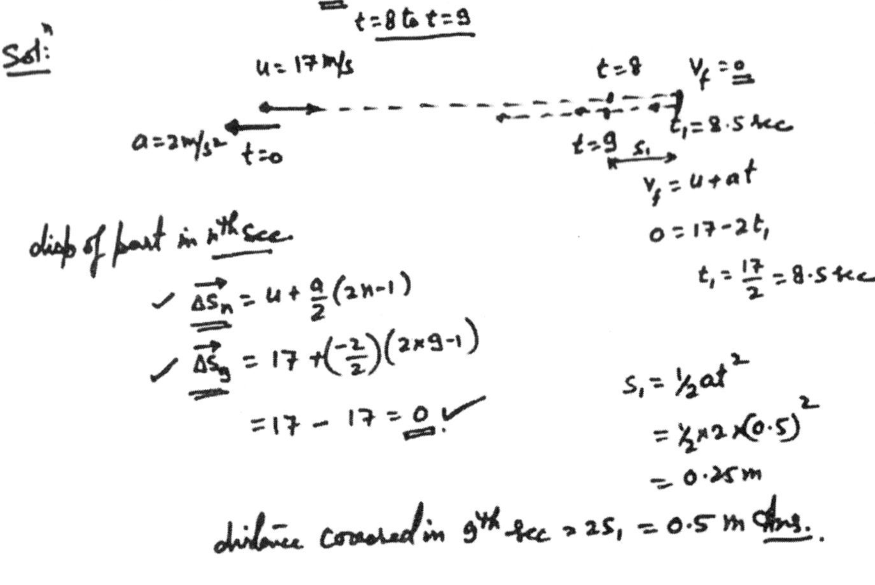

distance covered in 9th sec $= 2s_1 = 0.5$ m Ans.

Scan for Video Explanation

Web Reference at www.physicsgalaxy.com

Module-12: Solved Example-8

Ex : A car and a truck starts from same point along same direction, car with initial speed 2 m/s & acceleration 2 m/s^2 and truck with a constant speed 20 m/s^2. Find the time after which car will overtake the truck.

Sol:

Car $u = 2$ m/s, $a = 2$ m/s^2

Truck $u_T = 20$ m/s

Car, Truck, $t = t_0$, $t = 18$ sec

displacements: Truck $S_T = 20t_0$

Car $S_c = 2t_0 + \frac{1}{2}(2)t_0^2$

for overtaking $S_T = S_c$

$20t_0 = 2t_0 + t_0^2$

$t_0 = 18$ sec Ans.

Scan for Video Explanation

Web Reference at www.physicsgalaxy.com

Module-13: Solved Example-9

Ex : **Find the ratio of distances travelled in 1st, 2nd, & 3rd second by a particle started from rest with uniform acceleration.**

Sol:

$\xrightarrow{a}$ $u=0$, $t=0$ —— s_1 —— $t=1$ —— s_2 —— $t=2$ —— s_3 —— $t=3$

$s_1 : s_2 : s_3 = ?$

$$\vec{\Delta S_n} = \vec{u} + \frac{\vec{a}}{2}(2n-1)$$

$$S_1 = \frac{a}{2}(2-1) = a/2$$

$$S_2 = \frac{a}{2}(3) = 3a/2$$

$$S_3 = \frac{a}{2}(5) = 5a/2$$

$S_1 : S_2 : S_3 = 1 : 3 : 5$ Ans.

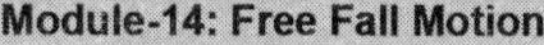

Module-14: Free Fall Motion

Free Fall Motion:

Motion of a body moving freely under Earth's gravity is called free fall motion

under free fall acc^n = $g\downarrow$

$\downarrow a = g$ ground

if we take downward dir +ve $a = +g$

$$v = u + gt$$
$$s = ut + \frac{1}{2}gt^2$$
$$v^2 = u^2 + 2gh$$
$$\Delta h_n = u + \frac{g}{2}(2n-1)$$

if we take upward dir +ve $a = -g$.

$$v = u - gt$$
$$s = ut - \frac{1}{2}gt^2$$
$$v^2 = u^2 - 2gh$$
$$\Delta h_n = u - g/2(2n-1)$$

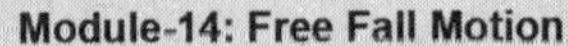

Ex : A boy throws a ball up at speed u. Find :
(a) time to reach max height.
(b) max height attained.

Sol^n:

we use $v = u + at$

$0 = u + (-g)t_f$

(a) $\boxed{t_f = u/g}$ Ans.

we use $v^2 = u^2 + 2as$

$0 = u^2 + 2(-g)H$

(b) $\boxed{H = \frac{u^2}{2g}}$ Ans.

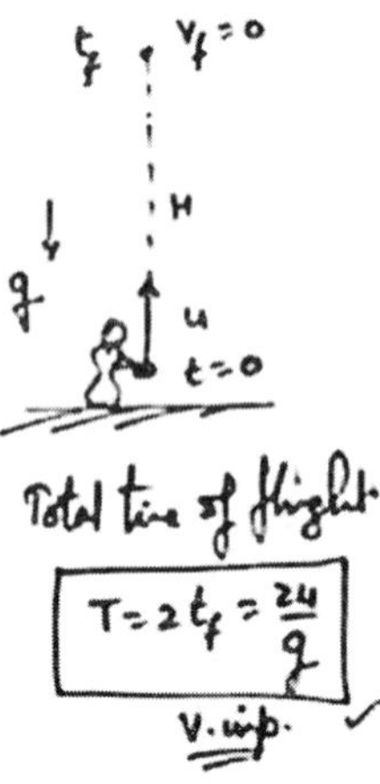

Total time of flight

$\boxed{T = 2t_f = \frac{2u}{g}}$

V. imp.

Scan for Video Explanation

Web Reference at www.physicsgalaxy.com

Module-15: Solved Example-10

Ex : A stone is released from rest from a height above the ground. It covers a distance 6 m in last second of its motion. Find the height from which it was dropped.

Sol^n: let stone falls for n sec.

$\Rightarrow$ in n^{th} sec.

$\Delta S_n = u + \frac{a}{2}(2n-1)$

$\Delta S_n = 6 = \frac{g}{2}(2n-1)$

$2n - 1 = 6/5$

$n = \frac{11}{10}$ sec.

t = 0, a = g, h, n-1, 6m, n, ground

$(g = 10\ m/s^2)$

Total height

$h = \frac{1}{2}gt^2$

$= \frac{1}{2} \times 10 \times \left(\frac{11}{10}\right)^2 = \frac{121}{20}$ m Ans.

Scan for Video Explanation

Web Reference at www.physicsgalaxy.com

Module-16: Concept of Relative Motion

Concept of Relative Motion:

Relative Motion → observation w.r.to a given reference.

Case-I: When bodies move in same dir

A v_A → B v_B →

$$v_{BA} = v_B - v_A$$

↑ relative vel of Body B w.r.to body A.

Case-II: When bodies move in opp. dir

A v_A → ← v_B B

$$v_{BA} = v_B + v_A$$

→ Same concept of Relative motion can be applied to acc^n of bodies also.

Web Reference at www.physicsgalaxy.com

Scan for Video Explanation

Module-16: Concept of Relative Motion

Ex : **In the situation shown in figure if both the boys throw balls at same time, find the time when the balls will collide.**

B
20 m/s ↓ g
100 m
5 m/s ↓ g
A (rest)

Sol^n:

Relative vel of B w.r.to A

$$v_{BA} = 20 + 5 = 25 \text{ m/s.}$$

$$a_{BA} = g - g = 0$$

time when B will meet A is $t = \frac{\text{distance}}{\text{vel}} = \frac{100}{25} = 4 \text{ sec.}$

Ans.

Web Reference at www.physicsgalaxy.com

Scan for Video Explanation

Module-16: Concept of Relative Motion

Ex : Two cars moving toward each other at velocities v_A and v_B are at a separation d. At this instant both are retarded with acceleration a_A and a_B respectively. Find minimum value of d such that no collision occurs.

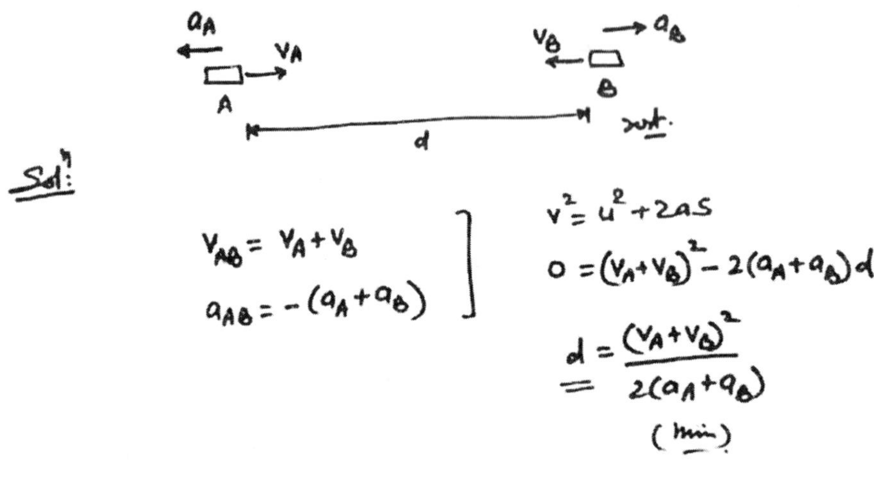

Scan for Video Explanation

Web Reference at www.physicsgalaxy.com

Module-17: Solved Example-11

Ex : A balloon is rising up at 20 m/s and a stone is released from it, when it is at a height 100 m above ground. Find the time after which the stone will hit the ground.

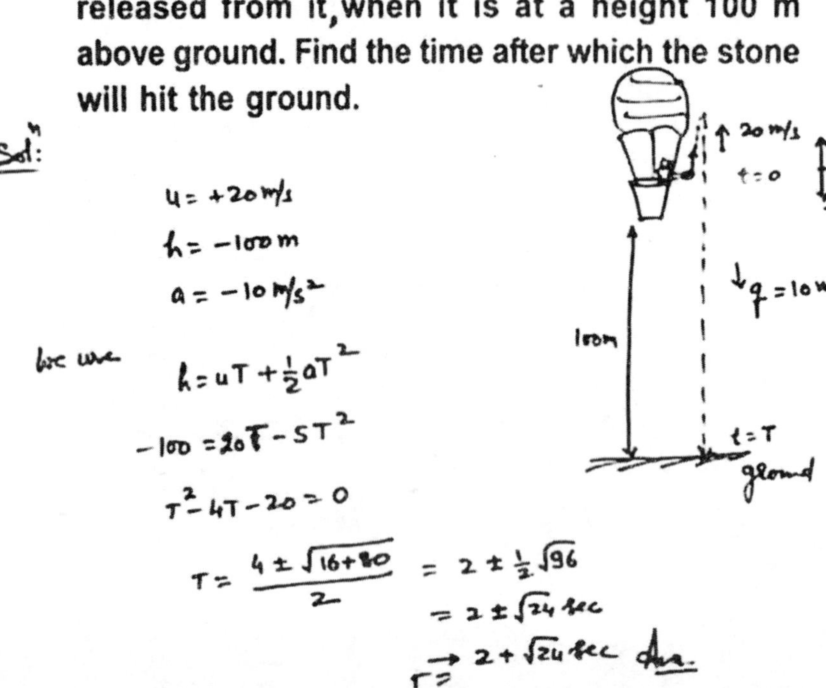

Scan for Video Explanation

Web Reference at www.physicsgalaxy.com

Module-18: Solved Example-12

Ex : **Inside a lift accelerating up at 2 m/s^2 a loose bolt falls from its ceiling. If height of lift is 2m find the speed of bolt with which it hits the floor. Initial speed of lift is 5 m/s in upward direction.**

Sol^n:

Initial speed of bolt w.r.to lift is

$u = 0$

acc^n of bolt w.r.to lift

$a_{BL} = 10 + 2 = 12\ m/s^2$

$u = 5\ m/s$, $a = 2\ m/s^2$, 2m, lift

in reference of lift $h = ut + \frac{1}{2}at^2$

$2 = \frac{1}{2} \times 12 \times t_1^2 \Rightarrow t_1^2 = \frac{1}{3} \Rightarrow t_1 = \frac{1}{\sqrt{3}}$ sec

vel of bolt as seen from lift $v_1 = u + at = 12 \times \frac{1}{\sqrt{3}} = 4\sqrt{3}\ m/s$

net vel w.r.to ground. $v_2 = u + at = 5 - 10\left(\frac{1}{\sqrt{3}}\right) = 5 - \frac{10}{\sqrt{3}}\ m/s$ Ans

Web Reference at www.physicsgalaxy.com | Scan for Video Explanation

Module-19: Graphical Analysis of Motion

Graphical Analysis of Motion:

Rectilinear motion → 3 types of graphs are used in motion analysis.

(1) Displacement v/s time → distance v/s time

(2) Velocity v/s time → speed v/s time

(3) Acc^n v/s time

Web Reference at www.physicsgalaxy.com | Scan for Video Explanation

Module-19: Graphical Analysis of Motion

Displacement v/s Time Graphs:

Position v/s time.

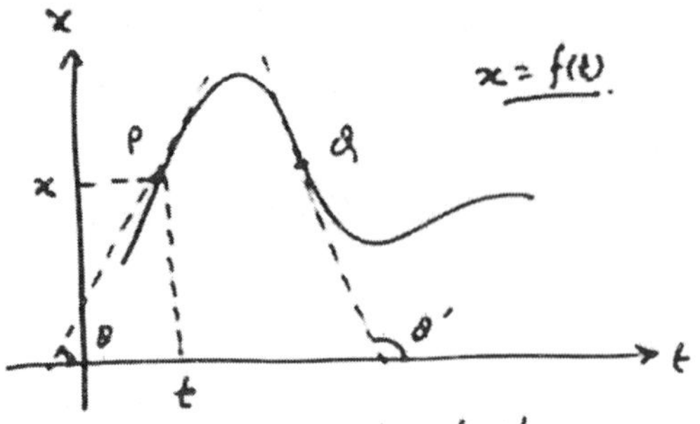

$x = f(t)$

Slope at pt P

$$\frac{dx}{dt} = \tan\theta = v_P$$

$v_P = \tan\theta = +ve.$ $\quad v_Q = \tan\theta' = -ve.$

Pract. Situation

A part moves → 1st accelerates, uniformly, retards 2nd

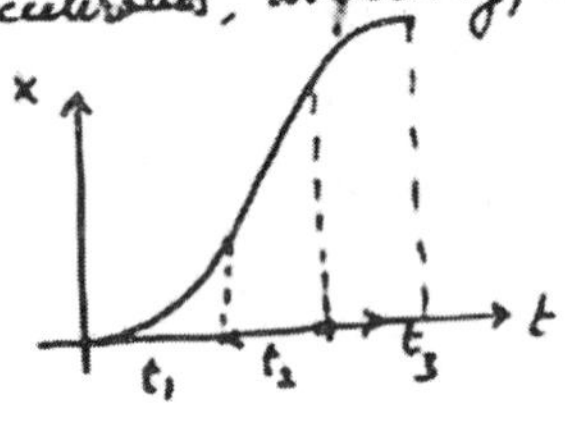

Scan for Video Explanation

Web Reference at www.physicsgalaxy.com

Module-19: Graphical Analysis of Motion

Exp.

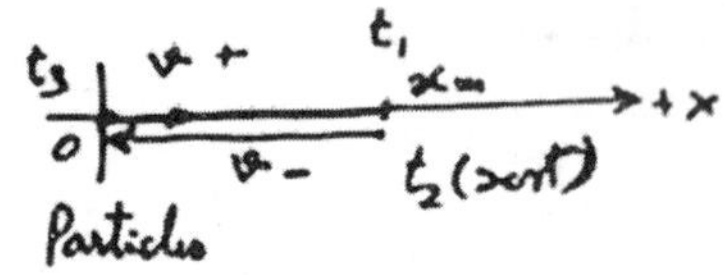

Particle

Pos-time graph:

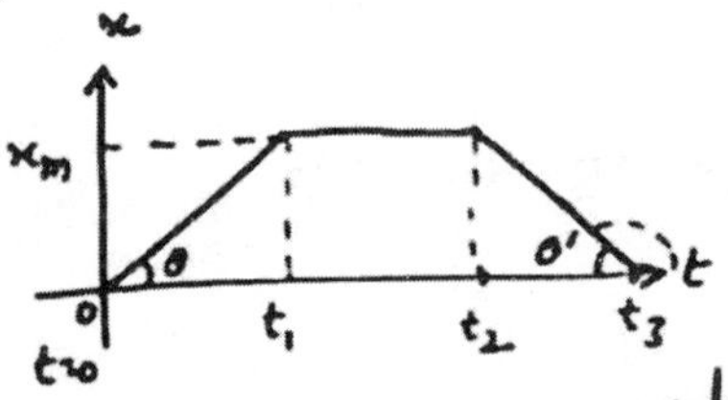

$\tan\theta = v$

$\tan\theta' = v$

distance-time graph. (distance)

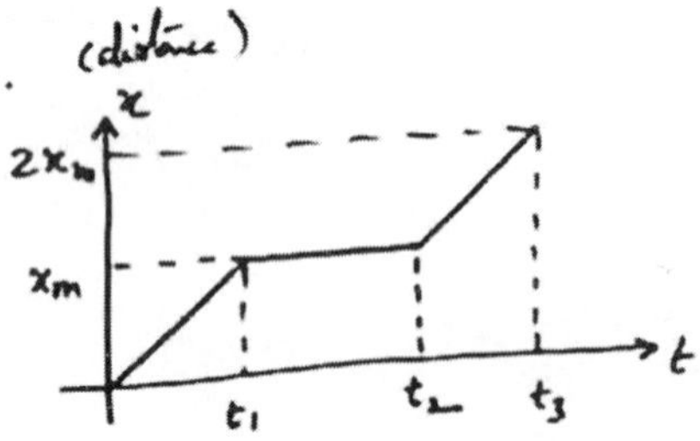

Scan for Video Explanation

Web Reference at www.physicsgalaxy.com

Module-19: Graphical Analysis of Motion

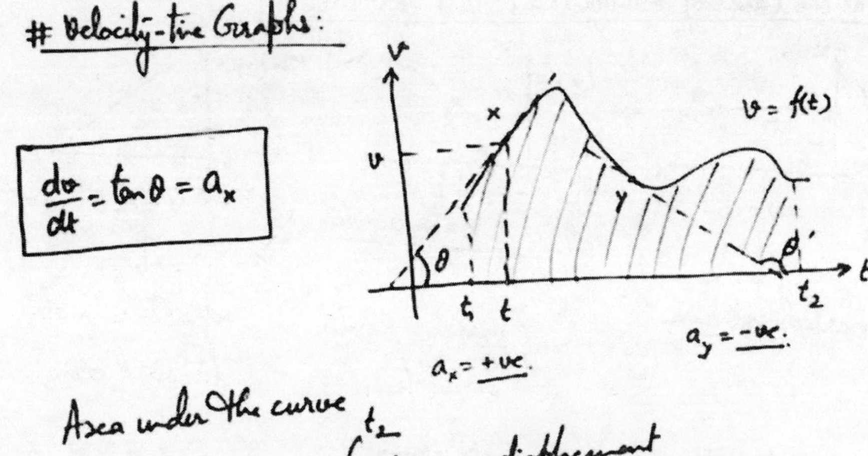

Area under the curve

$$\text{Area} = \int_{t_1}^{t_2} v\,dt \rightarrow \text{displacement of particle from } t = t_1 \text{ to } t_2.$$

Module-19: Graphical Analysis of Motion

Motion Situation:

v, +ve, S_1, t_2, t, t_1, t=0, -ve, S_2, -ve

Total displacement of particle from $t = 0$ to t_2 is

$$\text{disp} = S_1 - S_2$$

$$\text{distance travelled} = S_1 + S_2$$

Accⁿ time graphs:

$$A = \int_{t_1}^{t_2} a\,dt \rightarrow \text{net change in vel of part from } t_1 \text{ to } t_2.$$

a, t, t_1, t_2, area: A

Web Reference at www.physicsgalaxy.com

Scan for Video Explanation

Module-20: Displacement-Time Graphs

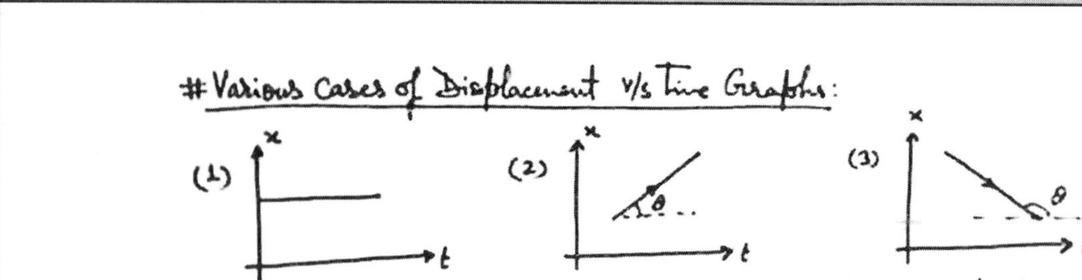

$v = 0$

↓

particle at Rest.

$v = \tan\theta$ +ve

↓

a particle moving away from Origin at Constant vel.

$v = \tan\theta = -ve.$

↓

a particle moving toward origin at Constant vel.

Scan for Video Explanation

Web Reference at www.physicsgalaxy.com

Module-20: Displacement-Time Graphs

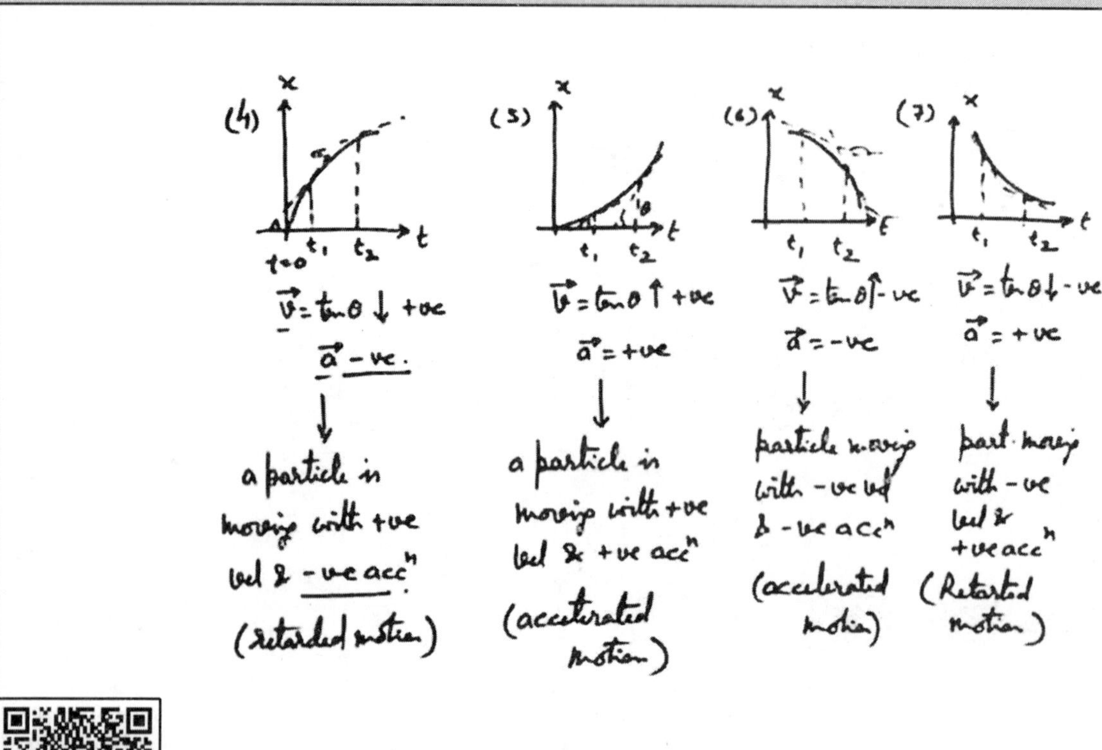

Scan for Video Explanation

Web Reference at www.physicsgalaxy.com

Module-20: Displacement-Time Graphs

Ex : A boy on top of a tower of height H throws a ball up with initial speed u, taking upward direction positive draw the displacement v/s time curve for ball's motion till it hits the ground.

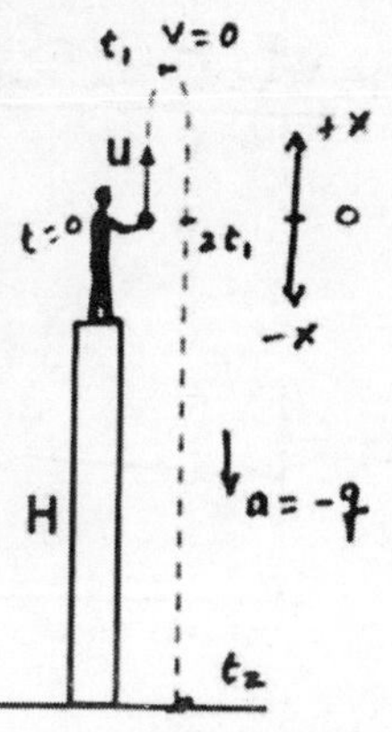

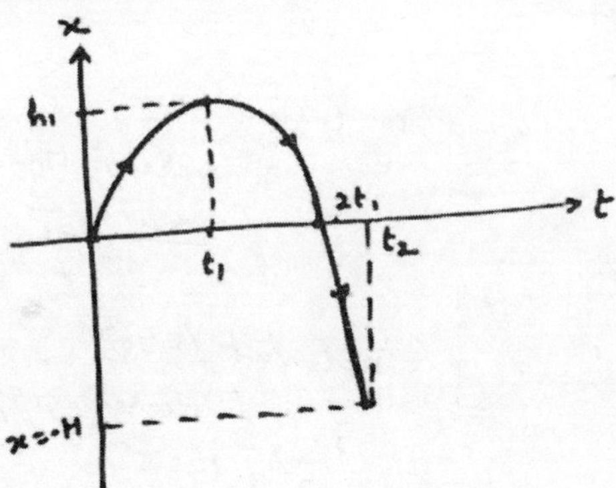

Web Reference at www.physicsgalaxy.com

Scan for Video Explanation

Module-20: Displacement-Time Graphs

Ex : A car moves at speed v_0. If at t = 0 driver sees a need to apply brakes and applies the brakes at a reaction time t_R and finally comes to rest in a distance s after brakes are applied. Draw position time curve for car's motion.

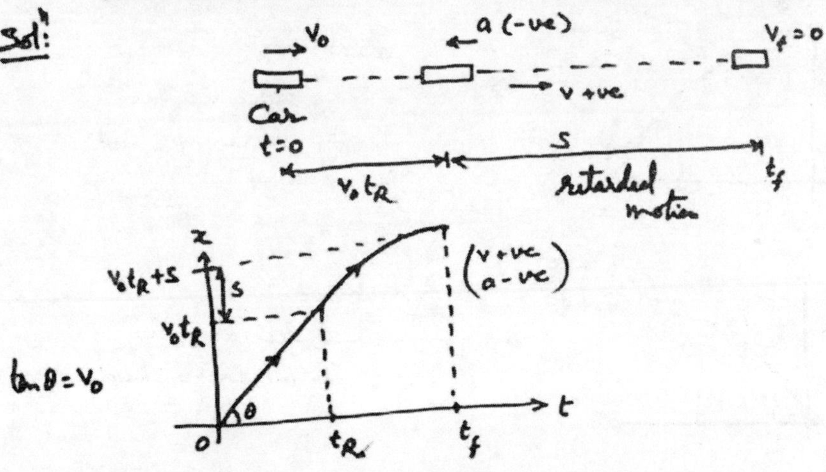

Web Reference at www.physicsgalaxy.com

Scan for Video Explanation

Module-21: Velocity-Time Graphs

Velocity v/s Time Graphs:

slope → Acceleration
Area → Displacement

(1) ⇒ $a = 0$, uniform motion (const vel)

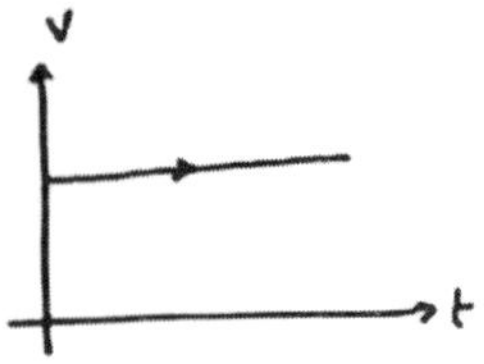

(2) ⇒ a = Constant (+ve)
increasing speed.
$\vec{a}$ + ve ⊕ $\vec{v}$ + ve

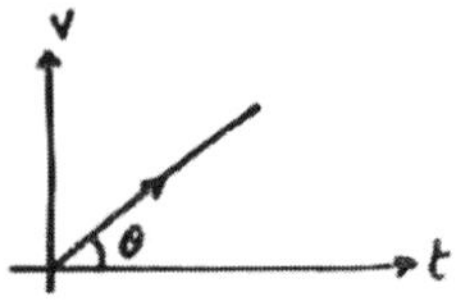

(3) ⇒ a = Constant (−ve)
decreasing speed.
$\vec{a}$ − ve ⊕ $\vec{v}$ + ve

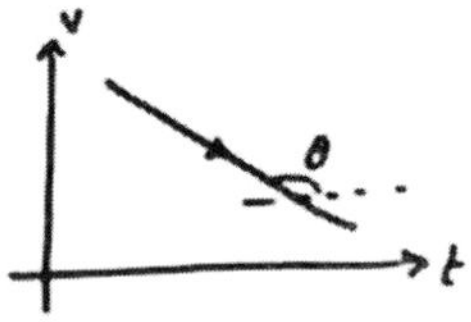

Scan for Video Explanation

Module-21: Velocity-Time Graphs

(4) $\vec{v}$ + ve, $\vec{a}$ + ve ⇒ variable acc^n
→ increasing acc^n
→ increasing speed

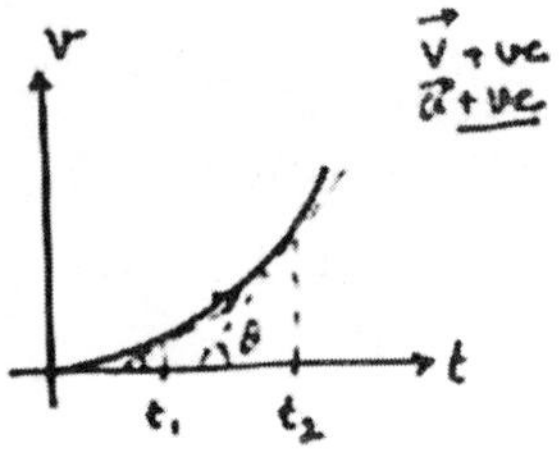

(5) $\vec{a}$ − ve, $\vec{v}$ + ve ⇒ variable acc^n
→ increasing acc^n
→ decreasing speed.

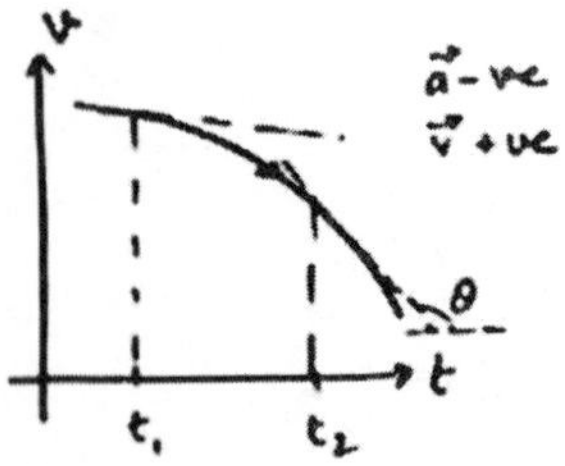

(6) $\vec{a}$ + ve, $\vec{v}$ + ve ⇒ variable acc^n
→ decreasing acc^n
→ increasing speed.

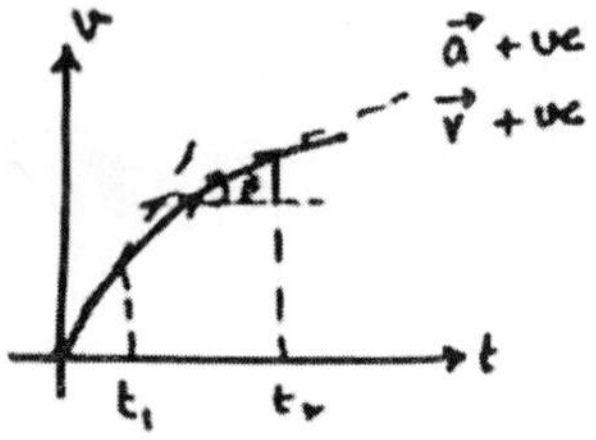

Scan for Video Explanation

Web Reference at www.physicsgalaxy.com

Module-21: Velocity-Time Graphs

Ex : A boy on top of a tower of height H throws a ball up with initial speed u, taking upward direction positive draw the velocity v/s time curve for ball's motion till it hits the ground.

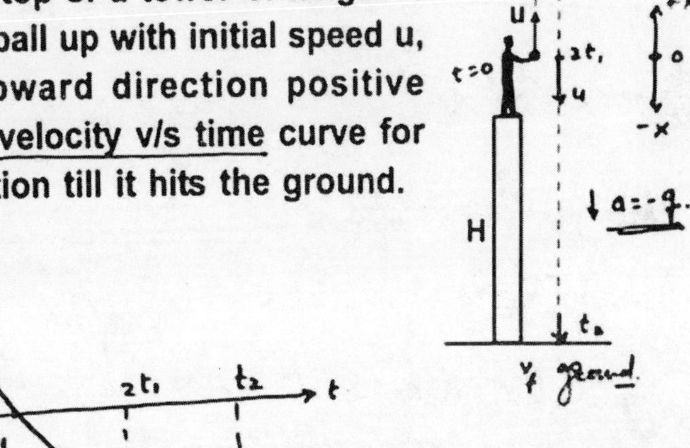

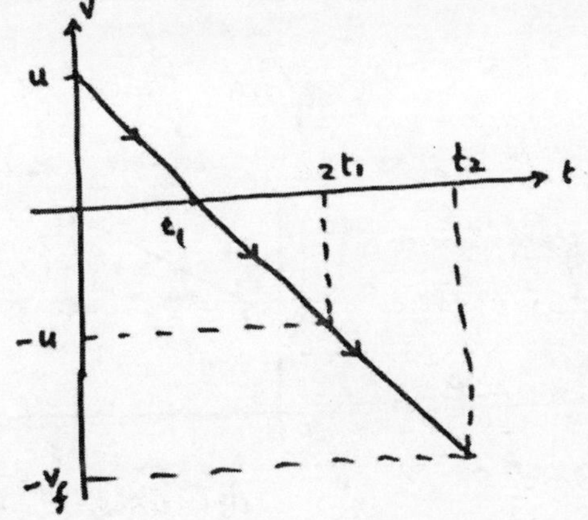

Web Reference at www.physicsgalaxy.com

Scan for Video Explanation

Module-21: Velocity-Time Graphs

Ex : A ball is dropped at t = 0 from a height H as shown, it collides elastically with floor and rebounds to same height. Draw velocity v/s time graph for ball's motion taking downward direction positive.

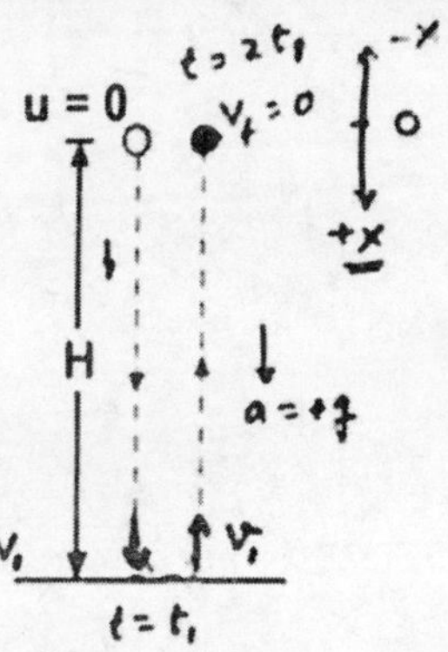

Sol: elastic collision → no energy is lost.

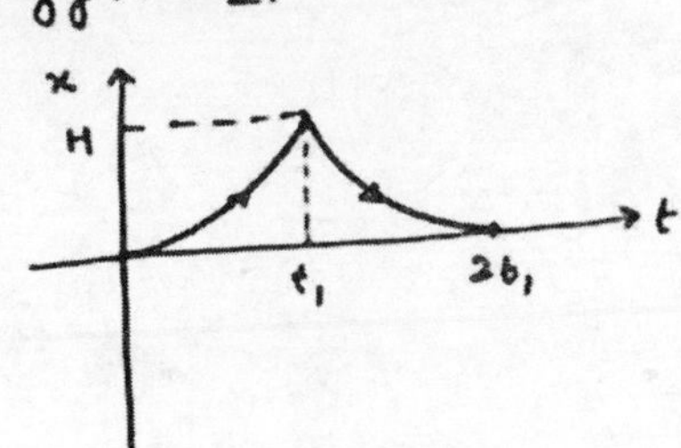

Web Reference at www.physicsgalaxy.com

Scan for Video Explanation

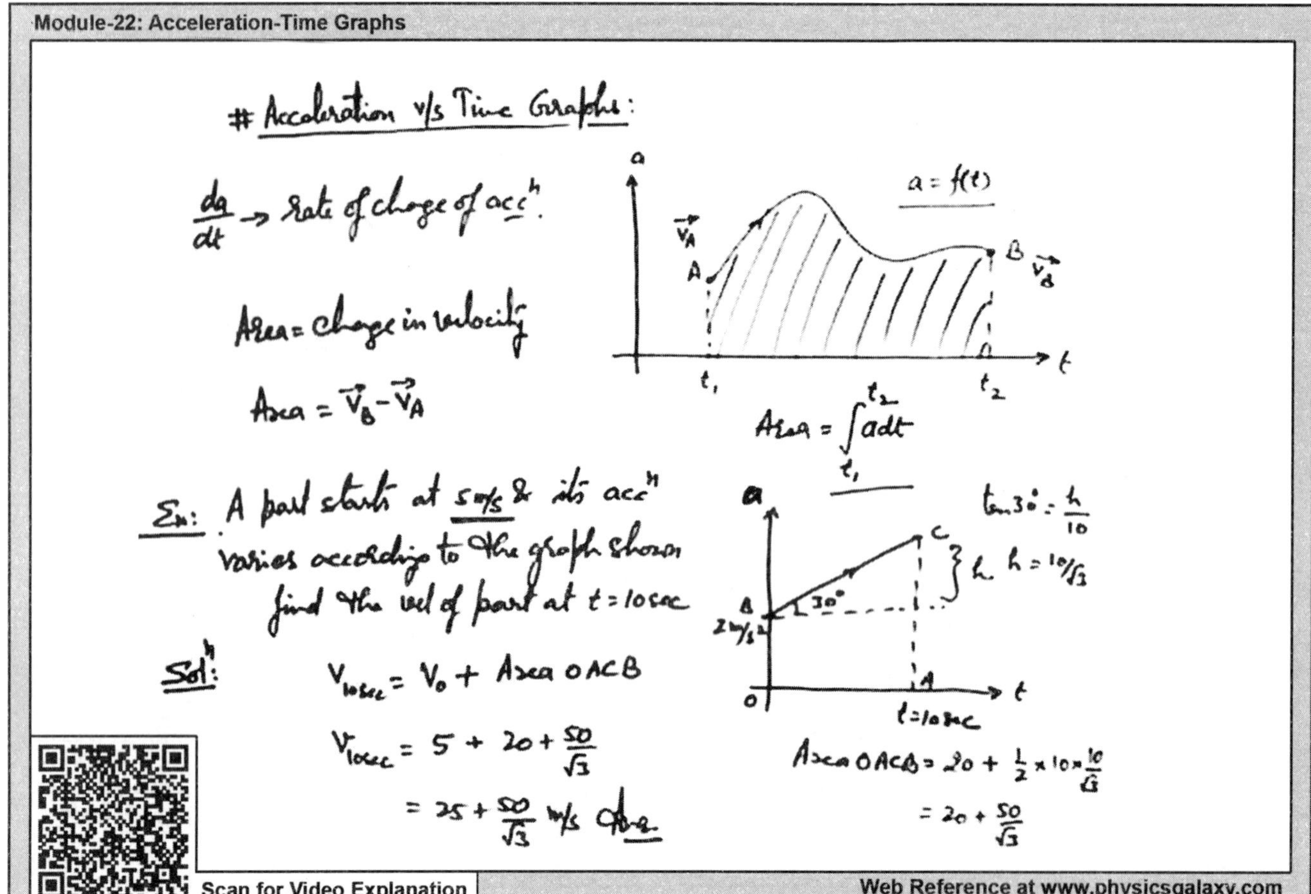
Module-22: Acceleration-Time Graphs
Acceleration v/s Time Graphs:
da/dt → Rate of change of accn.
Area = change in velocity
Area = VB − VA
a = f(t)
Area = ∫ adt (t1 to t2)
Ex: A part starts at 5 m/s & its accn varies according to the graph shown find the vel of part at t = 10 sec
Sol:
V10sec = V0 + Area OACB
V10sec = 5 + 20 + 50/√3
= 25 + 50/√3 m/s Ans.
tan 30° = h/10
h = 10/√3
Area OACB = 20 + 1/2 × 10 × 10/√3
= 20 + 50/√3
2 m/s²
t = 10 sec
Scan for Video Explanation
Web Reference at www.physicsgalaxy.com

Chapter 2
Motion in Two Dimensions

Lecture Notes Modules

Module-1: Introduction
Module-2: Solved Example-1
Module-3: Solved Example-2
Module-4: Solved Example-3
Module-5: Trajectory of a 2D motion
Module-6: Projectile Motion Under Gravity
Module-7: Velocity of a Particle During Projectile
Module-8: Position and Trajectory of Projectile
Module-9: Solved Example-4
Module-10: Solved Example-5
Module-11: Solved Example-6
Module-12: Solved Example-7
Module-13: Projectile in Moving Reference Frame
Module-14: Projectile on Inclined Plane

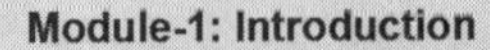

Module-1: Introduction

Motion in Two Dimensions : Motion in a Plane.

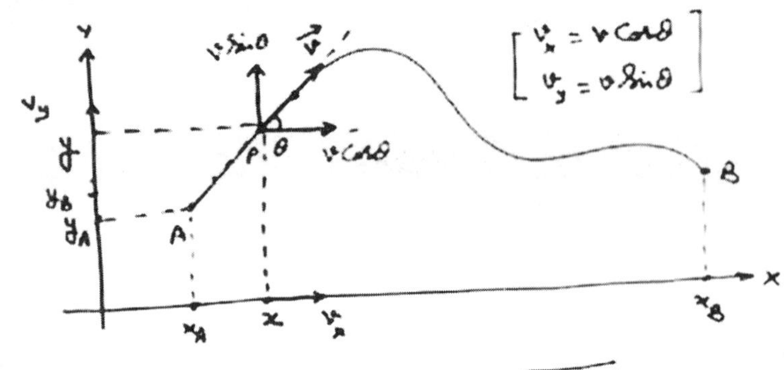

$$\vec{v} = v_x\hat{i} + v_y\hat{j}$$

$$v = \sqrt{v_x^2 + v_y^2}$$

$$\tan\theta = \frac{v_y}{v_x} \quad \text{or} \quad \theta = \tan^{-1}\left(\frac{v_y}{v_x}\right)$$

NOTE: A 2D motion can be analyzed by splitting it into two ⊥ 1D motions with t as a common variable.

Scan for Video Explanation

Web Reference at www.physicsgalaxy.com

Module-1: Introduction

In 2D motion all the analysis of 1D motion can be applied along x and Y directions simultaneously.

along x-dir $\quad v_x = \frac{dx}{dt} \quad \& \quad a_x = \frac{dv_x}{dt} = v_x\frac{dv_x}{dx}$

along y-dir $\quad v_y = \frac{dy}{dt} \quad \& \quad a_y = \frac{dv_y}{dt} = v_y\frac{dv_y}{dy}$.

Ex: A particle moves in a 2D motion such that its position depends on time as -

$$x = 4t^2 + 2t + 3$$
$$y = 5t + 7$$

Find the vel of particle at t = 2s.

Soln: $v_x = \frac{dx}{dt} = 8t + 2$, $\quad v_y = \frac{dy}{dt} = 5$

At t = 2 sec: $v_x = 18$ m/s, $v_y = 5$ m/s

$\vec{v} = 18\hat{i} + 5\hat{j}$

$v = \sqrt{(18)^2 + (5)^2}$

$\theta = \tan^{-1}(5/18)$ Ans.

Scan for Video Explanation

Web Reference at www.physicsgalaxy.com

Module-2: Solved Example-1

Ex : A particle starts in a 2D motion such that its position vector at any instant can be given as

$$\vec{r} = (2t^3 + 4t)\,\hat{i} + (3t^2 + 7)\,\hat{j}$$

Find the velocity and acceleration of particle at t = 1 sec.

Sol^n:

$x = 2t^3 + 4t \longrightarrow v_x = 6t^2 + 4 \longrightarrow a_x = 12t$

$y = 3t^2 + 7 \longrightarrow v_y = 6t \longrightarrow a_y = 6$

$t = 1\,\text{sec}$ $\quad \vec{v} = 10\hat{i} + 6\hat{j}$ $\quad \vec{a} = 12\hat{i} + 6\hat{j}$

$v = \sqrt{100 + 36}$ $\quad a = \sqrt{144 + 36}$

$= \sqrt{136}\ \text{m/s}$ $\quad = \sqrt{180}\ \text{m/s}^2$

Ans.

Web Reference at www.physicsgalaxy.com

Scan for Video Explanation

Module-3: Solved Example-2

Ex : A particle starts from origin such that its velocity along Y direction remains constant at 2 m/s and in X direction it is imparted an acceleration which varies with time as $a_x = 3t + 2\ \text{m/s}^2$. Find the position vector of particle at t = 2 sec.

Sol^n:

$u_y = 2\ \text{m/s}$

$a_x = 3t + 2\ \text{m/s}$

$y = u_y t$

$= 2 \times 2 = 4\,\text{m}.$

in x dir $\quad \dfrac{dv_x}{dt} = 3t + 2$

$\displaystyle\int_0^{v_x} dv_x = \int_0^t (3t + 2)\,dt$

$v_x = \dfrac{3t^2}{2} + 2t$

$\dfrac{dx}{dt} = \dfrac{3t^2}{2} + 2t$

$\displaystyle\int_0^x dx = \int_0^t \left(\frac{3t^2}{2} + 2t\right) dt$

$x = \dfrac{t^3}{2} + t^2$

at $t = 2$ $\quad x = 4 + 4 = 8\,\text{m}.$

Position at t = 2 sec is (8, 4)

$\vec{r} = 8\hat{i} + 4\hat{j}$ Ans.

Web Reference at www.physicsgalaxy.com

Scan for Video Explanation

Module-4: Solved Example-3

Ex : A particle is moving in 2D such that in x and y directions its velocities are given as

$$V_x = 5t^2 + 7t + 3$$

$$V_y = 2t^3$$

Find the angle between direction of velocity and acceleration at t = 1 sec.

Sol^n: at t = 1 sec $\quad \vec{V} = 15\hat{i} + 2\hat{j} \quad \hat{v} = \frac{\vec{v}}{v} = \frac{15\hat{i} + 2\hat{j}}{\sqrt{229}}$

$$\vec{a} = \frac{d\vec{v}}{dt} = (10t + 7)\hat{i} + (6t^2)\hat{j}$$

at t = 1 sec $\quad \vec{a} = 17\hat{i} + 6\hat{j} \quad \hat{a} = \frac{\vec{a}}{a} = \frac{17\hat{i} + 6\hat{j}}{\sqrt{325}}$

If θ is the angle between $\vec{v}$ & $\vec{a}$ at t = 1 sec

$$\theta = \cos^{-1}(\hat{v} \cdot \hat{a}) = \text{-----} \quad \text{Ans.}$$

Scan for Video Explanation

Web Reference at www.physicsgalaxy.com

Module-5: Trajectory of a 2D motion

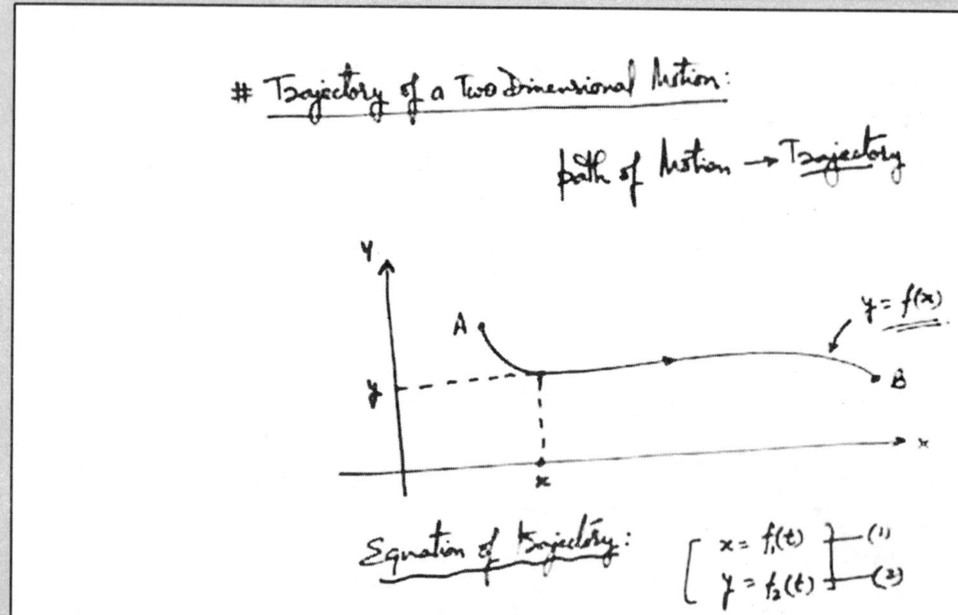

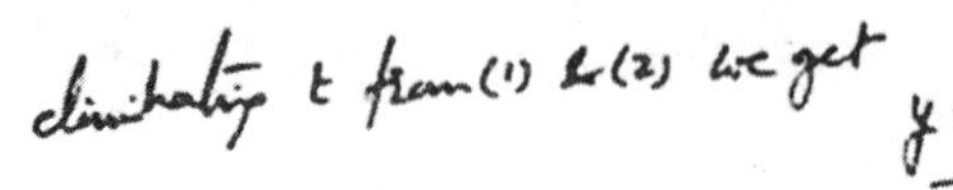

Scan for Video Explanation

Web Reference at www.physicsgalaxy.com

Module-5: Trajectory of a 2D motion

Ex : **If a particle travels in 2D with velocity given as**

$$\vec{V} = 4t\hat{i} + 5\hat{j}$$

Find the path of motion of particle and its equation of trajectory if it starts from origin.

Soln:

$$\vec{v} = 4t\hat{i} + 5\hat{j}$$

$v_x = 4t$ m/s

$$\int_0^x dx = \int_0^t 4t\,dt$$

$$x = 2t^2 \quad \text{—(1)}$$

$v_y = 5$ m/s

$$y = 5t \quad \text{—(2)}$$

$$t = y/5$$

from eqn (1) $\quad x = 2(y/5)^2$

$$x = 2y^2/25 \quad \text{parabolic Path.}$$

eqn of traj of part. $\rightarrow y = 5\sqrt{x/2}$ Ans.

Web Reference at www.physicsgalaxy.com | Scan for Video Explanation

Module-5: Trajectory of a 2D motion

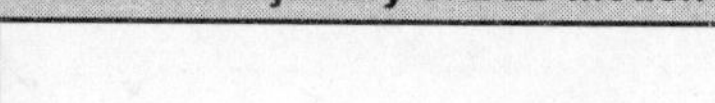

Distance Travelled by a particle in 2D Motion :

↓

length of path.

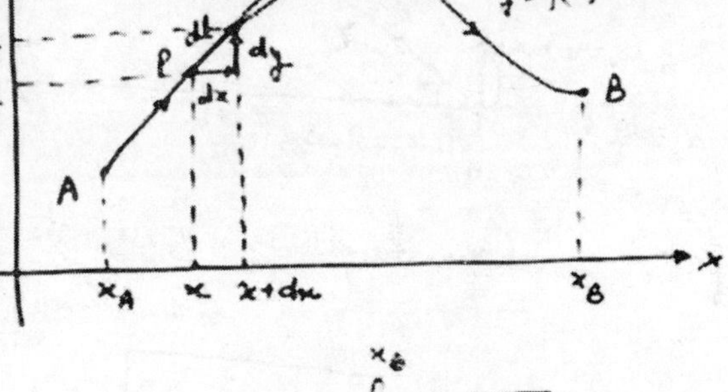

length of path

$$l_{AB} = \int dl$$

$$= \int \sqrt{dx^2 + dy^2}$$

$$= \int \sqrt{1 + \left(\frac{dy}{dx}\right)^2}\,.\,dx$$

$$\boxed{l_{AB} = \int_{x_A}^{x_B} \sqrt{1 + \left(\frac{dy}{dx}\right)^2}\,dx}$$

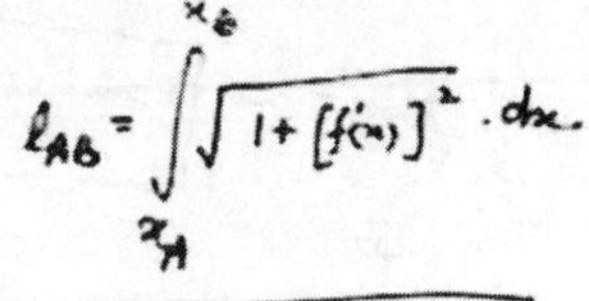

$$l_{AB} = \int_{x_A}^{x_B} \sqrt{1 + [f'(x)]^2}\,.\,dx$$

Web Reference at www.physicsgalaxy.com | Scan for Video Explanation

Module-6: Projectile Motion Under Gravity

Projectile Motion:

Motion of a body after its projection is called Projectile motion

projection ↓ to impart some initial velocity

Projectile Motion under gravity:

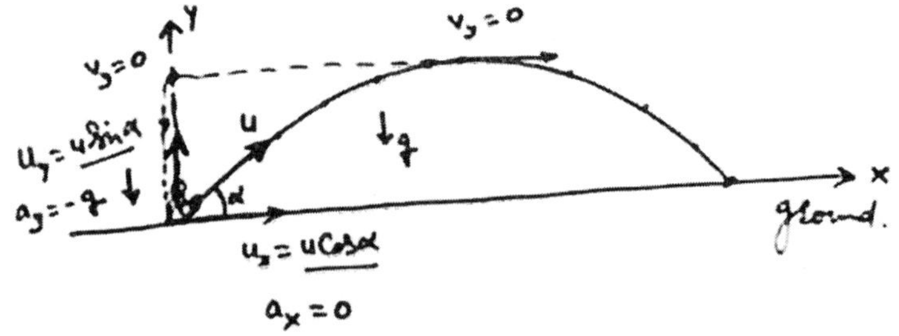

$v_y = 0$, $u_y = u\sin\alpha$, $a_y = -g$ ↓, u, α, ↓g, $v_y = 0$, $u_x = u\cos\alpha$, $a_x = 0$, X, Y, ground.

Scan for Video Explanation

Web Reference at www.physicsgalaxy.com

Module-6: Projectile Motion Under Gravity

Std. Parameters of Projectile Motion on Horizontal Plane:

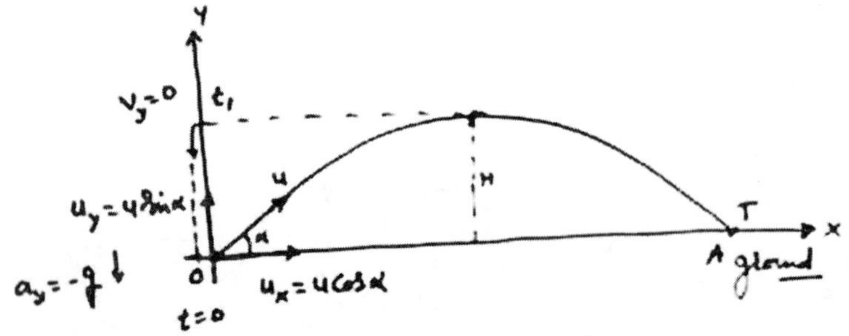

Y, X, $v_y = 0$, t_1, $u_y = u\sin\alpha$, u, α, H, T, A, O, $a_y = -g$ ↓, $u_x = u\cos\alpha$, $t = 0$, ground

* Time to reach max height → $v_y = u_y - gt_1$

$0 = u\sin\alpha - gt_1 \Rightarrow \boxed{t_1 = \frac{u\sin\alpha}{g}}$

* Time of flight → $\boxed{T = 2t_1 = \frac{2u\sin\alpha}{g}}$

* Max. height attained by projectile → $h = ut - \frac{1}{2}gt^2$

$H = u\sin\alpha\left(\frac{u\sin\alpha}{g}\right) - \frac{1}{2}g\frac{u^2\sin^2\alpha}{g^2}$

$v^2 = u^2 - 2gh$ → $\boxed{H = \frac{u^2\sin^2\alpha}{2g}}$

Scan for Video Explanation

Web Reference at www.physicsgalaxy.com

Module-6: Projectile Motion Under Gravity

Range of Projectile on Horizontal Plane:

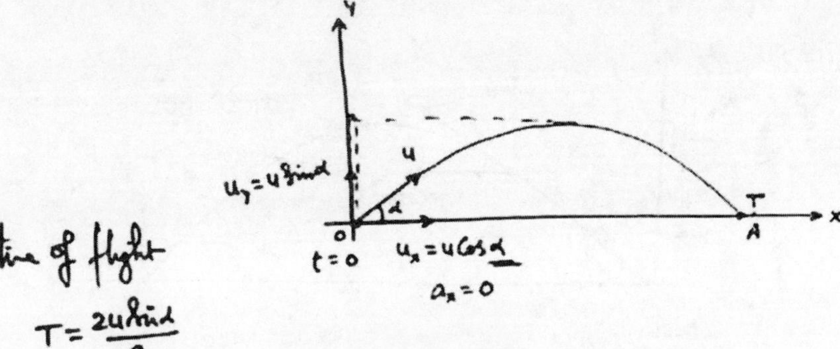

time of flight

$$T = \frac{2u\sin\alpha}{g}$$

Range of projectile = OA

$$R = u\cos\alpha \times T = u\cos\alpha \times \frac{2u\sin\alpha}{g}$$

$$\boxed{R = \frac{u^2\sin 2\alpha}{g}}$$

Web Reference at www.physicsgalaxy.com | Scan for Video Explanation

Module-6: Projectile Motion Under Gravity

Range Analysis of Projectile Motion:

$$R = \frac{u^2\sin 2\alpha}{g}$$

$(\sin 2\alpha)_{max} = 1$

$2\alpha = 90^\circ$

$\alpha = 45^\circ$

$$R_{max} = \frac{u^2}{g}$$

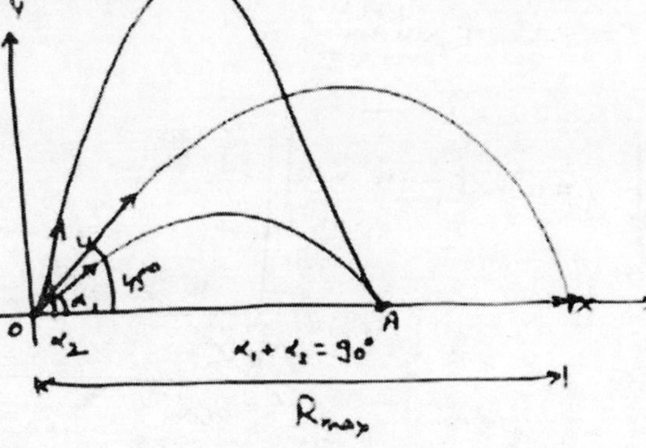

at proj angles $\alpha \neq 45^\circ$ always there exist two angles for which the range of proj on horizontal ground are equal. These angles are complimentary angle such that $\alpha_1 + \alpha_2 = 90^\circ$

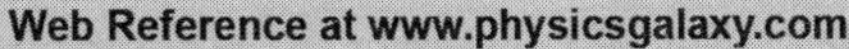

Web Reference at www.physicsgalaxy.com | Scan for Video Explanation

Module-7: Velocity of a Particle During Projectile

Velocity of a Particle during Projectile:

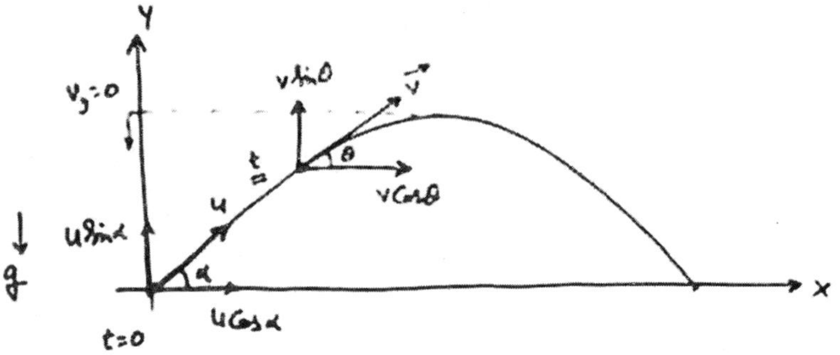

Initial vel vector $\vec{u} = (u\cos\alpha)\hat{i} + (u\sin\alpha)\hat{j}$

along x dir. $v\cos\theta = u\cos\alpha$ —(1)

along y dir $v\sin\theta = u\sin\alpha - gt$ —(2) $[v_y = u_y - gt]$

vel after time t of projectile $\boxed{\vec{v} = (u\cos\alpha)\hat{i} + (u\sin\alpha - gt)\hat{j}}$

Scan for Video Explanation

Web Reference at www.physicsgalaxy.com

Module-8: Position and Trajectory of Projectile

Position of Particle and Trajectory during Projectile Motion:

Position of part at time t

$$\begin{bmatrix} x = u\cos\alpha . t & —(1) \\ y = u\sin\alpha t - \frac{1}{2}gt^2 & —(2) \end{bmatrix}$$

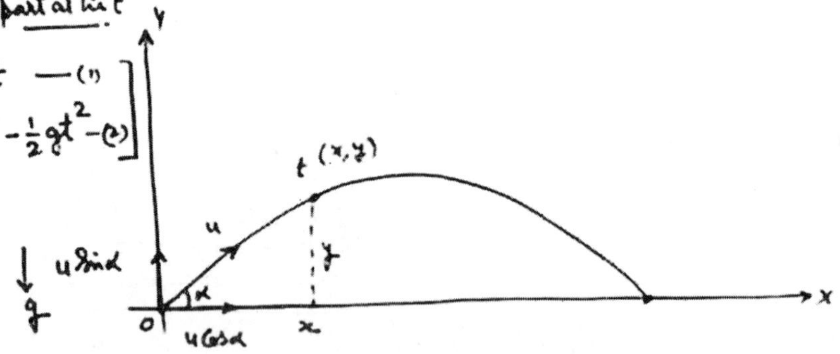

Equation of Trajectory from eq(1) $t = \frac{x}{u\cos\alpha}$

from eq^n(2) $y = u\sin\alpha\left(\frac{x}{u\cos\alpha}\right) - \frac{1}{2}g\left(\frac{x}{u\cos\alpha}\right)^2$

$$\boxed{y = x\tan\alpha - \frac{gx^2}{2u^2\cos^2\alpha}}$$ v. imp.

Scan for Video Explanation

Web Reference at www.physicsgalaxy.com

Module-8: Position and Trajectory of Projectile

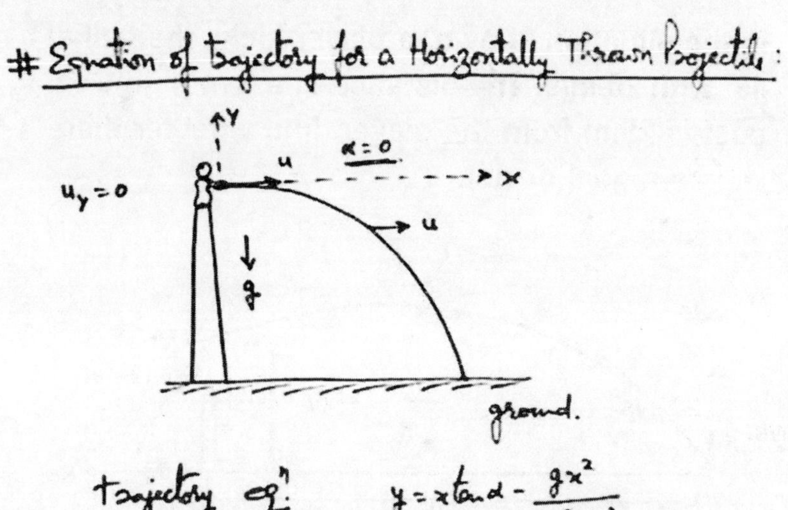

Trajectory eqⁿ $\quad y = x\tan\alpha - \dfrac{gx^2}{2u^2\cos^2\alpha}$

$\alpha = 0 \qquad \boxed{y = -\dfrac{gx^2}{2u^2}}$ v.imp.

Web Reference at www.physicsgalaxy.com | Scan for Video Explanation

Module-9: Solved Example-4

Ex : If initial velocity of a particle projected from ground is $\vec{u} = 6\hat{i} + 8\hat{j}$ m/s, find the horizontal range of projectile.

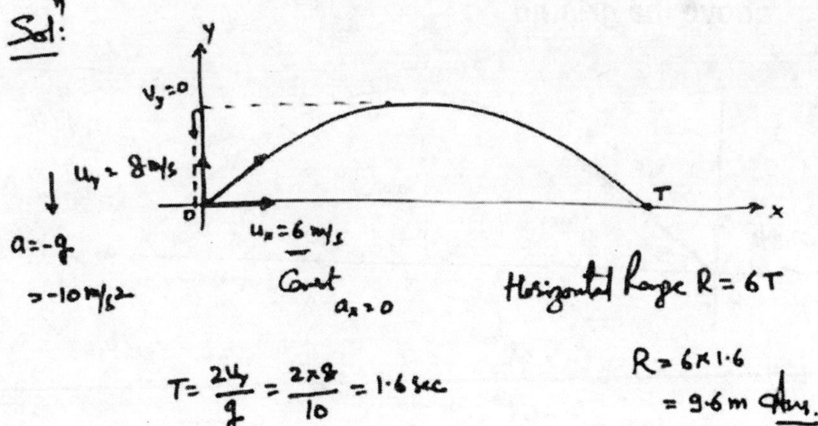

Web Reference at www.physicsgalaxy.com | Scan for Video Explanation

Module-10: Solved Example-5

Ex : **In the situation shown, a player kicks the ball at 45° with 20 m/s. The distance of a 3 m high Goal post is 25 m from the player, find whether there will be a goal or not.**

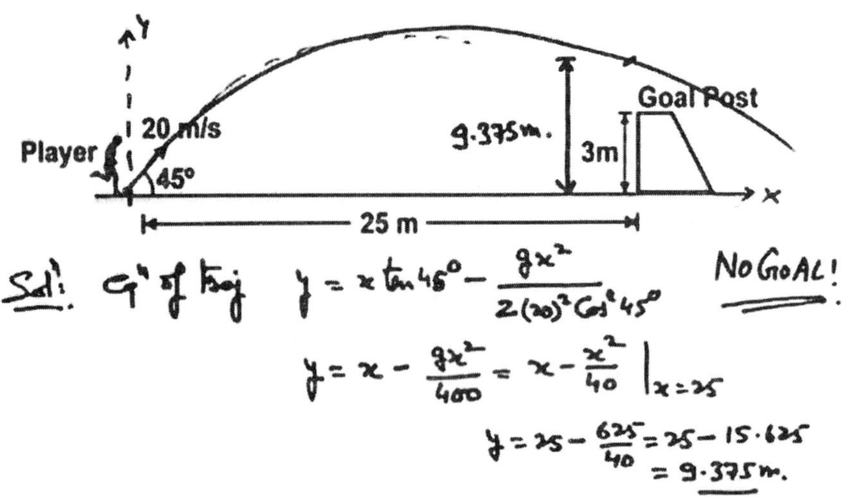

Scan for Video Explanation

Web Reference at www.physicsgalaxy.com

Module-11: Solved Example-6

Ex : **A particle is thrown from ground at an angle 30° with horizontal at 40 m/s. Find the time duration for which it will be at a height more them 10 m above the ground.**

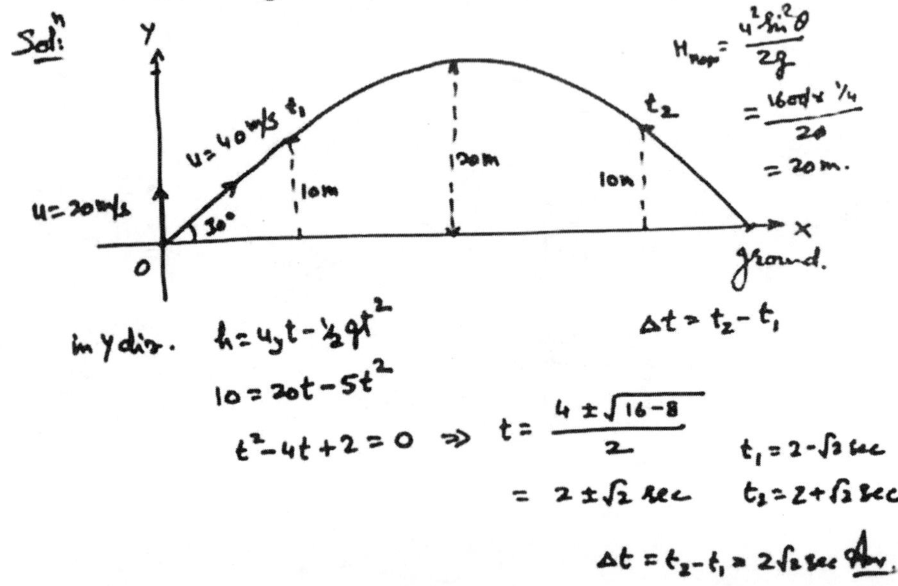

Scan for Video Explanation

Web Reference at www.physicsgalaxy.com

Module-12: Solved Example-7

Ex : A body is projected horizontally from top of a high tower at speed 20 m/s. Find the displacement of body at t = 10 sec.

20 m/s

t=0, $u_y = 0$, g, → 20 m/s, t = 10 sec

Sol^n: Position of body at t = 10 sec

$u_x = 20$ m/s $\qquad x = u_x t$

$= 20 \times 10 = 200$ m.

$u_y = 0 \qquad a_y = g \qquad y = \frac{1}{2} g t^2$

$y = \frac{1}{2} \times 10 \times 100 = 500$ m.

$r = \sqrt{x^2 + y^2} = \sqrt{(200)^2 + (500)^2}$

$= 100\sqrt{4 + 25} = 100\sqrt{29}$ m Ans.

Web Reference at www.physicsgalaxy.com

Scan for Video Explanation

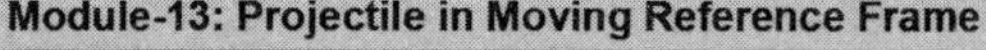

Module-13: Projectile in Moving Reference Frame

Projectile from a moving refrence frame:

Initial vel Components of ball's motion

$u_x = u\cos\alpha + v$

$u_y = u\sin\alpha$

Time of flight $\quad T = \dfrac{2u_y}{g} = \dfrac{2u\sin\alpha}{g}$

Horizontal Range $\quad R = u_x \times T$

$= (u\cos\alpha + v) \cdot \left(\dfrac{2u\sin\alpha}{g}\right)$

Web Reference at www.physicsgalaxy.com

Scan for Video Explanation

Module-13: Projectile in Moving Reference Frame

Ex : **A boy in an automobile throws a ball at 40 m/s at an angle 45° from horizontal as shown. Just after throw, boy jumps and start running in same direction to catch the ball. Find the speed at which boy should run to catch the ball and the time and position at which he will catch the ball.**

Sol^n:

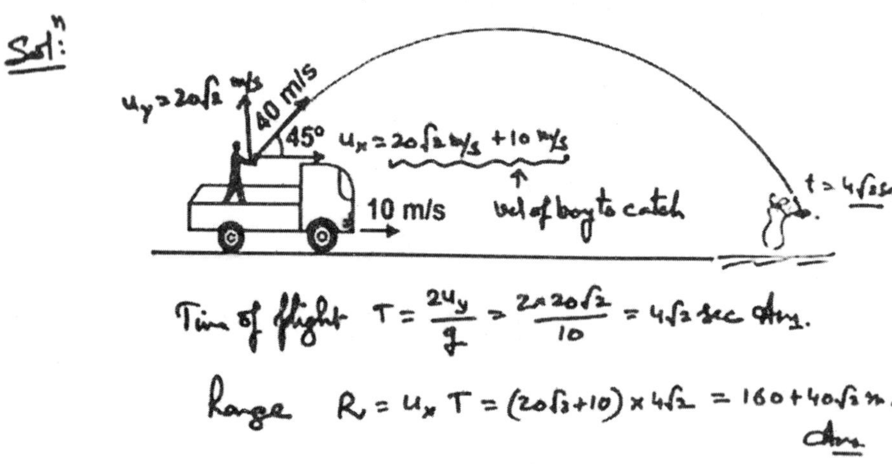

Time of flight $T = \frac{2u_y}{g} = \frac{2\times 20\sqrt{2}}{10} = 4\sqrt{2}$ sec Ans.

Range $R = u_x T = (20\sqrt{2}+10)\times 4\sqrt{2} = 160 + 40\sqrt{2}$ m. Ans.

Scan for Video Explanation

Web Reference at www.physicsgalaxy.com

Module-14: Projectile on Inclined Plane

Projectile Motion on Inclined Plane:

Case-I: Projection up the Plane

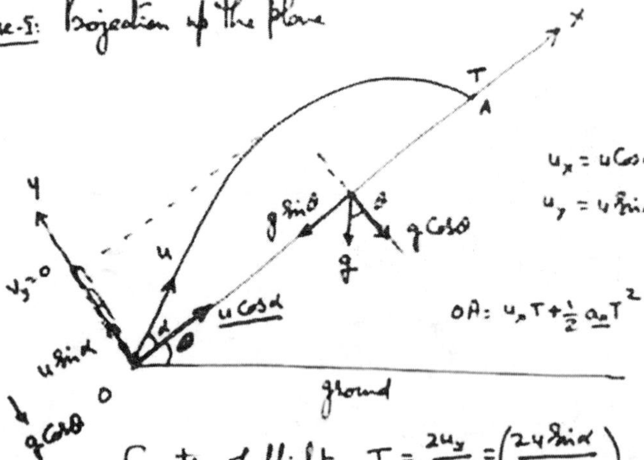

$u_x = u\cos\alpha \quad a_x = -g\sin\theta$

$u_y = u\sin\alpha \quad a_y = -g\cos\theta$

$OA = u_x T + \frac{1}{2} a_x T^2$

$v_y^2 = u_y^2 - 2gh.$

$0 = u_y^2 - 2g\cos\theta\, H$

$[v_y = u_y - a_y T]$

Time of flight $T = \frac{2u_y}{a_y} = \left(\frac{2u\sin\alpha}{g\cos\theta}\right)$

Max. height $H = \frac{u_y^2}{2a_y} = \left(\frac{u^2\sin^2\alpha}{2g\cos\theta}\right)$

Range of proj $R = u\cos\alpha(T) - \frac{1}{2} g\sin\theta (T)^2 = \ldots$

Scan for Video Explanation

Web Reference at www.physicsgalaxy.com

Module-14: Projectile on Inclined Plane

Case-II: Projection down the Plane

Time of flight $T = \frac{2u_y}{a_y} = \frac{2u\sin\alpha}{g\cos\theta}$

Max. height $H = \frac{u_y^2}{2a_y} = \frac{u^2\sin^2\alpha}{2g\cos\theta}$

Range along inclined Plane.

$$R = u\cos\alpha(T) + \frac{1}{2}g\sin\theta(T)^2$$

$$= - - - \checkmark$$

Web Reference at www.physicsgalaxy.com

Scan for Video Explanation

Module-14: Projectile on Inclined Plane

Maximum Range of Projectile on inclined Plane:

$$R = u_x T \pm \frac{1}{2}a_x T^2 \qquad a_x = g\sin\theta.$$

R will be max when $\frac{dR}{d\alpha} = 0$

↓

max Range along inclined Plane. $R_{max} = \frac{u^2}{g(1 \pm \sin\theta)}$

$\theta \to$ angle of inc.

+ sign → proj up the plane.

− sign → proj down the plane.

$\theta = 0 \to$ horiz. ground $\quad R_{max} = \frac{u^2}{g}. \quad \theta = 0, \ \alpha = 45°$

Web Reference at www.physicsgalaxy.com

Scan for Video Explanation

Chapter 3
Concept of Relative Motion

Lecture Notes Modules

Module-1: Introduction to Relative Motion

Relative Motion:

Motion of a body as seen from a reference frame which may be at rest or in motion is called relative motion of the body w.r.t. the frame.

A $\vec{V}_A = 20\hat{i}$ m/s

B $\vec{V}_B = 13\hat{i}$ m/s

→ relative velocity of A relative to B is

$$\boxed{\vec{V}_{AB} = \vec{V}_A - \vec{V}_B}$$

$= 20\hat{i} - 13\hat{i}$

$= 7\hat{i}$ m/s Ans.

Scan for Video Explanation

Web Reference at www.physicsgalaxy.com

Module-1: Introduction to Relative Motion

Relative Motion → It is the motion as seen by someone.

v_A v_B

A → ← B

velocity of B relative to A $\vec{V}_{BA} = \vec{V}_B - \vec{V}_A$

$= (-v_B) - (v_A)$

$= -(v_A + v_B)$

in same dir of two bodies

relative speed $= |v_1 - v_2|$.

in opp dir motion of two bodies

relative speed $= v_1 + v_2$.

Scan for Video Explanation

Web Reference at www.physicsgalaxy.com

Module-1: Introduction to Relative Motion

Ex : On a straight road cyclist are riding one after the other at a separation of 30 m at a speed of 10 m/s. In the same direction boys are running at a separation of 20 m at speed 5 m/s. If an old man is walking in opposite direction, find his speed so that he will meet each cycle and boy together.

Sol:

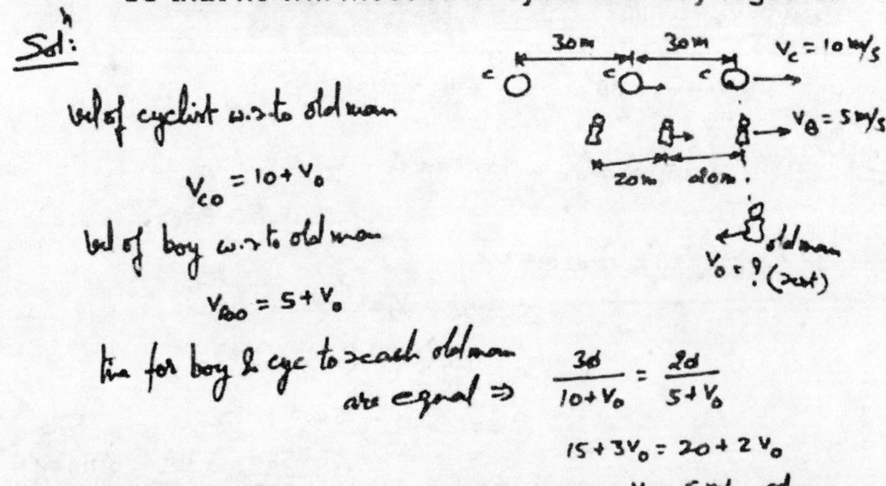

Web Reference at www.physicsgalaxy.com | Scan for Video Explanation

Module-2: Solved Example-1

Ex : A thief is running away on a straight road at 9 m/s. A policeman chases him on a motor cycle at 10 m/s. If the separation between them is 100 m, how long will it take for policeman to catch the thief ?

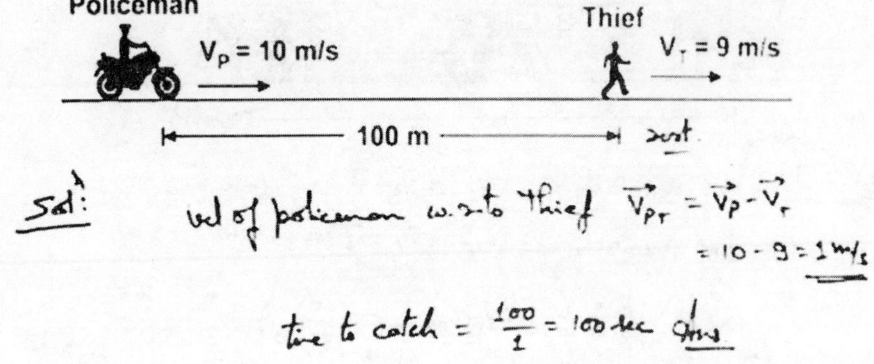

Web Reference at www.physicsgalaxy.com | Scan for Video Explanation

Module-3: Solved Example-2

Ex : A bus is moving at 10 m/s on a straight road. A scooterist 80 m behind moving at 5 m/s wishes to overtake the bus in 100 sec. Find the acceleration required for scooterist to do this.

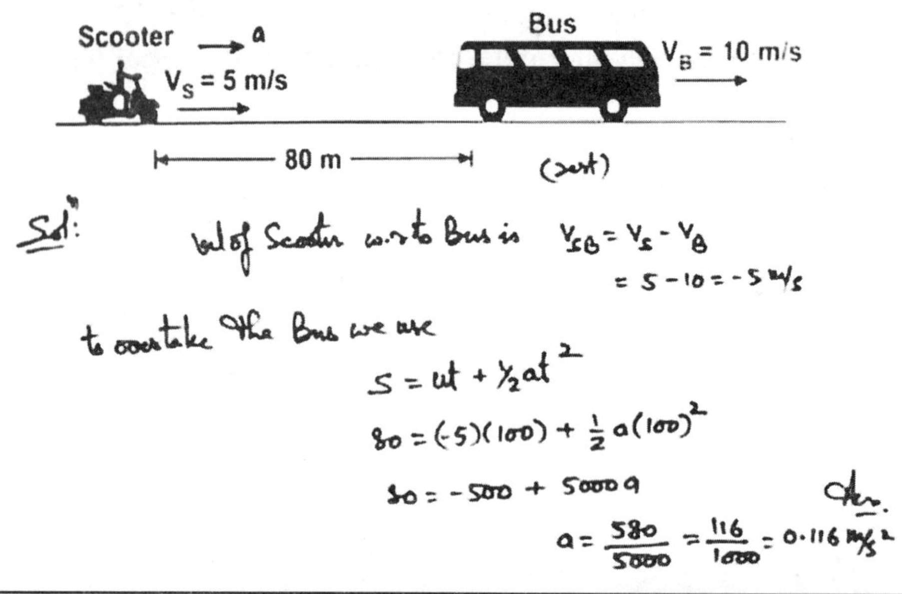

Scan for Video Explanation

Web Reference at www.physicsgalaxy.com

Module-4: Solved Example-3

Ex : Three elephants A, B and C are moving along a straight line as shown with constant speeds. When B catches C the separation between A and C becomes 3d. Find speed of B.

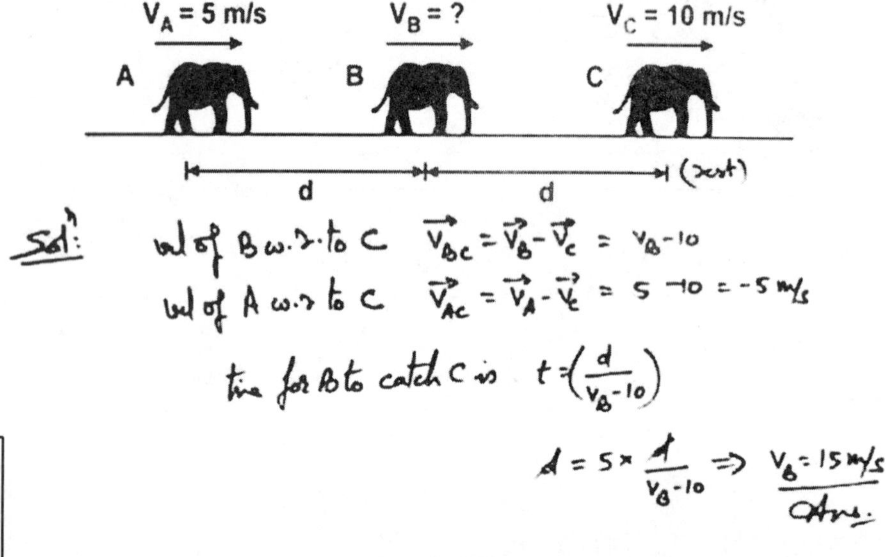

Scan for Video Explanation

Web Reference at www.physicsgalaxy.com

Module-5: Motion of a Body in Moving Ref Frame

Motion of a body in a moving reference frame:

Basic Ex:

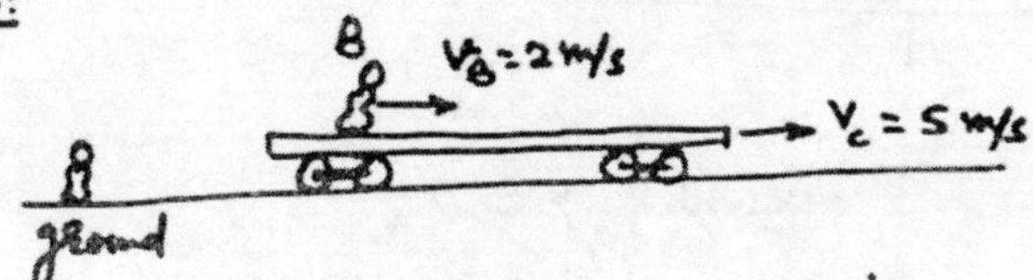

$v_B = 2$ m/s

$v_c = 5$ m/s

ground

vel of swimmer w.r.to ground $v_{BG} = v_B + v_C$

$= 2 + 5 = 7$ m/s

Ex:

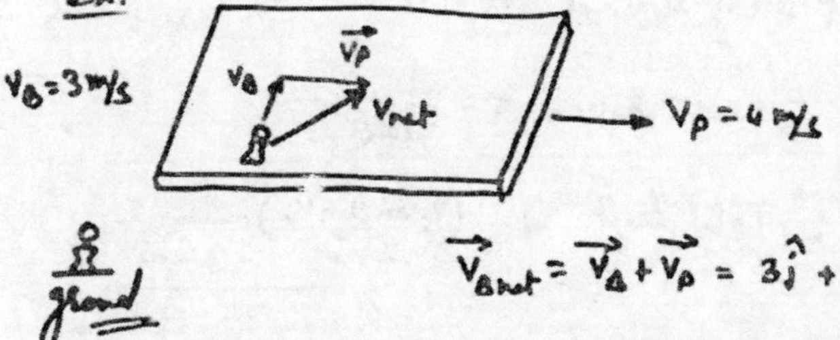

$v_B = 3$ m/s

$v_p = 4$ m/s

$\vec{v}_p = 4\hat{i}$

$\vec{v}_B = 3\hat{j}$

ground

$\vec{V}_{Bnet} = \vec{V}_B + \vec{V}_p = 3\hat{j} + 4\hat{i}$

$V_{Bnet} = 5$ m/s $\angle \tan^{-1} 3/4 = 5 \angle 37°$ m/s

Web Reference at www.physicsgalaxy.com

Scan for Video Explanation

Module-5: Motion of a Body in Moving Ref Frame

Motion of a Swimmer in a River:

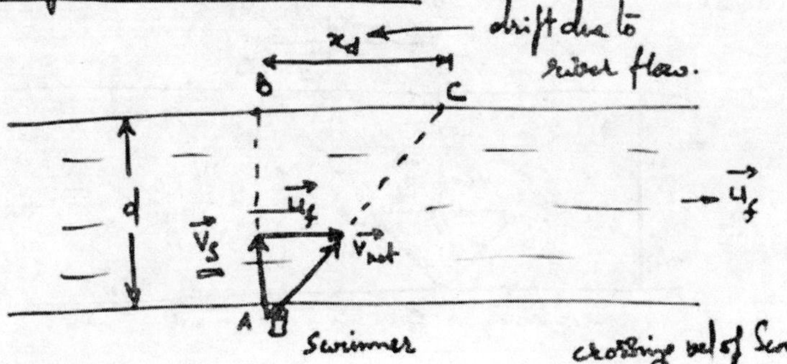

x_d ← drift due to river flow.

$\vec{u}_f$

$\vec{V}_{net}$

Swimmer

$\vec{v}_s$ → vel of swimmer relative to water

crossing vel of Swimmer $= v_s$

Drift vel of Swimmer $= u_f$

net vel of swimmer w.r.to ground is

$\vec{V}_{s\,net} = \vec{v}_s + \vec{u}_f$

$V_{s\,net} = \sqrt{v_s^2 + u_f^2}$

time to cross river $t = \frac{d}{v_s}$

Drift $x_d = u_f \times t = \left(u_f \frac{d}{v_s}\right)$

$t = \frac{d}{v_s} = \frac{AC}{\sqrt{v_s^2 + u_f^2}}$

Web Reference at www.physicsgalaxy.com

Scan for Video Explanation

Module-5: Motion of a Body in Moving Ref Frame

Downstream Swimming in a Flowing River:

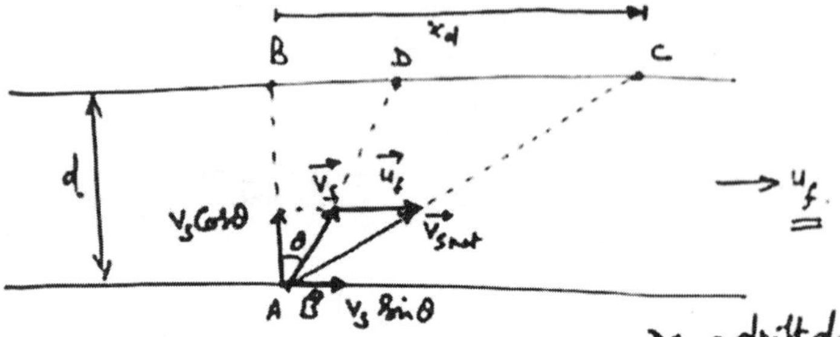

DC → drift due to river flow.

$$DC = u_f \cdot \frac{d}{v_s \cos\theta}$$

crossing vel of Swimmer $v_c = v_s \cos\theta$

Total drift vel of Swimmer $v_D = v_s \sin\theta + u_f$

time to cross river $t = \frac{d}{v_s \cos\theta}$

Total drift $x_d = (v_s \sin\theta + u_f) \cdot \frac{d}{v_s \cos\theta}$

Scan for Video Explanation

Web Reference at www.physicsgalaxy.com

Module-5: Motion of a Body in Moving Ref Frame

Upstream Swimming in a Flowing River:

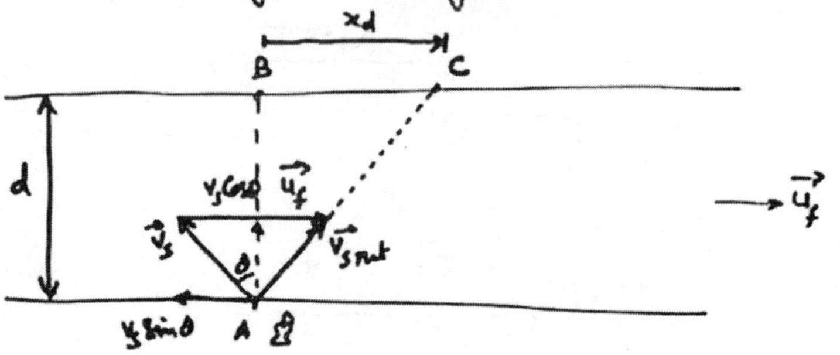

crossing vel $v_c = v_s \cos\theta$

Total drift vel $v_D = u_f - v_s \sin\theta$

time to cross river $t = \frac{d}{v_s \cos\theta} = \frac{AC}{v_{s\,net}}$

Total drift $x_d = (u_f - v_s \sin\theta) \cdot \frac{d}{v_s \cos\theta}$

Scan for Video Explanation

Web Reference at www.physicsgalaxy.com

Module-6: Solved Example-4

Ex : A swimmer wishes to cross a river flowing at 3 kph in minimum time. Find the direction in which he should swim to achieve this if he can swim at 5 kph relative to water.

Sol^n:

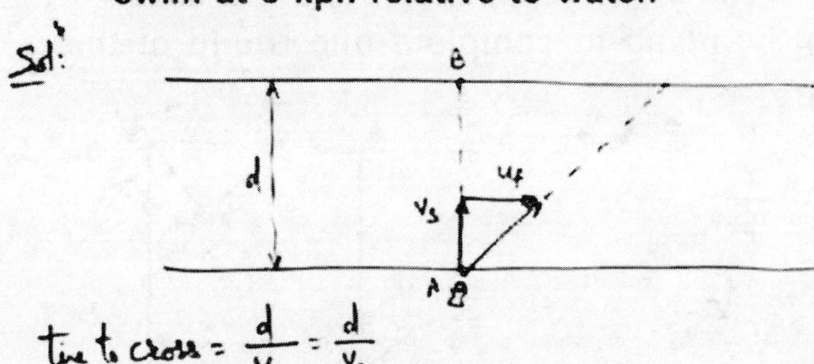

$$\text{time to cross} = \frac{d}{V_c} = \frac{d}{V_s}$$

NOTE: To minimize time to cross the river swimmer must swim in the dir perpendicular to river current.

Ans.

Web Reference at www.physicsgalaxy.com

Scan for Video Explanation

Module-7: Solved Example-5

Ex : If a swimmer wishes to cross a river in the shortest path find the direction in which he should swim to achieve this. The velocity of river current is 4 kph and the swimmer can swim relative to water at 5 kph.

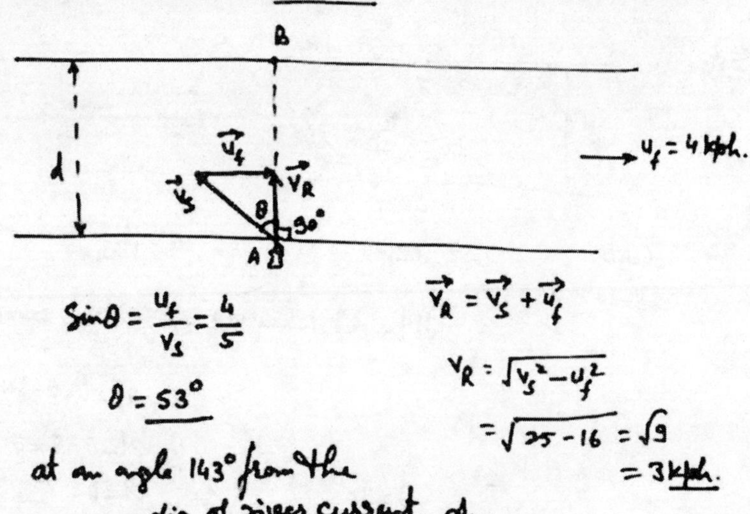

$= 3$ kph.

at an angle 143° from the dir of river current. Ans.

Web Reference at www.physicsgalaxy.com

Scan for Video Explanation

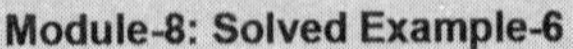

Module-8: Solved Example-6

Ex : An Aeroplane which flies at speed V_p tracks a horizontal square of side l as seen from ground. Given that wind exist in direction parallel to one side of the square at speed V_w. Find the time taken by plane to complete one round of the square.

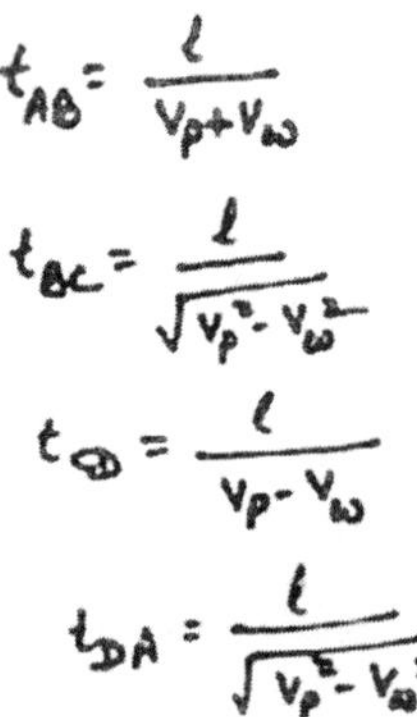

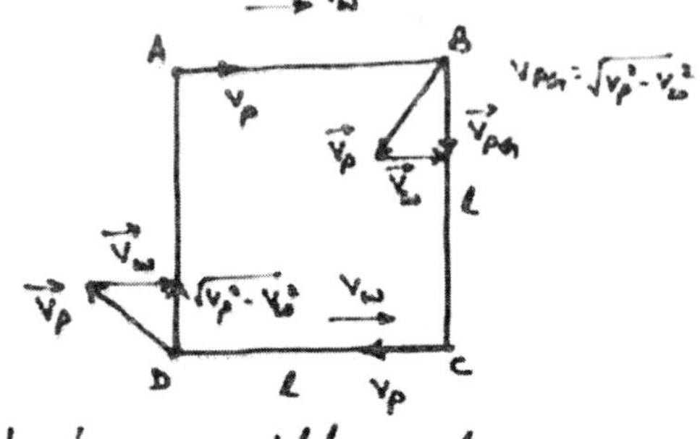

time for one Complete round is

$$T = \frac{l}{V_p + V_w} + \frac{2l}{\sqrt{V_p^2 - V_w^2}} + \frac{l}{V_p - V_w} \quad \text{Ans.}$$

Scan for Video Explanation

Web Reference at www.physicsgalaxy.com

Module-9: Solved Example-7

Ex : A river flows at 20 m/s in which a swimmer jumps from one bank of river who can swim at 10 m/s relative to water. Find the direction from normal to bank of river at which he should swim so as to minimize his drift along river flow.

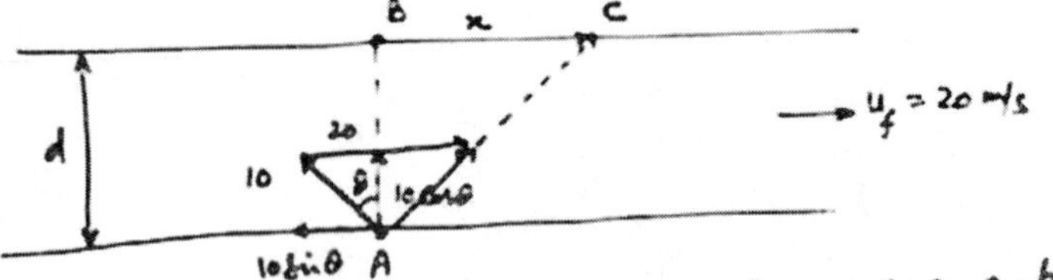

$V_c = 10\cos\theta$

$V_D = 20 - 10\sin\theta$

drift $x = (20 - 10\sin\theta)\frac{d}{10\cos\theta} = (2\sec\theta - \tan\theta)d$

x will be min when $\frac{dx}{d\theta} = 0$; $\frac{dx}{d\theta} = 2\sec\theta\tan\theta - \sec^2\theta = 0$

$\sec\theta[2\tan\theta - \sec\theta] = 0$

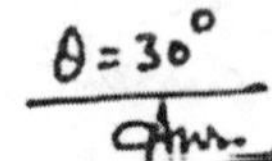

$\Leftarrow \sin\theta = 1/2$

Scan for Video Explanation

Web Reference at www.physicsgalaxy.com

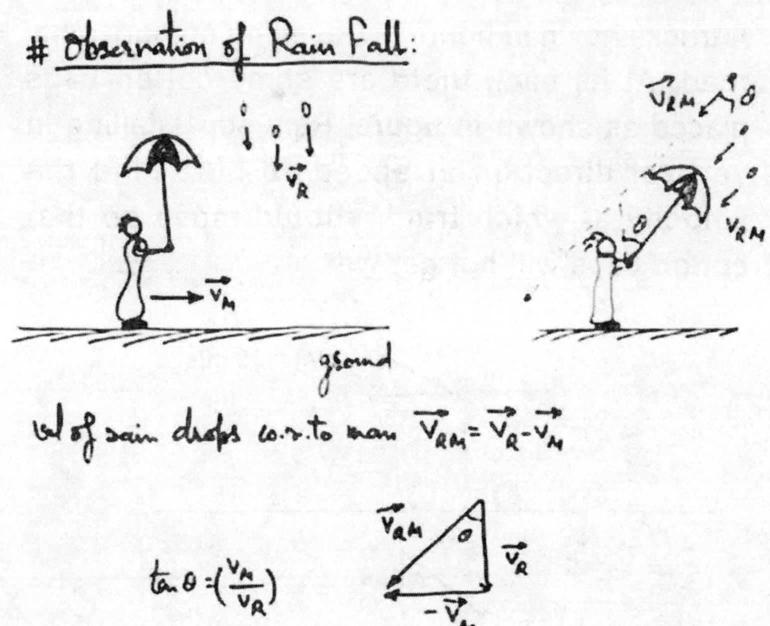

Web Reference at www.physicsgalaxy.com

Scan for Video Explanation

Module-10: Rain Fall Cases

Ex : A man is standing on ground with an umbrella hat as shown. Suddenly rain fall starts at speed V_R = 20 m/s at an angle 30° with the vertical. Find the speed and direction in which man should start running so as to save himself.

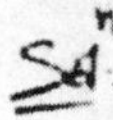

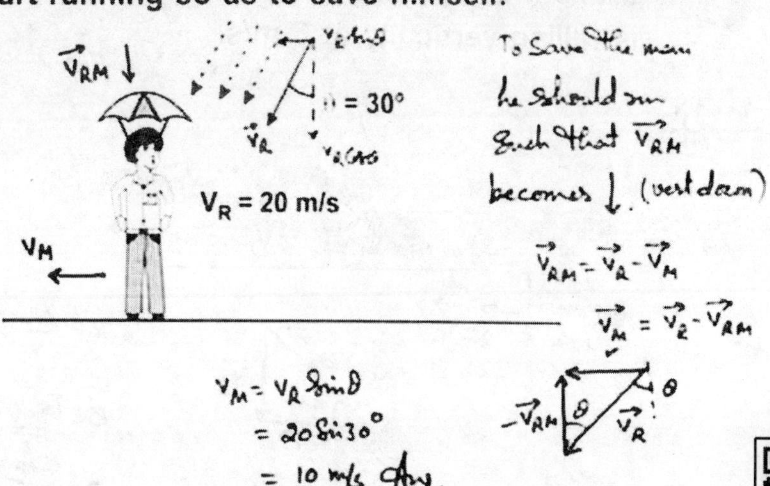

Web Reference at www.physicsgalaxy.com

Scan for Video Explanation

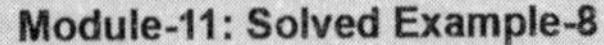

Module-11: Solved Example-8

Ex : A truck shown in figure is travelling on horizontal road. At its back there are some cotton bags placed as shown in figure. Rain starts falling in vertical direction at speed 10 m/s. Find the velocity at which truck should move so that cotton bags will not get wet.

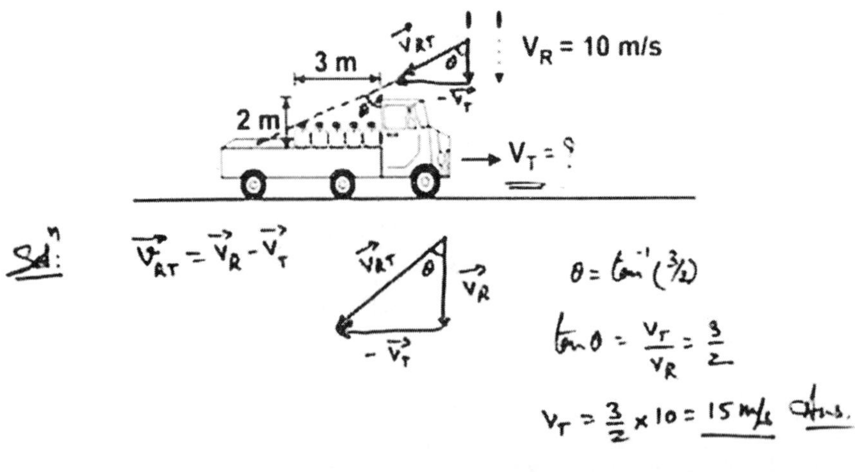

Scan for Video Explanation

Web Reference at www.physicsgalaxy.com

Module-12: Solved Example-9

Ex : A pipe which can rotate in vertical plane is mounted on a cart as shown. The cart travels along the horizontal path at 2 m/s. At what angle α to the horizontal the pipe be placed so that rain drops move parallel to the walls of pipe, if rain is falling vertically at 6 m/s.

Sol^n:

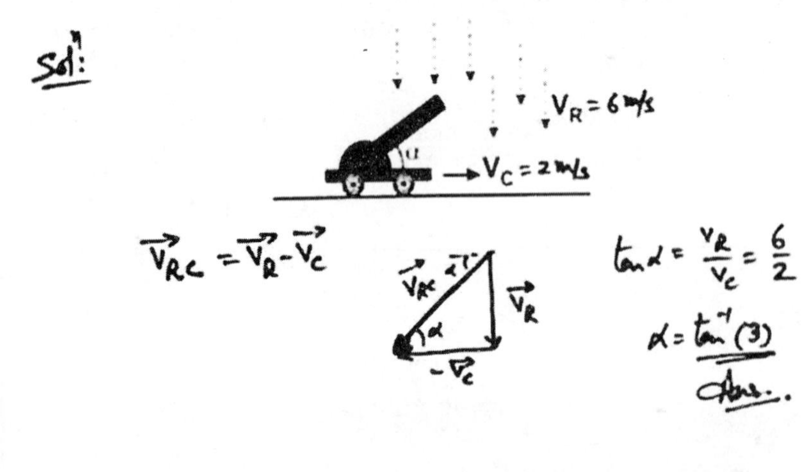

Scan for Video Explanation

Web Reference at www.physicsgalaxy.com

Module-13: Solved Example-10

Ex : **A man wearing a hat of extended length 12 cm is running in rain falling vertically down at 10 m/s. Find the maximum speed with which he can run so that rain drops does not fall on his face as shown.**

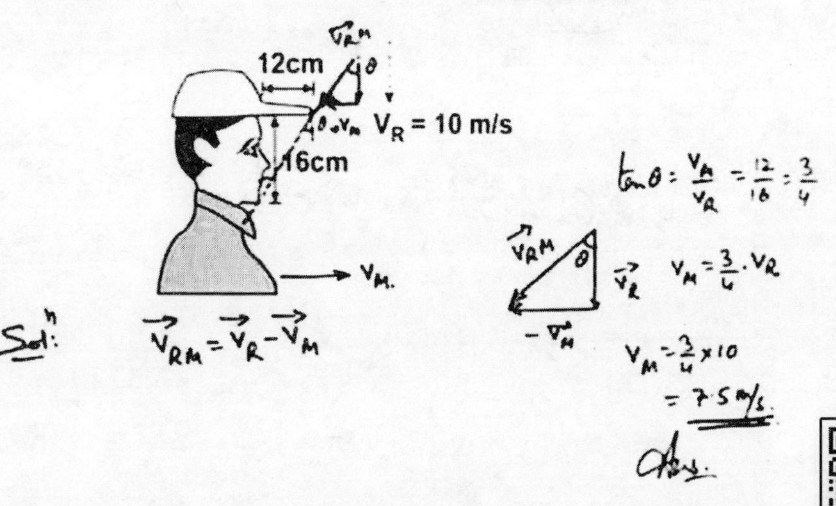

Module-14: Condition of Collision of Two Particle

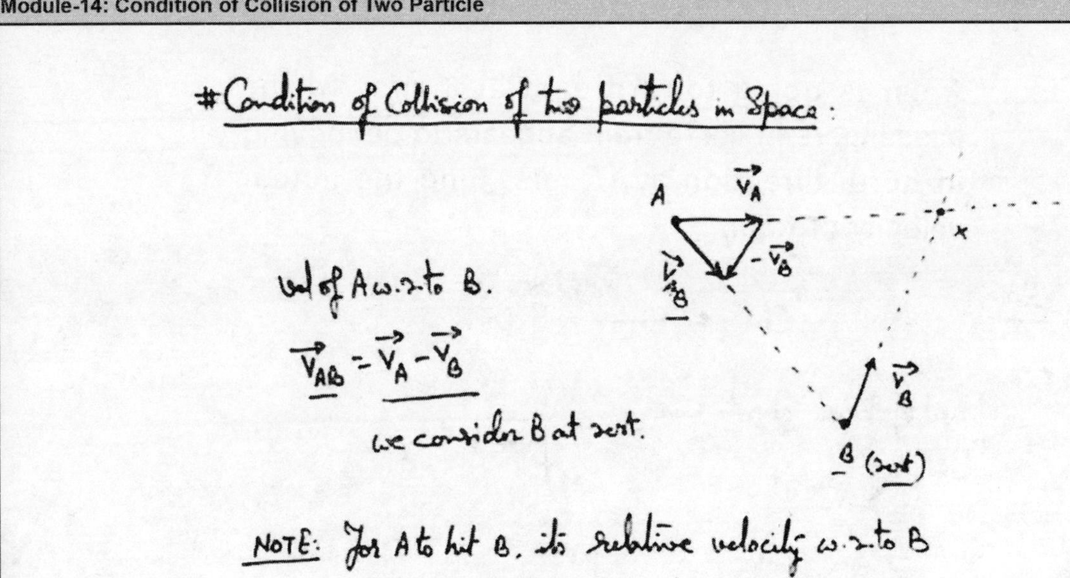

NOTE: For A to hit B, its relative velocity w.r.to B must be directed along line joining A to B.

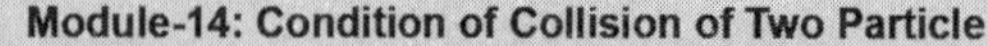

Module-14: Condition of Collision of Two Particle

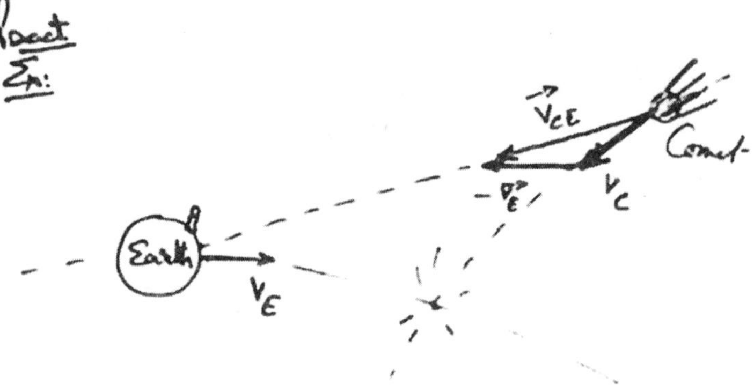

Scan for Video Explanation

Web Reference at www.physicsgalaxy.com

Module-15: Solved Example-11

Ex : A car is going toward east at 8 m/s. To the passengers in car, a train appears to be moving in north direction at 15 m/s. Find the actual velocity of train.

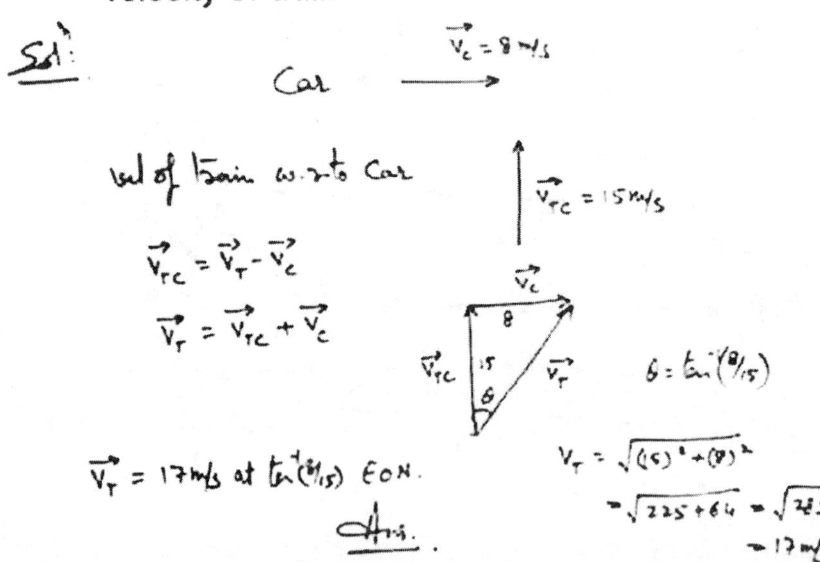

Scan for Video Explanation

Web Reference at www.physicsgalaxy.com

Module-16: Solved Example-12

Ex : A helicopter is flying toward south at 50 kph. A train is moving with same speed toward east. Find velocity of helicopter as seen by passengers in train.

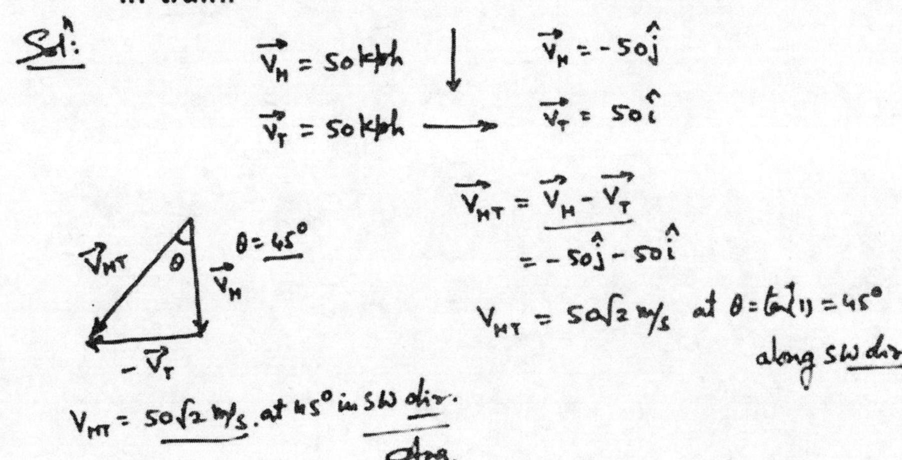

Web Reference at www.physicsgalaxy.com | Scan for Video Explanation

Module-17: Solved Example-13

Ex : An airplane flies toward west at 240 kph and after 1 Hr it is at a position which is 300 km west and 80 km south from its starting point. Find the wind speed and its direction.

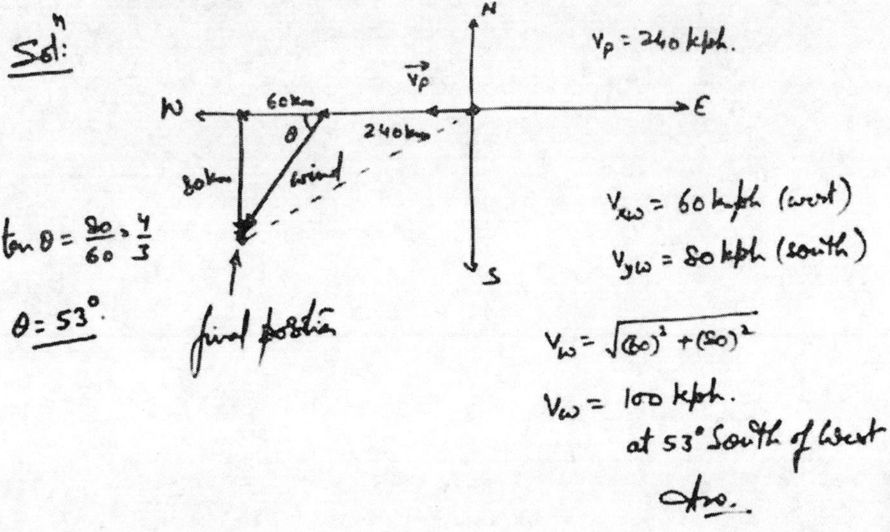

Web Reference at www.physicsgalaxy.com | Scan for Video Explanation

Chapter 4
Constrained Motion

Lecture Notes Modules

Module-1: Constrained Motion

Constrained Motion:

Motion of a body restricted under some physical conditions or governed by some mathematical rules is called Constrained Motion

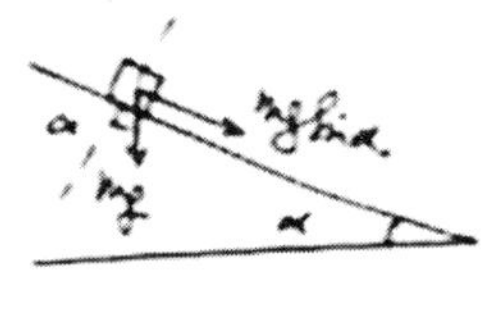

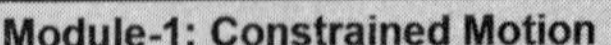

Scan for Video Explanation

Web Reference at www.physicsgalaxy.com

Module-1: Constrained Motion

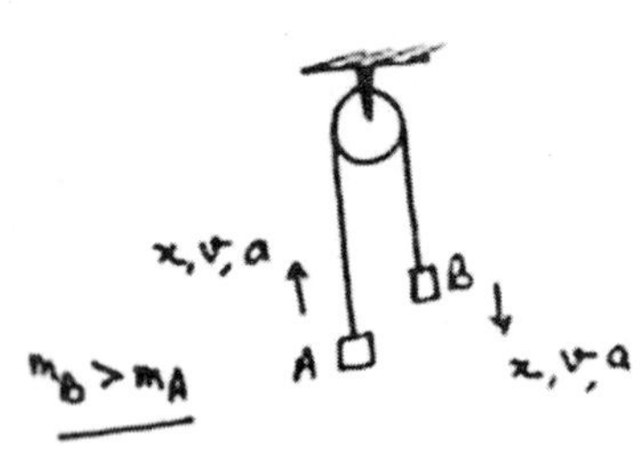

$m_B > m_A$

blocks A & B are Constrained to move with same speed & same acc^n mag.

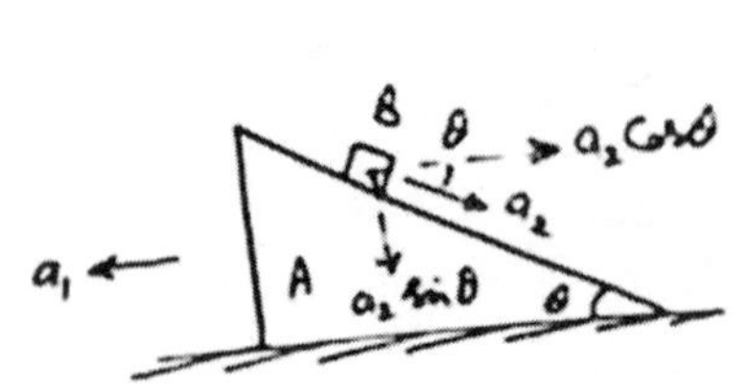

Block B is Constrained to move on Surface of A.

for B.

in x dir $a_x = a_2 \cos\theta - a_1$

$a_y = a_2 \sin\theta$.

net acc^n of block B $a_B = \sqrt{a_x^2 + a_y^2} = ---$

Scan for Video Explanation

Web Reference at www.physicsgalaxy.com

Module-1: Constrained Motion

Constrained Relations:

Mathematical relations by which motion of two or more bodies are related, are called Constraind Relations.

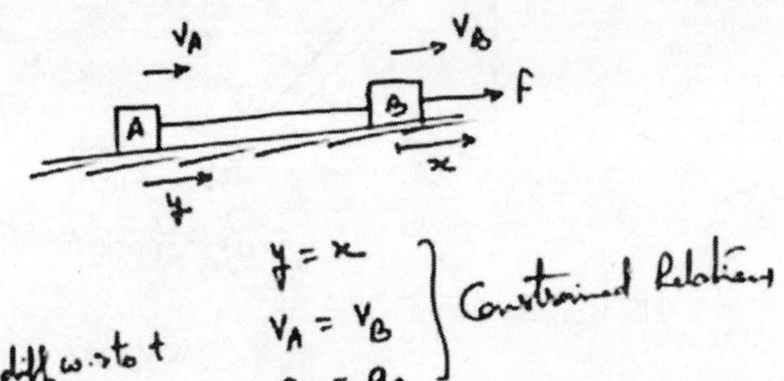

$$y = x$$

diff w.r.to t

$$v_A = v_B$$

$$a_A = a_B$$

} Constrained Relations

NOTE: To develop Constrained rel of vel & accⁿ try to relate displacement of bodies & diff w.r.to time.

Web Reference at www.physicsgalaxy.com

Scan for Video Explanation

Module-2: Solved Example-1

Ex : **Find velocity of end A when rod is inclined at θ with horizontal.**

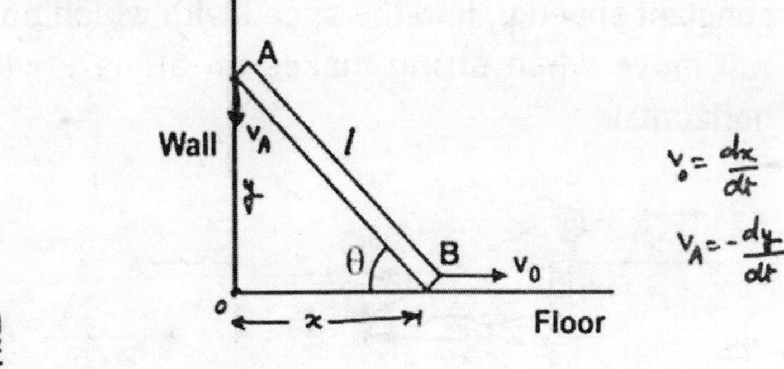

$v_0 = \frac{dx}{dt}$

$v_A = -\frac{dy}{dt}$

Sol:

rel in x in y $\quad x^2 + y^2 = l^2$

diff w.r.to t $\quad 2x\frac{dx}{dt} + 2y\frac{dy}{dt} = 0$

$$x v_0 - y v_A = 0 \Rightarrow v_A = \frac{x}{y} v_0$$

$$v_A = v_0 \cot\theta \quad \text{Ans.}$$

Web Reference at www.physicsgalaxy.com

Scan for Video Explanation

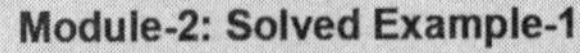

Module-2: Solved Example-1

Alternative method :

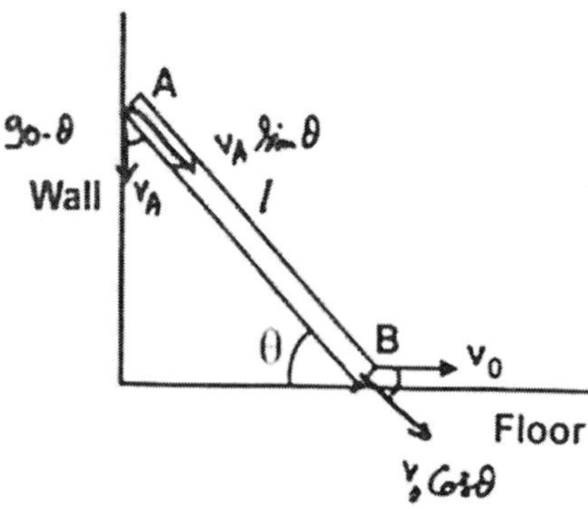

For l to be constant

$$v_A \sin\theta = v_0 \cos\theta$$

$$v_A = v_0 \cot\theta \quad \text{Ans.}$$

v. imp.

NOTE: For two pts, if their separation is constant then during motion their velocity components along the line joining these pts always remain equal.

Scan for Video Explanation

Web Reference at www.physicsgalaxy.com

Module-3: Solved Example-2

Ex : A toy boat in a swimming pool is pulled by a boy by a string as shown. If boy pulls the string at a constant speed u, find the speed with which boat will move when string makes an angle θ with horizontal.

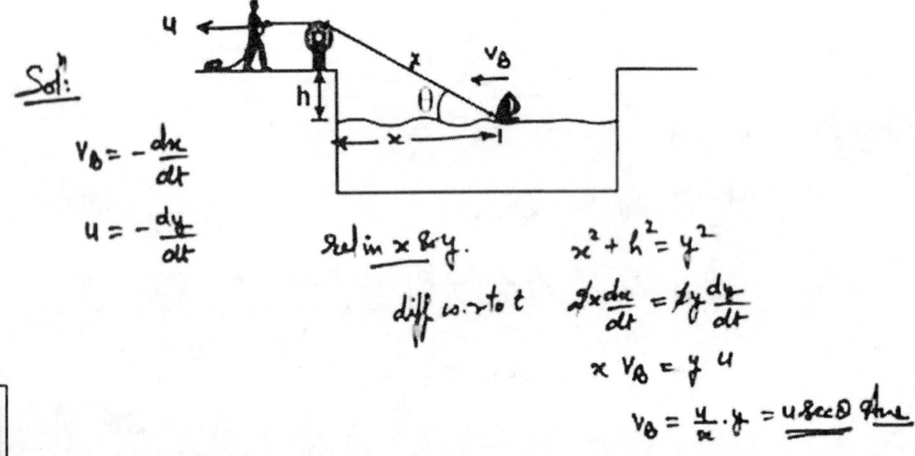

Sol^n:

$$v_B = -\frac{dx}{dt}$$

$$u = -\frac{dy}{dt}$$

Rel in x & y. $\quad x^2 + h^2 = y^2$

diff w.r.t. t $\quad 2x\frac{dx}{dt} = 2y\frac{dy}{dt}$

$$x v_B = y u$$

$$v_B = \frac{u}{x} \cdot y = u\sec\theta \quad \text{Ans.}$$

Scan for Video Explanation

Web Reference at www.physicsgalaxy.com

Module-3: Solved Example-2

Alternative method :

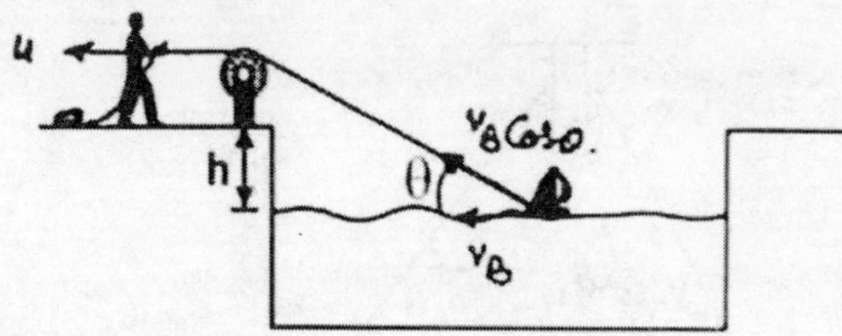

for strig to remain tight $u = v_B \cos\theta$

$v_B = u \sec\theta$. Ans.

NOTE: For an inextensible strig always velocity Components of all points on strig along its length Remain same (equal).

Web Reference at www.physicsgalaxy.com Scan for Video Explanation

Module-4: Solved Example-3

Ex : In the system shown in figure block A is pulled toward left at speed v_1, find velocity of block B when string makes an angle θ with horizontal.

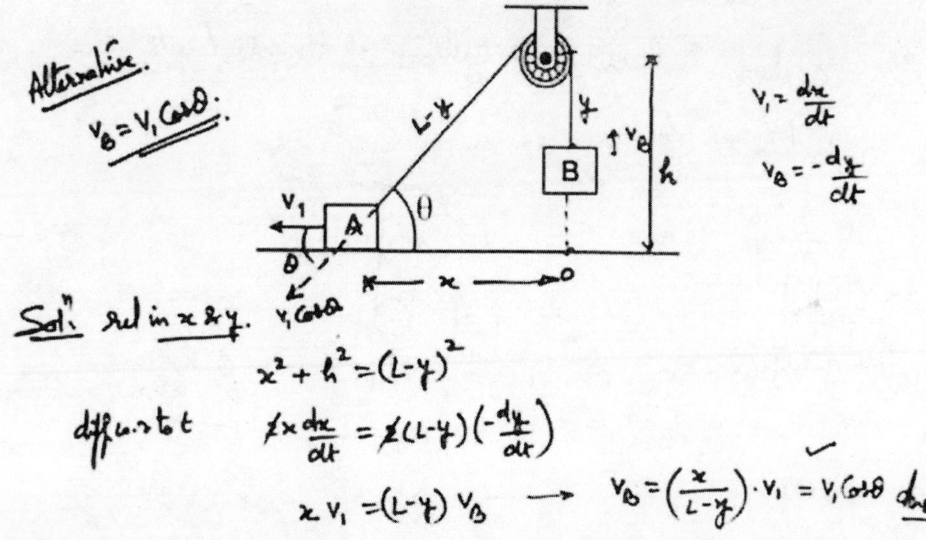

Sol^n rel in x & y.

$$x^2 + h^2 = (L-y)^2$$

diff w.r.t t $\quad 2x\frac{dx}{dt} = 2(L-y)\left(-\frac{dy}{dt}\right)$

$$x v_1 = (L-y)\, v_B \longrightarrow v_B = \left(\frac{x}{L-y}\right)\cdot v_1 = v_1\cos\theta \text{ Ans}$$

Web Reference at www.physicsgalaxy.com Scan for Video Explanation

Module-5: Solved Example-4

Ex : In the system shown in figure. Find velocity of block A, if B is pulled toward right speed v_0.

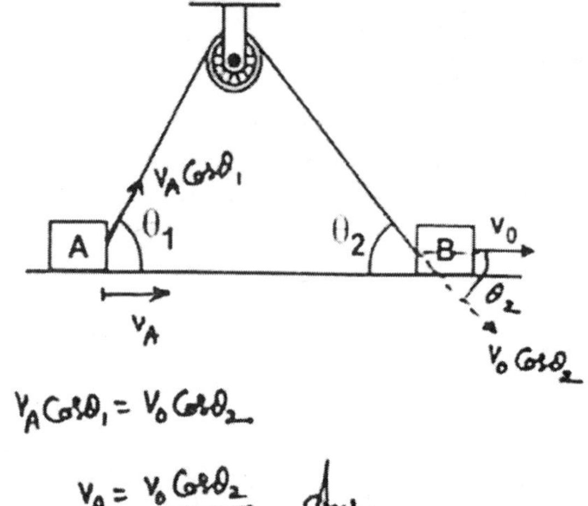

Sol:

$$v_A \cos\theta_1 = v_0 \cos\theta_2$$

$$v_A = \frac{v_0 \cos\theta_2}{\cos\theta_1} \quad \text{Ans.}$$

Scan for Video Explanation

Web Reference at www.physicsgalaxy.com

Module-6: Simple Pulley Constrained Motion

Simple Pulley-Block Constrained Relations:

In pulley system there are developed by analyzing loosing & tighting of strings due to motion of blocks.

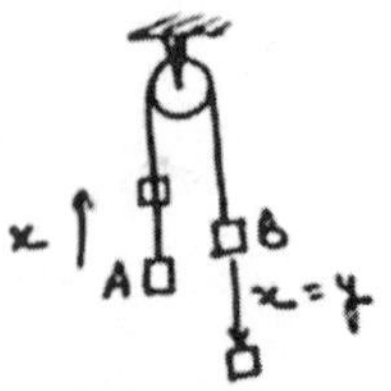

x ↑ A B ↓ $x = y$

$y = x$

$v_B = v_A$

$a_B = a_A$

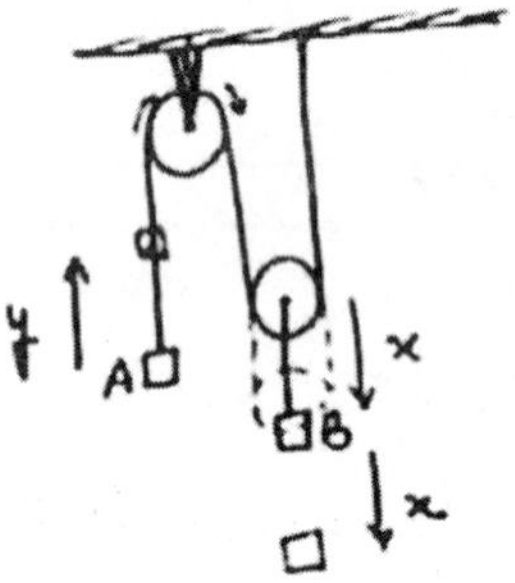

y ↑ A B ↓ x

$y = 2x$

$v_A = 2v_B$

$a_A = 2a_B$

Scan for Video Explanation

Web Reference at www.physicsgalaxy.com

Module-6: Simple Pulley Constrained Motion

Ex : In the system shown in figure, if block A moves upward at 3 m/s, find speed of block B.

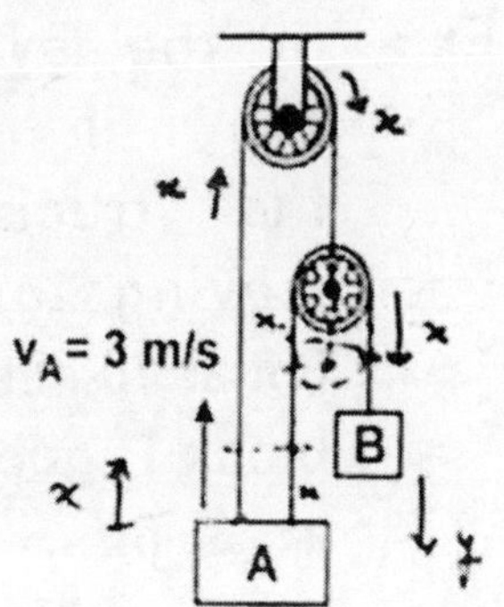

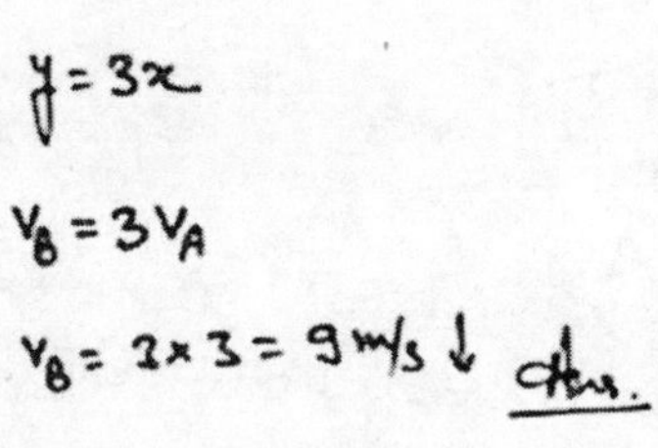

Web Reference at www.physicsgalaxy.com

Scan for Video Explanation

Module-7: Solved Example-5

Ex : In the system shown in figure find speed of block C.

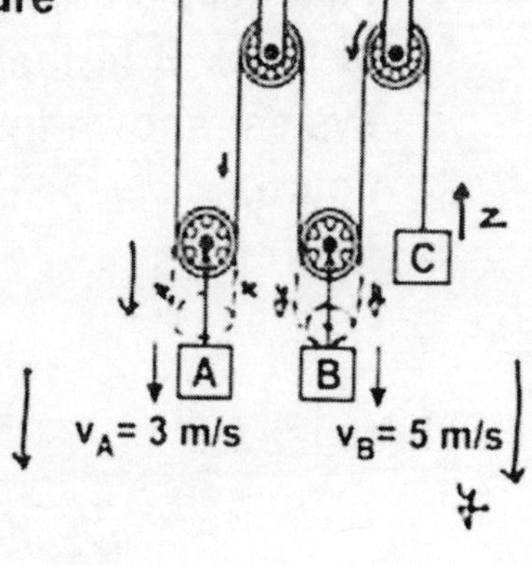

$$z = 2x + 2y$$

$$V_C = 2V_A + 2V_B$$

$$= 2\times 3 + 2\times 5$$

$$= 16 \text{ m/s} \uparrow \text{ Ans.}$$

Web Reference at www.physicsgalaxy.com

Scan for Video Explanation

Module-8: Solved Example-6

Ex : In the system shown in figure, the truck is moving toward left at 10 m/s and block P goes up at 3 m/s. Find speed of block Q.

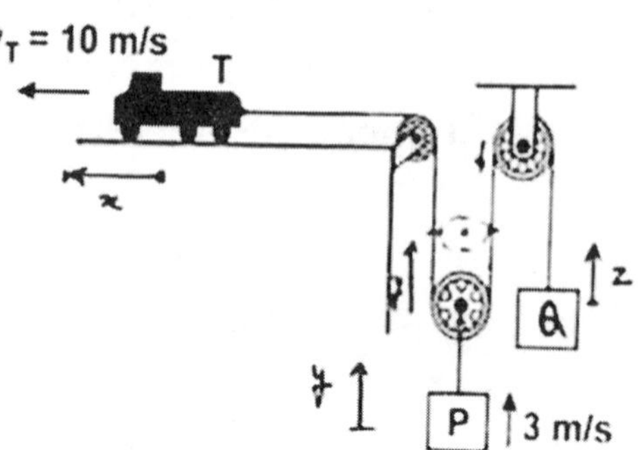

Sol:

$$x = 2y + z$$

$$v_T = 2v_P + v_Q$$

$$v_Q = v_T - 2v_P$$

$$= 10 - 6 = 4 \text{ m/s} \uparrow \quad \text{Ans.}$$

Scan for Video Explanation

Web Reference at www.physicsgalaxy.com

Module-9: Solved Example-7

Ex : Find acceleration of block B in the system shown in figure.

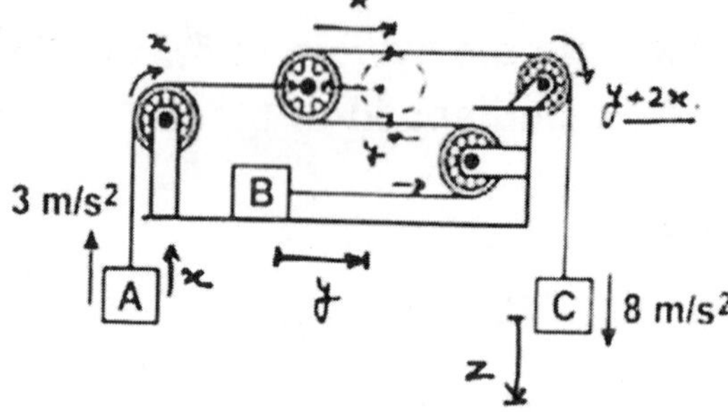

Sol:

$$z = 2x + y$$

$$a_C = 2a_A + a_B$$

$$a_B = a_C - 2a_A$$

$$a_B = 8 - 6 = 2 \text{ m/s}^2 \rightarrow \quad \text{Ans.}$$

Scan for Video Explanation

Web Reference at www.physicsgalaxy.com

Module-10: Wedge Constrained Motion

Wedge Constrained Motion:

Whenever a body moves over another body under some constrained rules then such motion are called Wedge Constrained Motions.

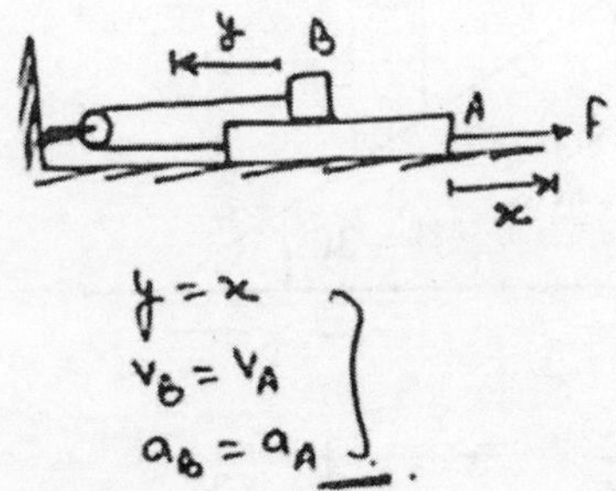

$$y = x$$
$$v_B = v_A$$
$$a_B = a_A$$

Scan for Video Explanation

Module-10: Wedge Constrained Motion

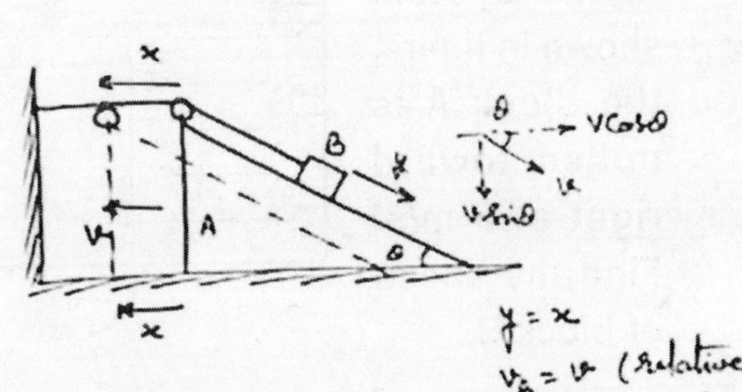

$y = x$

$v_B = v$ (Relative to wedge A)

For B. $v_x = v - v\cos\theta$

$v_y = v\sin\theta$

$$v_B = \sqrt{v_x^2 + v_y^2} = \sqrt{v^2(1-\cos\theta)^2 + v^2\sin^2\theta}$$
$$= \sqrt{v^2 + v^2 - 2v^2\cos\theta}$$
$$= \sqrt{v^2}\sqrt{2 - 2\cos\theta}$$
$$= 2v\sin\theta/2$$

Scan for Video Explanation

Module-11: Solved Example-8

Ex : **In the system shown in figure, the block A moves toward left at 2 m/s^2, find acceleration of rod B which is constrained to move vertically over the wedge.**

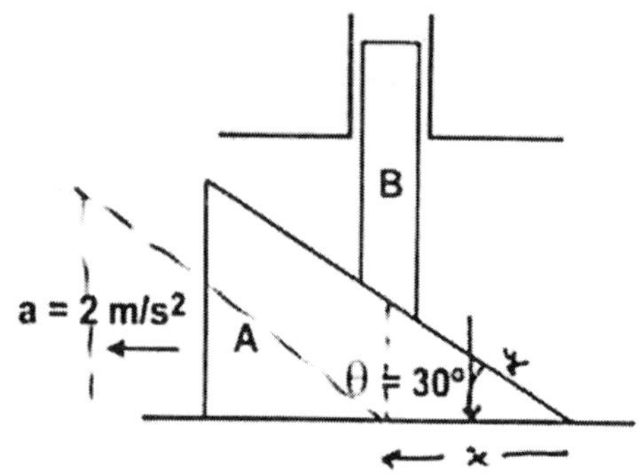

$$\tan 30^\circ = \frac{y}{x} \Rightarrow y = \frac{x}{\sqrt{3}}$$

$$a_B = \frac{a_A}{\sqrt{3}} = \frac{2}{\sqrt{3}} \text{ m/s}^2 \text{ Ans.}$$

Scan for Video Explanation

Web Reference at www.physicsgalaxy.com

Module-12: Solved Example-9

Ex : **In the system shown in figure, the block A is pulled toward right at 5 m/s. Find the speed of block B.**

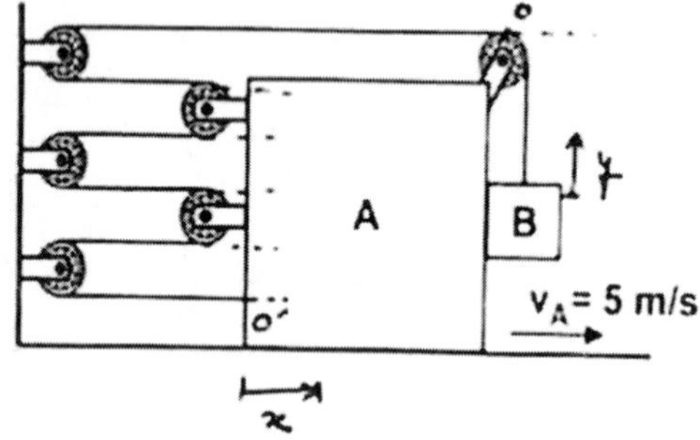

$$y = 6x$$

$$v_{By} = 6v_A = 6 \times 5 = 30 \text{ m/s}$$

$$v_{Bx} = 5 \text{ m/s}$$

$$v_B = \sqrt{v_{Bx}^2 + v_{By}^2} = \sqrt{25 + 900}$$

$$v_B = \sqrt{925} \text{ m/s Ans.}$$

Scan for Video Explanation

Web Reference at www.physicsgalaxy.com

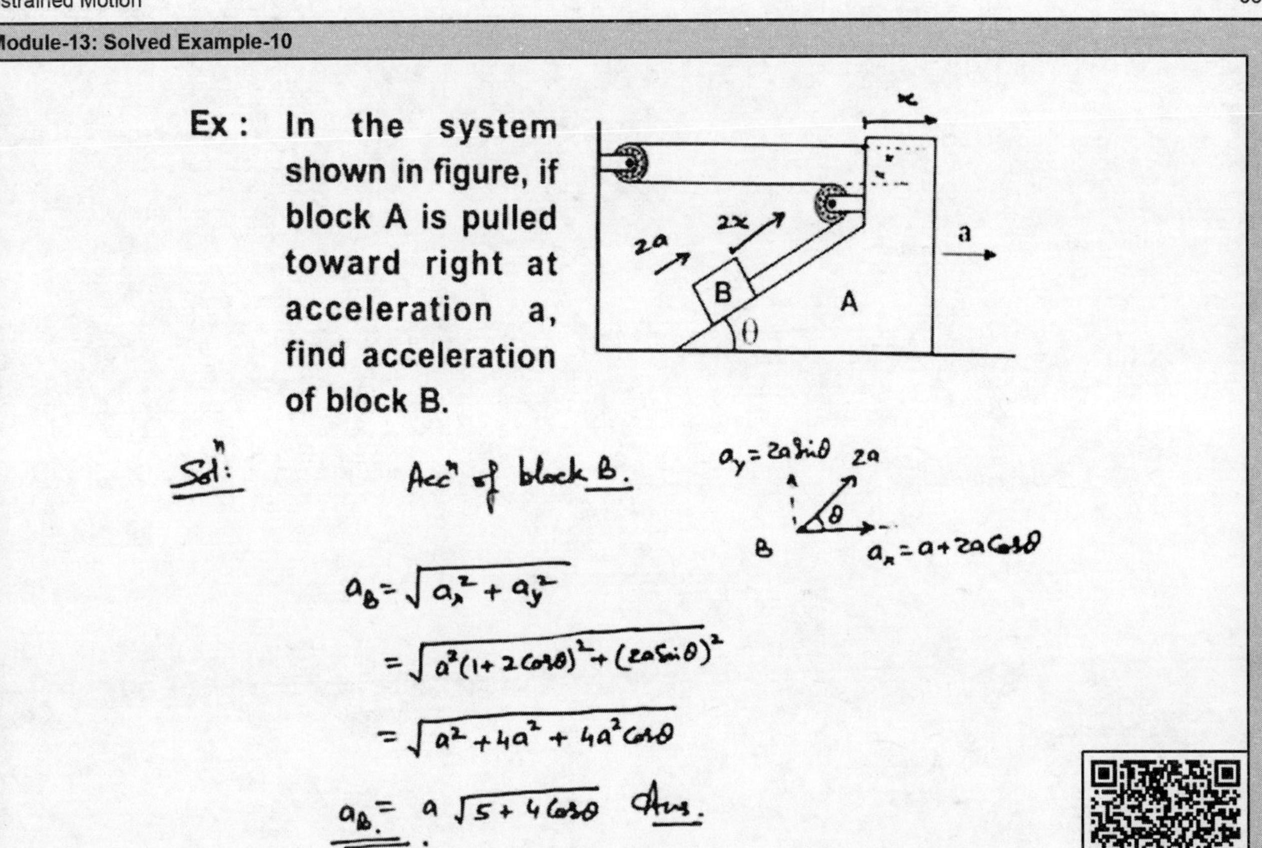
Module-13: Solved Example-10
Ex : In the system shown in figure, if block A is pulled toward right at acceleration a, find acceleration of block B.
x
2x
2a
a
B
A
θ
Solⁿ:
Accⁿ of block B.
a_y = 2a sinθ
2a
θ
B
a_x = a + 2a cosθ
a_B = √(a_x² + a_y²)
= √(a²(1 + 2cosθ)² + (2a sinθ)²)
= √(a² + 4a² + 4a² cosθ)
a_B = a √(5 + 4cosθ) Ans.
Web Reference at www.physicsgalaxy.com
Scan for Video Explanation

Chapter 5
Newton's Laws of Motion

Lecture Notes Modules

Module-1: Forces of Nature

Force:

A push or pull which can cause change in state of motion, is called a force.

state of motion → $\vec{v}$ → velocity

Force can change $\vec{v}$ → magnitude / direction

All forces of Nature are classified in 4 fundamental Categories.

Scan for Video Explanation

Web Reference at www.physicsgalaxy.com

Module-1: Forces of Nature

Fundamental Forces of Nature:

(1) Electromagnetic forces
(2) Gravitational forces (weakest)
→ long range forces.

Nuclear range forces:
(3) Strong forces
(4) Weak forces
→ Short range force. (appear only at separation $< 10^{-12}$ m / 10^{-15} m)

Scan for Video Explanation

Web Reference at www.physicsgalaxy.com

Module-1: Forces of Nature

Relative Strength of Fundamental forces.

For a given pair of particles at short range

(1) Grav. force → reference.

(2) Weak forces → 10^{25} times stronger than grav. forces

(3) Electromagnetic forces → 10^{36} times stronger than grav. force

(4) Strong forces → 10^{38} times stronger than grav. forces.

Scan for Video Explanation

Module-2: Force can Change the State of Motion

Force can change State of Motion:

↓ $\vec{v}$

Force causes acceleration ⇒ change in $\vec{v}$.

$\vec{F}$ → m → $\vec{v}$ — $v\uparrow$ — mag is increasing

$\vec{F}$ ↓ m → $\vec{v}$ — dir of $\vec{v}$ is changing

a parallel force → causes change in mag of $\vec{v}$

a normal force → causes change in dir of $\vec{v}$

Scan for Video Explanation

Module-2: Force can Change the State of Motion

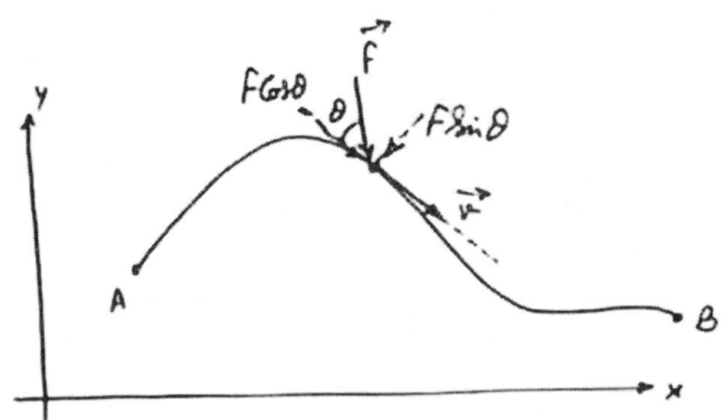

[F Cosθ → responsible for change in mag of $\vec{v}$
F Sinθ → responsible for change in dir of $\vec{v}$]

Scan for Video Explanation

Web Reference at www.physicsgalaxy.com

Module-3: Balanced & Unbalanced Forces

Classification of Group of Forces:

When two or more forces act on a body, then based on its state of motion, these forces are classified in two categories.

(1) Balanced Forces: $\Sigma\vec{F}=0 \Rightarrow \vec{a}=0$, $\vec{v}$ = Constant < rest / uniform motion

↓ Equilibrium

(2) Unbalanced Forces: $\Sigma\vec{F}\neq 0$

accelerated motion $\vec{a}=\left(\frac{\Sigma\vec{F}}{m}\right)$

$\vec{v}$ changes.

Scan for Video Explanation

Web Reference at www.physicsgalaxy.com

Module-3: Balanced & Unbalanced Forces

Static Equilibrium:

When under the action of two or more forces a body is at rest then it is said to be in 'Static Equilibrium'

$$\Sigma \vec{F} = 0.$$

F_1 ← rest → F_2 ⇒ $F_1 = F_2$

rest, F, mg: $F = mg.$

Web Reference at www.physicsgalaxy.com | Scan for Video Explanation

Module-3: Balanced & Unbalanced Forces

When a body is under the state of Equilibrium in the influence of 3 forces then these forces must successively represent the sides of a triangle.

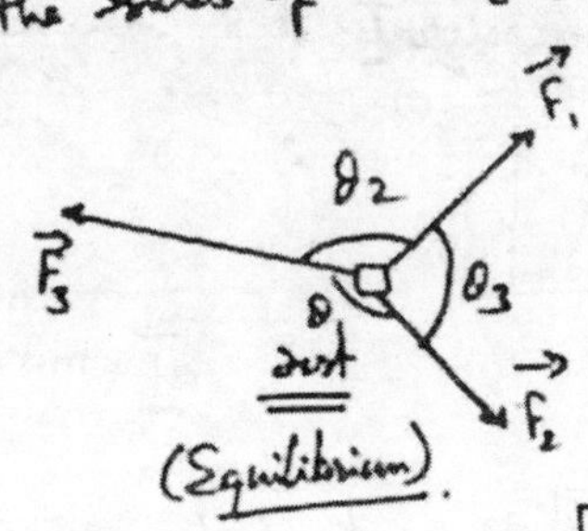

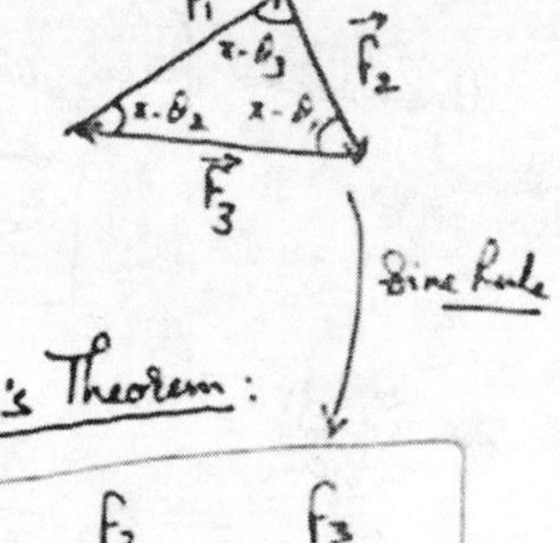

Lami's Theorem:

$$\frac{F_1}{\sin\theta_1} = \frac{F_2}{\sin\theta_2} = \frac{F_3}{\sin\theta_3}$$

Web Reference at www.physicsgalaxy.com | Scan for Video Explanation

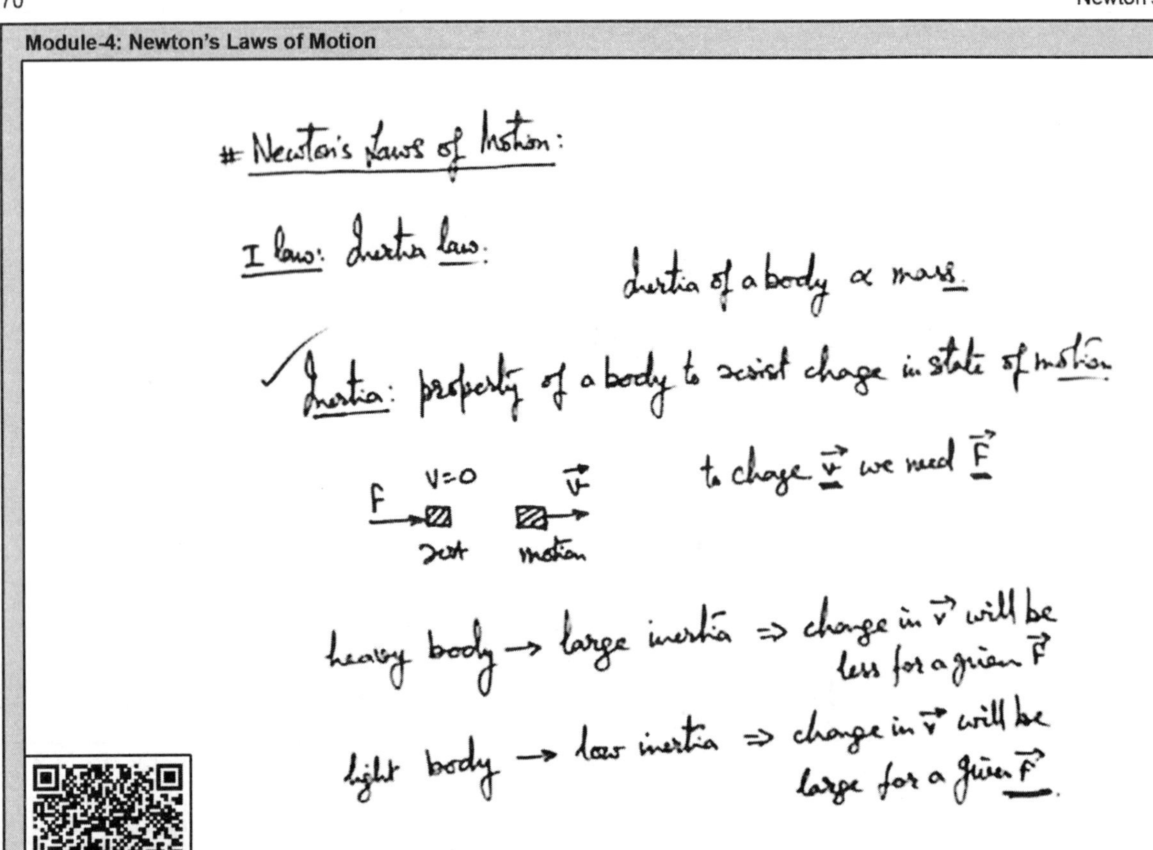

Module-4: Newton's Laws of Motion

Newton's Laws of Motion:

I law: Inertia law:

Inertia of a body $\propto$ mass.

Inertia: property of a body to resist change in state of motion

to change $\vec{v}$ we need $\vec{F}$

heavy body → large inertia ⇒ change in $\vec{v}$ will be less for a given $\vec{F}$

light body → low inertia ⇒ change in $\vec{v}$ will be large for a given $\vec{F}$.

Scan for Video Explanation

Web Reference at www.physicsgalaxy.com

Module-4: Newton's Laws of Motion

II law: law of unbalanced forces.

Force causes acceleration

Unbalanced forces on a body accelerates it & we use

$$\boxed{\Sigma \vec{F} = m\vec{a}}$$

$\vec{a} = \frac{d\vec{v}}{dt}$ $\qquad \Sigma \vec{F} = m\frac{d\vec{v}}{dt}$ $\qquad d\vec{p} = m\,d\vec{v}$

$$\boxed{\Sigma \vec{F} = \frac{d\vec{p}}{dt}}$$ ← rate of change of momentum.

Scan for Video Explanation

Web Reference at www.physicsgalaxy.com

Module-4: Newton's Laws of Motion

III law: Law of Actions & Reaction

✓ → Force always act in pairs
↓
Whenever a force is applied, always there exist an equal & opposite Reaction

$$\left[\begin{array}{l} |\vec{F_1}| = |\vec{F_2}| \\ \vec{F_1} = -\vec{F_2} \end{array}\right]$$

✓ → Action & Reaction are always equal & opposite

✓ → Action & Reaction both always act on different bodies.

Web Reference at www.physicsgalaxy.com | Scan for Video Explanation

Module-4: Newton's Laws of Motion

Commonly used Forces in Mechanics:

In study of Rest & Motion most Commonly used forces are –

Electromagnetic in Nature ← { (1) Normal Reaction at Contacts (N)
(2) Tension in a String (T) }

Web Reference at www.physicsgalaxy.com | Scan for Video Explanation

Module-5: Free Body Diagram

Free Body Diagram: (FBD)

A diagram showing all forces acting on a body using arrows, considering body as a point mass, is called FBD of body.

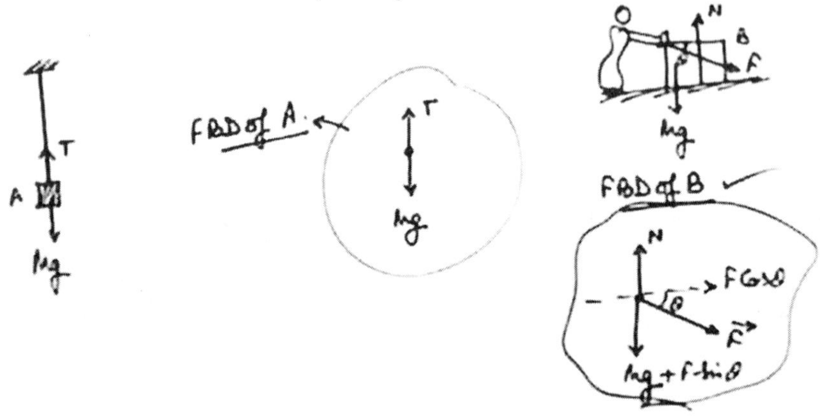

FBD of A

T

A

Mg

FBD of B

N

B

F

$F\cos\theta$

θ

$\vec{F}$

$Mg + F\sin\theta$

Scan for Video Explanation

Web Reference at www.physicsgalaxy.com

Module-6: Normal Reaction

Normal Reaction:

→ It is a force which exist when two bodies are in contact and one pushes the other.

→ It always act in the direction normal to the surfaces in contact.

N

N

Mg

FBD of body

N

Mg

Scan for Video Explanation

Web Reference at www.physicsgalaxy.com

Module-6: Normal Reaction

Ex : Show all forces acting on the block & rod in their free body diagrams.

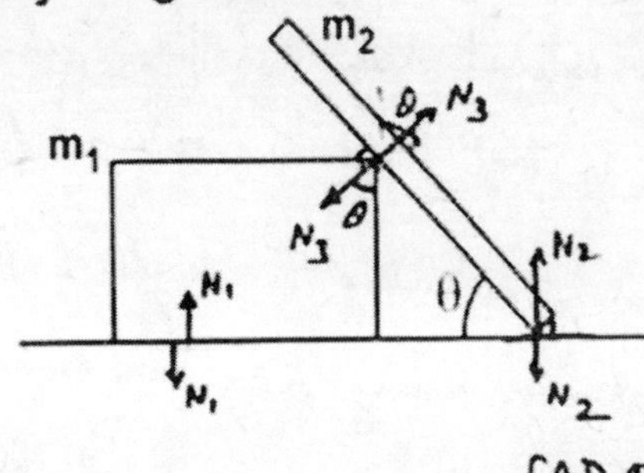

FBD of m_1

N_1

$N_3 \sin\theta$

N_3

$m_1 g + N_3 \cos\theta$

FBD of m_2

$N_2 + N_3 \cos\theta$

N_3

$N_3 \sin\theta$

$m_2 g$

Scan for Video Explanation

Module-6: Normal Reaction

NOTE: In case of a circular, Spherical or cylindrical object, normal reaction always pass through the centre of object.

FBD of cylinder

$N_1 + N_2 \sin\theta$

N_2

T

$N_2 \cos\theta$

mg

FBD of ball

N_1

N_2

mg

Scan for Video Explanation

Module-7: Tension in String

Tension in a String:

It is an internal molecular force which appear in a string when it is taut by some external force.

→ force of tension always act along the length of string
→ dir of tension is always away from tied ends or pts of contact of string
→ tension always has pulling tendency.
→ In an ideal string (↓ massless & frictionless) always, throughout its length the tension remains constant.

Scan for Video Explanation

Web Reference at www.physicsgalaxy.com

Module-7: Tension in String

Ex : **Draw free body diagram of all blocks shown in figure.**

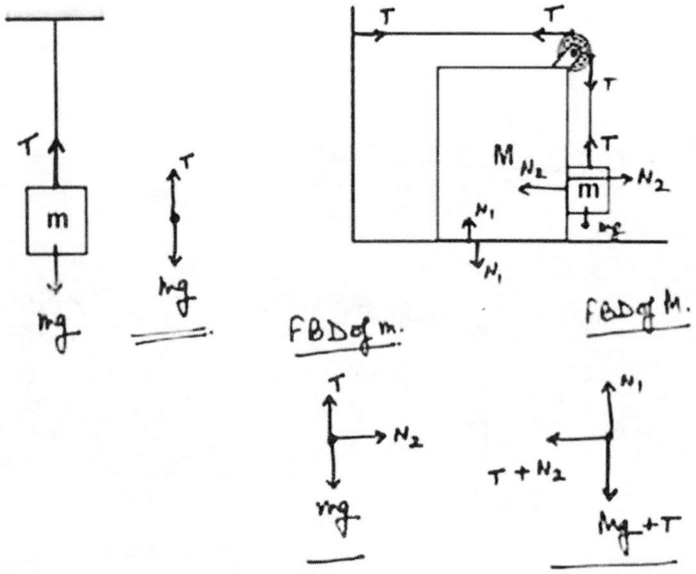

T, m, mg, T, mg

T, T, T, T, M, N_2, m, N_2, N_1, mg, N_1

FBD of m.

T, N_2, mg

FBD of M.

N_1, $T + N_2$, $Mg + T$

Scan for Video Explanation

Web Reference at www.physicsgalaxy.com

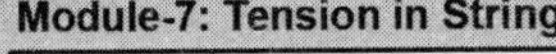

Module-7: Tension in String

Ex : Draw free body diagram of all blocks shown in figure.

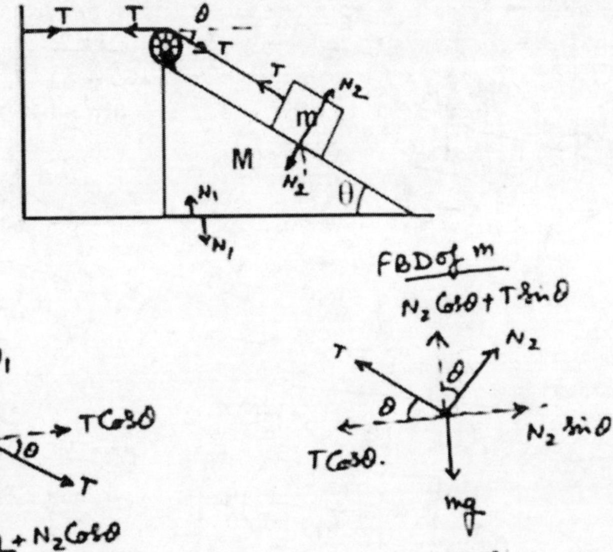

Module-7: Tension in String

Ex : Draw free body diagram of all blocks shown in figure.

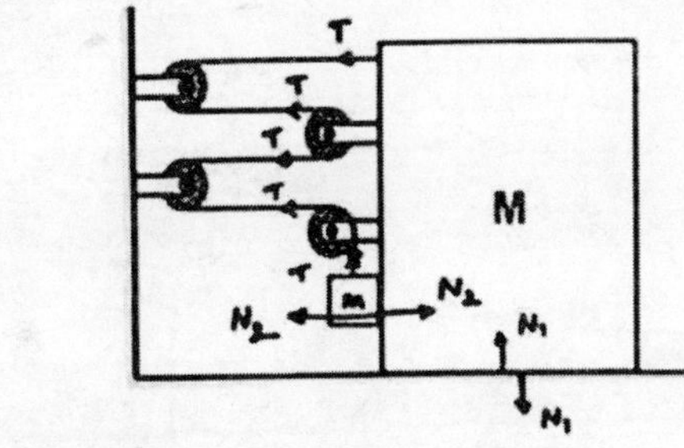

Sol^n:

FBD of M.

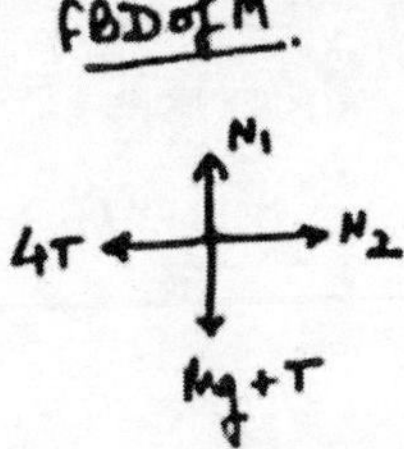

FBD of m

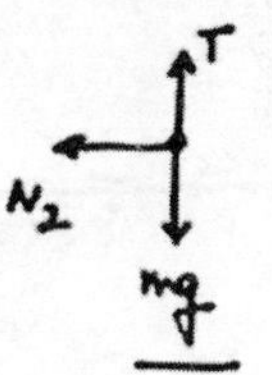

Module-8: Applications of Newton's Second Law

Applications of Newton's Second Law:

$$\Sigma \vec{F} = m\vec{a}$$

Working of Atwood's machine:

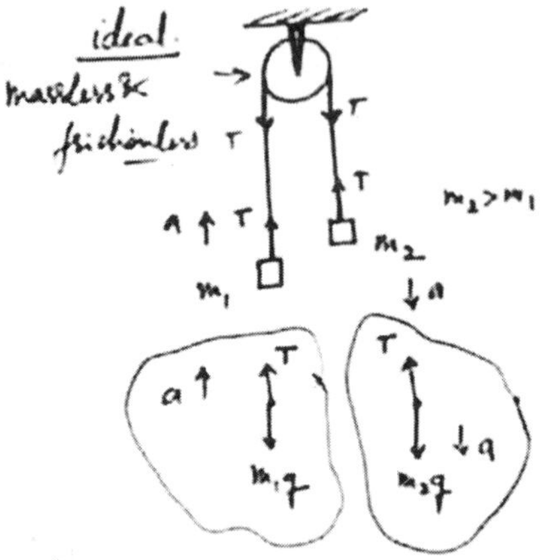

ideal massless & frictionless

$m_2 > m_1$

Eqⁿ of motion of m_1 and m_2.

$$T - m_1 g = m_1 a \quad \text{—(1)}$$

$$m_2 g - T = m_2 a \quad \text{—(2)}$$

$$(m_2 - m_1) g = (m_1 + m_2) a$$

v. imp.

$$a = \left(\frac{m_2 - m_1}{m_1 + m_2}\right) g$$

from (1)

$$T - m_1 g = m_1 \left(\frac{m_2 - m_1}{m_1 + m_2}\right) g$$

$$T = \left(\frac{m_1 m_2 - m_1^2}{m_1 + m_2}\right) g + m_1 g$$

$$T = \frac{2 m_1 m_2}{m_1 + m_2} g$$

Scan for Video Explanation

Web Reference at www.physicsgalaxy.com

Module-8: Applications of Newton's Second Law

Ex : Find acceleration of blocks when released from rest.

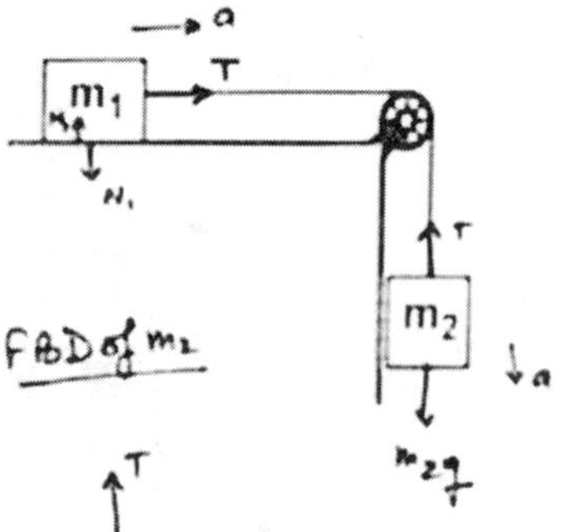

Sol: FBD of m_1 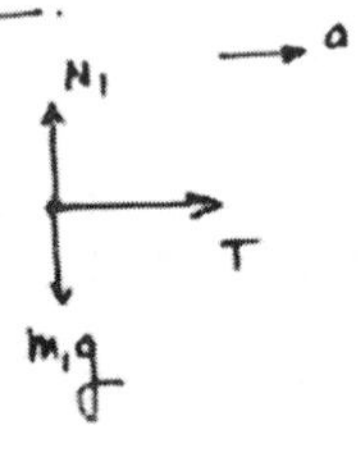 — FBD of m_2

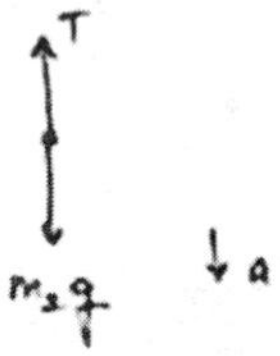

Eqⁿ of motions

$$T = m_1 a \quad \text{—(1)}$$

$$m_2 g - T = m_2 a \quad \text{—(2)}$$

$$(1) + (2) \Rightarrow \quad m_2 g = (m_1 + m_2) a$$

$$a = \frac{m_2 g}{m_1 + m_2} \quad \text{Ans.}$$

Scan for Video Explanation

Web Reference at www.physicsgalaxy.com

Module-8: Applications of Newton's Second Law

Ex : **Find acceleation of m_1 and m_2 in the system shown in figure.**

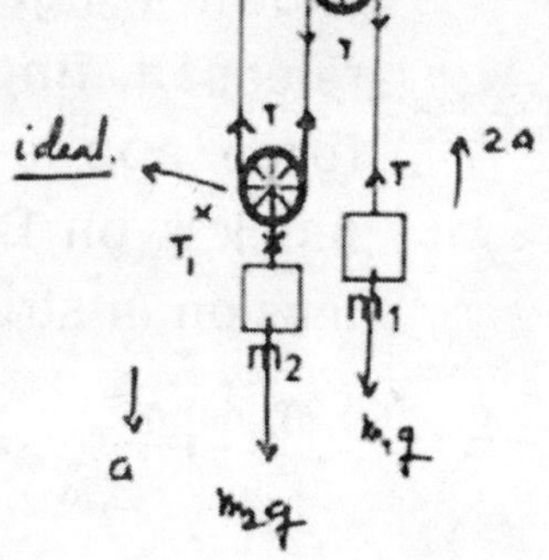

Sol^n:

NOTE: For a massless body, always Sum of all forces acting on it is zero.

$$\Sigma\vec{F} = m\vec{a} = 0$$

for pulley x we use $T_1 = 2T$

eq^n of motions for m_1 & m_2 ⟶

$$T - m_1 g = m_1(2a) \times 2$$

$$m_2 g - 2T = m_2 a$$

$$(m_2 - 2m_1)g = (m_2 + 4m_1)a$$

$a_{m_2} = a \downarrow$

$a_{m_1} = 2a \uparrow$

$$a = \left(\frac{m_2 - 2m_1}{m_2 + 4m_1}\right)g \quad \text{Ans}$$

Web Reference at www.physicsgalaxy.com | Scan for Video Explanation

Module-9: Solved Example-1

Ex : Three blocks A, B and C of masses shown in figure are pulled by applying a force F = 60 N on 6 kg block. During motion find the tensions in string X and Y.

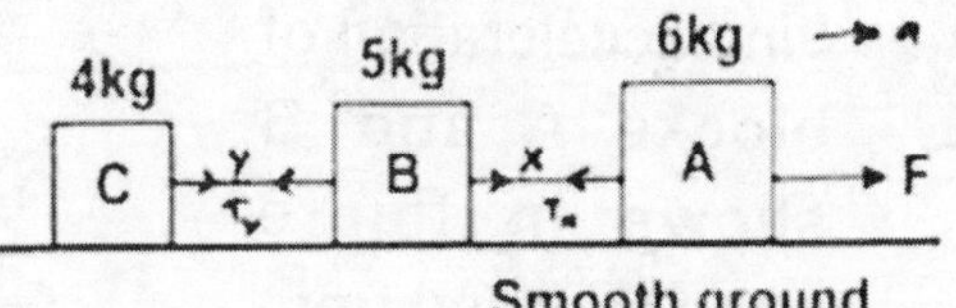

Sol^n: Common acc^n of blocks $a = \frac{F}{M} = \frac{60}{15} = 4\ m/s^2$

FBD of A.

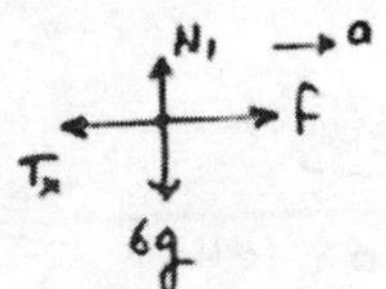

$$F - T_x = 6 \times 4$$

$$F - T_x = 24$$

$$T_x = 60 - 24 = 36\ Nt. \quad \text{Ans}$$

FBD of C

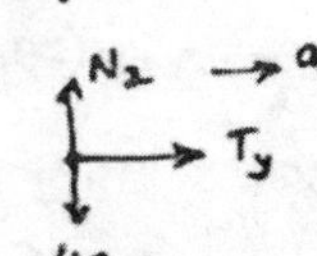

$$T_y = 4 \times 4 = 16\ Nt \quad \text{Ans}$$

Web Reference at www.physicsgalaxy.com | Scan for Video Explanation

Module-10: Solved Example-2

Ex : When the system shown in figure is released, find the force applied by block A on B and tension in string.

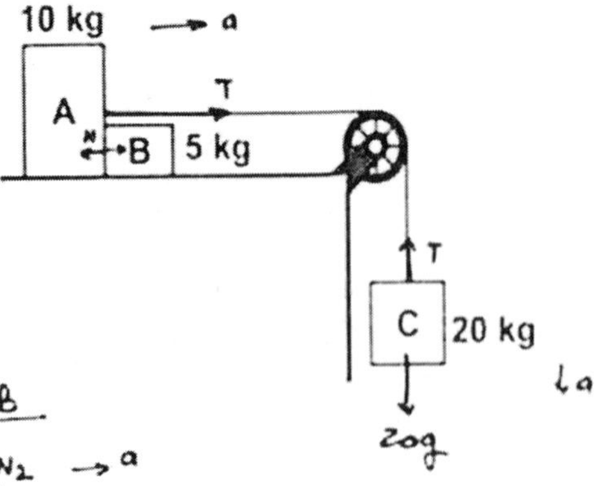

Sol^n: FBD for A; B; C

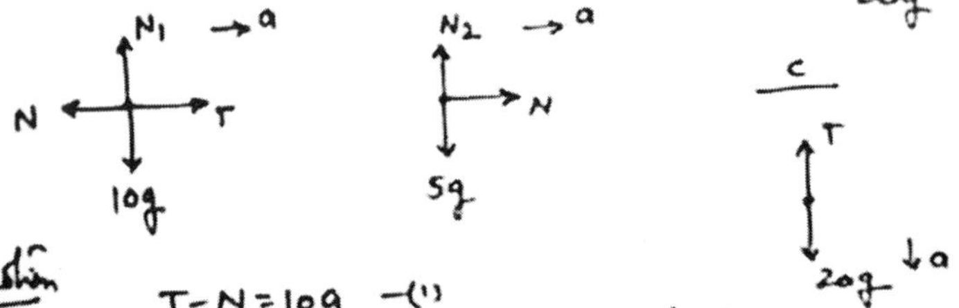

Eq^n of Motion

$T - N = 10a$ —(1)

$N = 5a$ —(2) → $N = 5\left(\frac{4g}{7}\right) = \frac{200}{7}$ Nt Ans.

$20g - T = 20a$ —(3)

$20g = 35a$ → $\left(a = \frac{4g}{7}\right)$

from (1) $T = 10a + N = \frac{400}{7} + \frac{200}{7} = \frac{600}{7}$ Nt Ans.

Scan for Video Explanation

Web Reference at www.physicsgalaxy.com

Module-11: Solved Example-3

Ex : Find acceleration of blocks A and B shown in figure when released from rest.

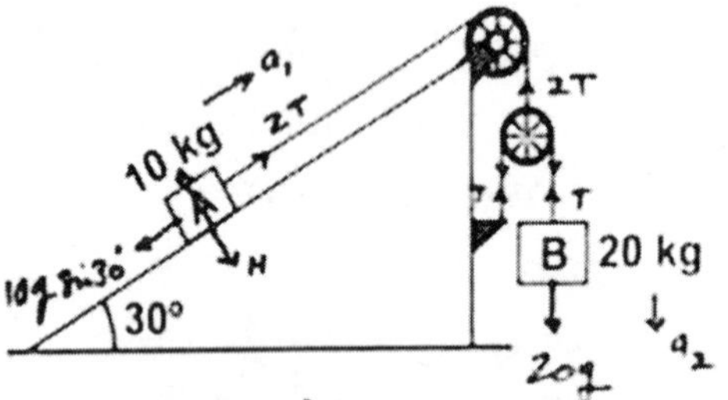

Sol^n: FBD of A. FBD of B

$a_2 = 2a_1$

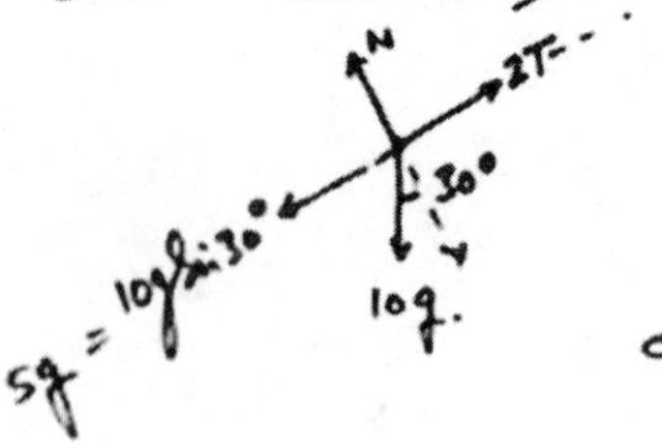

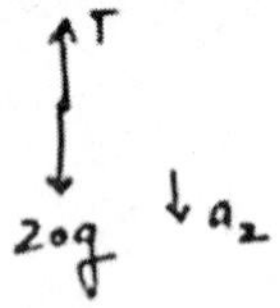

Eq^n of Motion.

$2T - 5g = 10a_1$ —(1)

$20g - T = 20(2a_1)$ —(2)×2

$35g = 90a_1$

$a_1 = \frac{35g}{90} = \frac{35}{9}$ m/s²

$a_A = \frac{35}{9}$ m/s²

$a_B = \frac{70}{9}$ m/s²

Ans.

Scan for Video Explanation

Web Reference at www.physicsgalaxy.com

Module-12: Solved Example-4

Ex : In the system shown in figure if it is released find the acceleration of the rod which is free to move vertically. Given that mass of wedge A is 2 m and that of rod B is m.

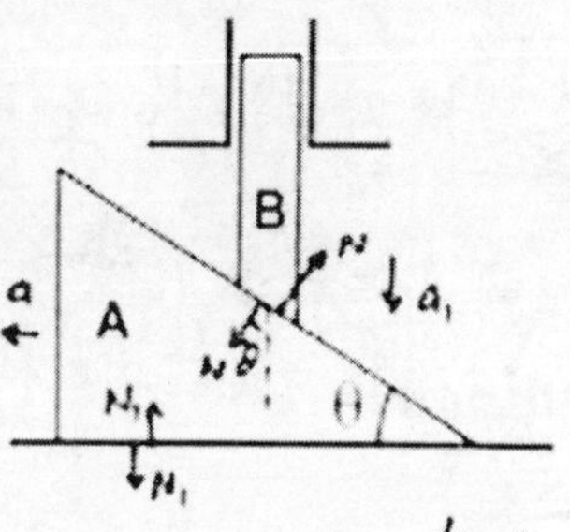

$\underline{a_1 = a\tan\theta}$

Sol^n: FBD of A

a ←, N_1, $N\sin\theta$, θ, N, $2mg + N\cos\theta$

FBD of B

$N\cos\theta$, θ, N, mg, ↓ $a\tan\theta$

$$a_B = \frac{g\tan\theta}{\tan\theta + 2\cot\theta}$$ Ans.

eq^n of motions

$$N\sin\theta = 2ma \longrightarrow N = \frac{2ma}{\sin\theta}$$

$$mg - N\cos\theta = ma\tan\theta$$

$$mg - 2ma\cot\theta = ma\tan\theta \Rightarrow \boxed{a_A = \frac{g}{\tan\theta + 2\cot\theta}}$$ Ans

Web Reference at www.physicsgalaxy.com | Scan for Video Explanation

Module-13: Solved Example-5

Ex : Find acceleration of masses shown in the figure when this system is released from rest.

Sol^n: FBD of 5m

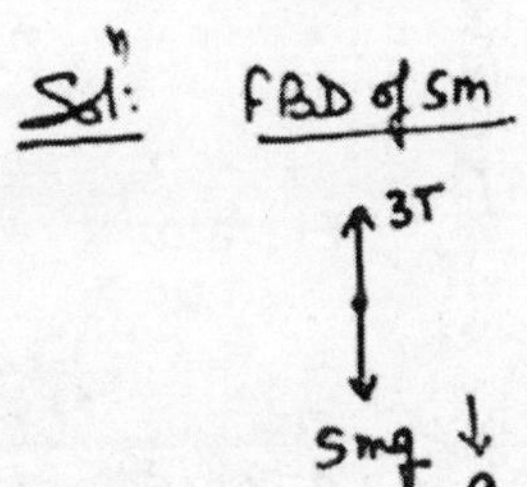

FBD of m

↑T ↑3a

mg

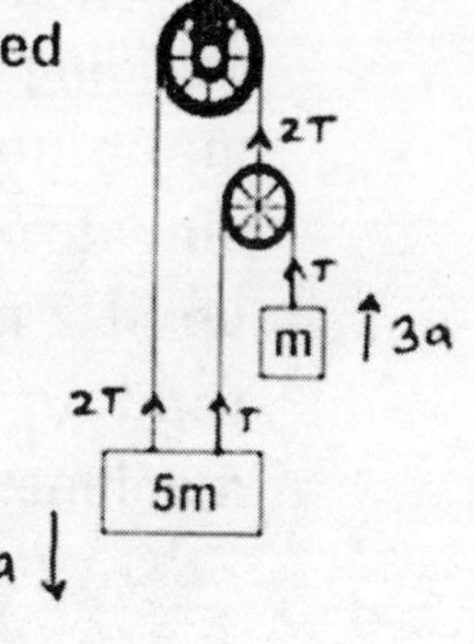

eq^n of motions

$$5mg - 3T = 5ma \quad -(1)$$

$$T - mg = m(3a) - (2) \times 3$$

$$2mg = 14ma$$

$$a = g/7$$

$$a_{5m} = g/7 \downarrow$$
$$a_m = 3g/7 \uparrow$$ Ans.

Web Reference at www.physicsgalaxy.com | Scan for Video Explanation

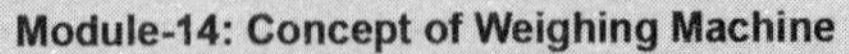

Module-14: Concept of Weighing Machine

Concept of Weighing Machine:

A weighing machine always measures the normal reaction acting on it in kgf.

$1\,kgf = g$ Newton.

If N is the normal reaction acting on a weighing machine then its reading will be

$$\text{Reading} = \left(\frac{N}{g}\right) kg$$

weighing M/c.

FBD of man

rest

$N = mg$

$$\text{Reading} = \frac{N}{g} = m$$

Scan for Video Explanation

Web Reference at www.physicsgalaxy.com

Module-14: Concept of Weighing Machine

Ex : A man of mass 60 kg is standing on a weighing machine inside an elevator accelerating up at 2 m/s^2. Find the reading of weighing machine.

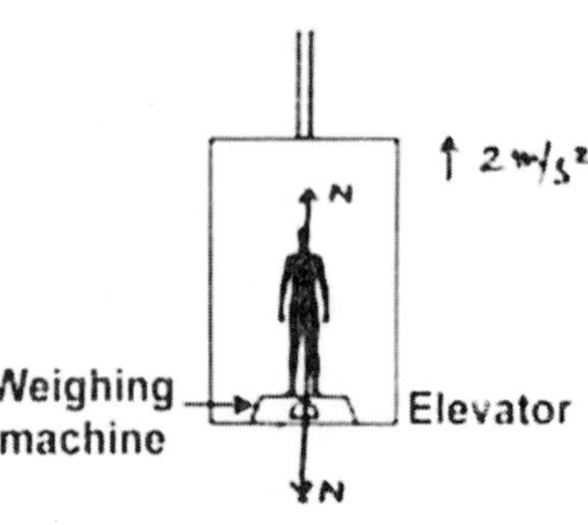

FBD of man.

$N \uparrow \quad \uparrow a = 2\,m/s^2$

$60g$

Sol:

eq^n of motion

$$N - 60g = 60a$$

$$N = 60(g+a) = 60 \times 12$$

$$= 720\,Nt.$$

$$\text{Reading of Machine} = \frac{N}{g} = \frac{720}{10} = 72\,kg.$$

Scan for Video Explanation

Web Reference at www.physicsgalaxy.com

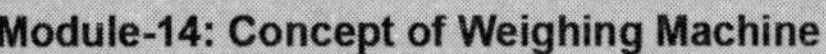
Module-14: Concept of Weighing Machine

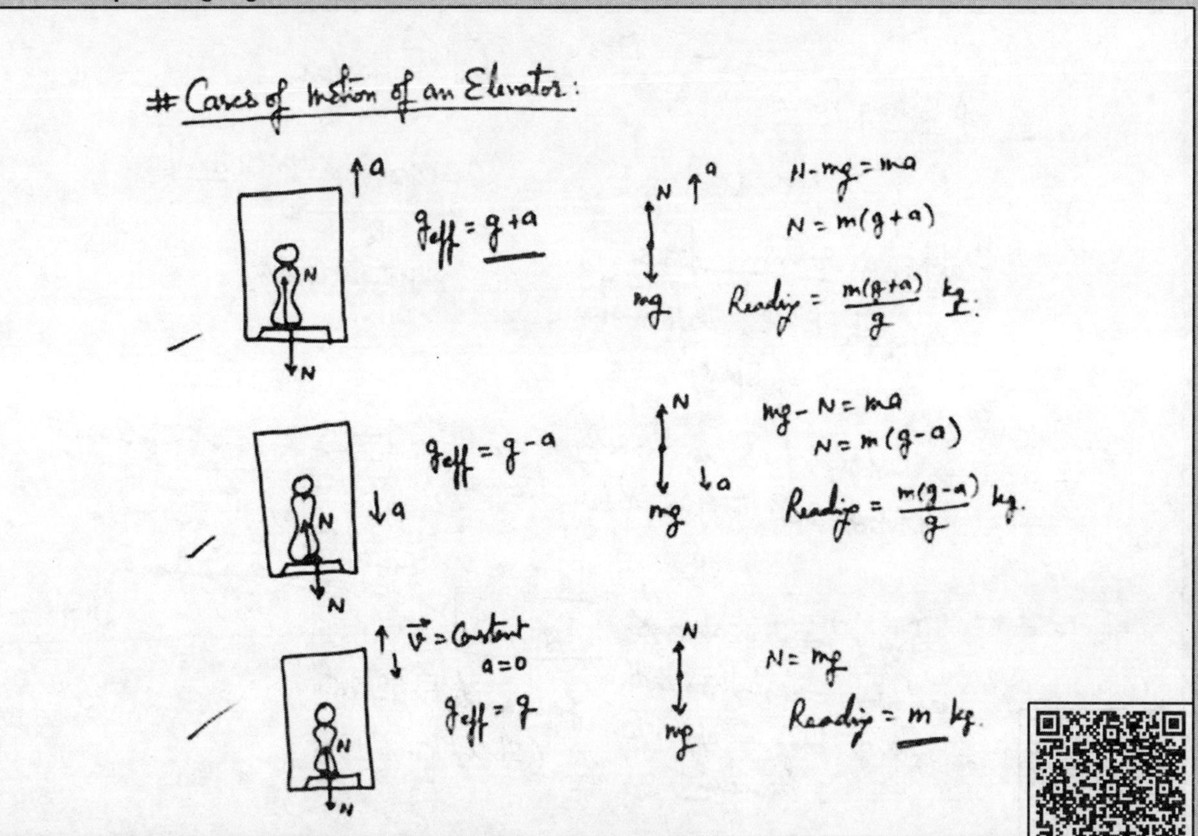

Web Reference at www.physicsgalaxy.com | Scan for Video Explanation

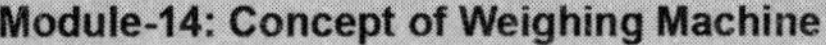
Module-14: Concept of Weighing Machine

Ex : In the figure a man of mass 80 kg is holding the cabin of mass 40 kg, in which he is standing on a weighing machine. Find the reading of weighing machine.

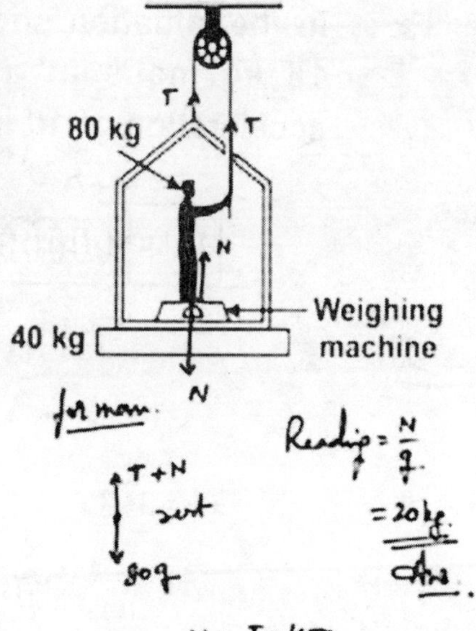

Sol:

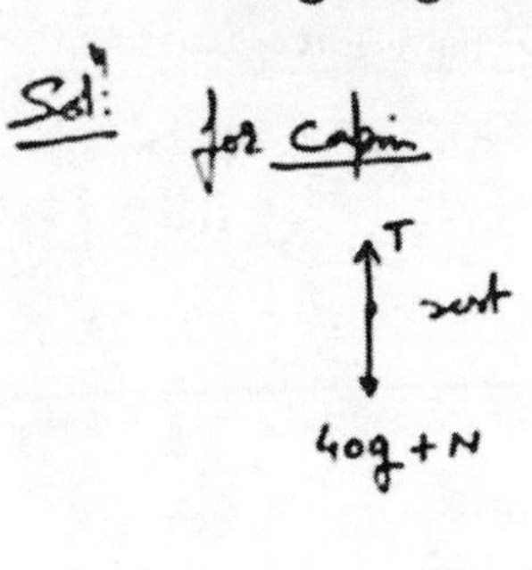

for man.

T + N
rest
80g

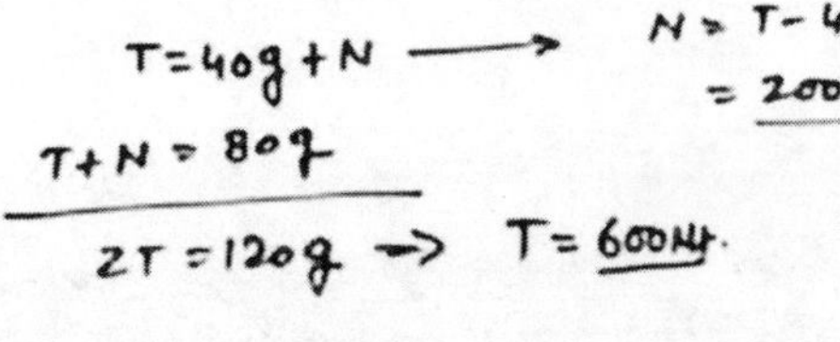

Web Reference at www.physicsgalaxy.com | Scan for Video Explanation

Module-15: Spring Force

Spring Force:

ideal → massless.

→ Spring has a tendency to apply a restoring force opposite to the deformation of spring.

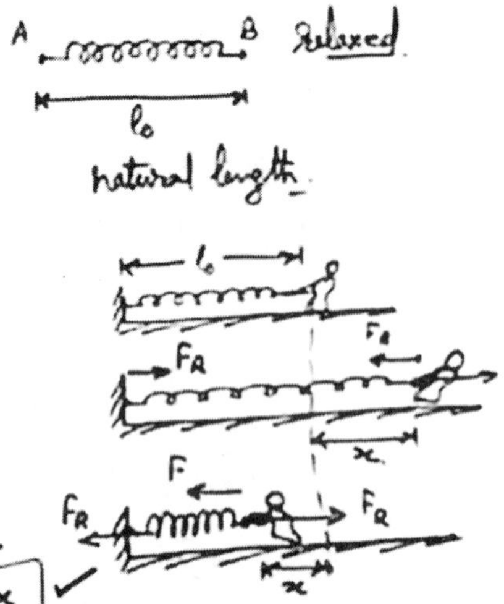

A ~~~~~ B Relaxed

l_0 natural length.

→ Restoring force is directly proportional to the deformation length.

$F_R \propto x$

$F_R = kx$ → force constant of spring (Spring constant)

→ Restoring force is always exerted on both ends of spring in opposite direction.

Scan for Video Explanation

Web Reference at www.physicsgalaxy.com

Module-15: Spring Force

Ex : In the situation shown in figure if acceleration 15 kg mass at an instant is 2 m/s^2, find acceleration of 10 kg mass at that instant.

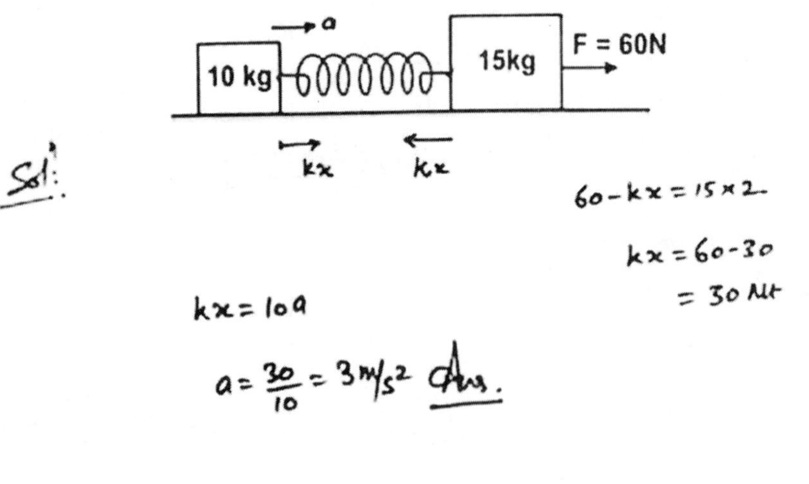

Scan for Video Explanation

Web Reference at www.physicsgalaxy.com

Ex : In the situation shown in figure all surfaces are smooth. When the system is set in motion under gravity, find the extension in spring under the state of uniform acceleration of block.

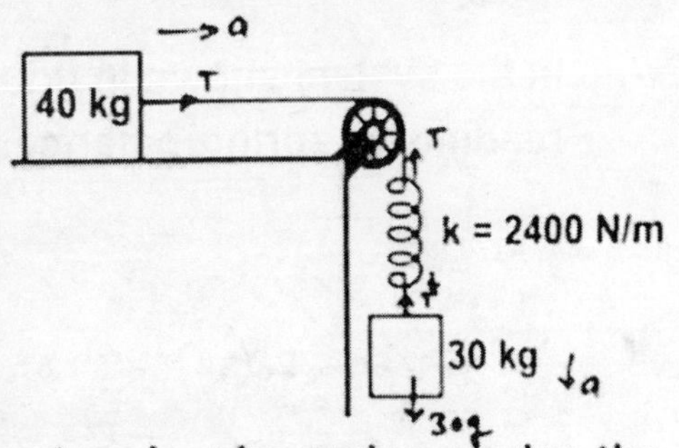

Sol: if x is the extension in spring $\Rightarrow$ $T = kx$

$$30g - T = 30a$$
$$T = 40a \longrightarrow T = \frac{120g}{7} = \frac{1200}{7}\ N$$
$$30g = 70a$$
$$a = \frac{3g}{7}$$

$$kx = \frac{1200}{7}$$
$$2400x = \frac{1200}{7} \Rightarrow x = \frac{1}{14}\ m \text{ Ans}$$

Web Reference at www.physicsgalaxy.com

Scan for Video Explanation

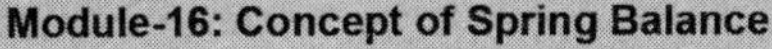

Concept of Spring Balance:

A spring balance always measures the tension in the string connected to it in units of kgf.

Reading of Sp. balance $= \left(\frac{T}{g}\right)$ kg.

Reading, T, T, M, eqm, $T = Mg$, Mg

Ex:

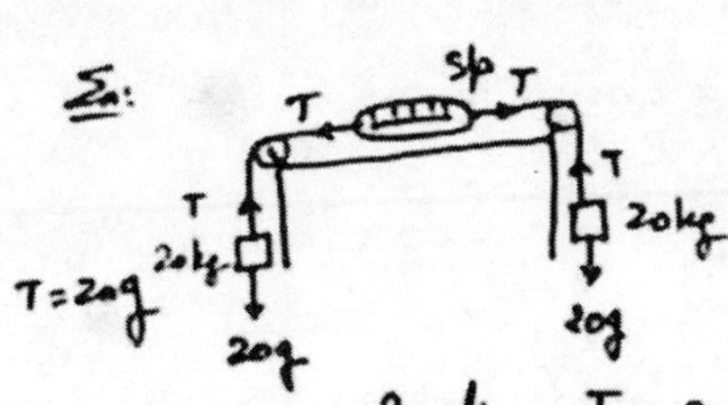

Reading $= \frac{T}{g} = 20$ kg.

Ex:

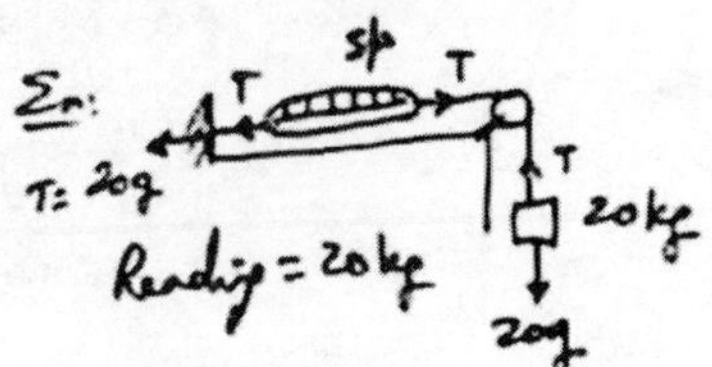

Web Reference at www.physicsgalaxy.com

Scan for Video Explanation

Module-16: Concept of Spring Balance

Ex : In the system shown in figure. Find the reading of spring balance.

Sol: Eqⁿ of Motion

$$T - 20g = 20(3a) \quad \text{—(1)} \times 3$$

$$80g - 3T = 80a \quad \text{—(2)}$$

$$20g = 260a$$

$$a = \frac{2g}{26} = \frac{g}{13}$$

eqⁿ (1)

$$T = 20g + 60a$$

$$= 20g + 60(g/13) = \frac{320g}{13} = \frac{3200}{13}\text{ Nt}$$

$$\text{Reading of sp} = \frac{2T}{g} = \frac{6400}{13 \times 10} = \frac{640}{13}\text{ kg. Ans.}$$

Scan for Video Explanation

Web Reference at www.physicsgalaxy.com

Module-17: Concept of Pseudo Force

Concept of Pseudo Force:

Pract. Illustration

FBD of 5kg block w.r.t. to boy on plank

$2\,m/s^2 \leftarrow$

5kg

F = 10N

Pseudo force ← (not an actual force)

Scan for Video Explanation

Web Reference at www.physicsgalaxy.com

Module-17: Concept of Pseudo Force

NOTE: Pseudo force appear to act on a body when seen by an accelerating observer.

$a \leftarrow$ [m] rest

obs. $\rightarrow$ acc^n a

to this observer a pseudo force appear to act on mass m.

- $\rightarrow$ Pseudo force = mass of object × acc^n of observer
- $\rightarrow$ Dir of Pseudo force is opp. to the dir of acc^n of observer.

Web Reference at www.physicsgalaxy.com | Scan for Video Explanation

Module-17: Concept of Pseudo Force

Pseudo Force does not obey Newton's laws:

$a_1 \leftarrow$ [m] rest

M $\rightarrow$ F

$a_1 = F/M$

I law $\rightarrow$ × without force block started accelerating

II law $\rightarrow$ $\Sigma\vec{F} = m\vec{a}$ × with force mass is accelerating

III law $\rightarrow$ × No reaction exist for Pseudo force.

NOTE: Based on acc^n of observer, ref. frames are classified in two categories. These are –

(i) Inertial ref. frames $\rightarrow a_{obs} = 0 \rightarrow$ uniform motion or Rest.

(ii) Non-inertial ref frames $\rightarrow a_{obs} \neq 0$. (Pseudo forces)

Web Reference at www.physicsgalaxy.com | Scan for Video Explanation

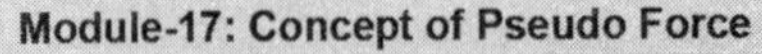

Module-17: Concept of Pseudo Force

Inertial & Non-inertial Refrence frames:

Inertial ref frame are those which are at rest or in uniform motion. In Inertial ref. frames all Newton's laws are directly applicable.

The ref. frames which have some non zero acc^n are called NI ref frames & in these frames NL's are not directly applicable. The observer in such frames sees a Pseudo force on all objects in dir opp to ref frame acc^n.

Pseudo force = mass of body × acc^n of Ref. frame

Scan for Video Explanation

Web Reference at www.physicsgalaxy.com

Module-18: Solved Example-6

Ex : Find the magnitude of F for which the blocks A and B will remain at rest w.r. to the bigger block.

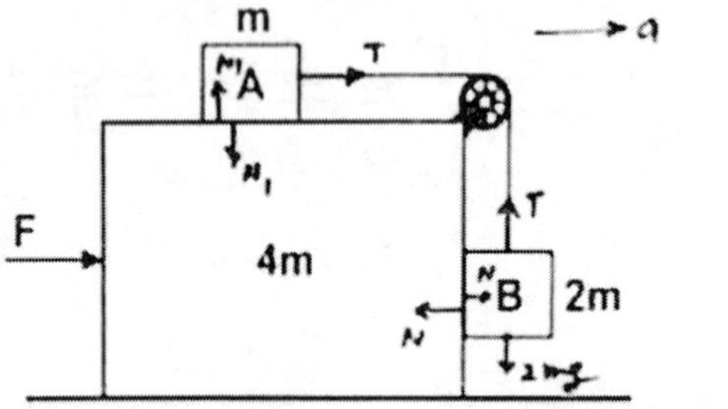

m, A, T, a, N_1, 4m, F, T, B, 2m, N, 2mg

Sol^n:

Common acc^n of blocks $a = \frac{F}{7m}$

w.r.t 4m. FBD of A.

N_1, T, ma, mg

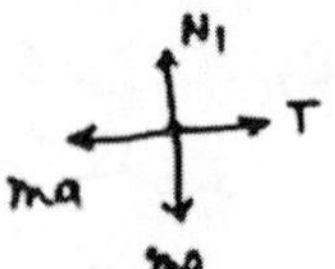

$$\begin{bmatrix} T = ma \\ N_1 = mg \end{bmatrix}$$

w.r.t 4m FBD of B.

T, N, 2ma, 2mg

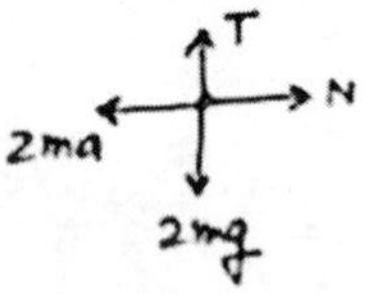

$$\begin{bmatrix} T = 2mg \\ N = 2ma \end{bmatrix}$$

$ma = 2mg$

$a = 2g$.

$F = 14mg$ Ans.

Scan for Video Explanation

Web Reference at www.physicsgalaxy.com

Module-19: Solved Example-7

Ex : When the system shown in figure is released from rest, find acceleration of 2m.

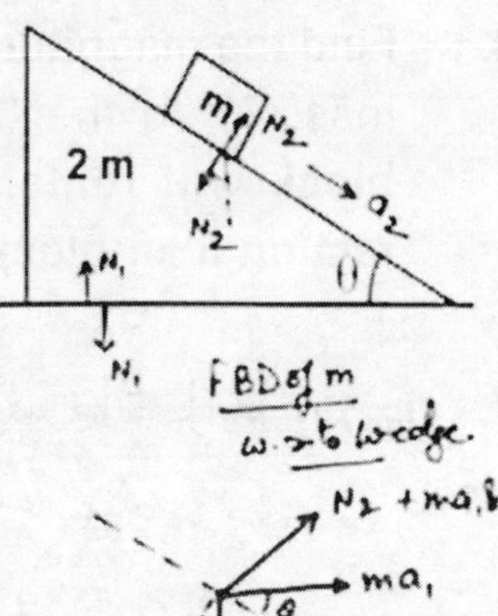

Sol^n:

FBD of 2m

a_1, N_1, $N_2 \sin\theta$, θ, N_2, $2mg + N_2\cos\theta$

FBD of m w.r.to wedge

$N_2 + ma_1\sin\theta$, ma_1, θ, a_2, $mg\cos\theta$, mg, $ma_1\cos\theta + mg\sin\theta$

eq^n $N_2\sin\theta = 2ma_1$ —(1)

eq^n $ma_1\cos\theta + mg\sin\theta = ma_2$ —(2)

$N_2 + ma_1\sin\theta = mg\cos\theta$ —(3)

(1)&(3) $\Rightarrow$ $\frac{2a_1}{\sin\theta} + a_1\sin\theta = g\cos\theta$

$$a_1 = \left(\frac{g\sin\theta\cos\theta}{2+\sin^2\theta}\right) \text{ Ans.}$$

Web Reference at www.physicsgalaxy.com | Scan for Video Explanation

Module-20: Solved Example-8

Ex : Find the value of F for which block of mass m will remain at rest over the wedge.

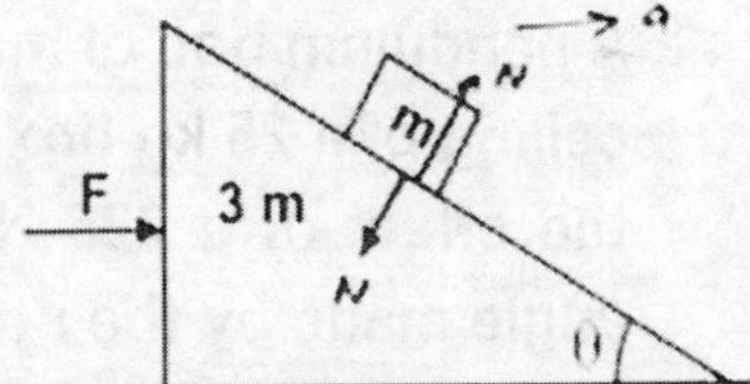

Sol^n:

Common acc^n of system $a = \frac{F}{4m}$

FBD of m w.r.to 3m.

N, $ma\cos\theta$, θ, ma, θ, $mg\sin\theta$, mg, $mg\cos\theta + ma\sin\theta$

$g\sin\theta = a\cos\theta$

$a = g\tan\theta$ v.imp.

$F = 4mg\tan\theta$ Ans.

Web Reference at www.physicsgalaxy.com | Scan for Video Explanation

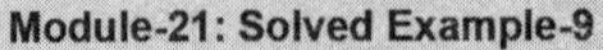

Module-21: Solved Example-9

Ex : Find the magnitude of mass M so that 2 kg block will remain at rest on 5 kg block.

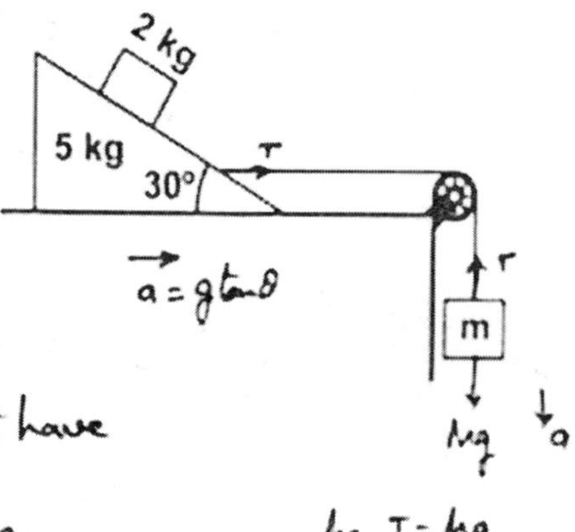

Sol: for 2kg block to be at rest on 5kg wedge we must have

$\vec{a} = g\tan\theta$

$a = g\tan 30° = g/\sqrt{3}$

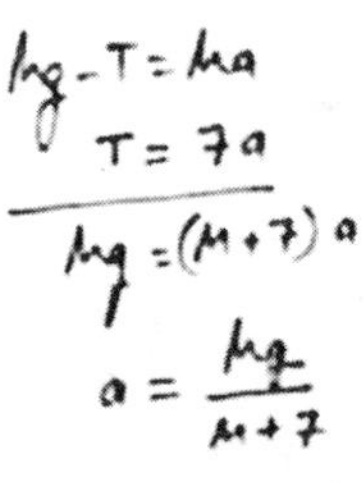

$Mg - T = Ma$

$T = 7a$

$Mg = (M+7)a$

$a = \frac{Mg}{M+7}$

$\frac{g}{\sqrt{3}} = \frac{M}{M+7} \cdot g$

$M + 7 = \sqrt{3}M$

$M = \left(\frac{7}{\sqrt{3}-1}\right)$ kg Ans.

Scan for Video Explanation

Web Reference at www.physicsgalaxy.com

Module-22: Solved Example-10

Ex : A pendulum bob of mass 5 kg is hanging from the ceiling of a 25 kg box car, which is moving under the effect of a 225 N force as shown. Find the angle made by the string of pendulum inside the moving car.

Sol^n:

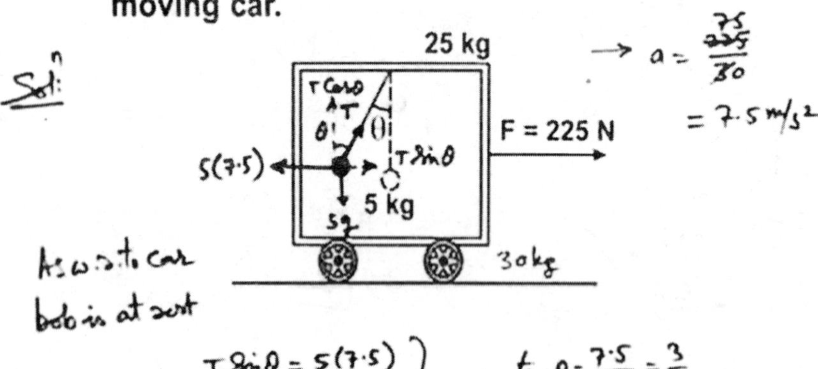

$\rightarrow a = \frac{225}{30} = 7.5 \text{ m/s}^2$

As w.r.t. car bob is at rest

$T\sin\theta = 5(7.5)$
$T\cos\theta = 5(10)$

$\rightarrow \tan\theta = \frac{7.5}{10} = \frac{3}{4}$

$\theta = \tan^{-1}(3/4) = 37°$ Ans.

Scan for Video Explanation

Web Reference at www.physicsgalaxy.com

Chapter 6
Friction

Lecture Notes Modules

Module-1: Friction and its Classification
Module-2: Types of Friction-Static Friction
Module-3: Limiting & Kinetic Friction
Module-4: Solved Example-1
Module-5: Solved Example-2
Module-6: Solved Example-3
Module-7: Solved Example-4
Module-8: Angle of Friction & Angle of Repose
Module-9: Cases of Sliding on Rough Surface
Module-10: Solved Example-6
Module-11: Solved Example-7

Module-1: Friction and its Classification

Friction: The force which opposes motion or tendency of motion is called friction. Based on opposition process, friction is divided in two categories –

(1) Dry friction – due to irregularities of surfaces in contact.

(2) Wet friction – due to the continuous collisions of medium particles on body.

Ex: air friction

Scan for Video Explanation

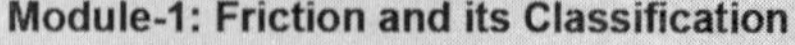

Web Reference at www.physicsgalaxy.com

Module-1: Friction and its Classification

Dry friction:

friction due to roughness of surfaces.

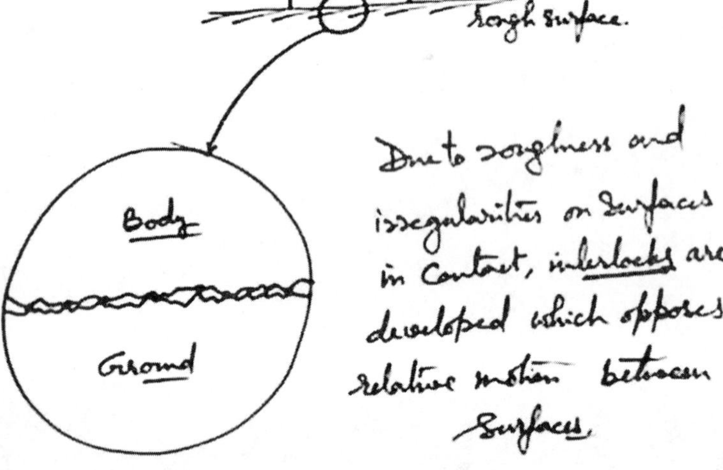

Due to roughness and irregularities on surfaces in contact, interlocks are developed which opposes relative motion between surfaces.

Scan for Video Explanation

Web Reference at www.physicsgalaxy.com

Module-1: Friction and its Classification

Due to these interlocks at various pts of Contact the Contact forces are distributed in various direction over the surface

body

N_1 N_2

ground

N_1

friction → Cumulative effect of horizontal Components of all Contact forces between the surface.

F N f R N f

net Contact force betw^n body & ground.

Web Reference at www.physicsgalaxy.com

Scan for Video Explanation

Module-2: Types of Friction-Static Friction

Types of friction between two Surfaces in Contact :

When two Surfaces are in Contact the friction between these surfaces Can be classified in 3 categories. –

(1) Static friction → acts when body is at rest

(2) Limiting friction → max limit of Static friction

(3) Kinetic friction → when body is in motion

Web Reference at www.physicsgalaxy.com

Scan for Video Explanation

Module-2: Types of Friction-Static Friction

Static Friction: body is at rest.
& some external force is acting on it

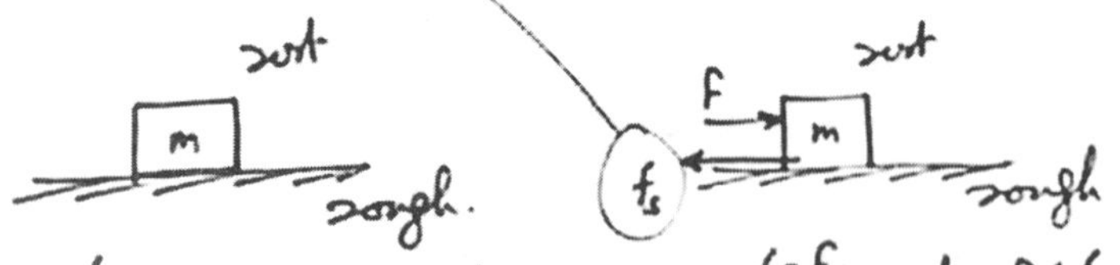

rest rest

m F → m

rough. f_s rough

$f = 0$. $f_s = F$. for $F < f_L$

no friction Static friction.

max limit upto which the static friction balances the external force acting on body is termed as "Limiting Friction"

Limiting $f_s = f_L$

body will start moving when $F \geq f_L$

Scan for Video Explanation

Web Reference at www.physicsgalaxy.com

Module-3: Limiting & Kinetic Friction

Magnitude of Limiting Friction:

magnitude depends on two factors

(1) Normal Reaction between surfaces

(2) Nature of roughness.

$$f_L \propto N$$

$$\boxed{f_L = \mu_s N}$$

μ_s → Coefficient of Static friction (depends on roughness of surfaces)

Scan for Video Explanation

Web Reference at www.physicsgalaxy.com

Module-3: Limiting & Kinetic Friction

Practical Illustration:

5kg

$N = 5g = 50\,Nt$

limiting fr. $f_L = \mu_s N$

$= 0.3 \times 50$

$= 15\,Nt.$

$\mu_s = 0.3$

$F =$	5N	12N	14.99N	15N
$f_s =$	5N	12N	14.99N	f_k → Kinetic friction
State of motion →	rest	rest	rest	motion

rest, rest, rest → Static friction

$f_k < f_L$

Module-3: Limiting & Kinetic Friction

Kinetic Friction: It acts when body is in motion

→ no external force is necessary for kinetic friction

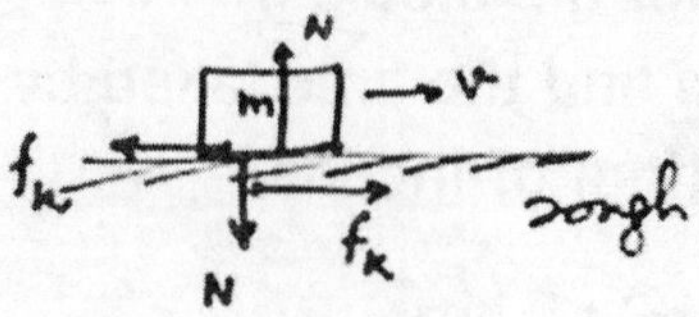

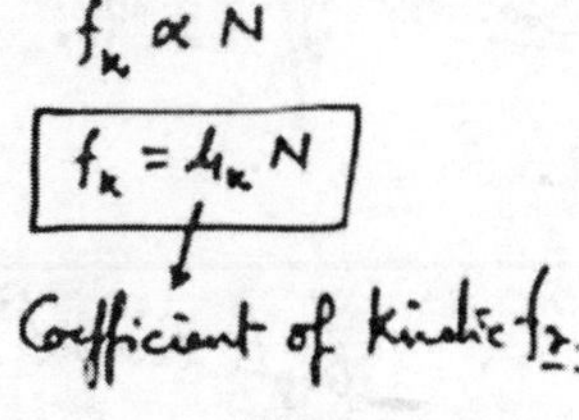

NOTE: When a body starts moving due to less interlocking between surfaces $f_k < f_L$

$\mu_k < \mu_s$.

Module-4: Solved Example-1

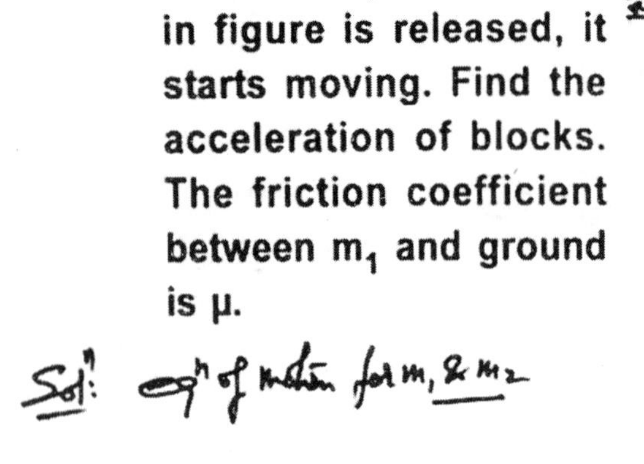

Ex : When the system shown in figure is released, it starts moving. Find the acceleration of blocks. The friction coefficient between m_1 and ground is μ.

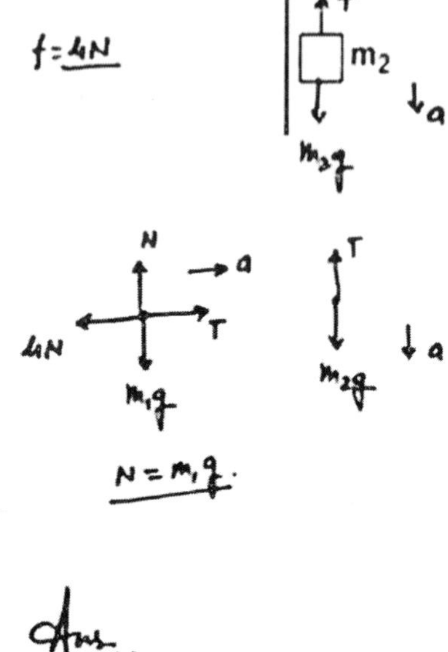

Sol^n: eq^n of motion for m_1 & m_2

$$m_2 g - T = m_2 a \quad —(1)$$

$$T - \mu m_1 g = m_1 a \quad —(2)$$

$$(1) + (2) \Rightarrow \quad (m_2 - \mu m_1) g = (m_1 + m_2) a$$

$$a = \left(\frac{m_2 - \mu m_1}{m_1 + m_2}\right) g. \quad \text{Ans.}$$

Scan for Video Explanation

Web Reference at www.physicsgalaxy.com

Module-5: Solved Example-2

Ex : A block of mass m is placed and released from the top of an inclined plane of length *l* which has a friction coefficient μ for the block. If it slides down, find the time taken by the block to reach the bottom of incline.

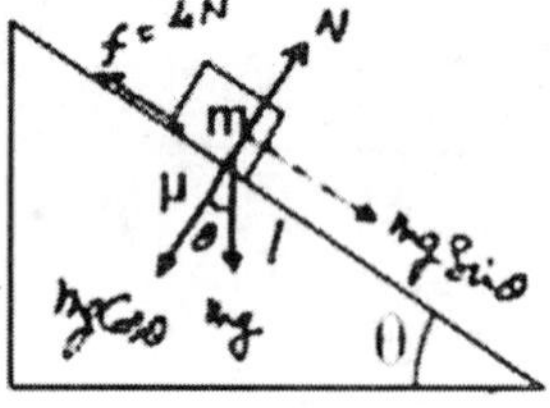

$$N = mg \cos\theta$$

Sol^n: If a is the acc^n of block

$$mg \sin\theta - \mu mg \cos\theta = ma$$

$$a = g \sin\theta - \mu g \cos\theta$$

length covered $l = \frac{1}{2} a t^2$

$$t = \sqrt{\frac{2l}{a}} = \sqrt{\frac{2l}{g(\sin\theta - \mu \cos\theta)}} \quad \text{Ans.}$$

Scan for Video Explanation

Web Reference at www.physicsgalaxy.com

Module-6: Solved Example-3

Ex : In the situation shown in figure a block of mass m is supported on the front surface of a bigger block of mass 3 m. The friction coefficient between vertical surface of 3 m and m is μ. Find a minimum magnitude of horizontal force F required to be applied so that m will remain at rest w.r. to 3 m.

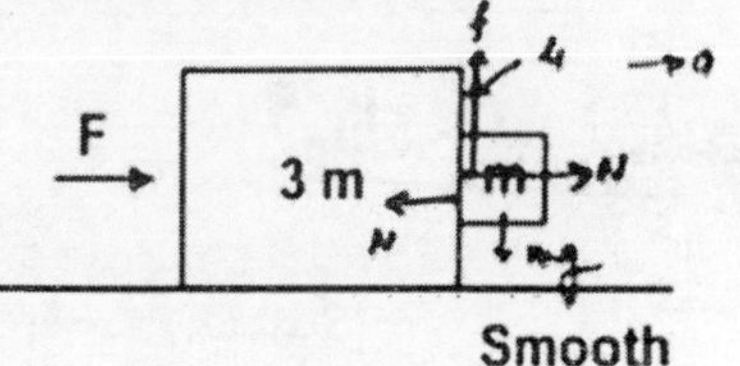

Sol^n: block will remain at rest

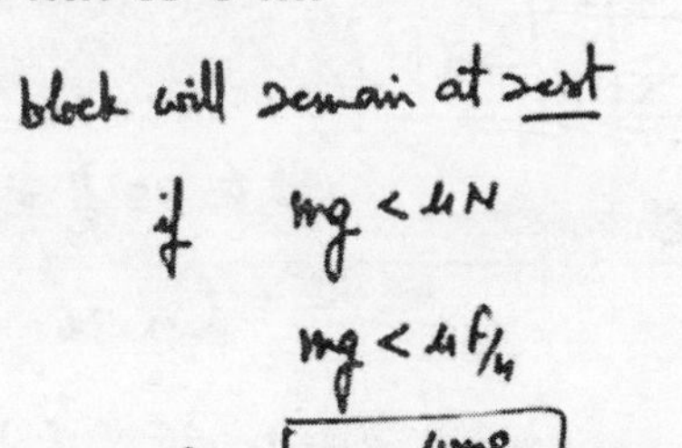

if $mg < \mu N$

$mg < \mu F/4$

or $\boxed{F > \frac{4mg}{\mu}}$ Ans.

Common acc^n

$a = \frac{F}{4m}$

for m.

$N = ma = m\left(\frac{F}{4m}\right)$

$N = \frac{F}{4}$

Web Reference at www.physicsgalaxy.com

Scan for Video Explanation

Module-7: Solved Example-4

Ex : A block of mass m is placed on a rough horizontal surface having friction coefficient μ. Find minimum force required to slide the block. Also find the direction θ at which this force is to be applied.

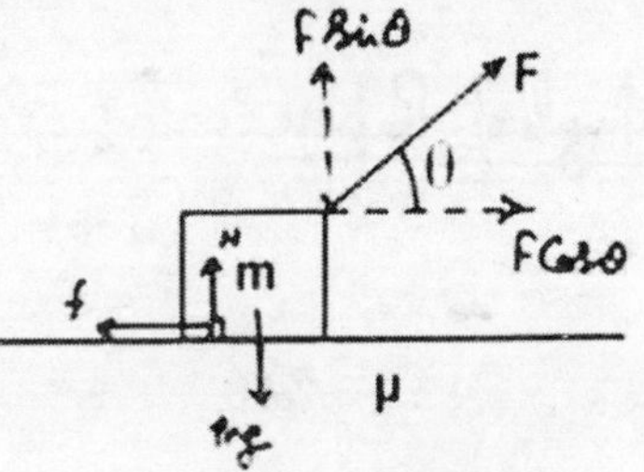

Sol^n: block will slide when $F\cos\theta \geq \mu N$

in vert dir.

$N + F\sin\theta = mg$

$N = mg - F\sin\theta$

$F\cos\theta = \mu(mg - F\sin\theta)$

$$F = \frac{\mu mg}{\cos\theta + \mu\sin\theta} \quad \text{---(1)}$$

F is min when

$\frac{dF}{d\theta} = 0 \Rightarrow -\sin\theta + \mu\cos\theta = 0$

$\tan\theta = \mu$

$\theta = \tan^{-1}\mu$ (Ans)

$$F_{min} = \frac{\mu mg}{\left(\frac{1}{\sqrt{1+\mu^2}}\right) + \mu\left(\frac{\mu}{\sqrt{1+\mu^2}}\right)}$$

$$F_{min} = \frac{\mu mg}{\sqrt{1+\mu^2}} \text{ Ans.}$$

Web Reference at www.physicsgalaxy.com

Scan for Video Explanation

Module-8: Angle of Friction & Angle of Repose

Angle of Friction:

When a body is at the verge of sliding, the angle between the normal reaction and total contact force is termed as angle of friction

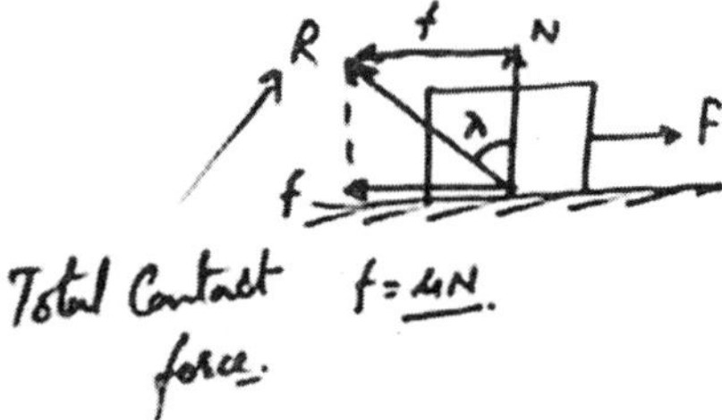

Total Contact force. $f = \mu N$.

$$\tan\lambda = \frac{f}{N} = \frac{\mu N}{N}$$

$$\tan\lambda = \mu$$

Angle of friction $\rightarrow \lambda = \tan^{-1}(\mu)$

Scan for Video Explanation

Web Reference at www.physicsgalaxy.com

Module-8: Angle of Friction & Angle of Repose

Angle of Repose:

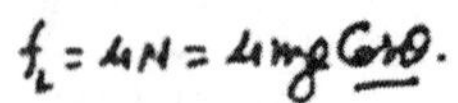

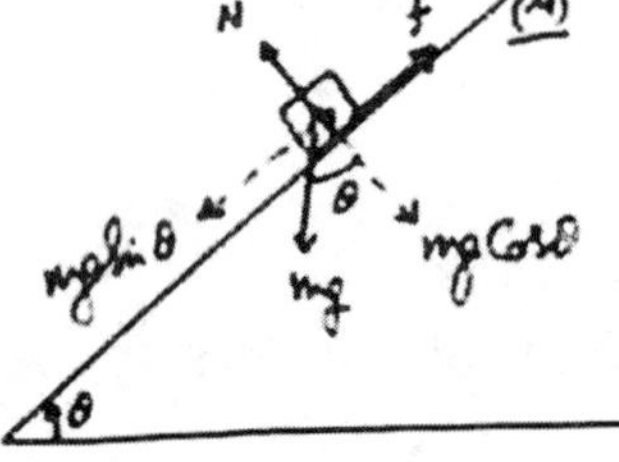

$N = mg\cos\theta$

if m is at rest

$\Rightarrow f = mg\sin\theta$.

block will start sliding down at an angle of inclination

$$\theta = \theta_R$$

when $mg\sin\theta_R = \mu mg\cos\theta_R$

$$\tan\theta_R = \mu$$

Angle of Repose. $\leftarrow \theta_R = \tan^{-1}(\mu)$

Scan for Video Explanation

Web Reference at www.physicsgalaxy.com

Cases of Sliding on Rough Surfaces:

On a rough surface a body at rest will slide only if by some external force, friction approaches to the value μN. (Limiting friction)

$f = F = \mu N \Rightarrow$ body will start sliding

$N = mg$ (μ) Smooth.

Common acc^n $a = \frac{F}{M+m}$

for m $f = m\left(\frac{F}{M+m}\right)$

m will slide over M when

$F = \mu(M+m)g \leftarrow f = \frac{mF}{M+m} = \mu mg$

Module-9: Cases of Sliding on Rough Surface

Ex : Find mass M such that on releasing the system, block A will start sliding on B.

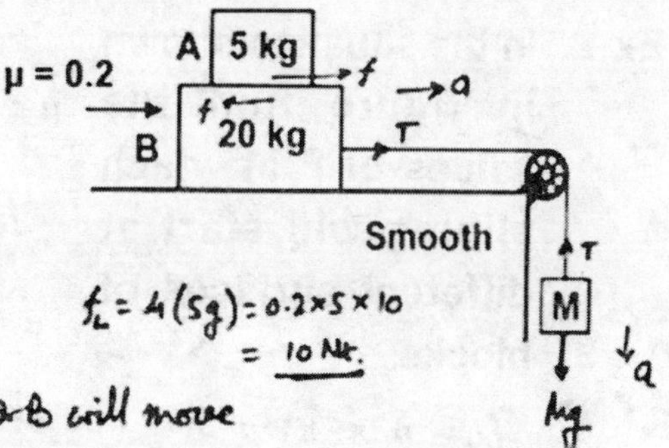

$f_L = \mu(5g) = 0.2 \times 5 \times 10 = 10$ Nt.

Sol^n: for low values of M, A & B will move together

$Mg - T = Ma.$
$T = 25a$ $\Big] \rightarrow Mg = (25 + M)a$

$a = \left(\frac{M}{25+M}\right)g$

A →a →f for block A.

$f = 5\left(\frac{Mg}{M+25}\right) = 10$

$5M = M + 25$

$M = \frac{25}{4} = 6.25$ kg. Ans.

Module-10: Solved Example-6

Ex : In figure the friction coefficient between 4 kg block and ground is 0.2 and that between the two blocks is 0.3. A horizontal force F is applied on 4 kg block as shown, if F is gradually increased, find values of F at which sliding starts at bottom surface and then between the two blocks.

2 kg; 4 kg; $\mu = 0.3$; $\mu_1 = 0.2$; F; f_1; f_2

Solⁿ:

$f_{LB} = 0.2 \times 6 \times 10 = 12N$

$f_{LM} = 0.3 \times 2 \times 10 = 6N$

for $F > 12N$, both blocks start together with accⁿ $a = \frac{F-12}{6}$ m/s²

for 2kg block. $f_2 = 2\left(\frac{F-12}{6}\right) = 6$ (Cond for sliding of 2kg block)

$F - 12 = 18$

$F = 30Nt$ Ans.

Scan for Video Explanation

Web Reference at www.physicsgalaxy.com

Module-11: Solved Example-7

Ex : In the situation shown in figure find the values of F at which sliding will start at different surfaces of blocks.

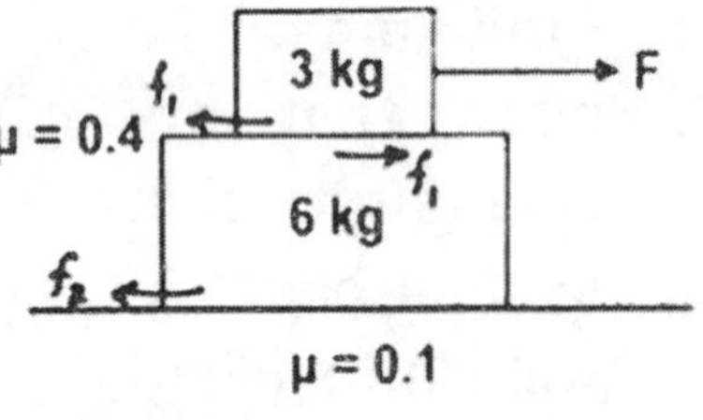

Solⁿ:

$f_{LB} = 0.1 \times 9 \times 10 = 9N$

$f_{LM} = 0.4 \times 3 \times 10 = 12N.$

at $F = 9N$, Sliding at bottom Surface will start.

for $F > 9$, Common accⁿ of blocks $a = \frac{F-9}{9}$ m/s²

for 3kg block $F - f_1 = 3\left(\frac{F-9}{9}\right)$

3kg will start sliding when $f_1 \to 12N$

$F - 12 = \frac{F-9}{3}$

$3F - 36 = F - 9 \Rightarrow 2F = 27$

$F = 13.5 Nt$ Ans.

Scan for Video Explanation

Web Reference at www.physicsgalaxy.com

Chapter 7
Work Energy Power

Lecture Notes Modules

Module-1: Work & its Calculation

Work :

Work → transfer of Energy.

→ Work is done when a force produces some displacement

work = Force × disp of pt. of appⁿ of force in the dir of force.

$= \underline{F.S}$ Joule.

Scan for Video Explanation

Web Reference at www.physicsgalaxy.com

Module-1: Work & its Calculation

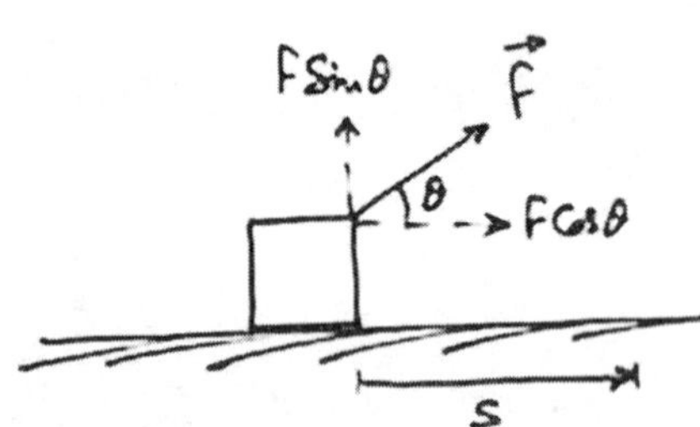

Work done by $\vec{F}$ $W = F\cos\theta \times s = Fs\cos\theta$

vect $W = \vec{F}.\vec{s}$

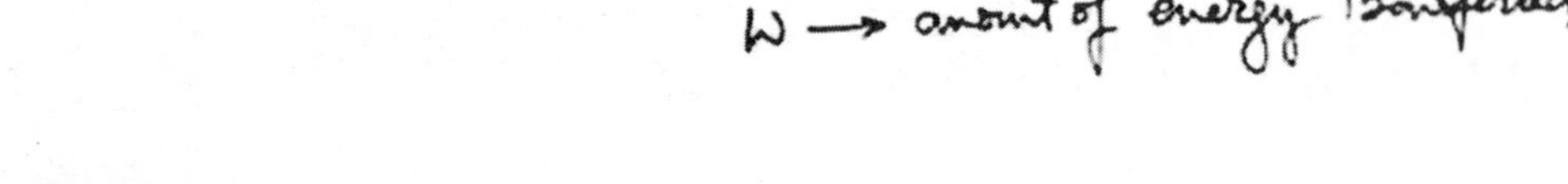

W → amount of energy transferred.

Scan for Video Explanation

Web Reference at www.physicsgalaxy.com

Module-1: Work & its Calculation

Positive & Negative Work:

Work Done by boy $W = F.S$ (+ve)

W/D by block $W = -FS$ (-ve)

+ve work ⇒ Supply of Energy.

-ve work ⇒ Gain of Energy

Web Reference at www.physicsgalaxy.com | Scan for Video Explanation

Module-2: Work Done by a Variable Force

Work Done by a variable Force:

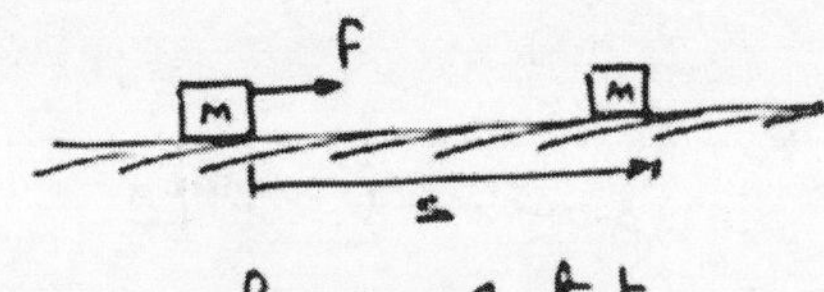

When F → Constant

Work = F.S

$W = \vec{F}.\vec{S}$

if $F = f(x)$

$F = f(x)$

$x = x_1$ x $x + dx$ $x = x_2$

work done in elemental disp dx is $dW = \vec{F}.\vec{dx}$

Total work in disp from $x = x_1$ to $x = x_2$ $W = \int dW = \int_{x_1}^{x_2} \vec{F}.\vec{dx}$

Web Reference at www.physicsgalaxy.com | Scan for Video Explanation

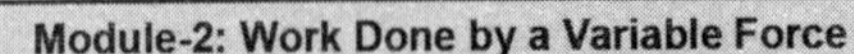

Ex : A block of mass 5 kg is pulled by an external force which depends on its position x as

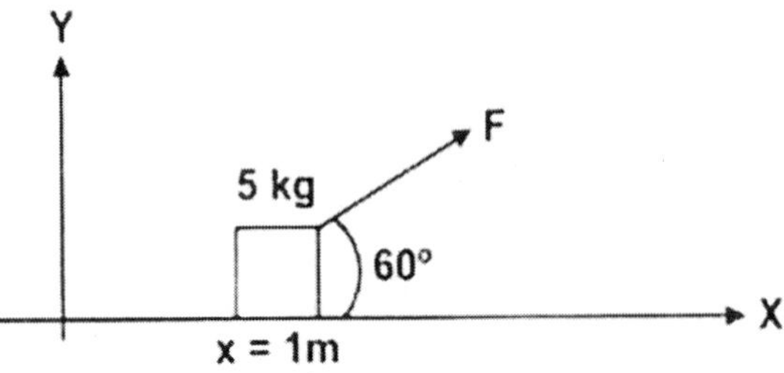

$$F = 4x^2 + 2x + 1 \text{ N}$$

Find work done by this force is displacing the block to the position x = 2m.

Sol:

$$W = \int \vec{F}\cdot\vec{dx} = \int F dx \cos 60^\circ$$

$$= \frac{1}{2}\int_1^2 (4x^2 + 2x + 1) dx$$

$$= \frac{1}{2}\left[\frac{4x^3}{3} + x^2 + x\right]_1^2 = \frac{1}{2}\left[\left(\frac{32}{3} + 4 + 2\right) - \left(\frac{4}{3} + 1 + 1\right)\right]$$

$$= \frac{20}{3} \text{ J Ans.}$$

Scan for Video Explanation

Web Reference at www.physicsgalaxy.com

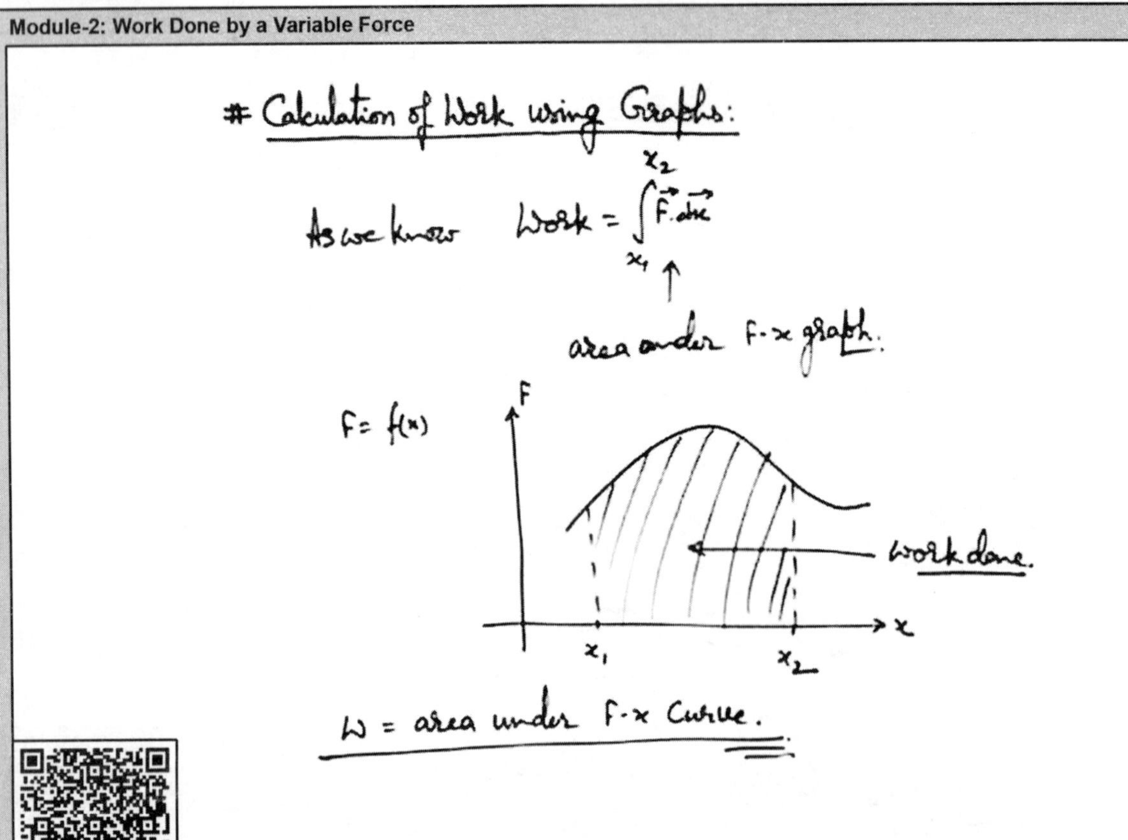

Module-3: Solved Example-1

Ex : A body is constrained to move in Y direction. A force $\vec{F} = (-2\hat{i} + 15\hat{j} + 6\hat{k})$N is applied on it. What is the work done by the force in moving the body by 10 m in +Y direction.

Sol^n: Displacement vect $\vec{s} = 10\hat{j}$ m.

force $\vec{F} = -2\hat{i} + 15\hat{j} + 6\hat{k}$ N

Work Done by force $W = \vec{F} \cdot \vec{s}$

$= 150$ J Ans.

Web Reference at www.physicsgalaxy.com | Scan for Video Explanation

Module-4: Solved Example-2

Ex : Find work done by a variable force in displacing the body from x = 0 to x = 35 m.

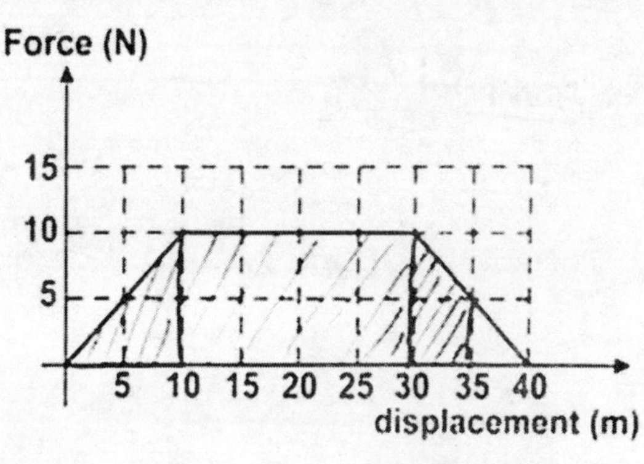

The force varies with displacement according to the graph shown.

Sol^n: Work = Area under the curve from x = 0 to x = 35 m.

$$W = \frac{1}{2} \times 10 \times 10 + 20 \times 10 + \frac{1}{2} \times 15 \times 5$$

$$= 50 + 200 + 37.5 = 287.5 \text{ J Ans.}$$

Web Reference at www.physicsgalaxy.com | Scan for Video Explanation

Module-5: Energy & its Types

Energy & its Types:

Energy → ability to do work.
↑
required to develop a force.

Types of Energies → There are two ways in which energies can be classified, these are -

(i) Kinetic Energy: due to motion in a body.

$KE = \frac{1}{2}mv^2$

(ii) Potential Energy: Stored form of Energy which can be used in doing work.

Scan for Video Explanation

Web Reference at www.physicsgalaxy.com

Module-5: Energy & its Types

Dissipated Energy:

Work Done ⇒ Transfer of Energy.
→ Kinetic Energy
→ Potential Energy
→ lost to surrounding in form of heat, Sound etc.

Can not be returned back to the system. ← Dissipated Energy. ← [lost to surrounding in form of heat, Sound etc.

f = μmg, s, rough ground (μ), m, F

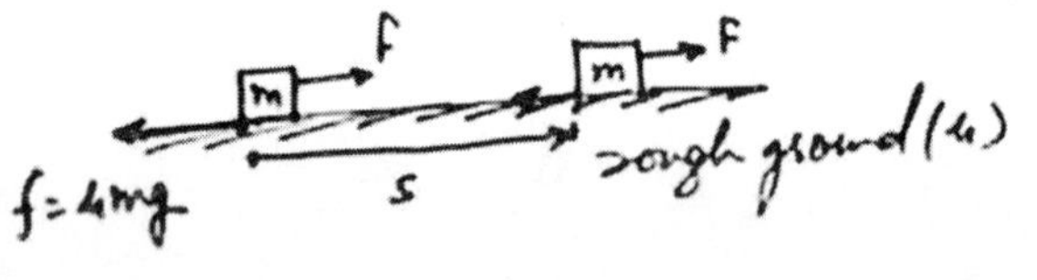

Work done by friction

$W = -\mu mgS$
↓
lost to surroundings (Dissipated).

Scan for Video Explanation

Web Reference at www.physicsgalaxy.com

Module-6: Conservative & Non-Conservative Forces

Classification of forces on the basis of Energy Transfer:

Based on the energy Transfer during W/D force can be classified in two categories.

→ (i) Conservative Forces

→ (ii) Non-Conservative Forces.

Conservative Forces:

→ these are the forces which never dissipates energy.

→ whenever these forces do work always this energy changes the potential energy of system.

+ve work ⇒ dec. in PE of System

−ve work ⇒ increase in PE of system.

Web Reference at www.physicsgalaxy.com | Scan for Video Explanation

Module-6: Conservative & Non-Conservative Forces

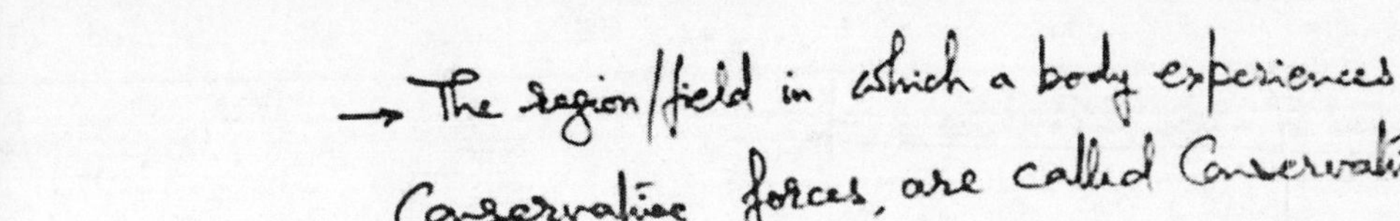

→ The region/field in which a body experiences Conservative forces, are called Conservative fields.

→ In Conservative fields always W/D depend on initial & final position of body & is independent from the path along which work is done.

W/D by the field forces.

$$W = U_A - U_B$$

W/D by ext agent

$$W = U_B - U_A$$

Web Reference at www.physicsgalaxy.com | Scan for Video Explanation

Module-6: Conservative & Non-Conservative Forces

Non-Conservative Forces:

These are forces of which W/D is always dissipated and the system energy always decreases

In non conservative field we never talk about Potential Energy.

Ex: friction.

Scan for Video Explanation

Web Reference at www.physicsgalaxy.com

Module-7: Potential Energy Stored in a Spring

Potential Energy Stored in a Spring:

Force of an ideal Spring → Conservative Force.

Work done on a spring → Stored in form of Elastic Potential Energy

As spring is massless

$F = kx$

W/D in Compression of spring by x

$$W = \int_0^x kx \cdot dx$$

$$= \frac{1}{2}kx^2 \leftarrow \text{PE stored in spring}$$

Scan for Video Explanation

Web Reference at www.physicsgalaxy.com

Module-7: Potential Energy Stored in a Spring

If a spring is elongated then also it

Stores energy $\longrightarrow \frac{1}{2}kx^2$

$\rightarrow$ under deformed state (Compressed / Elongated)

$\downarrow$

Spring has some PE stored ($\frac{1}{2}kx^2$)

Initially $PE = \frac{1}{2}kx^2$

k, m, $F_R = kx$, x, v

smooth

def $= x$.

Final $PE = 0$

spring is doing work on block

$\downarrow$

block gains KE

$$\frac{1}{2}mv^2 = \frac{1}{2}kx^2 \Rightarrow v = \sqrt{\frac{k}{m}}\,x.$$

Web Reference at www.physicsgalaxy.com | Scan for Video Explanation

Module-8: Work-Energy Theorem

Work-Energy Theorem:

Whenever work is done on an object or a system of particles, its energy increases and the inc in energy is equal to WD on system/object.

In case of rigid body. $\longrightarrow \Delta W = \Delta K$ (inc in KE)

In Conservative fields $\longrightarrow \Delta W = \Delta U$ (inc in PE)

For system of bodies $\longrightarrow \Delta W = \Delta U + \Delta K$

Web Reference at www.physicsgalaxy.com | Scan for Video Explanation

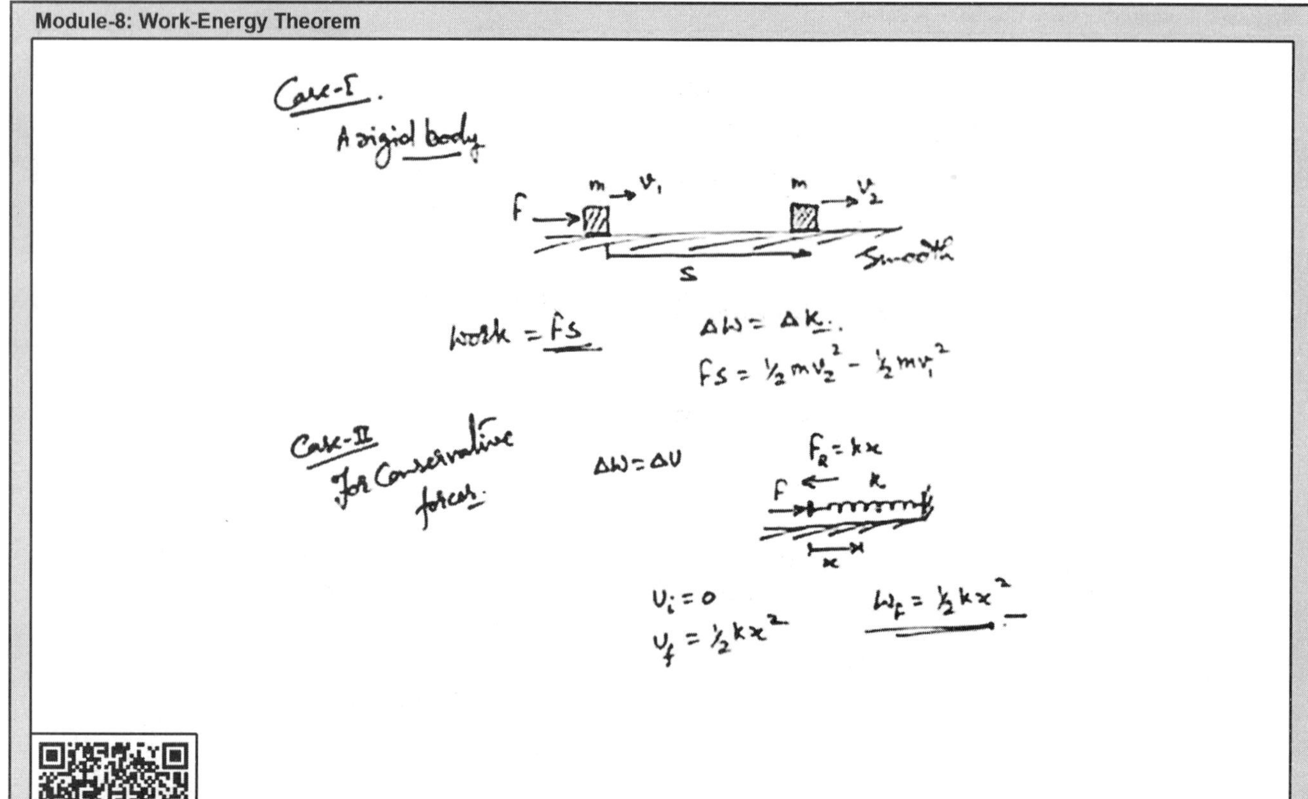

Module-8: Work-Energy Theorem

Case-I.

A rigid body

F
m
v_1
m
v_2
s
Smooth

work = Fs

$\Delta W = \Delta K$.

$Fs = \frac{1}{2}mv_2^2 - \frac{1}{2}mv_1^2$

Case-II

For Conservative forces.

$\Delta W = \Delta U$

$F_R = kx$
F
k
x

$U_i = 0$

$U_f = \frac{1}{2}kx^2$

$W_F = \frac{1}{2}kx^2$

Scan for Video Explanation

Web Reference at www.physicsgalaxy.com

Module-8: Work-Energy Theorem

Case-III

System of bodies (mixed)

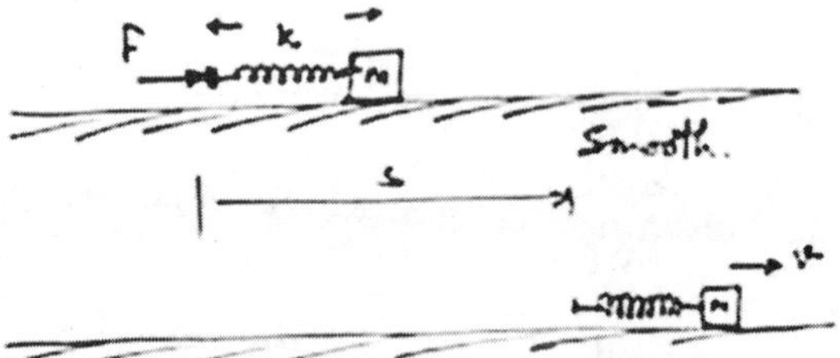

F
k
m
Smooth.
s
v
m

def = x

W/D by external force

$W_F = \frac{1}{2}mv^2 + \frac{1}{2}kx^2$

$$\boxed{W_F = \Delta K + \Delta U}$$

Scan for Video Explanation

Web Reference at www.physicsgalaxy.com

Module-8: Work-Energy Theorem

Ex : In a region potential energy of a body is given as

$$U = 4x^2 + 3x - 5 \text{ J}$$

Find work done by an external agent in slowly moving the body from point (3, 2) to (–1, 4).

Solⁿ:

$$U_i = 4(3)^2 + 3(3) - 5 = 40 \text{ J}$$

$$U_f = 4(-1)^2 + 3(-1) - 5 = -4 \text{ J}$$

W/D by ext. agent $W = U_f - U_i$

$$= (-4) - (40) = -44 \text{ J} \quad \text{Ans. } (-ve)$$

⇒ In this process external agent will gain energy

Web Reference at www.physicsgalaxy.com

Scan for Video Explanation

Module-9: Relation in Force & Potential Energy

Relation in Potential Energy & Forces:

Potential Energy ⇒ Conservative Forces.

$$\Delta W = \Delta U$$

Cons. field

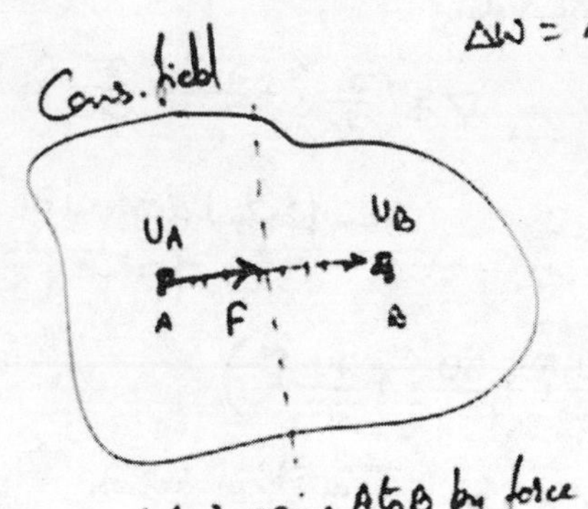

$U_A > U_B$

× Release.

mg

$U_x > U_y$

y

ground

W/D in going A to B by force $\Delta W = U_A - U_B$. grav. → Cons. field

$$\Delta W = \int_A^B \vec{F} \cdot d\vec{x} = -\Delta U$$

Web Reference at www.physicsgalaxy.com

Scan for Video Explanation

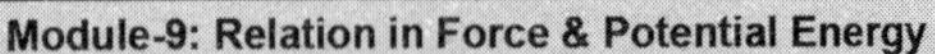

Module-9: Relation in Force & Potential Energy

$U = f(x)$

A, dx, B, F, X

In displacing the body by dx, let dU be the decrease in PE of System then we can use

$$-dU = F\,dx$$

$$dU = -F\,dx$$

or $$F = -\frac{dU}{dx}$$

vectorially $$\vec{F} = -\frac{dU}{dx}\hat{i}$$ for unidirectional variation in PE.

Scan for Video Explanation

Web Reference at www.physicsgalaxy.com

Module-9: Relation in Force & Potential Energy

In free space or 3D variation of PE we use

$$\vec{F} = -\nabla U = -\text{gradient of } U$$

(∇ → gradient operator.)

$$\nabla \equiv \left(\frac{\partial}{\partial x}\hat{i} + \frac{\partial}{\partial y}\hat{j} + \frac{\partial}{\partial z}\hat{k}\right)$$

∂ → partial derivative operator

$$\vec{F} = -\frac{dU}{dx}\hat{i}$$

$$\vec{F} = -\left(\frac{\partial U}{\partial x}\hat{i} + \frac{\partial U}{\partial y}\hat{j} + \frac{\partial U}{\partial z}\hat{k}\right)$$

Ex: If in a region $U = 4x^3 + 3y^2 z$ find $\vec{F}$ in this region

Sol: $$\vec{F} = -(12x^2)\hat{i} - (6yz)\hat{j} - (3y^2)\hat{k} = -12x^2\hat{i} - 6yz\hat{j} - 3y^2\hat{k}$$ Ans.

Scan for Video Explanation

Web Reference at www.physicsgalaxy.com

Module-10: Solved Example-3

Ex : **In a region, potential energy of a particle of mass 4 kg depends on its x-coordinate as**

$$U = 5x^3 + 4x + 7 \text{ Joule}$$

Find the acceleration of particle at position (2, 4).

As we know, force on a particle

$$F = \left|\frac{dU}{dx}\right| = 15x^2 + 4 \text{ N}$$

at $x = 2$, force on particle is

$$F = 15(2)^2 + 4 = 64 \text{ N}$$

$$a = \frac{F}{m} = \frac{64}{4} = 16 \text{ m/s}^2 \text{ Ans.}$$

Web Reference at www.physicsgalaxy.com | **Scan for Video Explanation**

Module-11: Solved Example-4

Ex : In a region potential energy of a particle of mass 2 kg is given by

$$U = 3x^2 + 4y^2 \text{ J}$$

Find the acceleration of particle when it is released from (1, 1)

Sol: force on particle $\vec{F} = -\nabla U = -\left(\frac{\partial U}{\partial x}\hat{i} + \frac{\partial U}{\partial y}\hat{j}\right)$

$$\vec{F} = -6x\hat{i} - 8y\hat{j}$$

for (1, 1)

$$\vec{F} = -6\hat{i} - 8\hat{j}$$

$$\vec{a} = \frac{\vec{F}}{m} = -\frac{(6\hat{i} + 8\hat{j})}{2} = -3\hat{i} - 4\hat{j} \text{ m/s}^2$$

$$a = \sqrt{3^2 + 4^2} = 5 \text{ m/s}^2$$

at an angle 53° with −x dir (in III quad) Ans.

$\theta = \tan^{-1}(4/3) = 53°$

-3, -4, X, Y, θ, 5

Web Reference at www.physicsgalaxy.com | **Scan for Video Explanation**

Module-12: Solved Example-5

Ex : In a conservative force field, work done in carrying a body from point P to Q is 5J and that from Q to R is 2J. Find work done in carrying the body from P to R.

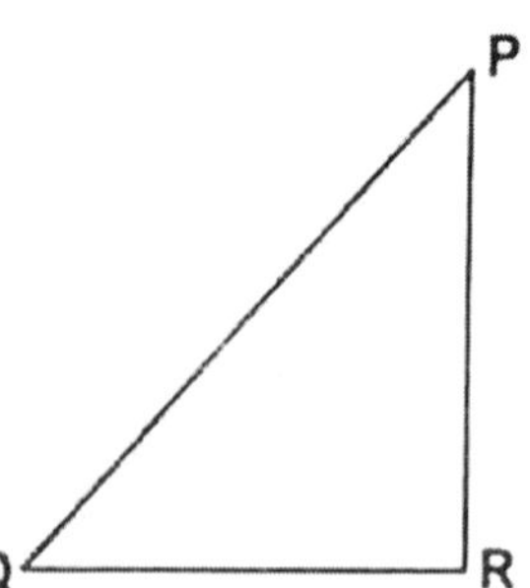

Sol^n:

$$W = U_f - U_i$$

$$W_{PQ} = U_Q - U_P = 5J \quad -(1)$$

$$W_{QR} = U_R - U_Q = 2J \quad -(2)$$

$$W_{PR} = U_R - U_P = 7J. \text{ Ans.}$$

Scan for Video Explanation

Web Reference at www.physicsgalaxy.com

Module-13: Work-Energy Equation for Rigid Bodies

Work-Energy Equation for rigid bodies:

For rigid bodies. → KE

$\Delta W = \Delta K$

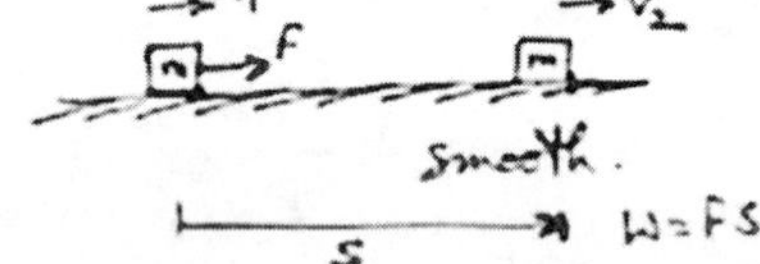

$K_i \qquad K_f$

$$\frac{1}{2}mv_1^2 + FS = \frac{1}{2}mv_2^2$$

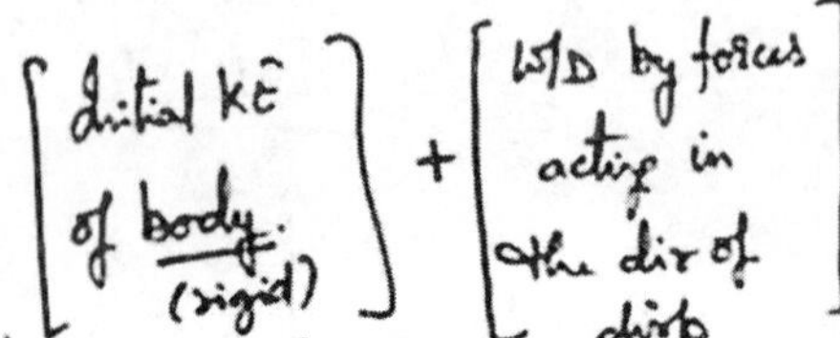
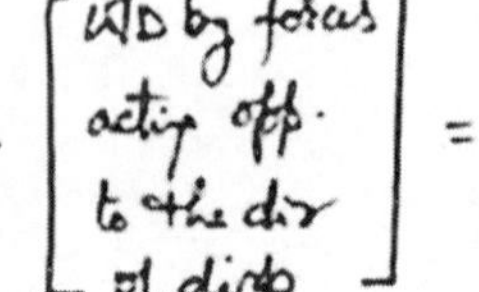
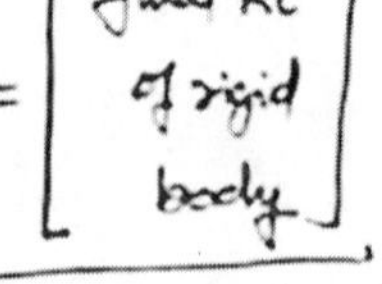

[Initial KE of body (rigid)] + [W/D by forces acting in the dir of disp] − [W/D by forces acting opp. to the dir of disp] = [Final KE of rigid body]

W-E Eq. for motion of a rigid body.

Scan for Video Explanation

Web Reference at www.physicsgalaxy.com

Module-13: Work-Energy Equation for Rigid Bodies

Ex:

$f = \mu mg$, s , rough (μ)

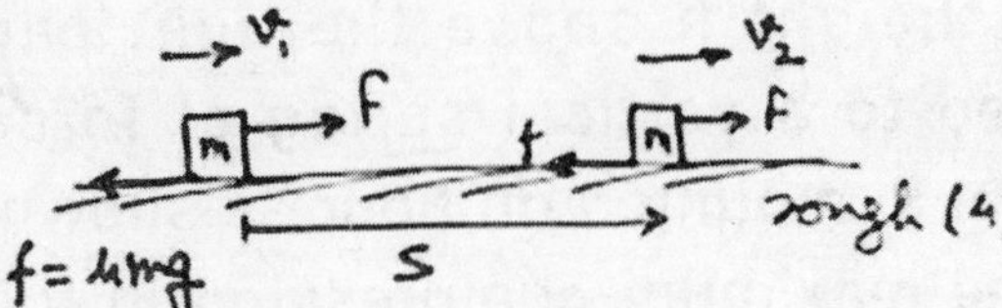

W-E eqⁿ for this motion

$$\frac{1}{2}mv_1^2 + Fs - \mu mgs = \frac{1}{2}mv_2^2$$

Ex: Find the speed when body hits the ground.

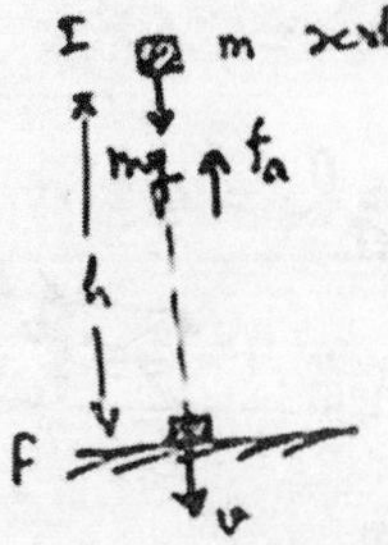

Solⁿ: W-E eqⁿ between I & F pos.

$$0 + mgh - f_a \cdot h = \frac{1}{2}mv^2$$

$$v = \sqrt{\frac{2(mgh - f_a h)}{m}}$$

Web Reference at www.physicsgalaxy.com | Scan for Video Explanation

Module-13: Work-Energy Equation for Rigid Bodies

Ex : A rigid block of mass m moves at speed v toward an ideal spring of force constant k as shown, find the maximum distance to which the spring will be compressed by the block.

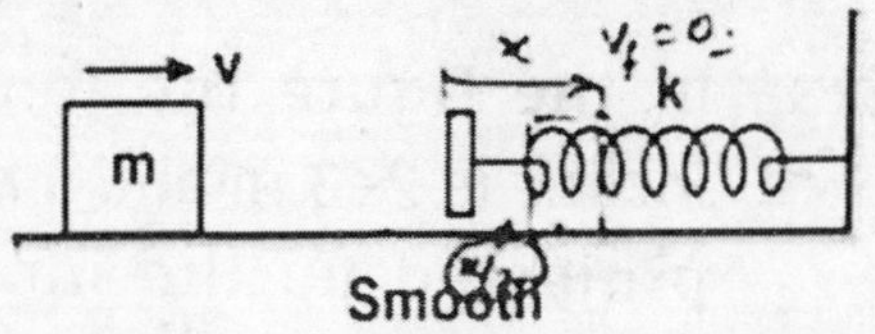

Smooth

Solⁿ. Let finally spring is compressed by x.

using W-E eqⁿ we have

$$\frac{1}{2}mv^2 - \frac{1}{2}kx^2 = 0$$

$$\frac{1}{2}mv^2 = \frac{1}{2}kx^2$$

$$x = \sqrt{\frac{m}{k}}\,v \quad \text{Ans.}$$

if we wish to find vel of block when compression in spring is $x/2$ then we use → $\frac{1}{2}mv^2 - \frac{1}{2}k\left(\frac{x}{2}\right)^2 = \frac{1}{2}mv_1^2$ $v_1 = \ldots$

Web Reference at www.physicsgalaxy.com | Scan for Video Explanation

Module-14: Solved Example-6

Ex : A block of mass m is released from rest from a height h above the light pan attached to a vertical spring of force constant k, mounted on floor as shown. Find the maximum compression in the spring by the block.

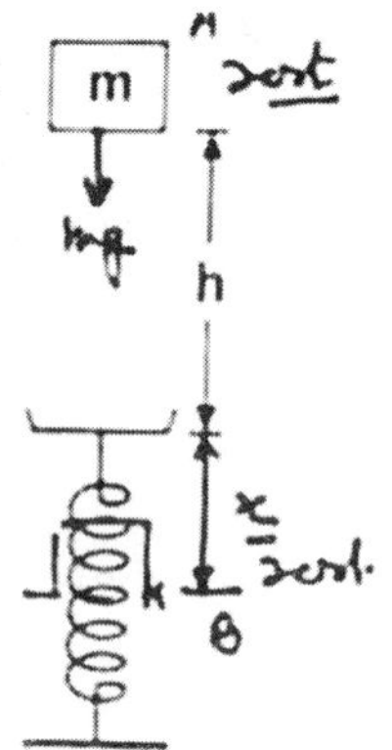

Sol^n: using WE eq^n from A to B.

$$\underset{K_i}{0} + mg(h+x) - \frac{1}{2}kx^2 = \underset{K_f}{0}$$

$$kx^2 - 2mgx - 2mgh = 0$$

$$x = \left(\frac{2mg + \sqrt{4m^2g^2 + 8mghk}}{2k}\right) \text{ Ans.}$$

Scan for Video Explanation

Module-15: Solved Example-7

Ex : In the figure the length of incline is $2\sqrt{3}$ m and a block is projected up the incline at speed 10 m/s. Find the speed with which block will move off the top of incline plane.

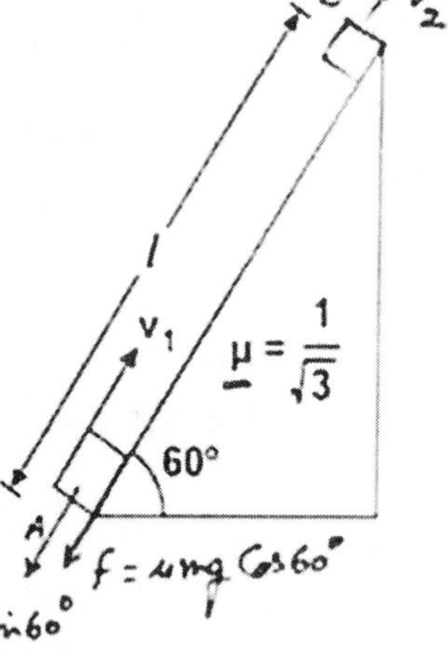

Sol^n: W-E eq^n from A to B.

$$\frac{1}{2}mv_1^2 - mg\sin60^\circ \times l - \mu mg\cos60^\circ \times l = \frac{1}{2}mv_2^2$$

$$\frac{(10)^2}{2} - 10 \times \frac{\sqrt{3}}{2} \times 2\sqrt{3} - \frac{1}{\sqrt{3}} \times 10 \times \frac{1}{2} \times 2\sqrt{3} = \frac{1}{2}v_2^2$$

$$50 - 30 - 10 = \frac{1}{2}v_2^2 \Rightarrow v_2 = \sqrt{20} \text{ m/s. Ans.}$$

Scan for Video Explanation

Module-16: Solved Example-8

Ex : A pendulum bob is projected horizontally as shown, find the speed of pendulum bob when string is at an angle θ with vertical. Also find the maximum angle to which string will be deflected.

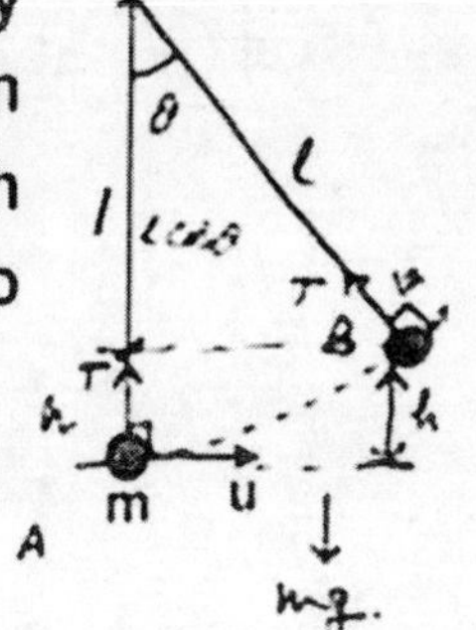

Sol^n: using W-E eq^n betw^n pts A and B.

$$\frac{1}{2}mu^2 - mg\,l(1-\cos\theta) = \frac{1}{2}mv^2$$

$h = l - l\cos\theta = l(1-\cos\theta)$

$$v = \sqrt{u^2 - 2gl(1-\cos\theta)} \text{ Ans.}$$

If $\theta = \phi$ is the max angle to which string is deflected
$\Rightarrow$ at $\theta = \phi$, $v = 0$.

$$0 = u^2 - 2gl(1-\cos\phi)$$

$$\cos\phi = \frac{2gl - u^2}{2gl} \Rightarrow \phi = \cos^{-1}\left(\frac{2gl-u^2}{2gl}\right) \text{ Ans.}$$

Web Reference at www.physicsgalaxy.com | Scan for Video Explanation

Module-17: Solved Example-9

Ex : A block B of mass 1 kg is attached to a spring of natural length 7 cm and force constant 2000 N/m of which other end is attached to a fixed point A. Initially the block B is placed at a position where the distance AB = 10 cm. If block B is released, find the maximum speed attained by the block during its motion.

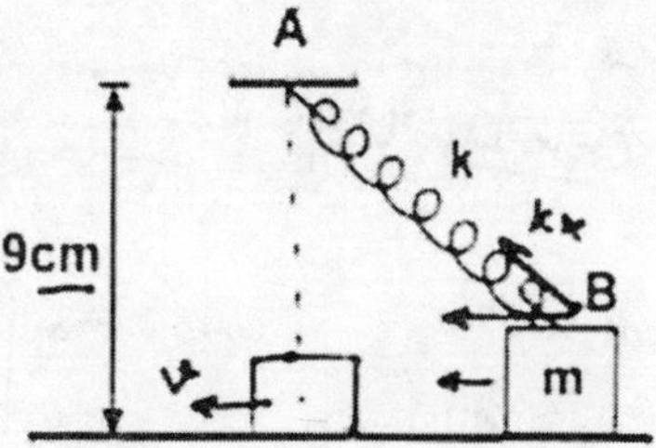

Sol^n: $U_{s_i} = \frac{1}{2}k(0.03)^2$ $\quad U_{s_f} = \frac{1}{2}k(0.02)^2$

WE eq^n

$$0 + \left[\frac{1}{2}k(0.03)^2 - \frac{1}{2}k(0.02)^2\right] = \frac{1}{2}mv^2$$

$$v = \sqrt{\frac{k}{m}(5\times10^{-4})} = \sqrt{\frac{2000}{1}\times5\times10^{-4}} = 1 \text{ m/s Ans.}$$

Web Reference at www.physicsgalaxy.com | Scan for Video Explanation

Module-18: Concept of Equilibrium

Concept of Equilibrium:

Equilibrium $\Rightarrow$ $\Sigma\vec{F} = 0$

In Conservative field.

$$\vec{F} = -\frac{dU}{dx}\hat{i}$$

When a body is under the state of eq^n in Cons. field

$$F = \left|\frac{dU}{dx}\right| = 0$$

(1) If U = Constant (2) If U → maximum (3) If U → minimum

Scan for Video Explanation

Web Reference at www.physicsgalaxy.com

Module-18: Concept of Equilibrium

Case-I: U → maximum U = f(x)

at x = x₁

$$F = \left|\frac{dU}{dx}\right| = 0$$

at $x = x_1{+}$ $\vec{F} = -\frac{dU}{dx}\hat{i}$ (+ve)

at $x = x_1{-}$ $\vec{F} = -\frac{dU}{dx}\hat{i}$ (−ve)

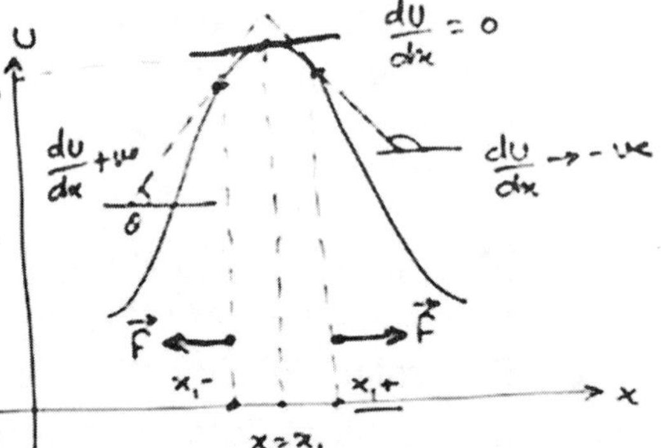

at $x = x_1$ ⟶ body is said to be in "Unstable Equilibrium".

Scan for Video Explanation

Web Reference at www.physicsgalaxy.com

Module-18: Concept of Equilibrium

Case-II: $U \rightarrow$ minimum $\quad U = f(x)$

at $x = x_1$

$$\vec{F} = -\frac{dU}{dx}\hat{i} = 0.$$

at $x = x_1+$

$$\vec{F} = -\frac{dU}{dx}\hat{i} \; (-ve)$$

at $x = x_1-$

$$\vec{F} = -\frac{dU}{dx}\hat{i} \; (+ve)$$

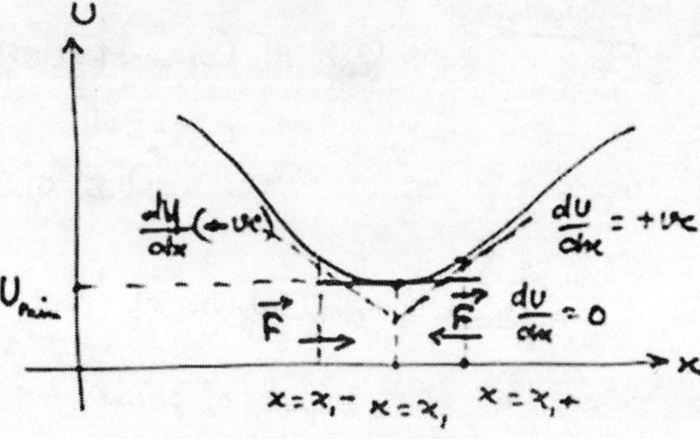

Stable Equilibrium
↓
minimum PE.

Web Reference at www.physicsgalaxy.com

Scan for Video Explanation

Module-18: Concept of Equilibrium

Case-III: $U \rightarrow$ Constant

everywhere

$$U = Const$$

$$F = \left|\frac{dU}{dx}\right| = 0$$

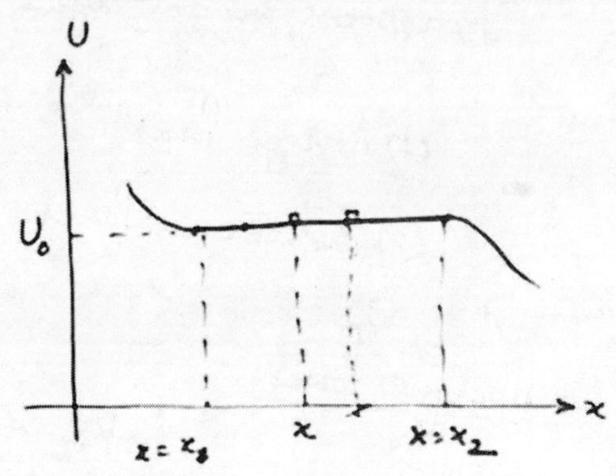

Neutral Equilibrium

for all positions $x_1 \leq x \leq x_2$

Web Reference at www.physicsgalaxy.com

Scan for Video Explanation

Module-19: Power

Power:

Rate of Consumption of Energy

OR

Rate of Doing work

→ Power is a measure of how fast one can do work.

unit of power → J/sec or watt

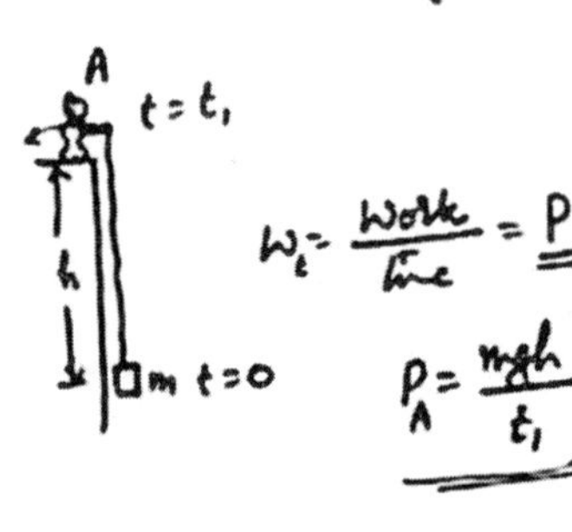

$W_t = \frac{\text{Work}}{\text{time}} = P$

$P_A = \frac{mgh}{t_1}$

B $t = t_2$ $\quad t_2 < t_1$

h

m $t = 0$

$P_B = \frac{mgh}{t_2}$

$P_B > P_A$

Scan for Video Explanation

Web Reference at www.physicsgalaxy.com

Module-19: Power

For a process we can define power in two ways -

(1) Average Power

(2) Instantaneous Power.

Average Power:

$$\langle P \rangle_{avg} = \frac{\text{Total work done}}{\text{time taken}} = \frac{\Delta W}{\Delta t}$$

For a rigid body always $\Delta W = \Delta K$ $\quad \langle P_{avg} \rangle = \frac{\Delta K}{\Delta t}$

* Power associated with a force can be +ve or -ve.

+ Power ⇒ Supply of Energy/sec

- Power ⇒ Gain of Energy/sec.

Scan for Video Explanation

Web Reference at www.physicsgalaxy.com

Module-19: Power

Ex : **Find average power of gravity in motion of a projectile of mass m from starting points O to the highest point of trajectory A as shown in figure.**

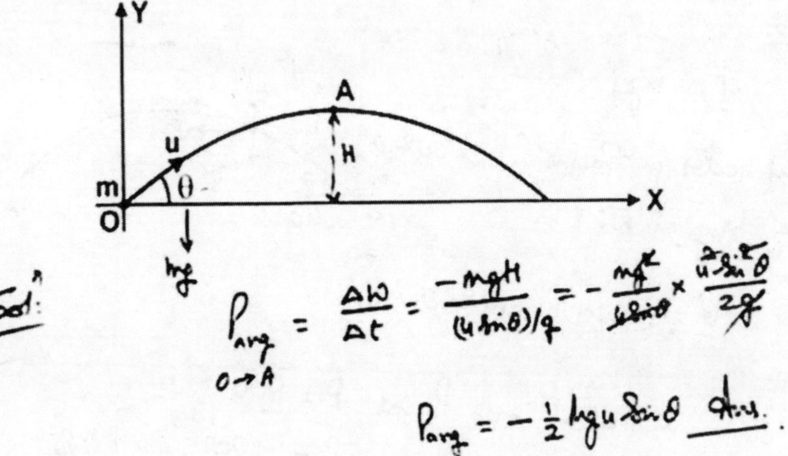

Sol^n:

$$P_{\underset{O\to A}{avg}} = \frac{\Delta W}{\Delta t} = \frac{-mgH}{(u\sin\theta)/g} = -\frac{mg^2}{u\sin\theta} \times \frac{u^2\sin^2\theta}{2g}$$

$$P_{avg} = -\frac{1}{2} mgu\sin\theta \quad \text{Ans.}$$

Web Reference at www.physicsgalaxy.com

Scan for Video Explanation

Module-19: Power

Instantaneous Power:

In a process of doing work if for an elemental duration dt, W/D is dW then for this instant, instantaneous power is defined as

$$P = \frac{dW}{dt}$$

if $\vec{F}$ is the force associated $\Rightarrow$ $dW = \vec{F}\cdot\vec{dx}$

$$P = \frac{\vec{F}\cdot\vec{dx}}{dt} = \vec{F}\cdot\vec{v} = Fv\cos\theta$$

$$\boxed{P = \vec{F}\cdot\vec{v}}$$

[for supporting forces P is +ve
for opposing forces P is −ve.]

Web Reference at www.physicsgalaxy.com

Scan for Video Explanation

Module-19: Power

Ex : A body of mass m is thrown at an angle θ with the horizontal with initial velocity u. Find the instantaneous power developed by gravity as function of time.

Sol:

$\vec{F} = -mg\hat{j}$

vel vector in the motion of proj at time t is

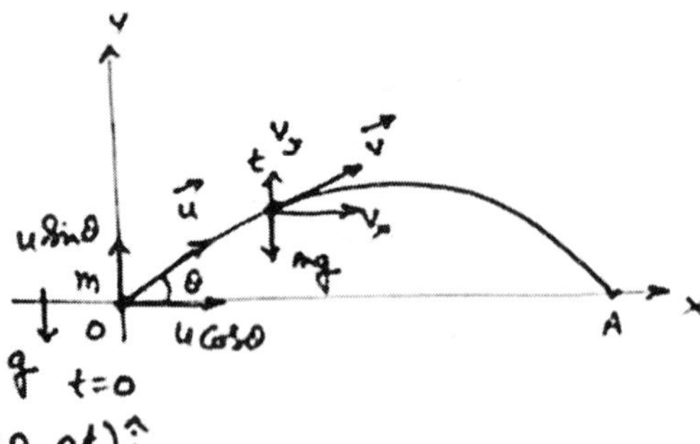

$\vec{v} = (u\cos\theta)\hat{i} + (u\sin\theta - gt)\hat{j}$

Instantaneous Power $P = \vec{F}\cdot\vec{v}$

$P = -mgu\sin\theta + mg^2t$. Ans.

Scan for Video Explanation

Web Reference at www.physicsgalaxy.com

Module-20: Solved Example-10

Ex : A man lifts 100 stones to a height of 6 m in 2 minutes. If mass of each stone is 1 kg what is the average power of man. (Take g = 10 m/s^2)

Sol:

Total W/D by man in 120 sec is

$W = 100 \times mgh$

$= 100 \times 1 \times 10 \times 6 = 6000\,J$

Avg power of man $\langle P \rangle_{avg} = \frac{\Delta W}{\Delta t} = \frac{6000}{120} = 50$ Watt Ans.

Scan for Video Explanation

Web Reference at www.physicsgalaxy.com

Module-21: Solved Example-11

Ex : **A block of mass m is placed at rest on a rough horizontal surface with fiction coefficient μ. A constant horizontal force is applied on it so that it starts accelerating with acceleration a. Find the power of the applied force at time t.**

Solⁿ:

for motion of block

$F - \mu mg = ma$

$F = ma + \mu mg$.

$f = \mu mg$. (μ)

vel of block at time t is $v = at$.

Instantaneous Power of force F at time t is $P = Fv$

$= m(a + \mu g)at$

Ans.

Scan for Video Explanation

Chapter 8
Circular Motion

Lecture Notes Modules

Module-1: Circular Motion and Angular Properties

Circular Motion:

Motion of a particle along a circular path.

→ It is an accelerated motion.

In general CM is defined in two categories –

(1) Uniform Circular Motion (UCM) → $|\vec{v}|$ = Constant

(2) Non-Uniform Cir Motion (NUCM) → $|\vec{v}| \neq$ Constant

Scan for Video Explanation

Web Reference at www.physicsgalaxy.com

Module-1: Circular Motion and Angular Properties

Standard Properties of Angular Motion:

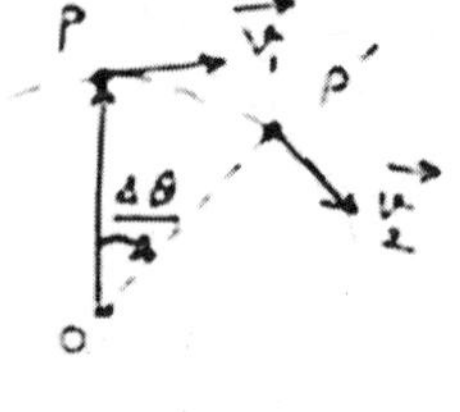

(1) Angular Displacement: (in rad)

Angle traversed by p.v. of particle w.r.t. a ref point (Centre of Circle)

(2) Angular velocity: rate of change of angular displacement.
(in rad/sec)

(3) Angular Acceleration: rate of change of angular velocity.
(in rad/sec²)

NOTE: Dir of angular vectors are given by Right Hand Thumb Rule.

Scan for Video Explanation

Web Reference at www.physicsgalaxy.com

Module-1: Circular Motion and Angular Properties

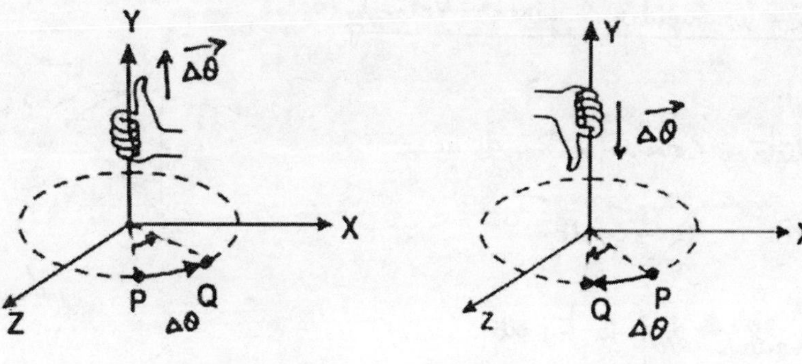

\# Angular Displacement : → $\vec{\Delta\theta}$

\# Angular Velocity → $\vec{\omega} = \frac{\vec{\Delta\theta}}{\Delta t}$ rad/sec

↑ Avg ang. velocity

Instantaneous ang vel $\omega = \frac{d\theta}{dt}$

Web Reference at www.physicsgalaxy.com

Scan for Video Explanation

Module-1: Circular Motion and Angular Properties

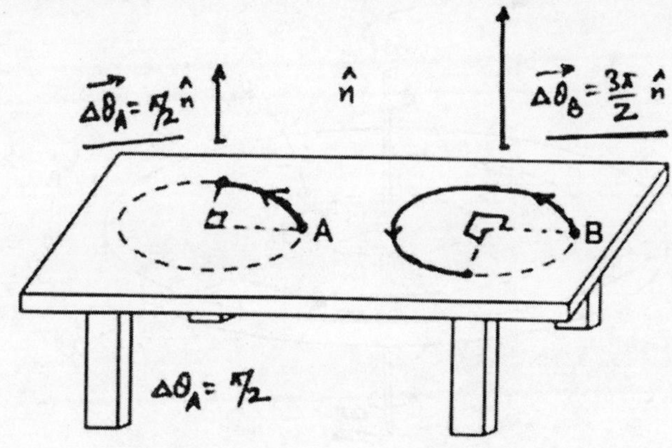

$\Delta\theta_B = \frac{3\pi}{2}$.

Actual dir of Angular disp → ckwise ↓ OR ackwise ↑

Web Reference at www.physicsgalaxy.com

Scan for Video Explanation

Module-2: Relation in Linear and Angular Velocity

Relation in Angular & Linear Velocity:

distance covered in time dt is

$$dS = v\,dt$$

Angular disp in time dt

$$d\theta = \frac{dS}{R} = \frac{v\,dt}{R}$$

$$\frac{d\theta}{dt} = \frac{v}{R}$$

Ang. vel. $\boxed{\omega = v/R}$ or $\boxed{v = R\omega}$

$\vec{\omega} \rightarrow$ Dir is given by RHTR.

t, $\vec{v}$, t + dt, R, dθ, C, ω

Scan for Video Explanation

Web Reference at www.physicsgalaxy.com

Module-2: Relation in Linear and Angular Velocity

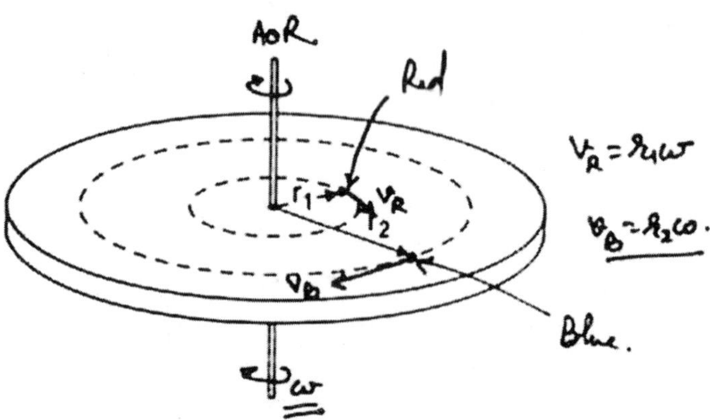

NOTE: When a body rotates at an angular speed ω then all of its particles revolve in cir. motion at same ang. speed ω.

Scan for Video Explanation

Web Reference at www.physicsgalaxy.com

Module-3: Angular Acceleration

Angular Acceleration: (denoted by 'α'.)

Acceleration → rate of change of velocity

Angular Acceleration → rate of change of ang. vel.

$$a = \frac{dv}{dt} \quad \text{OR} \quad a = v\frac{dv}{dx} \longrightarrow \alpha = \frac{d\omega}{dt} \times \frac{d\theta}{d\theta} = \frac{d^2\theta}{dt^2} \quad \text{OR} \quad \alpha = \omega\frac{d\omega}{d\theta}$$

As we know $v = R\omega$

diff w.r.to t $\frac{dv}{dt} = R.\frac{d\omega}{dt}$

tangential acceleration $\boxed{a_t = R\alpha}$

Web Reference at www.physicsgalaxy.com | Scan for Video Explanation

Module-3: Angular Acceleration

Speed Equations for Constant Angular Acceleration:

for linear motion with Constant acc^n we use -

$$v = u + at$$
$$s = ut + \frac{1}{2}at^2$$
$$v^2 = u^2 + 2as$$
$$\Delta s_n = u + \frac{a}{2}(2n-1)$$

Similarly for uniform ang. acc^n in Circular motion we use angular speed equations, given as-

$$\omega = \omega_0 + \alpha t$$
$$\theta = \omega_0 t + \frac{1}{2}\alpha t^2$$
$$\omega^2 = \omega_0^2 + 2\alpha\theta$$
$$\Delta\theta_n = \omega_0 + \frac{\alpha}{2}(2n-1)$$

ω_0 → Initial ang. vel

ω → Final ang. vel

α → Ang. acc^n

θ → ang. disp

$\Delta\theta_n$ → ang disp in n^{th} sec

t → time

Web Reference at www.physicsgalaxy.com | Scan for Video Explanation

Module-3: Angular Acceleration

If in a Case ang acc^n is variable Then we use

$$\left[\alpha = \frac{d\omega}{dt} \quad \text{or} \quad \alpha = \omega\frac{d\omega}{d\theta} \qquad \omega = \frac{d\theta}{dt}\right]$$

$$a = \frac{dv}{dt} \text{ or } a = \frac{v\,dv}{dx} \qquad v = \frac{dx}{dt}$$

Ex: If a body rotates such that its ang. acc^n varies with time as-

$$\alpha = 4t^3 + 2t \ \text{rad/s}^2$$

Find ang. speed of body at $t = 2$ sec if it starts from rest.

Sol^n:

$$\frac{d\omega}{dt} = 4t^3 + 2t$$

$$\int_0^{\omega} d\omega = \int_0^2 (4t^3 + 2t)\,dt \Rightarrow \omega = [t^4 + t^2]_0^2$$

$$\omega = 16 + 4 = 20 \text{ rad/sec}$$

Ans.

Scan for Video Explanation

Web Reference at www.physicsgalaxy.com

Module-4: Solved Example-1

Ex : A solid body rotates about a stationary axis with an angular retardation $\alpha = k\sqrt{\omega}$, where ω is the angular velocity of body. Find the time after which body will come to rest if at t = 0, angular velocity of body was ω_0.

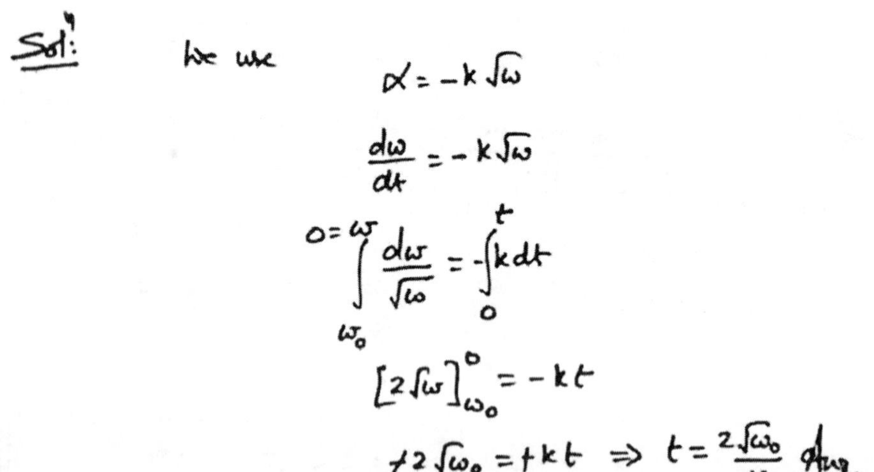

Scan for Video Explanation

Web Reference at www.physicsgalaxy.com

Module-5: Solved Example-2

Ex : A wheel is subjected to uniform angular acceleration about its axis. Initially it was at rest. In first 2 seconds it rotates through angle θ_1. In next 2 seconds, it rotates through angle θ_2. Find the ratio of θ_2/θ_1.

Sol: As initially wheel was at rest then at time t after starts its ag. disp is -

$$\theta = \omega_0 t + \frac{1}{2}\alpha t^2 \qquad [\text{As } \omega_0 = 0]$$

$$\theta = \frac{1}{2}\alpha t^2$$

at $t = 2\,s$ $\quad \theta_1 = \frac{1}{2}\alpha(2)^2 = 2\alpha$

at $t = 4\,s$ $\quad \theta_1 + \theta_2 = \frac{1}{2}\alpha(4)^2 = 8\alpha$

$\theta_2 = 6\alpha$

$$\frac{\theta_2}{\theta_1} = 3 \text{ Ans.}$$

Web Reference at www.physicsgalaxy.com | Scan for Video Explanation

Module-6: Solved Example-3

Ex : The length of second's hand in a watch is 1 cm. Find the magnitude of change in velocity of its tip in 15 second. Also find the magnitude of average acceleration during this interval.

Sol^n: Time period of second's hand $T = 60$ sec

$\Rightarrow$ Ang vel $\omega = \frac{2\pi}{T} = \frac{\pi}{30}$ rad/s

vel of tip of Second's hand is $v = R\omega = \frac{\pi}{30}$ cm/s

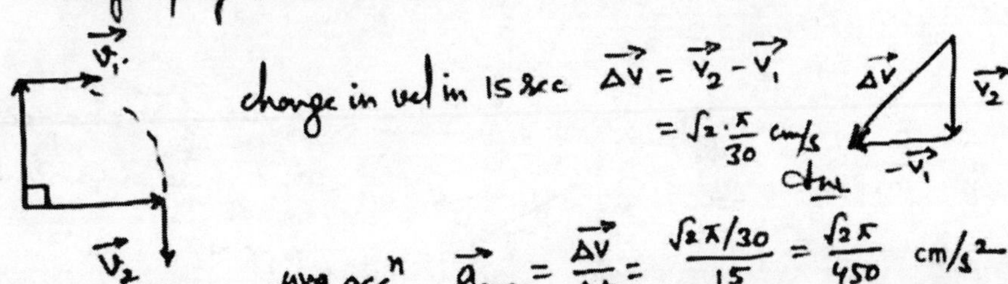

change in vel in 15 sec $\vec{\Delta v} = \vec{v_2} - \vec{v_1}$

$= \sqrt{2}\cdot\frac{\pi}{30}$ cm/s Ans

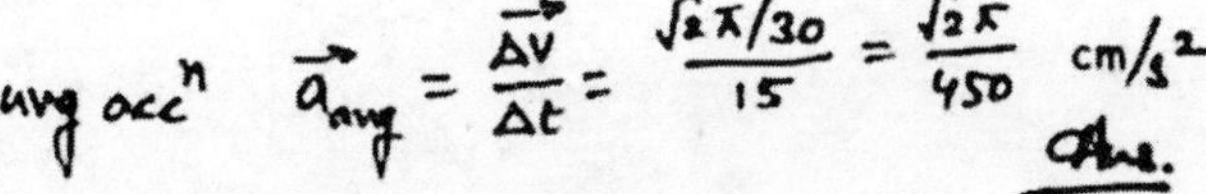

avg acc^n $\vec{a}_{avg} = \frac{\vec{\Delta v}}{\Delta t} = \frac{\sqrt{2}\pi/30}{15} = \frac{\sqrt{2}\pi}{450}$ cm/s^2 Ans.

Web Reference at www.physicsgalaxy.com | Scan for Video Explanation

Module-7: Solved Example-4

Ex : A particle starts moving in a circular path of radius 2 m with initial speed 2 m/s at constant angular acceleration. After two complete revolutions, its speed becomes 8 m/s. Find the angular acceleration of the particle.

Soln:

Initial ang speed $\omega_0 = \frac{v_i}{R} = \frac{2}{2} = 1$ rad/s

Final ang speed $\omega = \frac{v_f}{R} = \frac{8}{2} = 4$ rad/s.

We use $\omega^2 = \omega_0^2 + 2\alpha\theta$

$$\alpha = \frac{\omega^2 - \omega_0^2}{2\theta} = \frac{(4)^2 - (1)^2}{2(4\pi)} = \frac{15}{8\pi} \text{ rad/s}^2$$

Ans.

Scan for Video Explanation

Web Reference at www.physicsgalaxy.com

Module-8: Analysis of Acceleration in 2D Motion

Analysis of Acceleration of a particle in 2D motion:

$\vec{a} \rightarrow$ change in $\vec{v}$ → magnitude, Direction

$\vec{a} = \frac{\vec{F}}{m}$ — mag of $\vec{v}$ increases

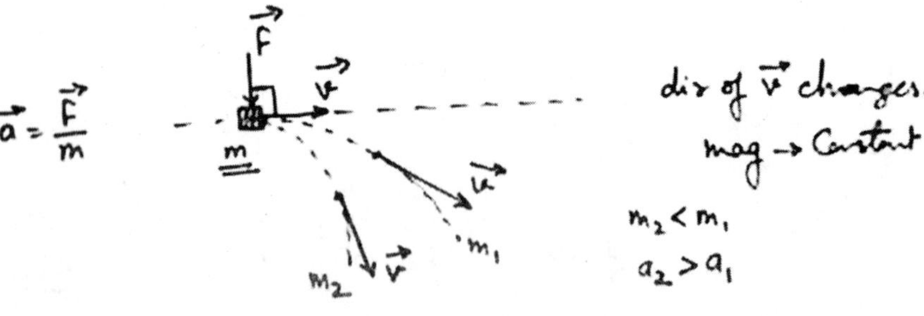

$\vec{a} = \frac{\vec{F}}{m}$ — dir of $\vec{v}$ changes. mag → Constant

$m_2 < m_1$

$a_2 > a_1$

Scan for Video Explanation

Web Reference at www.physicsgalaxy.com

Module-8: Analysis of Acceleration in 2D Motion

$\vec{F}$ $F\sin\theta$ $\vec{v}$ θ $F\cos\theta$ m

acceleration along $\vec{v}$ $\quad a_{\parallel} = \frac{F\cos\theta}{m}$ ← responsible for change in magnitude of velocity.

acceleration normal to $\vec{v}$ $\quad a_{\perp} = \frac{F\sin\theta}{m}$ ← responsible for change in direction of velocity.

net acc^n $\quad \vec{a}_T = \vec{a}_{\parallel} + \vec{a}_{\perp}$

Web Reference at www.physicsgalaxy.com | Scan for Video Explanation

Module-8: Analysis of Acceleration in 2D Motion

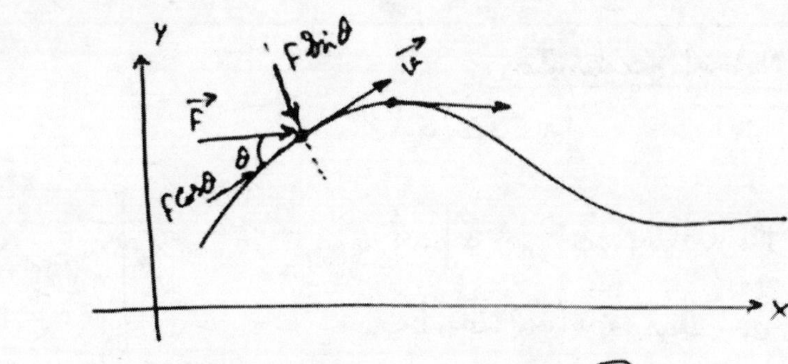

✓ Tangential Acc^n of Particle $\quad a_t = \frac{F\cos\theta}{m}$

✓ Normal Acc^n of Particle $\quad a_N = \frac{F\sin\theta}{m}$

Total acc^n of Particle $\quad \boxed{a_T = \sqrt{a_t^2 + a_N^2}}$

Web Reference at www.physicsgalaxy.com | Scan for Video Explanation

Module-9: Tangential and Normal Acceleration

Tangential Acceleration:

for Circular Motion

for UCM → $|\vec{v}|$ = Constant

$a_t = 0$

for NUCM → $a_t \neq 0$

$$\left[\begin{array}{l} a_t = \frac{dv}{dt} = \frac{d}{dt}|\vec{v}| \\ a_t = v\frac{dv}{ds} \end{array}\right]$$

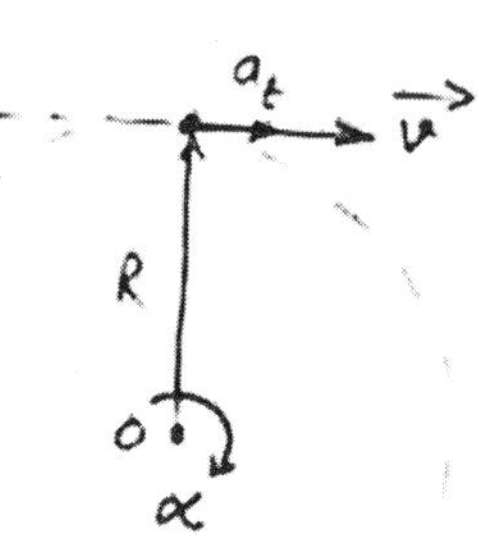

$$\boxed{a_t = R\alpha}$$

Scan for Video Explanation

Web Reference at www.physicsgalaxy.com

Module-9: Tangential and Normal Acceleration

Normal Acceleration:

for Circular Motion

The normal acc^n for a particle in circular motion can be given as-

$$\boxed{a_N = \frac{v^2}{R}}$$

$$a_N = \frac{(R\omega)^2}{R} = \omega^2 R$$

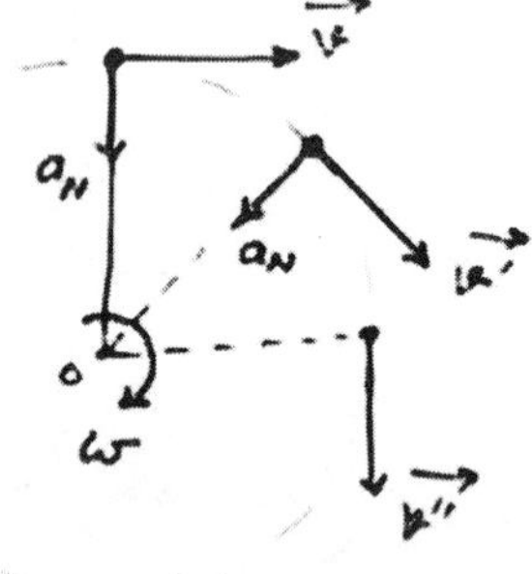

$v = R\omega$

Scan for Video Explanation

Web Reference at www.physicsgalaxy.com

Module-9: Tangential and Normal Acceleration

$$a_N = \frac{v^2}{R} = \omega^2 R$$

Vel. vect of particle at time t is

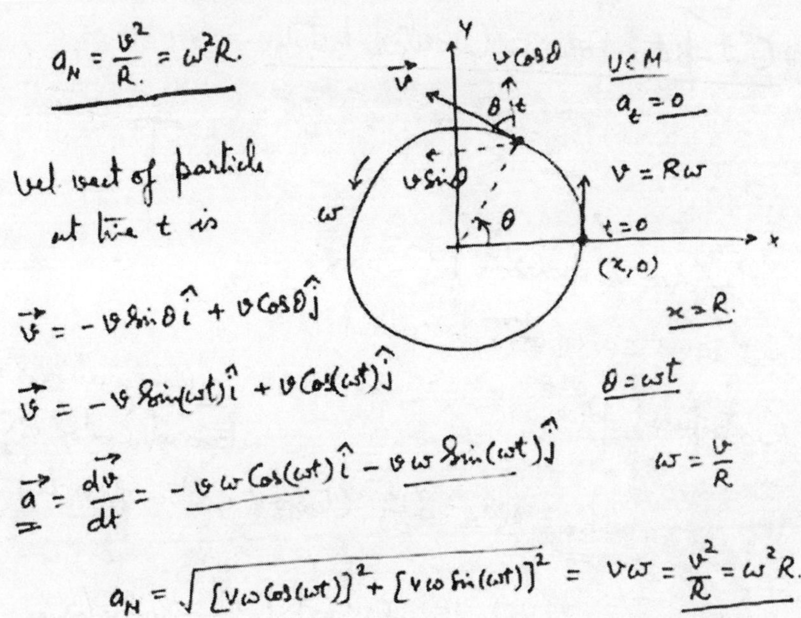

$x = R$

$\theta = \omega t$

$\omega = \frac{v}{R}$

$$\vec{v} = -v\sin\theta\,\hat{i} + v\cos\theta\,\hat{j}$$

$$\vec{v} = -v\sin(\omega t)\,\hat{i} + v\cos(\omega t)\,\hat{j}$$

$$\vec{a} = \frac{d\vec{v}}{dt} = -v\omega\cos(\omega t)\,\hat{i} - v\omega\sin(\omega t)\,\hat{j}$$

$$a_N = \sqrt{[v\omega\cos(\omega t)]^2 + [v\omega\sin(\omega t)]^2} = v\omega = \frac{v^2}{R} = \omega^2 R$$

Module-9: Tangential and Normal Acceleration

Normal Acceleration for a particle in 2D motion:

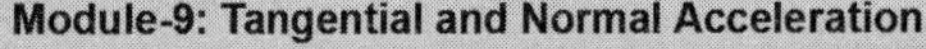

$$\text{rad. of curv. } r = \frac{\left[1+\left(\frac{dy}{dx}\right)^2\right]^{3/2}}{|d^2y/dx^2|}$$

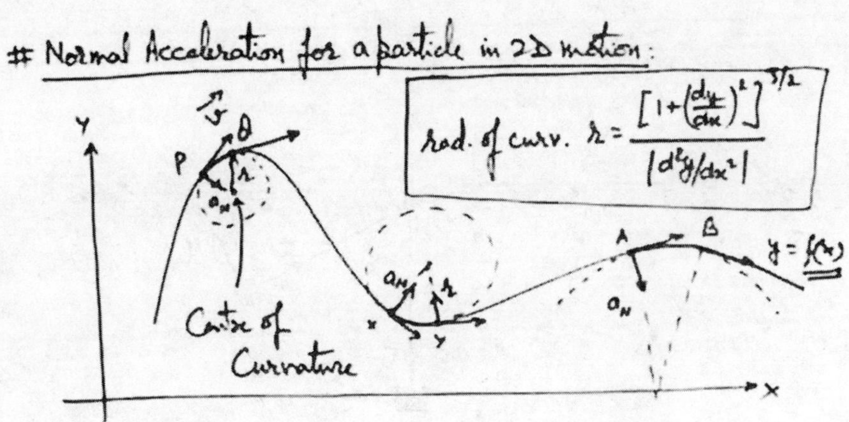

r – radius of curvature

If at a position on curve where rad. of curvature is r & a particle is moving at speed v then its normal acc^n at this pos. can be given as $\boxed{a_N = \frac{v^2}{r}}$ ← Centripetal acc^n

Module-9: Tangential and Normal Acceleration

Centripetal Force in Circular Motion:

$$a_N = \frac{v^2}{R}$$

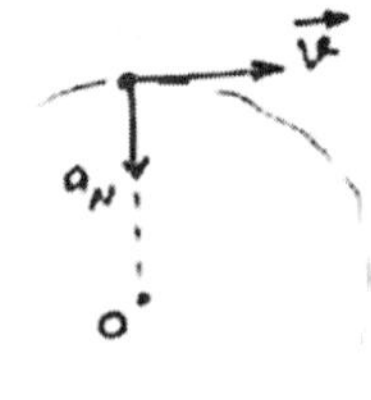

The force responsible for normal acc^n in a cir. motion is called Centripetal force.

C.P. force always act toward Centre of Circle.

$$F_{cp} = m a_N = \frac{mv^2}{R} \text{ (toward centre of circle)}$$

NOTE: For circular Motion of a particle Centripetal force is necessary.

Scan for Video Explanation

Web Reference at www.physicsgalaxy.com

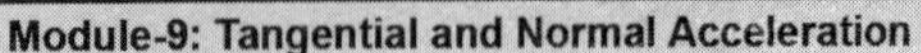

Module-9: Tangential and Normal Acceleration

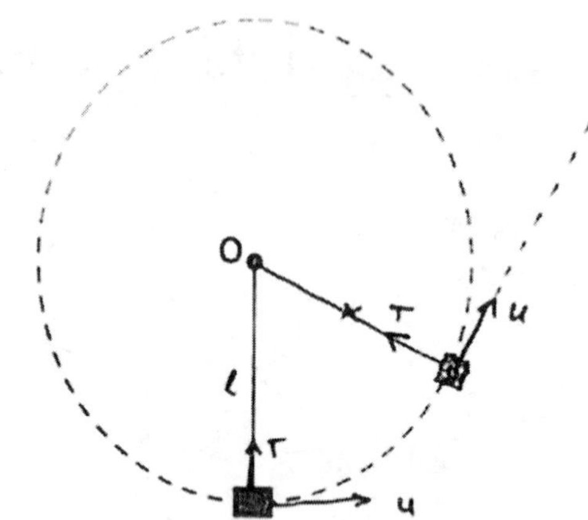

Here $T = \frac{mu^2}{l}$.

Scan for Video Explanation

Web Reference at www.physicsgalaxy.com

Module-9: Tangential and Normal Acceleration

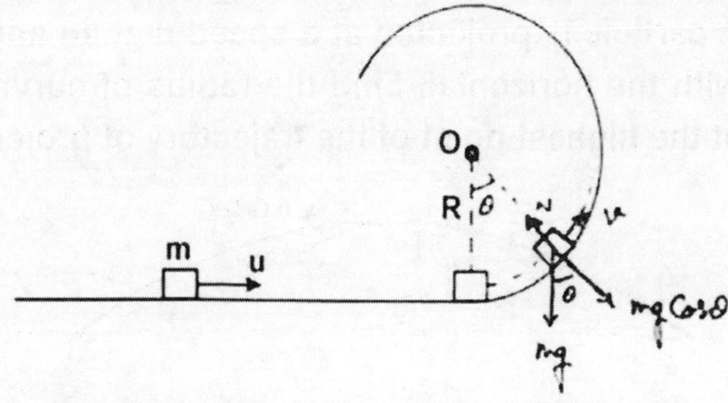

Here we use

$$N - mg\cos\theta = \frac{mv^2}{R}$$

in a CM net radially inward force $= \frac{mv^2}{R}$

Centripetal force.

Web Reference at www.physicsgalaxy.com | Scan for Video Explanation

Module-10: Solved Example-5

Ex : **A particle moves in a circular path of radius 3m at a speed given as v = 3t² m/s. Find at t = 2 sec.**

(a) Tangential acceleration of particle.

(b) Normal acceleration of particle.

(c) Total acceleration of particle.

Solⁿ: $v = 3t^2$ m/s

(a) $a_t = \frac{dv}{dt} = 6t = 6\times 2 = 12\ m/s^2$ Ans.

(b) $a_N = \frac{v^2}{R} = \frac{(3t^2)^2}{R} = \frac{9t^4}{3}\Big|_{t=2} = 3\times 16 = 48\ m/s^2$ Ans.

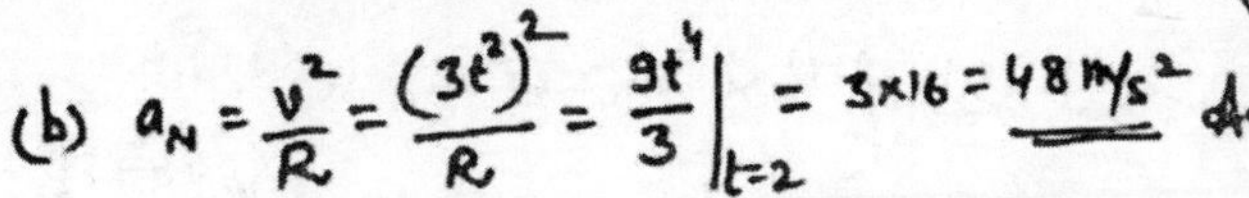

(c) $a_T = \sqrt{a_t^2 + a_N^2} = \sqrt{(12)^2+(48)^2} = 12\sqrt{17}\ m/s^2$ Ans.

Web Reference at www.physicsgalaxy.com | Scan for Video Explanation

Module-11: Solved Example-6

Ex : A particle is projected at a speed u at an angle θ with the horizontal. Find the radius of curvature at the highest point of the trajectory of projectile.

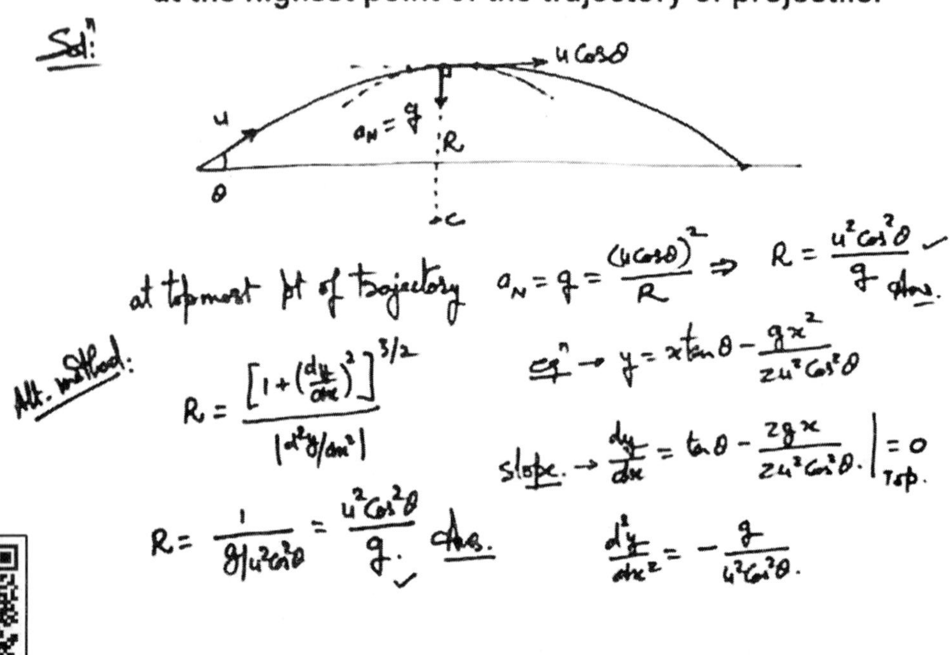

Scan for Video Explanation

Web Reference at www.physicsgalaxy.com

Module-12: Solved Example-7

Ex : A particle moves in a circular path of radius 1 m with an angular speed

$$\omega = 2t^2 + 1 \text{ rad/sec}$$

Find the angle between total acceleration and normal acceleration at t = 1 sec.

Sol: Ang. accn of particle $\alpha = \frac{d\omega}{dt} = 4t$ rad/s²

tangential accn of Part $a_t = R\alpha = 4t\big|_{t=1s} = 4 \text{ m/s}^2$

Normal accn of Part $a_N = \omega^2 R = (2t^2+1)^2 R$

$= 4t^4 + 4t^2 + 1\big|_{t=1sec}$

$= 9 \text{ m/s}^2$

$\tan\theta = \frac{a_t}{a_N} = \frac{4}{9}$

$\theta = \tan^{-1}\left(\frac{4}{9}\right)$ Ans.

Scan for Video Explanation

Web Reference at www.physicsgalaxy.com

Module-13: Solved Example-8

Ex : **A stone is thrown horizontally from top of a tower at 10 m/s. Find the radius of curvature of its trajectory at the end of 3 sec after the projection. (Take g = 10 m/s^2)**

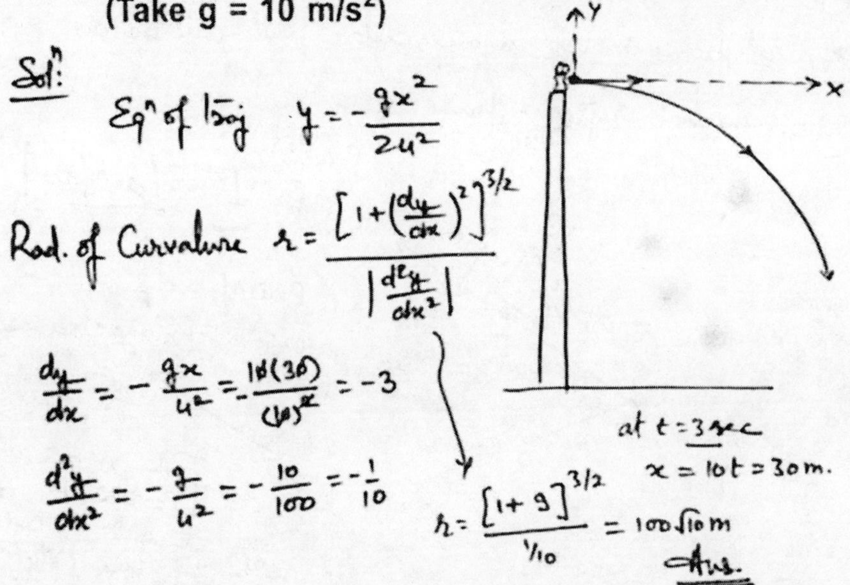

Scan for Video Explanation

Module-14: Horizontal Circular Motion of a Conical Pendulum

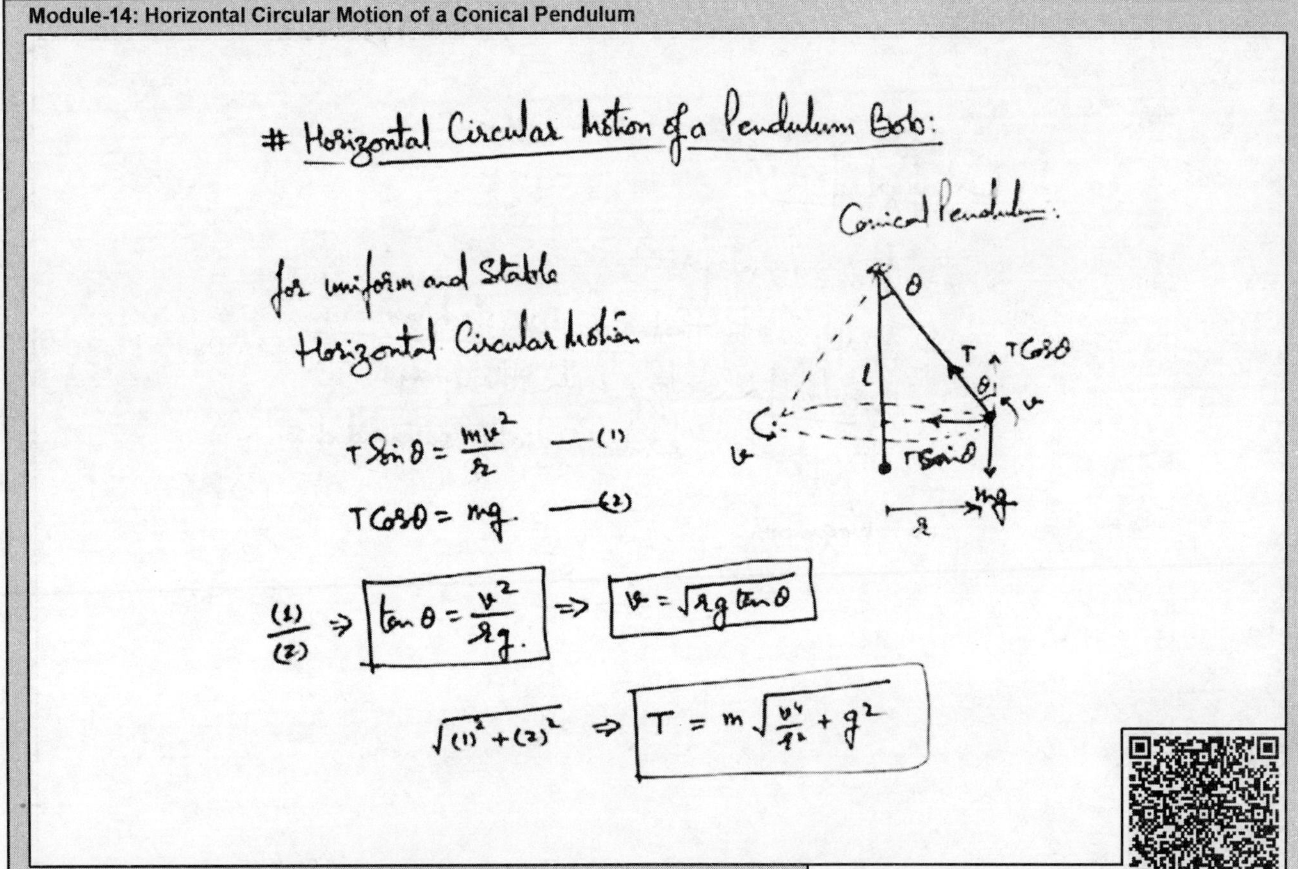

Scan for Video Explanation

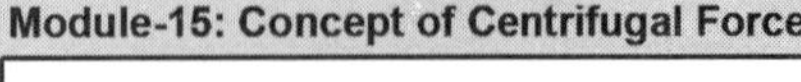

Module-15: Concept of Centrifugal Force

Concept of Centrifugal force:

→ Circular Motion is an accelerated Motion

→ A ref. frame moving in a circular path will be a non-inertial refrence frame.

Pseudo force.

$F = \left(\frac{mv^2}{R}\right)$ [Centrifugal force].

$\vec{v}$, $\vec{v}$, $a_N = v^2/R$, T, O, R.

FBD of Body w.r.to revolving observer

$\frac{mv^2}{R}$, rest., T

$$T = \frac{mv^2}{R}$$

Ans in the ref frame of obs.

Scan for Video Explanation

Web Reference at www.physicsgalaxy.com

Module-15: Concept of Centrifugal Force

Centrifugal force:

→ It is a Pseudo force

→ It appears to that observer which moves in circular path along with the body in C.M.

→ It appears to act in radially outward direction

→ magnitude $F = \frac{mv^2}{R}$.

Scan for Video Explanation

Web Reference at www.physicsgalaxy.com

Module-15: Concept of Centrifugal Force

Analysis of Conical Pendulum by Centrifugal Force:

FBD of bob as seen by an observer in rotating ref frame,

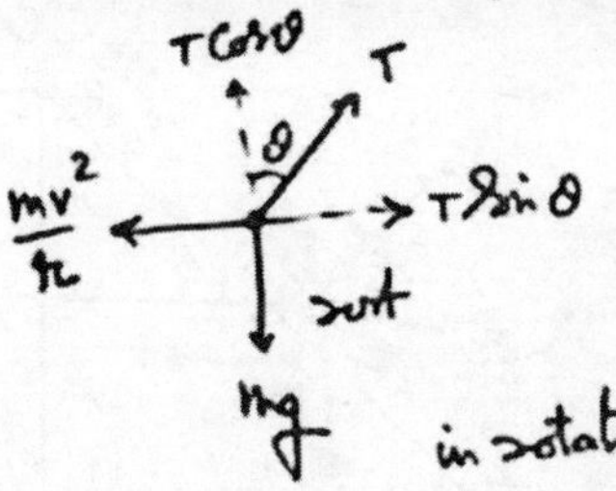

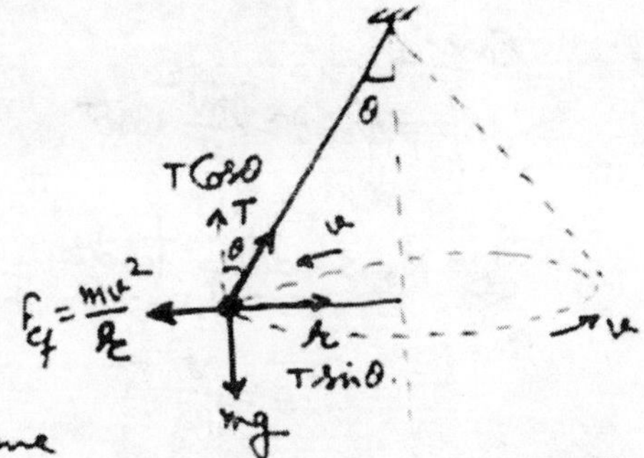

$T\cos\theta$, T, θ, $\frac{mv^2}{r}$, $T\sin\theta$, rest, mg

$T\cos\theta$, T, θ, v, $f_{cf} = \frac{mv^2}{R}$, R, $T\sin\theta$, mg, v

in rotating ref frame as body is at rest

$$T\sin\theta = \frac{mv^2}{R} \quad \text{—(1)}$$

$$T\cos\theta = mg \quad \text{—(2)}$$

$$\tan\theta = \frac{v^2}{Rg}$$

$$v = \sqrt{Rg\tan\theta}$$

$$T = m\sqrt{\frac{v^4}{R^2} + g^2}$$

Web Reference at www.physicsgalaxy.com

Scan for Video Explanation

Module-16: Turning of an Automobile on a Road

Skidding of an automobile while taking a turn:

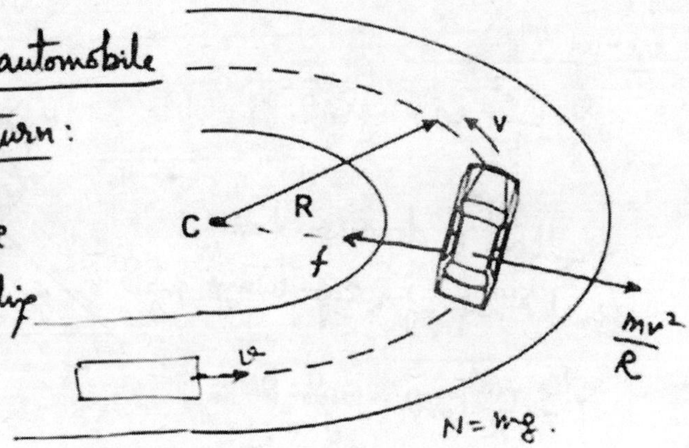

v, R, C, f, $\frac{mv^2}{R}$, v

for safe turning without skidding

$$f = \frac{mv^2}{R}$$

↑ static friction

$N = mg$.

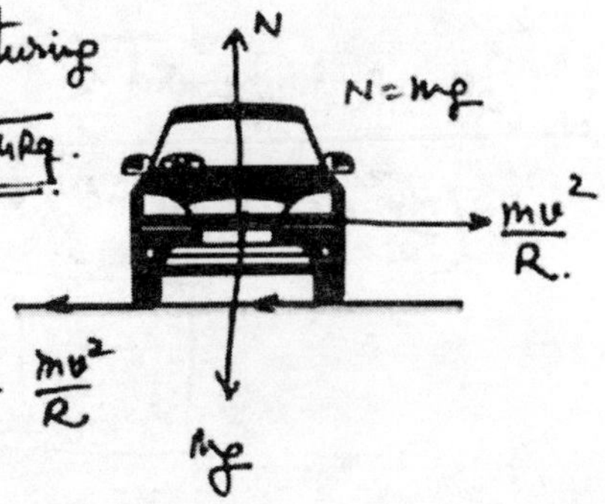

for safe turning

$$v < \sqrt{\mu Rg}.$$

N, $N = mg$, $\frac{mv^2}{R}$, mg

$$f = \frac{mv^2}{R}$$

for skidding

$$\frac{mv^2}{R} \geq \mu N$$

$$\frac{mv^2}{R} \geq \mu mg$$

$$v \geq \sqrt{\mu Rg}$$

Web Reference at www.physicsgalaxy.com

Scan for Video Explanation

Module-16: Turning of an Automobile on a Road

Skidding of an automobile while taking a turn on Banked Road:

Case-I:

if $mg\sin\theta = \frac{mv^2}{R}\cos\theta$

$\Rightarrow$ No skidding tendency

$$\tan\theta = \frac{v^2}{Rg}$$

$$\theta = \tan^{-1}\left(\frac{v^2}{Rg}\right)$$

angle of banking suitable for a speed v.

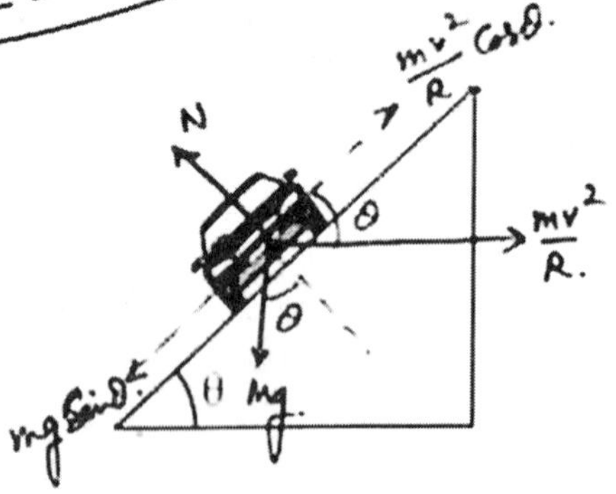

N, $\frac{mv^2}{R}\cos\theta$, $\frac{mv^2}{R}$, θ, $mg\sin\theta$, mg

Scan for Video Explanation

Web Reference at www.physicsgalaxy.com

Module-16: Turning of an Automobile on a Road

Case-II:

If $\frac{mv^2}{R}\cos\theta > mg\sin\theta$.

f will act in downward dir such that for safe turning

$$f = \frac{mv^2}{R}\cos\theta - mg\sin\theta$$

N, $\frac{mv^2}{R}\cos\theta$, $\frac{mv^2}{R}$, θ, $mg\sin\theta$, f, mg, $mg\cos\theta + \frac{mv^2}{R}\sin\theta$

Car will skid upward if

$$\left(\frac{mv^2}{R}\cos\theta - mg\sin\theta\right) = \mu\left(mg\cos\theta + \frac{mv^2}{R}\sin\theta\right)$$

$$v = \sqrt{\frac{Rg(\sin\theta + \mu\cos\theta)}{(\cos\theta - \mu\sin\theta)}}$$

max speed limit for safe turning

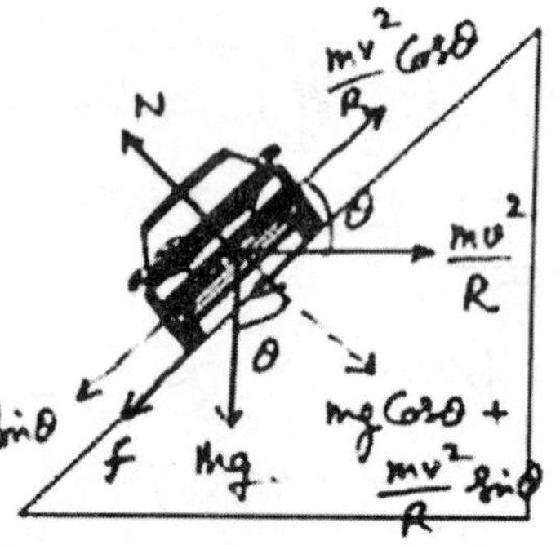

Scan for Video Explanation

Web Reference at www.physicsgalaxy.com

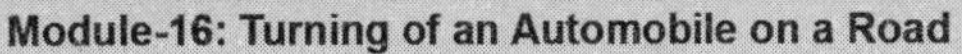

Module-16: Turning of an Automobile on a Road

Case-III

If $mg\sin\theta > \frac{mv^2}{R}\cos\theta$

f will act in upward dir

Such that

Static fr $f = mg\sin\theta - \frac{mv^2}{R}\cos\theta$

$N = mg\cos\theta + \frac{mv^2}{R}\sin\theta$

Car will skid downward if

$$\left(mg\sin\theta - \frac{mv^2}{R}\cos\theta\right) = \mu\left(mg\cos\theta + \frac{mv^2}{R}\sin\theta\right)$$

$$v = \sqrt{\frac{Rg(\sin\theta - \mu\cos\theta)}{\cos\theta + \mu\sin\theta}}$$

minimum speed limit for safe turning

if $\theta >$ Angle of Repose.

Web Reference at www.physicsgalaxy.com

Scan for Video Explanation

Module-17: Solved Example-9

Ex : **A horizontal disc which is free to rotate about its vertical central axis is initially at rest. At a distance r from axis, a coin is placed on disc and the friction coefficient between coin and disc is μ. Find the angular speed at which disc should be rotated so that coin will start slipping.**

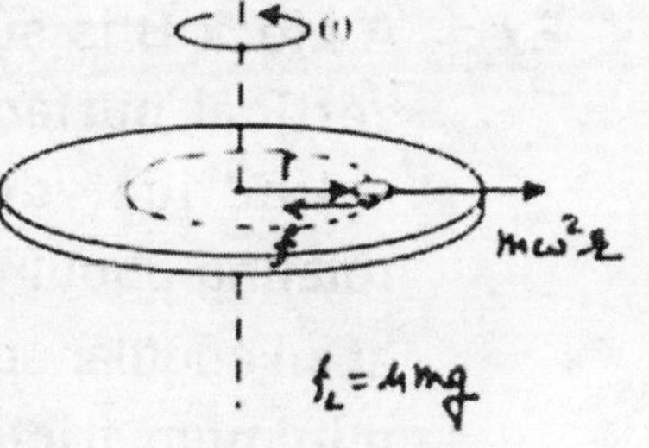

Sol: when coin is at rest on disc

$$f = m\omega^2 r$$

the coin will slip when $f = \mu mg$.

$$\mu mg = m\omega^2 r \Rightarrow \omega = \sqrt{\frac{\mu g}{r}} \text{ Ans}$$

Web Reference at www.physicsgalaxy.com

Scan for Video Explanation

Module-18: Solved Example-10

Ex : In a horizontal disc of radius R a smooth groove is cut along its radius as shown and a small bead is placed at a distance a from the centre of disc. If disc is set in rotation at angular speed ω, the bead will slide out. Find the speed with which bead will slide out from the edge of disc.

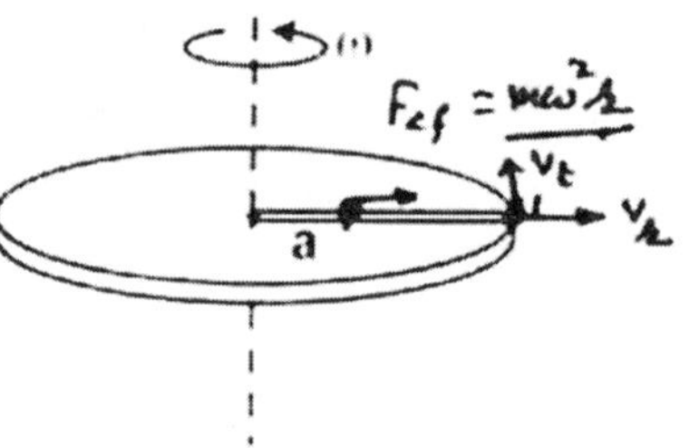

Sol^n: When bead will move off the edge of disc its tangential speed $v_t = R\omega$ w.r.t. disc. If a is the acc^n of bead we use

$m\omega^2 r = ma \Rightarrow v\frac{dv}{dr} = \omega^2 r$

$$\int_0^{v_r} v\,dv = \int_a^R \omega^2 r\,dr \rightarrow \frac{v_r^2}{2} = \frac{\omega^2}{2}(R^2-a^2)$$

$$v_r = \omega\sqrt{R^2-a^2}$$

$$v_{bead} = \sqrt{v_t^2+v_r^2} = \sqrt{2\omega^2R^2-\omega^2a^2}$$ Ans.

Scan for Video Explanation

Web Reference at www.physicsgalaxy.com

Module-19: Solved Example-11

Ex : A block B is supported at the vertical surface of a hollow cylindrical drum which is rotating about its vertical axis at an angular speed ω. Find the minimum friction coefficient between block and wall of cylinder so that block will not fall during circular motion.

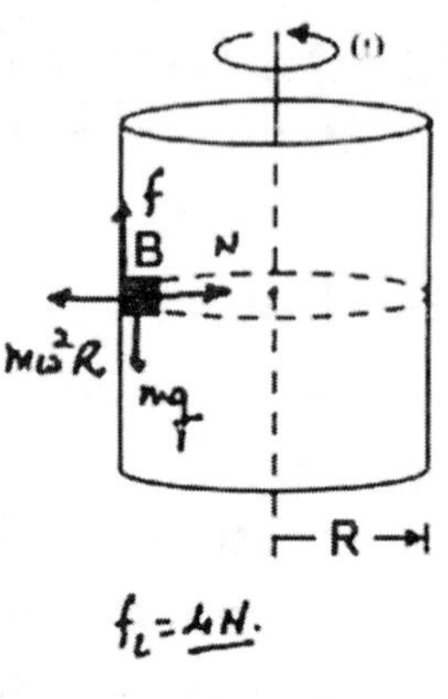

Sol^n: Normal Reaction on Block is $N = m\omega^2 R$

for block not to slide down $mg < \mu N$

$$mg < \mu m\omega^2 R$$

or $$\mu > \frac{g}{\omega^2 R}$$ Ans.

Scan for Video Explanation

Web Reference at www.physicsgalaxy.com

Module-20: Solved Example-12

Ex : **On a smooth horizontal table a block is attached to a point C through a string as shown and it is set in circular motion with a uniform angular speed such that tension in string is T_0. Now length of string and angular speed of revolution are doubled find new tension in the string.**

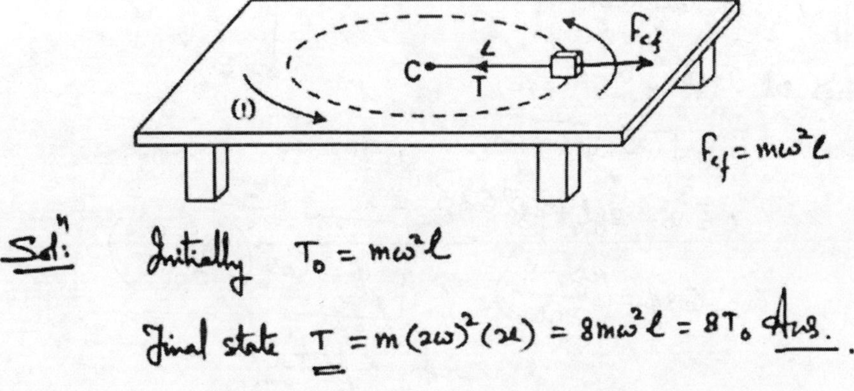

Web Reference at www.physicsgalaxy.com | Scan for Video Explanation

Module-21: Vertical Circular Motion of a Pendulum Bob

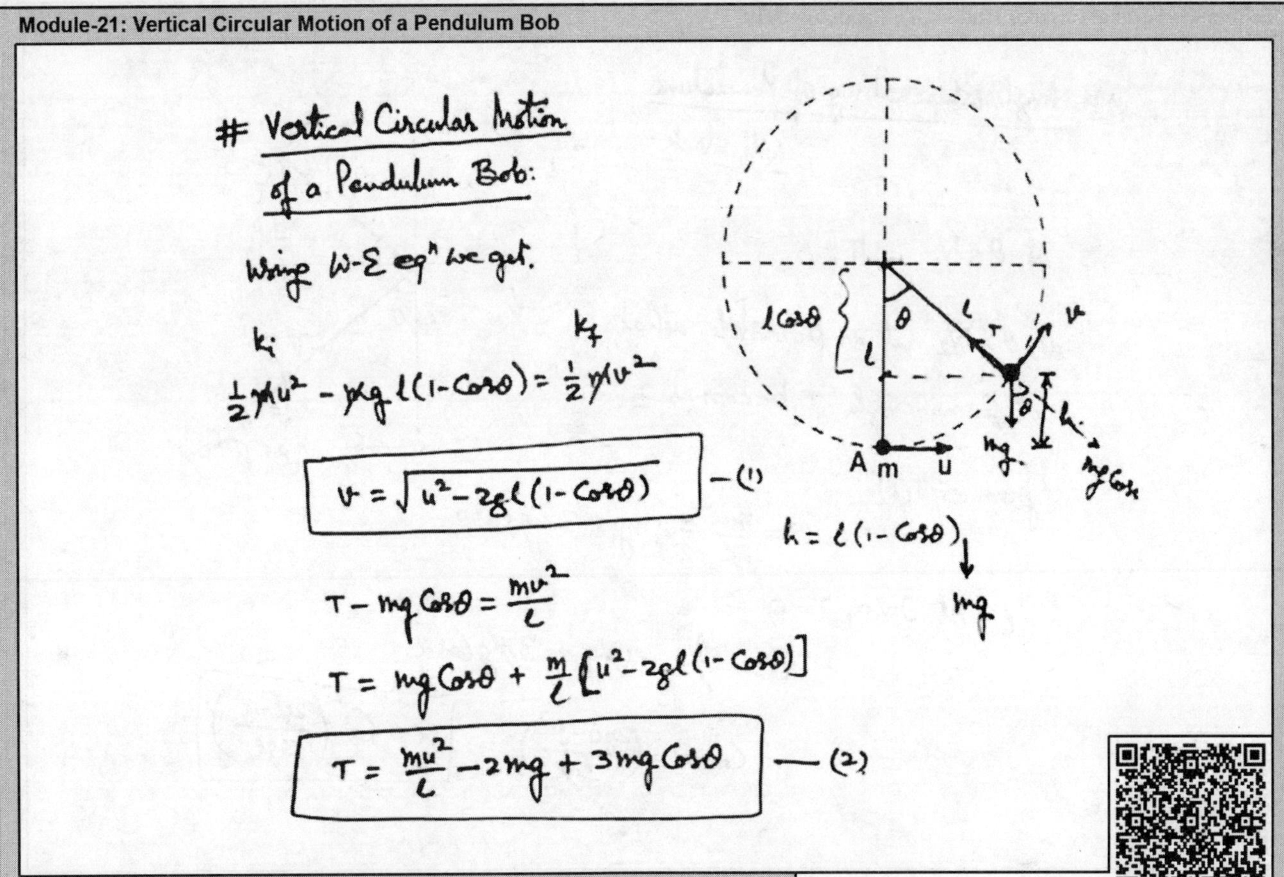

Web Reference at www.physicsgalaxy.com | Scan for Video Explanation

Module-21: Vertical Circular Motion of a Pendulum Bob

'Angular Amplitude' of Pendulum:

from eq^n (1)

$$v = \sqrt{u^2 - 2gl(1-\cos\theta)}$$

If ϕ is the angular amplitude

$\Rightarrow$ at $\theta = \phi$, $v = 0$

$$0 = \sqrt{u^2 - 2gl(1-\cos\phi)}$$

$$0 = u^2 - 2gl + 2gl\cos\phi$$

$$\cos\phi = \left(\frac{2gl - u^2}{2gl}\right) \Rightarrow \boxed{\phi = \cos^{-1}\left(\frac{2gl - u^2}{2gl}\right)}$$

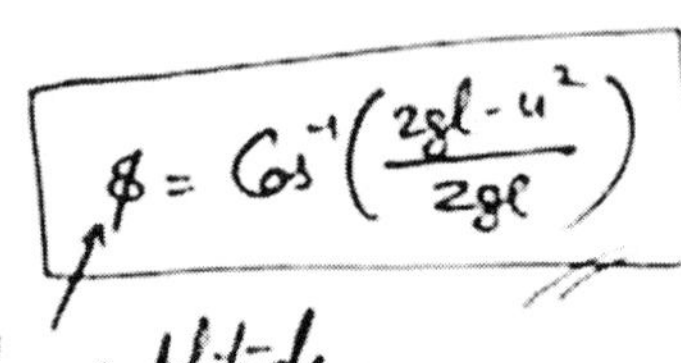

Ang. amplitude.

Scan for Video Explanation

Web Reference at www.physicsgalaxy.com

Module-21: Vertical Circular Motion of a Pendulum Bob

Angle where string of Pendulum will slack:

at $\theta < \pi/2$, $T \neq 0$

at $\theta > \pi/2$ it is possible that at some angle T becomes 0.

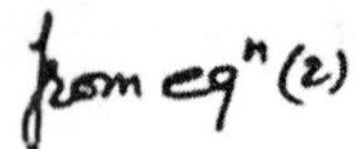

from eq^n (2)

$$T = \frac{mu^2}{l} - 2mg + 3mg\cos\theta$$

let at $\theta = \alpha$, $T = 0 \Rightarrow$

$$0 = \frac{mu^2}{l} - 2mg + 3mg\cos\alpha.$$

$$\cos\alpha = \left(\frac{2gl - u^2}{3gl}\right) \Rightarrow \boxed{\alpha = \cos^{-1}\left(\frac{2gl - u^2}{3gl}\right)}$$

Scan for Video Explanation

Web Reference at www.physicsgalaxy.com

Module-22: Cases of Projection of a Pendulum Bob

Cases of Projection of a Pendulum Bob:

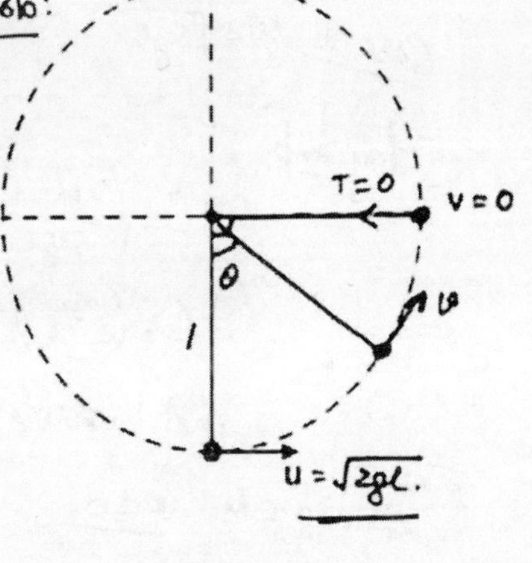

Case I: $u = \sqrt{2gl}$

Ang. Amp.

$$\phi = \cos^{-1}\left(\frac{2gl - u^2}{2gl}\right)$$

$$= \cos^{-1}(0) = \pi/2$$

let at $\theta = \alpha$, $T = 0$

$$\Rightarrow \quad \alpha = \cos^{-1}\left(\frac{2gl - u^2}{3gl}\right)$$

$$= \cos^{-1}(0) = \pi/2.$$

At $u = \sqrt{2gl}$, vel of bob & tension in string becomes zero simultaneously when $\theta = \pi/2$ / string becomes horizontal.

Web Reference at www.physicsgalaxy.com | Scan for Video Explanation

Module-22: Cases of Projection of a Pendulum Bob

Case-II: $u = \sqrt{4gl}$

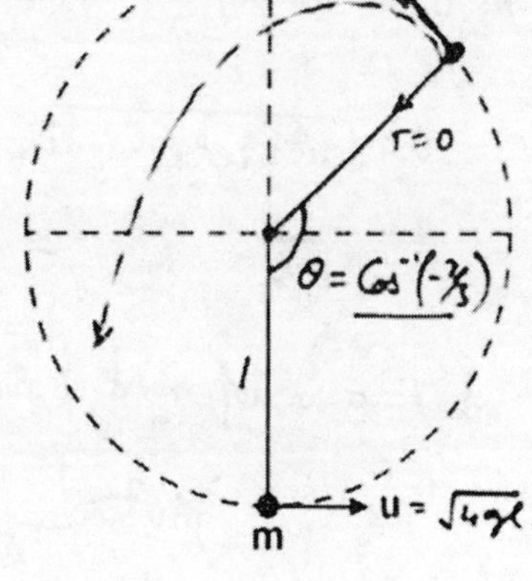

Ang. Amp. $\phi = \cos^{-1}\left(\frac{2gl - u^2}{2gl}\right)$

$$= \cos^{-1}(-1)$$

$$= \pi$$

At $\theta = \alpha$ if $T = 0$

$$\alpha = \cos^{-1}\left(\frac{2gl - u^2}{3gl}\right)$$

$$= \cos^{-1}(-2/3) = 131^\circ.$$

NOTE: If $u = \sqrt{4gl}$ then this speed is sufficient to carry the bob to the topmost pt of vertical circle. but tension in string is not supporting beyond $\theta = \cos^{-1}(-2/3)$.

Web Reference at www.physicsgalaxy.com | Scan for Video Explanation

Module-22: Cases of Projection of a Pendulum Bob

Case-III : $u = \sqrt{5gl}$

Ang. Amp:

$$\phi = \cos^{-1}\left(\frac{2gl - u^2}{2gl}\right)$$

$$= \cos^{-1}\left(-3/2\right)$$

(not possible)

During CM $v \neq 0$.

let at $\theta = \alpha$, $T = 0 \Rightarrow \alpha = \cos^{-1}\left(\frac{2gl - u^2}{3gl}\right)$

$$= \cos^{-1}(-1) = \pi.$$

At bottommost pos. if $u = \sqrt{5gl}$, it is the min speed required to Complete vertical circular motion.

$\sqrt{gl} = v$

$v = \sqrt{u^2 - 2gl(2)} = \sqrt{gl}$.

$T = 0$

l

$u = \sqrt{5gl}$

Scan for Video Explanation

Web Reference at www.physicsgalaxy.com

Module-22: Cases of Projection of a Pendulum Bob

at $\theta = \pi$ then from eq^n(1)

$$v = \sqrt{u^2 - 2gl(1 - (-1))}$$

$$= \sqrt{gl}$$

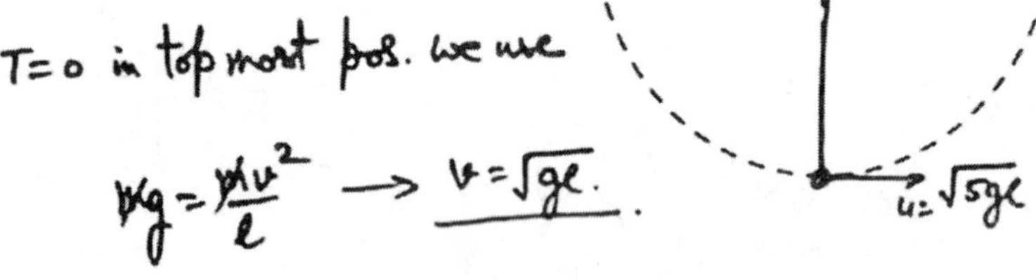

at $T = 0$ in top most pos. we use

$$mg = \frac{mv^2}{l} \longrightarrow v = \sqrt{gl}.$$

$\sqrt{gl} = v$

$T + mg$ ($T \to 0$)

$u = \sqrt{5gl}$

* Condition to Complete vertical circular path by a bob:

$T = 0$ at the top most pt

$T \geq 0$.

Scan for Video Explanation

Web Reference at www.physicsgalaxy.com

Module-23: Vertical Circular Motion of a Pendulum with a Rod

Vertical Circular Motion of a Pendulum with light rigid rod:

If $u = \sqrt{4gl}$, in case of a light rigid rod, bob will complete the circle as rod will never slack.

$v = 0$

$\theta = \cos^{-1}(-2/3)$

l

$u = \sqrt{4gl}$

NOTE: After $\theta = \cos^{-1}(-2/3)$ the dir of force by rod on bob changes from inward to outward.

Web Reference at www.physicsgalaxy.com | Scan for Video Explanation

Module-24: Circular Motion inside a Vertical Circular Track

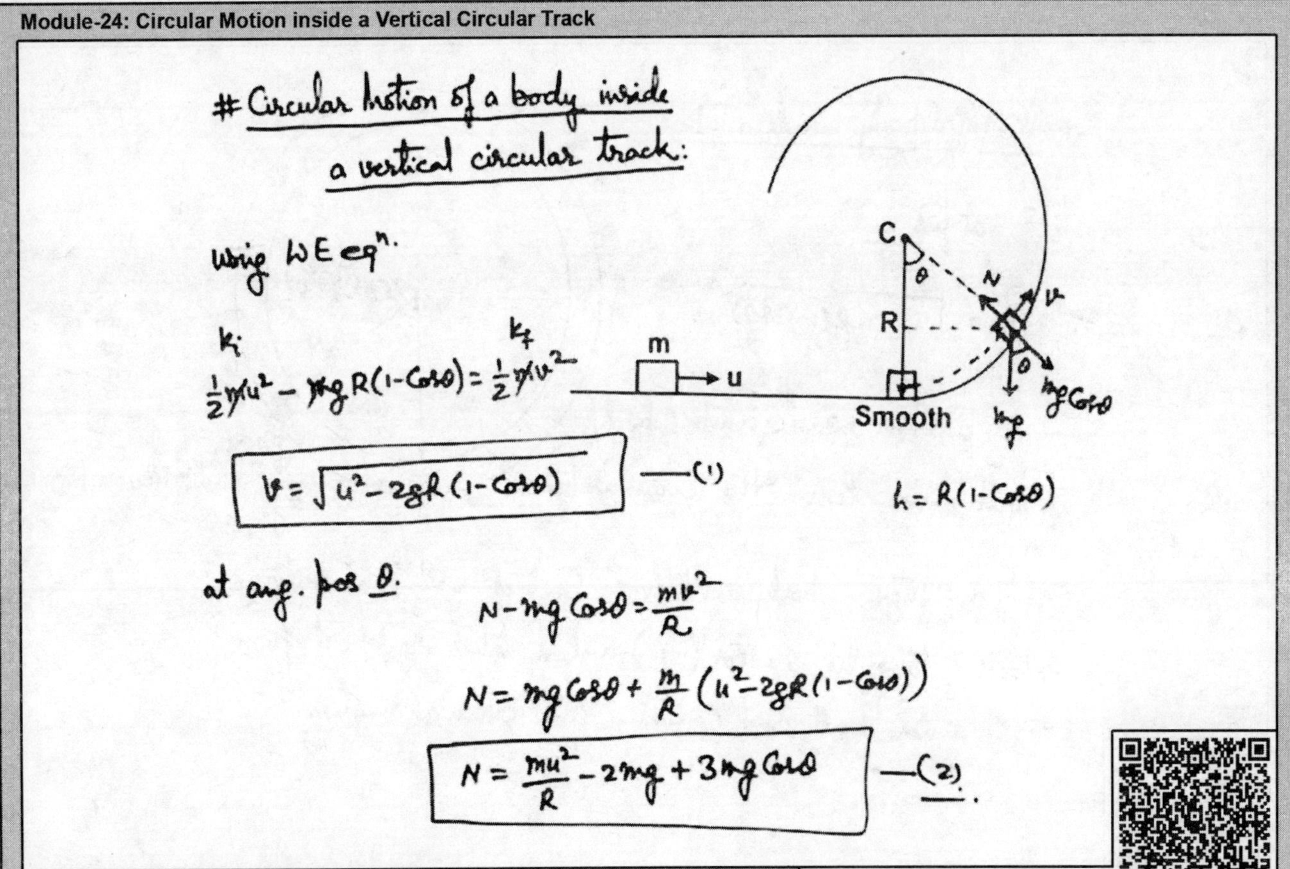

Module-24: Circular Motion inside a Vertical Circular Track

Cases of Projection:

→ at $u = \sqrt{2gR}$, body will reach pt B & return

→ at $u = \sqrt{4gR}$, body will leave the circular track at $\theta = \cos^{-1}(-2/3)$ & follow proj motion.

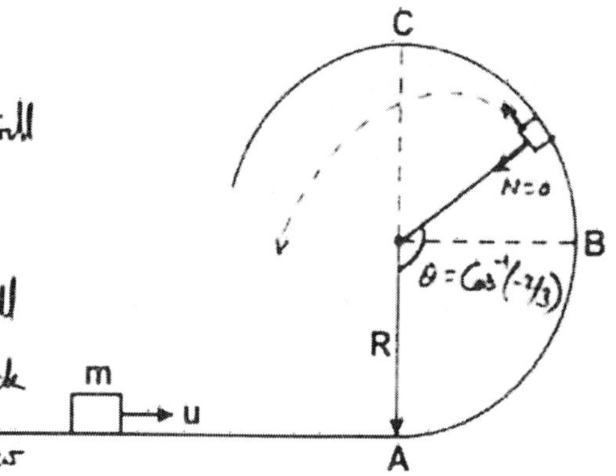

→ at $u = \sqrt{5gR}$, at top most pt $N = 0$ & $v = \sqrt{gR}$ & body will Complete the cir track.

→ at $\sqrt{5gR} > u > \sqrt{2gR}$, body will leave the track ($N = 0$) somewhere betn pt B & C.

C
N=0
B
$\theta = \cos^{-1}(-2/3)$
R
m
u
A

Scan for Video Explanation

Web Reference at www.physicsgalaxy.com

Module-25: Vertical Circular Motion inside a Tube

VCM of a body inside a Tube:

at pos. B.

$$v = \sqrt{u^2 - 2gR(1-\cos\theta)}$$

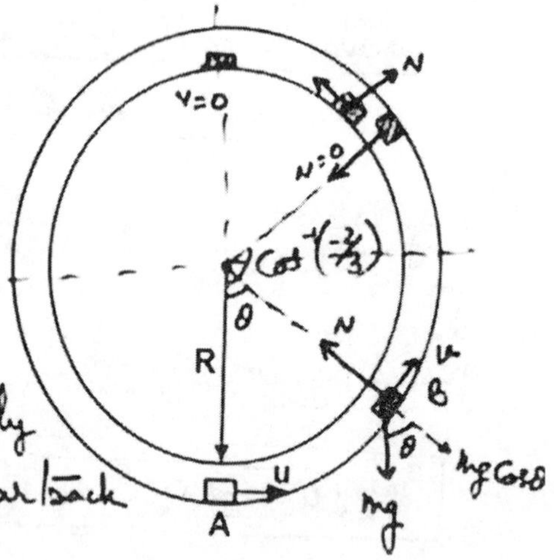

→ As path is inside a tube, body will never leave the circular track

→ If $u = \sqrt{4gR}$ body will loose Contact with the outer wall of tube at $\theta = \cos^{-1}(-2/3)$ and it takes support from the inner wall and Continue the circular motion.

v=0
N
N=0
$\cos^{-1}\left(\frac{-2}{3}\right)$
θ
N
R
v
B
θ
$mg\cos\theta$
u
A
mg

Scan for Video Explanation

Web Reference at www.physicsgalaxy.com

Module-26: Vertical Circular Motion outside a Track

VCM Outside a circular track:

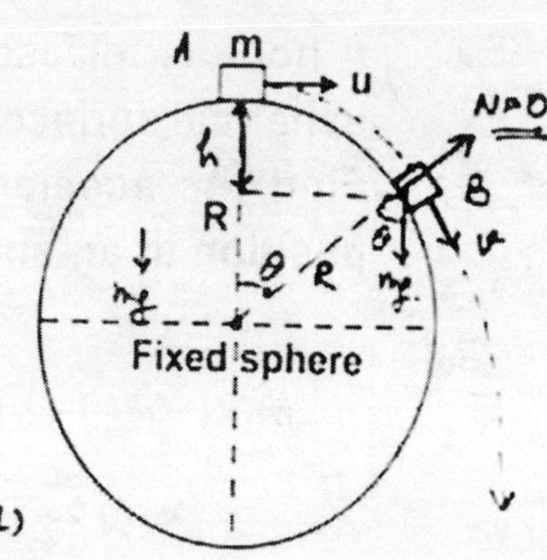

W-E eqⁿ from A to B.

$$\frac{1}{2}mu^2 + mgR(1-\cos\theta) = \frac{1}{2}mv^2$$

$$v = \sqrt{u^2 + 2gR(1-\cos\theta)} \quad \text{—(1)}$$

at pt B.

$$mg\cos\theta - N = \frac{mv^2}{R}$$

$$N = mg\cos\theta - \frac{mv^2}{R}$$

$$N = mg\cos\theta - \frac{m}{R}\left[u^2 + 2gR(1-\cos\theta)\right]$$

$$N = 3mg\cos\theta - 2mg - \frac{mu^2}{R} \quad \text{—(2)}$$

Web Reference at www.physicsgalaxy.com | Scan for Video Explanation

Module-26: Vertical Circular Motion outside a Track

→ at some pt $\theta = \beta$ on track $N=0$ and body will leave the circular track

from eqⁿ (2)

$$0 = 3mg\cos\beta - 2mg - \frac{mu^2}{R}$$

$$\cos\beta = \left(\frac{2gR + u^2}{3gR}\right)$$

$$\beta = \cos^{-1}\left(\frac{2gR + u^2}{3gR}\right)$$

Web Reference at www.physicsgalaxy.com | Scan for Video Explanation

Module-27: Solved Example-13

Ex : A body is released from rest from top of a fixed spherical surface such that it starts sliding down. Find the acceleration of body when it is at a position at an angle 30° from the initial position.

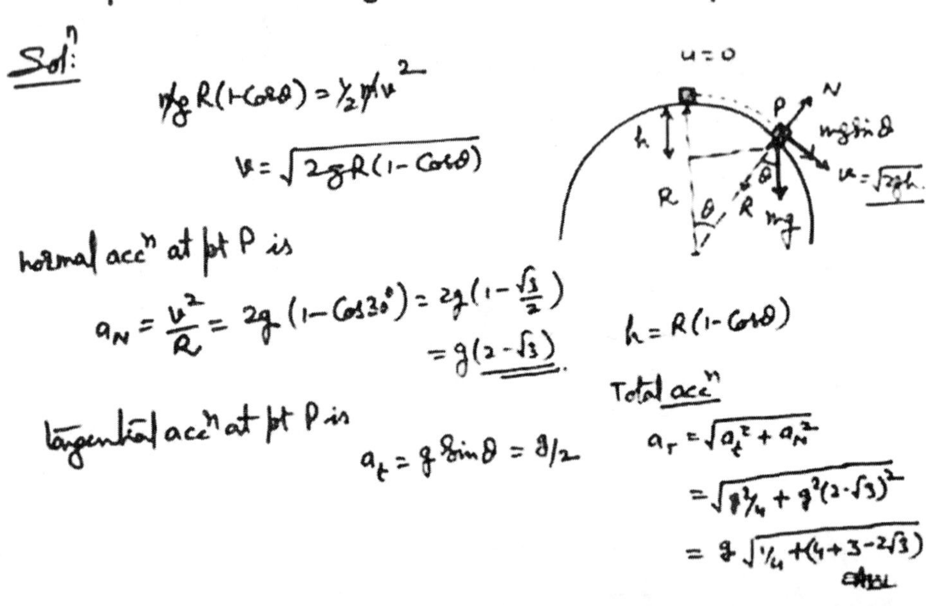

Scan for Video Explanation

Web Reference at www.physicsgalaxy.com

Module-28: Solved Example-14

Ex : Figure shows a loop track of radius r. A block B starts from an inclined plane connected to the track at a distance h above the top of the track. Find the minimum value of h for successful looping.

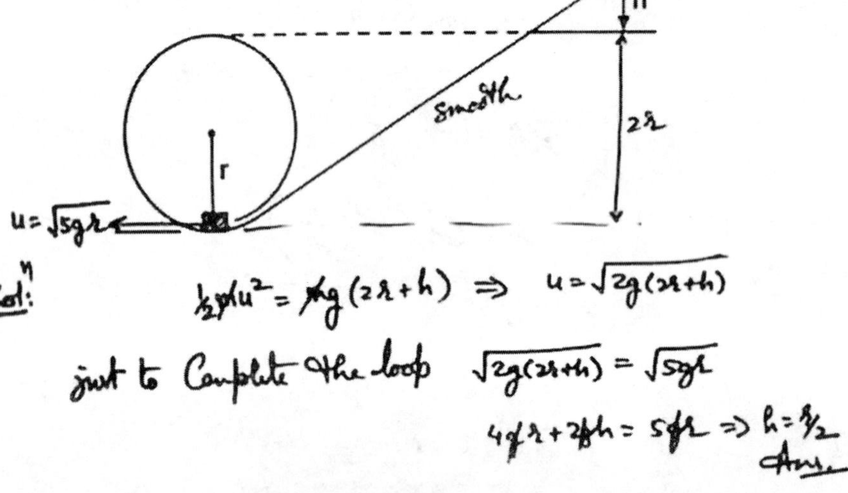

Scan for Video Explanation

Web Reference at www.physicsgalaxy.com

Module-29: Solved Example-15

Ex : **A simple pendulum bob (length = l) is projected horizontally with speed $u = \sqrt{gl}$ from the bottom position. Find the speed of particle and the inclination of string with the vertical at the instant when tension in string is equal to the weight of bob.**

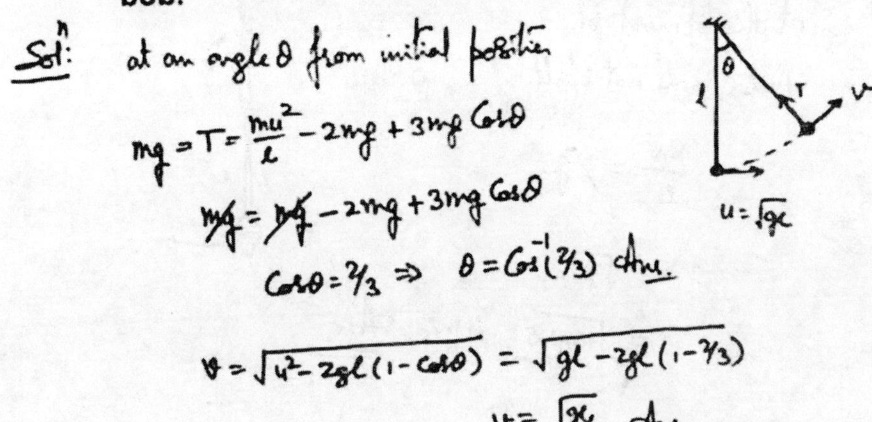

Web Reference at www.physicsgalaxy.com | Scan for Video Explanation

Module-30: Solved Example-16

Ex : **A simple pendulum oscillates in a vertical plane. When it passes through the mean position, tension in string is 3 times the weight of bob. What is the maximum angular displacement of string from vertical during oscillations.**

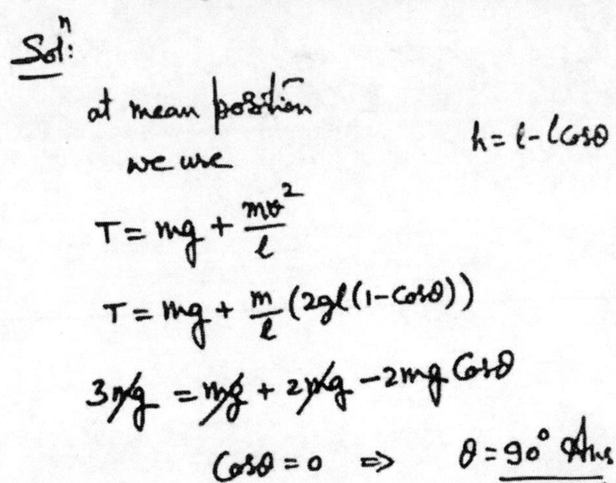

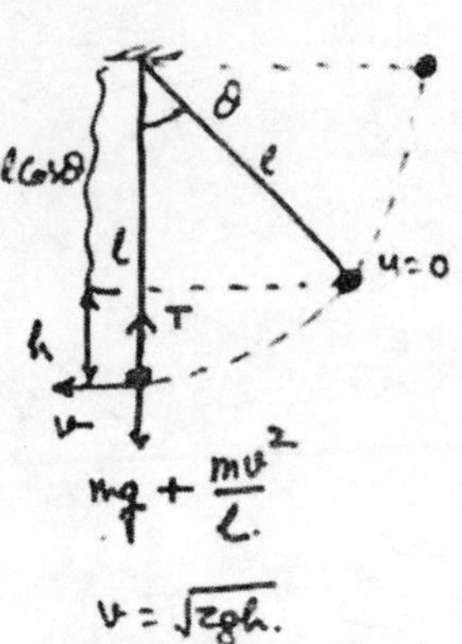

Web Reference at www.physicsgalaxy.com | Scan for Video Explanation

Module-31: Solved Example-17

Ex : **A bucket tied at the end of a 1.6 m long rod is whirled in a vertical circle with constant speed. What should be the minimum speed so that water from the bucket does not spill, when the bucket is at the height position. (Take g = 10 m/s^2)**

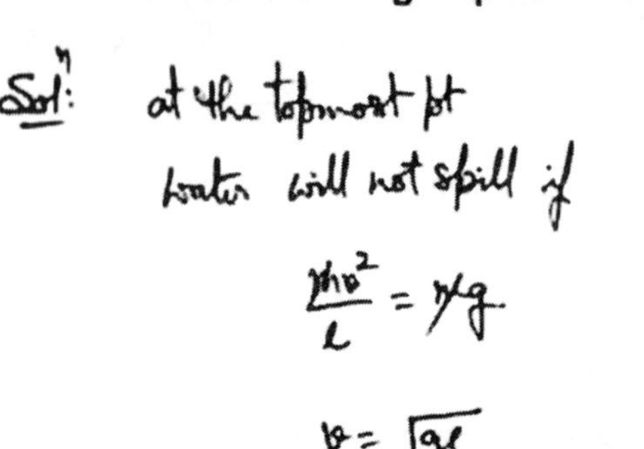

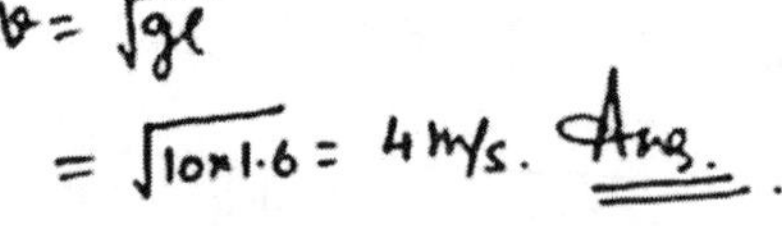

Scan for Video Explanation

Web Reference at www.physicsgalaxy.com

Chapter 9
System of Particle-I

Lecture Notes Modules

Module-1: Centre of Mass
Module-2: How to Locate Centre of Mass
Module-3: Centre of Mass of Multiple Objects
Module-4: Solved Example-1
Module-5: Solved Example-2
Module-6: Solved Example-3
Module-7: Centre of Mass of Subtractive Objects
Module-8: Centre of Mass of Continuous Extended Bodies
Module-9: Centre of Mass of a Uniform Half Ring
Module-10: Centre of Mass of a Uniform Half Disc
Module-11: Centre of Mass of a Uniform Hollow Hemisphere
Module-12: Centre of Mass of a Uniform Solid Hemisphere
Module-13: Centre of Mass of a Uniform Hollow Cone
Module-14: Centre of Mass of a Uniform Solid Cone
Module-15: Solved Example-4
Module-16: Solved Example-5
Module-17: Solved Example-6
Module-18: Displacement of Centre of Mass
Module-19: Velocity and Acceleration of Centre of Mass
Module-20: Solved Example-7
Module-21: Solved Example-8

Module-1: Centre of Mass

Centre of Mass:

It is a pt associated with a SoP where all the masses of system are supposed to be Concentrated.

→ For uniform bodies → COM is located at Geometric Centre of bodies.

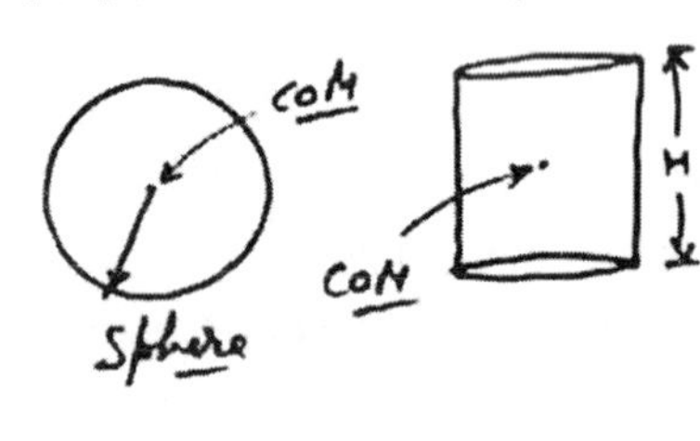

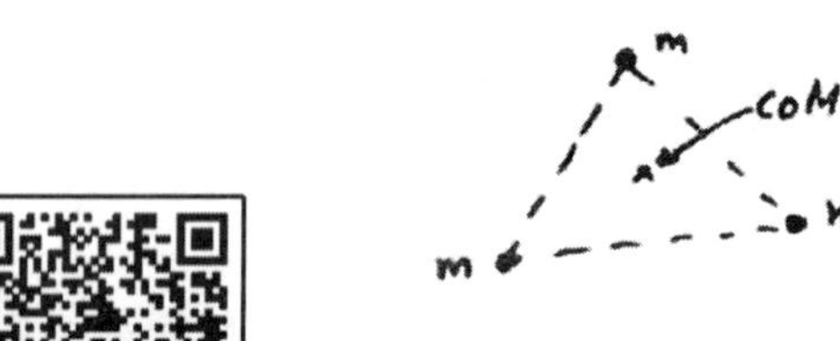

Scan for Video Explanation

Web Reference at www.physicsgalaxy.com

Module-1: Centre of Mass

Types of System of Particles:

Every physical System in nature] ← System of Particle

Based on relative location of particles in a system SoP can be classified in two Categories -

(1) Discrete object System

(2) Continuous object System.

Scan for Video Explanation

Web Reference at www.physicsgalaxy.com

Module-1: Centre of Mass

DOS : → SoP with Several independent objects

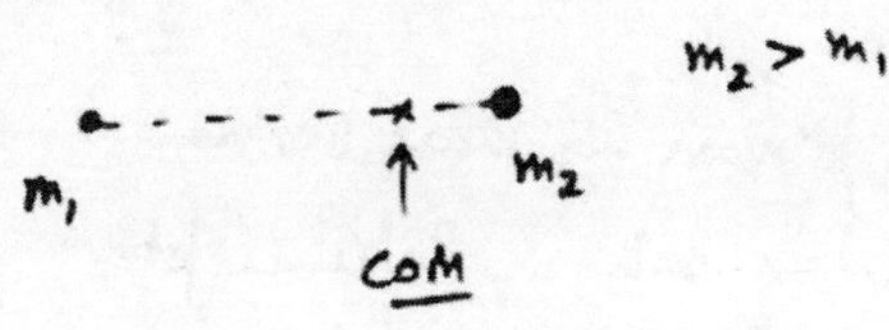

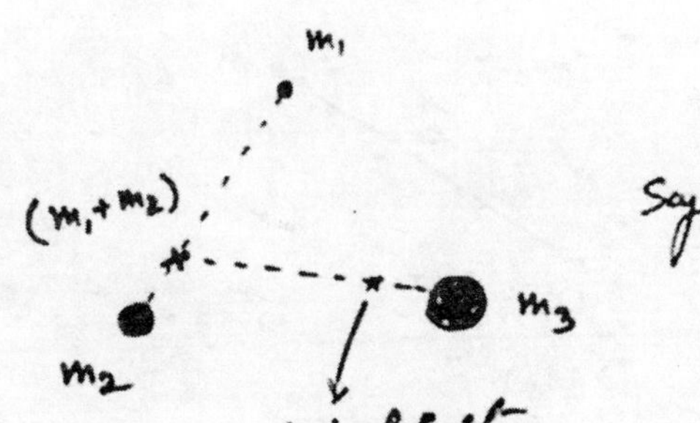

Say $m_3 > (m_1+m_2)$

Web Reference at www.physicsgalaxy.com

Scan for Video Explanation

Module-1: Centre of Mass

COS. → SoP with all particles linked together to form an extended body.

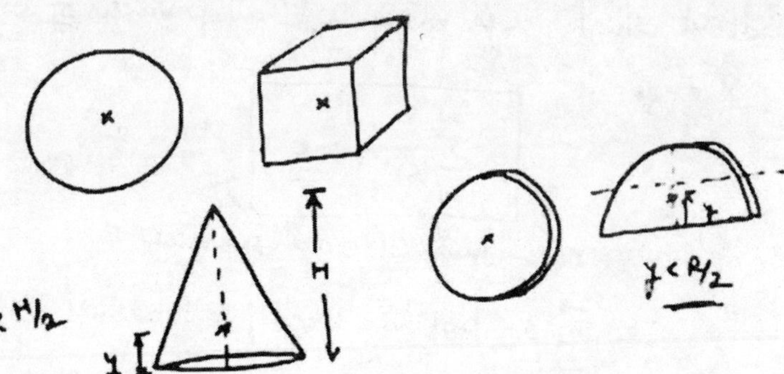

Web Reference at www.physicsgalaxy.com

Scan for Video Explanation

Module-2: How to Locate Centre of Mass

How to locate Centre of Mass of a SOP:

* Mass Moment:

For a given pt mass its mass moment is always calculated w.r.to a Refrence pt.

Mass moment of "m" w.r.to pt O is given as-

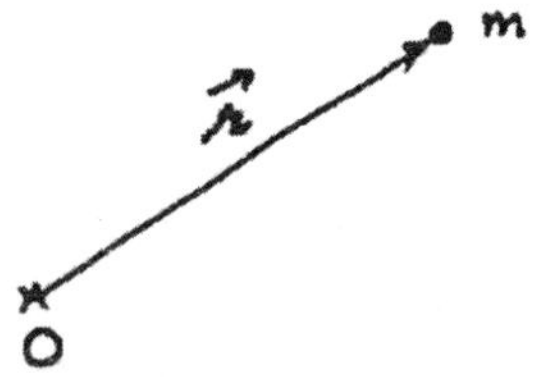

$$\vec{Z}_{mo} = m\vec{r}$$

Scan for Video Explanation

Web Reference at www.physicsgalaxy.com

Module-2: How to Locate Centre of Mass

Centre of Mass in terms of Mass Moments:

In a SOP, Centre of Mass is defined as a point about which mass moments of all particles of SOP is 0.

$$\sum_{i=1}^{N} m_i \vec{r_i} = 0$$

m_i ← mass of each particle

$\vec{r_i}$ ← position vec of ith particle w.r.to COM.

Scan for Video Explanation

Web Reference at www.physicsgalaxy.com

Module-2: How to Locate Centre of Mass

COM of a Two Particle System :

$m_1 > m_2$

$-x$ — 0 — $+x$

m_1 —— x —— COM —— $l-x$ —— m_2 (separation l)

by mass-moment definition of COM we use

$$\sum_{i=1}^{2} m_i \vec{r}_i = 0$$

$$m_2(l-x)\hat{i} + m_1(-x)\hat{i} = 0$$

$$m_2 l = (m_1 + m_2)x$$

$$x = \frac{m_2 l}{m_1 + m_2}$$

Web Reference at www.physicsgalaxy.com

Scan for Video Explanation

Module-2: How to Locate Centre of Mass

Ex : **Find location of center of mass of this system from 2 kg mass.**

2 kg —— x —— COM —— 5 kg (10 m)

Sol^n:

$$x = \frac{5 \times 10}{2+5} = \frac{50}{7}\text{ m. Ans.}$$

Web Reference at www.physicsgalaxy.com

Scan for Video Explanation

Module-2: How to Locate Centre of Mass

Ex : Find co-ordinates of centre of mass in the system shown in figure.

y, (4, 3), 4 kg, (x_c, y_c) COM, r_c, y_c, 3, 37^0, x_c, O, 2 kg, 4, A, x

Solⁿ:

$$r_c = \frac{m_2 r}{m_1 + m_2}$$

$$= \frac{4 \times 5}{6} = \frac{10}{3}\text{ m.}$$

co-ordinates of COM are

$$x_c = r_c \cos 37^0 = \frac{10}{3} \times \frac{4}{5} = \frac{8}{3}\text{ m}$$

$$y_c = r_c \sin 37^0 = \frac{10}{3} \times \frac{3}{5} = 2$$

COM → (8/3, 2) Ans.

Scan for Video Explanation

Web Reference at www.physicsgalaxy.com

Module-3: Centre of Mass of Multiple Objects

Centre of Mass of a SOP with Multiple Objects:

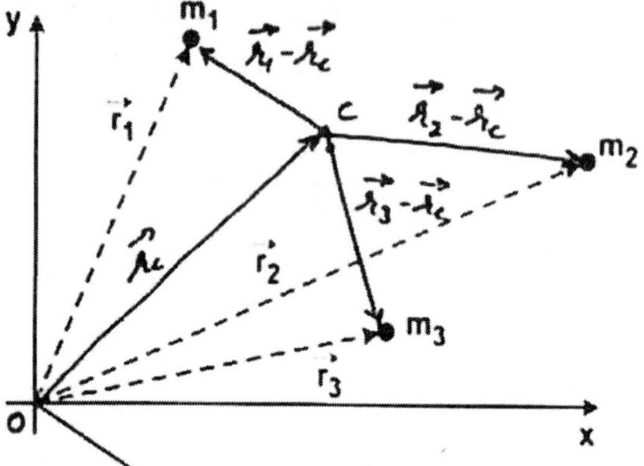

By definition of Centre of Mass

$$m_1(\vec{r}_1 - \vec{r}_c) + m_2(\vec{r}_2 - \vec{r}_c) + m_3(\vec{r}_3 - \vec{r}_c) = 0$$

$$(m_1 + m_2 + m_3)\vec{r}_c = m_1\vec{r}_1 + m_2\vec{r}_2 + m_3\vec{r}_3$$

z

$$\vec{r}_c = \frac{m_1\vec{r}_1 + m_2\vec{r}_2 + m_3\vec{r}_3}{m_1 + m_2 + m_3} = \frac{\sum_{i=1}^{N} m_i \vec{r}_i}{\sum_{i=1}^{N} m_i}$$

Scan for Video Explanation

Web Reference at www.physicsgalaxy.com

Module-3: Centre of Mass of Multiple Objects

$$\vec{r}_1 = x_1\hat{i} + y_1\hat{j}$$

$$\vec{r}_2 = x_2\hat{i} + y_2\hat{j}$$

$$\vdots$$

$$\vec{r}_c = \frac{m_1\vec{r}_1 + m_2\vec{r}_2 + \cdots}{m_1 + m_2 + \cdots} = \frac{m_1(x_1\hat{i} + y_1\hat{j}) + m_2(x_2\hat{i} + y_2\hat{j}) + \cdots}{m_1 + m_2 + \cdots}$$

$$x_c\hat{i} + y_c\hat{j} = \left(\frac{m_1x_1 + m_2x_2 + \cdots}{m_1 + m_2 + \cdots}\right)\hat{i} + \left(\frac{m_1y_1 + m_2y_2 + \cdots}{m_1 + m_2 + \cdots}\right)\hat{j}$$

$$x_c = \frac{\sum_{i=1}^{N} m_i x_i}{\sum_{i=1}^{N} m_i} \; ; \quad y_c = \frac{\sum_{i=1}^{N} m_i y_i}{\sum_{i=1}^{N} m_i}$$

$$\left[z_c = \sum_{i=1}^{N} m_i z_i \Big/ \sum_{i=1}^{N} m_i\right]$$

Web Reference at www.physicsgalaxy.com | Scan for Video Explanation

Module-4: Solved Example-1

Ex : Figure shows a co-ordinate system in which 8 uniform cubes of side a are placed as shown. If masses of cubes 1, 2, 3 & 4 is m each & 2m for remaining cubes, find location of centre of mass of this system.

Sol^n:

$$x_c = \frac{\Sigma m_i x_i}{\Sigma m_i} = \frac{5m \times a/2 + 3m \times \frac{3a}{2} + 3m \times \frac{5a}{2} + m \times \frac{7a}{2}}{12m}$$

$$= \frac{18}{12}a = \frac{3a}{2}$$

$$y_c = \frac{\Sigma m_i y_i}{\Sigma m_i} = \frac{4m \times a/2 + 6m \times 3a/2 + 2m \times \frac{5a}{2}}{12m}$$

$$= \frac{16}{12}a = \frac{4}{3}a.$$

COM $\rightarrow \left(\frac{3a}{2}, \frac{4}{3}a\right)$ Ans.

Web Reference at www.physicsgalaxy.com | Scan for Video Explanation

Module-5: Solved Example-2

Ex : Figure shows a uniform plate of shape E as shown. Find the co-ordinates of centre of mass of this structure.

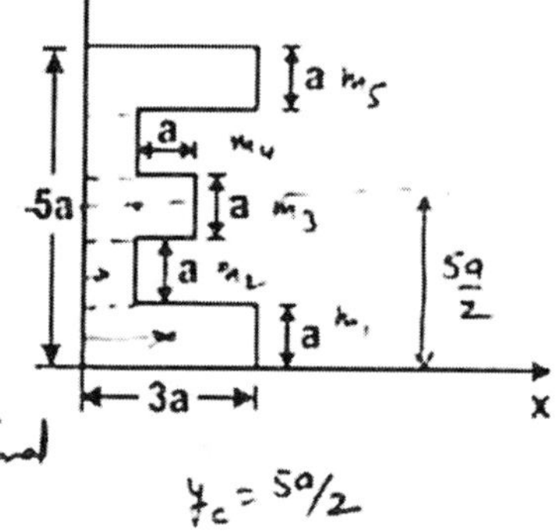

Solⁿ: As plate is 2D object its mass is uniform so it is proportional to its area.

$y_c = 5a/2$

$m_1 = 3a^2$

$m_2 = a^2$

$m_3 = 2a^2$

$m_4 = a^2$

$m_5 = 3a^2$

$$x_c = \frac{m_1x_1 + m_2x_2 + \cdots}{m_1 + m_2 + \cdots}$$

$$x_c = \frac{2\times 3a^2\times \frac{3a}{2} + a^2\times a/2 + 2a^2\times a + a^2\times a/2}{10a^2}$$

$$x_c = \frac{12a}{10} = 6a/5 \qquad \text{CoM} \rightarrow \left(\frac{6a}{5}, \frac{5a}{2}\right)$$

Scan for Video Explanation

Web Reference at www.physicsgalaxy.com

Module-6: Solved Example-3

Ex : Figure shows a uniform two dimensional T-shaped structure. Find co-ordinates of centre of mass of this object.

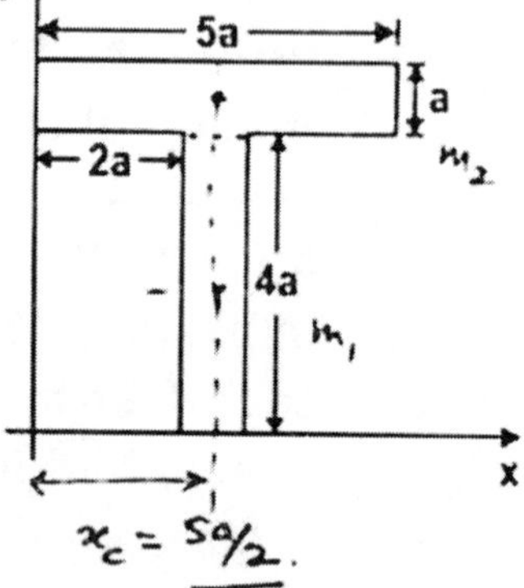

Solⁿ:

$m_1 = 4a^2$

$m_2 = 5a^2$

$x_c = 5a/2$

$$y_c = \frac{m_1y_1 + m_2y_2}{m_1 + m_2}$$

$$y_c = \frac{4a^2\times 2a + 5a^2\times 9a/2}{9a^2} = \frac{61a}{18}$$

$$\text{CoM} \rightarrow \left(\frac{5a}{2}, \frac{61a}{18}\right)$$

Scan for Video Explanation

Web Reference at www.physicsgalaxy.com

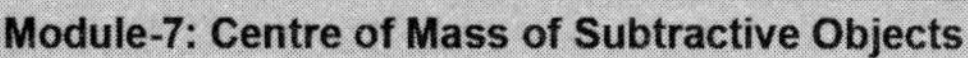

Module-7: Centre of Mass of Subtractive Objects

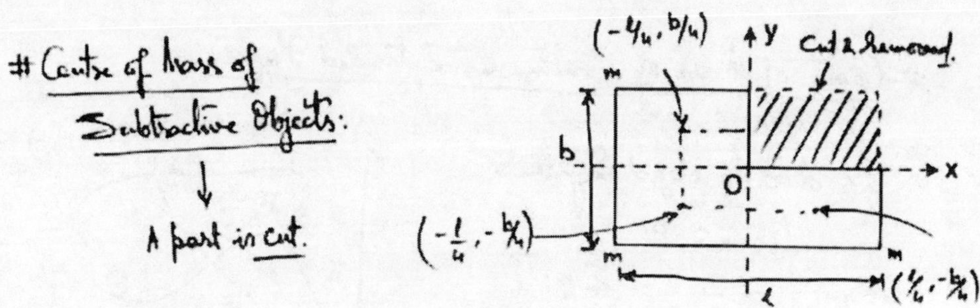

Que: Find COM of the uniform plate shown in fig if 1/4th of its part is cut & removed as shown.

Sol^n: COM of remaining object is

$$x_c = \frac{m(-l/4) + m(-l/4) + m(l/4)}{3m} = -l/12$$

$$y_c = \frac{m(b/4) + m(-b/4) + m(-b/4)}{3m} = -b/12$$

$$COM = (-l/12, -b/12) \text{ Ans.}$$

Web Reference at www.physicsgalaxy.com | Scan for Video Explanation

Module-7: Centre of Mass of Subtractive Objects

Ex : **Figure shows a uniform disc of radius R with centre C_1 and from this disc a small disc of radius R/2 is cut with centre at C_2 as shown. Find the distance of centre of mass from C_1 of the remaining part of disc.**

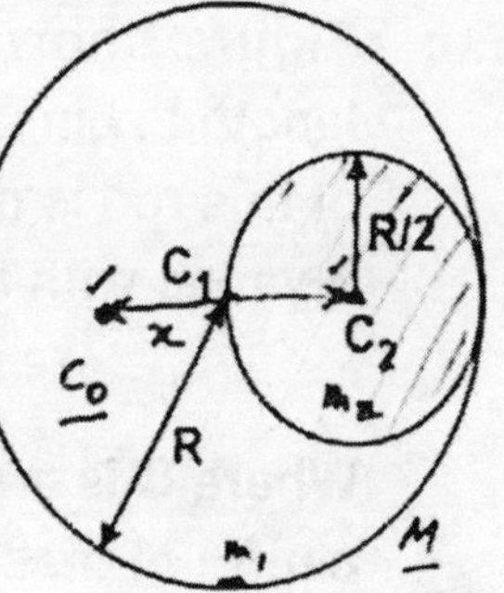

Sol^n: By property of mass moments we use

$$m_2 = \pi(R/2)^2 = \frac{\pi R^2}{4} = \frac{M}{4}$$

$$m_1 = M - m_2 = \frac{3M}{4}$$

$$m_2(R/2) - m_1 x = 0$$

$$\frac{M}{4} \cdot R/2 = \frac{3M}{4} \cdot x \Rightarrow x = R/6 \text{ Ans.}$$

Web Reference at www.physicsgalaxy.com | Scan for Video Explanation

Module-8: Centre of Mass of Continuous Extended Bodies

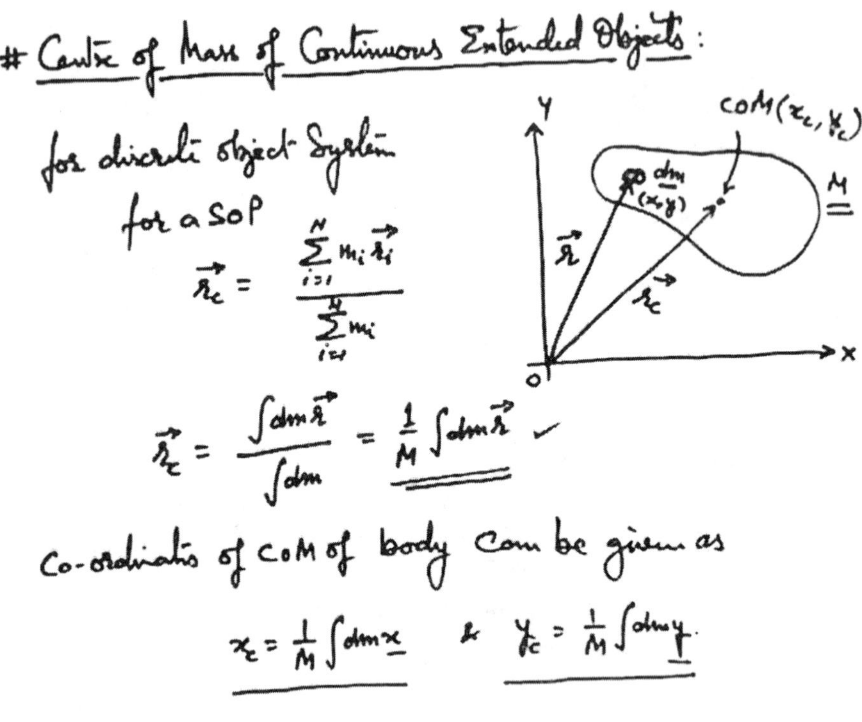

Scan for Video Explanation

Web Reference at www.physicsgalaxy.com

Module-8: Centre of Mass of Continuous Extended Bodies

Ex : Figure shows a rod AB of length L. Linear mass density of this rod is non-uniform and it varies with the distance x from end A of rod as

$$\lambda = Cx^2 \text{ kg/m}$$

Where C is a positive constant. Find distance of centre of mass of this rod from end A of rod.

Soln:

$$x_c = \frac{1}{M}\int dm\,x$$

$$= \frac{1}{M}\int_0^L \lambda dx . x$$

$$dm = \lambda dx$$

$$M = \int dm = \int_0^L Cx^2 dx$$

$$M = \frac{CL^3}{3}$$

$$x_c = \frac{1}{M}\int_0^L Cx^3 dx = \frac{CL^4}{4M} = \frac{CL^4}{4\left(\frac{CL^3}{3}\right)} = \frac{3L}{4} \text{ Ans.}$$

Scan for Video Explanation

Web Reference at www.physicsgalaxy.com

Module-9: Centre of Mass of a Uniform Half Ring

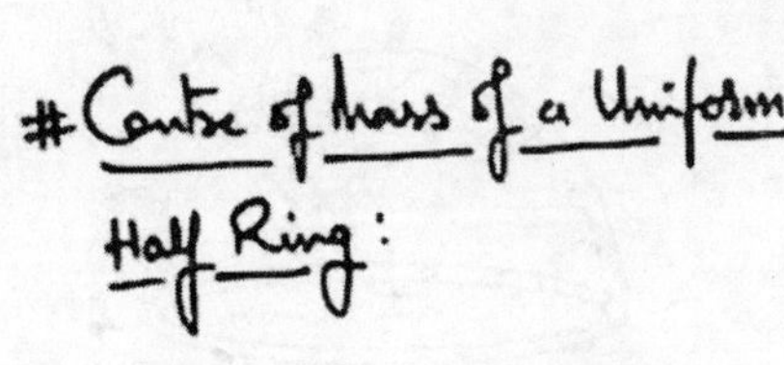

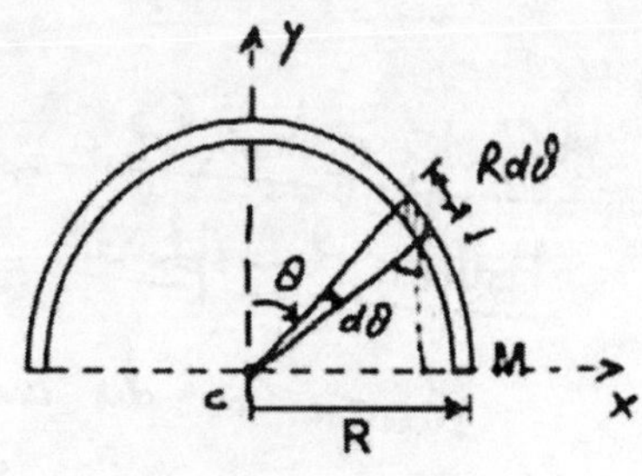

First we Consider an elemental mass dm on Ring.

$$dm = \frac{M}{\pi}.d\theta$$

y co-ordinate of dm is $y = R\cos\theta$

y-coordinate of COM is $y_c = \frac{1}{M}\int dm\,y = \frac{1}{M}\int_{-\pi/2}^{+\pi/2}\frac{M}{\pi}\,d\theta\,(R\cos\theta)$

$$y_c = \frac{R}{\pi}\int_{-\pi/2}^{+\pi/2}\cos\theta\,d\theta = \frac{R}{\pi}[\sin\theta]_{-\pi/2}^{+\pi/2}$$

$$y_c = \frac{R}{\pi}[1+1] = \frac{2R}{\pi}$$

$y_c = \frac{2R}{\pi}$, R

Web Reference at www.physicsgalaxy.com | Scan for Video Explanation

Module-10: Centre of Mass of a Uniform Half Disc

Centre of Mass of a Uniform Half Disc:

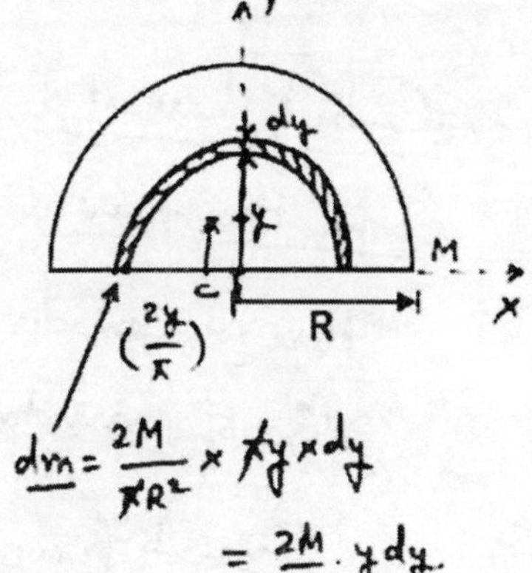

Here we take an elemental half ring of mass dm.

$$dm = \frac{2M}{\pi R^2}\times\pi y\times dy = \frac{2M}{R^2}.y\,dy$$

$$y_c = \frac{1}{M}\int dm\,y$$

$$= \frac{1}{M}\int_0^R \frac{2M}{R^2}.y\,dy\times\left(\frac{2y}{\pi}\right) = \frac{4}{\pi R^2}\int_0^R y^2\,dy$$

$$= \frac{4}{\pi R^2}\left[\frac{y^3}{3}\right]_0^R = \frac{4}{\pi R^2}\times\frac{R^3}{3}$$

$$\left[y_c = \frac{4R}{3\pi}\right]$$

$y_c = \frac{4R}{3\pi}$, R

Web Reference at www.physicsgalaxy.com | Scan for Video Explanation

Module-11: Centre of Mass of a Uniform Hollow Hemisphere

Centre of Mass of a Hollow Hemisphere:

Here we Consider an elemental strip ring of mass dm.

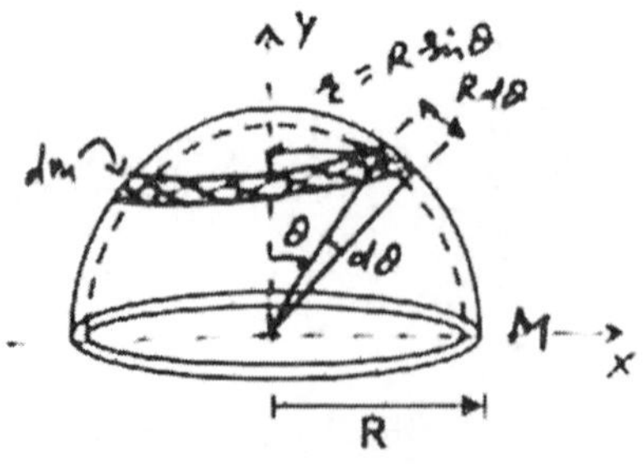

$$dm = \frac{M}{2\pi R^2} \times 2\pi R \sin\theta . R d\theta$$

$$dm = M \sin\theta d\theta$$

$$y_c = \frac{1}{M}\int dm\, y$$

$$= \frac{1}{M}\int_0^{\pi/2} M \sin\theta d\theta . (R\cos\theta) \times \frac{2}{2}$$

$$= \frac{R}{2}\int_0^{\pi/2} \sin 2\theta\, d\theta = \frac{R}{2}\left[-\frac{\cos 2\theta}{2}\right]_0^{\pi/2}$$

$$= \frac{R}{2}\left[\frac{1}{2}+\frac{1}{2}\right] = R/2$$

$y_c = R/2$.

Scan for Video Explanation

Web Reference at www.physicsgalaxy.com

Module-12: Centre of Mass of a Uniform Solid Hemisphere

Centre of Mass of a Solid Hemisphere:

Here we Consider an elemental disc of mass dm

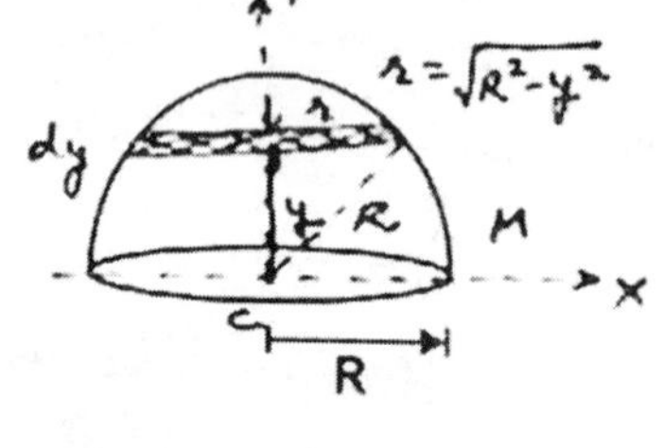

$$dm = \frac{3M}{2\pi R^3} \times \pi r^2 dy$$

$$= \frac{3M}{2\pi R^3} \times \pi (R^2 - y^2) dy$$

$$y_c = \frac{1}{M}\int dm\, y$$

$$= \frac{1}{M}\int_0^R \frac{3M}{2R^3}(R^2-y^2)\, dy \times y$$

$$= \frac{3}{2R^3}\int_0^R (R^2 y - y^3)\, dy$$

$$= \frac{3}{2R^3}\left[\frac{R^2y^2}{2} - \frac{y^4}{4}\right]_0^R = \frac{3}{2R^3}\left[\frac{R^4}{2}-\frac{R^4}{4}\right] = \frac{3R}{8}$$

Scan for Video Explanation

Web Reference at www.physicsgalaxy.com

Module-13: Centre of Mass of a Uniform Hollow Cone

Centre of Mass of a Uniform Hollow Cone:

we consider a strip ring of mass dm as an element

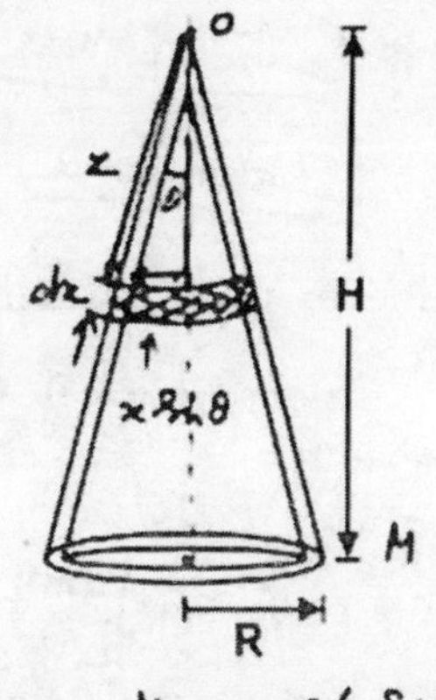

$$y_c = \frac{1}{M}\int dm\, y$$

$$= \frac{1}{M}\int_0^{\sqrt{R^2+H^2}} \frac{2M}{H^2+R^2}\cdot x\,dx \cdot \left[x\left(\frac{H}{\sqrt{H^2+R^2}}\right)\right]$$ ($\cos\theta$)

$$= \frac{2H}{(H^2+R^2)^{3/2}}\int_0^{\sqrt{R^2+H^2}} x^2\,dx$$

$$= \frac{2H}{(H^2+R^2)^{3/2}}\left[\frac{x^3}{3}\right]_0^{\sqrt{R^2+H^2}}$$

$$dm = \frac{M}{\pi R\sqrt{H^2+R^2}} \times 2\pi x \sin\theta\, dx$$

$$dm = \frac{M}{R\sqrt{H^2+R^2}} \cdot 2x \frac{R}{\sqrt{H^2+R^2}}\, dx$$

$$dm = \frac{2M}{H^2+R^2}\cdot x\,dx.$$

Scan for Video Explanation

Module-13: Centre of Mass of a Uniform Hollow Cone

$$y_c = \frac{2H}{(H^2+R^2)^{3/2}} \times \frac{(R^2+H^2)^{3/2}}{3}$$

$$y_c = \frac{2H}{3}$$

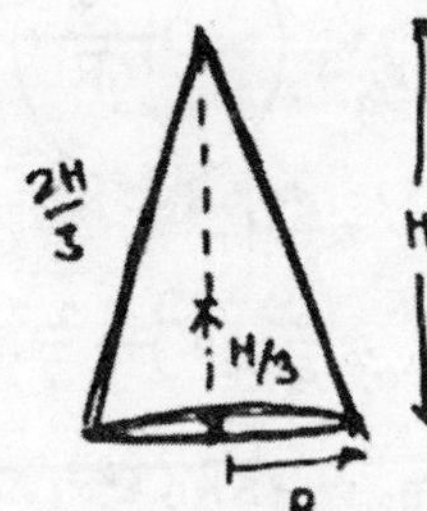

$$y_{c_{base}} = H/3.$$

Web Reference at www.physicsgalaxy.com

Scan for Video Explanation

Module-14: Centre of Mass of a Uniform Solid Cone

Centre of Mass of a Uniform Solid Cone:

We consider an elemental disc of mass dm,

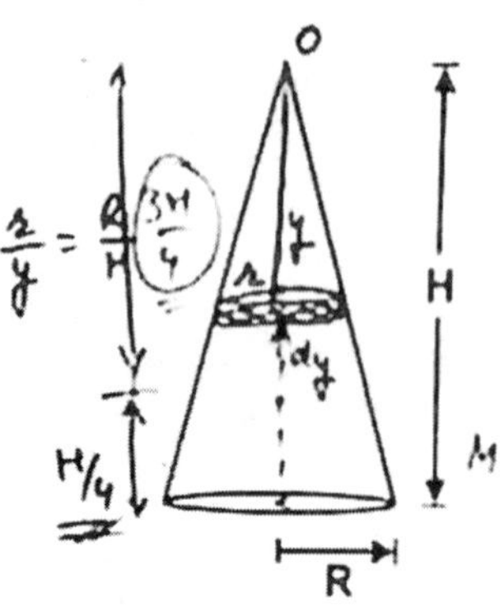

$$y_c = \frac{1}{M}\int dm\, y$$

$$= \frac{1}{M}\int_0^H \frac{3My^2}{H^3}.dy \times y$$

$$= \frac{3}{H^3}\int_0^H y^3 dy = \frac{3}{H^3}\left[\frac{y^4}{4}\right]_0^H$$

$$= \frac{3}{H^3}.\frac{H^4}{4} = \frac{3H}{4}$$

$$dm = \frac{3M}{\pi R^2 H} \times \pi r^2 dy$$

$$dm = \frac{3M}{\pi R^2 H} \times \pi\left(\frac{Ry}{H}\right)^2 dy$$

$$dm = \frac{3My^2}{H^3}dy$$

Scan for Video Explanation

Web Reference at www.physicsgalaxy.com

Module-15: Solved Example-4

Ex : **Find centre of mass of a uniformly dense object which consist of a hemisphere joined at the base of a cone as shown.**

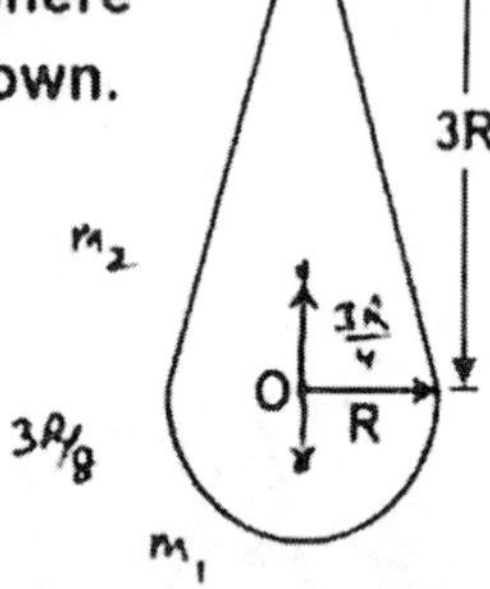

$$y_c = \frac{m_2\left(\frac{3R}{4}\right) - m_1\left(\frac{3R}{8}\right)}{m_1 + m_2}$$

$$y_c = \frac{m\left(\frac{3R}{4}\right) - \frac{2}{3}m.\frac{3R}{8}}{\frac{5m}{3}}$$

$$y_c = \frac{3R}{10} \text{ Ans.}$$

$$m_1 = \frac{2}{3}\pi R^3 \rightarrow \frac{2}{3}m$$

$$m_2 = \frac{1}{3}\pi R^2(3R)$$

$$= \pi R^3 \rightarrow m$$

Scan for Video Explanation

Web Reference at www.physicsgalaxy.com

Module-16: Solved Example-5

Ex : Figure shows a square plate of side a from which a semicircular disc is removed as shown. Find the centre of mass of the remaining object.

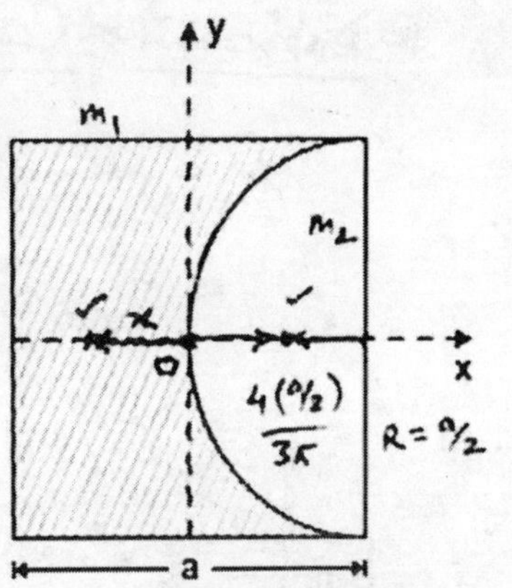

Sol^n:

CoM of $m_1 \rightarrow -x$

CoM of $m_2 \rightarrow \frac{a}{2} - \frac{2a}{3\pi}$

$$m_1 + m_2 = a^2$$

$$m_2 = \frac{\pi(a/2)^2}{2} = \frac{\pi a^2}{8}$$

$$m_1 = a^2 - \frac{\pi a^2}{8}$$

$$m_2\left(\frac{a}{2} - \frac{2a}{3\pi}\right) = m_1 x$$

$$x = \frac{m_2 a}{m_1}\left(\frac{1}{2} - \frac{2}{3\pi}\right)$$

$$x = \frac{a(3\pi - 4)}{6(8-\pi)} \quad \text{Ans}$$

Web Reference at www.physicsgalaxy.com | Scan for Video Explanation

Module-17: Solved Example-6

Ex : From a uniform cylinder of height 2R and radius R, a hemisphere is cut as shown. Find centre of mass of the remaining object.

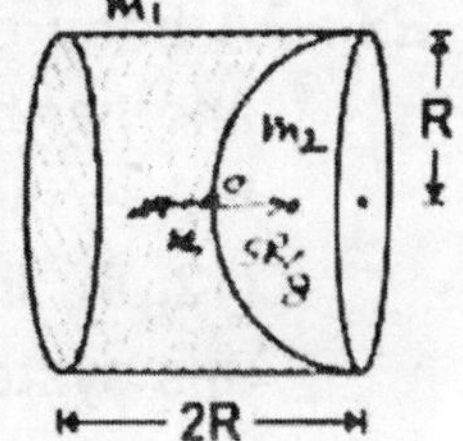

Sol^n:

$$m_2 = \frac{2}{3}\pi R^3 \rightarrow m$$

$$m_1 = \pi R^2(2R) - \frac{2}{3}\pi R^3 = \frac{4}{3}\pi R^3 \rightarrow 2m$$

by def. of CoM using mass moments

$$m_2(5R/8) - m_1 x = 0$$

$$x = \frac{5R}{8} \times \frac{m_2}{m_1} = \frac{5R}{16} \quad \text{Ans.}$$

Web Reference at www.physicsgalaxy.com | Scan for Video Explanation

Module-18: Displacement of Centre of Mass

Displacement of Centre of Mass of a SOP:

for a given SOP

$$\vec{r}_c = \frac{m_1\vec{r}_1 + m_2\vec{r}_2 + \cdots}{m_1 + m_2 + \cdots}$$

If $\Delta\vec{r}_1, \Delta\vec{r}_2, \ldots$ are the displacements in position of masses $m_1, m_2, m_3 \ldots$ then disp in pos. of COM can be given as.

$$\Delta\vec{r}_c = \frac{m_1\Delta\vec{r}_1 + m_2\Delta\vec{r}_2 + \cdots}{m_1 + m_2 + \cdots}$$

Scan for Video Explanation

Web Reference at www.physicsgalaxy.com

Module-18: Displacement of Centre of Mass

Ex : A body of A mass 5 kg is placed at (5, 0) and another body B of mass 10 kg is placed at (8, 0). If A is displaced to (7, 0) and B is displaced to (12, 0), find displacement of centre of mass of this system.

Sol:

5 kg: $\Delta x_1 = 2$ units

10 kg: $\Delta x_2 = 4$ units

$$\Delta x_c = \frac{m_1\Delta x_1 + m_2\Delta x_2}{m_1 + m_2}$$

$$= \frac{5\times 2 + 10\times 4}{15} = \frac{50}{15} = \frac{10}{3} \text{ units Ans.}$$

Scan for Video Explanation

Web Reference at www.physicsgalaxy.com

Module-19: Velocity and Acceleration of Centre of Mass

Velocity & Acceleration of Centre of Mass of a SOP:

As we know for a SOP, p.v of COM is given as

$$\vec{r}_c = \left(\frac{m_1\vec{r}_1 + m_2\vec{r}_2 + \cdots}{m_1 + m_2 + \cdots}\right)$$

Velocity of COM can be given as-

$$\left[\vec{v}_c = \frac{d\vec{r}_c}{dt} = \left(\frac{m_1\vec{v}_1 + m_2\vec{v}_2 + \cdots}{m_1 + m_2 + \cdots}\right) = \frac{\vec{P}_{system}}{\sum_{i=1}^{n} m_i}\right]$$

$$\left[\text{vel of COM} = \frac{\text{Total momentum of SOP}}{\text{Sum of masses.}}\right]$$

Web Reference at www.physicsgalaxy.com | **Scan for Video Explanation**

Module-19: Velocity and Acceleration of Centre of Mass

Acceleration of COM of a SOP

$$\vec{a}_c = \frac{d\vec{v}_c}{dt} = \left(\frac{m_1\vec{a}_1 + m_2\vec{a}_2 + \cdots}{m_1 + m_2 + \cdots}\right)$$

$$\left[\vec{a}_c = \frac{\vec{F}_{ext}}{\sum_{i=1}^{n} m_i}\right]$$

$$\left[\text{Acc}^n \text{ of COM} = \frac{\text{Net External force on a SOP}}{\text{Sum of masses.}}\right]$$

Web Reference at www.physicsgalaxy.com | **Scan for Video Explanation**

Module-20: Solved Example-7

Ex : A body of mass 4 kg moves along +X direction at speed 20 m/s. Find the speed with which a 10 kg mass should move along +Y direction such that their centre of mass travels along line x = y. Assume both particle starts at the same time from origin.

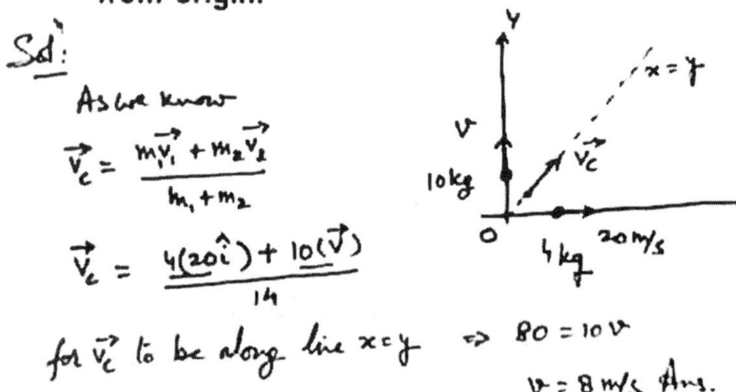

Scan for Video Explanation

Web Reference at www.physicsgalaxy.com

Module-21: Solved Example-8

Ex : Two blocks of masses 3 kg and 5 kg are connected by an ideal spring and placed on a smooth surface as shown. A force of 40 N is applied on 3 kg block and it is observed that at an instant acceleration of 3 kg mass is 2 m/s^2. Find acceleration of 5 kg mass at this instant.

5kg —k— 3kg → F

Sol^n. As F is the only ext force present

acc^n of COM $a_c = \frac{F}{8} = \frac{40}{8} = 5 \text{ m/s}^2$

As we know $a_c = \frac{m_1a_1 + m_2a_2}{m_1+m_2}$ ⇒ $5 = \frac{3\times2 + 5a}{8}$

$5a = 40 - 6 = 34$

$a = \frac{34}{5} \text{ m/s}^2$ Ans.

Scan for Video Explanation

Web Reference at www.physicsgalaxy.com

Chapter 10
System of Particle-II

Lecture Notes Modules

Module-1: Conservation of Momentum
Module-2: Solved Example-1
Module-3: Solved Example-2
Module-4: Solved Example-3
Module-5: Effect of Internal Forces
Module-6: Solved Example-4
Module-7: Solved Example-5
Module-8: Solved Example-6
Module-9: Solved Example-7
Module-10: Solved Example-8
Module-11: Impulse & Conservation of Momentum
Module-12: Solved Example-9
Module-13: Solved Example-10
Module-14: Solved Example-11
Module-15: Collisions
Module-16: Types of Collisions Based on Material Properties
Module-17: Collision of Bodies of Different Materials
Module-18: Coefficient of Restitution
Module-19: Head-on Collisions
Module-20: Solved Example-12
Module-21: Partial Elastic Head-on Collision
Module-22: Solved Example-13
Module-23: Solved Example-14
Module-24: Solved Example-15
Module-25: Solved Example-16
Module-26: Solved Example-17
Module-27: Oblique Collision of a Ball on a Flat Surface
Module-28: Oblique Collision in a 2D Plane
Module-29: Solved Example-18
Module-30: Solved Example-19
Module-31: Solved Example-20
Module-32: Mass Variation Cases
Module-33: Super Elastic Collision

Module-1: Conservation of Momentum

Law of Conservation of Momentum:

for a SoP

$$\vec{V}_{CM} = \frac{\vec{P}_{system}}{\Sigma m_i} \quad \& \quad \vec{a}_{CM} = \frac{\vec{F}_{ext}}{\Sigma m_i}$$

if on a SoP $\vec{F}_{ext} = 0 \Rightarrow \vec{a}_{CM} = 0 \Rightarrow \vec{V}_{CM} = \text{Constant}$

$$\Downarrow$$

$$\vec{P}_{system} = \text{Constant}$$

["If on a SoP, no external force is acting, then the total momentum of SoP remain Conserved"]

Scan for Video Explanation

Web Reference at www.physicsgalaxy.com

Module-1: Conservation of Momentum

if $\vec{F}_{ext} = 0 \Rightarrow \vec{P}_{system} = \text{Constant}$

Recoiling of a Gun:

before firing $\vec{P}_s = 0$

$v_G \leftarrow$ M (gun) ... m $\rightarrow v_B$

by Cons. of Momentum we write

before shot   after shot

$$0 = mv_B - Mv_G$$

$$mv_B = Mv_G$$

Scan for Video Explanation

Web Reference at www.physicsgalaxy.com

Module-1: Conservation of Momentum

Adding a mass on a moving mass:

$m_1 \rightarrow v_0$ m_2 (placed on) m_1 $\rightarrow v_f$

No ext. force.

by Cons. of momentum

$$m_1 v_0 = (m_1 + m_2) v_f$$

find speed of blocks is $v_f = \frac{m_1 v_0}{m_1 + m_2}$.

Web Reference at www.physicsgalaxy.com | Scan for Video Explanation

Module-2: Solved Example-1

Ex : A bullet of mass 5 kg is fired toward a 20 kg block at speed 30 m/s placed on smooth ground. It is observed that the bullet penetrates the block and comes out at a speed 10 m/s. Find the speed acquired by the block in this process.

5 kg, $u = 30$ m/s, 20 kg, $\rightarrow v$, 10 m/s

Sol^n: no F_{ext} is present.

$\Rightarrow$ by Cons. of momentum we use

$$5 \times 30 = 20v + 5 \times 10$$

$$v = \frac{100}{20} = 5 \text{ m/s} \quad \text{Ans.}$$

Web Reference at www.physicsgalaxy.com | Scan for Video Explanation

Module-3: Solved Example-2

Ex : A pendulum bob of mass 2 kg is hanging from a string of length 1 m as shown. A bullet of mass 0.5 kg moving at 10 m/s strikes the bob and gets embedded into it. Find the maximum deflection angle from vertical to which the string will be deflected.

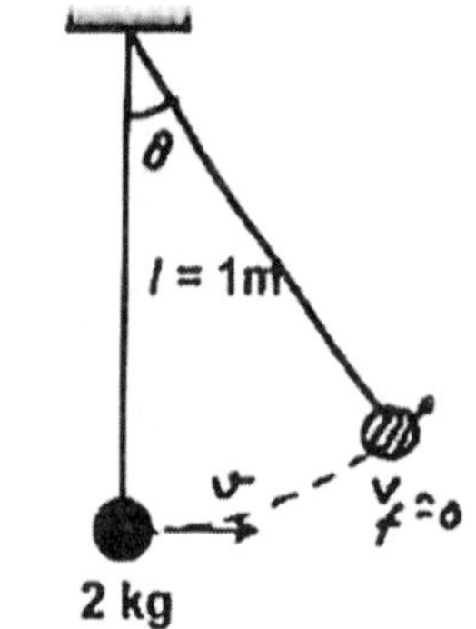

$g = 10 m/s^2$

Solⁿ: no F_{ext} is present.

$0.5 \times 10 = 2.5 \times v \Rightarrow v = 2 m/s$

As we know for any amplitude $\cos\theta = \frac{2gl - u^2}{2gl}$

$\cos\theta = \frac{2 \times 10 - 4}{2 \times 10} = \frac{16}{20} = \frac{4}{5}$

$\theta = \cos^{-1}(4/5) = 37°$ Ans.

Scan for Video Explanation

Web Reference at www.physicsgalaxy.com

Module-4: Solved Example-3

Ex : A shell is fired from a canon with a speed of 100 m/s at 60° with horizontal. At the highest point of its trajectory, the shell explodes into two equal fragments. One of these moves along horizontal backward direction at 50 m/s, find the speed of other fragment at the time of explosion.

Solⁿ:

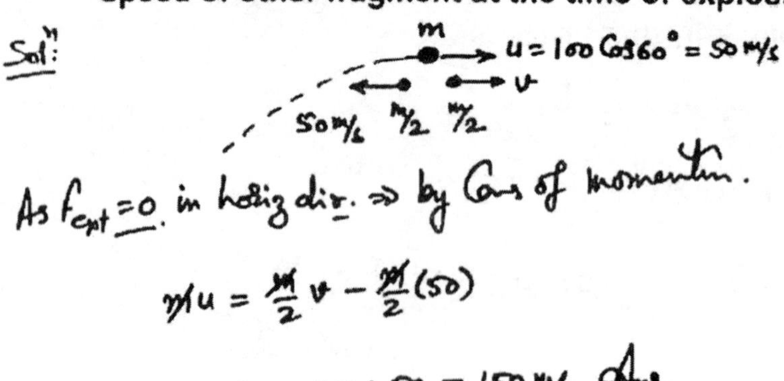

As $F_{ext} = 0$ in horiz dir. ⇒ by Cons of momentum.

$mu = \frac{m}{2}v - \frac{m}{2}(50)$

$v = 2u + 50 = 150 m/s$ Ans.

Scan for Video Explanation

Web Reference at www.physicsgalaxy.com

Module-5: Effect of Internal Forces

Effect of Internal Forces:

If in a SOP, Centre of mass of System is at rest.

$\Rightarrow \vec{V}_{cm} = 0 = \text{Const.}$

& if no external forces are acting on the SOP then

COM of System will remain at rest.

OR.

v. imp.

Only Internal forces of a System can never

Cause any motion in COM of a SOP

if it is at rest.

Web Reference at www.physicsgalaxy.com | Scan for Video Explanation

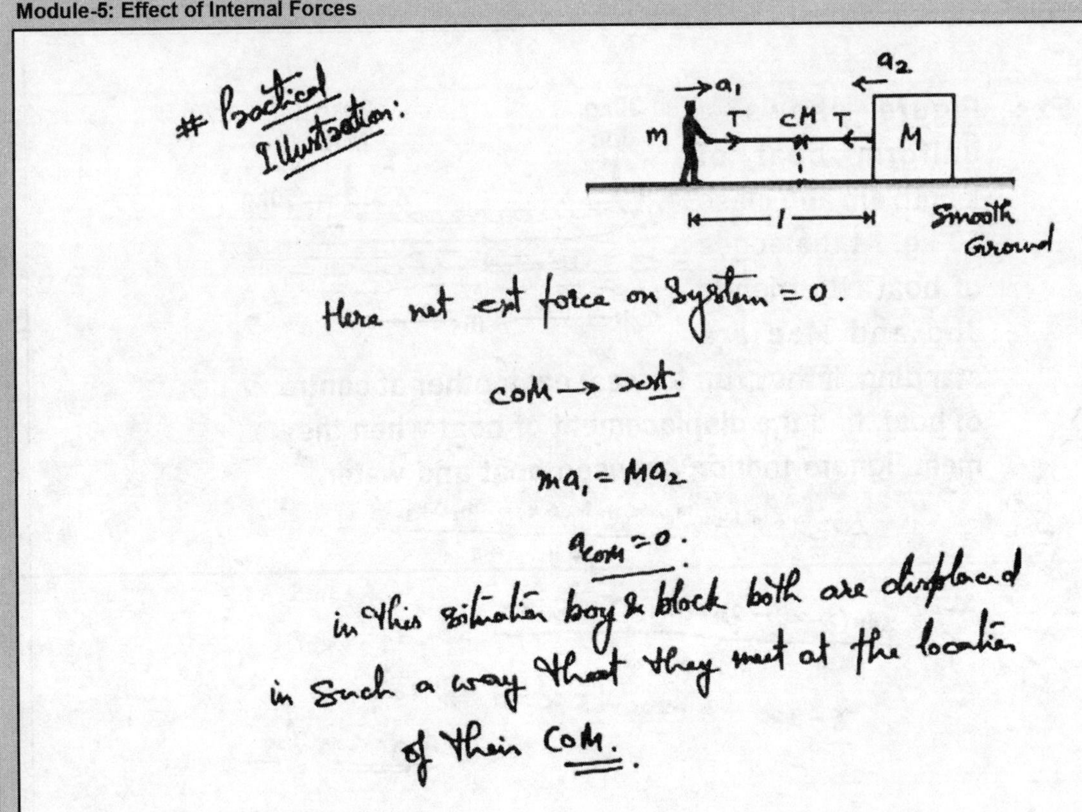

Module-5: Effect of Internal Forces

Pactical Illustration:

Here net ext force on System = 0.

COM → rest.

$ma_1 = Ma_2$

$a_{com} = 0.$

in this situation boy & block both are displaced in such a way that they meet at the location of their COM.

Web Reference at www.physicsgalaxy.com | Scan for Video Explanation

Module-5: Effect of Internal Forces

Ex : **A monkey holds an umbrella and this system is floating in air at <u>rest</u> due to buoyancy on balloon. If monkey starts climbing the string at speed u relative to string, find the speed with which balloon will move.**

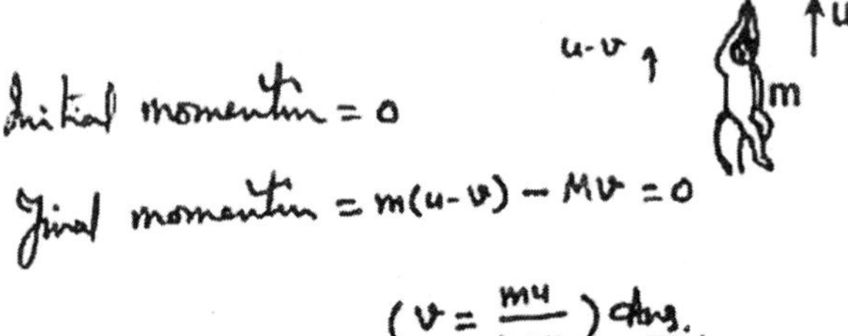

Initial momentum = 0

Final momentum $= m(u-v) - Mv = 0$

$$\left(v = \frac{mu}{M+m}\right) \text{Ans.}$$

Scan for Video Explanation

Web Reference at www.physicsgalaxy.com

Module-6: Solved Example-4

Ex : **Figure shows a uniform boat of length 4m and mass 50 kg. At the edges of boat two friends Joc and Mac are standing. If they run to meet each other at centre of boat, find the displacement of boat when they meet. Ignore friction between boat and water.**

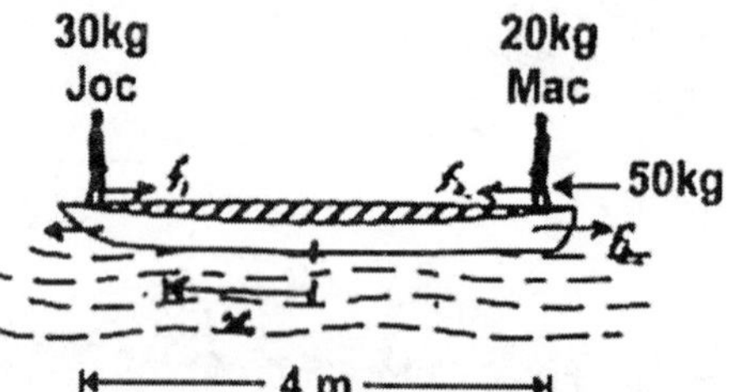

Sol^n:

$$\Delta x_{com} = 0 = \frac{m_1 \Delta x_1 + m_2 \Delta x_2 + m_3 \Delta x_3}{m_1 + m_2 + m_3}$$

$$0 = \frac{30 \times (2-x) - 20 \times (2+x) - 50 \times x}{100}$$

$$6 - 3x - 4 - 2x - 5x = 0 \Rightarrow 10x = 2$$

$$x = 0.2\text{ m Ans.}$$

Scan for Video Explanation

Web Reference at www.physicsgalaxy.com

Module-7: Solved Example-5

Ex : **A flat car of mass M is at rest on a frictionless floor with a child of mass m standing at the edge. If child jumps off from the car toward right with initial velocity u, with respect to car, find the velocity of car after the jump.**

Sol^n. by Cons. of momentum, we use.

$$0 = m(u-v) - Mv$$

$$v = \frac{mu}{m+M} \quad \text{Ans.}$$

Web Reference at www.physicsgalaxy.com

Scan for Video Explanation

Module-8: Solved Example-6

Ex : **A flat car of mass M with a child of mass m is moving at speed v_1. The child jumps in the direction of motion of car with a velocity u with respect to car. Find the final velocities of the child and that of car after jump.**

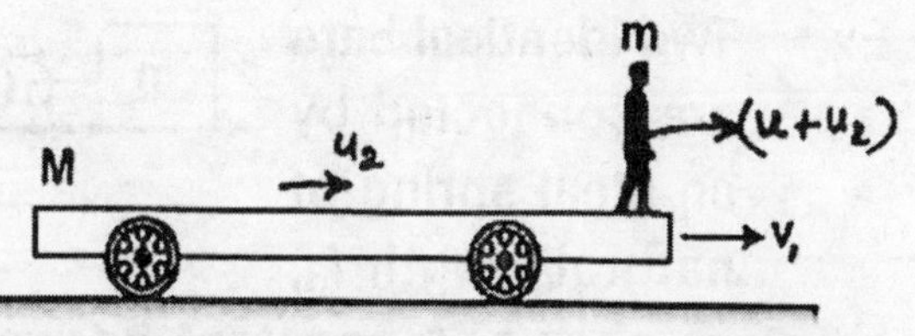

Sol^n. by Cons. of momentum

$$(M+m)v_1 = m(u+u_2) + Mu_2.$$

Vel of Car $\quad u_2 = \dfrac{(M+m)v_1 - mu}{m+M}$ Ans.

Vel of child $\quad u+u_2 = \dfrac{(M+m)v_1 + Mu}{m+M}$ Ans.

Web Reference at www.physicsgalaxy.com

Scan for Video Explanation

Module-9: Solved Example-7

Ex : A shell at rest at origin explodes into three fragments of masses 1kg, 2kg and m kg. The fragments of masses 1kg and 2 kg fly off with speeds 12 m/s along X-axis and 8 m/s along Y-axis respectively. If m kg flies off with speed 40 m/s then find the total mass of the shell.

Sol^n:

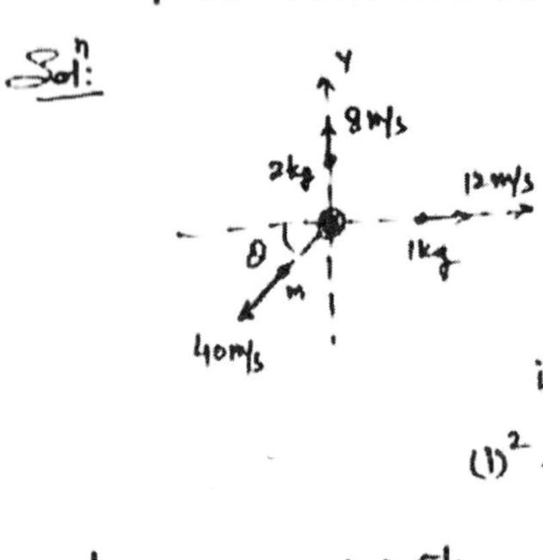

Initial momentum = 0

In x dir.

$m(40\cos\theta) = 1\times 12$ —(1)

in Y dir $m(40\sin\theta) = 2\times 8 = 16$ —(2)

$(1)^2 + (2)^2 \Rightarrow m^2(40)^2 = (12)^2 + (16)^2$

$m^2 = \frac{144+256}{1600} = \frac{1}{4}$

$m = \frac{1}{2} = 0.5$ kg.

$M_{shell} = 1 + 2 + 0.5$ kg

$= 3.5$ kg Ans.

Scan for Video Explanation

Web Reference at www.physicsgalaxy.com

Module-10: Solved Example-8

Ex : Two identical bars are connected by an ideal spring of natural length l_0, as shown. A constant horizontal force F starts acting on one of the bars as shown. Find the maximum and minimum separation between the bars during their motion.

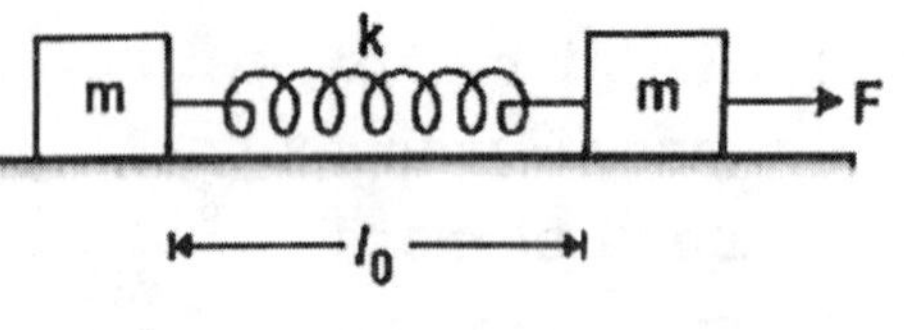

Sol^n:

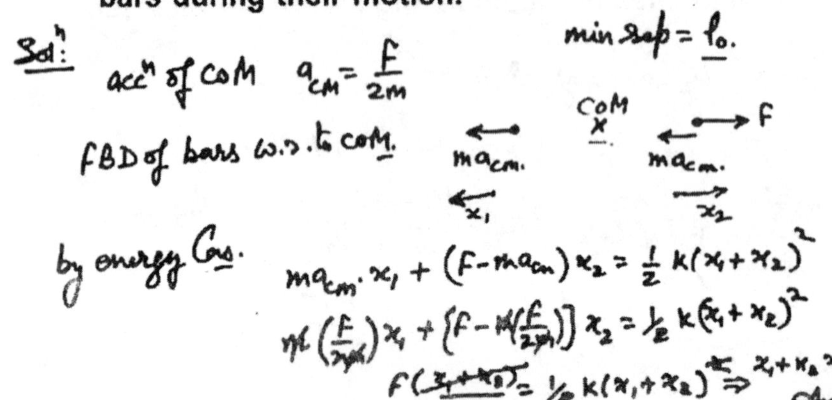

acc^n of COM $a_{CM} = \frac{F}{2m}$

min sep = l_0.

FBD of bars w.r.t. COM.

ma_{cm} ← COM → ma_{cm} ← → F

x_1 ← → x_2

by energy Cons.

$ma_{cm}\cdot x_1 + (F - ma_{cm})x_2 = \frac{1}{2}k(x_1+x_2)^2$

$m\left(\frac{F}{2m}\right)x_1 + \left[F - m\left(\frac{F}{2m}\right)\right]x_2 = \frac{1}{2}k(x_1+x_2)^2$

$F\frac{(x_1+x_2)}{2} = \frac{1}{2}k(x_1+x_2)^2 \Rightarrow x_1+x_2 = \frac{F}{k}$ Ans.

Scan for Video Explanation

Web Reference at www.physicsgalaxy.com

Module-11: Impulse & Conservation of Momentum

Impulse & Conservation of Momentum:

As we know $F = \frac{dp}{dt}$

$$dp = F\,dt$$
$$\Delta p = \int F\,dt$$

] Impulse → momentum imparted by a force in a given time.

(Impulse = force × time duration)

Work: for const force $W = F.\Delta s$; for var. force $W = \int F\,dx$

Impulse: $J = F\Delta t$ (for a constant F); $J = \int F\,dt$ (for a time varying F)

Web Reference at www.physicsgalaxy.com | Scan for Video Explanation

Module-11: Impulse & Conservation of Momentum

Impulse - Momentum Equation:

$F \rightarrow$ [m] $\rightarrow v_1$ at $t=0$; [m] $\rightarrow v_2$ at $t=T$; Smooth Ground.

Initial Momentum + Impulse Imparted = Final momentum

$$mv_1 + Ft = mv_2$$

External force ⇒ Continuous change in momentum.

Web Reference at www.physicsgalaxy.com | Scan for Video Explanation

Module-11: Impulse & Conservation of Momentum

Ex : A body of mass 10 kg is pulled from rest with a time varying force $F = 2t^2$ N on a rough surface having friction coefficient $\mu = 0.2$. Find the speed of block after 6 seconds.

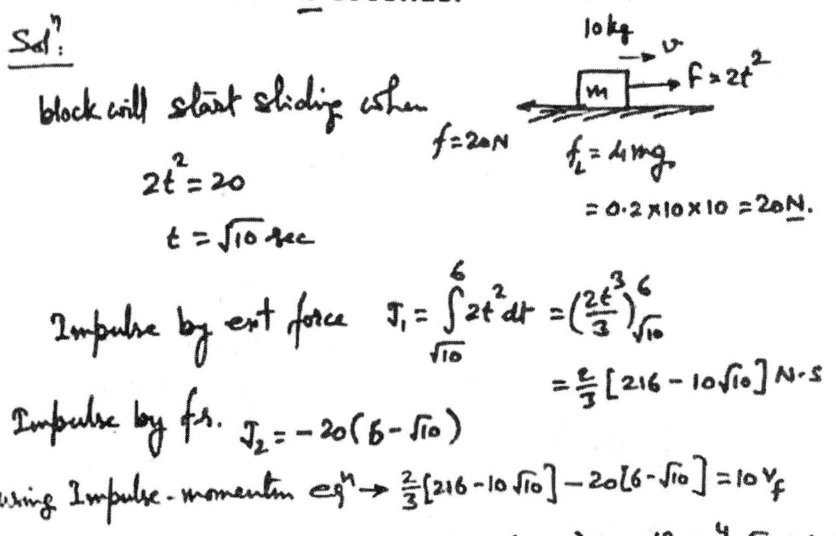

Sol^n:

block will start sliding when $f = 20N$

$f_L = \mu mg = 0.2 \times 10 \times 10 = 20N$.

$2t^2 = 20$

$t = \sqrt{10}$ sec

Impulse by ext force $J_1 = \int_{\sqrt{10}}^{6} 2t^2 dt = \left(\frac{2t^3}{3}\right)_{\sqrt{10}}^{6}$

$= \frac{2}{3}[216 - 10\sqrt{10}]$ N-s

Impulse by fr. $J_2 = -20(6 - \sqrt{10})$

using Impulse-momentum eq^n → $\frac{2}{3}[216 - 10\sqrt{10}] - 20[6 - \sqrt{10}] = 10 v_f$

$v_f = (24 + \frac{40}{3}\sqrt{10})/10 = \frac{12}{5} + \frac{4}{3}\sqrt{10}$ m/s Ans.

Scan for Video Explanation

Web Reference at www.physicsgalaxy.com

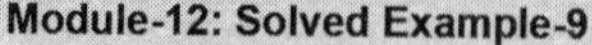

Module-12: Solved Example-9

Ex : A block A is released from rest from top of a wedge block of height h as shown in figure.

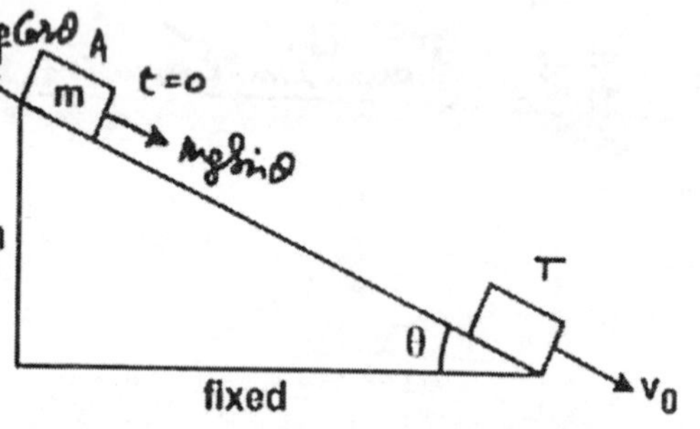

If velocity of block when it reaches the bottom of incline is v_0, find the time of sliding. Friction coefficient on inclined plane is μ.

Sol^n: net downward force on block along incline is

$F_{down} = mg\sin\theta - \mu mg\cos\theta$

W-E th.: $(mg\sin\theta - \mu mg\cos\theta) \times h\,\text{Cosec}\,\theta = \frac{1}{2} m v_0^2$ —(1)

by Imp eq^n: $(mg\sin\theta - \mu mg\cos\theta) \times T = m v_0$ —(2)

$\frac{(2)}{(1)}$ $\frac{T}{h\,\text{Cosec}\,\theta} = \frac{2}{v_0} \Rightarrow T = \frac{2h\,\text{Cosec}\,\theta}{v_0}$ Ans.

Scan for Video Explanation

Web Reference at www.physicsgalaxy.com

Module-13: Solved Example-10

3kg k 2kg → F = 5t

Smooth

Ex : **Figure shows a spring block system on which time varying force 5t is applied on 2kg mass. After 10 second, velocity of 3 kg mass is 30 m/s. Find velocity of 2 kg mass at this instant.**

Sol^n: Total impulse by external force in 10s is $J = \int_0^{10} F\,dt$

$$= \int_0^{10} 5t\,dt = 250 \text{ N-S.}$$

$$(\Sigma m)v_{CM} = 250.$$

$$v_{CM} = 250/5 = 50 \text{ m/s}.$$

$$v_{CM} = \frac{m_1v_1 + m_2v_2}{m_1 + m_2} = \frac{3\times 30 + 2\times v_2}{5} = 50$$

$$\Rightarrow v_2 = \frac{160}{2} = 80 \text{ m/s} \quad \text{Ans.}$$

Web Reference at www.physicsgalaxy.com | Scan for Video Explanation

Module-14: Solved Example-11

Ex : **Figure shows a smooth L-shaped block of mass M placed on a smooth plane. If a small mass m is thrown on it with speed u as shown, find the minimum speed u such that it is able to reach the topmost point B on block.**

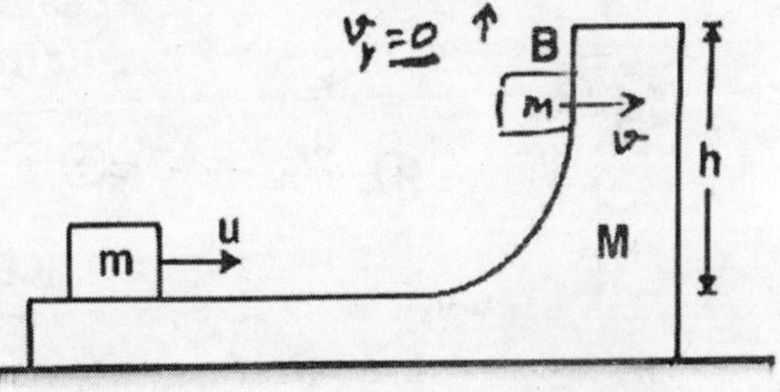

Sol^n: As no F_{ext} is present $\Rightarrow$ $mu = (m+M)v$

$$v = \frac{mu}{m+M}$$

by W/E theo-

$$\frac{1}{2}mu^2 - mgh = \frac{1}{2}(m+M)\left(\frac{mu}{m+M}\right)^2 \Rightarrow \frac{1}{2}mu^2\left[1 - \frac{m}{m+M}\right] = mgh$$

$$u = \sqrt{\frac{2gh(M+m)}{M}} \quad \text{Ans.}$$

Web Reference at www.physicsgalaxy.com | Scan for Video Explanation

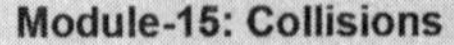

Module-15: Collisions

Collision:

It is a process of momentum transfer by internal forces of a System.

F_e ← u_1 ↓ ... F_e → u_2 ↑ ... F_e ← r_{min} → F_e ... v_1 ... v_2

m_1 ... m_2

Say $u_1 > u_2$

$t = 0$

State of min KE during Collision

$v_2 > v_1$

$t = T$

Impact ↓ physical Contact occurs

Scan for Video Explanation

Web Reference at www.physicsgalaxy.com

Module-15: Collisions

F_e ← u_1 ... F_e → u_2 ... r_{min} u u ... v_1 ... v_2

m_1 m_2

$u_1 > u_2$

KE_{min}

$v_2 > v_1$

As no external force is present in the above case

⇒ Total momentum of System will remain Conserved.

$$m_1u_1 + m_2u_2 = m_1v_1 + m_2v_2$$

Scan for Video Explanation

Web Reference at www.physicsgalaxy.com

Module-15: Collisions

Impact between two bodies:

↓

Physical Contact

N $\vec{u}$, $u_1 \downarrow$ N $u_2 \uparrow$

$m_1 \rightarrow u_1$ $m_2 \rightarrow u_2$ $\vec{u}$ $\vec{u}$ v_1 v_2

$u_1 > u_2$ "SC" KE_{min} $v_2 > v_1$

As no external force is present

$$m_1u_1 + m_2u_2 = m_1v_1 + m_2v_2$$

Web Reference at www.physicsgalaxy.com

Scan for Video Explanation

Module-16: Types of Collisions Based on Material Properties

Types of Collisions based on material properties:

Based on types of material, collisions can be classified in 3 categories - These are -

		during Collision
$KE_f = KE_i$	(1) Elastic Collision	→ KE loss = 0
$KE_f < KE_i$	(2) Partial Elastic Collision	→ Some KE loss
$KE_f < KE_i$ (min)	(3) Inelastic Collisions	→ KE loss → max.

u_1 u_2 $\vec{u}$ $\vec{u}$ v_1 v_2

m_1 m_2

$u_1 > u_2$ $KE_{min.}$ $KE_f.$

KE_i

Web Reference at www.physicsgalaxy.com

Scan for Video Explanation

Module-16: Types of Collisions Based on Material Properties

Classification of Solids:

(1) Elastic material
(2) Partially elastic material
(2) Inelastic materials (plastic)

(1) Elastic Material: which deform on application of external force & regains original shape on removal of force.

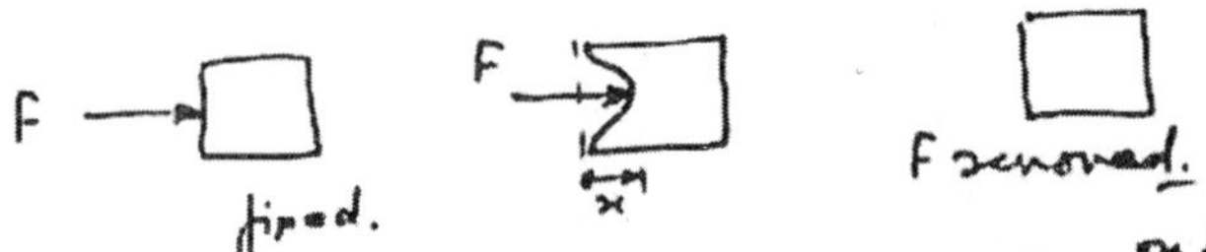

F → [fixed] ; F → (deformed, x) ; F removed.

Deformation ⇒ PE is stored. → on removal of force this PE is released

Scan for Video Explanation

Web Reference at www.physicsgalaxy.com

Module-16: Types of Collisions Based on Material Properties

Partially Elastic Material:

W/D in Deformation → partly stored in form of PE & remaining energy is dissipated.

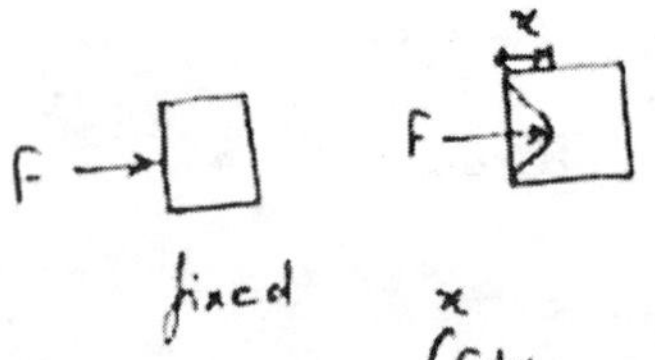

F → [fixed] ; F → (deformed, x)

$PE < \int_0^x F dx$ → on removal of ext force only the stored PE will be released.

Scan for Video Explanation

Web Reference at www.physicsgalaxy.com

Module-16: Types of Collisions Based on Material Properties

Inelastic Materials:

WD in deformation → Completely dissipated
&
No PE is stored
⇓
on removal of force object remain in deformed state.

F → □   F → ▷□   ⊐

No restoring force exist in Inelastic materials

Web Reference at www.physicsgalaxy.com

Scan for Video Explanation

Module-17: Collision of Bodies of Different Materials

Collision of bodies of different materials:

$m_1 \xrightarrow{u_1}$ ... $m_2 \xrightarrow{u_2}$ ... $(m_1)(m_2)$ $\xrightarrow{u_1}$ $\xrightarrow{u_2}$

$(u_1 > u_2)$

$F_R \leftarrow \rightarrow F_R$

PE → max

KE → min

$m_1 \xrightarrow{u}$ $m_2 \xrightarrow{u}$

$m_1 \xrightarrow{v_1}$ ... $m_2 \xrightarrow{v_2}$

for elastic or partially elastic materials bodies will separate.

$$m_1u_1 + m_2u_2 = (m_1 + m_2)u$$

$$\left[u = \frac{m_1u_1 + m_2u_2}{m_1 + m_2}\right]$$

$(m_1)(m_2) \xrightarrow{u}$

inelastic material along line of motion bodies do not separate.

Web Reference at www.physicsgalaxy.com

Scan for Video Explanation

Module-18: Coefficient of Restitution

Coefficient of Restitution:

When two bodies collide then this is a constant parameter which accounts for the elasticity of material of bodies.

def:

$$e = \frac{\text{velocity of separation along line of Impact}}{\text{velocity of approach along line of Impact}}$$

u_1 u_2 v_1 v_2

$u_1 > u_2$

$v_{ap} = u_1 - u_2$

$$e = \left(\frac{v_2 - v_1}{u_1 - u_2}\right)$$

$v_2 > v_1$

sep vel $v_{sep} = v_2 - v_1$

Scan for Video Explanation

Web Reference at www.physicsgalaxy.com

Module-18: Coefficient of Restitution

For different type of material of bodies value of 'e' is different -

for elastic collision $e = 1$

for partial elastic collision $0 < e < 1$

Inelastic collisions $e = 0 = \frac{v_{sep}}{v_{app}}$

bodies do not separate along line of impact.

Scan for Video Explanation

Web Reference at www.physicsgalaxy.com

Module-18: Coefficient of Restitution

Types of Collisions:

Based on material of bodies involved in collision. These are categories in 3 ways.

(1) <u>Elastic Collisions</u>: In such cases before & after collision no energy loss takes place in deformation of bodies.

$$\underline{KE_{iB}} = \underline{KE_{fA}} \quad (e=1)$$

(2) <u>Partially Elastic Collisions</u>: In such cases some energy loss takes place during collision under deformation of bodies $\quad KE_{iB} > KE_{fA} \quad [0<e<1]$

Web Reference at www.physicsgalaxy.com

Scan for Video Explanation

Module-18: Coefficient of Restitution

(3) <u>Inelastic Collision</u>:

In such cases loss in energy during collision will be maximum and after collision no restoring force exist for separation of bodies. $\quad (\underline{e=0})$

<u>Classification of Collisions based on motion direction</u>:

<u>Two Categories</u>:

(1) Head-on Collisions

(2) Oblique Collisions

Web Reference at www.physicsgalaxy.com

Scan for Video Explanation

Module-19: Head-on Collisions

Head-on Collisions :

--- m_1 → u_1 --- m_2 → u_2 --- (collision: N ⟷ N) --- m_1 → v_1 --- m_2 → v_2 ---

When line of motion of two bodies before and after collision are same it is termed as Head-on Collision.

As no ext force is present ⇒

$$m_1u_1 + m_2u_2 = m_1v_1 + m_2v_2 \quad \text{—(1)}$$

COR $e = 1$.

Scan for Video Explanation

Web Reference at www.physicsgalaxy.com

Module-19: Head-on Collisions

$$m_1u_1 + m_2u_2 = m_1v_1 + m_2v_2 \quad \text{—(1)}$$

$e = 1. = \frac{v_{sep}}{v_{app}}$

$$v_{sep} = v_{app}$$

$$v_2 - v_1 = u_1 - u_2 \quad \text{—(2)}$$

As collision is elastic ⇒ $KE_i = KE_f$.

$$\frac{1}{2}m_1u_1^2 + \frac{1}{2}m_2u_2^2 = \frac{1}{2}m_1v_1^2 + \frac{1}{2}m_2v_2^2 \quad \text{—(3)}$$

Solving any two eq^n of (1), (2) & (3) we'll get values of v_1 and v_2 ....

Scan for Video Explanation

Web Reference at www.physicsgalaxy.com

Module-19: Head-on Collisions

from eq^n (2)

$$v_2 = u_1 - u_2 + v_1$$

from eq^n (1)

$$m_1u_1 + m_2u_2 = m_1v_1 + m_2(u_1 - u_2 + v_1)$$

On solving, we get

v.imp.

$$\vec{v}_1 = \left(\frac{m_1 - m_2}{m_1 + m_2}\right)\vec{u}_1 + \left(\frac{2m_2}{m_1 + m_2}\right)\vec{u}_2 \quad \text{—(A)}$$

$$\vec{v}_2 = \left(\frac{m_2 - m_1}{m_1 + m_2}\right)\vec{u}_2 + \left(\frac{2m_1}{m_1 + m_2}\right)\vec{u}_1 \quad \text{—(B)}$$

Web Reference at www.physicsgalaxy.com

Scan for Video Explanation

Module-19: Head-on Collisions

Special Cases of Head-on elastic Collisions :

$$\vec{v}_1 = \left(\frac{m_1 - m_2}{m_1 + m_2}\right)\vec{u}_1 + \left(\frac{2m_2}{m_1 + m_2}\right)\vec{u}_2$$

$$\vec{v}_2 = \left(\frac{m_2 - m_1}{m_1 + m_2}\right)\vec{u}_2 + \left(\frac{2m_1}{m_1 + m_2}\right)\vec{u}_1$$

Case-I: If $m_1 = m_2$.

$\Rightarrow$ $\vec{v}_1 = \vec{u}_2$ & $\vec{v}_2 = \vec{u}_1$ } after collision vel are swapped.

A u_1 → - - - - B $u_2 = 0$

rest

A B → u_1

Web Reference at www.physicsgalaxy.com

Scan for Video Explanation

Module-19: Head-on Collisions

Case-II : If $m_1 >> m_2$

$$\vec{v}_1 = \left(\frac{m_1 - m_2}{m_1 + m_2}\right)\vec{u}_1 + \left(\frac{2m_2}{m_1 + m_2}\right)\vec{u}_2$$

$$\boxed{\vec{v}_1 = \vec{u}_1}$$

$$\vec{v}_2 = \left(\frac{m_2 - m_1}{m_1 + m_2}\right)\vec{u}_2 + \left(\frac{2m_1}{m_1 + m_2}\right)\vec{u}_1$$

$$\boxed{\vec{v}_2 = 2\vec{u}_1 - \vec{u}_2}$$

Scan for Video Explanation

Web Reference at www.physicsgalaxy.com

Module-19: Head-on Collisions

Case-III : If $m_2 >> m_1$

$$\vec{v}_1 = \left(\frac{m_1 - m_2}{m_1 + m_2}\right)\vec{u}_1 + \left(\frac{2m_2}{m_1 + m_2}\right)\vec{u}_2$$

$$\boxed{\vec{v}_1 = 2\vec{u}_2 - \vec{u}_1}$$

$$\vec{v}_2 = \left(\frac{m_2 - m_1}{m_1 + m_2}\right)\vec{u}_2 + \left(\frac{2m_1}{m_1 + m_2}\right)\vec{u}_1$$

$$\boxed{\vec{v}_2 = \vec{u}_2}$$

Scan for Video Explanation

Web Reference at www.physicsgalaxy.com

Module-19: Head-on Collisions

Ex : A horizontal platform is going up at a speed of 10 m/s and a small elastic ball falls on it at a speed of 5 m/s. Find the height to which ball will bounce after collision above the point of collision.

Sol^n:

$u_2 = -5$ m/s, $v_f = 0$, $u_1 = 10$ m/s, $g = 10$ m/s^2

$$\vec{v_2} = 2\vec{u_1} - \vec{u_2}$$
$$= 2\times10 - (-5)$$
$$= 25 \text{ m/s}$$

$$h = \frac{v_2^2}{2g} = \frac{(25)^2}{2\times10} = \frac{625}{20} = 31.25 \text{ m. Ans.}$$

Web Reference at www.physicsgalaxy.com | Scan for Video Explanation

Module-20: Solved Example-12

Ex : A neutron moving at a speed v undergoes a head-on elastic collision with a neucleus of mass number A at rest. Find the ratio of kinetic energies of neutron after and before collision.

Sol^n:

K_i: neutron (m) $u_1 = v$; Nucleus (mA) (rest) $u_2 = 0$; K_f: v_1, v_2

After head-on elastic collision speed of neutron is -

$$v_1 = \left(\frac{m_1 - m_2}{m_1 + m_2}\right)u_1 + \left(\frac{2m_2}{m_1 + m_2}\right)u_2$$

$$v_1 = \left(\frac{m - mA}{m + mA}\right)v = \left(\frac{1-A}{1+A}\right)v$$

$$r = \frac{K_f}{K_i} = \frac{\frac{1}{2}mv_1^2}{\frac{1}{2}mv^2} = \left(\frac{1-A}{1+A}\right)^2 \text{ Ans.}$$

Web Reference at www.physicsgalaxy.com | Scan for Video Explanation

Module-21: Partial Elastic Head-on Collision

Partially elastic Head-on Collision: $(0<e<1)$

u_1, u_2, v_1, v_2

$v_{app} = u_1 - u_2$ $\qquad$ $v_{sep} = v_2 - v_1$

by Cons. of momentum $\quad m_1u_1 + m_2u_2 = m_1v_1 + m_2v_2 \quad$ —(1)

using COR — $\quad v_2 - v_1 = e(u_1 - u_2) \quad$ —(2)

from eq^n (1) $\quad m_1u_1 + m_2u_2 = m_1v_1 + m_2(v_1 + eu_1 - eu_2)$

on Simplifying

$$\vec{v}_1 = \left(\frac{m_1 - em_2}{m_1 + m_2}\right)\vec{u}_1 + \left(\frac{m_2(1+e)}{m_1+m_2}\right)\vec{u}_2 \quad \text{(A)}$$

$$\vec{v}_2 = \left(\frac{m_2 - em_1}{m_1 + m_2}\right)\vec{u}_2 + \left[\frac{m_1(1+e)}{m_1+m_2}\right]\vec{u}_1 \quad \text{(B)}$$

$e = 1$ ✓ &

Scan for Video Explanation

Web Reference at www.physicsgalaxy.com

Module-21: Partial Elastic Head-on Collision

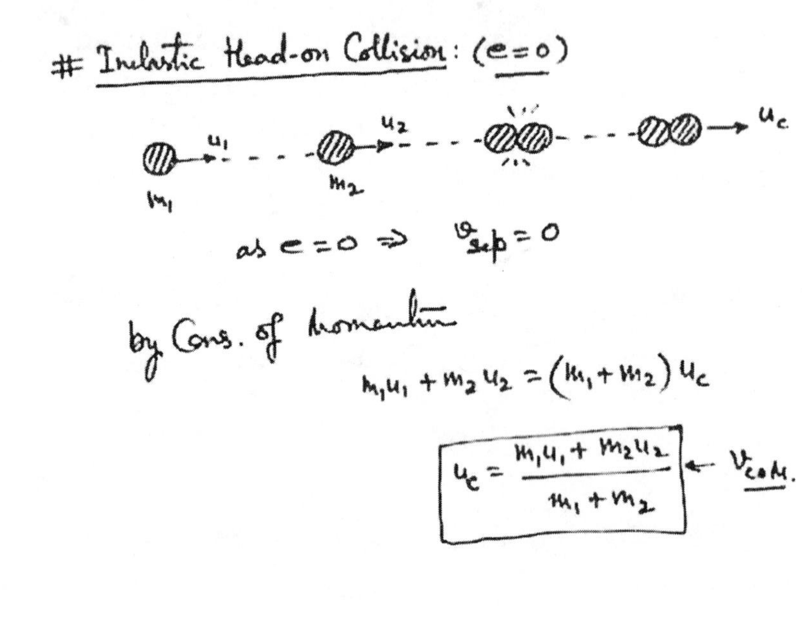

Scan for Video Explanation

Web Reference at www.physicsgalaxy.com

Module-21: Partial Elastic Head-on Collision

Ex : A 3 kg ball moving at 10 m/s collides head-on inelastically with another ball of mass 2 kg moving toward the first ball at 20 m/s. After collision balls will stick to each other, find the amount of total energy loss in this collision.

Sol^n:

3kg 10 m/s 20 m/s 2kg → x

$\vec{p}_1 = 30\hat{i}$

$\vec{p}_2 = -40\hat{i}$

$-10\hat{i}$

5kg, $v = 2$ m/s

$v = \frac{10}{5} = 2$ m/s

$$KE_i = \frac{1}{2}(3)(10)^2 + \frac{1}{2}(2)(20)^2 = 150 + 400 = 550\text{J}$$

$$KE_f = \frac{1}{2}(5)(2)^2 = 10\text{J}$$

loss in energy $\Delta E_L = KE_i - KE_f$

$= 550 - 10 = 540\text{J}$ Ans.

Web Reference at www.physicsgalaxy.com | Scan for Video Explanation

Module-22: Solved Example-13

Ex : A ball is dropped on a floor from a height h. If coefficient of restitution is e, find the height to which ball will rise after rebound.

Sol^n:

using the speed eq^n

$$v^2 = u^2 + 2as$$

$$0 = (e\sqrt{2gh})^2 - 2gh_1$$

$$h_1 = e^2 h. \text{ Ans.}$$

$v_f = 0$, h, h_1, $-g$, u, $v = eu$, e

$u = \sqrt{2gh}$ $\quad e = \frac{v}{u}$

$v = eu$

Web Reference at www.physicsgalaxy.com | Scan for Video Explanation

Module-23: Solved Example-14

Ex : A ball is released from a height h above a floor with coefficient of restitution e between floor & ball. Find the number of bounces ball will take before coming to rest. Also find the total time after which ball will come to rest.

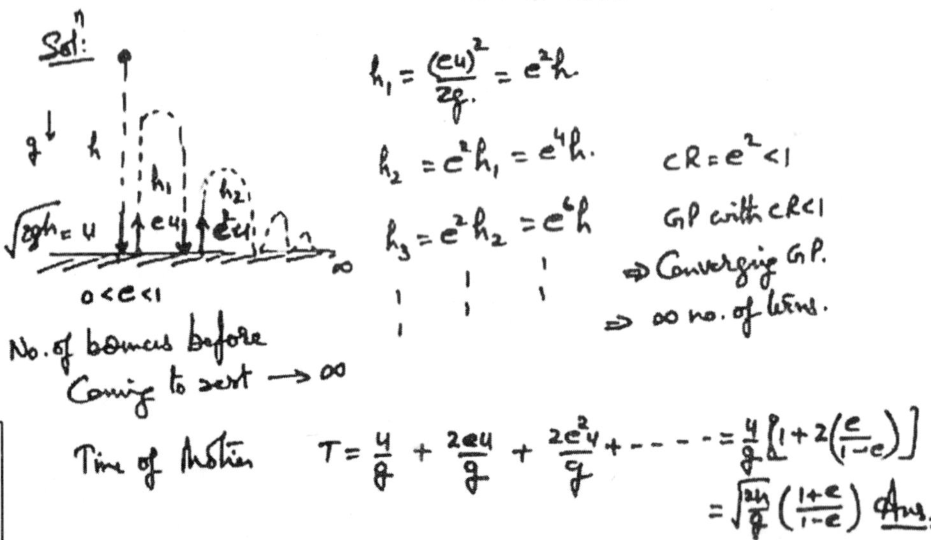

Scan for Video Explanation

Web Reference at www.physicsgalaxy.com

Module-24: Solved Example-15

Ex : Figure shows a U-shaped block of mass M placed on smooth ground in which an ideal spring of force constant k is attached as shown. If a ball of mass m moving at speed u strikes the spring, find the maximum fraction of kinetic energy which will be stored in spring in the process of collision.

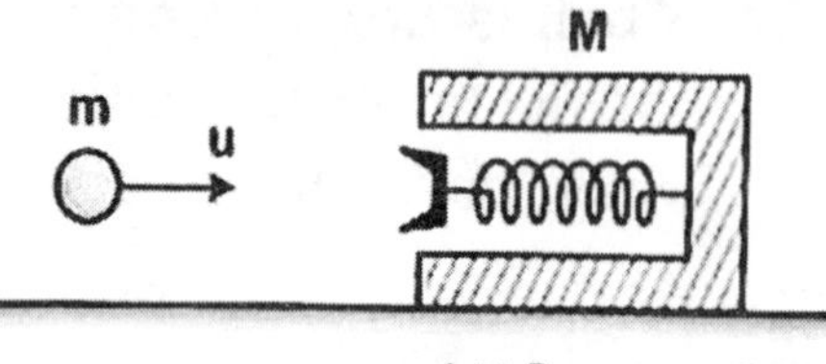

$(KE_{min}) \to v_f$

Soln: by Cons. of momentum $mu = (m+M)v_f \Rightarrow v_f = \frac{mu}{m+M}$

$$f = \frac{\Delta K_L}{K_i} = \frac{\frac{1}{2}mu^2 - \frac{1}{2}(m+M)v_f^2}{\frac{1}{2}mu^2} = 1 - \frac{m+M}{m}\cdot\frac{v_f^2}{u^2} = 1 - \frac{m}{m+M}$$

$$f = \frac{M}{m+M} \quad \text{Ans.}$$

Scan for Video Explanation

Web Reference at www.physicsgalaxy.com

Module-25: Solved Example-16

Ex : A ball of mass m moving at speed v makes a head-on collision with an identical ball at rest. The kinetic energy of the balls after the collision is three fourth of original. Find the coefficient of restitution.

Soln:

$m_1 = m_2 = m$.

m_1 with $u_1 = v$ → m_2 at rest, $u_2 = 0$; after collision: 1 → v_1, 2 → v_2

$$v_1 = \left(\frac{m_1 - em_2}{m_1 + m_2}\right)u_1 + \frac{m_2(1+e)}{m_1+m_2}.u_2 = \left(\frac{1-e}{2}\right)v$$

$$v_2 = \left(\frac{m_2 - em_1}{m_1 + m_2}\right)u_2 + \frac{m_1(1+e)}{m_1+m_2}u_1 = \left(\frac{1+e}{2}\right)v$$

$$K_f = \frac{3}{4}\left(\frac{1}{2}mv^2\right)$$

$$\frac{1}{2}m\left(\frac{1-e}{2}\right)^2v^2 + \frac{1}{2}m\left(\frac{1+e}{2}\right)^2v^2 = \frac{3}{4}\left(\frac{1}{2}mv^2\right) \Rightarrow 2+2e^2 = 3$$

$$e = \frac{1}{\sqrt{2}} \text{ Ans.}$$

Web Reference at www.physicsgalaxy.com | Scan for Video Explanation

Module-26: Solved Example-17

Ex : A steel ball of mass m falls from a height on a horizontal surface. Find the cumulative momentum that the ball inparts to surface after numerous bounces, if coefficient of restitution is e.

Soln: Total momentum imparted to surface can be given as-

(h; u, eu, eu, e^2u; $e<1$; $u = \sqrt{2gh}$)

first hit $\Delta P_1 = mu + m(eu)$

Second hit $\Delta P_2 = m(eu) + m(e^2u)$

$$\Delta P_T = mu + 2emu + 2e^2mu + \cdots$$

$$= mu[1 + 2e + 2e^2 + \cdots] \quad \text{[Conv. G.P.]}$$

$$= mu\left[1 + \frac{2e}{1-e}\right] = mu\left(\frac{1+e}{1-e}\right) = m\sqrt{2gh}\left(\frac{1+e}{1-e}\right)$$

Ans.

Web Reference at www.physicsgalaxy.com | Scan for Video Explanation

Module-27: Oblique Collision of a Ball on a Flat Surface

Oblique Collision of a ball on a flat surface:

Case-I : Elastic Collision

$e = 1$

$v_{app} = v_{sep}$

$u\cos\theta = v\cos\phi \quad -(1)$

$u\sin\theta = v\sin\phi \quad -(2)$

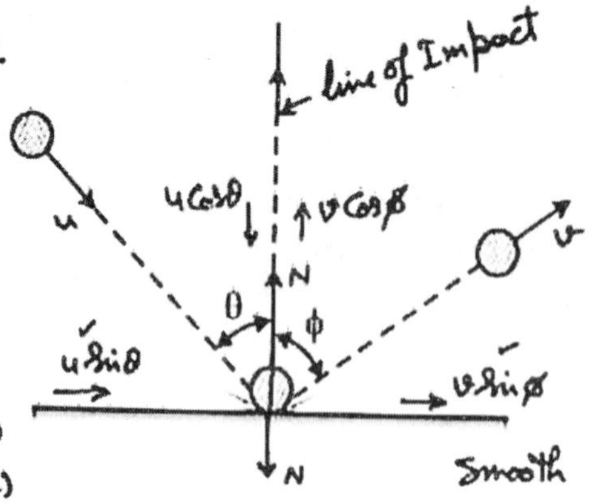

from (1) & (2) $\quad v = u \;\&\; \phi = \theta$

Angle of Reflection = Angle of Incidence.

Scan for Video Explanation

Web Reference at www.physicsgalaxy.com

Module-27: Oblique Collision of a Ball on a Flat Surface

Case-II: Partial Elastic Collision

$(0 < e < 1)$

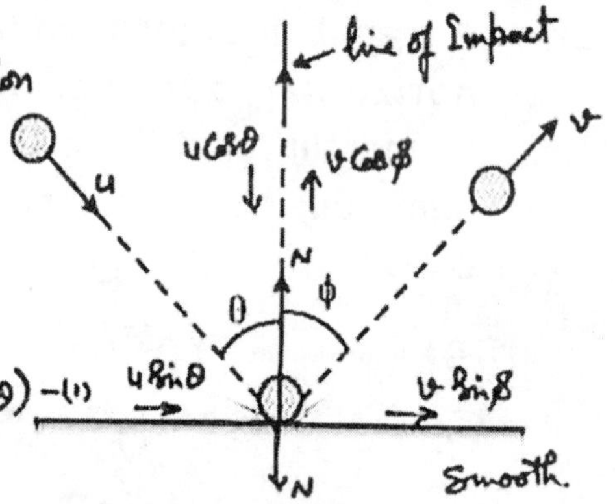

Along line of impact

$v_{sep} = e\, v_{app}$

$v\cos\phi = e(u\cos\theta) \quad -(1)$

Along the surface

$v\sin\phi = u\sin\theta \quad -(2)$

$\sqrt{(1)^2+(2)^2}$ $\quad \boxed{v = u\sqrt{\sin^2\theta + e^2\cos^2\theta}}$ $\quad$ for $e = 1$ $\Rightarrow \left[\begin{matrix} v = u \\ \phi = \theta \end{matrix}\right]$

$\frac{(2)}{(1)} \Rightarrow \boxed{\tan\phi = \frac{1}{e}\tan\theta}$

Scan for Video Explanation

Web Reference at www.physicsgalaxy.com

Module-27: Oblique Collision of a Ball on a Flat Surface

Case-III: Inelastic Collision
$(e=0)$

$\Rightarrow$ No separation

$v_{sep} = 0.$

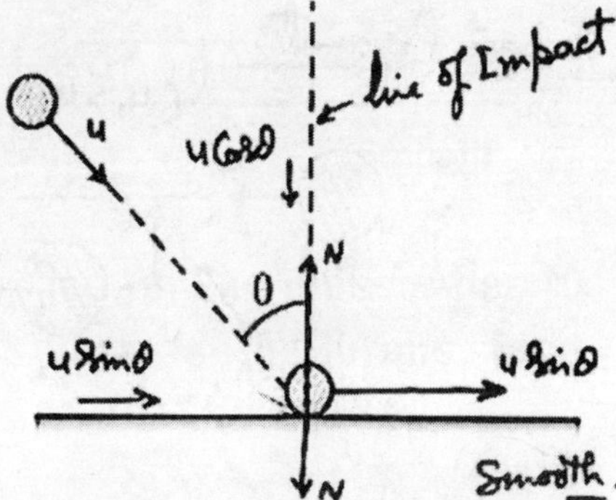

Web Reference at www.physicsgalaxy.com

Scan for Video Explanation

Module-28: Oblique Collision in a 2D Plane

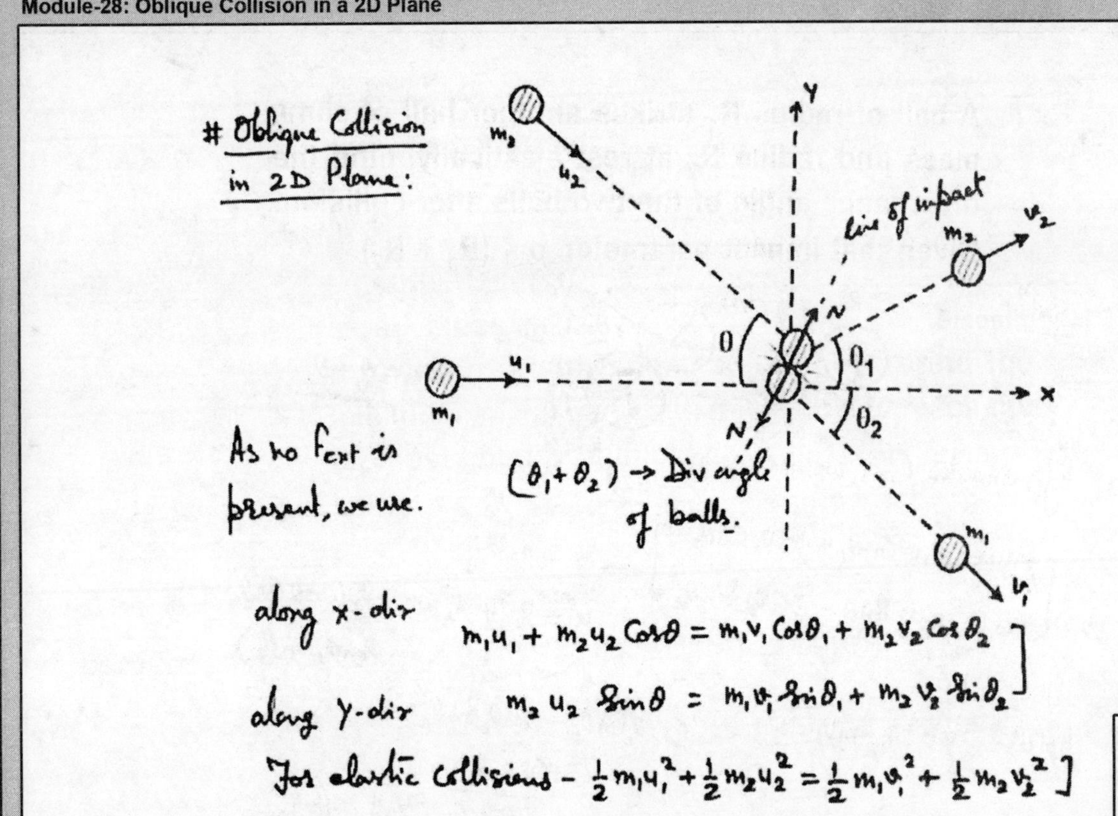

As no F_{ext} is present, we use.

$(\theta_1 + \theta_2) \rightarrow$ Div angle of balls.

along x-dir $\quad m_1u_1 + m_2u_2\cos\theta = m_1v_1\cos\theta_1 + m_2v_2\cos\theta_2$

along y-dir $\quad m_2u_2\sin\theta = m_1v_1\sin\theta_1 + m_2v_2\sin\theta_2$

For elastic collisions $- \frac{1}{2}m_1u_1^2 + \frac{1}{2}m_2u_2^2 = \frac{1}{2}m_1v_1^2 + \frac{1}{2}m_2v_2^2$

Web Reference at www.physicsgalaxy.com

Scan for Video Explanation

Module-28: Oblique Collision in a 2D Plane

Impact Parameter:

$(u_1 > u_2)$

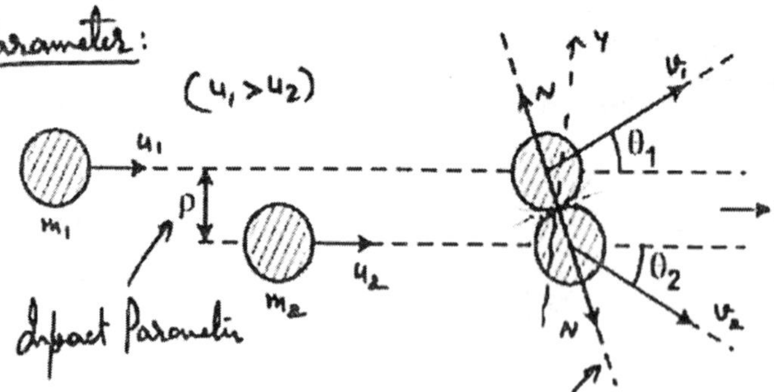

Labels in figure: m_1, u_1, ρ, m_2, u_2, Impact Parameter, N, Y, X, v_1, θ_1, θ_2, v_2, line of impact

$\theta_1 \rightarrow$ Scattering Angle of ball-1

$\theta_2 \rightarrow$ Scattering Angle of ball-2

$\theta_1 + \theta_2 \rightarrow$ Divergence Angle of two balls after collision

along x-dir $\quad m_1u_1 + m_2u_2 = m_1v_1\cos\theta_1 + m_2v_2\cos\theta_2$

along y-dir $\quad 0 = m_1v_1\sin\theta_1 - m_2v_2\sin\theta_2$

for elastic Collision $\quad \frac{1}{2}m_1u_1^2 + \frac{1}{2}m_2u_2^2 = \frac{1}{2}m_1v_1^2 + \frac{1}{2}m_2v_2^2$

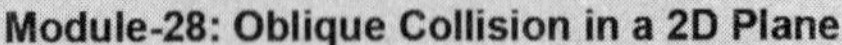

Scan for Video Explanation

Web Reference at www.physicsgalaxy.com

Module-28: Oblique Collision in a 2D Plane

Ex : A ball of radius R_1 strikes another ball of same mass and radius R_2 at rest elastically. Find the divergence angle of the two balls after collision. Given that impact parameter $\rho < (R_1 + R_2)$.

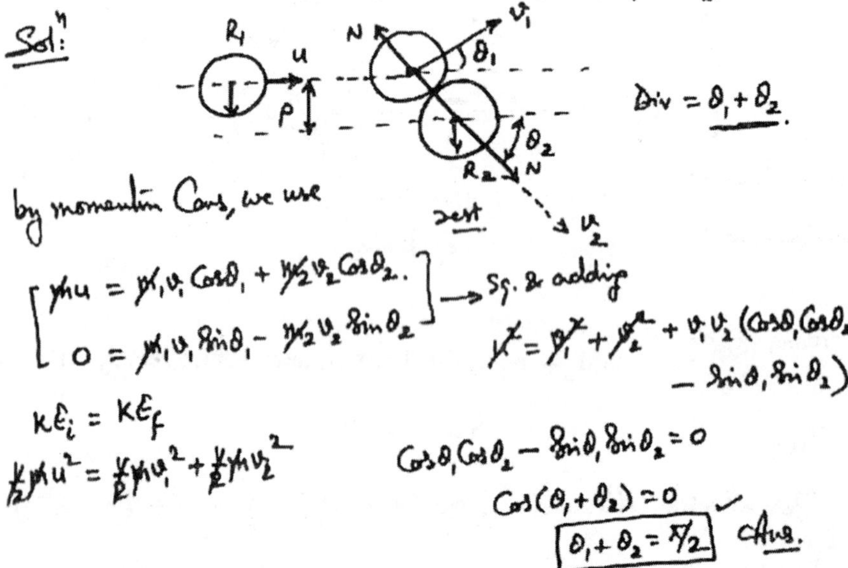

Scan for Video Explanation

Web Reference at www.physicsgalaxy.com

Module-29: Solved Example-18

Ex : A particle of mass m collides with a stationary particle of mass M is scattered at angle π/2 and M is recoiled at 30° to the initial direction of motion. Find the fraction of initial energy lost in collision if M = 5 m.

Sol^n: along x dir.

$$mu = Mv_2 \cos 30^\circ \quad (\cos 30^\circ = \sqrt{3}/2)$$

$$v_2 = \frac{2u}{5\sqrt{3}} \quad \text{—(1)}$$

along y-dir $\quad mv_1 = Mv_2 \sin 30^\circ \Rightarrow v_1 = \frac{5}{2}v_2$ —(2)

$$v_1 = \frac{5}{2}\left(\frac{2u}{5\sqrt{3}}\right) = \frac{u}{\sqrt{3}}$$

fraction of energy lost in collision

$$f = \frac{\frac{1}{2}mu^2 - \left(\frac{1}{2}mv_1^2 + \frac{1}{2}Mv_2^2\right)}{\frac{1}{2}mu^2} = \frac{u^2 - v_1^2 - 5v_2^2}{u^2} = 1 - \frac{1}{3} - \frac{4}{15}$$

$$= \frac{2}{5} \quad \text{Ans.}$$

Web Reference at www.physicsgalaxy.com

Scan for Video Explanation

Module-30: Solved Example-19

Ex : A ball with a speed 9 m/s strikes another identical ball at rest such that after collision the direction of each ball makes an angle 30° with the original line of motion. Find the speeds of the two balls after collision. Is kinetic energy conserved in this collision.

Sol^n:

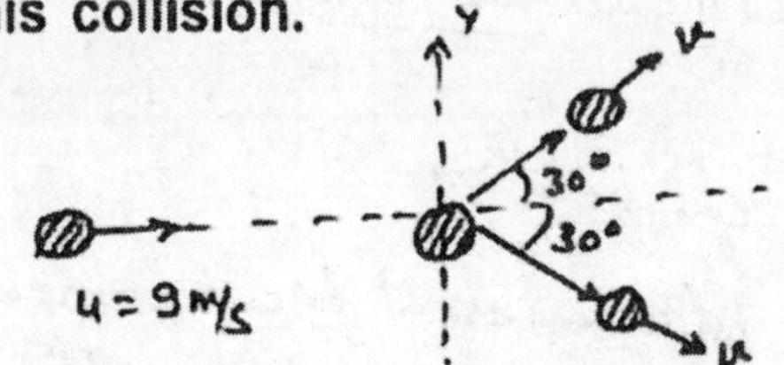

along x-dir $\quad mu = 2mv\cos 30^\circ \Rightarrow v = \frac{u}{\sqrt{3}} = 3\sqrt{3}$ m/s Ans.

Divergence angle $\neq \pi/2$ (it is 60°)

This collision is NOT elastic ⇒ KE will NOT be conserved. Ans.

Web Reference at www.physicsgalaxy.com

Scan for Video Explanation

Module-31: Solved Example-20

Ex : A ball of mass m, moving at speed u along x-axis, strikes another ball of mass 2m kept at rest. First ball comes to rest after collision and the other breaks into two equal parts. One of these starts moving along y-axis with a speed v, what will be the velocity of the other part.

Sol^n:

Along x-dir:

$mu = mv'\cos\theta$ — (1)

Along y dir

$mv = mv'\sin\theta$ — (2)

$\Rightarrow \sqrt{(1)^2+(2)^2}$

$v'^2 = u^2 + v^2$

$v' = \sqrt{u^2+v^2}$ Ans.

Scan for Video Explanation

Web Reference at www.physicsgalaxy.com

Module-32: Mass Variation Cases

Mass Variation Cases:

Whenever mass of a System (or bodies) changes with time during motion such cases can be handled by Concept of Impulse and Conservation of momentum.

Two cases can be there -

Case-I: When external force is absent.

Case-II: When external force is present

Scan for Video Explanation

Web Reference at www.physicsgalaxy.com

Module-32: Mass Variation Cases

Case-I: When F_{ext} is not present

Hint → In such cases we use Cons. of momentum at an intermediate time of motion from $\underline{t}$ to $\underline{t+dt}$

Ex of Rocket Propulsion:

$m \rightarrow v$, u ←, $\underline{r\ kg/sec}$, $t = t_1$

$u-(v+dv)$ ←, $dm = r\,dt$

$\rightarrow v+dv$, $(m-dm)$, $t = t+dt$

$u \leftarrow$ relative to rocket.

(t) (t+dt)

by Conservation of momentum → $mv = (m-dm)(v+dv) - dm(u-v-dv)$

Web Reference at www.physicsgalaxy.com | Scan for Video Explanation

Module-32: Mass Variation Cases

(t) (t+dt)

$$mv = (m-dm)(v+dv) - dm(u-v-dv)$$

$$\cancel{mv} = \cancel{mv} - \cancel{dm\,v} + m\,dv - dm\,u + \cancel{dm\,v}$$

$$m\frac{dv}{dt} = \frac{dm\,u}{dt}$$

$$\underline{ma = r.u}$$

$\rightarrow a$, ← $r\ kg/s$, $\rightarrow F_{th}$.

$$\boxed{F_{th} = r u.}$$

Web Reference at www.physicsgalaxy.com | Scan for Video Explanation

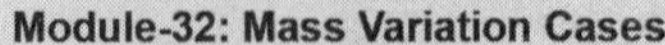

Module-32: Mass Variation Cases

Case-II: When F_{ext} is present

→ In such cases we use Impulse-momentum eq^n for the motion of body at $\underline{t}$ & $\underline{t+dt}$.

Ex: Find vel of tank as the function in the given situation.

M, $m = M - rt$, v, $v + dv$, $m - dm$, dm, F, r kg/sec, u (rel to tank), $t = 0$, $t = t$, $u - v - dv$, $t + dt$

Here we write impulse-momentum eq^n for tank -

$$mv + Fdt = (m - dm)(v + dv) - dm(u - v - dv)$$

$$mv + Fdt = mv - dmv + mdv - dmu + dmv$$

$$Fdt = mdv - dmu$$

Scan for Video Explanation

Web Reference at www.physicsgalaxy.com

Module-32: Mass Variation Cases

$$Fdt = mdv - dmu$$

$$m = M - rt$$

$$dm = rdt$$

$$Fdt = (M - rt)dv - rudt$$

$$(F + ru)dt = (M - rt)dv$$

$$\int_0^v dv = \int_0^t (F + ru)\frac{dt}{(M - rt)}$$

$$v = (F + ru)\left[-\frac{1}{r}\ln(M - rt)\right]_0^t$$

$$v = \frac{(F + ru)}{r}\ln\left(\frac{M}{M - rt}\right) \quad \text{Ans.}$$

Scan for Video Explanation

Web Reference at www.physicsgalaxy.com

Module-32: Mass Variation Cases

Alternative method

M

F

r kg/sec

u (rel to tank)

→ v

→ F + ru

tank

$$F + ru = m\frac{dv}{dt} \Rightarrow \int_0^v dv = \int_0^t \frac{dt}{(M - rt)}(F + ru)$$

$m = M - rt$

$v = - - - -$ ✓

Web Reference at www.physicsgalaxy.com

Scan for Video Explanation

Module-33: Super Elastic Collision

Super elastic Collisions :

Collisions in which $e > 1$ are termed as Super elastic.

When $e = 1$ → no dissipation of energy

$e < 1$ → energy loss

$e = 0$ → max. energy loss.

$e > 1$ ⇒ gain of energy.

KE_f after collision > KE_i before collision

⇒ $e > 1$ happens only when in a collision some energy is released. like the cases of explosion.

$v_{sep} > v_{app}$.

Web Reference at www.physicsgalaxy.com

Scan for Video Explanation

Chapter 11
Rigid Body Dynamics

Lecture Notes Modules

Module-1: Rotational Motion

Rotational Motion:

It is the motion of a rigid body about an AOR such that different particles of body move in different circular paths with all the centres lie on the AOR.

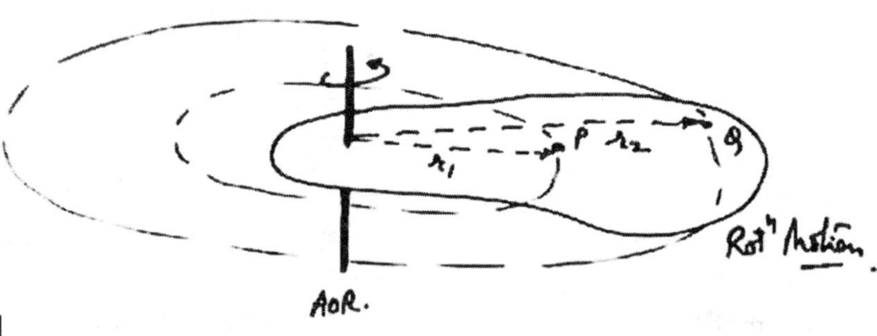

Scan for Video Explanation

Web Reference at www.physicsgalaxy.com

Module-1: Rotational Motion

Various Sections of Rigid Body Dynamics:

→ Moment of Inertia

→ Newton's II law for Rot^n Motion

→ Angular momentum & its Conservation

→ Kinetic Energy in Rot^n Motion

→ Work & Power in Rot^n Motion

→ Rolling Motion & its applications

—x—.

Scan for Video Explanation

Web Reference at www.physicsgalaxy.com

Module-2: Moment of Inertia

Moment of Inertia:

It is the same property analogous to inertia in rot^n motion

Inertia → mass. m.

$F = ma$
$a = \frac{F}{m}$ } for a given force $a \propto \frac{1}{m}$.

Similarly.

Moment of Inertia → mass & mass distribution w.r.to AOR.

$\tau = I\alpha$.

$\alpha = \frac{\tau}{I}$

$\alpha \propto \frac{1}{I}$ → change in state of rot^l motion.

Web Reference at www.physicsgalaxy.com | Scan for Video Explanation

Module-2: Moment of Inertia

Moment of Inertia of a point mass in Circular Motion:

MI of this particle is given as-

$$I = mr^2$$

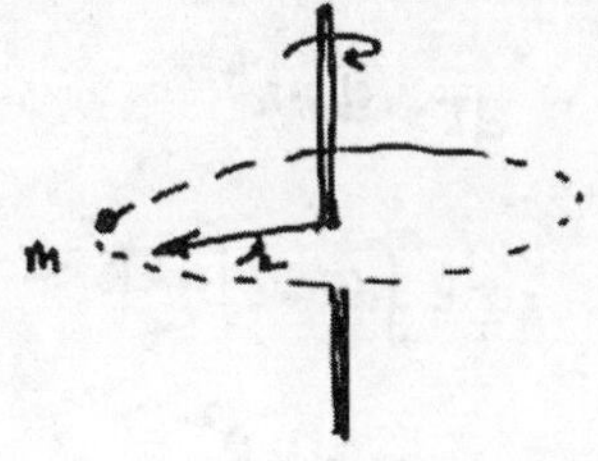

Web Reference at www.physicsgalaxy.com | Scan for Video Explanation

Module-2: Moment of Inertia

MI of an extended body in Rotational Motion:

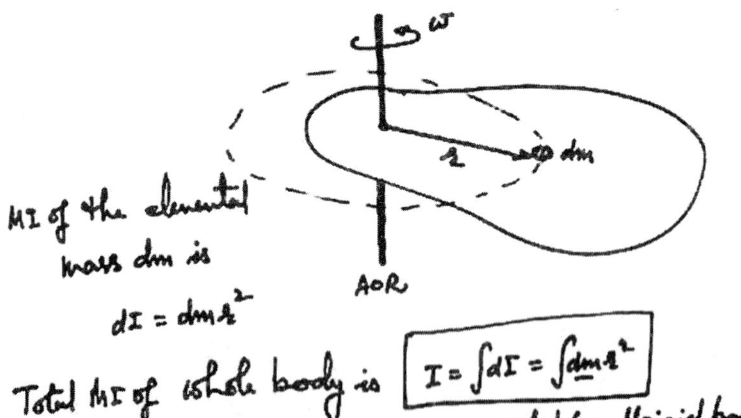

MI of the elemental mass dm is

$dI = dm\, r^2$

Total MI of whole body is $\boxed{I = \int dI = \int dm\, r^2}$ valid for all rigid bodies

NOTE: MI depends on location of AOR for a rotating body.

Scan for Video Explanation

Web Reference at www.physicsgalaxy.com

Module-3: Moment of Inertia of a Ring

Moment of Inertia of a Ring:

MI of elemental mass is

$dI = dm\, r^2$

$I = \int dI = \int dm\, R^2$

$I = MR^2$

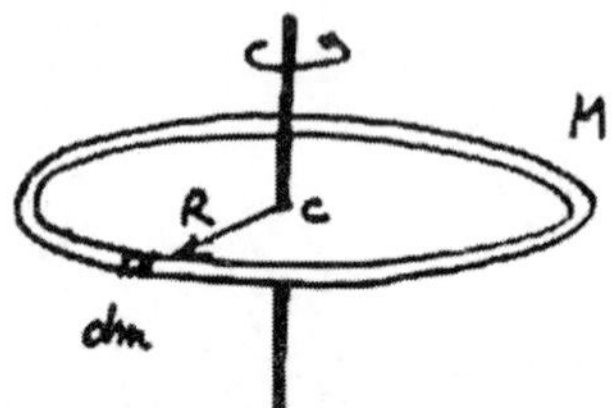

Scan for Video Explanation

Web Reference at www.physicsgalaxy.com

Module-4: Moment of Inertia of a Disc

Moment of Inertia of a Disc:

mass of elemental ring is

$$dm = \frac{M}{\pi R^2} \times 2\pi x\, dx$$

$$dm = \frac{M}{R^2} \cdot 2x\, dx$$

MI of the elemental ring $dI = dm\, x^2$

$$dI = \frac{2M}{R^2} \cdot x^3 dx$$

MI of whole disc $I = \int dI = \int_0^R \frac{2M}{R^2} \cdot x^3 dx$

$$= \frac{2M}{R^2}\left[\frac{x^4}{4}\right]_0^R = \frac{2M}{R^2}\left(\frac{R^4}{4} - 0\right)$$

$$I = \frac{1}{2} MR^2$$

Figure labels: R, dx, x, c, M, dm, AOR

Web Reference at www.physicsgalaxy.com | Scan for Video Explanation

Module-5: Moment of Inertia of a Hollow Sphere

Moment of Inertia of a Hollow Sphere:

mass of element $dm = \frac{M}{4\pi R^2} \times 2\pi R\cos\theta \cdot R\, d\theta$

$$dm = \frac{1}{2} M \cos\theta\, d\theta$$

MI of the element is $dI = dm (R\cos\theta)^2$

$$dI = \left(\frac{1}{2} M \cos\theta\, d\theta\right) \cdot R^2 \cos^2\theta$$

$$dI = \frac{1}{2} MR^2 \cos^3\theta\, d\theta$$

MI of Hollow sphere is $I = \int dI = \int_{-\pi/2}^{+\pi/2} \frac{1}{2} MR^2 \cos^3\theta\, d\theta$

$$I = \frac{1}{2} mR^2 \int_{-\pi/2}^{+\pi/2} \cos^3\theta\, d\theta = \frac{2}{3} MR^2$$

$t = \sin\theta$

Figure labels: $R\,d\theta$, R, $d\theta$, θ, c, $R\cos\theta$, M, AOR

Web Reference at www.physicsgalaxy.com | Scan for Video Explanation

Module-6: Moment of Inertia of a Solid Sphere

Moment of Inertia of a Solid Sphere:

mass of element $dm = \frac{M}{\frac{4}{3}\pi R^3} \times 4\pi x^2 dx$

$$dm = \frac{3M}{R^3} \cdot x^2 dx$$

MI of the element is $dI = \frac{2}{3} dm\, x^2$

$$dI = \frac{2}{3}\left(\frac{3M}{R^3} \cdot x^2 dx\right) x^2$$

$$dI = \frac{2M}{R^3} \cdot x^4 dx$$

MI of Solid Sphere $I = \int dI = \frac{2M}{R^3} \int_0^R x^4 dx$

$$= \frac{2M}{R^3} \cdot \frac{R^5}{5} = \frac{2}{5} MR^2$$

R, dx, x, M, AoR

Scan for Video Explanation

Web Reference at www.physicsgalaxy.com

Module-7: Moment of Inertia of a Hollow Cone

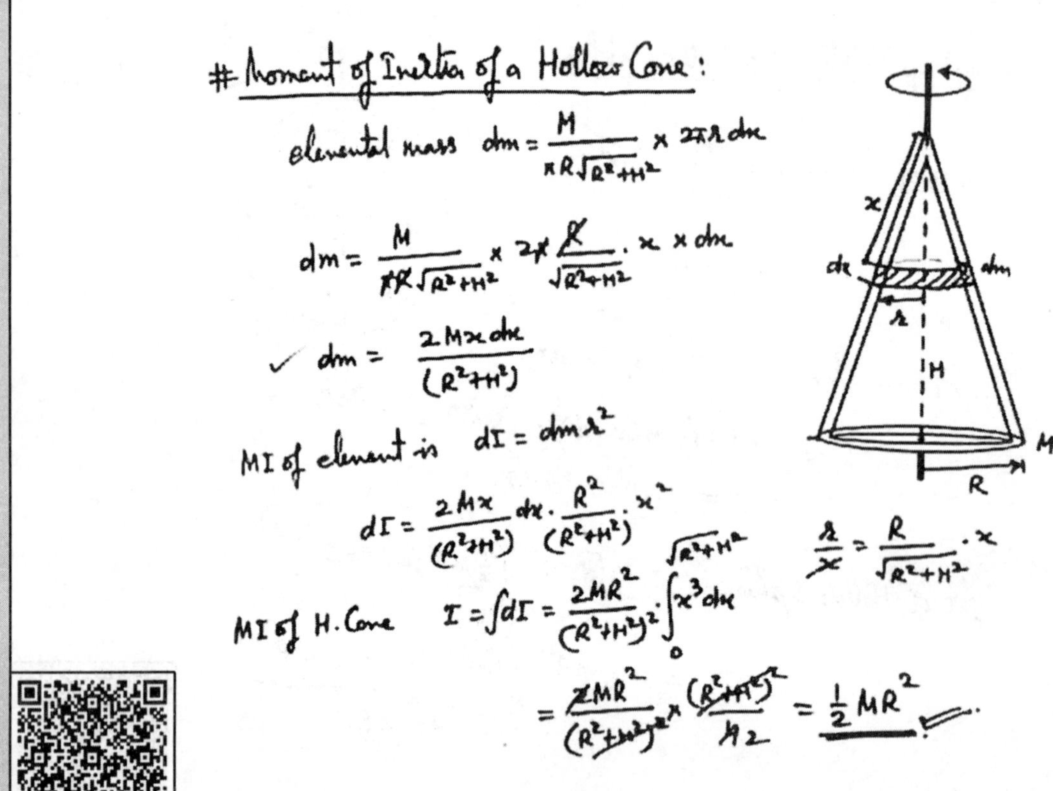

Scan for Video Explanation

Web Reference at www.physicsgalaxy.com

Module-8: Moment of Inertia of a Solid Cone

Moment of Inertia of a Solid Cone:

mass of elemental disc

$$dm = \frac{M}{\frac{1}{3}\pi R^2 H} \times \pi r^2 dx$$

$$dm = \frac{3M}{\pi R^2 H} \times \pi \left(\frac{R^2}{H^2} \cdot x^2\right) dx$$

$$dm = \frac{3M}{H^3} \cdot x^2 dx$$

$$\frac{r}{x} = \frac{R}{H}x$$

MI of the elemental disc $dI = \frac{1}{2} dm r^2$

$$dI = \frac{1}{2}\left(\frac{3M}{H^3} \cdot x^2 dx\right) \times \frac{R^2}{H^2} \cdot x^2 .$$

$$I = \int dI = \frac{3}{2}\frac{M}{H^5} \cdot R^2 \int_0^H x^4 dx = \frac{3}{2}\frac{M}{H^5} \cdot R^2 \left[\frac{x^5}{5}\right]_0^H$$

$$= \frac{3}{2}\frac{MR^2}{H^5} \times \frac{H^5}{5} = \frac{3}{10}MR^2$$

Web Reference at www.physicsgalaxy.com

Scan for Video Explanation

Module-9: Moment of Inertia of a Thin Rod

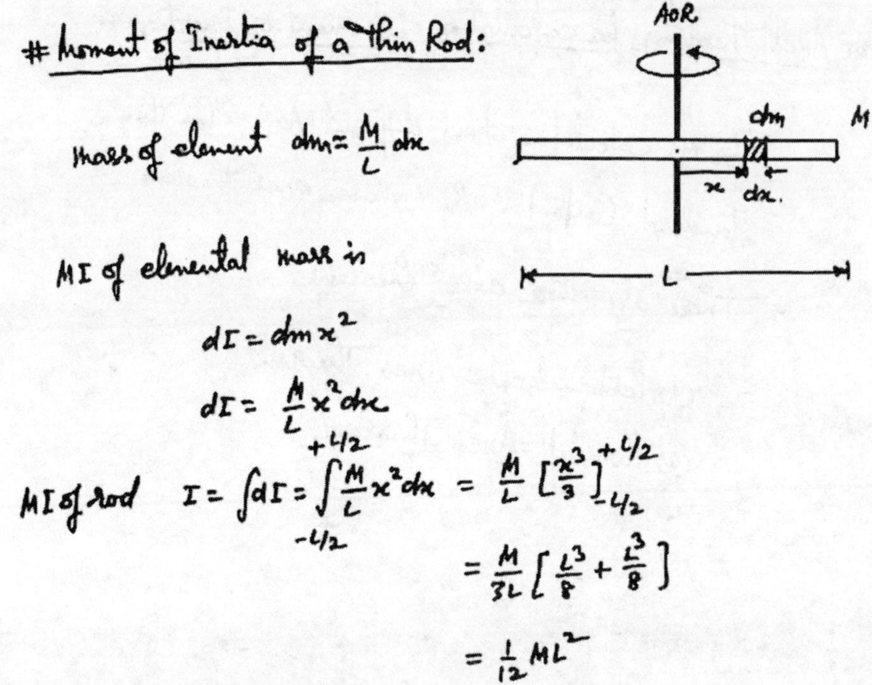

Moment of Inertia of a Thin Rod:

mass of element $dm = \frac{M}{L} dx$

MI of elemental mass is

$$dI = dm\, x^2$$

$$dI = \frac{M}{L} x^2 dx$$

MI of rod $I = \int dI = \int_{-L/2}^{+L/2} \frac{M}{L} x^2 dx = \frac{M}{L}\left[\frac{x^3}{3}\right]_{-L/2}^{+L/2}$

$$= \frac{M}{3L}\left[\frac{L^3}{8} + \frac{L^3}{8}\right]$$

$$= \frac{1}{12}ML^2$$

Web Reference at www.physicsgalaxy.com

Scan for Video Explanation

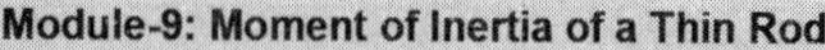

Module-9: Moment of Inertia of a Thin Rod

elemental mass $dm = \frac{M}{L} dx$

M
x
dx
L
AoR

MI of element is

$$dI = dm\,x^2 = \frac{M}{L} x^2 dx$$

MI of rod about side AoR is

$$I = \int dI = \int_0^L \frac{M}{L} x^2 dx$$

$$I = \frac{M}{L}\left[\frac{x^3}{3}\right]_0^L$$

$$\boxed{I = \frac{1}{3} ML^2}$$

$$\boxed{I = \frac{1}{12} ML^2}$$

Scan for Video Explanation

Web Reference at www.physicsgalaxy.com

Module-10: Axes Theorem-Perpendicular Axes Theorem

Axes Theorems for calculation of Moment of Inertia:

For MI Calculation about different AoR, other than standard Central AoR, we use axes theorems.

There are two axes theorems -

(1) Perpendicular Axes Theorem

(2) Parallel Axes Theorem.

Scan for Video Explanation

Web Reference at www.physicsgalaxy.com

Module-10: Axes Theorem-Perpendicular Axes Theorem

Perpendicular Axes Theorem:

This Theorem is applicable only for laminar bodies (2D structure)

Acc. to perpendicular axes theorem

$$I_z = I_x + I_y$$

Web Reference at www.physicsgalaxy.com

Scan for Video Explanation

Module-10: Axes Theorem-Perpendicular Axes Theorem

Proof of Perpendicular Axes Theorem:

$I_z = \int dm\, r^2$

$I_x = \int dm\, x^2$

$I_y = \int dm\, y^2$

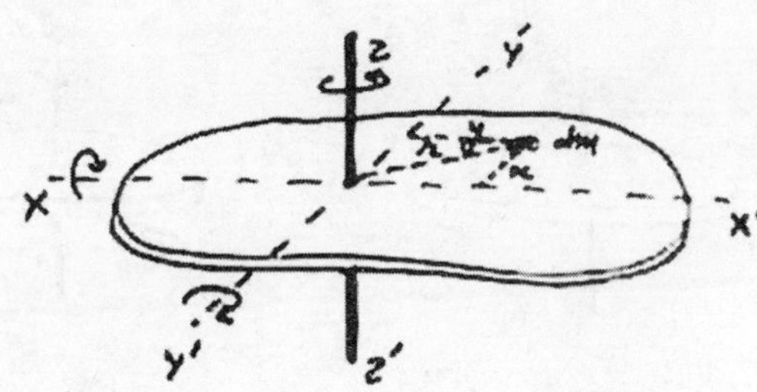

$$x^2 + y^2 = r^2$$

$$I_z = \int dm\, r^2 = \int dm (x^2 + y^2) = \int dm\, x^2 + \int dm\, y^2$$

$$I_z = I_x + I_y$$

Web Reference at www.physicsgalaxy.com

Scan for Video Explanation

Module-10: Axes Theorem-Perpendicular Axes Theorem

Applications of Perpendicular Axes Theorem:

Ring.

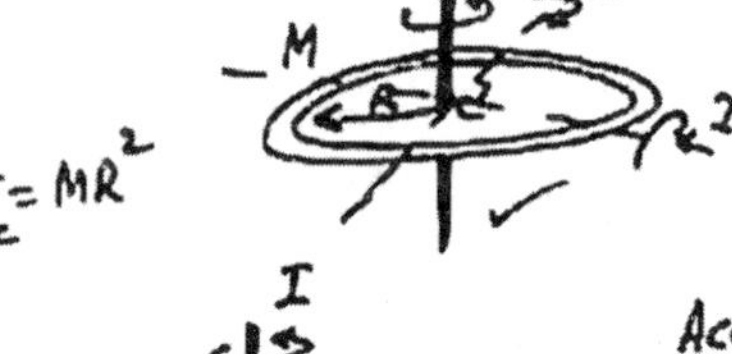

$I_c = MR^2$

Acc. to ⊥ axes theorem we use

$$I + I = MR^2$$

$$\boxed{I = \frac{1}{2}MR^2}$$

Scan for Video Explanation

Web Reference at www.physicsgalaxy.com

Module-10: Axes Theorem-Perpendicular Axes Theorem

Disc.

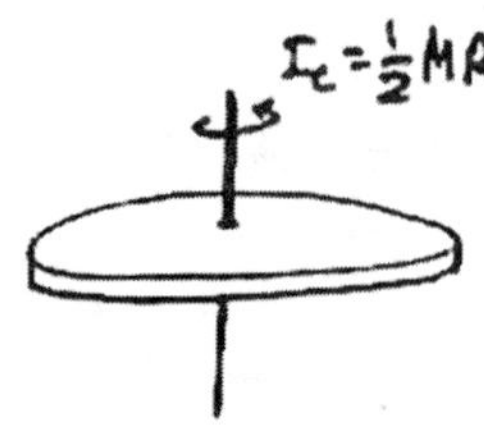

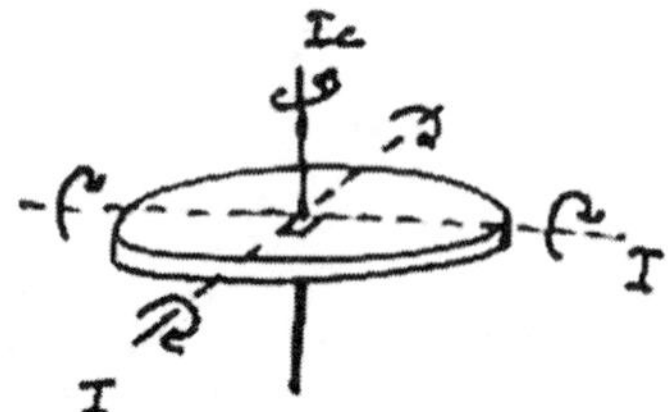

acc. to ⊥ axes theorem

$$I + I = \frac{1}{2}MR^2$$

$$\boxed{I = \frac{1}{4}MR^2}$$

Scan for Video Explanation

Web Reference at www.physicsgalaxy.com

Module-10: Axes Theorem-Perpendicular Axes Theorem

Thin rectangular plate:

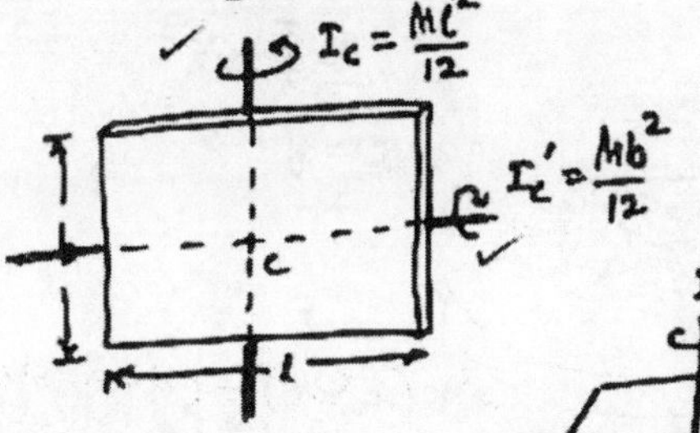

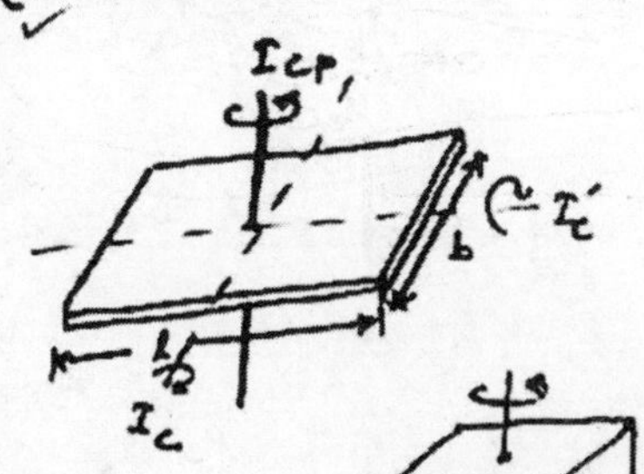

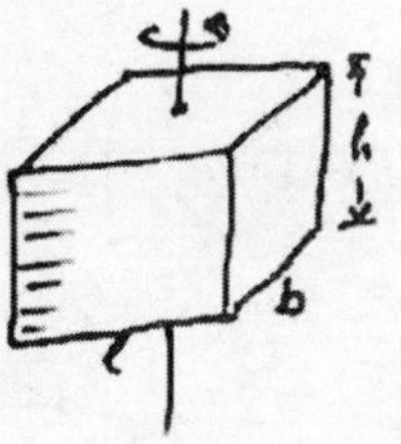

$I_c = \frac{Ml^2}{12}$

$I_c' = \frac{Mb^2}{12}$

I_{cp}, I_c', I_c, l, b, h

by ⊥ axes th.

$I_{cp} = I_c + I_c'$

$$I_{cp} = \frac{M}{12}(l^2 + b^2)$$

Module-11: Axes Theorem-Parallel Axes Theorem

Parallel Axes Theorem:

It is valid for all types of rigid bodies

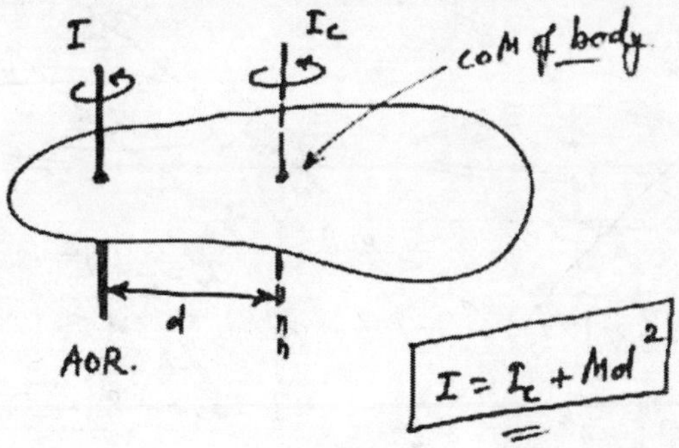

I, I_c, COM of body, d, AOR.

$$I = I_c + Md^2$$

Module-11: Axes Theorem-Parallel Axes Theorem

Proof of Parallel Axes Theorem:

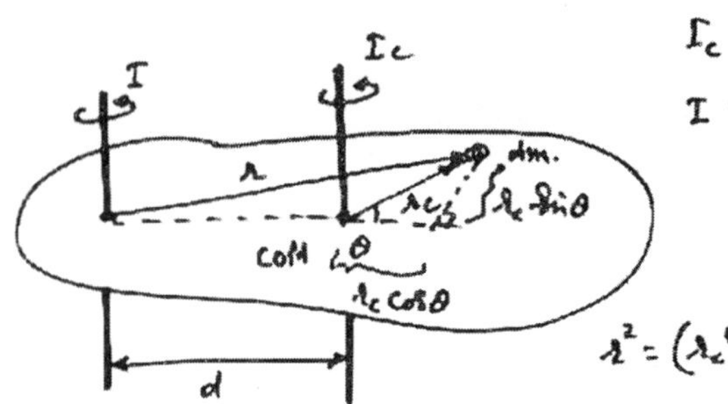

$I_c = \int dm\, r_c^2$

$I = \int dm\, r^2$

$r^2 = (r_c \sin\theta)^2 + (d + r_c \cos\theta)^2$

$r^2 = r_c^2 + d^2 + 2 d r_c \cos\theta$

$I = \int dm\, r^2 = \int dm\, r_c^2 + \int dm . d^2 + \int dm (2 d r_c \cos\theta)$

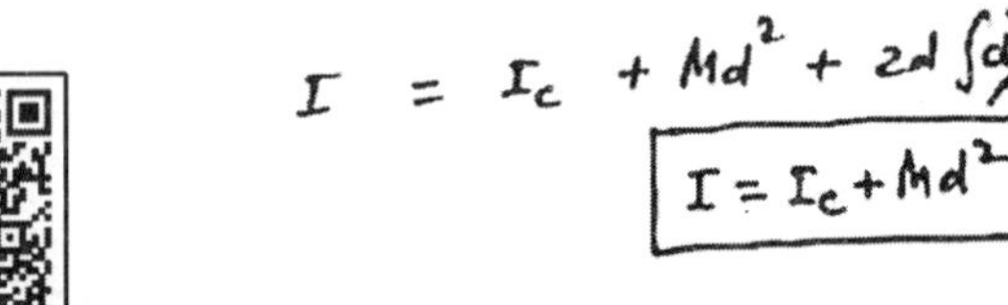

$I = I_c + Md^2 + 2d \int dm\, r_c \cos\theta$

$$\boxed{I = I_c + Md^2}$$

Scan for Video Explanation

Web Reference at www.physicsgalaxy.com

Module-11: Axes Theorem-Parallel Axes Theorem

Applications of Parallel Axes Theorem:

Ring.

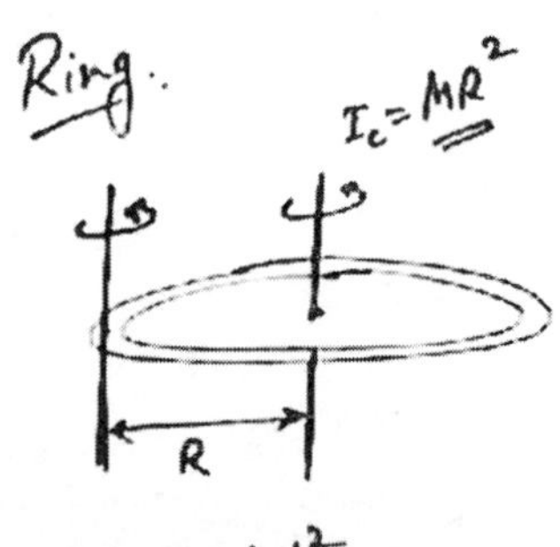

$I = I_c + Md^2$

$I = MR^2 + MR^2$

$$\boxed{I = 2MR^2}$$

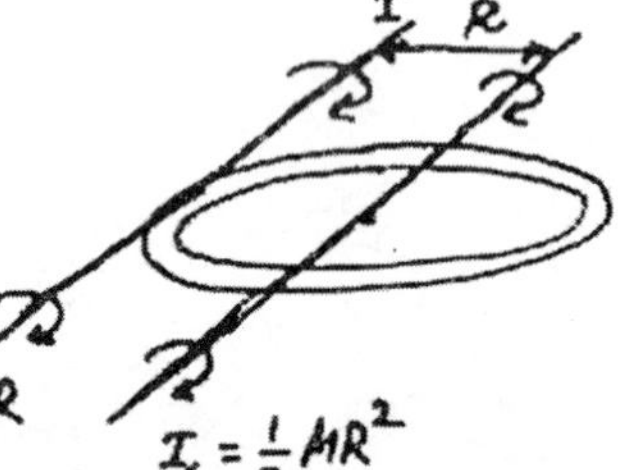

$I_c = \frac{1}{2} MR^2$

$I = I_c + Md^2$

$I = \frac{1}{2} MR^2 + MR^2$

$$\boxed{I = \frac{3}{2} MR^2}$$

Scan for Video Explanation

Web Reference at www.physicsgalaxy.com

Module-11: Axes Theorem-Parallel Axes Theorem

→ Disc.

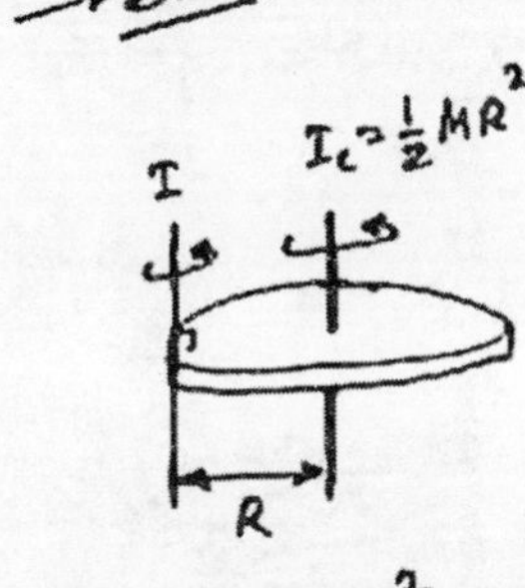

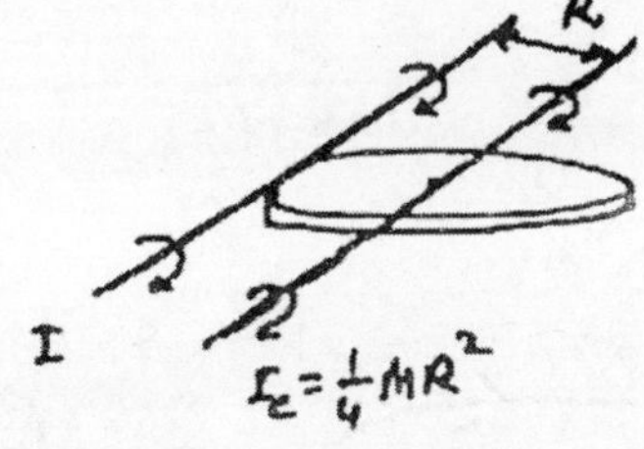

$I = I_c + Md^2$

$I = \frac{1}{2}MR^2 + MR^2$

$I = \frac{3}{2}MR^2$

$I = I_c + Md^2$

$I = \frac{1}{4}MR^2 + MR^2$

$I = \frac{5}{4}MR^2$

Web Reference at www.physicsgalaxy.com | Scan for Video Explanation

Module-11: Axes Theorem-Parallel Axes Theorem

→ MI of a hollow & Solid sphere abt tangential AOR.

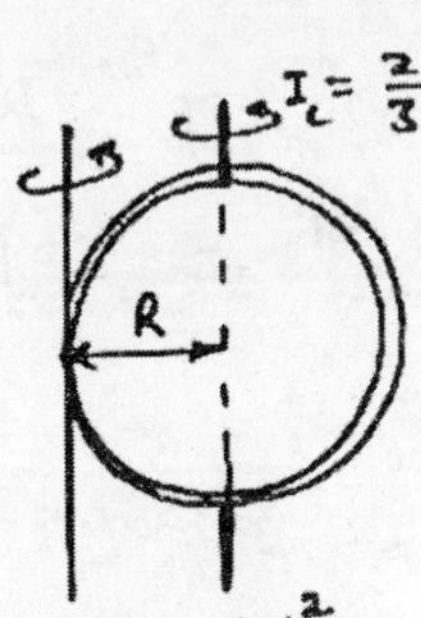

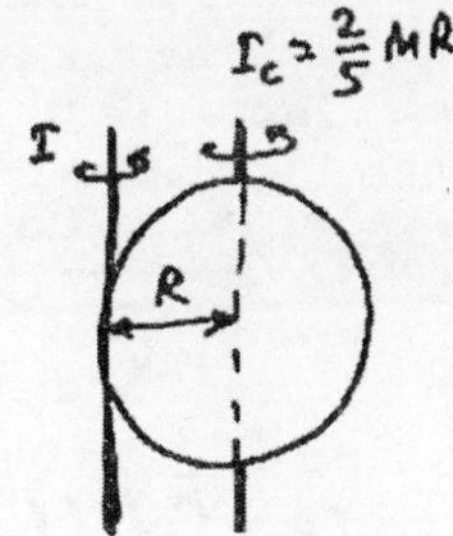

$I = I_c + Md^2$

$I = \frac{2}{3}MR^2 + MR^2$

$I = \frac{5}{3}MR^2$

$I = I_c + Md^2$

$I = \frac{2}{5}MR^2 + MR^2$

$I = \frac{7}{5}MR^2$

Web Reference at www.physicsgalaxy.com | Scan for Video Explanation

Module-12: Radius of Gyration

Radius of Gyration:

It is the eq. radius of cir. motion for a rigid body in rotation.

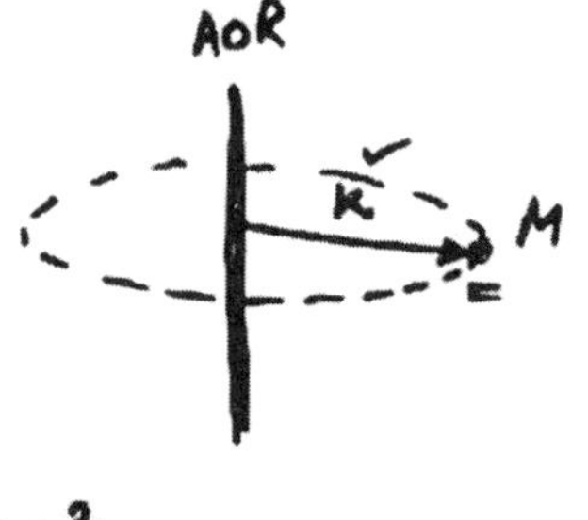

$I = Mk^2$

$$k = \sqrt{\frac{I}{M}}$$

Scan for Video Explanation

Web Reference at www.physicsgalaxy.com

Module-12: Radius of Gyration

for a Ring abt Central AOR $K = R$ $I = Mk^2$

abt Diametrical AOR $k = \frac{R}{\sqrt{2}}$

for a sphere abt Central AOR $I = \frac{2}{5}MR^2 = Mk^2$

$$k = \sqrt{\frac{2}{5}}R.$$

for a Solid Cone abt Central AOR $I = \frac{3}{10}MR^2 = Mk^2$

$$k = \sqrt{\frac{3}{10}}R.$$

Scan for Video Explanation

Web Reference at www.physicsgalaxy.com

Module-13: Solved Example-1

Ex : Find moment of inertia of a spherical ball of mass m, radius r with its centre attached at the end of a thin straight rod of mass M and length L about axis passing through the other end of rod is perpendicular to it.

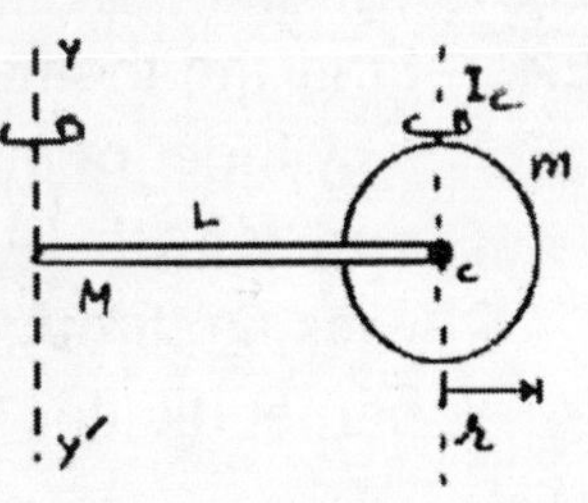

Sol:

$$I_{Rod} = \frac{ML^2}{3}$$

$$I_{sph_{YY'}} = I_c + mL^2 = \frac{2}{5}mr^2 + mL^2$$

$$I_{Tot_{YY'}} = I_{Rod} + I_{sph_{YY'}} = \frac{ML^2}{3} + \frac{2}{5}mr^2 + mL^2 \quad \text{Ans.}$$

Web Reference at www.physicsgalaxy.com | Scan for Video Explanation

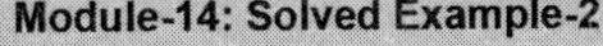

Module-14: Solved Example-2

Ex : Find moment of inertia of a half disc of radius R_2 from which a smaller half disc of radius R_1 is cut as shown in figure, about an axis of rotation passing through centre & perpendicular to plane of disc. Mass of this disc is M.

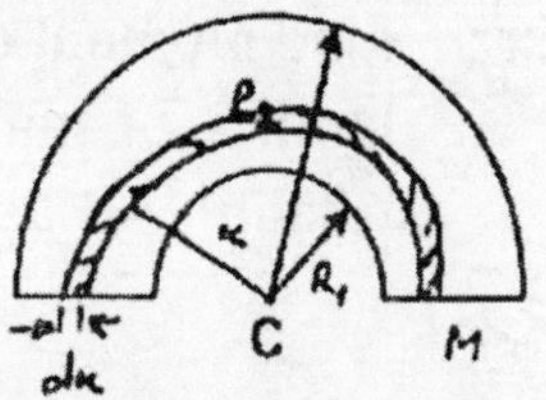

Sol:

mass of elemental half ring

$$dm = \frac{2M}{\pi(R_2^2 - R_1^2)} \times \pi x \times dx$$

MI of element $dI = dm\,x^2 = \frac{2M}{R_2^2 - R_1^2} \times x^3 dx$.

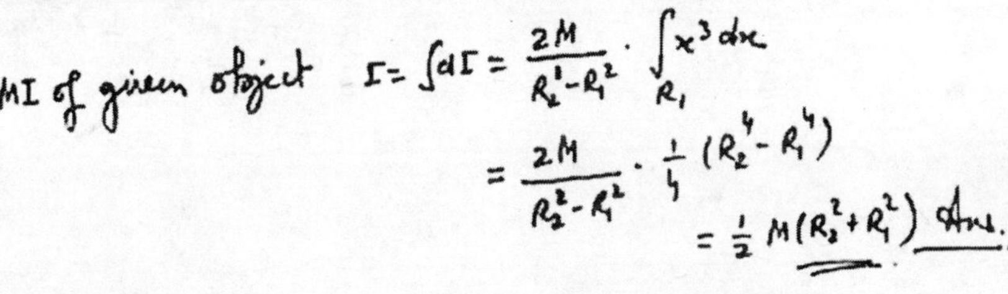

MI of given object $I = \int dI = \frac{2M}{R_2^2 - R_1^2} \cdot \int_{R_1}^{R_2} x^3 dx$

$$= \frac{2M}{R_2^2 - R_1^2} \cdot \frac{1}{4}(R_2^4 - R_1^4)$$

$$= \frac{1}{2}M(R_2^2 + R_1^2) \quad \text{Ans.}$$

Web Reference at www.physicsgalaxy.com | Scan for Video Explanation

Module-15: Solved Example-3

Ex : Find the moment of inertia of a cylinder of mass M, radius R and length L about an axis passing through its centre and perpendicular to its axis.

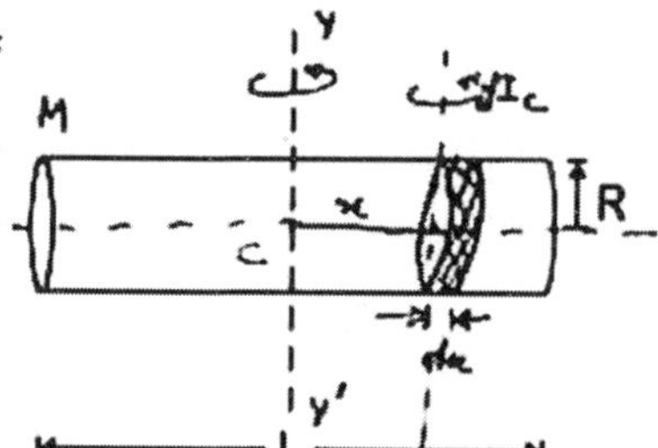

Sol^n: Mass of elemental disc is

$$dm = \frac{M}{L}dx$$

MI of disc about AOR YY'. $dI = dI_c + dm x^2$

$$dI = \frac{1}{4}dmR^2 + dm\,x^2$$

Total MI of cylinder $I = \int dI = \frac{1}{4}\int_{-L/2}^{+L/2}\frac{M}{L}R^2dx + \int_{-L/2}^{+L/2}\frac{M}{L}x^2dx$

$$I = \frac{1}{4}\frac{MR^2}{L}[x]_{-L/2}^{+L/2} + \frac{M}{L}\left[\frac{x^3}{3}\right]_{-L/2}^{+L/2}$$

$$I = \frac{1}{4}MR^2 + \frac{1}{12}ML^2 \text{ Ans.}$$

Scan for Video Explanation

Web Reference at www.physicsgalaxy.com

Module-16: Solved Example-4

Ex : Find moment of inertia of the triangular lamina of mass M about the axis of rotation AB as shown in figure.

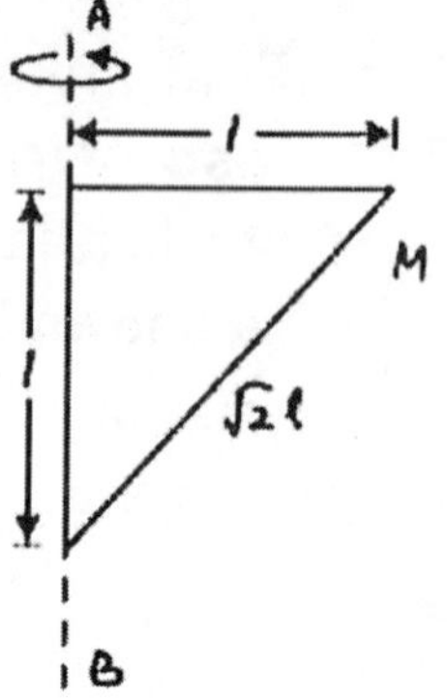

Sol^n:

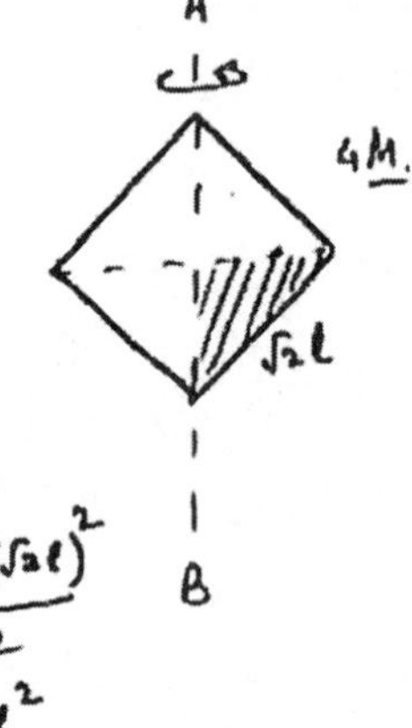

MI of this sq. is –

$$I = \frac{(4M)(\sqrt{2}l)^2}{12} = \frac{2}{3}Ml^2$$

$$I_{each} = \frac{1}{4}I$$

$$= \frac{\frac{2}{3}Ml^2}{4} = \frac{1}{6}Ml^2 \text{ Ans.}$$

Scan for Video Explanation

Web Reference at www.physicsgalaxy.com

Module-17: Newton's Second Law in Rotational Motion

Newton's Second Law in Rotational Motion:

As we know in T_x Motion

$$\Sigma \vec{F} = m\vec{a}$$

Similarly in R_x motion

$$\Sigma \vec{\tau} = I\vec{\alpha}$$

$F_1 > F_2$

F_1 → [m] ← F_2 → a

$$F_1 - F_2 = ma.$$

eq^n of motion

$$F_2 r_2 - F_1 r_1 = I\alpha.$$

Web Reference at www.physicsgalaxy.com | Scan for Video Explanation

Module-17: Newton's Second Law in Rotational Motion

Ex : **A uniform rod of length L & mass M which is hinged at topmost point is released from a position where it makes an angle θ with vertical as shown. Find the acceleration of the tip of rod just after it is released.**

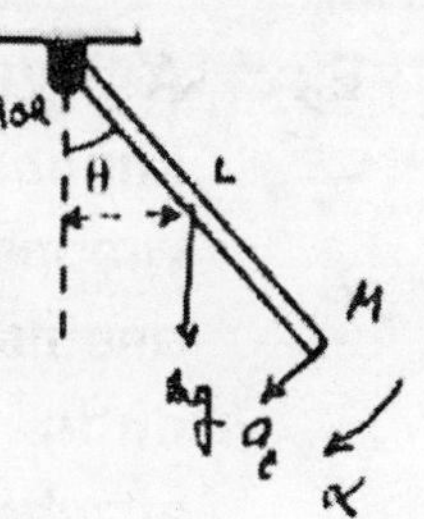

Sol^n: Torque on rod just after release

$$\tau = Mg \times \frac{L}{2}\sin\theta$$

ang acc^n $\alpha = \frac{\tau}{I} = \frac{Mg\frac{L}{2}\sin\theta}{\frac{ML^2}{3}} = \frac{3g}{2L}\sin\theta$

$$a_t = L\alpha = \frac{3g}{2}\sin\theta \quad \text{Ans.}$$

Web Reference at www.physicsgalaxy.com | Scan for Video Explanation

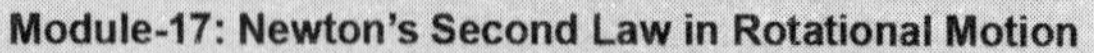

Module-17: Newton's Second Law in Rotational Motion

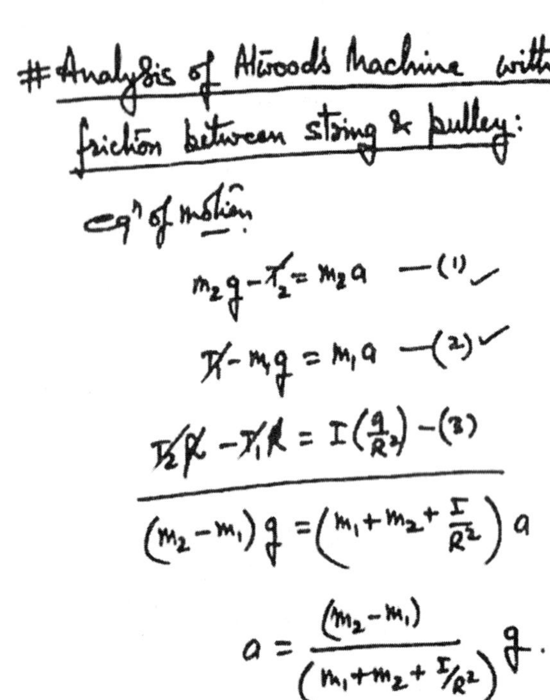

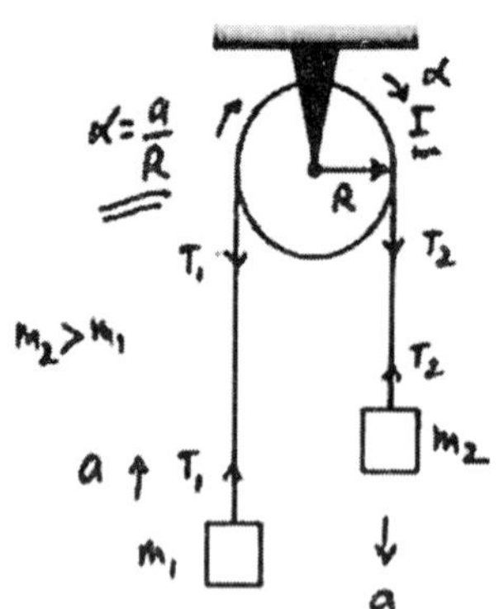

Scan for Video Explanation

Web Reference at www.physicsgalaxy.com

Module-18: Solved Example-5

Ex : **A cylinder of mass m suspended by two strings wrapped around the cylinder, one near each end, the free ends of the strings are attached to ceiling as shown. From rest cylinder is allowed to roll down under gravity. As strings unwind, find acceleration of falling cylinder & tension in strings.**

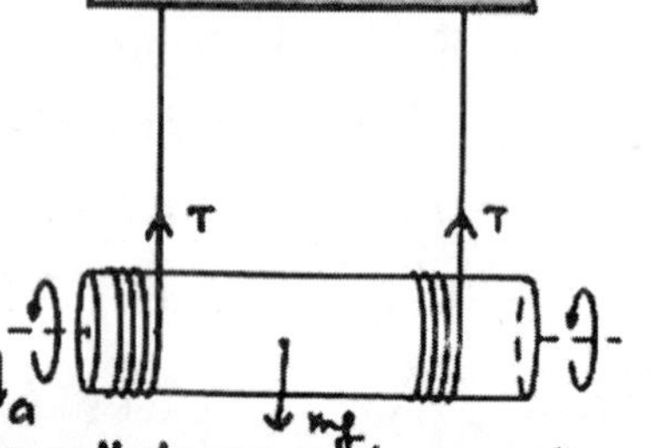

Solⁿ:

$mg - 2T = ma$ —(1)

$2TR = \frac{1}{2} m R^2 \left(\frac{a}{R}\right)$ —(2)

$mg = \frac{3}{2} m a$

$a = \frac{2g}{3}$ Ans.

$mg - 2T = \frac{2mg}{3}$

$2T = \frac{mg}{3}$

$T = \frac{1}{6} mg$ Ans.

Scan for Video Explanation

Web Reference at www.physicsgalaxy.com

Module-19: Solved Example-6

Ex : A uniform disc of radius R is first spinned about its axis to the angular speed ω and then carefully placed with its flat face on a rough horizontal surface. How long will the disc be rotating on the surface if the friction coefficient is equal to μ ?

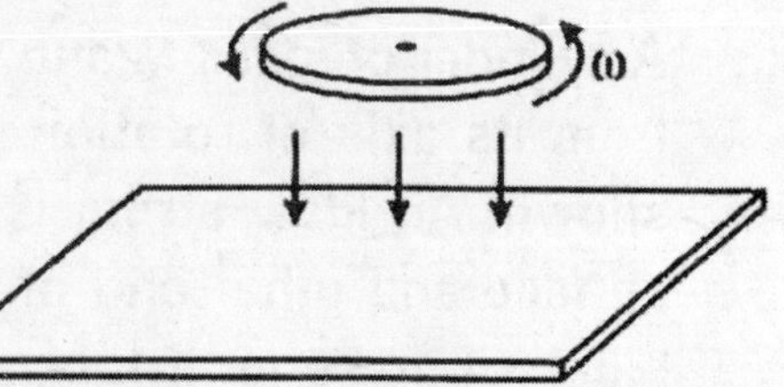

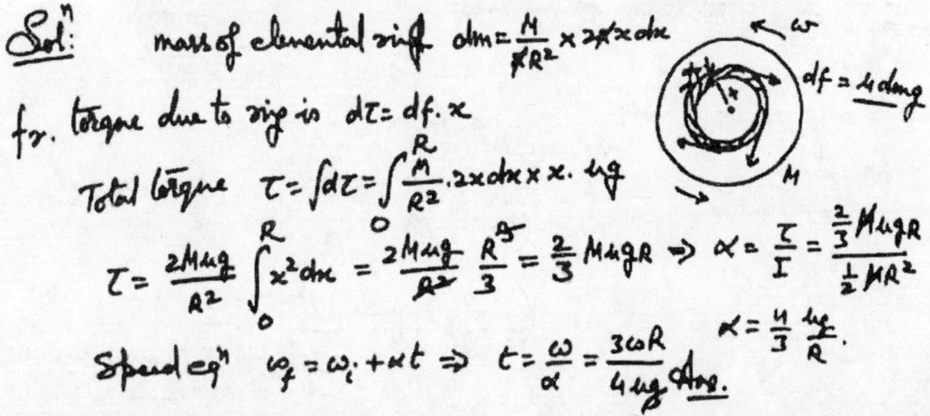

Web Reference at www.physicsgalaxy.com | Scan for Video Explanation

Module-20: Solved Example-7

Ex : A cylinder B of mass m and radius R is mounted on a massless mount A as shown. On cylinder an ideal string is wrapped, other end of which connected to a block C which hangs over an ideal pulley as shown. When the system is set free, find the acceleration of block C.

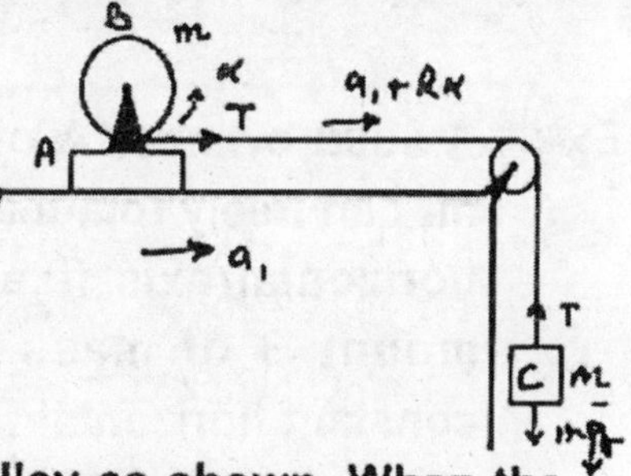

Sol^n: $a = a_1 + R\alpha$. —(1)

eq^n of motion for C. $mg - T = ma$. —(2)

for cylinder $T = ma_1$, $TR = \frac{1}{2}mR^2\alpha$.

$a_1 = \frac{1}{2}\frac{mR\alpha}{m} = \frac{R\alpha}{2}$

$mg - \frac{mR\alpha}{2} = \frac{3}{2}mR\alpha$

$a = \frac{1}{2}R\alpha + R\alpha = \frac{3}{2}R\alpha$.

$g = 2R\alpha$

$a = \frac{3}{2}R\left(\frac{g}{2R}\right) = \frac{3g}{4}$ Ans. $\alpha = \frac{g}{2R}$.

Web Reference at www.physicsgalaxy.com | Scan for Video Explanation

Module-21: Solved Example-8

Ex : A cylinder of mass M and radius R is hinged from its axis of rotation O from ceiling as shown. An ideal string is wrapped over its surface and other end of which is tied to a block of mass m. If this system is released from rest, find the acceleration of falling mass m.

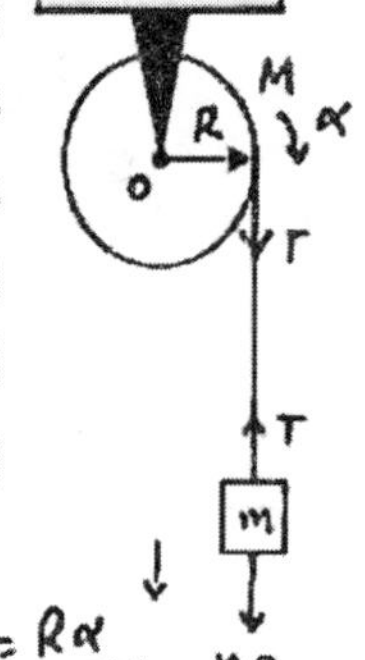

Sol^n: eq^n of motion for falling mass

$a = R\alpha$

$$mg - T = ma \quad \text{---(1)}$$

for cylinder

$$TR = \left(\frac{1}{2}MR^2\right)\left(\frac{a}{R}\right) \quad \text{---(2)}$$

$$mg = \left(m + \frac{M}{2}\right)a$$

$$a = \left(\frac{2m}{2m+M}\right)g \quad \text{Ans.}$$

Scan for Video Explanation

Web Reference at www.physicsgalaxy.com

Module-22: Solved Example-9

Ex : A solid cylinder A of mass m_1 can freely rotate about a horizontal axis fixed to a mount B of mass m_2. A constant horizontal force is applied to end P of a light string wound on the cylinder. Neglect friction anywhere, find the acceleration of point P.

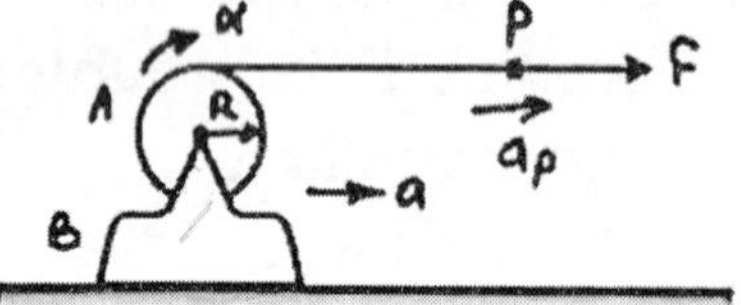

Sol^n:

$a_P = a + R\alpha$

$$F = (m_1 + m_2)a \longrightarrow a = \frac{F}{m_1 + m_2}$$

$$FR = \left(\frac{1}{2}m_1R^2\right)\alpha \longrightarrow \alpha = \frac{2F}{m_1 R}$$

$$a_P = a + R\alpha = \frac{F}{m_1 + m_2} + \frac{2F}{m_1} = \frac{F(3m_1 + 2m_2)}{m_1(m_1 + m_2)} \quad \text{Ans.}$$

Scan for Video Explanation

Web Reference at www.physicsgalaxy.com

Module-23: Angular Momentum

Angular Momentum:

Trans. Motion → Linear Momentum ($m\vec{v}$)

Rot^n Motion → Angular Momentum
↓
moment of linear momentum.
↓
The product of linear momentum with the shortest distance of line of motion from the pt about which angular momentum is taken.

Web Reference at www.physicsgalaxy.com | Scan for Video Explanation

Module-23: Angular Momentum

Different Cases for calculation of Angular Momentum:

Case-I: Ang. momentum of a particle moving in a st. line

$\vec{L}_{mx}$ ⊗ inward.

$d = r\sin\theta$

Ang momentum of m w.r.to x is

$L_{mx} = mv \times d$

$L_{mx} = mv \times r\sin\theta$

$\vec{L}_{mx} = m(\vec{r} \times \vec{v})$

Web Reference at www.physicsgalaxy.com | Scan for Video Explanation

Module-23: Angular Momentum

Case-II : Angular Momentum of a particle in Circular Motion

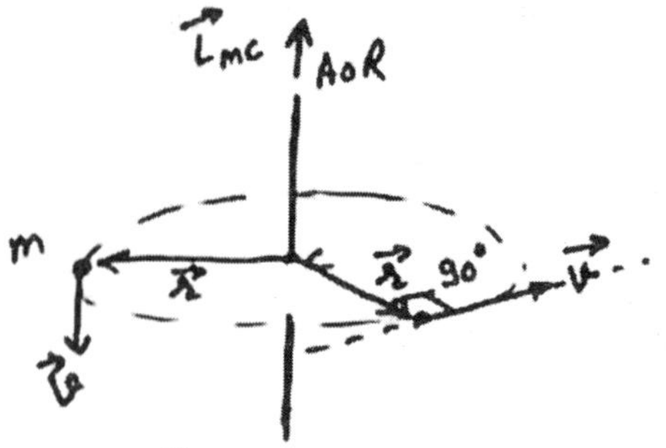

$\vec{L}_{mc}$ AoR

m, $\vec{r}$, $\vec{r}$, 90°, $\vec{v}$, $\vec{v}$

$$\vec{L}_{mc} = m(\vec{r} \times \vec{v})$$

$$L_{mc} = mvr.$$

$\vec{L}_{mP}$, P, $\vec{r'}$, C, $\vec{v}$

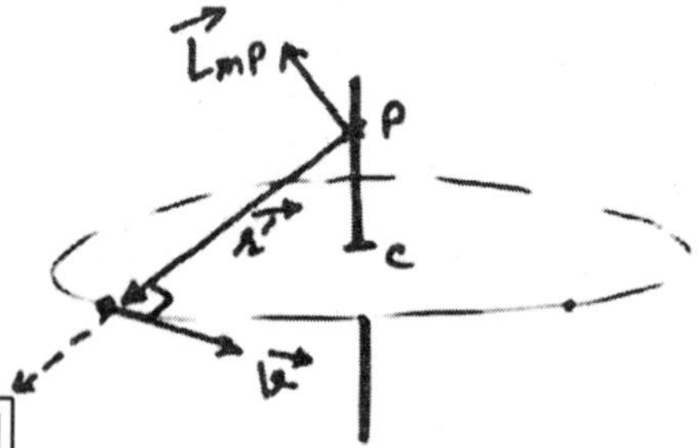

$$\vec{L}_{mp} = m(\vec{r'} \times \vec{v})$$

$$L_{mp} = mvr'$$

Scan for Video Explanation

Web Reference at www.physicsgalaxy.com

Module-23: Angular Momentum

Case-III : Angular Momentum of a Rigid Body in Rotation

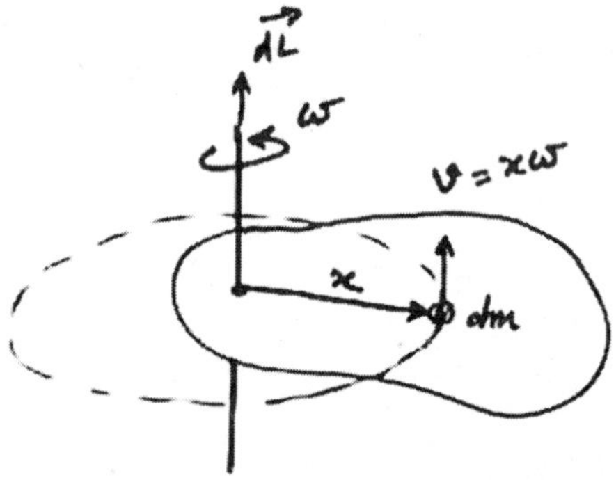

$\vec{dL}$, ω, $v = x\omega$, x, dm

L, v, m, r

$$L = mvr.$$

Ang momentum of dm about given AoR is

$$dL = dm\,v x = dm(x\omega)x$$

$$dL = dm\,x^2 . \omega$$

for whole body $L = \int dL = \int dm\,x^2 . \omega$

$$\boxed{\vec{L} = I\vec{\omega}}$$

Scan for Video Explanation

Web Reference at www.physicsgalaxy.com

Module-23: Angular Momentum

Case-IV: Angular Momentum of a Rotating Body about an AOR passing through CoM & moving translationally.

ω, $\vec{v_c}$, M, $\vec{r_c}$, P, $\vec{v_c}$, CoM

$$\vec{L_c} = I\vec{\omega}$$
$$\vec{L_T} = M(\vec{r_c} \times \vec{v_c})$$

Ang. momentum of this body w.r.to pt P is

$$\vec{L_{MP}} = \vec{L_c} + \vec{L_T}$$

imp.

$$\boxed{\vec{L_{MP}} = I\vec{\omega} + M(\vec{r_c} \times \vec{v_c})}$$

Web Reference at www.physicsgalaxy.com | Scan for Video Explanation

Module-24: Conservation of Angular Momentum

Law of Conservation of Angular Momentum:

For a rotating rigid body.

$$L = I\omega$$

diff. w.r.to t.

$$\frac{dL}{dt} = I\frac{d\omega}{dt} = I\alpha \leftarrow \tau$$

$$\tau = \frac{dL}{dt} \leftarrow \left(F = \frac{dp}{dt}\right)$$

Newton's II law for rot^n motion

"Rate of change of angular momentum of a rotating body is equal to net torque acting on it."

Web Reference at www.physicsgalaxy.com | Scan for Video Explanation

Module-24: Conservation of Angular Momentum

If for a system of bodies

$$\vec{\tau}_{ext} = 0.$$

$$\Rightarrow \frac{dL}{dt} = 0 \Rightarrow L = \text{Constant}$$

In absence of external torque on a system, total angular momentum of the system will remain Conserved.

Scan for Video Explanation

Web Reference at www.physicsgalaxy.com

Module-24: Conservation of Angular Momentum

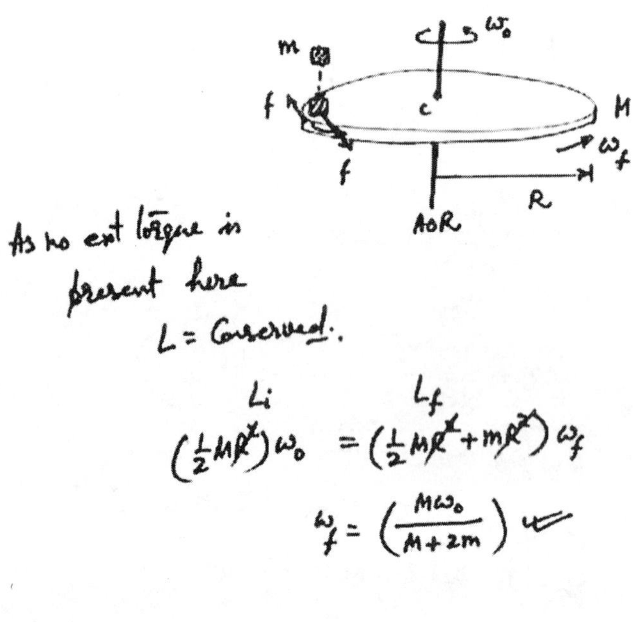

As no ext torque is present here

L = Conserved.

$$\underset{L_i}{\left(\frac{1}{2}MR^2\right)\omega_0} = \underset{L_f}{\left(\frac{1}{2}MR^2 + mR^2\right)\omega_f}$$

$$\omega_f = \left(\frac{M\omega_0}{M+2m}\right)$$

Scan for Video Explanation

Web Reference at www.physicsgalaxy.com

Module-25: Solved Example-10

Ex : **A rod AB of length L and mass M is hinged at the topmost point A as shown & it is free to rotate about this point. If ball of mass M/2, moving at speed u strikes the other end of rod and sticks to it, find the angular speed with which rod will move after collision.**

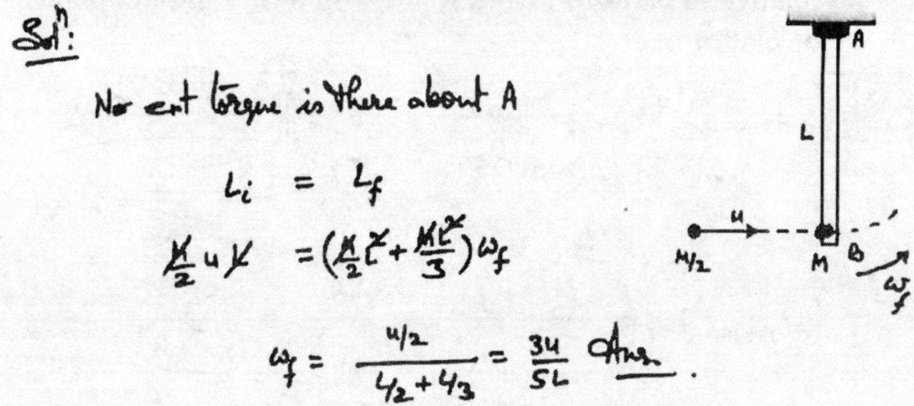

Web Reference at www.physicsgalaxy.com | **Scan for Video Explanation**

Module-26: Solved Example-11

Ex : **A child of mass m is standing on periphery of a circular platform of radius R, which can rotate about its central axis. The moment of inertia of platform is I. The child jumps off the platform with a velocity u relative to platform and tangential to it. Find the recoil angular speed of platform after jump.**

Sol^n: As no ext. torque is present about C

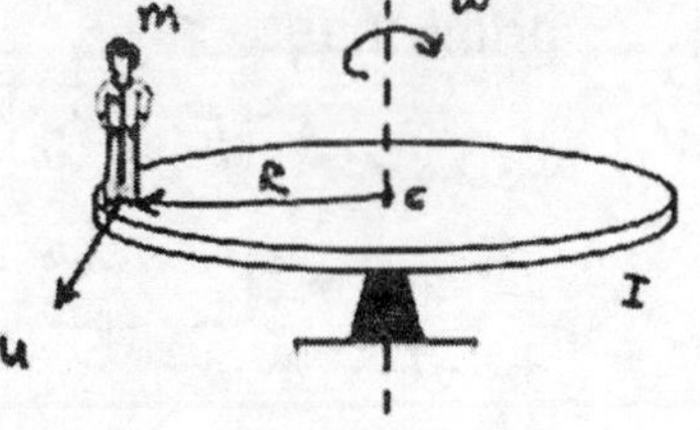

$$L_i = L_f$$

$$0 = m(u - R\omega)R - I\omega$$

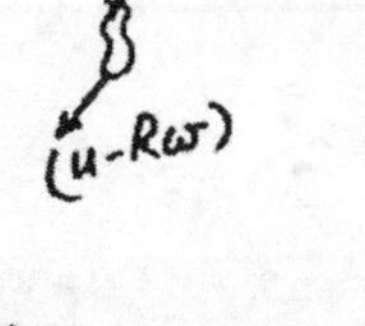

$$muR = (I + mR^2)\omega$$

$$\omega = \left(\frac{muR}{I + mR^2}\right) \text{ Ans.}$$

Web Reference at www.physicsgalaxy.com | **Scan for Video Explanation**

Module-27: Solved Example-12

Ex : **A horizontal circular platform of mass M, radius R and moment of inertia I which is free to rotate about a vertical axis passing through its centre, is rotating at an angular speed ω_1. A boy starts walking from rest long its periphery in opposite direction with speed u relative to platform, what will be the new angular speed of platform.**

Soln: As no ext torque is there abt pt C, we use

$$L_i = L_f.$$

$$(I + mR^2)\omega_1 = I\omega_2 - m(u - R\omega_2)R$$

$$\omega_2 = \frac{(I+mR^2)\omega_1}{(I+mR^2)} + \frac{muR}{(I+mR^2)} = \frac{(I+mR^2)\omega_1 + muR}{I+mR^2}$$ Ans.

Scan for Video Explanation

Web Reference at www.physicsgalaxy.com

Module-28: Solved Example-13

Ex : **A point mass is tied to one end of a cord other end of which passes through a hollow tube, caught in one hand. The point mass is being revolved in a horizontal circle of radius 2m with speed of 4 m/s. The cord is then pulled down so that the radius of circle reduces to 1m. Compute the new linear and angular velocities of the point mass.**

Soln: As no ext torque is present abt Centre of circle we can Cons. angular momentum of system -

$r_1 = 2m$, $u = 4 m/s$, $r_2 = 1m$.

$$L_i = L_f$$

$$mur_1 = mvr_2$$

$$v = \frac{ur_1}{r_2} = \frac{4 \times 2}{1} = 8 \text{ m/s} \quad \text{Ans.}$$

$$\omega = \frac{v}{r_2} = \frac{8}{1} = 8 \text{ rad/sec} \quad \text{Ans.}$$

Scan for Video Explanation

Web Reference at www.physicsgalaxy.com

Module-29: Concept of Angular Impulse

Concept of Angular Impulse:

for Translational motion $\Delta P = \int_0^t F dt$

As for rot^n motion $L = I\omega$

$$\tau = \frac{dL}{dt}$$

$$dL = \tau dt$$

Angular Impulse:
- For a Constant torque for a time Δt, $\Delta L = \tau \Delta t$
- For a time varying torque for a time 0 to T $\Delta L = \int_0^T \tau dt$

Web Reference at www.physicsgalaxy.com | Scan for Video Explanation

Module-29: Concept of Angular Impulse

Impulse - Momentum equation for Rotational Motion:

for T_r motion $P_i \pm J = P_f$

for R_r motion $L_i \pm J_R = L_f$.

$$J_R = \tau \Delta t \quad \text{or} \quad J_R = \int \tau dt$$

$\tau = Fr$

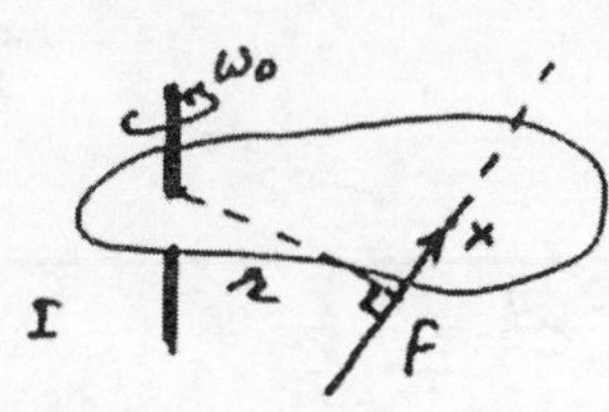

after time t if ang speed of body changes to ω_f

$$\left[I\omega_0 + Frt = I\omega_f \right]$$

Web Reference at www.physicsgalaxy.com | Scan for Video Explanation

Module-29: Concept of Angular Impulse

Ex : The wheel of radius R and moment of inertia I shown in figure is released from rest with a mass m tied to an ideal string wrapped on wheel. Find the speed of mass m after time t.

$\alpha = a/R$

Solⁿ: eqⁿ of motion

$$mg - T = ma.$$

$$T(R) = I\left(a/R\right)$$

$$mg = \left(m + \frac{I}{R^2}\right)a$$

$$a = \frac{mg}{m + I/R^2} = \frac{mgR^2}{mR^2 + I}$$

after t.

$$v = u + at$$

$$v = at.$$

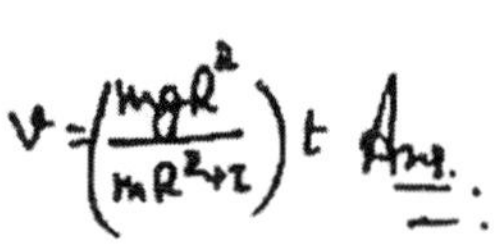

Scan for Video Explanation

Web Reference at www.physicsgalaxy.com

Module-29: Concept of Angular Impulse

Alternative Solution:

Solⁿ: we use Impulse eqⁿ as -

$$0 + mgt - Tt = mv \quad -(1)$$

$$0 + TRt = I\left(\frac{v}{R^2}\right) \quad -(2)$$

$$mgt = \left(m + \frac{I}{R^2}\right)v$$

$$v = \frac{mgR^2t}{I + mR^2} \quad \text{Ans}$$

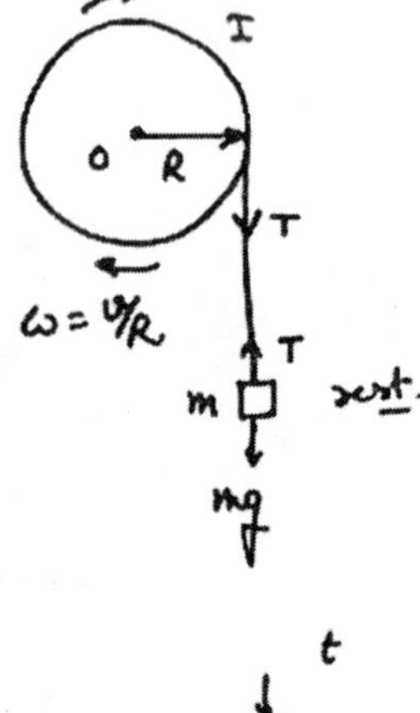

Scan for Video Explanation

Web Reference at www.physicsgalaxy.com

Module-30: Kinetic Energy of a Rigid body in Rotational Motion

Kinetic Energy of a Rigid Body in Rotation:

$K = \frac{1}{2}mv^2$

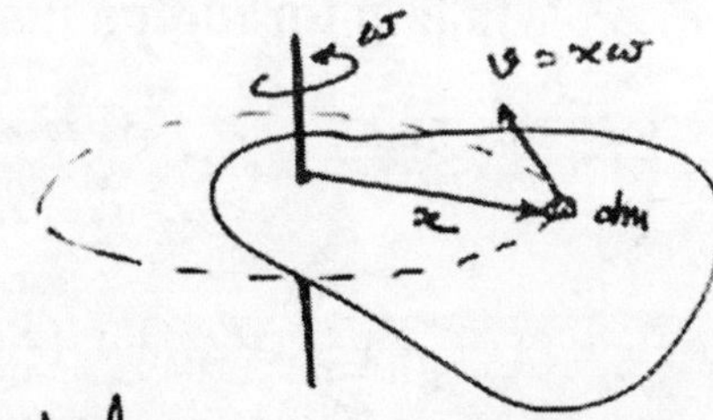

KE of dm is –

$$dK = \frac{1}{2}dm(x\omega)^2$$

$$= \frac{1}{2}dm\,x^2\omega^2$$

Total KE of rotating body is

$$K = \int dK = \int \frac{1}{2}dm\,x^2\omega^2 = \frac{1}{2}\omega^2 \int dm\,x^2$$

$$\boxed{K = \frac{1}{2}I\omega^2}$$

Web Reference at www.physicsgalaxy.com

Scan for Video Explanation

Module-30: Kinetic Energy of a Rigid body in Rotational Motion

KE of a rotating body about a moving AOR.

M, L, C, ω, v_c

$$K = K_{RC} + \frac{1}{2}Mv_c^2$$

$$\boxed{K = \frac{1}{2}I\omega^2 + \frac{1}{2}Mv_c^2}$$

v_c → vel. of COM.

Web Reference at www.physicsgalaxy.com

Scan for Video Explanation

Module-30: Kinetic Energy of a Rigid body in Rotational Motion

Ex : **A wheel of moment of Inertia I, and radius R is free to rotate about the horizontal axis O and an ideal a string is wrapped on it and attached to a small mass m as shown. If the system is released, find speed of mass m after falling through a distance h.**

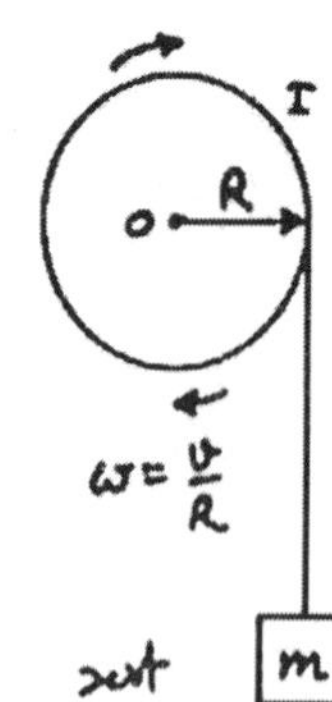

Sol^n: using W/E theorem ✓

$$\underset{k_i}{0} + mgh = \underset{k_f}{\frac{1}{2}mv^2 + \frac{1}{2}I\left(\frac{v^2}{R^2}\right)}$$

$$v = \sqrt{\frac{2mghR^2}{(I + mR^2)}} \quad \text{Ans.}$$

Scan for Video Explanation

Web Reference at www.physicsgalaxy.com

Module-31: Rolling Motion and Pure Rolling of a body on Inclined Plane

Rolling Motion:

for a round shaped object

Rolling motion = Rot^n motion + Tran. motion on a Surface.

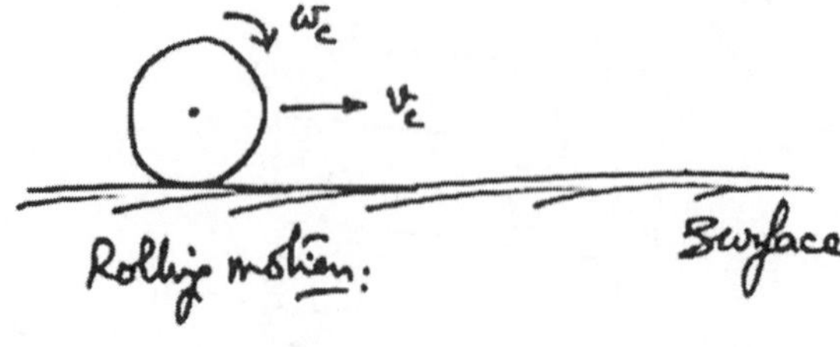

Scan for Video Explanation

Web Reference at www.physicsgalaxy.com

Module-31: Rolling Motion and Pure Rolling of a body on Inclined Plane

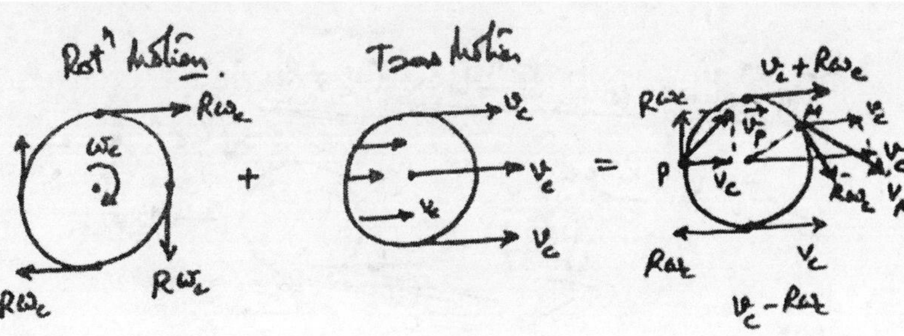

Types of Rolling:

two ways (i) Pure Rolling – (Rolling without Sliding)

(ii) Rolling with Sliding

Web Reference at www.physicsgalaxy.com | Scan for Video Explanation

Module-31: Rolling Motion and Pure Rolling of a body on Inclined Plane

Pure Rolling:

ω_c ; v_c ; $R\omega_c$

if $v_c = R\omega_c$ ⇒ the Contact pt will be at rest.

if F_{ext} is present ⇒ No Dynamic friction will act on body.

$f \rightarrow$ static

if No F_{ext} is present & friction if exist, will be static friction only.

$f = 0$. (No friction)

Web Reference at www.physicsgalaxy.com | Scan for Video Explanation

Module-31: Rolling Motion and Pure Rolling of a body on Inclined Plane

Rolling with Sliding: ($v_c \neq R\omega_c$)

Case-I: $v_c > R\omega_c$.

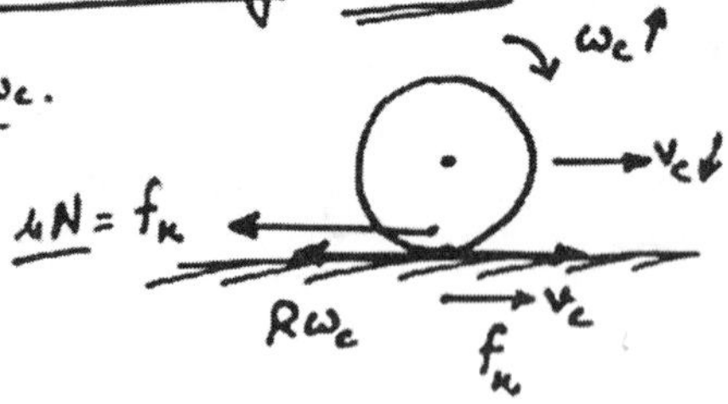

$\mu N = f_k$

$\omega_c \uparrow$, $v_c \downarrow$, $R\omega_c$, v_c, f_k

after some time $v_f = R\omega_f$

pure rolling will start ($f = 0$)

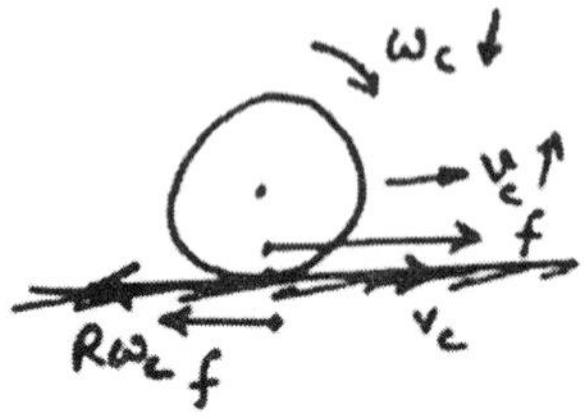

Case-II: $v_c < R\omega_c$

$\omega_c \downarrow$, $v_c \uparrow$, f, $R\omega_c$, f, v_c

after some time $v_f = R\omega_f$

pure rolling will start ($f = 0$)

Scan for Video Explanation

Web Reference at www.physicsgalaxy.com

Module-31: Rolling Motion and Pure Rolling of a body on Inclined Plane

Pure Rolling of a body on Inclined Plane:

for pure rolling $v = R\omega$.

using W/E theorem.

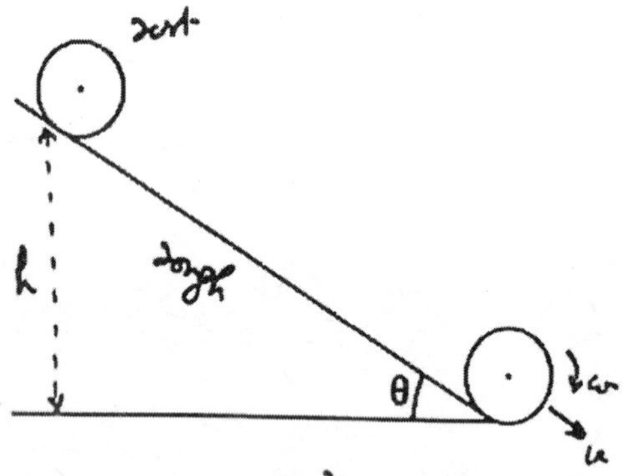

rest, h, rough, θ, ω, v

$$k_i \qquad k_f$$

$$0 + Mgh = \frac{1}{2}Mv^2 + \frac{1}{2}(MK^2)\omega^2$$

$$I = MK^2$$

$$2gh = v^2 + K^2\left(\frac{v^2}{R^2}\right)$$

$$v = \sqrt{\frac{2gh}{1 + K^2/R^2}}$$

Scan for Video Explanation

Web Reference at www.physicsgalaxy.com

Module-31: Rolling Motion and Pure Rolling of a body on Inclined Plane

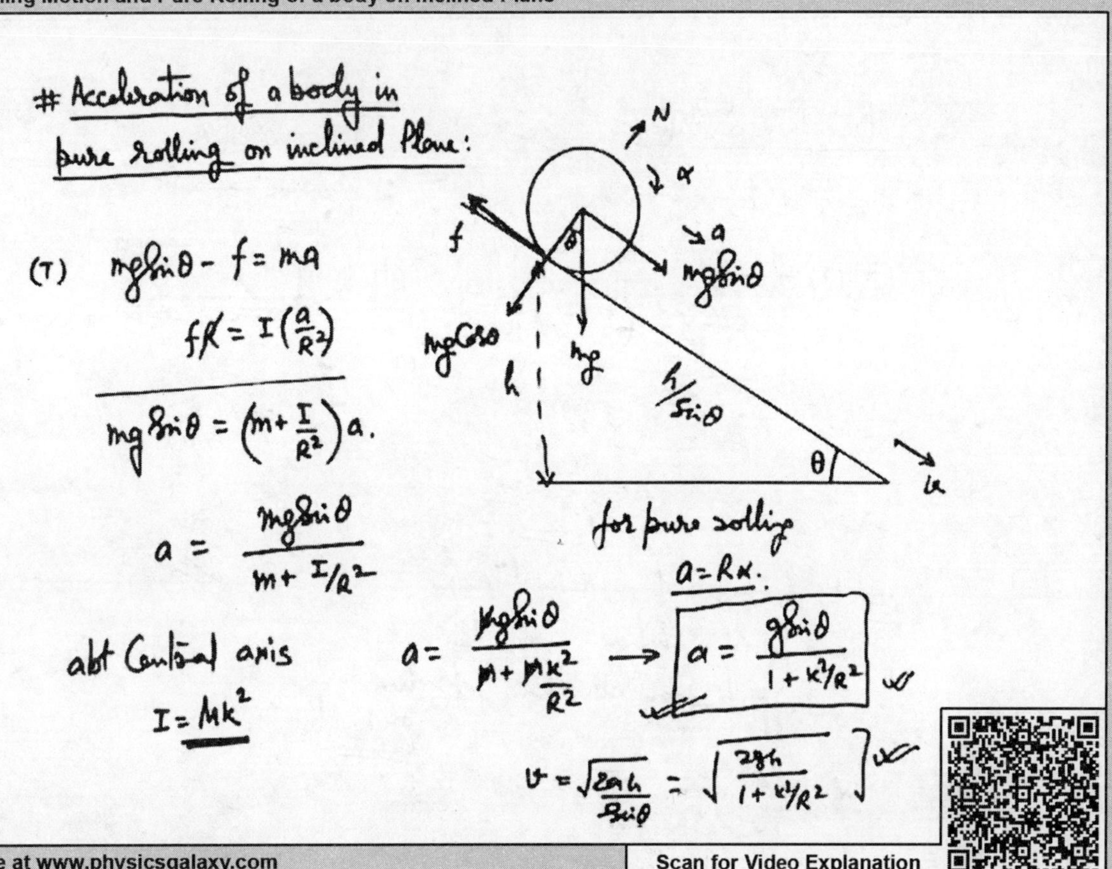

Web Reference at www.physicsgalaxy.com | Scan for Video Explanation

Module-32: Solved Example-14

Ex : **A force F is applied tangential at the topmost point of a sphere of mass M and radius R. If the ground is rough enough to prevent sliding, find the linear acceleration of sphere.**

Sol^n

eq^n of motion

$$F - f = Ma \quad \text{—(1)}$$

$$FR + fR = \left(\frac{2}{5}MR^2\right)\left(\frac{a}{R}\right) \quad \text{—(2)}$$

$$2F = \frac{7}{5}Ma$$

$$a = \frac{10F}{7M} \quad \text{Ans.}$$

M, F, α, a, R, f, rough

for pure rolling $\alpha = a/R$.

friction

$$f = F - Ma = F - \frac{10F}{7}$$

$$f = -\frac{3F}{7}$$

opposite dir.

Web Reference at www.physicsgalaxy.com | Scan for Video Explanation

Module-32: Solved Example-14

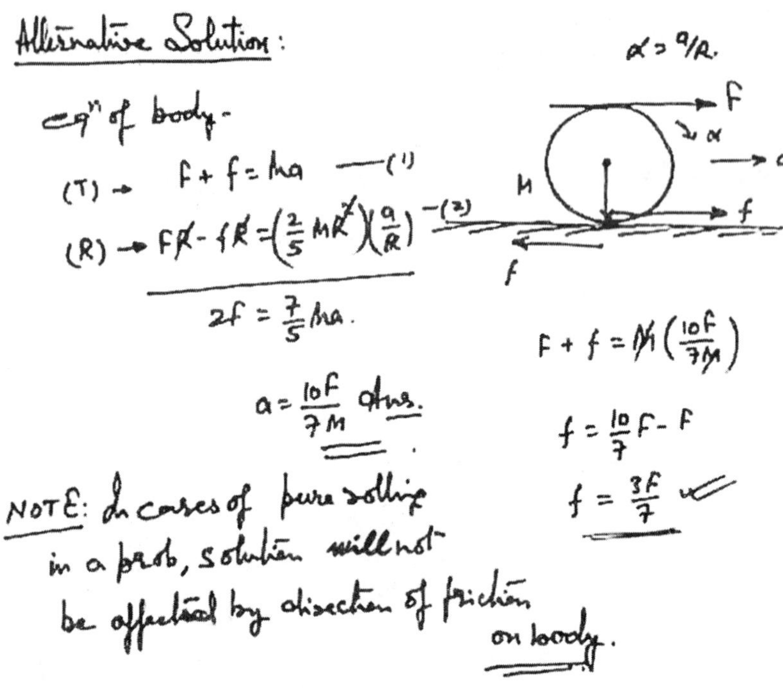

Scan for Video Explanation

Web Reference at www.physicsgalaxy.com

Module-33: Solved Example-15

Ex : **A cylinder of mass M and radius R rolls without slipping down an inclined plane of length *l* as shown. Find the linear acceleration of cylinder. Also find the minimum friction coefficient required on the inclined plane for which the cylinder does not slip.**

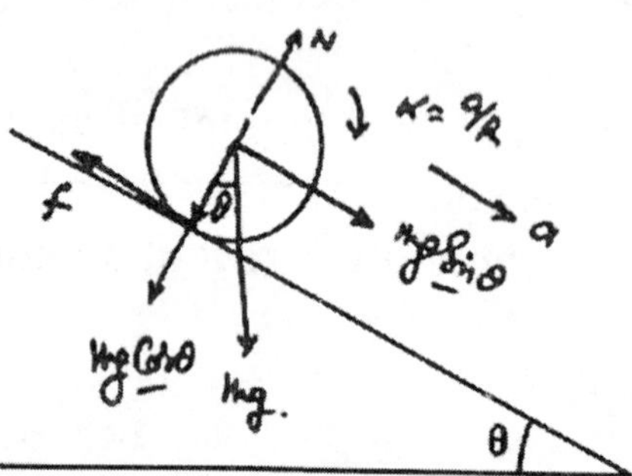

Sol^n: As we know $a = \frac{g\sin\theta}{1 + k^2/R^2} = \frac{g\sin\theta}{1 + 1/2}$ $\quad k = R/\sqrt{2}$

$a = \frac{2}{3} g\sin\theta$ Ans.

for pure rolling $f < f_L (\mu N)$

$mg\sin\theta - f = m\left(\frac{2}{3} g\sin\theta\right)$

$f = \frac{1}{3} mg\sin\theta$

$\frac{1}{3} mg\sin\theta < \mu\, mg\cos\theta$

$\mu > \frac{1}{3}\tan\theta.$

min $\mu = \frac{1}{3}\tan\theta$. Ans.

Scan for Video Explanation

Web Reference at www.physicsgalaxy.com

Module-34: Solved Example-16

Ex : Figure shows a cylinder on which a string is wrapped and other end of which is connected to a hanging mass m. If cylinder moves in pure rolling, find the acceleration of falling mass.

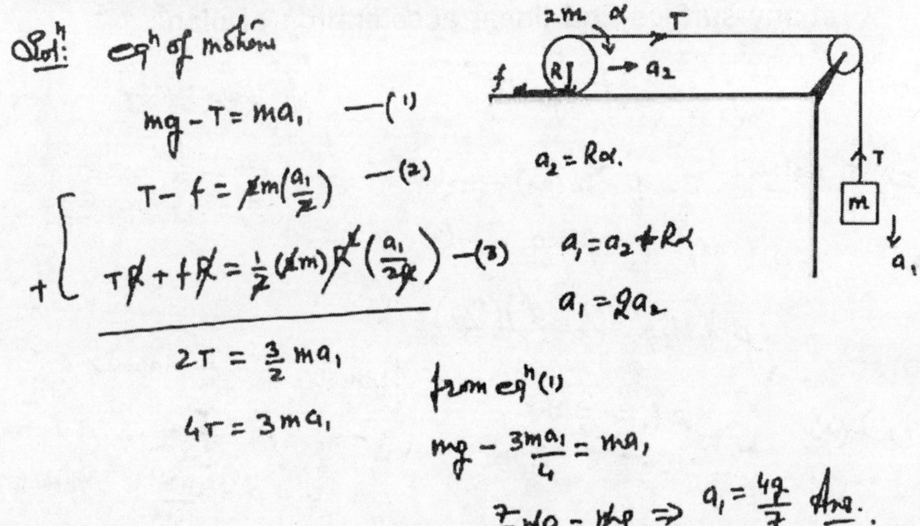

Solⁿ: eqⁿ of motion

$mg - T = ma_1$ —(1)

$T - f = 2m\left(\frac{a_1}{2}\right)$ —(2)

$TR + fR = \frac{1}{2}(2m)R^2\left(\frac{a_1}{2R}\right)$ —(3)

$a_2 = R\alpha$

$a_1 = a_2 + R\alpha$

$a_1 = 2a_2$

$2T = \frac{3}{2}ma_1$

$4T = 3ma_1$

from eqⁿ (1)

$mg - \frac{3ma_1}{4} = ma_1$

$\frac{7}{4}ma_1 = mg \Rightarrow a_1 = \frac{4g}{7}$ Ans.

Web Reference at www.physicsgalaxy.com | Scan for Video Explanation

Module-35: Solved Example-17

Ex : Figure shows a ball of mass m placed on rough surface of a plank of mass 4 m which is placed on a smooth ground. If plank is pulled by a horizontal force F. Find linear acceleration of plank and cylinder if cylinder is not slipping on plank.

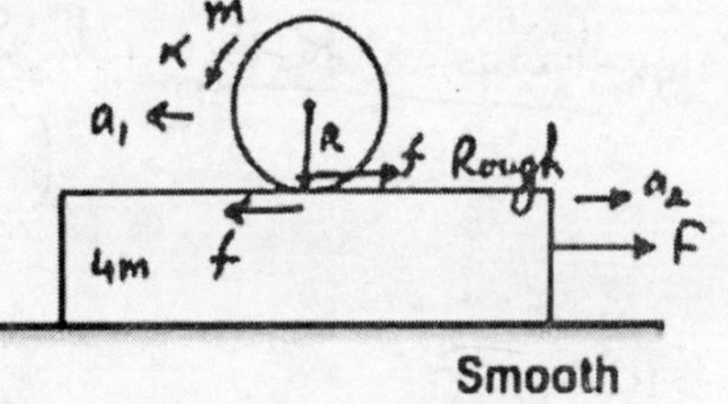

Solⁿ: eqⁿ of motion

$F - f = 4ma_2$

$f = m(a_2 - a_1)$

$F = 5ma_2 - ma_1$

$fR = \frac{2}{5}mR^2\left(\frac{a_1}{R}\right)$

for pure rolling of ball.

$a_1 = R\alpha$

$\frac{2}{5}ma_1 = ma_2 - ma_1$

$\frac{7}{5}a_1 = a_2$

$F = 5ma_2 - m\left(\frac{5}{7}a_2\right)$

$F = \frac{30}{7}ma_2$

$a_2 = \frac{7F}{30m}$ Ans.

Web Reference at www.physicsgalaxy.com | Scan for Video Explanation

Module-36: Solved Example-18

Ex : A plank of mass m is placed over a cylinder of mass m as shown. A horizontal force F is applied on plank, if slipping is not there at any surface find linear acceleration of plank.

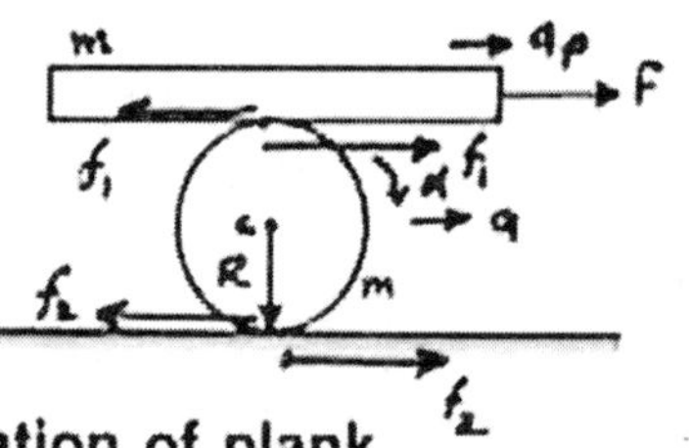

Sol^n: $f_1, f_2 \rightarrow$ static friction

for pure rolling

$a = R\alpha$

$a_p = a + R\alpha = 2a$

Eq^n of motion

$F - f_1 = m(2a)$ —(1)

$f_1 - f_2 = ma$ —(2)

$f_1 R + f_2 R = \left(\frac{1}{2}mR^2\right)\left(\frac{a}{R}\right)$ —(3)

(2) + (3) $\quad 2f_1 = \frac{3}{2}ma.$

from (1) $\quad F - \frac{3}{4}ma = 2ma$

$F = \frac{11}{4}ma.$

$a = \frac{4F}{11m}.$

acc^n of Plank $a_p = 2a = \frac{8F}{11m}$ **Ans.**

Scan for Video Explanation

Web Reference at www.physicsgalaxy.com

Module-37: Analysis of Rolling with Sliding

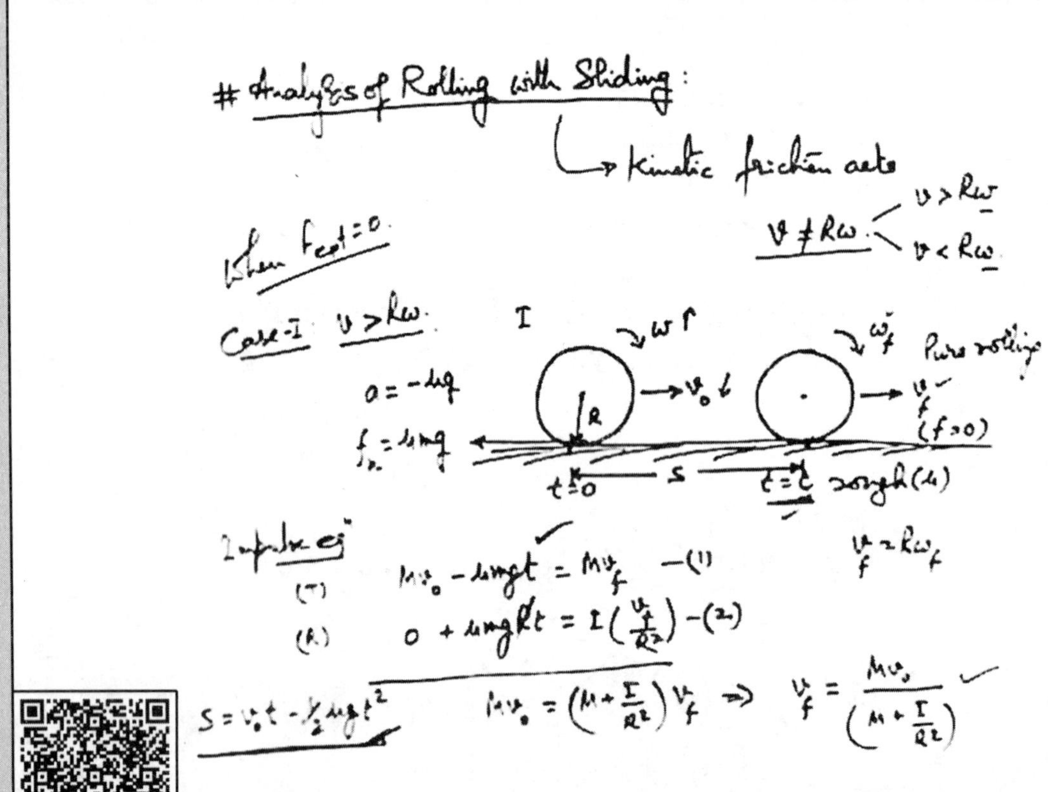

Scan for Video Explanation

Web Reference at www.physicsgalaxy.com

Module-37: Analysis of Rolling with Sliding

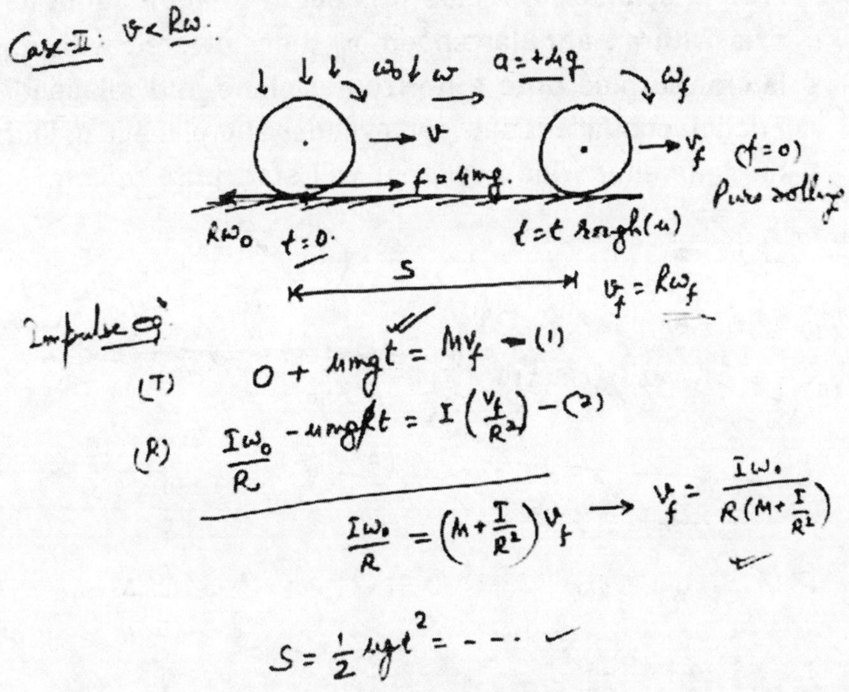

Web Reference at www.physicsgalaxy.com | Scan for Video Explanation

Module-38: Solved Example-19

Ex : A thin spherical shell of mass m and radius R lying on a rough surface is hit sharply by a cue horizontally as shown. Find h so that shell does not slip over the surface.

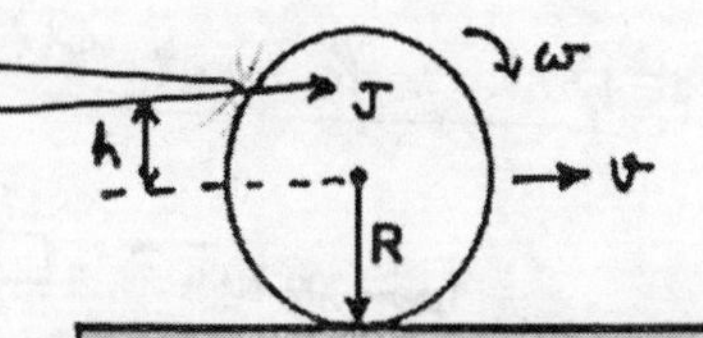

Solⁿ. Shell does not slip if from beginning it starts pure rolling.

$$v = R\omega.$$

Impulse eqⁿ:

$$J = Mv$$

$$Jh = \left(\frac{2}{3}MR^2\right)\left(\frac{v}{R}\right)$$

$$Mvh = \frac{2}{3}MRv \rightarrow h = \frac{2}{3}R \text{ Ans.}$$

Web Reference at www.physicsgalaxy.com | Scan for Video Explanation

Module-39: Solved Example-20

Ex : A solid cylinder of radius R is set in rotation about its axis with an angular speed ω_0 then lowered with its lateral surface onto a horizontal plane and released. Friction coefficient between cylinder and plane is μ, find the time after which cylinder will start pure rolling.

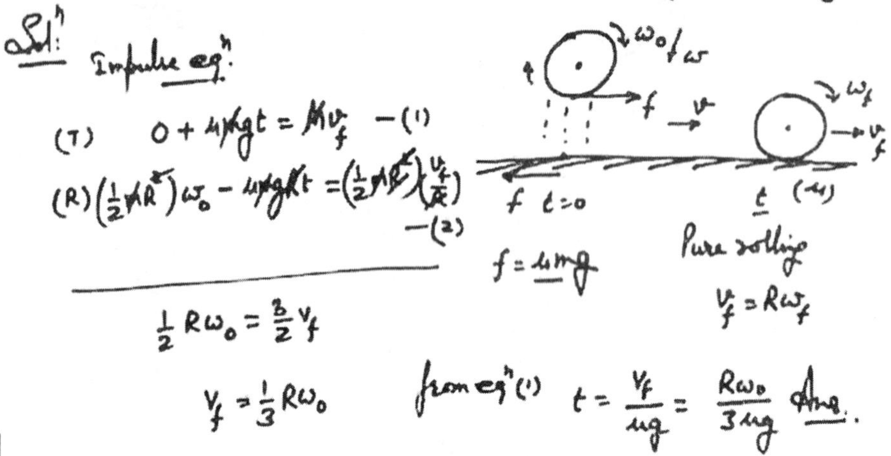

Scan for Video Explanation

Web Reference at www.physicsgalaxy.com

Module-40: Work & Power in Rotational Motion

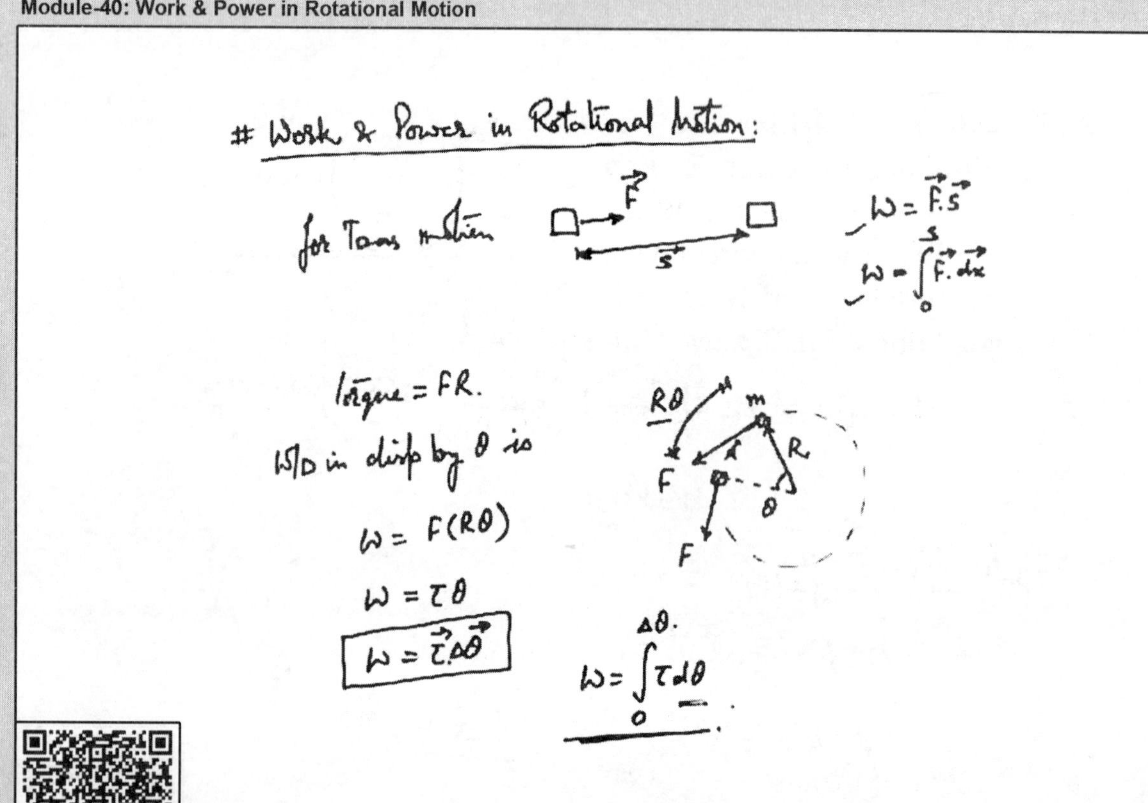

Scan for Video Explanation

Web Reference at www.physicsgalaxy.com

Module-40: Work & Power in Rotational Motion

Power → Rate of doing Work.

$$P = \frac{dW}{dt} = \frac{\tau d\theta}{dt} = \tau\omega$$

vector rep. $P = \vec{\tau} \cdot \vec{\omega}$

Avg Power → $\Delta W / \Delta t$

Instantaneous Power → dW/dt

Web Reference at www.physicsgalaxy.com | Scan for Video Explanation

Module-40: Work & Power in Rotational Motion

Ex : An electric motor of power P is connected with a pulley & a string to which a mass m is hanging. Find the maximum speed at which mass can be raised up.

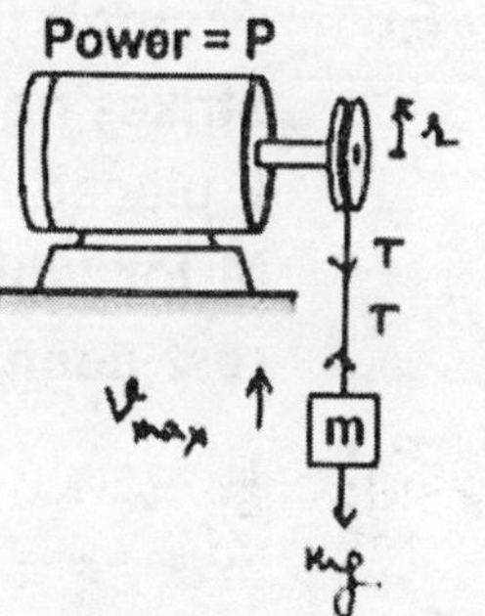

Soln: Torque on motor due to wt of block is

$$\tau = mg.r$$

max power of motor $P = mgr.\omega$ $(\tau).(\omega)$

$$\omega = \frac{P}{mgr}.$$

$$v_{max} = r\omega = \frac{P}{mg}. \text{ Ans.}$$

Web Reference at www.physicsgalaxy.com | Scan for Video Explanation

Module-41: Solved Example-21

Ex : A uniform rod of mass 3 m and length L is hanging from a hinge H as shown. A small ball of mass m moving horizontally at speed u strikes the end of rod elastically. Find the speed of ball and angular speed of rod just after collision.

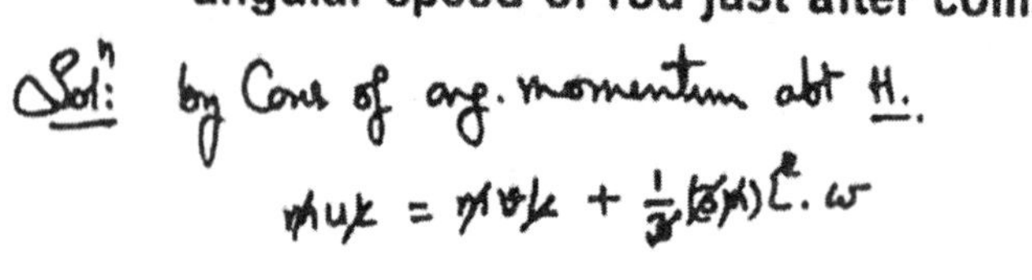

Solⁿ: by Cons of ang. momentum abt H.

$$muL = mvL + \frac{1}{3}(3m)L^2 \cdot \omega$$

$$e = 1 = \frac{v_{sep}}{v_{app}}$$

$$u = v + L\omega \quad —(1)$$

by $e = 1$ $\quad u = L\omega - v \quad —(2)$

$$2u = 2L\omega \Rightarrow \omega = u/L$$

from eqⁿ (1) $\quad u = v + u \Rightarrow v = 0.$ Ans.

Scan for Video Explanation

Web Reference at www.physicsgalaxy.com

Module-42: Solved Example-22

Ex : A small ball of mass m, moving at speed u strikes normally on a rod of mass M and length L placed on a smooth surface as shown. Find M for which after collision ball will come to rest,coefficient of restitution is e.

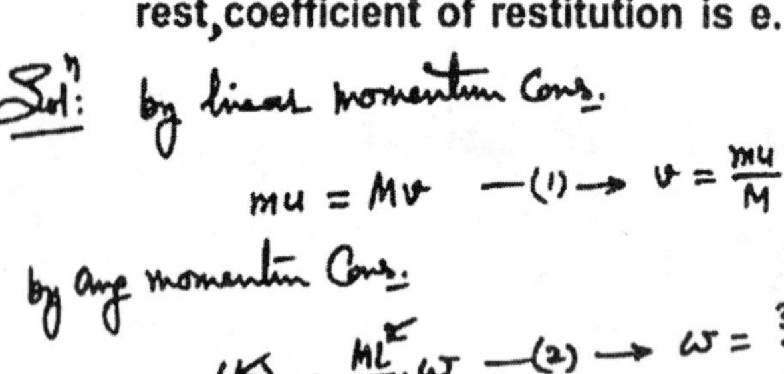

Solⁿ: by linear momentum Cons.

$$mu = Mv \quad —(1) \rightarrow v = \frac{mu}{M}$$

$$v_{sep} = e\, v_{app}$$

by ang momentum Cons.

$$mu\left(\frac{L}{4}\right) = \frac{ML^2}{12}\cdot\omega \quad —(2) \rightarrow \omega = \frac{3mu}{ML}$$

by CoR. $\quad e = \frac{v_{sep}}{v_{app}} = \frac{v + \frac{L}{4}\omega}{u} \Rightarrow v + \frac{L}{4}\omega = ue$

$$\frac{mu}{M} + \frac{L}{4}\left(\frac{3mu}{ML}\right) = ue \qquad M = \frac{7}{4}\frac{m}{e}$$

$$7m = 4eM \quad \text{Ans.}$$

Scan for Video Explanation

Web Reference at www.physicsgalaxy.com

Chapter 12
Fluid Statics

Lecture Notes Modules

Module-1: Introduction to Fluids
Module-2: Pressure in a Fluid
Module-3: Floatation of a Body due to Fluid Pressure
Module-4: Fluid Pressure due to Gravity
Module-5: Average Pressure on Side Walls of a Vessel
Module-6: Force on Side Walls of a Random Shaped Vessel
Module-7: Archimede's Principle
Module-8: Buoyant Force on a Body at the Interface of Two Liquids
Module-9: Apparent Weight of a Body Submerged in a Liquid
Module-10: Solved Example-1
Module-11: Solved Example-2
Module-12: Solved Example-3
Module-13: Solved Example-4
Module-14: Solved Example-5
Module-15: Pascal's Principle of Pressure Distribution
Module-16: Pressure at Different Levels in a Liquid
Module-17: Mechanism of a Hydraulic Lift
Module-18: Concept of Open tube Manometer
Module-19: Pressure Distribution in an Accelerated Frame
Module-20: Pressure Distribution in a Closed Accelerated Container
Module-21: Pressure Distribution in a Rotating tube Filled with a Liquid
Module-22: Solved Example-6
Module-23: Solved Example-7
Module-24: Solved Example-8
Module-25: Solved Example-9

Module-1: Introduction to Fluids

Fluids:

– Substances which do not have definite shape but have definite volume are called fluids (liq/gas) [almost constant density]

– A given amount of fluid is always separated by an interface from other solids or gases.

air (gas) — interfaces. — solid.

– The fluid interface bounded by a gas is called free surface of the fluid.

Scan for Video Explanation

Web Reference at www.physicsgalaxy.com

Module-2: Pressure in a Fluid

Pressure in a Fluid:

When an external force is applied on a fluid body, it develops an internally distributed pressure at all pts of fluid body. This pressure is called fluid pressure.

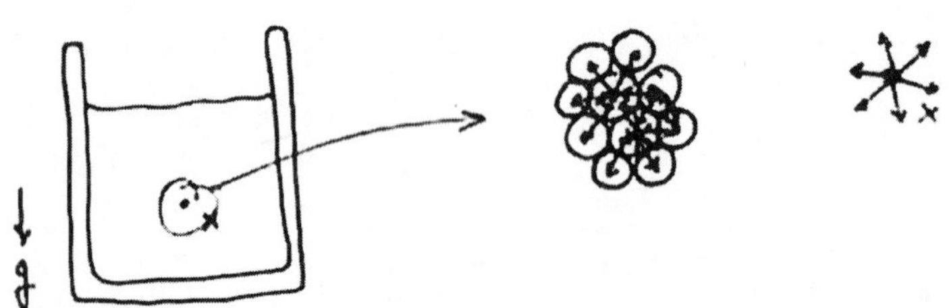

Scan for Video Explanation

Web Reference at www.physicsgalaxy.com

Module-2: Pressure in a Fluid

Some Important points about Fluid Pressure:

(1) It acts at all pts of fluid body. (distributed)

(2) At one point in fluid body it acts uniformly in all direction

(3) If fluid is in contact with any solid surface, fluid pressure will exert a force normal to that surface.

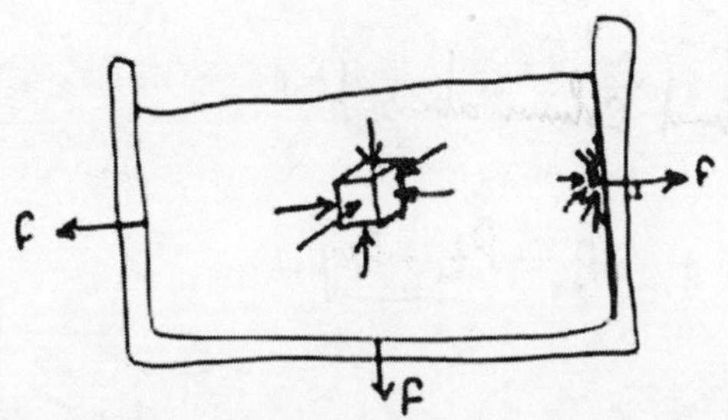

Web Reference at www.physicsgalaxy.com | Scan for Video Explanation

Module-3: Floatation of a Body due to Fluid Pressure

Floatation of a body due to Fluid Pressure:

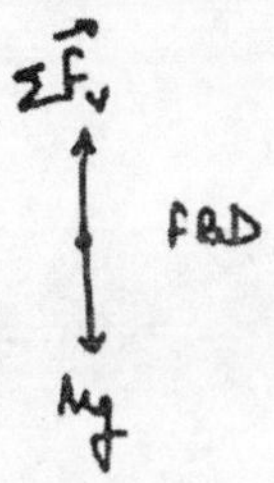

All the forces on body surface due to fluid pressure have their horizontal components balanced.

all vertical components of forces due to fluid pressure balance the wt. of body under floatation.

Web Reference at www.physicsgalaxy.com | Scan for Video Explanation

Module-4: Fluid Pressure due to Gravity

Fluid Pressure due to Gravity:

Fluid Pressure at pt A is due to the whole wt of liquid

Pressure at pt A is

$$P_A = \frac{Mg}{S} = \frac{(hS\rho)g}{S}$$

← Gauge pressure.

$$\boxed{P_A = h\rho g}$$

h → height of fluid column above pt A.

net pressure at pt A $P_{AT} = P_{atm} + h\rho g$.

P_{atm} P_{atm}

h

A

Surface area = S.

Scan for Video Explanation

Web Reference at www.physicsgalaxy.com

Module-4: Fluid Pressure due to Gravity

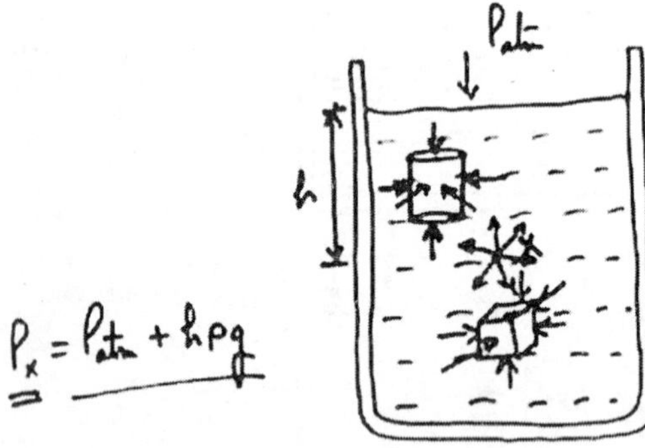

Scan for Video Explanation

Web Reference at www.physicsgalaxy.com

Module-4: Fluid Pressure due to Gravity

Fluid pressure does not depend on shape of Vessel:

$P_x = P_{atm} + h\rho g$

$P_A = P_B = P_C = P_D = P_{atm} + h\rho g$

$P_x = P_{atm} + h\rho g$

Web Reference at www.physicsgalaxy.com | Scan for Video Explanation

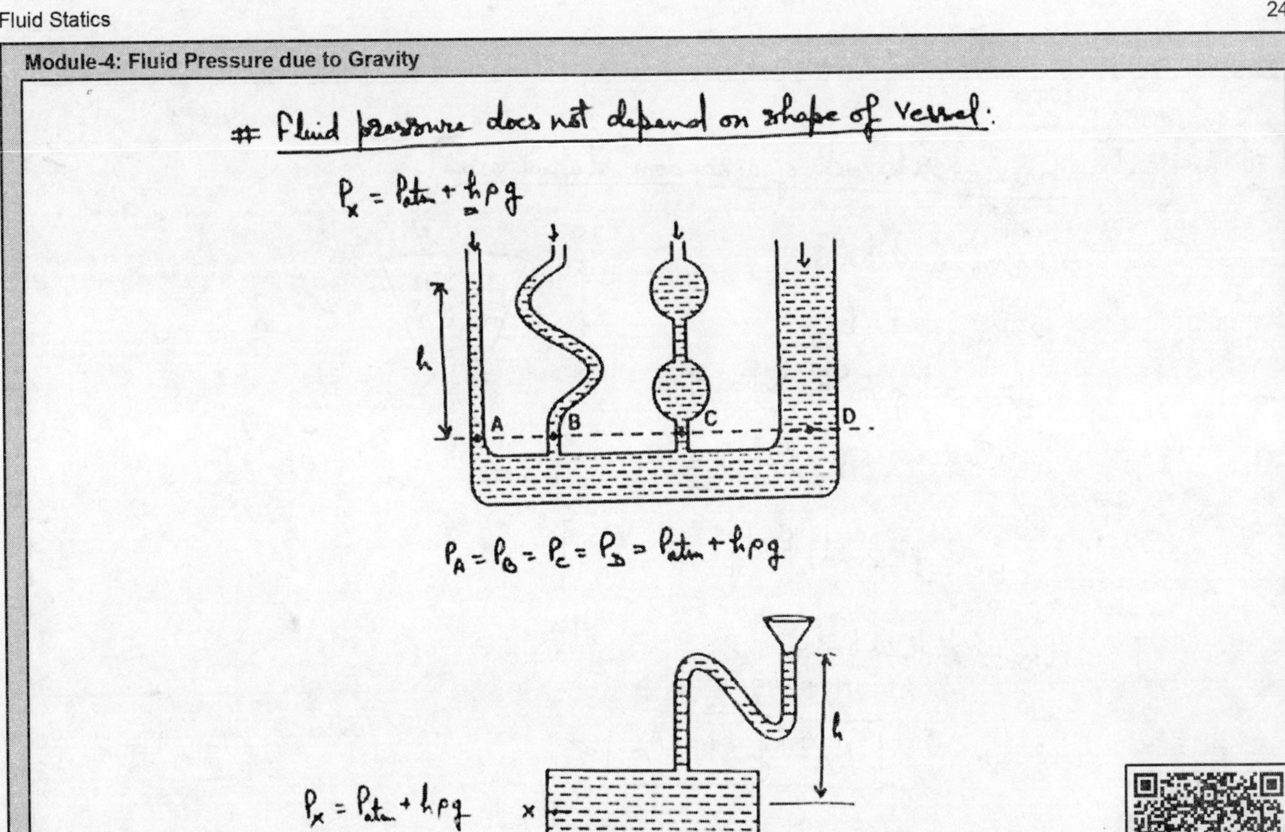

Module-5: Average Pressure on Side Walls of a Vessel

Average Pressure on side walls of a vessel:

Pressure due to fluid at a pt behind the elemental strip is

$P = y\rho g$

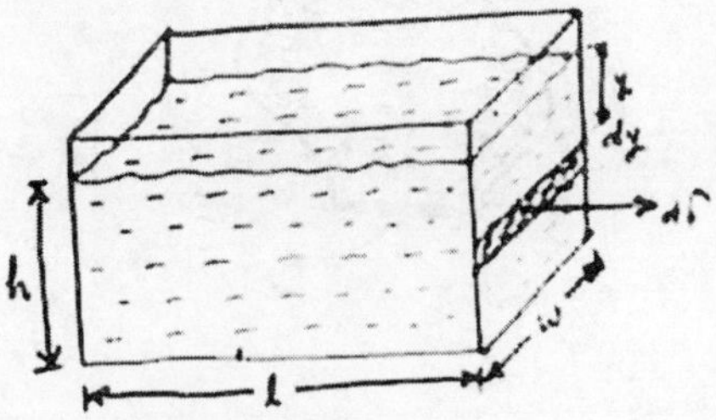

$P_p = h\rho g$.

outward force on elemental strip is

$dF = y\rho g \times w\,dy$

Total force on side wall of vessel due to fluid pressure -

$$F = \int dF = \int_0^h y\rho g w\,dy = \rho g w\left[\frac{y^2}{2}\right]_0^h = \frac{1}{2}\rho g w h^2$$

avg pressure on side wall is $P_{av} = \frac{F}{hw} = \frac{\frac{1}{2}\rho g w h^2}{hw} = \boxed{\frac{1}{2}h\rho g}$

half of the pressure which fluid exert on bottom

Web Reference at www.physicsgalaxy.com | Scan for Video Explanation

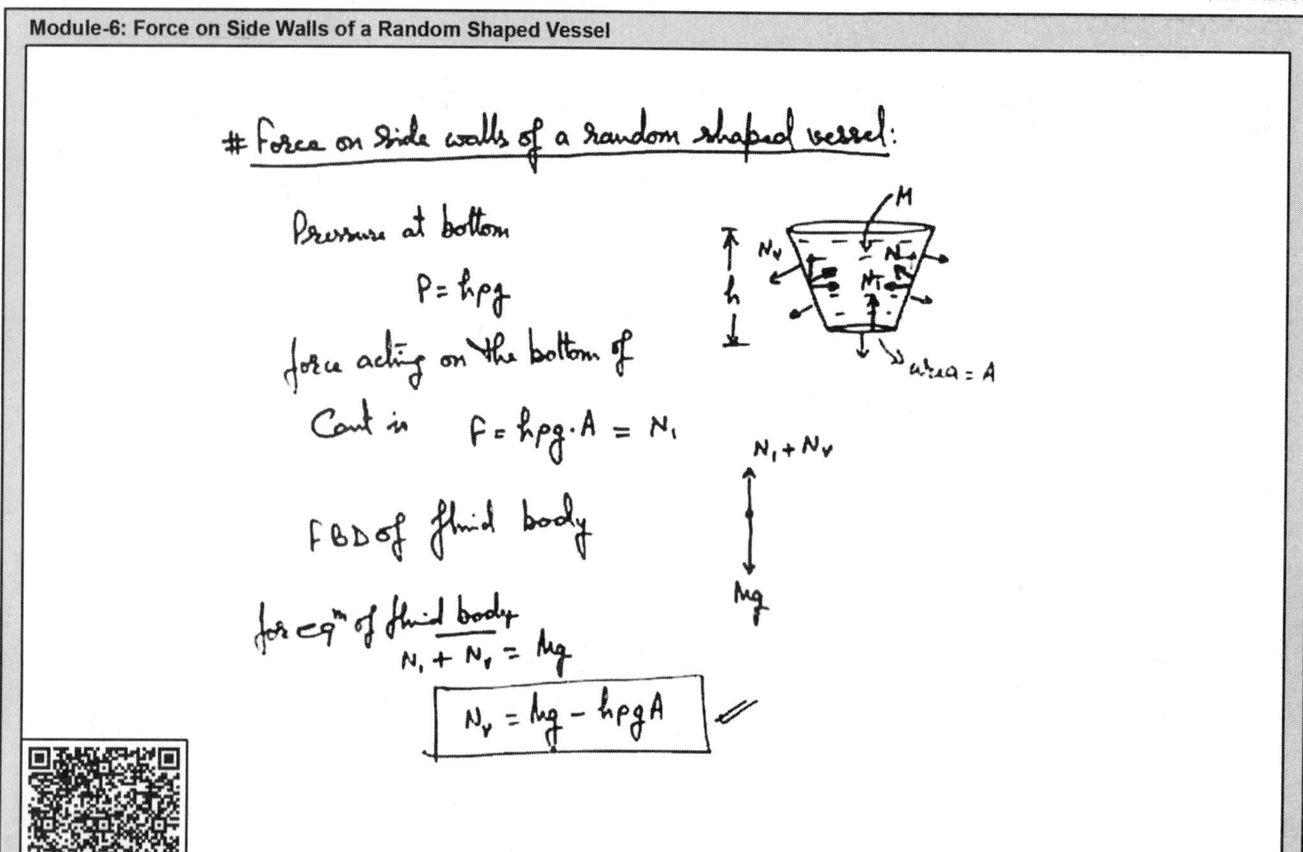

Module-6: Force on Side Walls of a Random Shaped Vessel

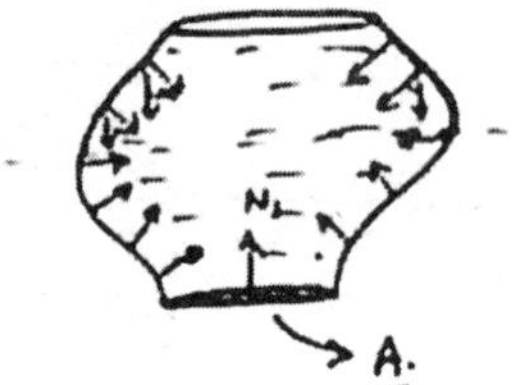

FBD.

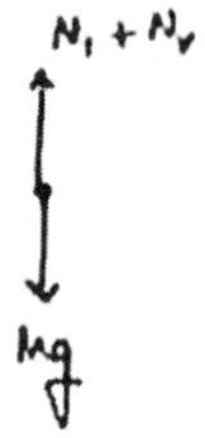

for eqᵐ

$N_1 + N_v = Mg$

$N_v = Mg - N_1$

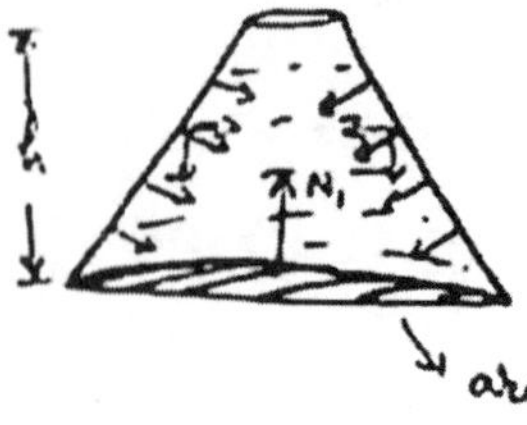

$N_1 + N_v$ / Mg

A.

$N_1 = h\rho g . A$

area = A

N_1 / $Mg + N_v$

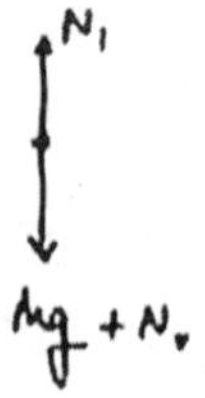

$N_1 = Mg + N_v$

$N_v = N_1 - Mg$

Scan for Video Explanation

Web Reference at www.physicsgalaxy.com

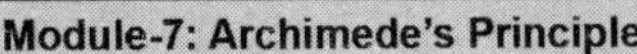

Archimede's Principle:

"A body whether partially or completely submerged in a fluid is buoyed upward by a force due to fluid pressure that is equal to the weight of displaced liquid."

Buoyant force on object

$F_B = F_2 - F_1$

$F_1 = (P_{atm} + l\rho g) \cdot S$

$F_2 = [P_{atm} + (l+h)\rho g] \cdot S$

$\rightarrow F_B = hS\rho g = V\rho g$ [wt of liq displaced by the object]

$P_x = P_{atm} + l\rho g$

$P_y = P_{atm} + (l+h)\rho g$

Web Reference at www.physicsgalaxy.com

Scan for Video Explanation

Module-7: Archimede's Principle

Law of Floatation:

$F_B = V\rho g$

for eq^n of floating object

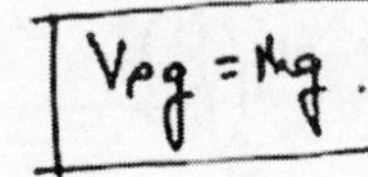

$V\rho g = mg$

Web Reference at www.physicsgalaxy.com

Scan for Video Explanation

Module-8: Buoyant Force on a Body at the Interface of Two Liquids

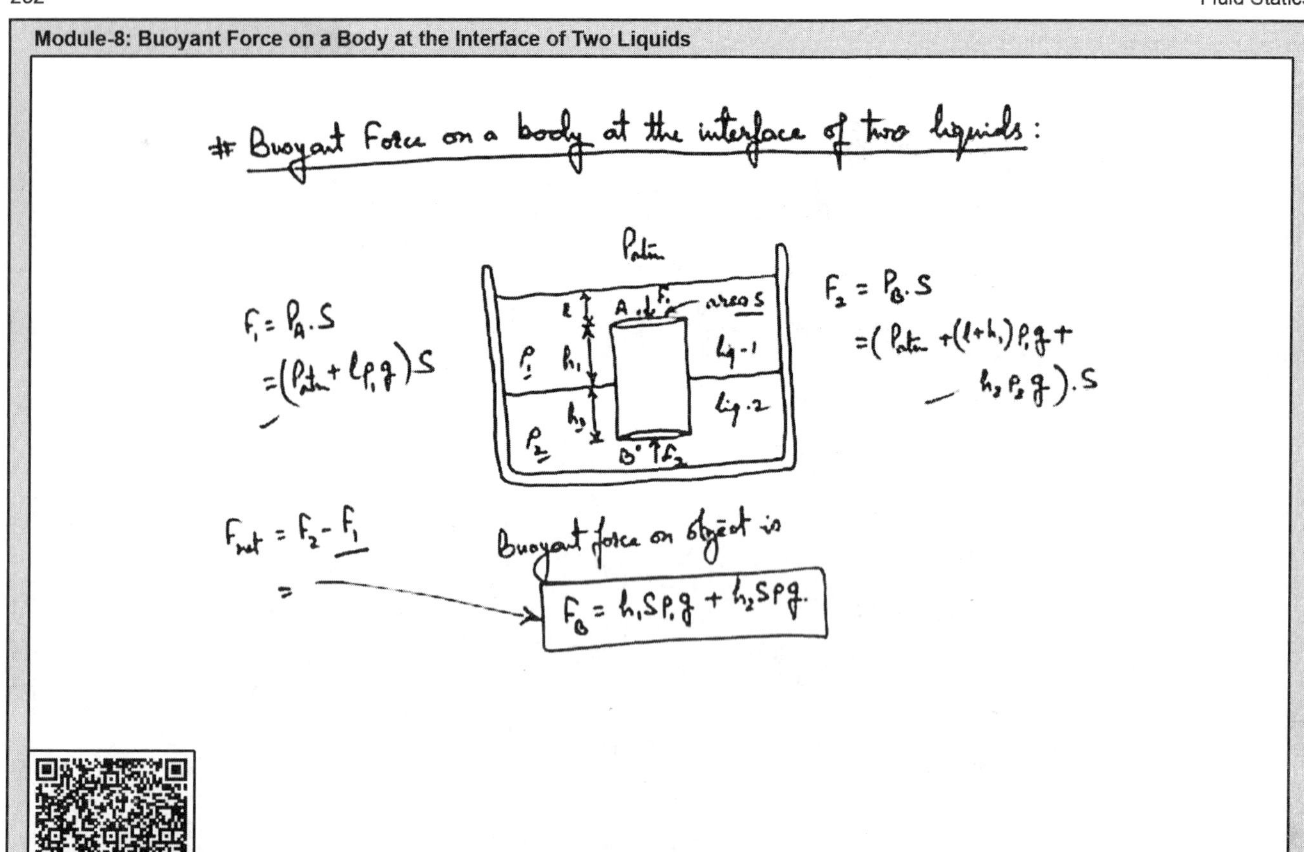

Scan for Video Explanation

Web Reference at www.physicsgalaxy.com

Module-9: Apparent Weight of a Body Submerged in a Liquid

Apparent weight of a body submerged in a liquid:

If mass M is hanging through Sp.

its reading $= \frac{T}{g} = M$ kgf.

Volume of weight $V = \left(\frac{M}{\rho_s}\right)$

Buoyant force on block $F_B = V \rho_l g$

for eqm of weight →

$$T + F_B = Mg$$

$$T = Mg - F_B = Mg - Mg\left(\frac{\rho_l}{\rho_s}\right)$$

apparent wt of object

$$T = Mg\left(1 - \frac{\rho_l}{\rho_s}\right) \rightarrow \text{Reading} = M\left(1 - \frac{\rho_l}{\rho_s}\right) \text{kgf}$$

Sp, T, M, $T = Mg$, Mg

Sp, F_B, M, ρ_s, Mg, ρ_l

eqn: $T + F_B$ ↑, Mg ↓

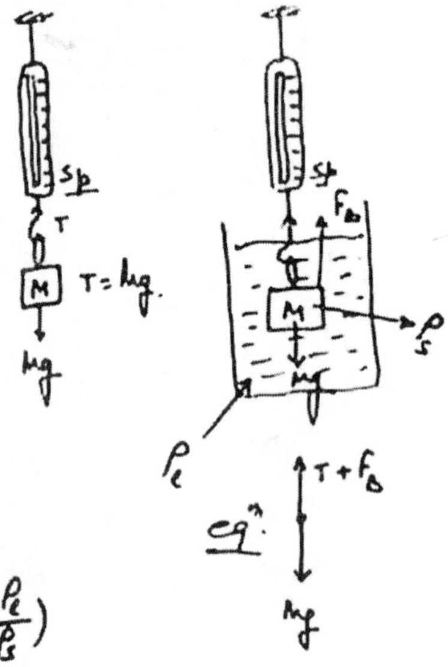

Scan for Video Explanation

Web Reference at www.physicsgalaxy.com

Module-10: Solved Example-1

Ex : **A tank containing water of mass M is placed on a weighing machine. A stone of weight W is hung and lowered in water without touching the sides. If volume of stone is V and density of water is ρ, what will be the reading of weighing machine now.**

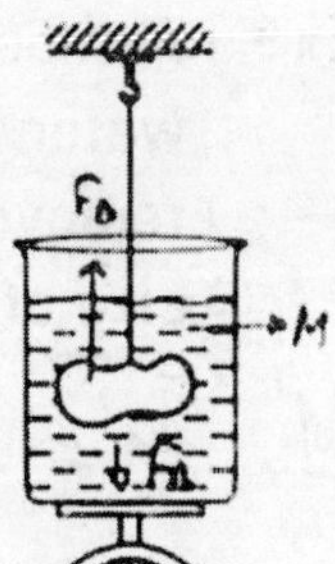

Sol:

Total force on weighing machine is

$$F = Mg + F_B$$

$$F_B = V\rho g$$

Reading of machine in kgf

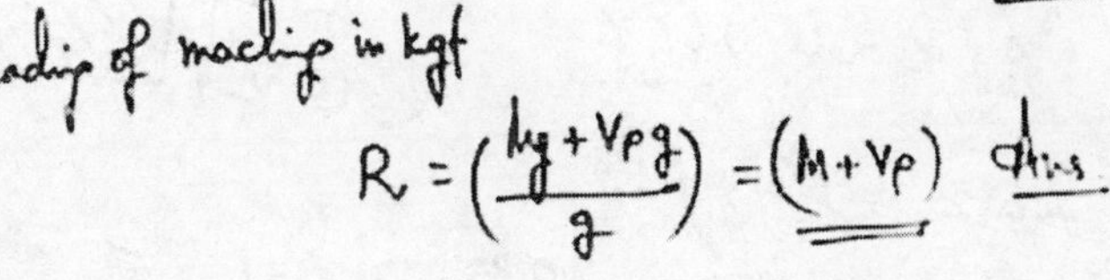

$$R = \left(\frac{Mg + V\rho g}{g}\right) = (M + V\rho) \quad \text{Ans.}$$

Web Reference at www.physicsgalaxy.com | Scan for Video Explanation

Module-11: Solved Example-2

Ex : **A rubber ball of mass m and radius r is submerged in water to a depth h. On releasing the ball, find to what height above the water surface ball will jump. Neglect the resistance of water. Take density of water ρ_ω.**

From pt (i) to (f) using W/E th we get

(f) $v_f = 0$, h_1

h, $F_B = \frac{4}{3}\pi r^3 \rho_\omega g$

(i) $v_i = 0$

$$\overset{k_i}{0} + F_B \cdot h - mg(h + h_1) = 0$$

$$h_1 = \left(\frac{F_B - mg}{mg}\right) h.$$

$$h_1 = \left(\frac{\frac{4}{3}\pi r^3 \rho_\omega - m}{m}\right) h. \quad \text{Ans.}$$

Web Reference at www.physicsgalaxy.com | Scan for Video Explanation

Module-12: Solved Example-3

Ex : A cube of wood supporting 200 gm mass just floats in water in fully submerged state. When the mass is removed cube rises by 2cm above water level. Find the size of cube ? (Take ρ_{water} = 1000 kg/m^3)

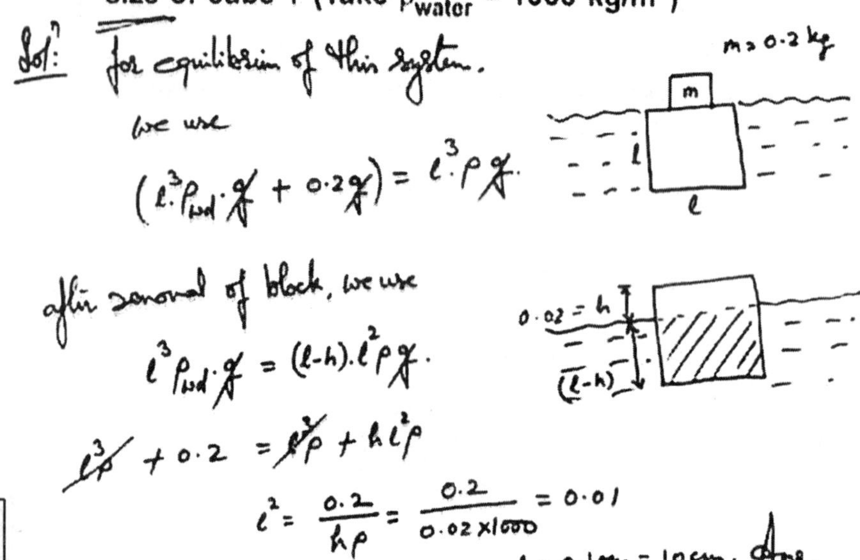

Scan for Video Explanation

Web Reference at www.physicsgalaxy.com

Module-13: Solved Example-4

Ex : A piece of alloy of mass 96gm is composed of two metals whose specific gravity are 11.4 and 7.4 respectively. If the weight of alloy is 86gm in water, find mass of each metal in alloy.

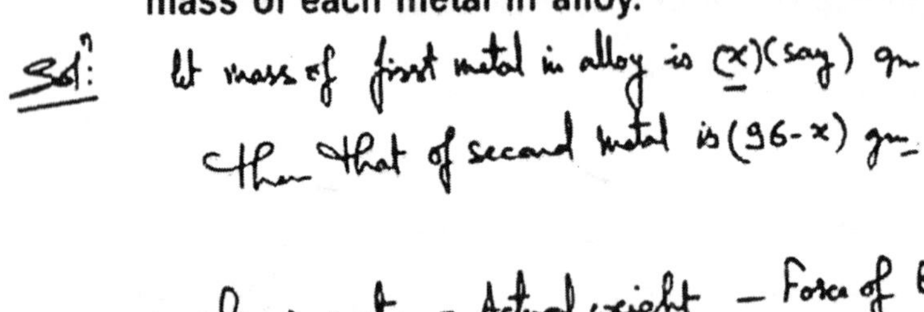

Scan for Video Explanation

Web Reference at www.physicsgalaxy.com

Module-14: Solved Example-5

Ex : **A piece of copper having an internal cavity weighs 264gm in air and 221gm in water. Find the volume of cavity. Take density of copper 8.8 gm/cm³.**

Sol^n:

apparent weight = actual weight − Buoyant force

$$W_{ap} = W - V\rho g$$

$$221 g = 264 g - \left[\frac{264}{8.8} + V_c\right] \cdot 1 \cdot g$$

$$221 = 264 - V_c - \frac{264}{8.8}$$

$$V_c = 13 \text{ cm}^3 \text{ Ans.}$$

Web Reference at www.physicsgalaxy.com | Scan for Video Explanation

Module-15: Pascal's Principle of Pressure Distribution

Pascal's Principle of Pressure Distribution:

" The pressure applied at one pt in an enclosed fluid body is transmitted uniformly to every part of fluid".

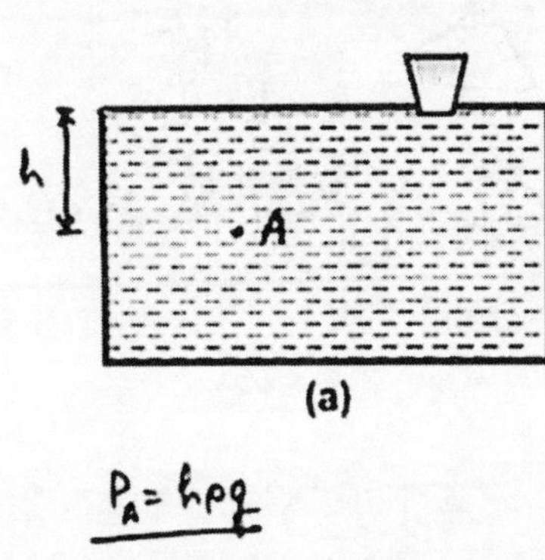

(a)

$P_A = h\rho g$

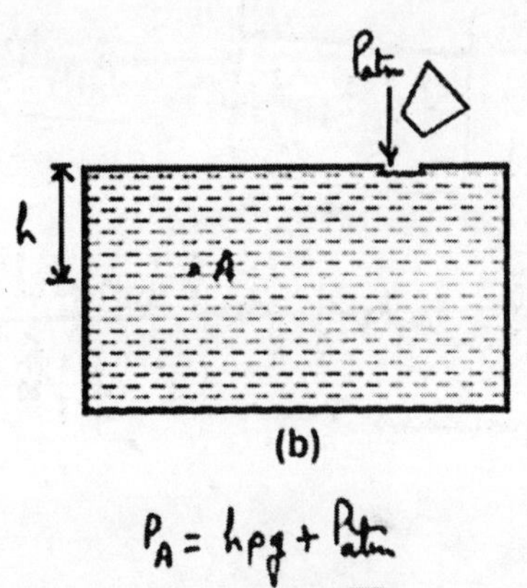

(b)

$P_A = h\rho g + P_{atm}$

Web Reference at www.physicsgalaxy.com | Scan for Video Explanation

Module-15: Pascal's Principle of Pressure Distribution

Applications of Hydraulic Forces:

A, B, F_1, F_2, area $= S_1$, area $= S_2$

$$P_1 = \frac{F_1}{S_1} \qquad P_2 = \frac{F_2}{S_2}$$

$$P_1 = P_2$$

$$\frac{F_1}{S_1} = \frac{F_2}{S_2} \Rightarrow F_1 = F_2\left(\frac{S_1}{S_2}\right)$$

$$\left[\text{if } S_1 > S_2 \Rightarrow F_1 > F_2\right]$$

Scan for Video Explanation

Web Reference at www.physicsgalaxy.com

Module-16: Pressure at Different Levels in a Liquid

Pressure at different levels in a liquid:

- In a static fluid, its free surface is always normal to the effective acceleration acting on the fluid.

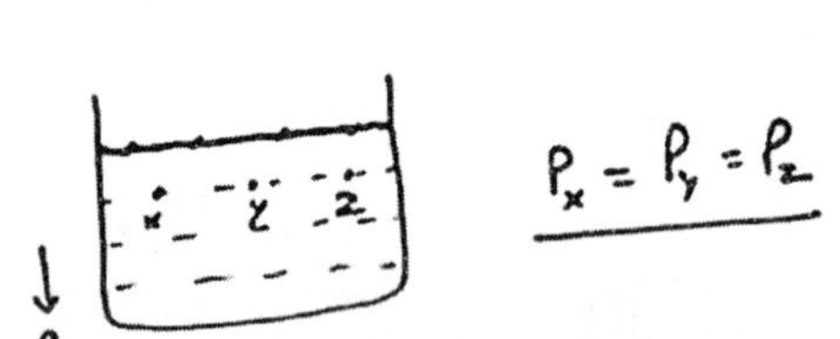

liq., A, B, C, g

$$P_A = P_B = P_C$$

- In a layer of fluid parallel to free surface of fluid, pressure remains same for all pts.

Scan for Video Explanation

Web Reference at www.physicsgalaxy.com

Module-16: Pressure at Different Levels in a Liquid

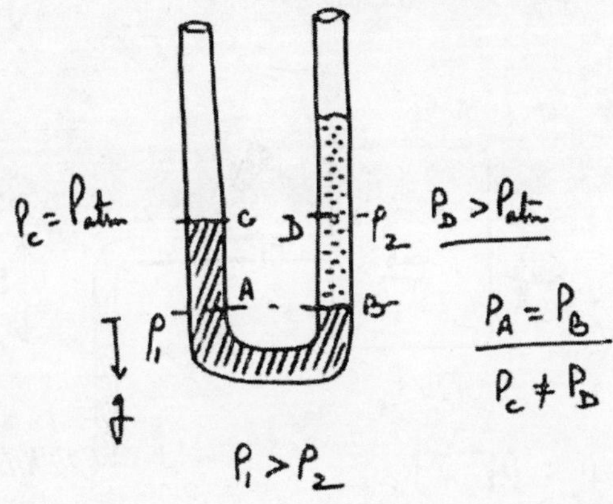

Web Reference at www.physicsgalaxy.com

Scan for Video Explanation

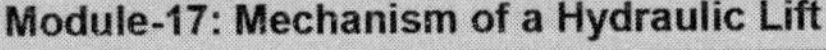

Module-17: Mechanism of a Hydraulic Lift

Mechanism of a Hydraulic Lift:

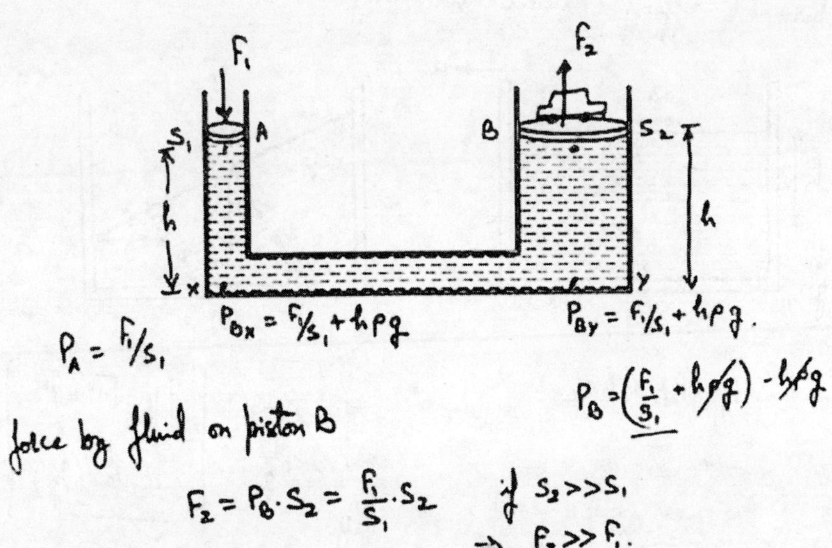

Web Reference at www.physicsgalaxy.com

Scan for Video Explanation

Module-18: Concept of Open tube Manometer

Concept of Open Tube Manometer:

used to measure pressure gauge.

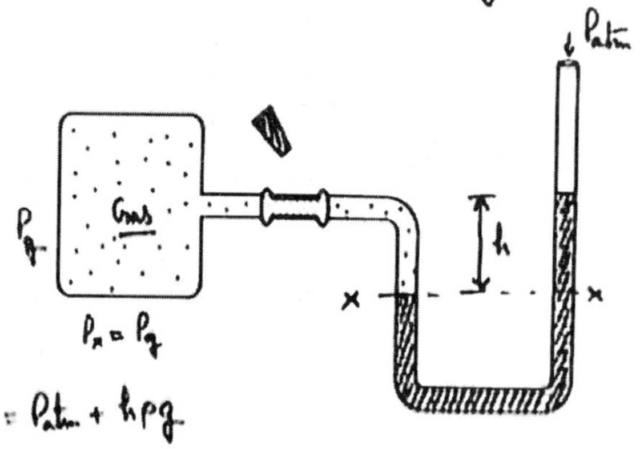

P_{atm}

Gas

P_g

h

x x

$P_x = P_g$

$P_x = P_{atm} + h\rho g$

$$P_g - P_{atm} = h\rho g$$

Scan for Video Explanation

Web Reference at www.physicsgalaxy.com

Module-19: Pressure Distribution in an Accelerated Frame

Pressure distribution in an accelerated frame:

In a static fluid free surface of fluid is always normal to effective acceleration acting on it.

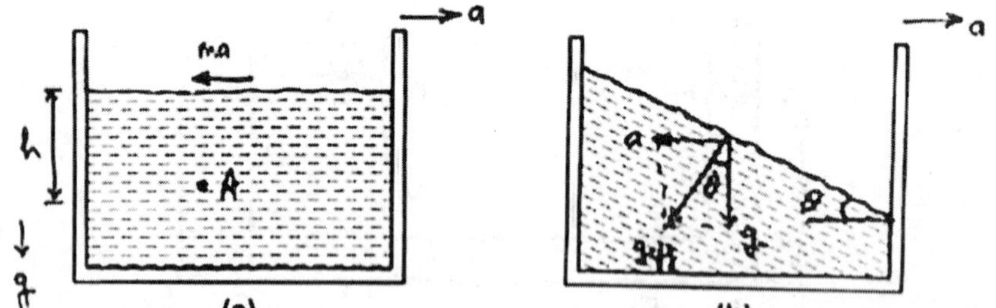

a

ma

h

A

g

(a)

a

a

θ

θ

g

g_{eff}

(b)

$P_A = P_{atm} + h\rho g$

a

θ

g

g_{eff}

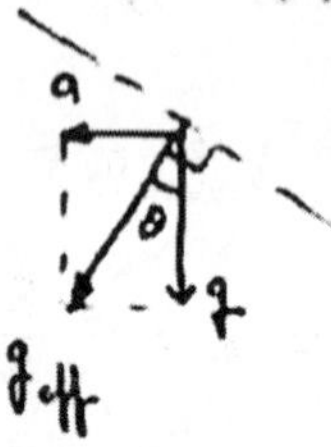

$$g_{eff} = \sqrt{a^2 + g^2}$$

$$\theta = \tan^{-1}(a/g)$$

Scan for Video Explanation

Web Reference at www.physicsgalaxy.com

Module-19: Pressure Distribution in an Accelerated Frame

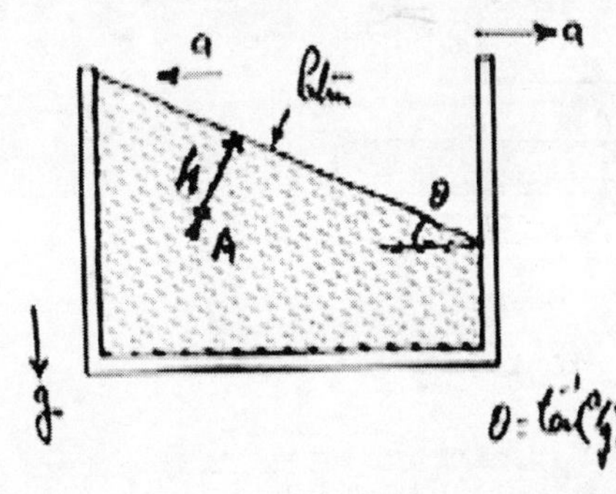

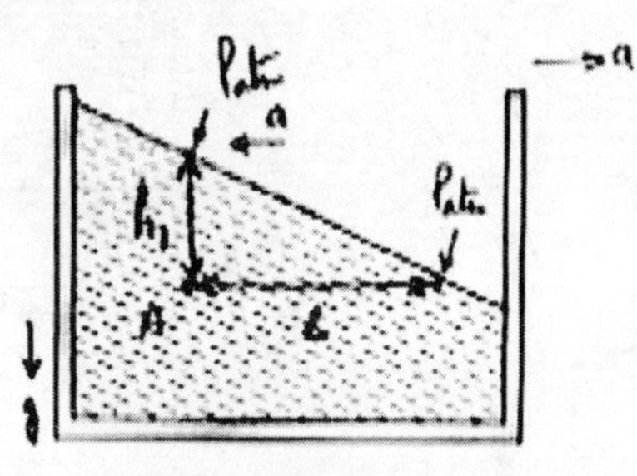

$\theta = \tan^{-1}(a/g)$

$P_A = P_{atm} + h_1 \rho g$ ✓

$P_A = P_{atm} + l \rho a$ ✓

$P_A = P_{atm} + h\rho\sqrt{g^2+a^2}$

Web Reference at www.physicsgalaxy.com | Scan for Video Explanation

Module-20: Pressure Distribution in a Closed Accelerated Container

Pressure distribution in a closed Accelerated container:

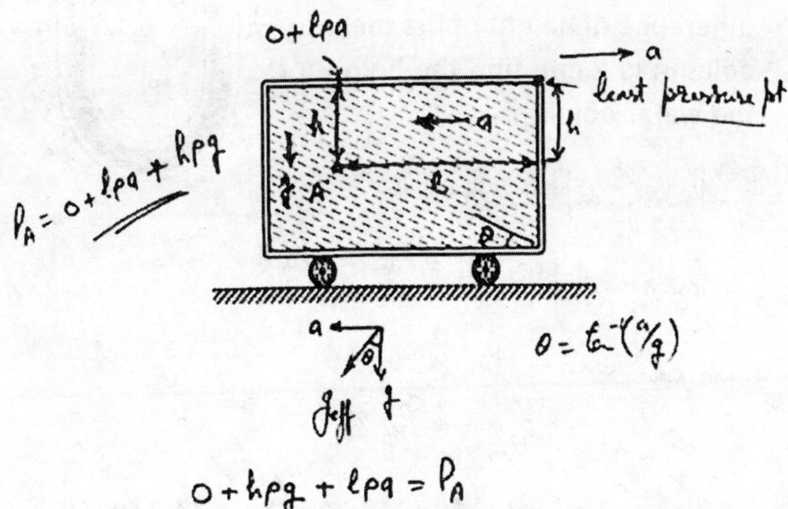

$0 + h\rho g + l\rho a = P_A$

$$\boxed{P_A = h\rho g + l\rho a}$$

Web Reference at www.physicsgalaxy.com | Scan for Video Explanation

Module-21: Pressure Distribution in a Rotating tube Filled with a Liquid

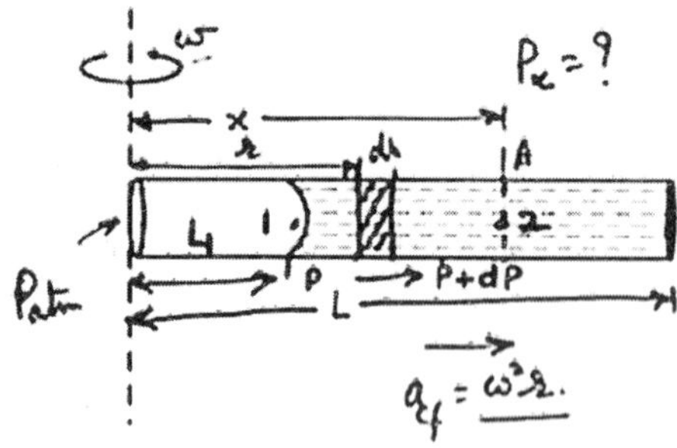

$$dP = dr \cdot \rho \cdot \omega^2 r$$

$$P_2 - P_1 = \int dP = \int_{L_1}^{x} \rho\omega^2 r\, dr = \rho\omega^2 \left[\frac{r^2}{2}\right]_{L_1}^{x}$$

$$P_2 - P_1 = \frac{1}{2}\rho\omega^2\left[x^2 - L_1^2\right]$$

$$\boxed{P_A = P_{atm} + \frac{1}{2}\rho\omega^2\left(x^2 - L_1^2\right)}$$

Scan for Video Explanation

Web Reference at www.physicsgalaxy.com

Module-22: Solved Example-6

Ex : The liquids shown in figure in the two arms are mercury (specific gravity = 13.6) and water. If the difference of height of the mercury column is 2 cm, find the height of the water column.

Pressure at pt A $\quad P_A = P_{atm} + h\rho_w g$

Pressure at pt B $\quad P_B = P_{atm} + h_1\rho_{Hg} g$

we can use $\quad P_A = P_B$

$$h\rho_w g = h_1\rho_{Hg} g$$

$$h = h_1 \times 13.6 = 2 \times 13.6 = 27.2\ \text{cm} \quad \text{Ans.}$$

Scan for Video Explanation

Web Reference at www.physicsgalaxy.com

Module-23: Solved Example-7

Ex : **An open U-tube of uniform cross section contains some mercury. When 40.8 cm length of water is poured in one arm of U-tube, find how high does the mercury rise in other arm from its initial level ? Take $\rho_\omega = 1 gm/cm^3$ and $\rho_{Hg} = 13.6 gm/cm^3$.**

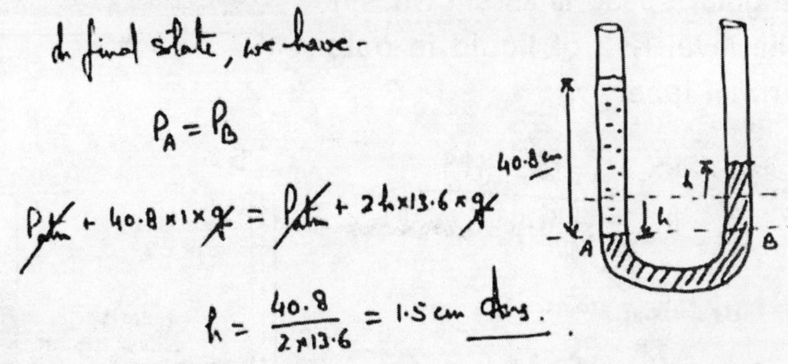

Web Reference at www.physicsgalaxy.com | **Scan for Video Explanation**

Module-24: Solved Example-8

Ex : **In the figure shown the liquid in manometer tube is of specific gravity 0.9. If the difference in levels of the liquid in tube is 40 cm, find the height difference of water level in the two tanks.**

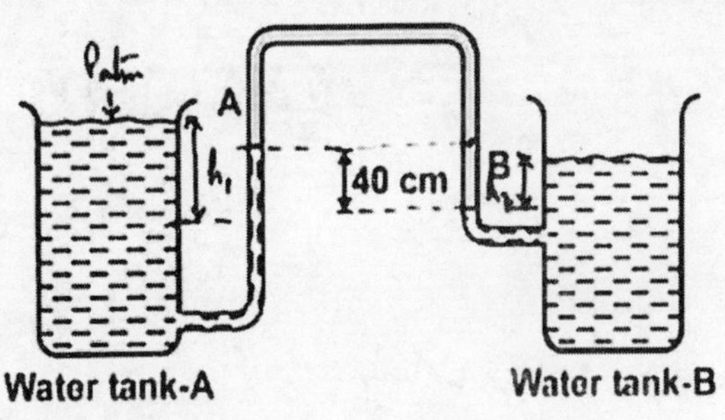

$$P_A + 40.\rho_\ell.g = P_B$$

$$P_{atm} + (h_1 - 40)\times 1\times g + 40\times 0.9.g = P_{atm} + h_2\times 1\times g$$

$$h_1 - 40 + 40\times 0.9 = h_2$$

$$h_1 - h_2 = 40\times 0.1 = 4\text{ cm Ans.}$$

Web Reference at www.physicsgalaxy.com | **Scan for Video Explanation**

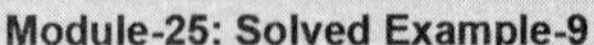
Module-25: Solved Example-9

Ex : Figure shows a U-tube of base length L in which a liquid of density ρ is filled such that it completely fills the base length only. If the tube is now rotated at angular speed ω as shown, find the level rise of liquid in outer arm of tube.

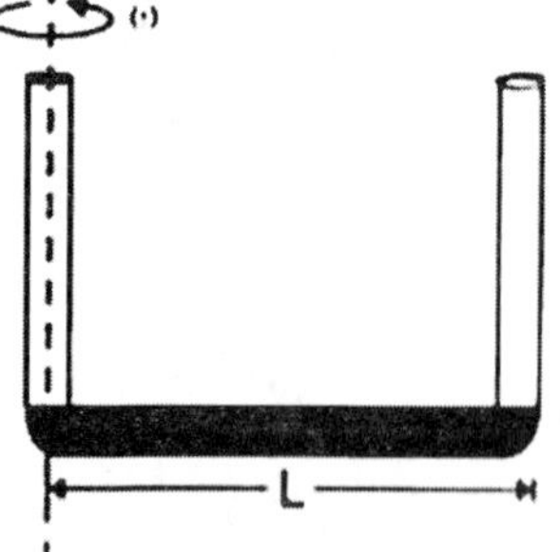

Sol: Pressure at x $P_x = P_{atm} + y\rho g$

on the base length of U-tube, we have

$$dP = dx.\rho.\omega^2 x$$

$$P_x - P_{atm} = \int_y^L dP = \int \rho\omega^2 x\,dx$$

$$P_x = P_{atm} + \frac{\rho\omega^2}{2}[L^2 - y^2] = P_{atm} + y\rho g$$

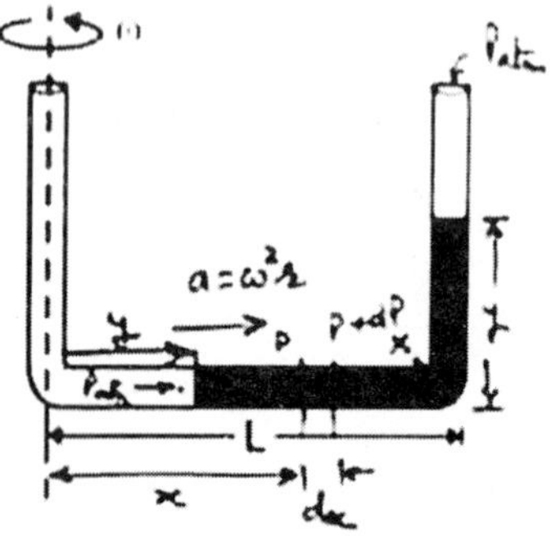

Scan for Video Explanation

Web Reference at www.physicsgalaxy.com

Module-25: Solved Example-9

$$\frac{\rho\omega^2}{2}[L^2 - y^2] = y\rho g$$

$$y^2 + \frac{2g}{\omega^2}y - L^2 = 0$$

on Solving

$$y = \frac{-\frac{2g}{\omega^2} + \sqrt{4g^2/\omega^4 + 4L^2}}{2} \quad \leftarrow \text{Ans.}$$

Scan for Video Explanation

Web Reference at www.physicsgalaxy.com

Chapter 13
Fluid Dynamics

Lecture Notes Modules

Module-1: Introduction to Fluid Dynamics
Module-2: Representation of Streamlines
Module-3: Velocity Profile of a Flowing Fluid
Module-4: Turbulent Flow
Module-5: Equation of Continuity
Module-6: Solved Example-1
Module-7: Bernoulli's Theorem
Module-8: Pressure-Velocity Trade-off
Module-9: Solved Example-2
Module-10: Solved Example-3
Module-11: Solved Example-4
Module-12: Solved Example-5
Module-13: Working and Application of Pitot Tube
Module-14: Working and Application of Venturimeter
Module-15: Solved Example-6
Module-16: Solved Example-7
Module-17: Torecelli's Theorem
Module-18: Solved Example-8
Module-19: Solved Example-9
Module-20: Cross-section of a Freely Falling Liquid
Module-21: Reaction due to Ejection of a Liquid
Module-22: Solved Example-10
Module-23: Solved Example-11

Module-1: Introduction to Fluid Dynamics

Fluid Dynamics: study & analyze motion of fluids.

For basic analysis we use ideal fluids instead of real fluids.

For an ideal fluid we make some assumptions –

(1) Streamline flow: Also termed as laminar flow.
at a point vel of fluid part does not change in mag/dir.

(2) Incompressible flow: we assume that during flow fluid density remain Constant

(3) Non viscous flow: For ideal fluids we neglect viscous forces between fluid layers.

(4) Irrotational flow: we assume that fluid particles do not impart any rotational motion to the uniform bodies in path of fluid which are moving along with fluid.

Scan for Video Explanation

Web Reference at www.physicsgalaxy.com

Module-2: Representation of Streamlines

Representation of Streamlines: hypothetical lines which represent fluid flow.

- Stream lines in a flowing fluid are the representation of fluid particles motion
- For a flowing fluid dir of flow vel of fluid part is given by the dir of stream lines & speed of fluid flow is meas by the density of streamlines
- In a region where flow vel is more ⇒ s. lines are denser & in a region where flow vel is less ⇒ s. lines are rarer.

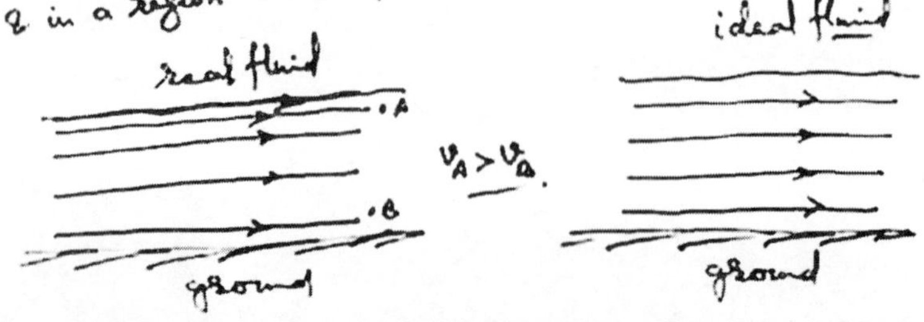

real fluid

ideal fluid

$v_A > v_B$.

ground

ground

Scan for Video Explanation

Web Reference at www.physicsgalaxy.com

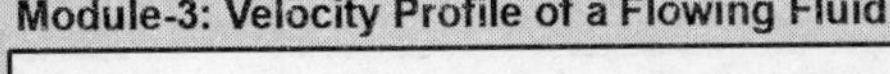

Module-3: Velocity Profile of a Flowing Fluid

Velocity Profile of a flowing fluid:

Due to friction between layers of a fluid, the particles which are close to walls/surface of a pipe tend to move slowly (due to fr) and those which are away from walls/surface move relatively fast.

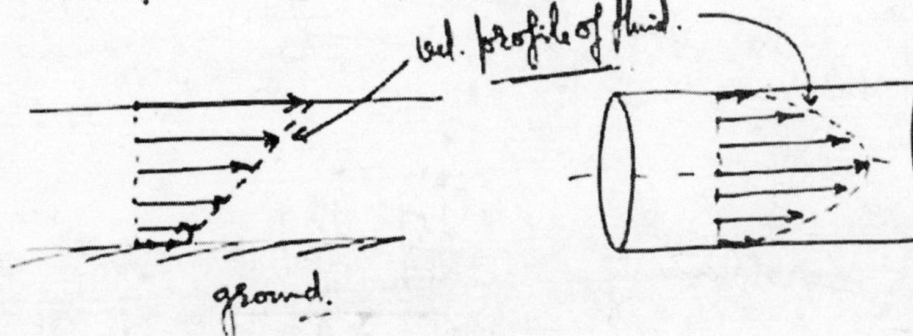

Web Reference at www.physicsgalaxy.com

Scan for Video Explanation

Module-4: Turbulent Flow

Turbulent Flow:

When in a streamline flow, flow vel of fluid increases, at a certain point flow particles become chaotic, no streamlines exist after this & this flow is called turbulent flow.

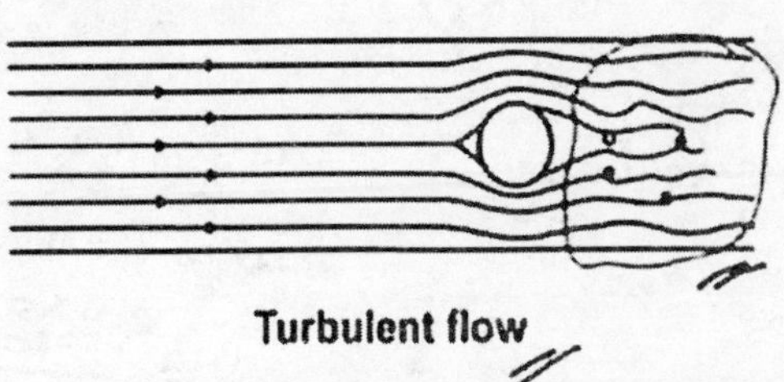

Turbulent flow

Web Reference at www.physicsgalaxy.com

Scan for Video Explanation

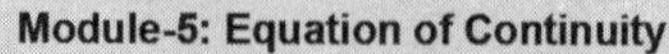

Module-5: Equation of Continuity

Equation of Continuity:

This eqn defines that for streamline flow for a fluid the mass entering per second at one end is equal the mass leaving/sec at the other end.

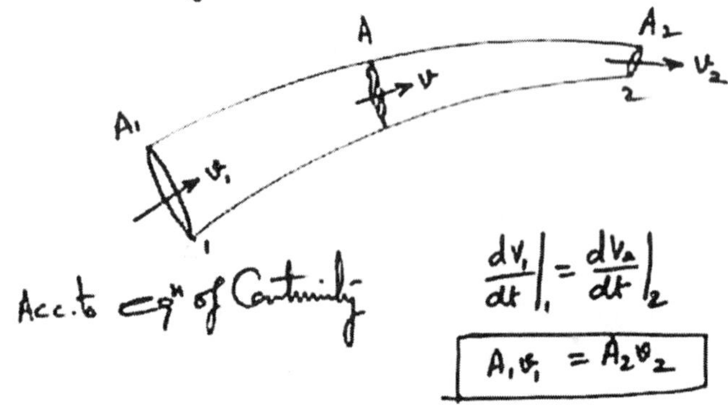

Acc. to eqn of Continuity

$$\left.\frac{dV_1}{dt}\right|_1 = \left.\frac{dV_2}{dt}\right|_2$$

$$\boxed{A_1v_1 = A_2v_2}$$

$$Av = \text{Constant}$$

Scan for Video Explanation

Web Reference at www.physicsgalaxy.com

Module-6: Solved Example-1

Ex : **A river of width 12 m flowing at 20 kph mixes with another river of width 8 m flowing at 16 kph and spreads in another stream of width 16 m. Find the flow velocity of water after mixing assuming the depth of rivers are same.**

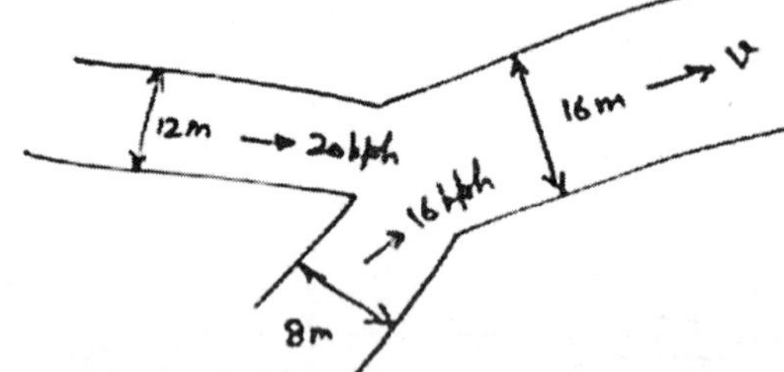

Acc. to Eqn of Continuity

$$A_1v_1 + A_2v_2 = A_3v_3$$

$$12\times 20 + 8\times 16 = 16\times v$$

$$v = \frac{12\times 20 + 8\times 16}{16}$$

$$= 15 + 8 = 23 \text{ kph Ans.}$$

Scan for Video Explanation

Web Reference at www.physicsgalaxy.com

Module-7: Bernoulli's Theorem

Bernoulli's Theorem:

This is a theorem about conservation of energy for a flowing fluid from one end to another in streamline flow.

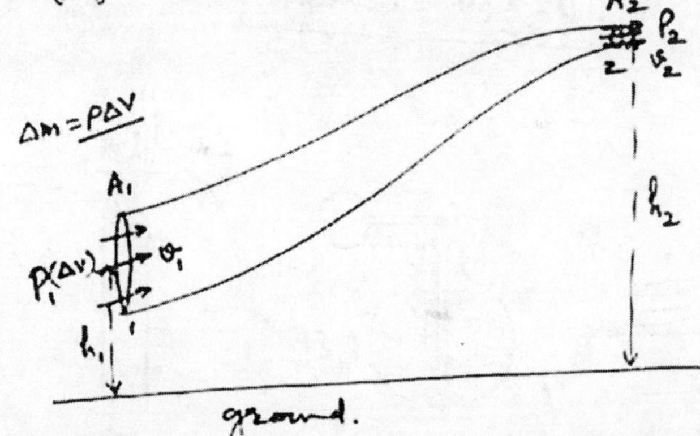

use W/E theorem for a volume ΔV of fluid from end 1 to end 2,

$$\frac{1}{2}[\rho \Delta V] v_1^2 + P_1 \Delta V - [\rho \Delta V] g(h_2 - h_1) - P_2 \Delta V = \frac{1}{2}[\rho \Delta V] v_2^2$$

(K_i … K_f)

Web Reference at www.physicsgalaxy.com

Scan for Video Explanation

Module-7: Bernoulli's Theorem

$$\frac{1}{2}[\rho \Delta V] v_1^2 + P_1 \Delta V - [\rho \Delta V] g(h_2 - h_1) - P_2 \Delta V = \frac{1}{2}[\rho \Delta V] v_2^2$$

$$\frac{1}{2}\rho v_1^2 + P_1 - \rho g h_2 + \rho g h_1 - P_2 = \frac{1}{2}\rho v_2^2$$

$$\frac{1}{2}\rho v_1^2 + P_1 + \rho g h_1 = \frac{1}{2}\rho v_2^2 + P_2 + \rho g h_2$$

at all sections of the flowing fluid body, we can use -

Bernoulli's Eqn → $\boxed{\frac{1}{2}\rho v^2 + P + \rho g h = \text{Constant}}$

- $\frac{1}{2}\rho v^2$ → KE per unit vol of fluid
- P → Pressure Energy per unit volume.
- $\rho g h$ → grav. PE per unit volume w.r.to given Ref.

Web Reference at www.physicsgalaxy.com

Scan for Video Explanation

Module-8: Pressure-Velocity Trade-off

Pressure-Velocity Trade-off:

For a fluid flowing at a horizontal level acc. to Bernoulli's theorem, we use –

$$P + \frac{1}{2}\rho v^2 = \text{Constant}$$

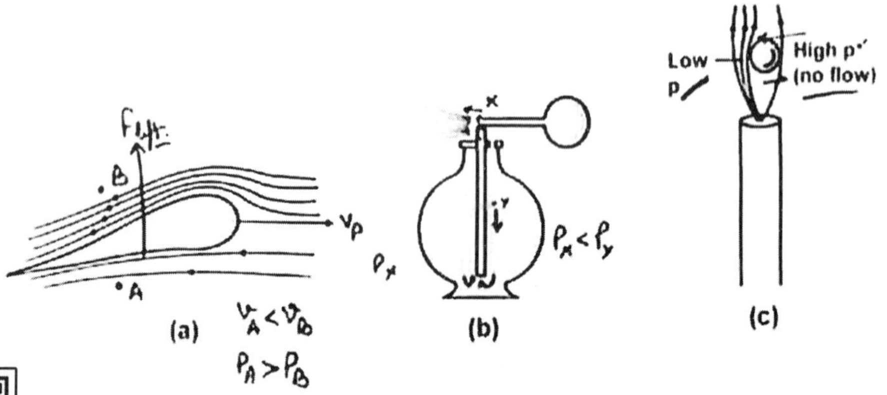

F_{lift}, B, A, v_p, P_x

(a) $v_A < v_B$

$P_A > P_B$

x, y, $P_x < P_y$

(b)

Low p, High p (no flow)

(c)

Scan for Video Explanation

Web Reference at www.physicsgalaxy.com

Module-9: Solved Example-2

Ex : In a horizontal pipe line, the flowing oil pressure falls by 8 N/m^2 between two points separated by 1 km. Find the change in kinetic energy per kg of oil at these points. Take density of oil 800 kg/m^3.

Sol^n: By using Bernoulli's theorem, we have

$$P_1 + \frac{1}{2}\rho v_1^2 = P_2 + \frac{1}{2}\rho v_2^2$$

$$\frac{1}{2}\rho(v_2^2 - v_1^2) = P_1 - P_2 = 8 \text{ N/m}^2$$

$$\text{change in KE/kg} = \frac{1}{2}(v_2^2 - v_1^2) = \frac{P_1 - P_2}{\rho} = \frac{8}{800} = 0.01 \text{ J/kg} \quad \text{Ans.}$$

Scan for Video Explanation

Web Reference at www.physicsgalaxy.com

Module-10: Solved Example-3

Ex : Calculate the gross lift force on an airplane wing of length 10 m and width 2 m. The air speed above the wing is 120 m/s and below the wing is 90 m/s. Take air density 1.3 kg/m^3.

Sol^n:

lift force $F = (P_B - P_T) \times A$

F_{lift}, P_T, v_T, T, B, v_B, P_B

$P_B > P_T$

we use Bernoulli's theorem at pts T & B –

$$P_T + \frac{1}{2}\rho v_T^2 = P_B + \frac{1}{2}\rho v_B^2$$

$$P_B - P_T = \frac{1}{2}\rho (v_T^2 - v_B^2)$$

$$= \frac{1}{2} \times 1.3 \times [(120)^2 - (90)^2] = 4.1 \times 10^3 \text{ N/m}^2$$

Gross lift force $F = (P_B - P_T) \times A$

$$= 4.1 \times 10^3 \times 20 = 8.2 \times 10^4 \text{ N} \quad \text{Ans.}$$

Web Reference at www.physicsgalaxy.com

Scan for Video Explanation

Module-11: Solved Example-4

Ex : Water flows through a tube which has one end A at a height 20 cm above ground and cross-sectional area 1 cm^2 and other end B at a height 15 cm above ground and cross-sectional area 0.5 cm^2. The speed of water at A is 10 cm/s find the speed at end B and pressure difference at A and B.

Using eq^n of Continuity

A (P_A), 1 cm^2, 10 cm/s, (P_B), B, 0.5 cm^2, v_B, h_1 = 20 cm, h_2 = 15 cm.

$$A_1 v_1 = A_2 v_2$$

$$1 \times 10 = 0.5 \times v_B$$

$$v_B = 20 \text{ cm/s} \quad \text{Ans.}$$

using Bernoulli's Eq^n at ends A & B.

$v_A = 0.1$

$v_B = 0.2$

$$P_A + \frac{1}{2}\rho v_A^2 + \rho g h_1 = P_B + \frac{1}{2}\rho v_B^2 + \rho g h_2$$

$$P_B - P_A = \rho g (h_1 - h_2) + \frac{1}{2}\rho (v_A^2 - v_B^2)$$

$$= 1000 \times 10 \times 0.05 + \frac{1}{2} \times 1000 [0.01 - 0.04] = 500 - 15$$

$$= 485 \text{ N/m}^2 \quad \text{Ans}$$

Web Reference at www.physicsgalaxy.com

Scan for Video Explanation

Module-12: Solved Example-5

Ex : In a bucket shown in figure a liquid of density 1.25×10^3 kg/m^3 is kept. Find speed at which liquid will be coming out if the bottom surface is removed and its top level is maintained by pouring the liquid through the tap.

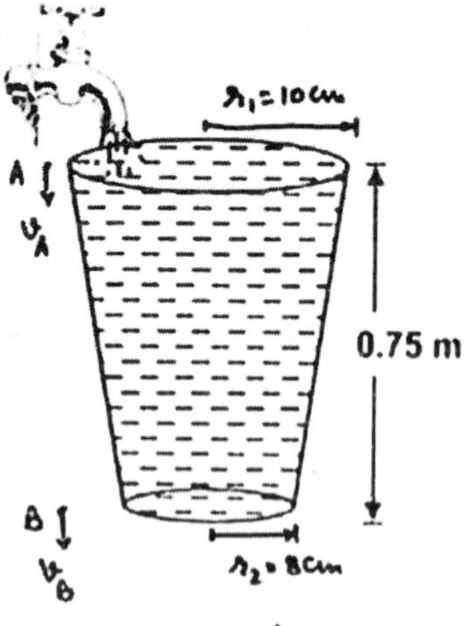

Sol^n: using Bernoulli's eq^n at A and B.

$$P_{atm} + \frac{1}{2}\rho v_A^2 + \rho g h = P_{atm} + \frac{1}{2}\rho v_B^2$$

$$A_A v_A = A_B v_B$$

$$v_B = v_A \cdot \frac{r_1^2}{r_2^2}$$

$$v_A = v_B \cdot \frac{r_2^2}{r_1^2}$$

$$v_B^2\left[1 - \frac{r_2^4}{r_1^4}\right] = 2gh$$

$$v_B = \sqrt{\frac{2gh}{1 - r_2^4/r_1^4}} = \sqrt{\frac{2 \times 10 \times 0.75}{1 - (0.8)^4}} = 6.45 \text{ m/s}$$

Ans.

Scan for Video Explanation

Web Reference at www.physicsgalaxy.com

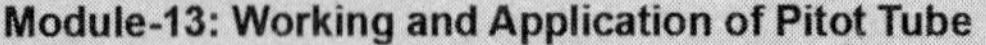

Module-13: Working and Application of Pitot Tube

Working and Application of a Pitot Tube:

A device used to meas flow vel of a fluid.

M, v, $\rightarrow v$, A, h, B, pitot tube, ρ

If flowing fluid is a gas.

$$P_A - P_B = h\rho g$$

$$P_A - P_B = h(\rho - \rho_l)g$$

If flowing fluid is a liquids

If we use Bernoulli's th at pts A & B in the flowing fluid

$$P_A + 0 = P_B + \frac{1}{2}\rho v^2 \Rightarrow v = \sqrt{\frac{2(P_A - P_B)}{\rho}}$$

Scan for Video Explanation

Web Reference at www.physicsgalaxy.com

Module-14: Working and Application of Venturimeter

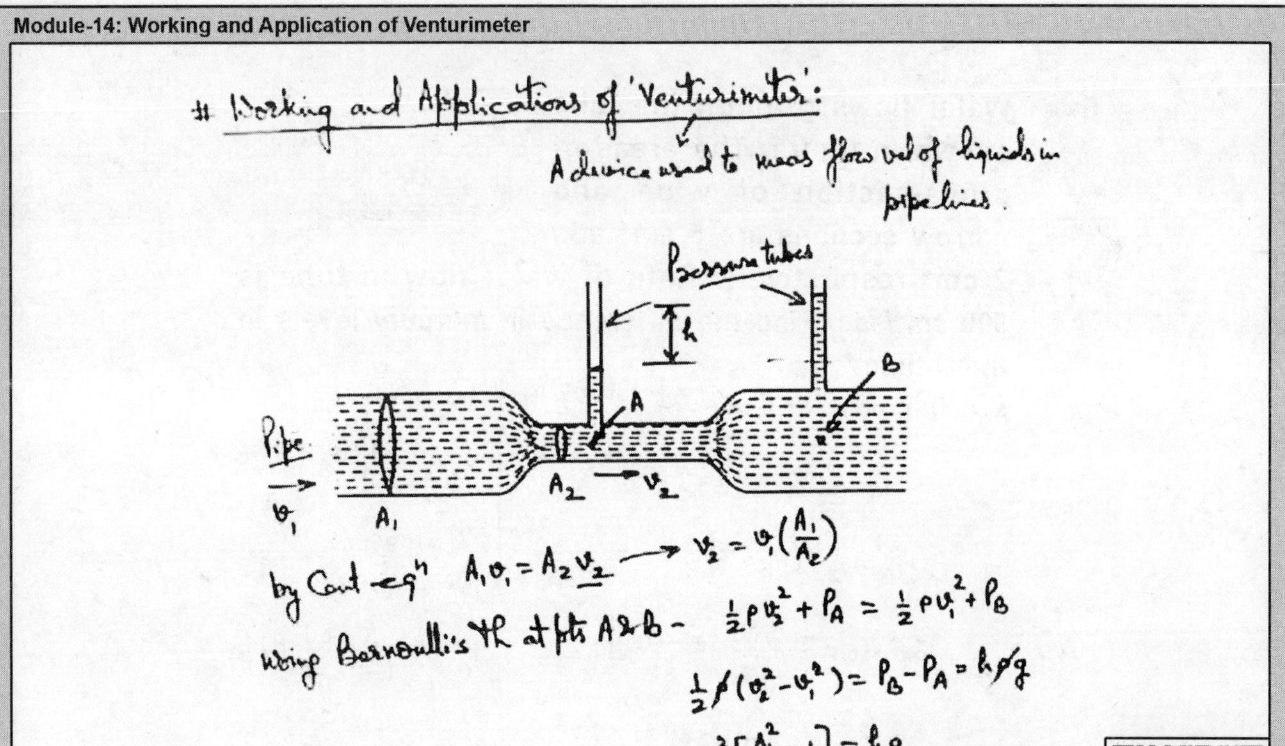

Web Reference at www.physicsgalaxy.com | Scan for Video Explanation

Module-15: Solved Example-6

Ex : In a venturi meter diameter of the pipe is 4 cm and that of constriction is 3 cm. When water flows the heights of water level in pressure tubes are 15 cm and 20 cm. Find the discharge rate of pipe. (Take g = 10 m/s²)

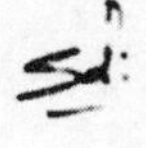

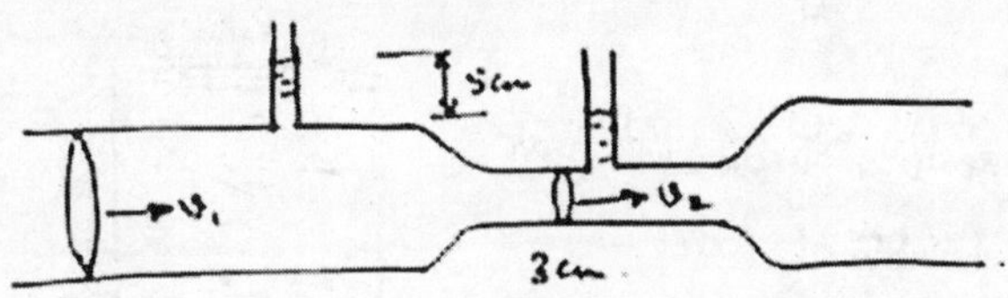

4cm

in venturimeter the flow vel of fluid in pipe is given as -

$$v_1 = \sqrt{\frac{2gh}{\left(\frac{A_1^2}{A_2^2} - 1\right)}} = \sqrt{\frac{2 \times 10 \times 0.05}{\left(\frac{4}{3}\right)^4 - 1}} = \sqrt{\frac{1}{\frac{256}{81} - 1}} = \frac{9}{5\sqrt{7}} \text{ m/s}$$

$$\text{Discharge Rate of pipe} = A_1v_1 = \pi(2)^2 \times \frac{900}{5\sqrt{7}}$$

$$= \frac{3600\pi}{5\sqrt{7}} \text{ cm}^3/\text{sec} \quad \text{Ans.}$$

Web Reference at www.physicsgalaxy.com | Scan for Video Explanation

Module-16: Solved Example-7

Ex : Water flows through the tube shown in figure. The areas of cross-section of wide and narrow sections are 5 cm^2 and 2 cm^2 respectively. Rate of water flow in tube is 500 cm^3/sec. Find the difference in mercury levels in the U-tube

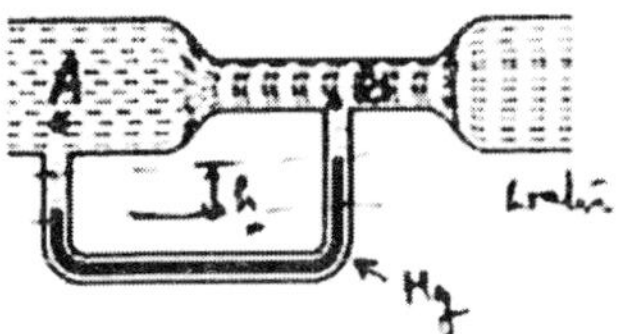

Sol^n Acc. to Bernoulli's theorem at pts A & B.

$$P_A + \frac{1}{2}\rho v_A^2 = P_B + \frac{1}{2}\rho v_B^2$$

$$P_A - P_B = \frac{1}{2}\rho(v_B^2 - v_A^2)$$

$$h(13600 - 1000) \times 10 = \frac{1}{2}\rho\left[(2.5)^2 - (1)^2\right]$$

$$h = \frac{5.25}{2 \times 126} = 0.0208\ m = 2.08\ cm \text{ Ans.}$$

Continuity eq^n -

$$A_A v_A = A_B v_B = 500$$

$v_A = 100$ cm/s

$v_B = 250$ cm/s.

$$P_A - P_B = h(\rho_{Hg} - \rho)g$$

Scan for Video Explanation

Web Reference at www.physicsgalaxy.com

Module-17: Torecelli's Theorem

Torricelli's Theorem:

This theorem is abt calculation of efflux vel of a fluid flowing out through a hole in a container.

If we use Bernoulli's theorem at just inside & outside pts of hole -

$$P_{atm} + \frac{1}{2}\rho v^2 = P_{atm} + h\rho g + 0$$

$$\boxed{v = \sqrt{2gh}}$$

Torricelli's eq^n of efflux vel.

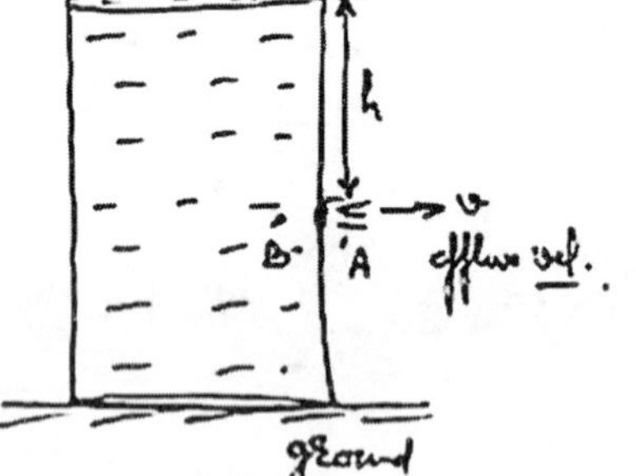

area of hole << area of Cont.

Scan for Video Explanation

Web Reference at www.physicsgalaxy.com

Module-18: Solved Example-8

Ex : **Water stands upto a height H in a tank as shown. A hole is made at a depth h below the open end of tank from which water ejects out. Find h for which the range of ejecting water on ground will be maximum.**

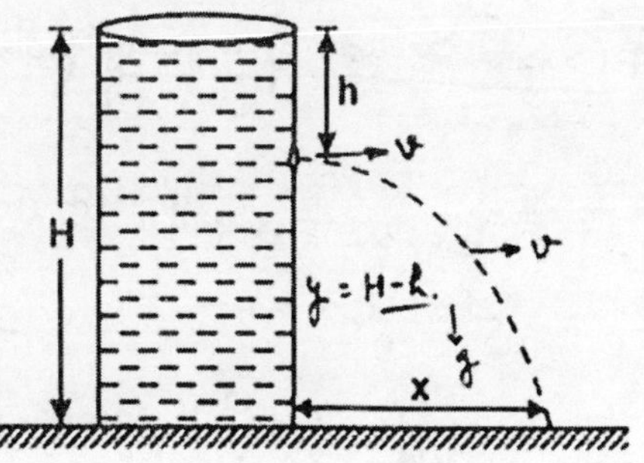

Sol^n: As we know, the efflux vel of water is $v = \sqrt{2gh}$.

time to reach ground level by water is $t = \sqrt{\frac{2y}{g}} = \sqrt{\frac{2(H-h)}{g}}$

horizontal range on ground $x = vt = \sqrt{2gh}\cdot\sqrt{\frac{2(H-h)}{g}} = 2\sqrt{h(H-h)}$

for x to be max $\frac{dx}{dh} = 0 \Rightarrow \frac{2}{2\sqrt{h(H-h)}} \times (H-2h) = 0$

$h = H/2$ Ans.

Web Reference at www.physicsgalaxy.com | Scan for Video Explanation

Module-19: Solved Example-9

Ex : **Figure shows a cylindrical tank of cross-sectional area A filled with water upto its full height H. A small hole of area a is made at its bottom through which water starts flowing. Find the time taken in which the tank will get empty to half volume.**

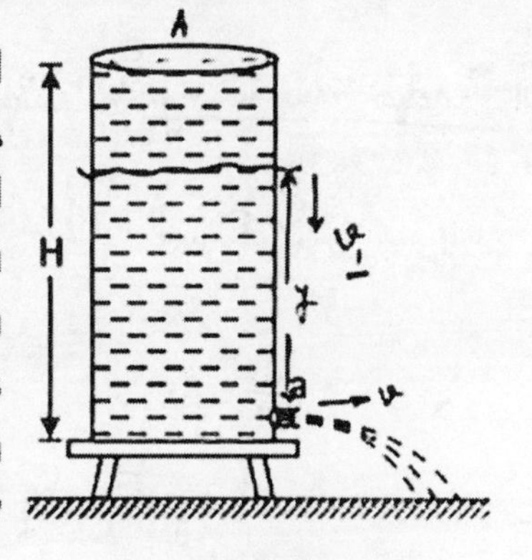

Sol^n: efflux vel $v = \sqrt{2gy}$

Acc to Cont eq^n

$Av_1 = a.v$

$v_1 = \frac{a}{A}.v = -\frac{dy}{dt}$

$\frac{dy}{dt} = -\frac{a}{A}\sqrt{2gy}$

$\int_H^{H/2}\frac{1}{\sqrt{y}}dy = -\frac{a}{A}\sqrt{2g}\int_0^t dt$

$\left[2\sqrt{y}\right]_H^{H/2} = -\frac{a}{A}\sqrt{2g}\,t$

$t = \frac{A}{a}\frac{1}{\sqrt{2g}}\left[2\sqrt{H} - \sqrt{H/2}\right]$

$t = \frac{A}{a}\sqrt{\frac{H}{g}}(\sqrt{2}-1)$ Ans.

Web Reference at www.physicsgalaxy.com | Scan for Video Explanation

Module-20: Cross-section of a Freely Falling Liquid

Cross- Section of a freely falling liquid:

we can use Bernoulli's Th at pts X & Y -

$$P_{atm} + \frac{1}{2}\rho v_0^2 + \rho gh = P_{atm} + \frac{1}{2}\rho v^2$$

$$v^2 = v_0^2 + 2gh$$

using eqⁿ of Continuity

$$v_0 A = v a$$

$$a = \frac{v_0}{v} A$$

$$\left[a = \frac{v_0 A}{\sqrt{v_0^2 + 2gh}} \right]$$

Scan for Video Explanation

Web Reference at www.physicsgalaxy.com

Module-21: Reaction due to Ejection of a Liquid

Reaction due to ejection of a liquid:

flow rate of liquid ejecting out is

$$\frac{dV}{dt} = Av$$

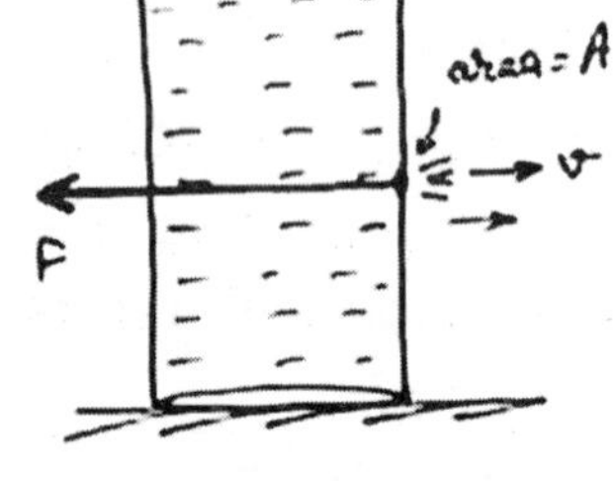

mass rate of ejecting liq is

$$\frac{dm}{dt} = \rho A v$$

momentum ejecting per second in fluid is

$$F = (\rho A v)v = \rho A v^2$$

force of reaction on Container due to ej of liq is $\boxed{F_R = \rho A v^2}$

Scan for Video Explanation

Web Reference at www.physicsgalaxy.com

Module-22: Solved Example-10

Ex : On the opposite sides of a wide vertical vessel filled with water, two identical holes are opened, each of area S. The height difference between them is Δh. Find the net force on vessel due to water flowing out of the vessel.

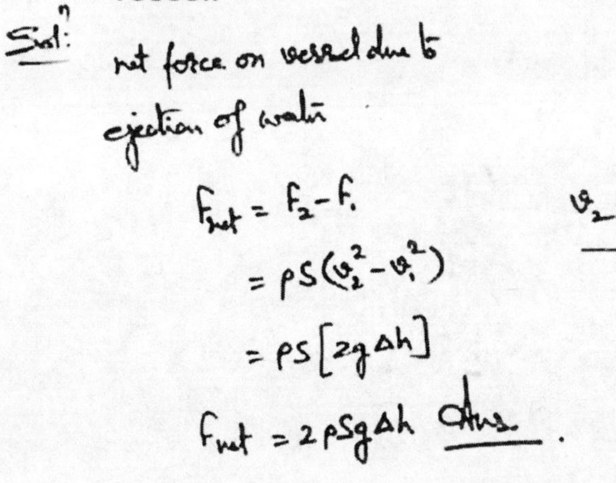

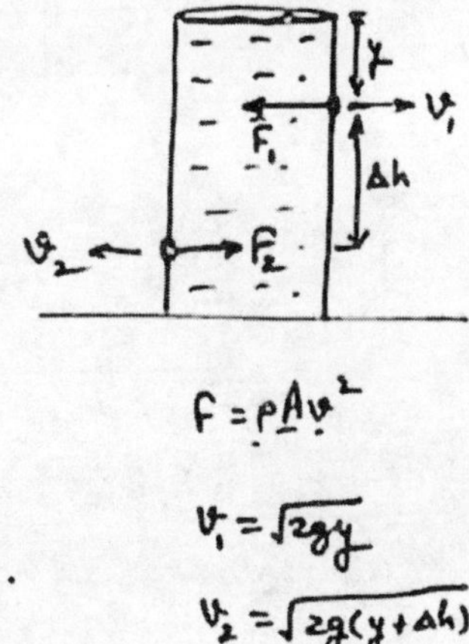

$F = \rho A v^2$

$v_1 = \sqrt{2gy}$

$v_2 = \sqrt{2g(y+\Delta h)}$

Web Reference at www.physicsgalaxy.com | Scan for Video Explanation

Module-23: Solved Example-11

Ex : A cylindrical vessel filled with water upto a height of 2m stand on a rough horizontal plane. At its bottom in its side wall a small hole is opened and it is found that the vessel slides on plane as water comes out. Find the diameter of hole if friction coefficient between vessel and plane is 0.4 and total mass of vessel with water is 100 kg.

Sol^n:

Reaction force due to ejection of water

$F = \rho A v^2$

100 kg. F $v = \sqrt{2gh}$ Rough.

to slide the vessel

$f_L = \mu Mg = 0.4 \times 100 \times 10 = 400\text{N}.$

$\rho A v^2 = 400$

$\rho\left(\frac{\pi d^2}{4}\right) v^2 = 400$

$d = \sqrt{\frac{4 \times 400}{\rho \pi \times 2g \times 2}} = \sqrt{\frac{4 \times 400}{1000 \times 3.14 \times 20 \times 2}} = 0.114\text{ m.}$ Ans.

Web Reference at www.physicsgalaxy.com | Scan for Video Explanation

Chapter 14
Surface Tension

Lecture Notes Modules

Module-1: Surface Tension

Surface Tension:

The prop of a liquid due to which its free surface tries to have min surface area and it behaves if it is under a tension like a stretched membrane is called Surface Tension.

– It is due to intermolecular force among liq. particles.

Scan for Video Explanation

Web Reference at www.physicsgalaxy.com

Module-2: Significance of Surface Tension

Significance of Surface Tension:

Surface tension is numerically defined as the force acting per unit length of a hypothetical line drawn on a liq. surface normal to it in either direction.

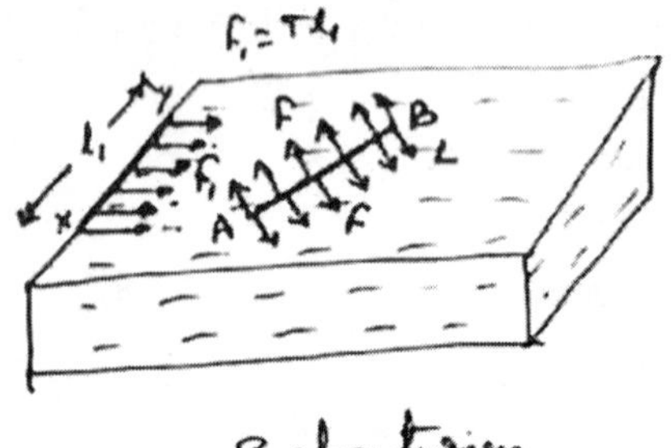

$f_1 = T l_1$

Surface tension

$T = \frac{F}{L}$ Nt/m.

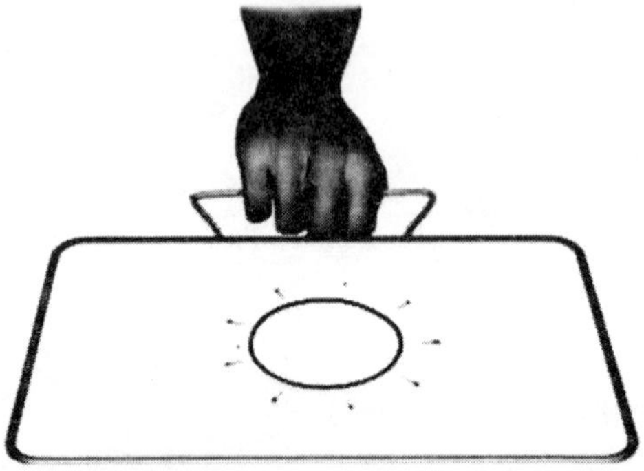

Scan for Video Explanation

Web Reference at www.physicsgalaxy.com

Module-3 Some Facts About Surface Tension

Some Facts about Surface Tension :

- It is a Scalar.
- It depends only on nature of liquid & its intermolecular forces.
- ST decreases with rise in temp & becomes 0 at critical temperature.
- It depends on impurities added to a liquid.
- For insoluble impurities ST decreases & for Soluble impurities it may increase or decrease.

Web Reference at www.physicsgalaxy.com | Scan for Video Explanation

Module-4 Solved Example-1

Ex : A thin wooden rod of mass M and length l is floating in water. Find the force required in vertically upward direction to lift the rod from water surface. Surface tension of water is T.

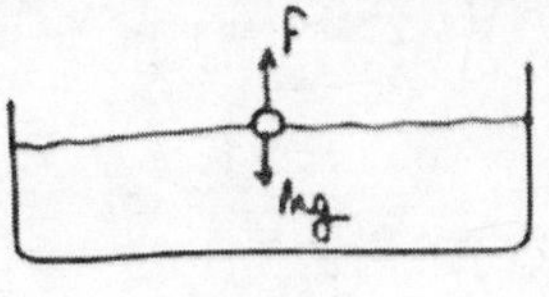

Sol: To lift the rod

$$F = Mg + 2Tl.$$ Ans.

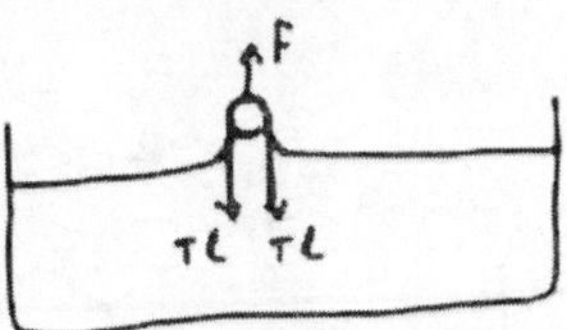

Web Reference at www.physicsgalaxy.com | Scan for Video Explanation

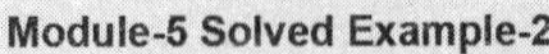

Module-5 Solved Example-2

Ex : A ring of radius R and mass m is kept at rest on the surface of a liquid of surface tension T by a string tied as shown in figure. Find the force required to lift the ring above the liquid.

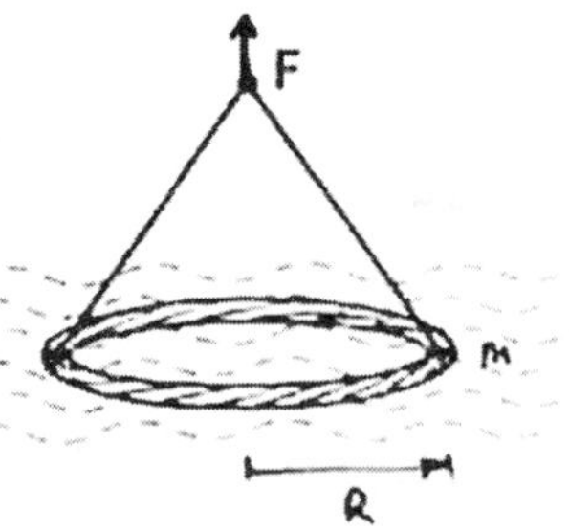

Sol^n: Force reqd to lift the ring

= wt of ring + force of ST

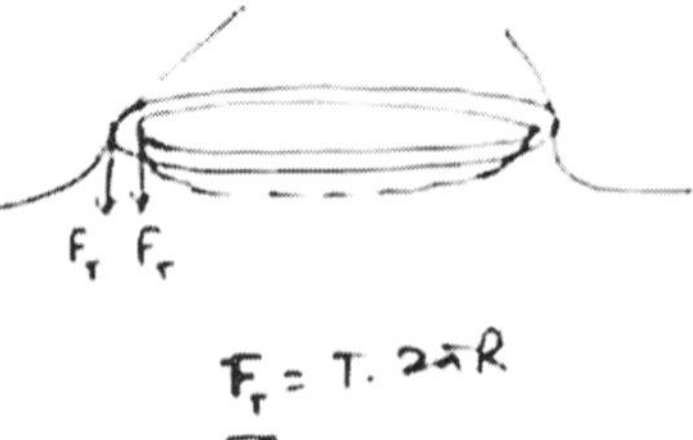

$F_T = T \cdot 2\pi R$

$F = mg + 2T(2\pi R)$

$F = mg + 4\pi RT$ Ans.

Scan for Video Explanation

Web Reference at www.physicsgalaxy.com

Module-6 Concept of Surface Energy

Concept of Surface Energy:

Stretched spring ⟶ stores some P.E in it.

free surface of a liquid ⟶ some PE is stored in it

↓

Surface energy.

force on slider due to ST is $F = 2Tl$

to slowly move the slider out $F_{ext} = 2Tl$

W/D in displacing slider by Δx is

$\Delta W = F_{ext} \cdot \Delta x = 2Tl\Delta x$

Soap film (ST = T)

inc in Surface area of film

$\Delta S = 2l\Delta x$

inc in Surface energy of film $\Rightarrow \Delta U = \Delta W = T\Delta S$

$T = \frac{\Delta U}{\Delta S}$ ← Surface energy per unit area.

Scan for Video Explanation

Web Reference at www.physicsgalaxy.com

Module-7 Solved Example-3

Ex : A soap bubble of radius R and film thickness t (t << R) coalesce to form a liquid drop. Find the rise in temperature of drop. Surface tension of soap solution is T, density of soap solution is ρ and its specific heat is S.

Sol^n: Initial surface area of bubble is $A_i = 2\times 4\pi R^2 = 8\pi R^2$

If radius of liq drop formed is r we use –

$$\frac{4}{3}\pi r^3 = 4\pi R^2 t \Rightarrow r = (3R^2t)^{1/3}$$

Final surface area $A_f = 4\pi r^2 = 4\pi(3R^2t)^{2/3}$

If temp of drop rises by $\Delta\theta$, we use

$$T(A_i - A_f) = ms\Delta\theta = \frac{4}{3}\pi r^3 \cdot \rho \cdot s\Delta\theta$$

$$\Delta\theta = \frac{T(8\pi R^2 - 4\pi(3R^2t)^{2/3})}{\frac{4}{3}\pi r^3 \rho s} = \frac{T[2R^2 - (3R^2t)^{2/3}]}{\rho S R^2 t} \quad \text{Ans.}$$

Web Reference at www.physicsgalaxy.com

Scan for Video Explanation

Module-8 Solved Example-4

Ex : A film of water is formed between two straight parallel wires each 10 cm long at a separation of 0.5 cm. Calculate the work required to increase their separation by 1 mm. Surface tension of water is 72 × 10^{-3} N/m.

Sol^n: Increase in surface area of film is

$$\Delta S = 2l\Delta x = 2\times 0.1\times 1\times 10^{-3} = 2\times 10^{-4}\,m^2$$

W/D in the process is equal to increase in surface energy

$$W = T\Delta S = 72\times 10^{-3}\times 2\times 10^{-4} = 144\times 10^{-7} = 14.44\,J \quad \text{Ans.}$$

Web Reference at www.physicsgalaxy.com

Scan for Video Explanation

Module-9 Excess Pressure Inside a Liquid Drop

Excess Pressure inside a liquid drop:

Due to ST, the surface of a liq drop tend to contract & compresses the enclosed matter due to which pressure inside increase

In eq^n of a drop, the diff in inside & outside pressure is called excess pressure (P_{ex})

$F = T.2\pi R$

$P_A > P_B$

for eq^n of the hemispherical section of drop.

$$T.(2\pi R) = P_{ex}.\pi R^2$$

$$\boxed{P_{ex} = \frac{2T}{R}}$$

Scan for Video Explanation

Web Reference at www.physicsgalaxy.com

Module-10 Excess Pressure Inside a Soap Bubble

Excess Pressure inside a Bubble:

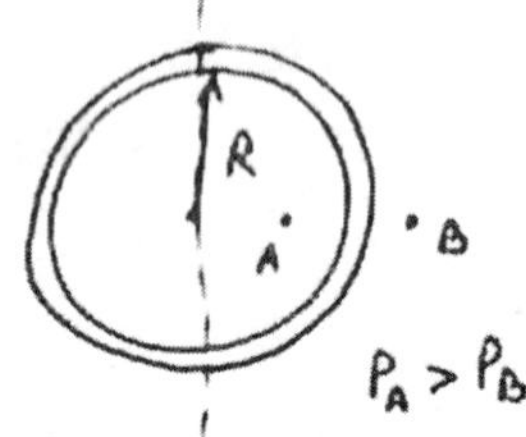

$P_A > P_B$

For eq^n of hemispherical section of the bubble, we can use

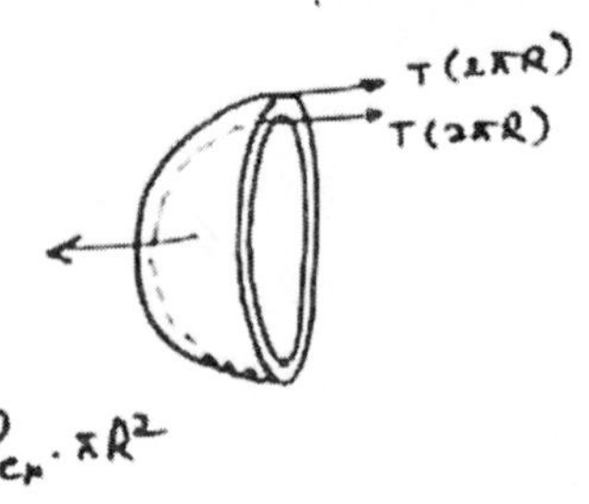

$F_{out} = P_{ex}.\pi R^2$

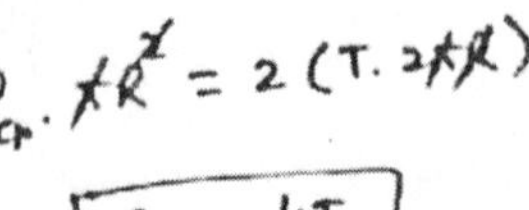

$$P_{ex}.\pi R^2 = 2(T.2\pi R)$$

$$\boxed{P_{ex} = \frac{4T}{R}}$$

Scan for Video Explanation

Web Reference at www.physicsgalaxy.com

Module-11 Excess Pressure Inside a Surface Having Two Curvatures

Excess Pressure inside a Surface having Two curvature:

net outward force on liq Surface is $F_{out} = (P_A - P_B) R_1 R_2 \theta \phi$

$\theta, \phi \to$ Small.

net inward force on liq surface due to ST is

$$F_{in} = T(R_2\phi)\sin\theta/2 \times 2 + T(R_1\theta)\sin\phi/2 \times 2$$

$$= T(R_2\phi)\cdot\theta + T(R_1\theta)\phi$$

$$F_{in} = T\phi\theta(R_1 + R_2)$$

Web Reference at www.physicsgalaxy.com | Scan for Video Explanation

Module-11 Excess Pressure Inside a Surface Having Two Curvatures

for eq^m of liq Surface

$$F_{out} = F_{in}$$

$$(P_A - P_B) R_1 R_2 \theta\phi = T\theta\phi(R_1 + R_2)$$

$$\boxed{P_{ex} = T\left[\frac{1}{R_1} + \frac{1}{R_2}\right]}$$

if this Surface is a film $P_{ex} = 2T\left[\frac{1}{R_1} + \frac{1}{R_2}\right]$

Excess Pressure inside a cylindrical Surface of liq.

$R_1 = R$

$R_2 = \infty$

$P_A - P_B = T/R$

$$P_{ex} = T\left[\frac{1}{R} + \frac{1}{\infty}\right] = T/R$$

for a cyl film $P_{ex} = 2T/R$.

Web Reference at www.physicsgalaxy.com | Scan for Video Explanation

Module-12 Connecting Soap Bubbles of Different Radii

Connecting Soap Bubbles of different Radii:

Pressure inside B_1, $P_1 = P_{atm} + \frac{4T}{R_1}$

Pressure inside B_2, $P_2 = P_{atm} + \frac{4T}{R_2}$

$P_1 > P_2$

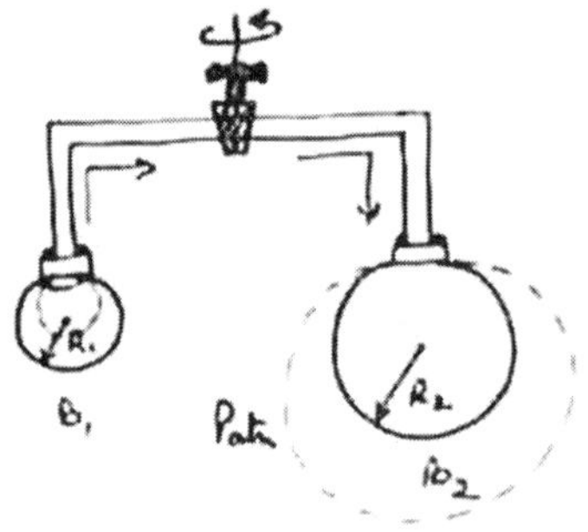

R_1 B_1 P_{atm} R_2 B_2

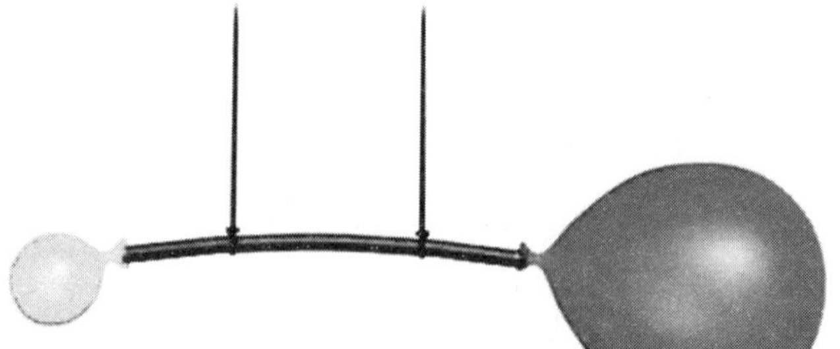

Scan for Video Explanation

Web Reference at www.physicsgalaxy.com

Module-13 Angle of Contact

Angle of Contact:

Cohesive forces → attractive forces between molecules of same substance

Adhesive forces → att. forces between molecules of diff substance

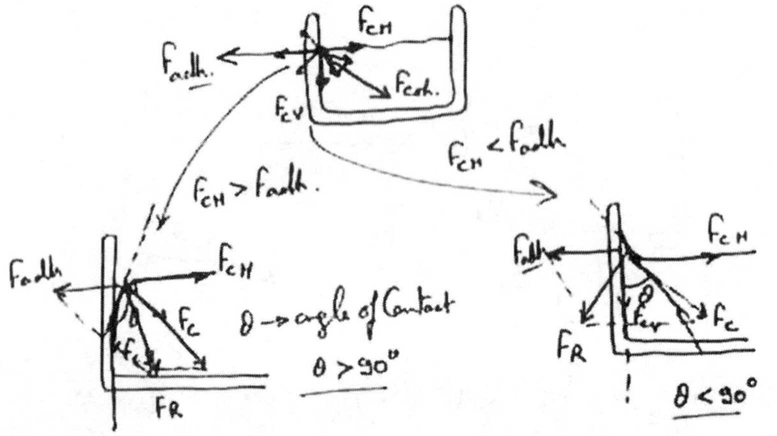

F_{cH} $F_{adh.}$ $F_{coh.}$ F_{cV}

$F_{cH} < F_{adh}$

$F_{cH} > F_{adh.}$

F_{adh} F_{cH} F_c F_{cv} F_R

θ → angle of Contact

$\theta > 90°$

F_{adh} F_{cH} F_R F_{cv} F_c

$\theta < 90°$

Scan for Video Explanation

Web Reference at www.physicsgalaxy.com

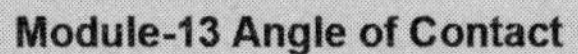

Module-13 Angle of Contact

for $\theta < 90^\circ$, liquid will wet the Solid surface.

$F_{adh} > F_{coh}$

liq drop

θ

water-glass.

for $\theta > 90^\circ$, liquid do not wet the solid Surface

liq drop

θ

Hg-glass.

Web Reference at www.physicsgalaxy.com

Scan for Video Explanation

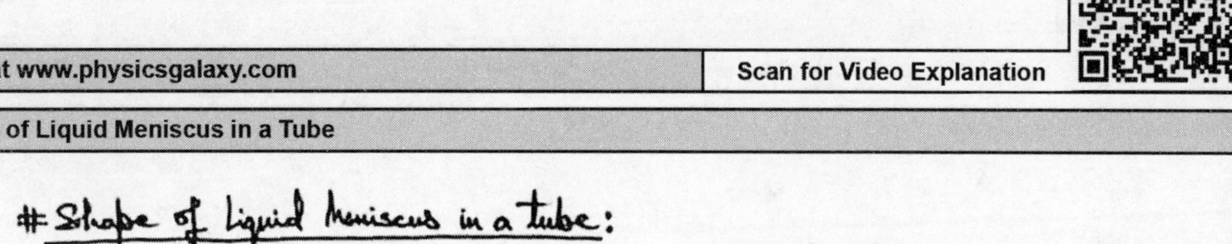

Module-14 Shape of Liquid Meniscus in a Tube

Shape of Liquid Meniscus in a tube:

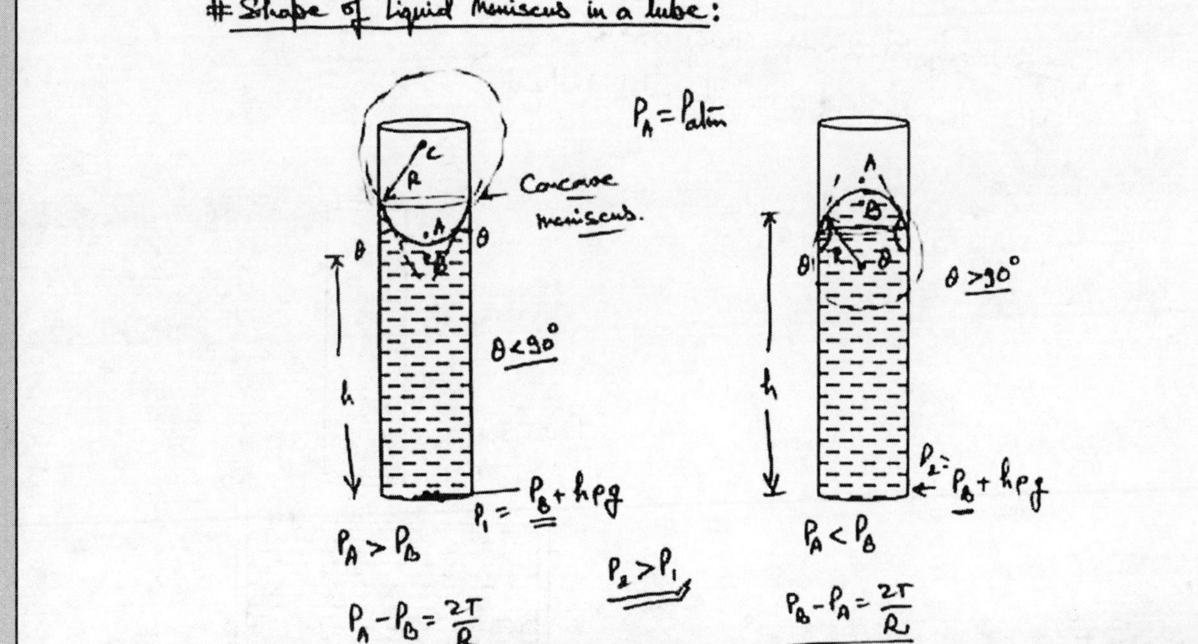

Web Reference at www.physicsgalaxy.com

Scan for Video Explanation

Module-15 Capillary Action

Capillary Action:

A tube of very narrow bore is called capillary.

When a capillary is dipped normally in a liquid it is found that inside capillary liquid level either ascend or descend relative to surrounding level of liq. This phenomenon is called Capillary action or capillarity.

$P_A = P_{atm}$

$P_B = P_{atm} - \frac{2T}{R}$

$P_C = P_{atm}$

$R = \frac{r}{\cos\theta}$

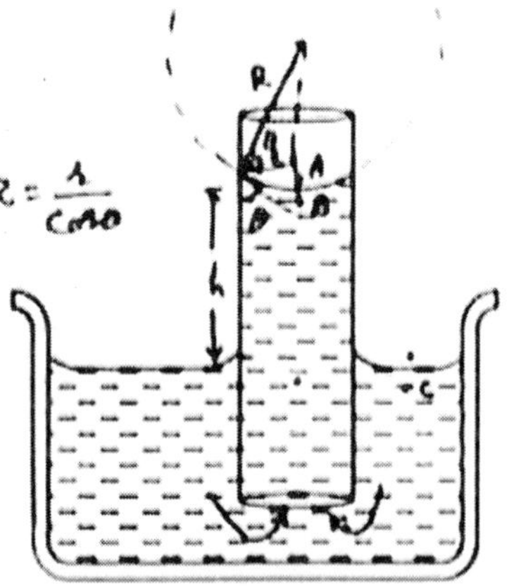

$P_C = P_B + h\rho g = P_{atm}$

$P_{atm} - \frac{2T}{R} + h\rho g = P_{atm} \rightarrow h = \frac{2T}{R\rho g}$

Capillary action height $h = \frac{2T\cos\theta}{r\rho g}$

Scan for Video Explanation

Web Reference at www.physicsgalaxy.com

Module-15 Capillary Action

Similarly when a liq having $\theta > 90°$ then the liq level in capillary tube will fall.

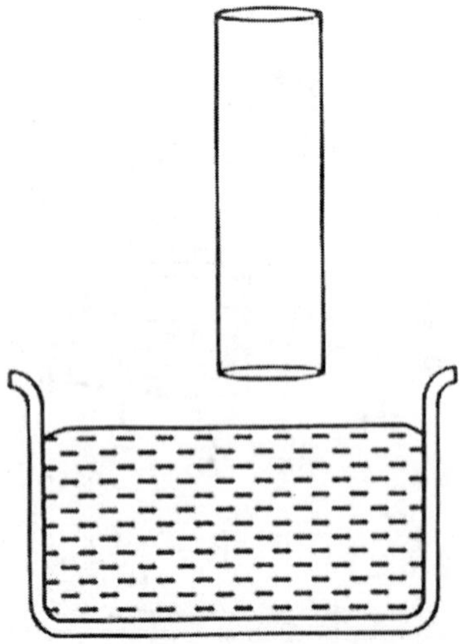

Scan for Video Explanation

Web Reference at www.physicsgalaxy.com

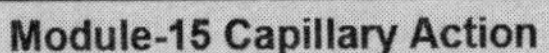

Module-15 Capillary Action

Similarly when a liq having $\theta > 90^\circ$
then the liq level in capillary tube will fall.

$P_A = P_{atm}$

$P_B = P_{atm} + \frac{2T}{R}$

$P_C = P_{atm}$

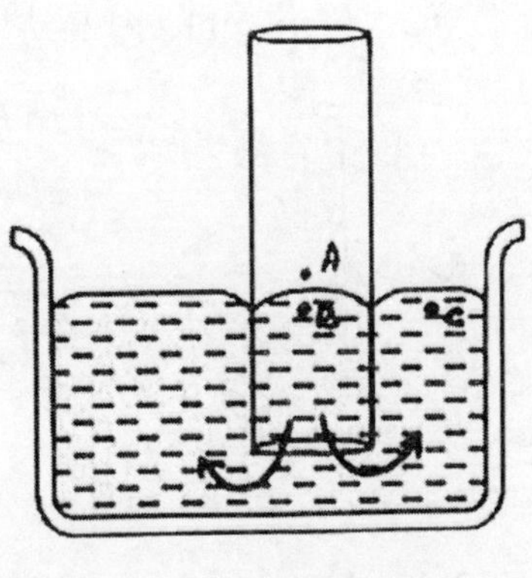

Web Reference at www.physicsgalaxy.com

Scan for Video Explanation

Module-15 Capillary Action

Similarly when a liq having $\theta > 90^\circ$
then the liq level in capillary tube will fall.

$P_A = P_{atm}$

$P_B = P_{atm} + \frac{2T}{R}$

$P_C = P_{atm}$

$P_D = P_{atm} + h\rho g = P_{atm} + \frac{2T}{R}$

$$h = \frac{2T}{R\rho g} = \frac{2T\cos\theta}{r\rho g}$$

$R = \frac{r}{\cos\theta}$

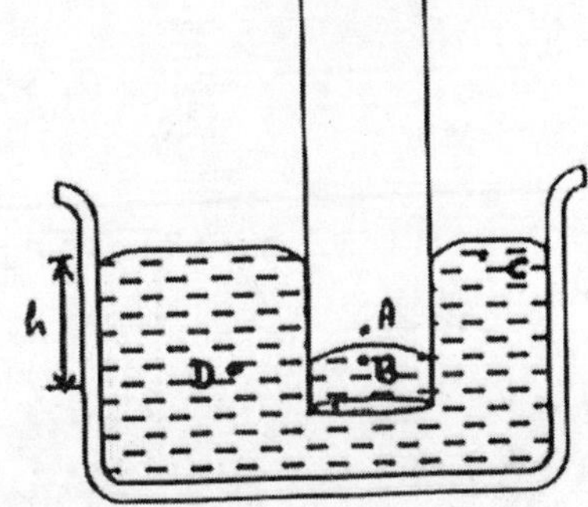

Web Reference at www.physicsgalaxy.com

Scan for Video Explanation

Module-16 Force Between Two Parallel Plates Due to Liquid Between Them

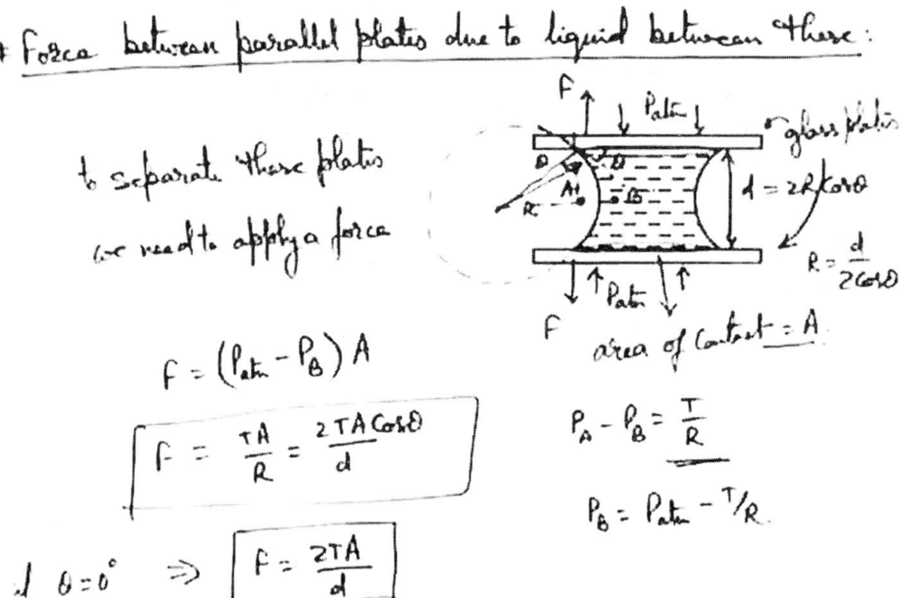

Scan for Video Explanation

Web Reference at www.physicsgalaxy.com

Module-17 Capillary Action with a Capillary of Insufficient Height

Capillary Action with a capillary of insufficient height:

As we know, Capillary height

$$h = \frac{2T\cos\theta}{r\rho g}$$

$$\frac{2T}{R} = h\rho g$$

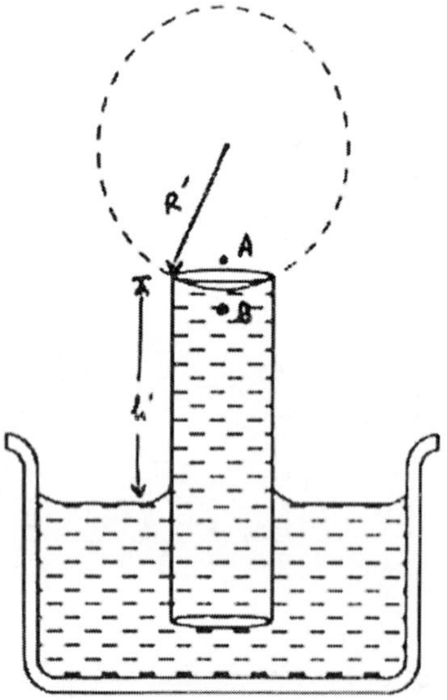

$$P_B = P_{atm} - \frac{2T}{R'}$$

$$P_{atm} - \frac{2T}{R'} + h'\rho g = P_{atm}$$

$$\frac{2T}{R'} = h'\rho g$$

$$hR = h'R'$$

$h' < h$

$R' > R$

liq will never overflow even if $h' < h$. because $R' > R$.

Scan for Video Explanation

Web Reference at www.physicsgalaxy.com

Module-18 Solved Example-5

Ex : A liquid of specific gravity 1.5 is observed to rise 3 cm in a capillary tube of diameter 0.5 mm and the liquid wets the surface of the tube. Calculate the excess pressure inside a spherical bubble of 1 cm diameter blown from the same liquid. Given that angle of contact is 0° and take g = 10 m/s^2.

Sol^n: As we know the surface tension of a liq is given as.

$$T = \frac{rh\rho g}{2\cos\theta} = \frac{0.25\times10^{-3}\times3\times10^{-2}\times1000\times10\times1.5}{2\times1}$$

$$= 56.25\times10^{-3}\ \text{N/m}$$

Excess Pressure inside the bubble is

$$P_{ex} = \frac{4T}{R} = \frac{4\times56.25\times10^{-3}}{0.5\times10^{-2}} = 45\ \text{Pa. Ans.}$$

Web Reference at www.physicsgalaxy.com | Scan for Video Explanation

Module-19 Solved Example-6

Ex : Two narrow bores of diameter 3 mm and 6 mm are joined together to make a U-tube open at both ends. If some water is poured in the tube find difference in level in two limbs. Take ST of water is 73 × 10^{-3} N/m, angle of contact 0°, g = 10 m/s^2 and water density = 1000 kg/m^3.

Pressure at A $\quad P_A = P_{atm} - \frac{2T}{R_1}$

Pressure at B $\quad P_B = P_{atm} - \frac{2T}{R_2}$

at level diff h, we can use

$$P_B - P_A = h\rho g$$

$$2T\left[\frac{1}{R_1} - \frac{1}{R_2}\right] = h\rho g$$

$$h = \frac{2T}{\rho g}\left[\frac{1}{R_1} - \frac{1}{R_2}\right] = \frac{2\times73\times10^{-3}}{1000\times10}\left[\frac{1}{1.5} - \frac{1}{3}\right]\times10^{3}$$

$$= 4.86\ \text{mm Ans.}$$

Web Reference at www.physicsgalaxy.com | Scan for Video Explanation

Module-20 Solved Example-7

Ex : In a cylindrical vessel at its bottom a round hole of diameter 1 mm is drilled and water is filled in it. Find the maximum height to which water can be filled in it without leakage. Take ST of water 75×10^{-3} N/m, density of water = 1000 kg/m^3, g = 10 m/s^2, and angle of contact 0°.

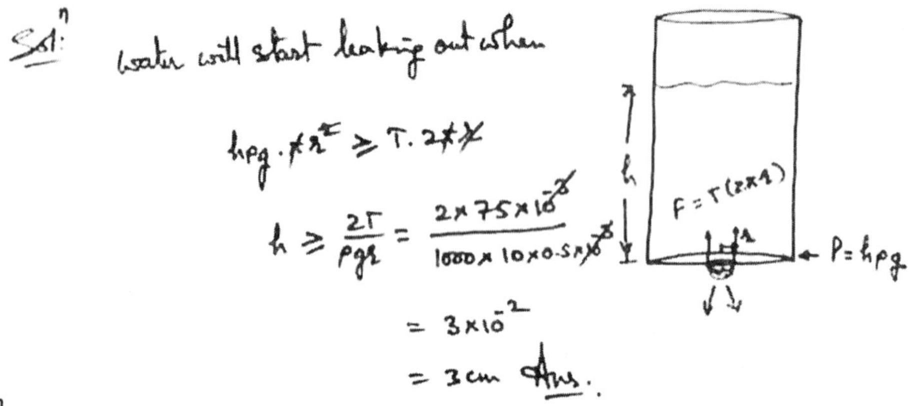

Scan for Video Explanation

Web Reference at www.physicsgalaxy.com

Module-21 Solved Example-8

Ex : The lower end of a capillary tube of diameter 2 mm is dipped 8 cm below the surface of water in a beaker. What is the pressure required in the tube to blow an air bubble at its end in water. Given that surface tension of water = 73×10^{-3} N/m^2 and $P_{atm} = 10^5$ Pa, g = 10 m/s^2.

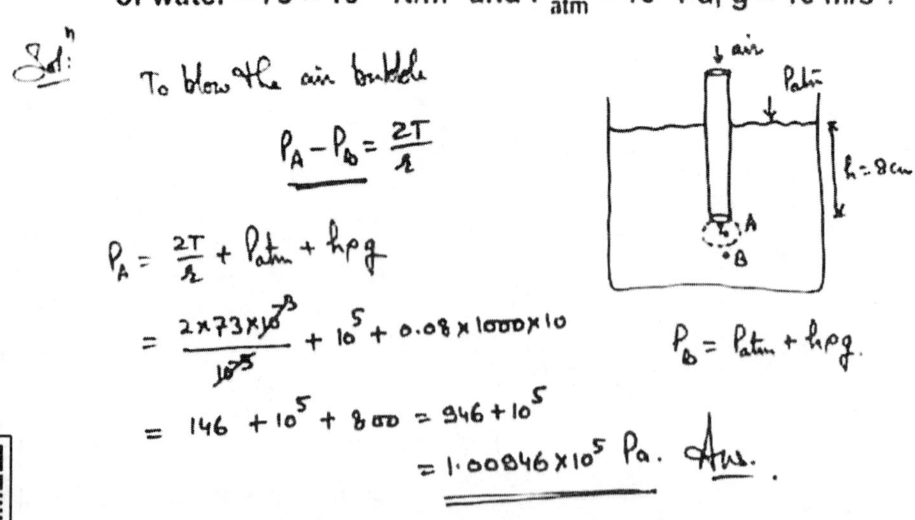

Scan for Video Explanation

Web Reference at www.physicsgalaxy.com

Module-22 Solved Example-9

Ex : **Two separate air bubbles of radii 2 mm and 4 mm formed of same soap solution of surface tension 70×10^{-3} N/m. When these bubble come in contact to form a double bubble, find the radius of curvature of the interface film which is common to both bubbles.**

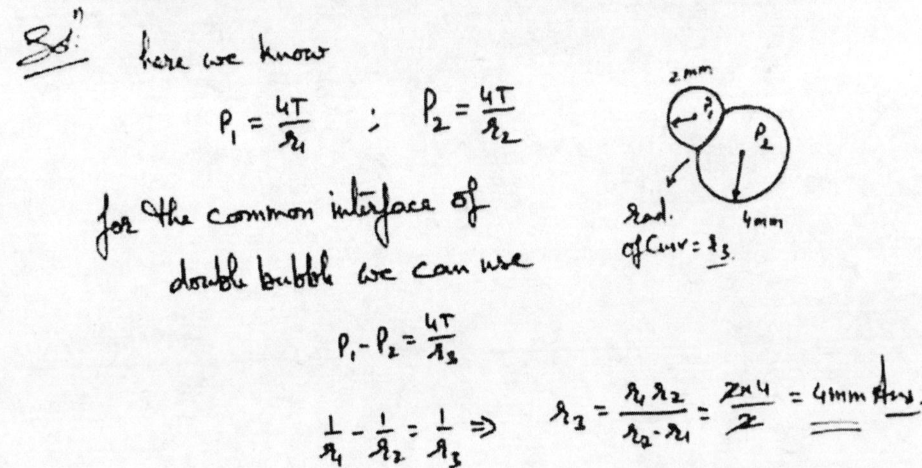

Web Reference at www.physicsgalaxy.com

Scan for Video Explanation

Chapter 15
Viscosity

Lecture Notes Modules

Module-1: Viscosity

Viscosity:

It is the prop of a fluid due to its intermolecular forces by which in case of fluid flow the relative motion between layer of fluid is opposed.

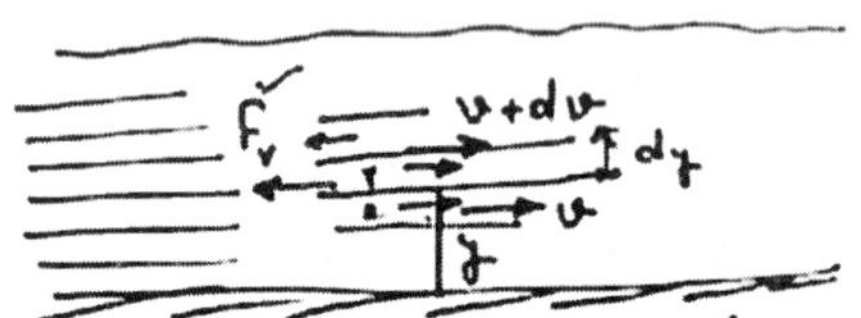

it is found that viscous force on a fluid layer mainly depend on two factors

① $F_v \propto A$ (surface area of layer)

② $F_v \propto \frac{dv}{dy}$ (velocity gradient of layer)

Scan for Video Explanation

Web Reference at www.physicsgalaxy.com

Module-1: Viscosity

(1) $F_v \propto A$ [Surface area of layer]

(2) $F_v \propto \frac{dv}{dy}$ [velocity gradient of layer]

viscous force on fluid layer is

$$\boxed{F_v = \eta A \frac{dv}{dy}}$$

η → Const of prop. called cofficient of Viscosity (depends on intermolecular prop of the fluid).

Scan for Video Explanation

Web Reference at www.physicsgalaxy.com

Module-2: Some Facts about Viscosity

Some Facts about Viscosity of a Fluid:

- Viscosity depends only on nature of fluid.
- $\eta_{liquids} >> \eta_{gases}$
- For liquids as density increases, viscosity also increases but in gases viscosity decrease with inc. in density.
- Units used for viscous Coefficient η is Poiseuille (Pl) in SI unit, in CGS units is poise, the rel is –

$$1\,Pl = 10\,poise$$

Web Reference at www.physicsgalaxy.com

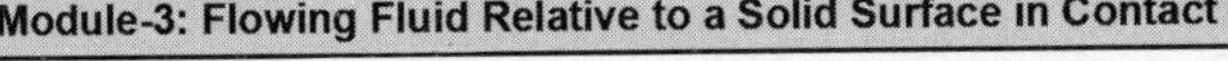

Scan for Video Explanation

Module-3: Flowing Fluid Relative to a Solid Surface in Contact

Flowing fluid relative to a Solid Surface in Contact:

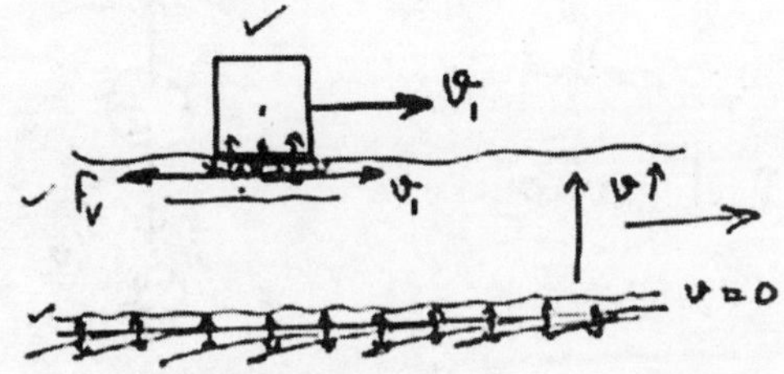

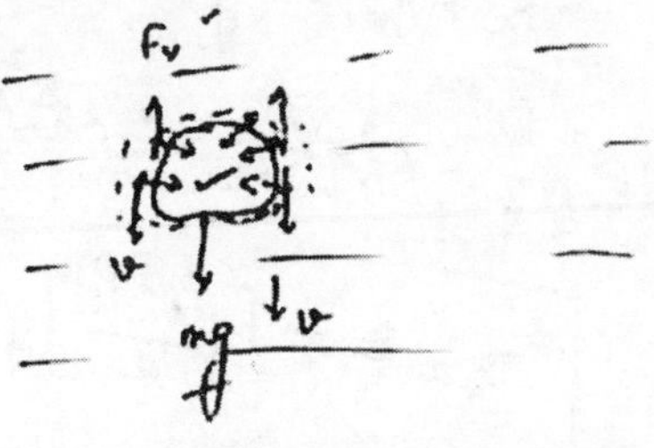

Web Reference at www.physicsgalaxy.com

Scan for Video Explanation

Module-4: Stoke's Law and Terminal Velocity

Stoke's Law and Terminal velocity:

When a body moves through a fluid, the fluid in contact with body is also dragged with it and the relative motion between fluid layer oppose the motion of body.

Acc. to Stokes Law the viscous force on a sphere of radius r moving with speed v through a fluid of coefficient of vis η is given as -

$$F_v = 6\pi\eta r v$$

Scan for Video Explanation

Web Reference at www.physicsgalaxy.com

Module-4: Stoke's Law and Terminal Velocity

When a sphere is dropped in a fluid.

Due to viscous forces, it attains a steady uniform speed v_T, called terminal speed at which $a = 0$.

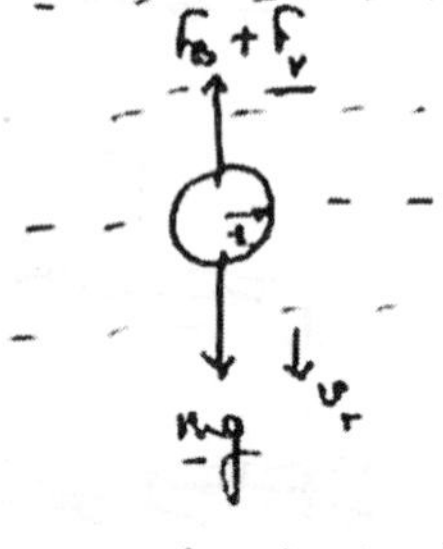

$\Rightarrow$

$$F_B + F_v = mg$$

$$\frac{4}{3}\pi r^3 \rho_l g + 6\pi\eta r v_T = \frac{4}{3}\pi r^3 \rho_s g$$

$$v_T = \frac{2}{9} r^2 \left[\frac{\rho_s - \rho_l}{\eta}\right] g.$$

terminal speed of sphere

$\rho_s \rightarrow$ density of sphere

$\rho_l \leftarrow$ density of liq.

$\eta \rightarrow$ vis coeff

Scan for Video Explanation

Web Reference at www.physicsgalaxy.com

Module-5: Critical Velocity and Reynold's Number

Critical Velocity and Reynold's Number:

As we know upto a specific flow vel, fluid flow remains streamline & beyond a critical vel it becomes turbulent.

Exp. it was established that this critical vel depends on some factors, these are -

(1) $v_c \propto \eta$

(2) $v_c \propto \frac{1}{\rho}$

(3) $v_c \propto \frac{1}{r}$

$$v_c = N_R\left(\frac{\eta}{r\rho}\right)$$

Reynold's Number.

Web Reference at www.physicsgalaxy.com

Scan for Video Explanation

Module-6: Poisueille's Equation

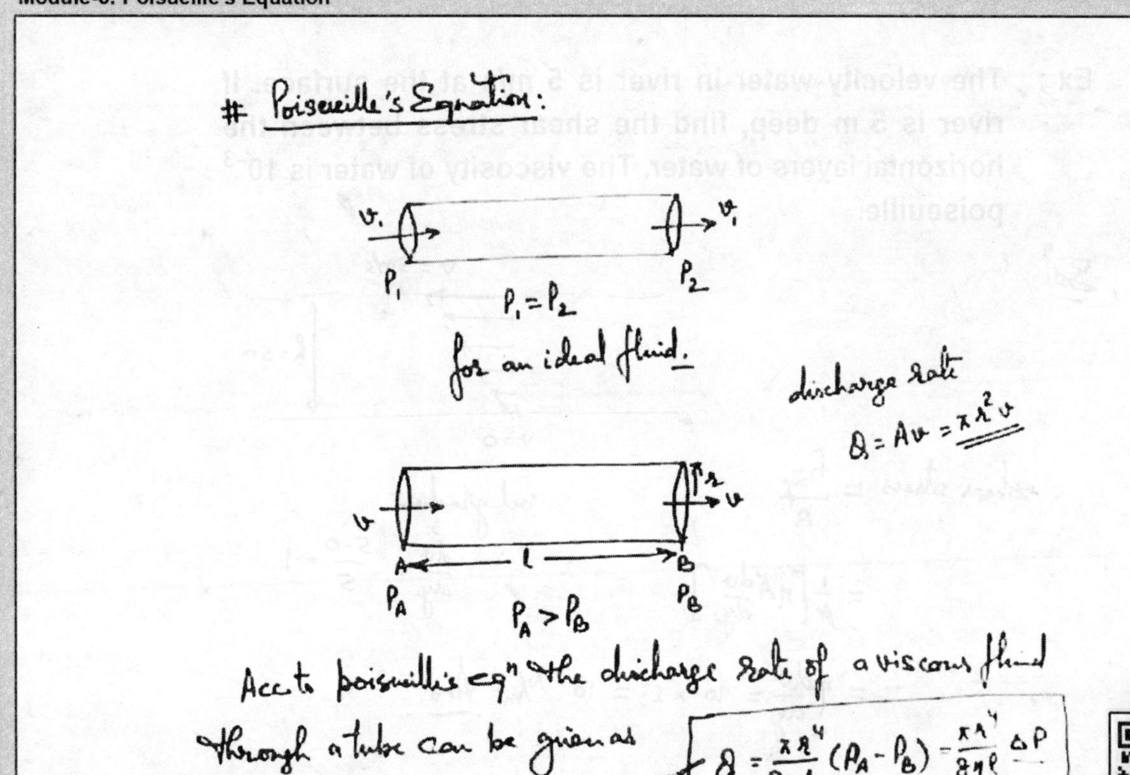

Web Reference at www.physicsgalaxy.com

Scan for Video Explanation

Module-7: Solved Example-1

Ex : An air bubble of radius 1 mm is allowed to rise through a long cylindrical column of a viscous liquid of radius 5 cm and travels at a steady rate of 2.1 cm/sec. If density of liquid is 1.5 gm/cm^3. Find its viscosity. Take g = 10 m/s^2 and neglect air density.

Sol^n:

for steady speed of bubble

$$F_B = F_v$$

$$\frac{4}{3}\pi r^3 \rho g = 6\pi\eta r v$$

$$\eta = \frac{2}{9}\frac{\rho r^2 g}{v} = \frac{2}{9} \times \frac{1.5 \times (10^{-1})^2 \times (1000)}{2.1}$$

$$= 1.58 \text{ poise Ans.}$$

Scan for Video Explanation

Web Reference at www.physicsgalaxy.com

Module-8: Solved Example-2

Ex : The velocity water in river is 5 m/s at the surface. If river is 5 m deep, find the shear stress between the horizontal layers of water. The viscosity of water is 10^{-3} poiseuille.

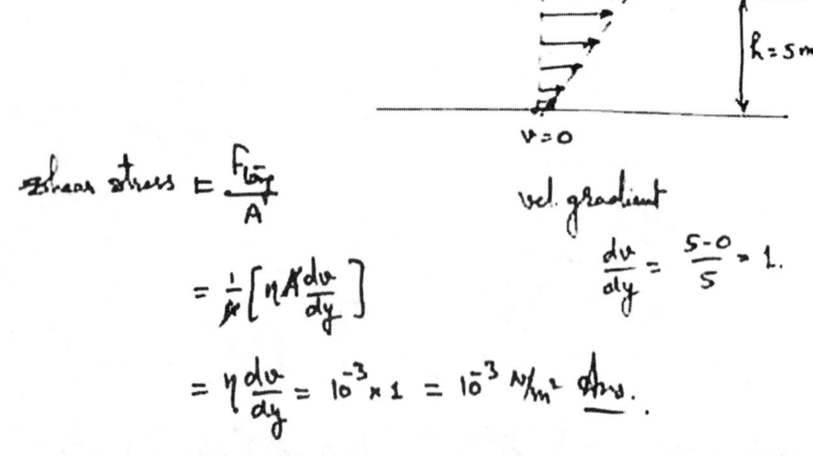

Shear stress $= \frac{F_{tg}}{A}$

$$= \frac{1}{A}\left[\eta A \frac{dv}{dy}\right]$$

$$= \eta \frac{dv}{dy} = 10^{-3} \times 1 = 10^{-3} \text{ N/m}^2 \text{ Ans.}$$

vel. gradient

$$\frac{dv}{dy} = \frac{5-0}{5} = 1.$$

Scan for Video Explanation

Web Reference at www.physicsgalaxy.com

Module-9: Solved Example-3

Ex : **Figure shows a cylindrical vessel of height H filled with a liquid of density ρ. At its bottom in a small hole a capillary tube of radius r and length L is fitted as shown. Find the flow rate of liquid when flow starts. Viscosity of fluid is η.**

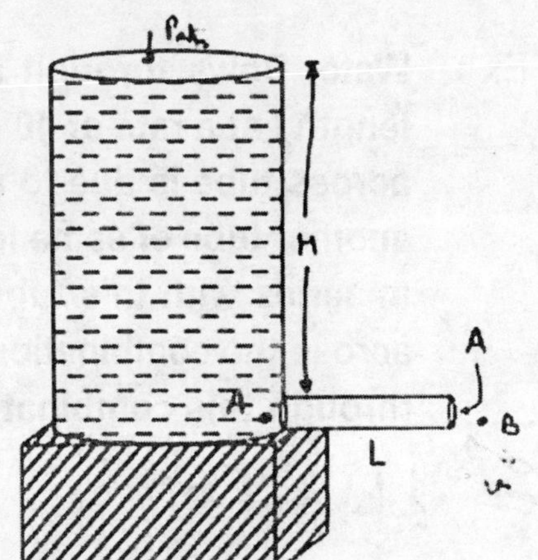

Solⁿ: Pressure diff across Capillary tube is $P_A - P_B = H\rho g$

$P_A = P_{atm} + H\rho g$

$P_B = P_{atm}$

acc. to Poiseuille's eqⁿ

flow rate $Q = \frac{\pi r^4}{8\eta l}(P_A - P_B) = \frac{\pi r^4 (H\rho g)}{8\eta L}$ Ans.

$v \pi r^2 = (\ldots) \rightarrow v = \ldots$

Scan for Video Explanation

Module-10: Solved Example-4

Ex : **Spherical dust particles of different radii are shaken up in water in a bottle and kept on a flat surface. If height of water in bottle is 10 cm find the radius of largest dust particle remain in suspension after 1 Hour. Take density of water 1000 kg/m^2, density of dust particles 1800 kg/m^3 and viscosity of water 10^{-2} poise and g = 10 m/s^2.**

Solⁿ: particle vel which reach bottom in 1Hr is $v = \frac{\Delta s}{\Delta t} = \frac{0.1}{3600} = \frac{10^{-3}}{36}$ m/s

As we know that term speed.

$$v = \frac{2}{9}\frac{g r^2}{\eta}(\rho_s - \rho_l)$$

$$r = \sqrt{\frac{9\eta v}{2g(\rho_s - \rho_l)}} = \sqrt{\frac{9 \times 10^{-3} \times 10^{-3}/36}{2 \times 10 \times 800}} = 3.95\ \mu m \text{ Ans.}$$

Scan for Video Explanation

Module-11: Solved Example-5

Ex : **Water flows through a capillary tube of radius r and length *l* at a rate of 40 ml/sec when pressure difference across tube is due to a height h of water column. Now another tube of same length and radius r/2 is connected in series with this tube with same pressure difference across the combination. Find the new flow rate of water through this combination.**

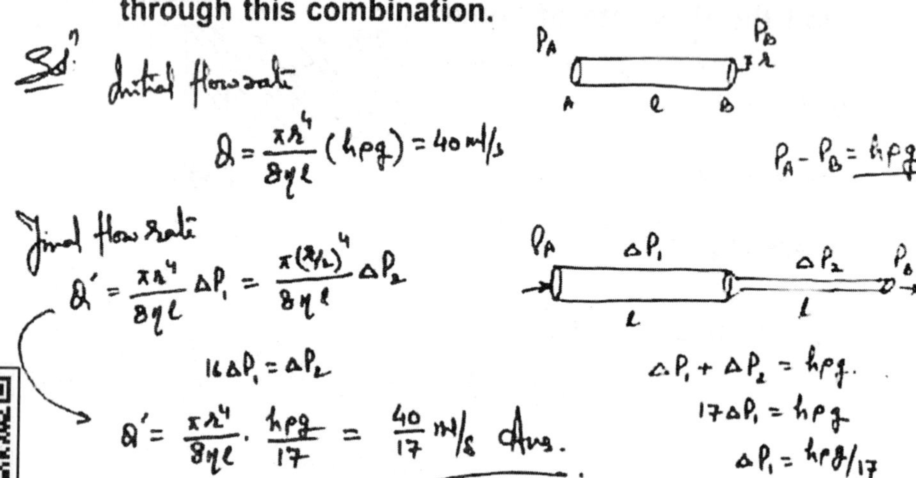

Scan for Video Explanation

Web Reference at www.physicsgalaxy.com

Chapter 16
Elasticity

Lecture Notes Modules

Module-1: Introduction to Elasticity

Elasticity:

The prop of matter by virtue of which a body tend to regain its original shape & size after deforming forces are removed is called elasticity.

Elasticity is due to intermolecular forces between constituent particles of body.

Scan for Video Explanation

Web Reference at www.physicsgalaxy.com

Module-2: Rigid Body

Rigid body:

A body in which the sep between its constituent particles does not change.

- it never gets deformed.
- in nature no body is perfectly rigid.

Scan for Video Explanation

Web Reference at www.physicsgalaxy.com

Module-3: Elastic and Partially Elastic Bodies

Elastic and Partially elastic Bodies:

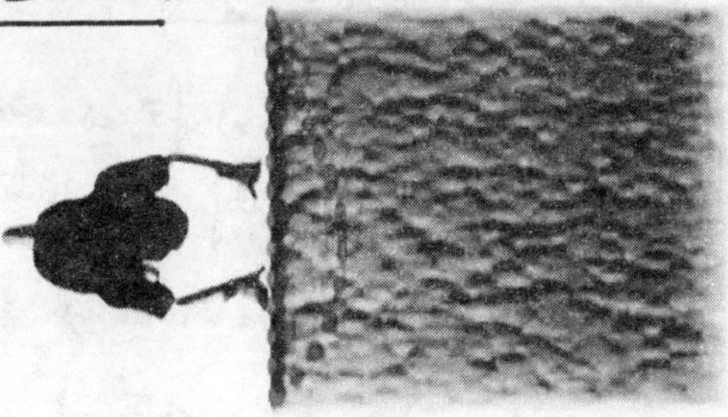

Elastic body:

it completely regains its original shape &

WD in def = stored PE in body.

Partially Elastic Body:

it does not completely regain its original shape &

WD in def → partly dissipated + partly stored as PE.

Web Reference at www.physicsgalaxy.com

Scan for Video Explanation

Module-4: Inelastic or Plastic Bodies

Inelastic or Plastic Bodies:

Such Bodies do not have any tendency to regain original shape &

WD in def → completely dissipated during def.

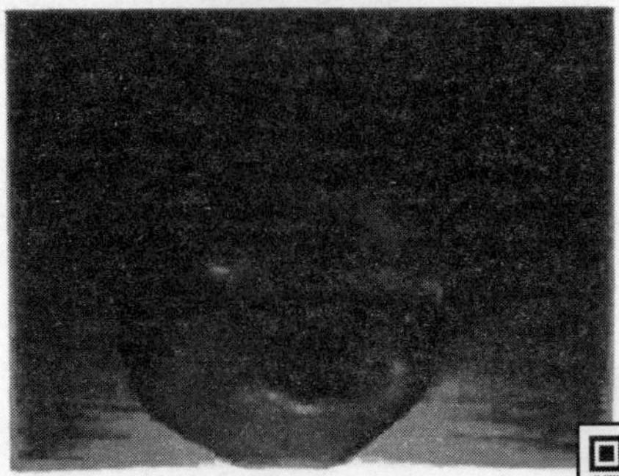

Web Reference at www.physicsgalaxy.com

Scan for Video Explanation

Module-5: Stress due to a Force

Stress due to a Force:

When ext forces are applied on a body, it gets deformed. Due to def, the intermolecular forces inside the body may develop some restoring forces within the volume of body which oppose the external deforming forces.

The internal restoring forces per unit cross-sect area of body is called 'Stress'.

under eqm state,

$$\text{STRESS} = \frac{\text{Deforming force}}{\text{Surface area of cross-section normal to force.}}$$

Scan for Video Explanation

Web Reference at www.physicsgalaxy.com

Module-6: Types of Stress

Types of Stress:

for solid bodies when stress normal to body surface, it is called normal stress & when stress is tangential to a body surface it is called shear stress.

Normal Stress = F/A.

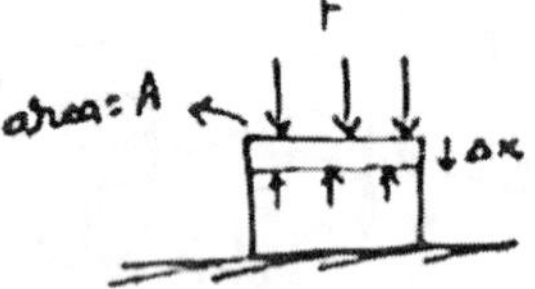

Shear stress = F/A

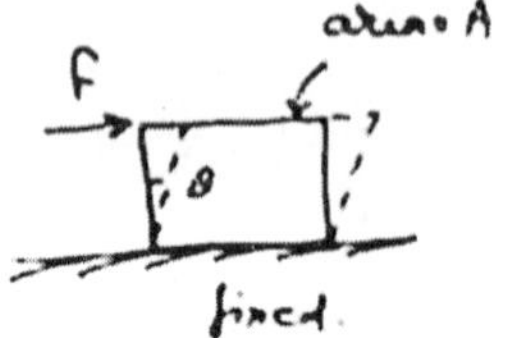

Scan for Video Explanation

Web Reference at www.physicsgalaxy.com

Module-6: Types of Stress

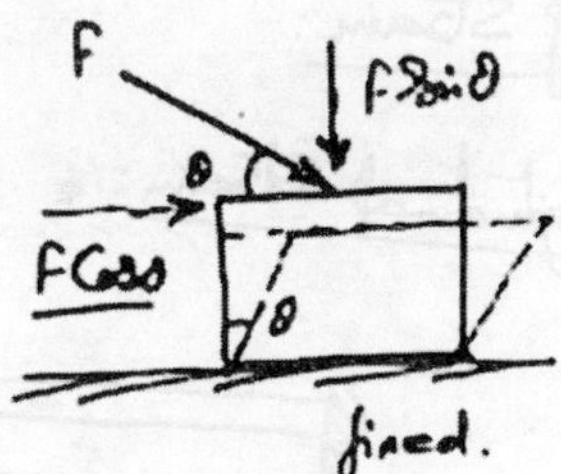

$$\text{Normal stress} = \frac{F\sin\theta}{A}$$

$$\text{Shear stress} = \frac{F\cos\theta}{A}$$

Web Reference at www.physicsgalaxy.com

Scan for Video Explanation

Module-7: Strain

Strain:

When applied forces on a body produce deformation stress is developed inside the body

The relative change in dimension of a body which is subjected to stress is called "Strain".

F, F, ΔD, D

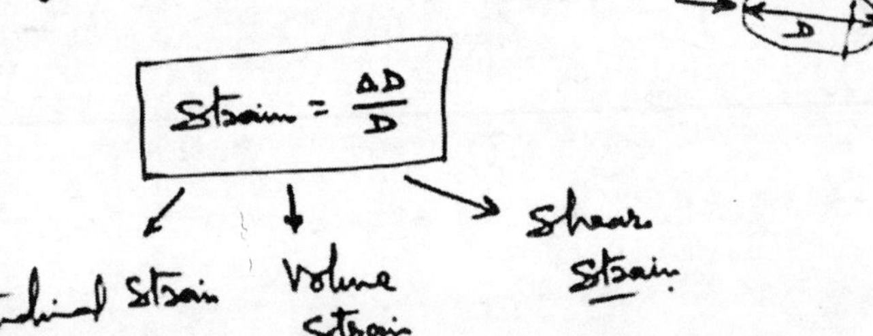

Web Reference at www.physicsgalaxy.com

Scan for Video Explanation

Module-8: Types of Strain

Types of Strain:

① Longitudinal Strain:

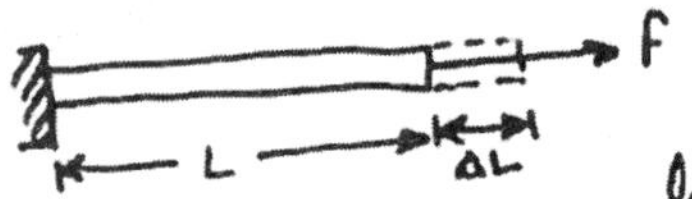

longitudinal strain $= \frac{\Delta L}{L}$ → elongation/compression

② Volume Strain: generally used in fluids.

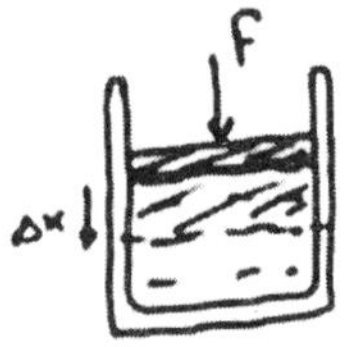

[volume strain $= \frac{\Delta V}{V}$].

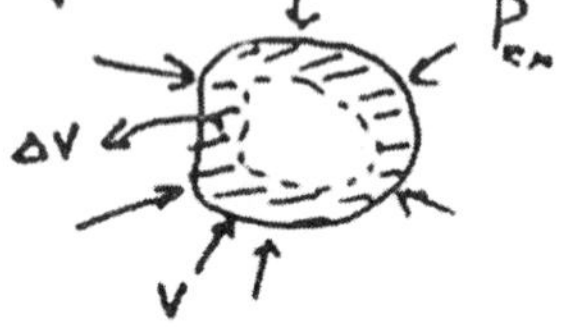

Scan for Video Explanation

Web Reference at www.physicsgalaxy.com

Module-8: Types of Strain

③ Shear Strain: tangential def in a body due to shear stress.

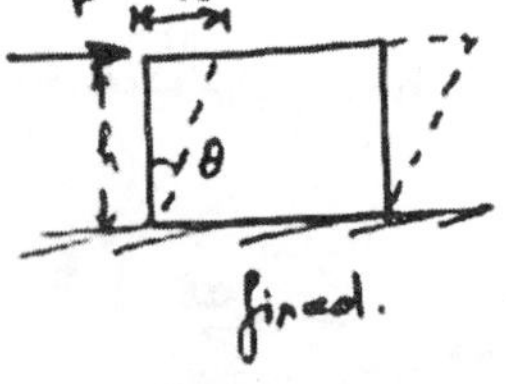

Shear strain $= \frac{x}{h} = \theta$ [small angle]

Scan for Video Explanation

Web Reference at www.physicsgalaxy.com

Module-9: Relation Between Stress and Strain

Relation between Stress and Strain:

It is observed experimentally that for small strain stress is proportional to strain in a body.

This is known as Hooke's law.

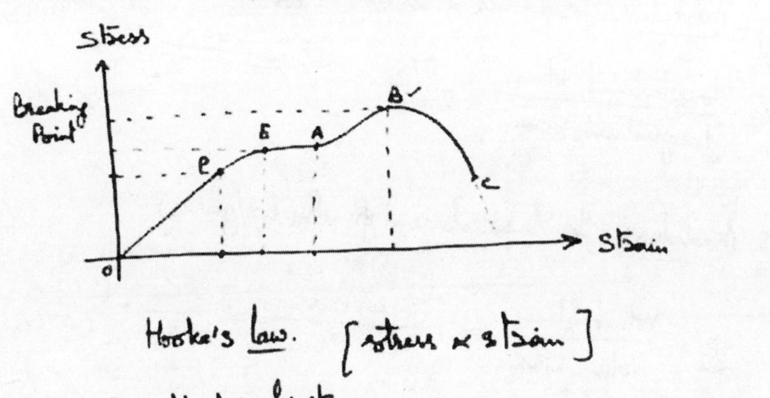

Hooke's law. [stress $\propto$ strain]

P ← Hooke's limit

Module-10: Hooke's Law and Modulus of Elasticity

Hooke's Law and Modulus of Elasticity:

Within Hooke's limit

$$\text{stress} \propto \text{strain}$$

$$\text{stress} = E(\text{strain})$$

$$\boxed{E = \left(\frac{\text{stress}}{\text{strain}}\right)}$$ { constant

↓

Modulus of elasticity for the material

↓

It is a measure of material elastic properties.

Module-11: Types of Modulus of Elasticity

Types of Modulus of Elasticity:

Depending on type of stress applied and resulting strain there are three types of elasticity Moduli.

(1) Young's Modulus: for solids it is given as

$$Y = \frac{\text{longitudinal stress}}{\text{longitudinal strain}} = \frac{F/S}{\Delta L/L}$$

F ←•—— L ——•→ F, ΔL, area = S

(2) Bulk Modulus: for solids and fluids (liq/gases)

$$B = \frac{\text{Volume Stress}}{\text{Volume Strain}} = \frac{\text{Excess Pressure}}{\text{Vol. Strain}} = \frac{\Delta P_{ex}}{|\Delta V/V|} = -\frac{\Delta P_{ex}}{(\Delta V/V)}$$

Scan for Video Explanation

Web Reference at www.physicsgalaxy.com

Module-11: Types of Modulus of Elasticity

(3) Shear Modulus: for solids it is defined as

$$\eta = \frac{\text{Shear stress}}{\text{Shear strain}}$$

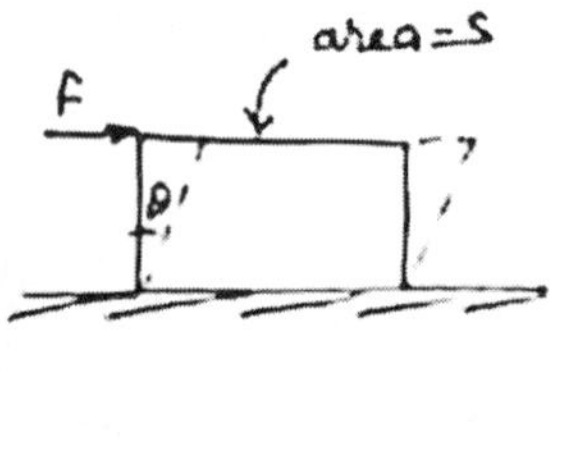

$$\eta = \left(\frac{F/S}{\theta}\right)$$

Compressibility of a material:

$$C = \frac{1}{B} = -\frac{\Delta V}{V \Delta P_{ex}}$$

$$\text{As } B = -\frac{\Delta P_{ex}}{\Delta V/V} = -\frac{V \Delta P_{ex}}{\Delta V}$$

Scan for Video Explanation

Web Reference at www.physicsgalaxy.com

Module-12: Solved Example-1

Ex : **The diameter of a brass rod is 4 mm and Young's modulus of brass is 9×10^{10} N/m^2. Find the force required to stretch it by 0.1% of its length.**

Sol^n: As we know

$$Y = \frac{\text{Stress}}{\text{Strain}} = \frac{F/A}{\Delta L/L}$$

$$\frac{\Delta L}{L} = 0.1 \times \frac{1}{100} = 0.001$$

$$F = \frac{YA\Delta L}{L}$$

$$F = 9\times10^{10} \times \pi(2\times10^{-3})^2 \times 0.001$$

$$F = 360\pi \text{ N} \quad \text{Ans.}$$

Web Reference at www.physicsgalaxy.com | Scan for Video Explanation

Module-13: Solved Example-2

Ex : **Calculate the elongation of the Copper and Aluminium wire shown in figure. Diameters of Cu and Al wires are 1.4 mm and 1 mm respectively. Given that $Y_{Cu} = 11 \times 10^{10}$ N/m^2 and $Y_{Al} = 7 \times 10^{10}$ N/m^2.** ($g = 10$ m/s^2)

Al 1m, M_2 4 kg, Cu 0.5 m, M_1 7 kg

Sol^n: Tension in Cu wire $T_1 = M_1 g = 70$ N

$$Y_{Cu} = \frac{\text{Stress}}{\text{Strain}} = \frac{T_1/A_1}{\Delta L_1/L_1} \Rightarrow \Delta L_1 = \frac{T_1 L_1}{Y_1 A}$$

$$= \frac{70\times0.5}{11\times10^{10}\times\pi(0.7\times10^{-3})^2}$$

$$= 0.2 \text{ mm} \quad \text{Ans.}$$

Tension in Al wire $T_2 = (M_1+M_2)g = 110$ N.

elongation in Al wire $\Delta L_2 = \dfrac{T_2 l_2}{Y_2 A_2} = \dfrac{110\times1}{7\times10^{10}\times\pi(0.5\times10^{-3})^2}$

$$= 2 \text{ mm}. \quad \text{Ans.}$$

Web Reference at www.physicsgalaxy.com | Scan for Video Explanation

Module-14: Solved Example-3

Ex : A steel wire is suspended vertically from a rigid support. When it is loaded by a weight in air, it is elongated by 5 mm and when the weight is submerged in water elongation is changed to 4 mm. Find the relative density of the material of weight.

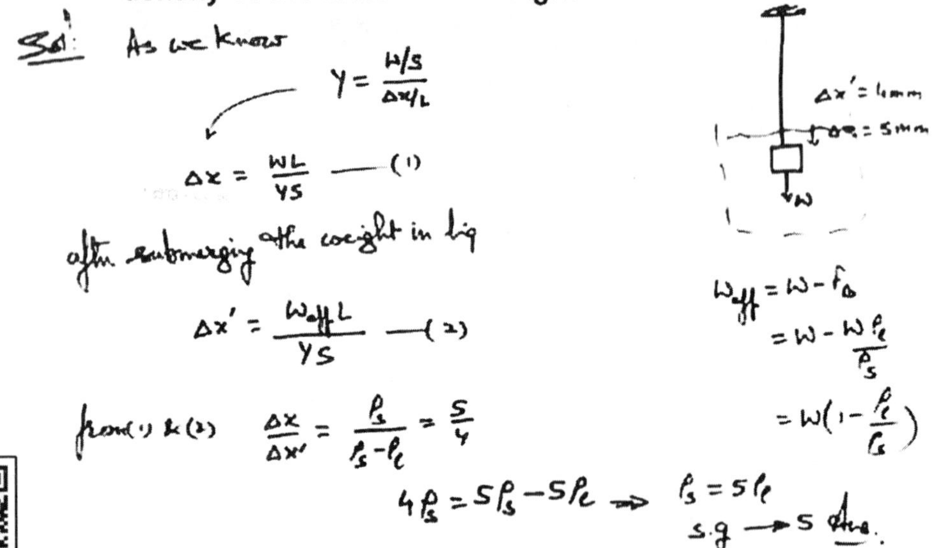

Scan for Video Explanation

Web Reference at www.physicsgalaxy.com

Module-15: Solved Example-4

Ex : When a metal block is placed in vacuum chamber from normal atmosphere find the fractional change in its volume. Given that atmospheric pressure is 10^5 N/m^2 and Bulk modulus of metal is 1.25×10^{11} N/m^2.

Sol: As Bulk mod. is given as

$$B = \left| \frac{\Delta P_{ex}}{\Delta V/V} \right|$$

$$\frac{\Delta V}{V} = \frac{\Delta P_{ex}}{B} = \frac{10^5}{1.25 \times 10^{11}} = 8 \times 10^{-7} \text{ Ans.}$$

Scan for Video Explanation

Web Reference at www.physicsgalaxy.com

Module-16: Solved Example-5

Ex : A rubber ball is taken to a depth of 200 m in a lake, its volume decreases by 0.1%. If density of water is 1000 kg/m^3 and g = 10 m/s^2. Find Bulk modulus of material of ball.

Sol^n:

Excess pressure at a depth of 200m is

$$\Delta P_{ex} = h\rho g$$

$$= 200 \times 1000 \times 10 = 2\times 10^6 \text{ N/m}^2$$

volume dec is $\Delta V = 0.1 \times \frac{V}{100} = 0.001V$

Bulk mod. $B = \left|\frac{\Delta P_{ex}}{\Delta V/V}\right| = \frac{2\times 10^6}{0.001} = 2\times 10^9 \text{ N/m}^2$ Ans.

Web Reference at www.physicsgalaxy.com | Scan for Video Explanation

Module-17: Solved Example-6

Ex : A wire of cross-sectional area A, Young's modulus Y and length 2L is stretched between two rigid poles. A weight of mass M is suspended at its middle. Find the angle made by string with horizontal.

Sol^n:

for eq^n of weight

$\sin\theta \simeq \theta = \frac{x}{L}$

$$2T\sin\theta = Mg \quad -(1)$$

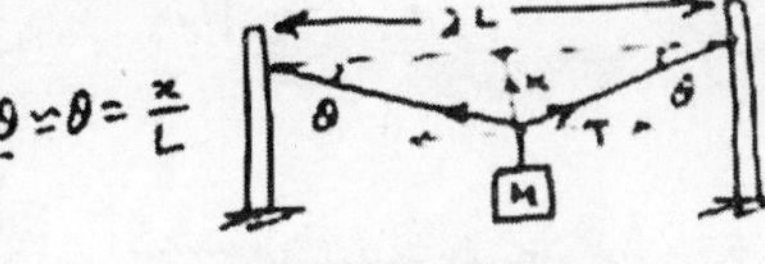

using def of Young's Mod -

$$Y = \frac{T/A}{\Delta L/L}$$

$$T = \frac{YAx^2}{2L^2}$$

elongation in wire

$$\Delta L = \left(\sqrt{L^2+x^2} - L\right)$$

$$= \left[L\left(1+\frac{x^2}{L^2}\right)^{1/2} - L\right]$$

for $x << L$

$$\Delta L = L\left(1+\frac{x^2}{2L^2}\right) - L$$

$$\Delta L = \frac{x^2}{2L}$$

from eq^n(1) $2\left(\frac{YAx^2}{2L^2}\right)\frac{x}{L} = Mg.$

$$\sin^3\theta = \frac{x^3}{L^3} = \frac{Mg}{YA} \rightarrow \theta = \sin^{-1}\left(\frac{Mg}{YA}\right)^{1/3} \text{ Ans.}$$

Web Reference at www.physicsgalaxy.com | Scan for Video Explanation

Module-18: Some Facts about Elasticity

Some Facts about Elasticity:

(1) For a material, modulus of elasticity is a constant and it is a measure of its stiffness or elasticity.

As $E = \frac{\text{stress}}{\text{strain}}$

for high value of E, then for large stress, strain will be less

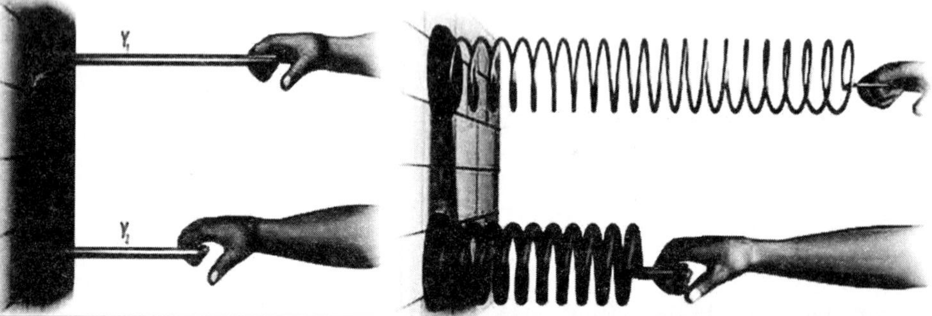

Scan for Video Explanation

Web Reference at www.physicsgalaxy.com

Module-18: Some Facts about Elasticity

(2) For solids, liquids & gases, we can use

$$E_{solids} > E_{liq} > E_{gases}$$

(3) As temp increases, intermolecular sep increases

$\Rightarrow$ restoring force decreases

& it lowers the value of E for the material.

Scan for Video Explanation

Web Reference at www.physicsgalaxy.com

Module-19: Elongation of Suspended Rod Under Self Weight

Elongation of a Suspended Rods under self Weight:

tension in rod at a dist x from bottom is

$$T = \left(\frac{M}{L}x\right)g$$

If dy is the elongation in elemental segment dx then we have

$$\left.\begin{array}{l}\text{Strain} = dy/dx \\ \text{Stress} = T/A\end{array}\right] \longrightarrow Y = \frac{\text{Stress}}{\text{Strain}} = \frac{T/A}{dy/dx}$$

$$dy = \frac{Mg}{YAL}x\,dx$$

$$\text{Total elongation } y = \int dy = \frac{Mg}{YAL}\int_0^L x\,dx = \frac{Mg}{YAL}\cdot\frac{L^2}{2} = \boxed{\frac{MgL}{2YA}}$$

Web Reference at www.physicsgalaxy.com | Scan for Video Explanation

Module-20: Metal Wires of Rods as Equivalent Spring

Metal wires or Rods as equivalent spring:

$$\left.\begin{array}{l}\text{Strain} = x/L \\ \text{Stress} = F/A\end{array}\right] \qquad Y = \frac{F/A}{x/L}$$

$$F = \left(\frac{YA}{L}\right)x = kx.$$

eq. force Constant for rod $k = \frac{YA}{L}$

Web Reference at www.physicsgalaxy.com | Scan for Video Explanation

Module-20: Metal Wires of Rods as Equivalent Spring

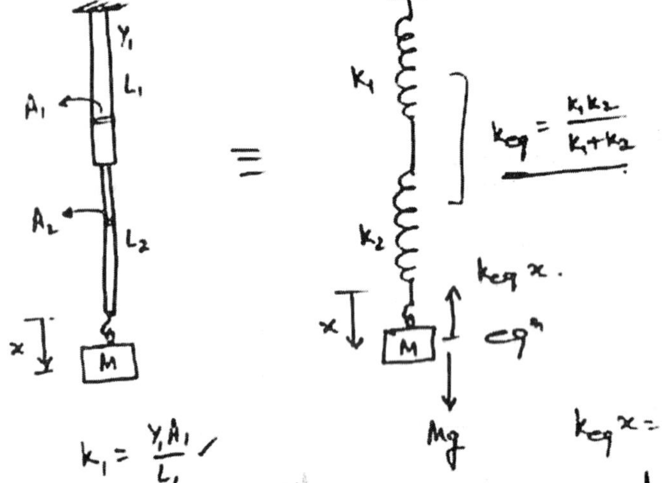

$$k_{eq} = \frac{k_1 k_2}{k_1 + k_2}$$

Y_1, L_1, A_1, A_2, L_2, x, M ≡ k_1, k_2, $k_{eq}x$, eqn, Mg

$$k_1 = \frac{Y_1 A_1}{L_1}$$

$$k_2 = \frac{Y_2 A_2}{L_2}$$

$$k_{eq} x = Mg$$

$$x = \frac{Mg}{K_{eq}}$$

Scan for Video Explanation

Web Reference at www.physicsgalaxy.com

Module-21: Elastic Potential Energy Stored due to Elasticity

Elastic Potential Energy stored due to elasticity:

When a solid is elongated, some work is done in this process & a part of this work is stored as PE in the material due to which restoring forces exist.

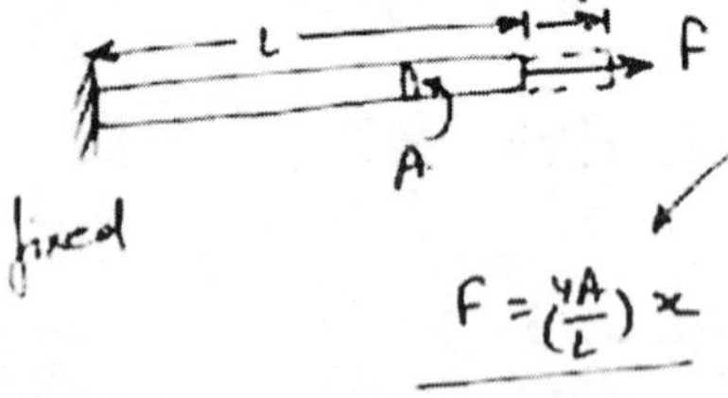

fixed, L, x, F, A

$$Y = \frac{F/A}{x/L}$$

$$x = \frac{FL}{YA}$$

$$F = \left(\frac{YA}{L}\right) x$$

equivalent force constant

Rod as if it is behaving like a spring is $\boxed{k = \frac{YA}{l}}$

PE stored in rod is $U = \frac{1}{2} k x^2 = \frac{1}{2}\left(\frac{YA}{l}\right) \times \left(\frac{FL}{YA}\right)^2 = \frac{1}{2} \frac{F^2 l}{YA}$

Scan for Video Explanation

Web Reference at www.physicsgalaxy.com

Module-21: Elastic Potential Energy Stored due to Elasticity

Density of elastic PE $= \frac{PE}{\text{Volume}}$

$$u_e = \frac{\frac{1}{2}\frac{F^2 l}{YA}}{Al} = \frac{1}{2}\frac{F^2}{A^2}\cdot\frac{1}{Y} = \boxed{\frac{1}{2}\frac{(\text{Stress})^2}{Y}} \ J/m^3$$

$$\boxed{u_e = \frac{1}{2}(\text{Stress})\times(\text{Strain})} \ J/m^3.$$

Web Reference at www.physicsgalaxy.com | Scan for Video Explanation

Module-22: Solved Example-7

Ex : Calculate the elastic potential energy stored in a brass rod of length 20 cm and area 1 cm^2 when it is elongated by a load of 5 kg mass. Given that Young's modulus of brass is 10^{11} N/m^2. $g = 10\ m/s^2$

Sol^n

Energy stored in rod $= u_e \times \text{volume}$

$$= \frac{1}{2}\frac{(\text{Stress})^2}{Y}\times \text{volume}$$

$$= \frac{1}{2}\frac{\left[50/10^{-4}\right]^2}{10^{11}} \times 0.2\times 10^{-4} \ J$$

$$= 2.5\times 10^{-5}\ J \ \text{Ans.}$$

Web Reference at www.physicsgalaxy.com | Scan for Video Explanation

Module-23: Solved Example-8

Ex : A 4m long cylindrical wire with cross section 1 cm^2 is suspended vertically from a rigid support and carries a bob of mass 100 kg at the other end. If the bob gets snapped, calculate the change in temperature of wire. Given that density of steel is 7800 kg/m^3, Young's modulus of steel is 2×10^{11} N/m^2 and specific heat of steel is 420 J/kg-K and g = 10 m/s^2.

Soln: Total energy stored in wire

$$E = \frac{1}{2}\frac{(\text{stress})^2}{Y} \times \text{volume}$$

$$= \frac{1}{2} \times \frac{(1000/10^{-4})^2}{2 \times 10^{11}} \times 4 \times 10^{-4} = 0.1\ J$$

If temp of rod inc by $\Delta T \Rightarrow 0.1 = ms\Delta T$

$$\Delta T = \frac{0.1}{L.A.\rho s} = \frac{0.1}{4 \times 10^{-4} \times 7800 \times 420} = 7.63 \times 10^{-5}\ K \quad \text{Ans}$$

Scan for Video Explanation

Web Reference at www.physicsgalaxy.com

Chapter 17
Gravitation Theory

Lecture Notes Modules

Module-1: Introduction to Gravitation

Gravitation:

Study, effects and analysis related to grav. field & forces in surrounding of masses & Earth.

Newton's law of Gravitation:

Acc. to this law –

(i) $F \propto m_1 m_2$

(ii) $F \propto \frac{1}{r^2}$

$\Rightarrow$

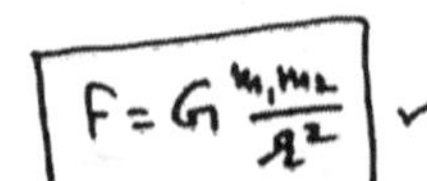

$$F = G\frac{m_1 m_2}{r^2}$$

G ← universal grav. Constant

$G = 6.67 \times 10^{-11}\ N \cdot m^2/kg^2$

Scan for Video Explanation

Web Reference at www.physicsgalaxy.com

Module-2: Limitations of Newton's Law of Gravitation

Limitations of Newton's law of Gravitation:

This law is only valid for pt. masses. On extended bodies it can not be directly applied.

F r F

m_1 m_2

$$F = \frac{G m_1 m_2}{r^2}$$

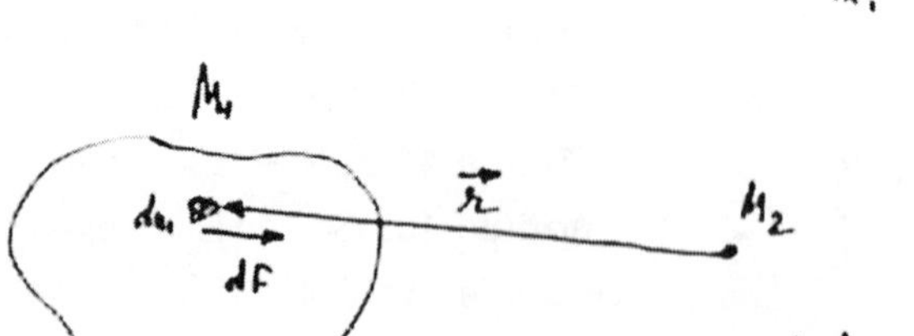

$$dF = \frac{G M_2\, dm}{r^2}$$

$$\vec{dF} = -\frac{G M_2\, dm}{r^2}\hat{r} = -\frac{G M_2\, dm}{r^3}\cdot\vec{r}$$

$$\vec{F} = \int \vec{dF} = -\int \frac{G M_2\, dm}{r^3}\cdot\vec{r}$$

Scan for Video Explanation

Web Reference at www.physicsgalaxy.com

Module-2: Limitations of Newton's Law of Gravitation

NOTE: For extended bodies NLG can be applied by taking small elements in extended body and integrate the exp. of force on element over the whole body.

$dm = \frac{M}{L}dx$

$$F \neq \frac{GmM}{(r+L/2)^2}$$

If dF be the grav force on m by $dm \Rightarrow dF = \frac{Gm\,dm}{x^2}$

Total force on m due to rod $F = \int dF = \int_r^{r+L} \frac{GmM\,dx}{Lx^2}$

$$F = \frac{GmM}{L}\left[-\frac{1}{x}\right]_r^{r+L}$$

Web Reference at www.physicsgalaxy.com

Scan for Video Explanation

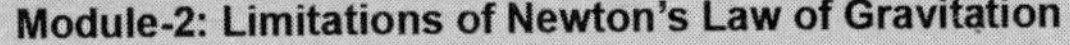

Module-2: Limitations of Newton's Law of Gravitation

$$F = \frac{GmM}{L}\left[-\frac{1}{x}\right]_r^{r+L}$$

$$F = \frac{GmM}{L}\left[\frac{1}{r} - \frac{1}{r+L}\right]$$

Web Reference at www.physicsgalaxy.com

Scan for Video Explanation

Module-3: Vector Representation of Gravitational Force

Vector Representation of gravitational force:

$$F = \frac{G m_1 m_2}{r^2}$$

$$\vec{F'} = -\frac{G m_1 m_2}{r^2}\hat{r}$$

$$\vec{F'} = -\frac{G m_1 m_2}{r^3}\cdot\vec{r}$$

$$\vec{F} = \frac{G m_1 m_2}{r^3}\vec{r}$$

m_1 ——— $\vec{r}$ ———> m_2

$\vec{F}$ $\vec{F'}$

$$\vec{F} = -\vec{F'}$$

$$|\vec{F}| = |\vec{F'}| = F$$

$$\hat{r} = \frac{\vec{r}}{r}$$

Scan for Video Explanation

Web Reference at www.physicsgalaxy.com

Module-4: Principle of Superposition of Forces

Principle of Superposition of Forces:

When there are more than two masses are there in a system then grav force on any mass can be obtained by vector sum of all individual forces acting on the mass due to all other masses of system.

Net grav force on M_0 as shown is

$$\vec{F}_{net} = \vec{F_1} + \vec{F_2} + \vec{F_3}$$

$$\vec{F}_{net} = \frac{G m_1 M_0}{r_1^2}\hat{r}_1 + \frac{G m_2 M_0}{r_2^2}\hat{r}_2 + \frac{G m_3 M_0}{r_3^2}\hat{r}_3$$

m_1, $\vec{r_1}$, $\vec{F_1}$, M_0, $\vec{F_2}$, $\vec{F_3}$, $\vec{r_2}$, $\vec{r_3}$, m_2, m_3

Scan for Video Explanation

Web Reference at www.physicsgalaxy.com

Module-5: Solved Example-1

Ex : **Two balls of mass m each are hung side by side by two long threads of equal length *l*. If the distance between upper ends is r, show that the distance r' between the centres of balls is given by**

$$gr'^2 (r - r') = 2lGm$$

Solⁿ: For eqⁿ of balls, we have

$$T\cos\theta = mg \quad \text{—(1)}$$

$$T\sin\theta = \frac{Gm^2}{r'^2} \quad \text{—(2)}$$

$$\frac{(2)}{(1)} \Rightarrow \tan\theta = \frac{Gm}{gr'^2} = \frac{r-r'}{2l} \qquad \left(\frac{r-r'}{2}\right)$$

$$F = \frac{Gm^2}{r'^2}$$

$$gr'^2(r-r') = 2Gml.$$

hence proved.

Web Reference at www.physicsgalaxy.com | Scan for Video Explanation

Module-6: Solved Example-2

Ex : **Two particles of equal mass go round a circle of radius R under the action of their mutual gravitational force. Find the speed of each particle.**

Solⁿ: For circular motion of masses

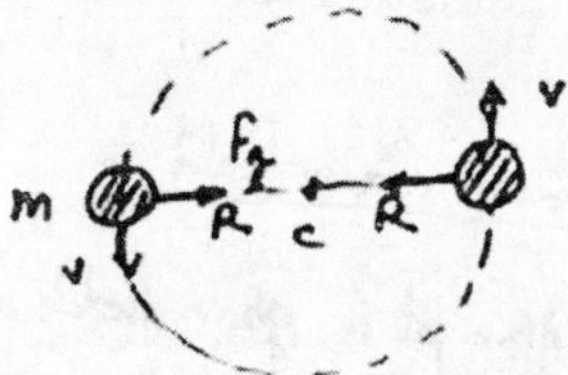

$$\frac{Gm^2}{(2R)^2} = \frac{mv^2}{R}$$

$$v = \sqrt{\frac{Gm}{4R}} \quad \text{Ans.}$$

Web Reference at www.physicsgalaxy.com | Scan for Video Explanation

Module-7: Solved Example-3

Ex : Find the gravitational attraction on mass m due to the quarter ring of same mass m and radius R as shown in figure.

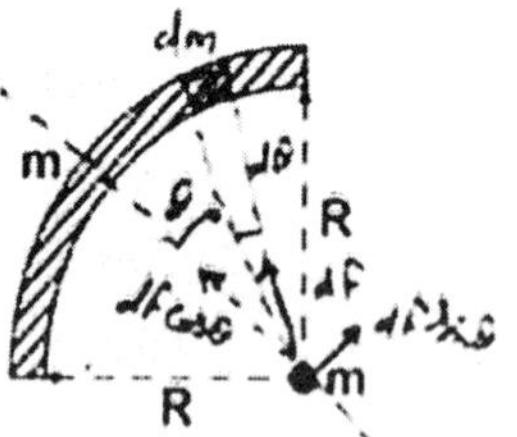

Sol^n: force on m due to dm on quarter ring is

$$dF = \frac{Gm\,dm}{R^2} = \frac{2Gm^2}{\pi R^2}\cdot d\theta \qquad dm = \frac{m}{\pi/2}\cdot d\theta = \frac{2m}{\pi}d\theta$$

net force on m will be

$$F = \int dF \cos\theta$$

$$= \frac{2Gm^2}{\pi R^2}\int_{-\pi/4}^{+\pi/4}\cos\theta\, d\theta$$

$$= \frac{2Gm^2}{\pi R^2}\left[\sin\theta\right]_{-\pi/4}^{+\pi/4}$$

$$= \frac{2Gm^2}{\pi R^2}\left[\frac{1}{\sqrt{2}} + \frac{1}{\sqrt{2}}\right]$$

$$F = \frac{2\sqrt{2}\,Gm^2}{\pi R^2} \quad \text{Ans.}$$

Scan for Video Explanation

Web Reference at www.physicsgalaxy.com

Module-8: Gravitational Field

Gravitational Field:

It is the region in surrounding of a mass where other masses experience a grav. force.

Strength of Grav. Field:

At a pt in grav. field, it is meas as force experienced by a unit mass. It is a vector qty & denoted by $\vec{g}$.

grav. field strength at pt P is

$$\vec{g}_P = \frac{\vec{F}}{m_o} \quad N/kg \text{ or } m/s^2$$

acceleration due to grav in the grav. field.

Scan for Video Explanation

Web Reference at www.physicsgalaxy.com

Module-9: Gravitational Field Strength due to a Point Mass and Extended Bodies

Gravitational Field Strength due to a point mass:

m ——— $\vec{x}$ ——— $\underline{F}$ m_0 P

$$F = \frac{Gmm_0}{x^2}$$

grav. field strength at P due to pt mass m is

$$g_P = \frac{F}{m_0} = \frac{Gm}{x^2}$$

vectorially

$$\vec{g}_P = -\frac{Gm}{x^2}\hat{x} = -\frac{Gm}{x^3}\cdot\vec{x}$$

Web Reference at www.physicsgalaxy.com | Scan for Video Explanation

Module-9: Gravitational Field Strength due to a Point Mass and Extended Bodies

Gravitational Field Strength due to extended bodies:

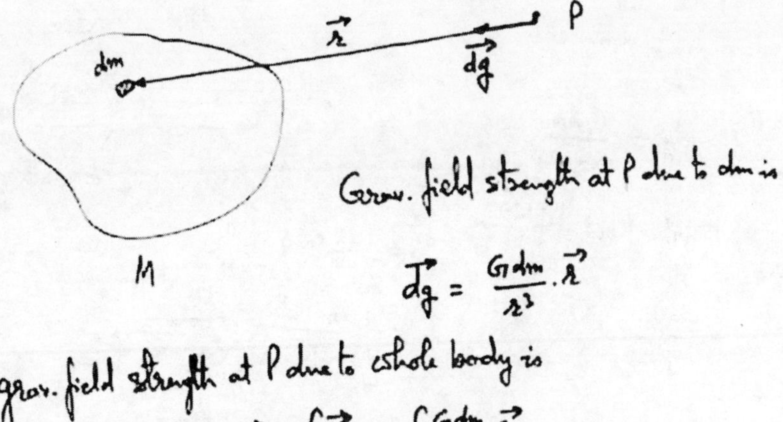

Grav. field strength at P due to dm is

$$\vec{dg} = \frac{G\,dm}{r^3}\cdot\vec{r}$$

grav. field strength at P due to whole body is

$$\vec{g}_P = \int\vec{dg} = \int_M \frac{G\,dm}{r^3}\cdot\vec{r}$$

Web Reference at www.physicsgalaxy.com | Scan for Video Explanation

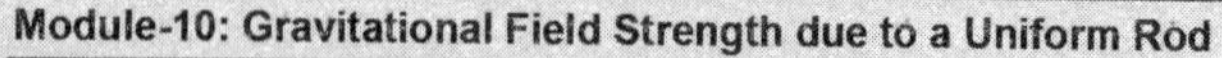

Module-10: Gravitational Field Strength due to a Uniform Rod

Gravitational Field Strength due to a uniform Rod:

Case-I: At an axial point of Rod.

grav. field strength at P due to dm is

$dm = \frac{M}{L}dx$

$$dg = \frac{G\,dm}{x^2} = \frac{GM}{Lx^2}dx$$

$$g_P = \int dg = \int_{r}^{r+L} \frac{GM}{Lx^2}dx$$

$$g_P = \frac{GM}{L}\left[-\frac{1}{x}\right]_{r}^{r+L}$$

$$\boxed{g_P = \frac{GM}{L}\left[\frac{1}{r} - \frac{1}{r+L}\right]}$$

Scan for Video Explanation

Web Reference at www.physicsgalaxy.com

Module-10: Gravitational Field Strength due to a Uniform Rod

Case-II: At an equatorial pt of rod.

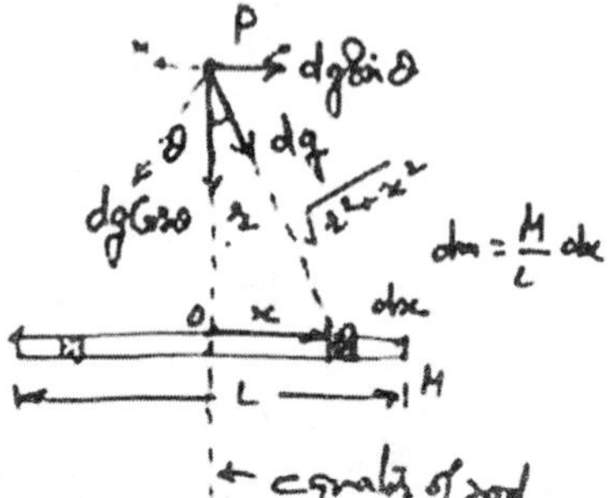

$dm = \frac{M}{L}dx$

If dg is grav field strength at P due to dm -

$$dg = \frac{G\,dm}{(r^2+x^2)}$$

net grav field at pt P is

$$g_P = \int dg \cos\theta$$

$$g_P = \int_{-L/2}^{+L/2} \frac{GM\,dx}{L(r^2+x^2)} \cdot \frac{r}{\sqrt{r^2+x^2}}$$

$$g_P = \frac{GMr}{L}\int_{-L/2}^{+L/2} \frac{dx}{(r^2+x^2)^{3/2}}$$

Scan for Video Explanation

Web Reference at www.physicsgalaxy.com

Module-10: Gravitational Field Strength due to a Uniform Rod

$$g_P = \frac{GMr}{L}\int_{-L/2}^{+L/2}\frac{dx}{(x^2+r^2)^{3/2}}$$

let $x = r\tan\theta$

$dx = r\sec^2\theta\, d\theta$

$$= \frac{GMr}{L}\int \frac{r\sec^2\theta\, d\theta}{r^3\sec^3\theta}$$

$$(r^2\tan^2\theta + r^2)^{3/2} = (r^2\sec^2\theta)^{3/2} = r^3\sec^3\theta$$

$$= \frac{GM}{Lr}\int \cos\theta\, d\theta$$

$$= \frac{GM}{Lr}[\sin\theta]$$

$$= \frac{GM}{Lr}\left[\frac{x}{\sqrt{x^2+r^2}}\right]_{-L/2}^{+L/2}$$

$$= \frac{GM}{Lr}\left[\frac{L/2}{\sqrt{L^2/4+r^2}}\times 2\right]$$

$$\boxed{g_P = \frac{2GM}{r\sqrt{L^2+4r^2}}}$$

Web Reference at www.physicsgalaxy.com

Scan for Video Explanation

Module-11: Gravitational Field Strength due to a Uniform Ring

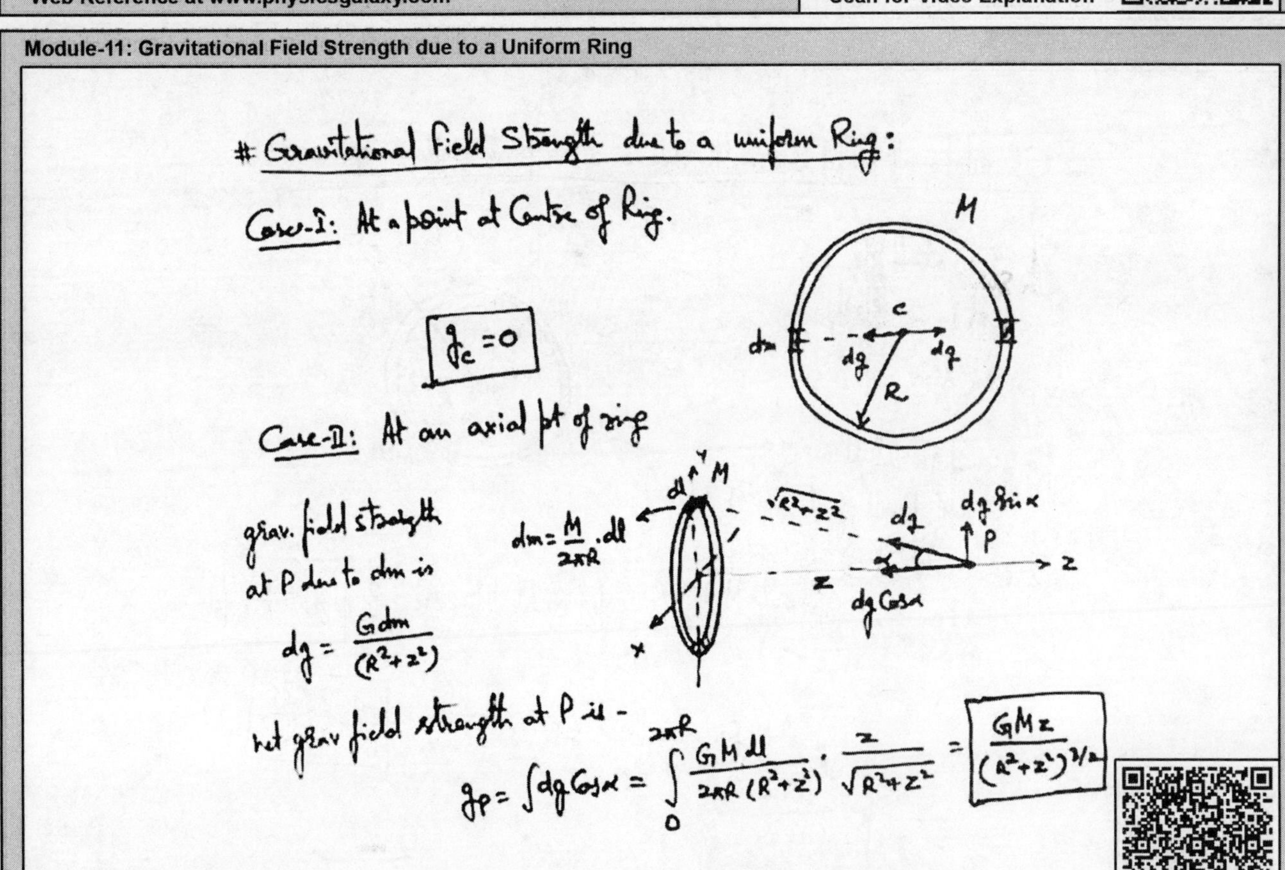

Module-12: Gravitational Field Strength due to a Circular Arc

Gravitational Field due to a Circular Arc:

$dm = \frac{M}{R\phi} R d\theta = \frac{M}{\phi} \cdot d\theta$

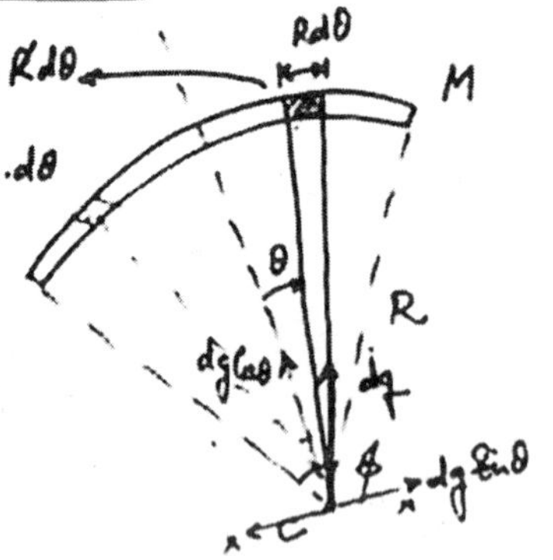

If dg be the grav field strength due to mass dm

$$dg = \frac{G\,dm}{R^2}$$

net grav field at pt C is

$$g_c = \int dg \cos\theta = \int_{-\phi/2}^{+\phi/2} \frac{GM\,d\theta}{\phi R^2} \cdot \cos\theta$$

$$g_c = \frac{GM}{\phi R^2} \int_{-\phi/2}^{+\phi/2} \cos\theta\, d\theta = \frac{GM}{\phi R^2} \left[\sin\theta\right]_{-\phi/2}^{+\phi/2}$$

$$\boxed{g_c = \frac{2GM \sin(\phi/2)}{\phi R^2}}$$

Scan for Video Explanation

Web Reference at www.physicsgalaxy.com

Module-13: Gravitational Field Strength due to a Hollow Sphere

Gravitational Field Strength due to a Uniform Hollow Sphere:

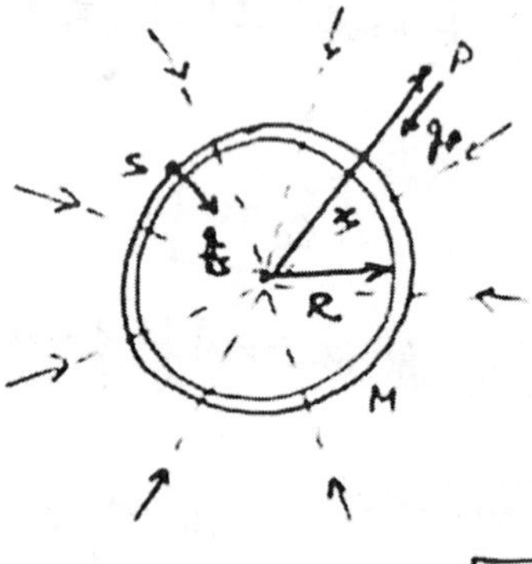

In surr at all pts $\vec{g}$ exist in radially inward dir.

for a uniform shell we can assume that all of its mass is concentrated at its centre (for outer pt.)

for outer pts $x > R$ $\quad \boxed{g_P = \frac{GM}{x^2}}$

for surface pts $x = R$ $\quad \boxed{g_s = \frac{GM}{R^2}}$

Scan for Video Explanation

Web Reference at www.physicsgalaxy.com

Module-13: Gravitational Field Strength due to a Hollow Sphere

grav field at pt P can be given

$$g_P = \int (dg_1 - dg_2)$$

$$= \int \frac{G\,dm_1}{x_1^2} - \frac{G\,dm_2}{x_2^2} = 0$$

$dm_1 = kx_1^2$

$dm_2 = kx_2^2$

at all interior pts of a uniform shell

for $x < R$.

$$\boxed{g_{in} = 0}$$

$g \propto \frac{1}{x^2}$

Web Reference at www.physicsgalaxy.com | Scan for Video Explanation

Module-14: Gravitational Field Strength due to a Solid Sphere

Gravitational Field Strength due to a uniform Solid Sphere:

for outer pts $x > R$

$$\boxed{g_P = \frac{GM}{x^2}}$$

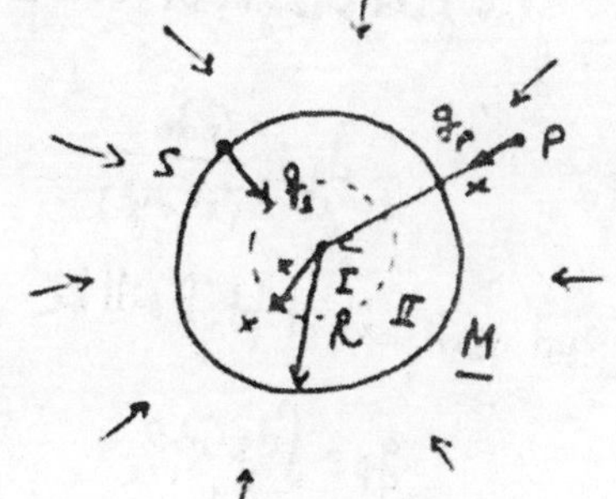

for surface pts $x = R$

$$\boxed{g_S = \frac{GM}{R^2}}$$

for interior pts $x < R$

mass enclosed in the inner sphere of rad x.

$$m = \frac{M}{\frac{4}{3}\pi R^3} \times \frac{4}{3}\pi x^3 = \frac{Mx^3}{R^3}$$

$$g_{in} = \frac{Gm}{x^2} = \frac{G}{x^2}\left[\frac{Mx^3}{R^3}\right]$$

$$\boxed{g_{in} = \frac{GMx}{R^3}}$$

Web Reference at www.physicsgalaxy.com | Scan for Video Explanation

Module-14: Gravitational Field Strength due to a Solid Sphere

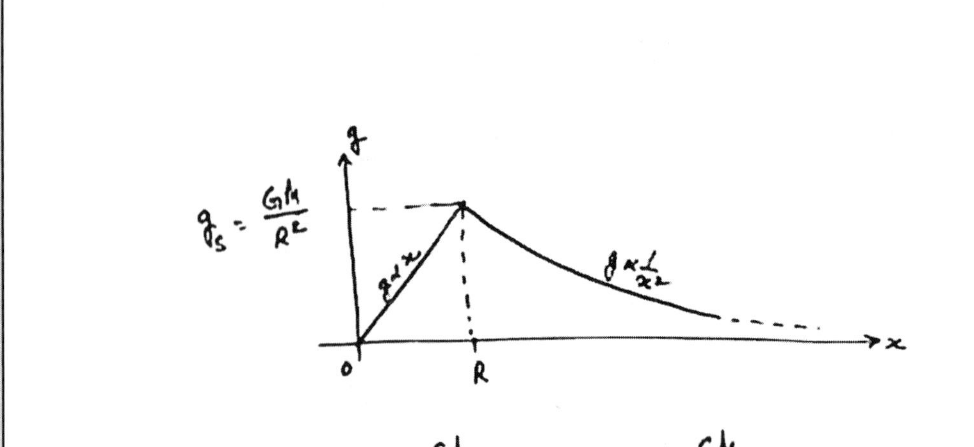

$$g_{in} = \frac{GMx}{R^3} \qquad g_{outer} = \frac{GM}{x^2}$$

Scan for Video Explanation

Web Reference at www.physicsgalaxy.com

Module-15: Gravitational Field Strength due to a Long Cylinder

Gravitational Field Strength due to a long thread:

grav. field strength at P due to dm is

$$dg = \frac{G\,dm}{(r^2+y^2)}$$

net grav. field at pt. P will be

$$g_P = \int dg\cos\theta$$

$$= \int_{-\infty}^{+\infty} \frac{G\lambda\,dy}{(r^2+y^2)}\cdot\frac{r}{\sqrt{r^2+y^2}} = \int_{-\infty}^{+\infty} \frac{G\lambda r\,dy}{(r^2+y^2)^{3/2}}$$

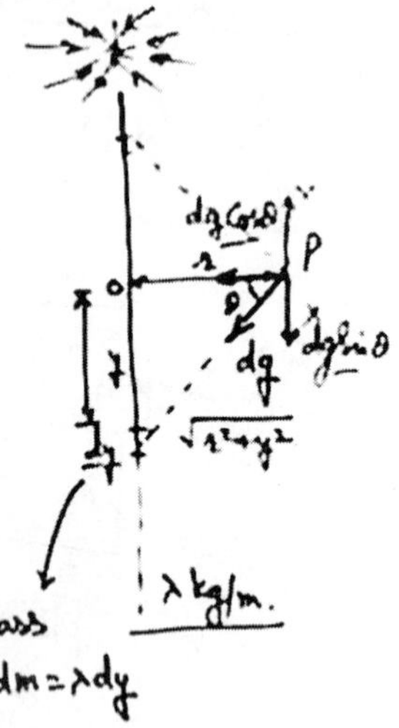

mass $dm = \lambda dy$

λ kg/m.

let $y = r\tan\theta$

$dy = r\sec^2\theta\,d\theta$

$$g_P = \int \frac{G\lambda r\cdot r\sec^2\theta\,d\theta}{r^3\sec^3\theta}$$

at $y = -\infty \rightarrow \theta = -\pi/2$

$y = \infty \rightarrow \theta = +\pi/2$

$$g_P = \frac{G\lambda}{r}\int_{-\pi/2}^{+\pi/2}\cos\theta\,d\theta = \frac{G\lambda}{r}\left[\sin\theta\right]_{-\pi/2}^{+\pi/2} = \frac{2G\lambda}{r}$$

$$\boxed{g_P = \frac{2G\lambda}{r}}$$

Scan for Video Explanation

Web Reference at www.physicsgalaxy.com

Module-16: Solved Example-4

Ex : Find the distance of a point from the earth's centre where the resultant gravitational field due to earth and moon is zero. The mass of earth is 6×10^{24} kg and that of moon is 7.4×10^{22} kg and the separation between earth and moon is 4×10^5 km.

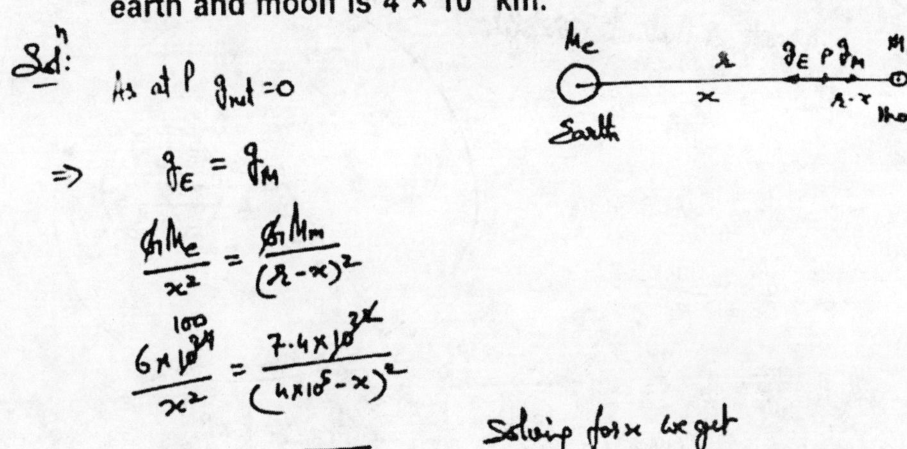

Web Reference at www.physicsgalaxy.com | Scan for Video Explanation

Module-17: Solved Example-5

Ex : A spherical hollow cavity is made in a lead sphere of radius R such that its surface touches the outside surface of lead sphere and passes through its centre. Find the gravitational field strength at the point P as shown. Given that mass of sphere before cavity is made was M.

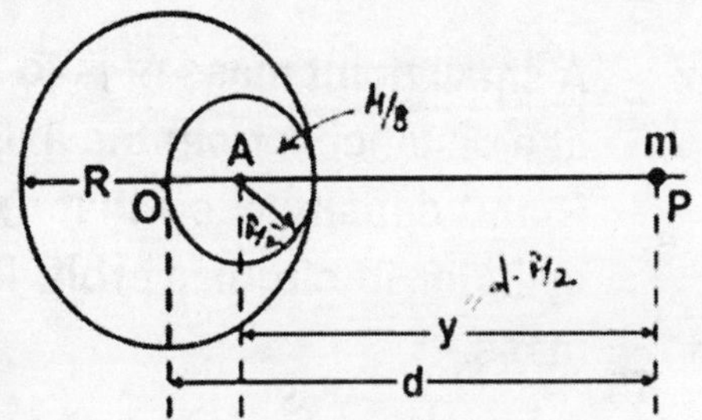

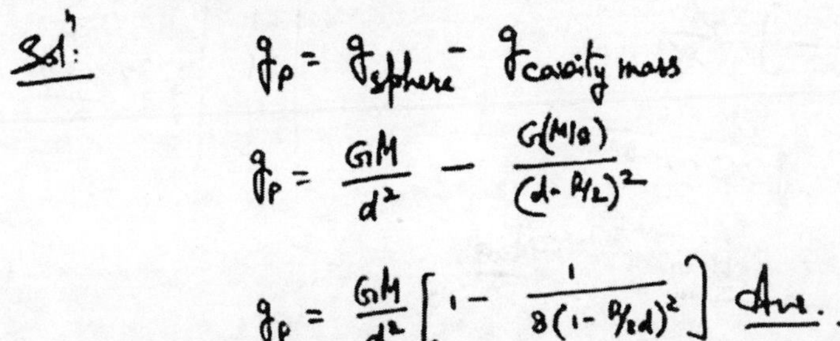

Web Reference at www.physicsgalaxy.com | Scan for Video Explanation

Module-18: Solved Example-6

Ex : **Inside a uniform sphere of density ρ, there is a spherical cavity whose centre is at a distance *l* from the centre of sphere. Find the strength of gravitational field inside the cavity.**

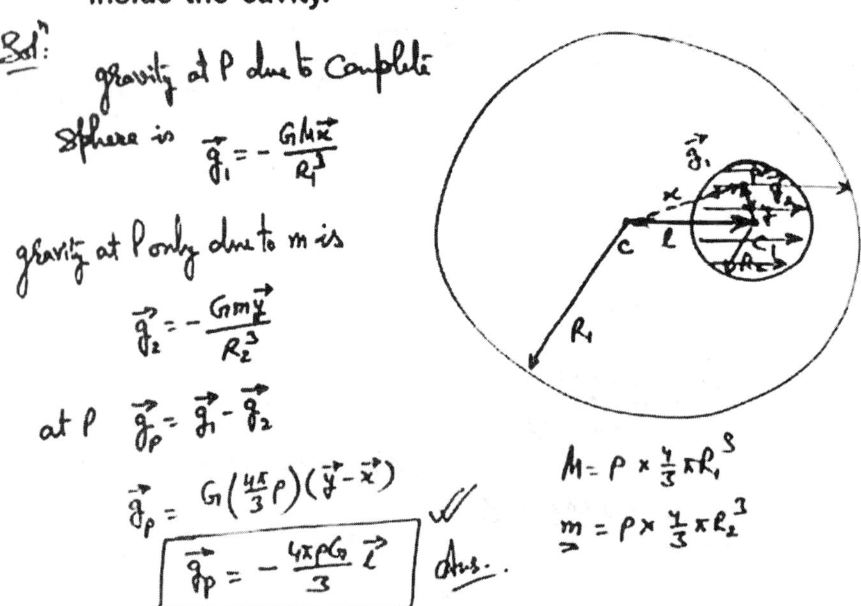

Scan for Video Explanation

Web Reference at www.physicsgalaxy.com

Module-19: Solved Example-7

Ex : A small point mass m is to be thrown with such a speed at a distance x from the axis of a long cylinder of radius R and density ρ, so that m starts revolving around the cylinder in circular orbit. Find the projection speed of mass.

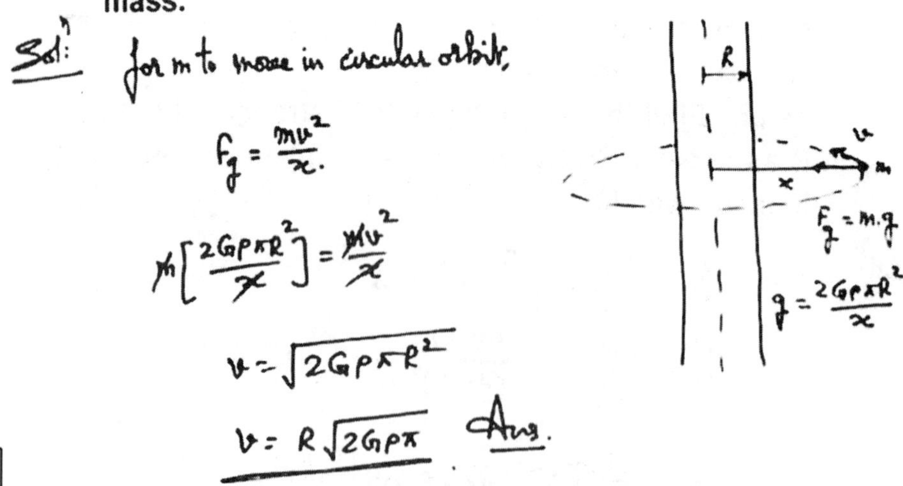

Scan for Video Explanation

Web Reference at www.physicsgalaxy.com

Module-20: Gravitational Lines of Forces

Gravitational Lines of Forces:

– These are hypothetical lines in grav. field which gives info about direction and magnitude of grav field strength at a point in the region.

– In a region these lines are drawn such that tangent to any point on a line gives the dir of $\vec{g}$ at that point & density of lines in the neighbourhood of a point are prop. to the magnitude of $\vec{g}$.

GLFs $|\vec{g}_A| > |\vec{g}_B|$

A $\vec{g}_A$

B $\vec{g}_B$

Web Reference at www.physicsgalaxy.com

Scan for Video Explanation

Module-20: Gravitational Lines of Forces

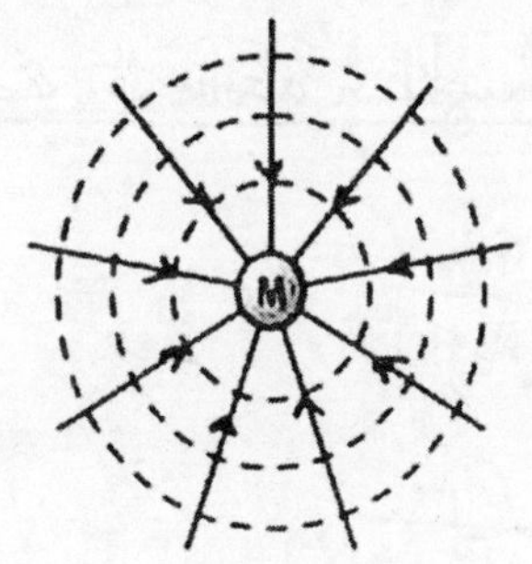

dir of $\vec{g}$ → tangent to GLF

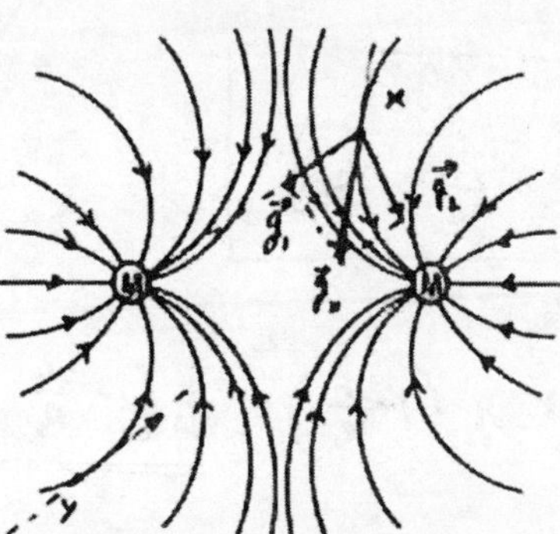

Web Reference at www.physicsgalaxy.com

Scan for Video Explanation

Module-21: Gravitational Field on Earth Surface

Gravitational Field on Earth Surface:

Earth → very large solid sphere.

$$g_s = \frac{GM_e}{R_e^2} = 9.8\ m/s^2$$

↓ acc^n due to gravity

Scan for Video Explanation

Web Reference at www.physicsgalaxy.com

Module-22: Value of g at a Height h Above Earth Surface

Value of g at a height h above the Earth Surface:

$$g_P = \frac{GM_e}{(R_e+h)^2}$$

$$g_h = \frac{GM_e}{R_e^2\left(1+\frac{h}{R_e}\right)^2}$$

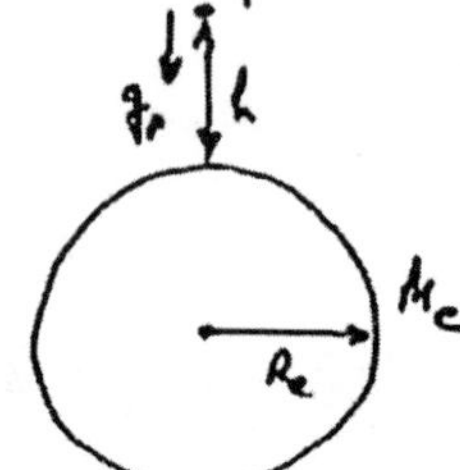

$$\boxed{g_h = \frac{g_s}{(1+h/R_e)^2}}$$

$R_e = 6400$ km.

for $h \ll R_e$

$$g_h = g_s\left(1+\frac{h}{R_e}\right)^{-2} = g_s\left(1-\frac{2h}{R_e}\right)$$

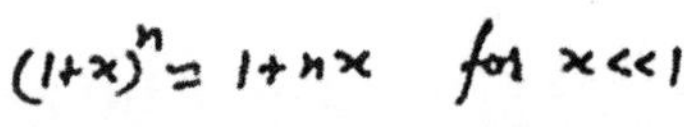

$$(1+x)^n \simeq 1+nx \quad \text{for } x \ll 1$$

Scan for Video Explanation

Web Reference at www.physicsgalaxy.com

Module-23: Value of g at a Height h Below Earth Surface

Value of g at a depth h inside the Earth Surface:

inside a solid sphere at a dist x

$$g = \frac{GMx}{R^3}$$

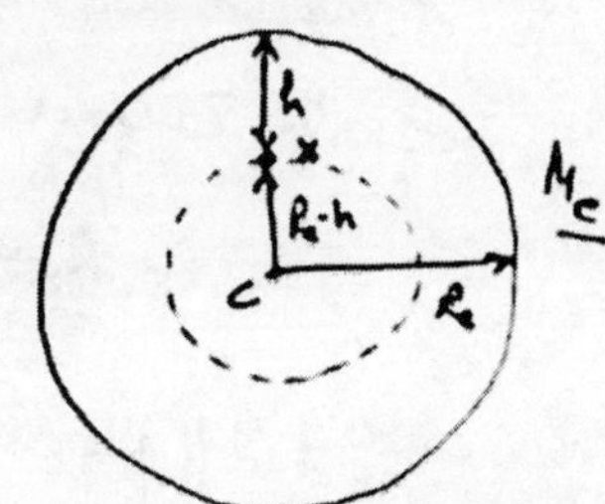

$$g_{in\,x} = \frac{GM_e(R_e - h)}{R_e^3}$$

$$\boxed{g_{in\,x} = g_s\left(1 - \frac{h}{R_e}\right)}$$

Web Reference at www.physicsgalaxy.com

Scan for Video Explanation

Module-24: Effect of Earth's Rotation on Value of g

Effect of Earth's Rotation on value of g:

for equilibrium of this body

$$N + m\omega_e^2 R_e \sin^2\lambda = mg_s$$

$$N = mg_s - m\omega_e^2 R_e \sin^2\lambda$$

$$mg_{eff} = W_{eff} = m(g_s - \omega_e^2 R_e \sin^2\lambda)$$

$$\boxed{g_{eff} = g_s - \omega_e^2 R_e \sin^2\lambda}$$

ω_e $T = 24\,hr = 86400\,sec$

N, $m\omega_e^2 R_e \sin\lambda$, $R_e \sin\lambda$, mg_s, R_e, λ

$$\omega_e = \frac{2\pi}{86400}\ rad/sec$$

at poles $\lambda = 0 \Rightarrow g_{poles} = g_s = 9.83\,m/s^2$

at equator $\lambda = \pi/2 \Rightarrow g_{eq} = g_s - \omega_e^2 R_e = 9.78\,m/s^2$

$g_{eq} < g_{poles}$.

Web Reference at www.physicsgalaxy.com

Scan for Video Explanation

Module-25: Effect of Shape of Earth on Value of g

Effect of Shape of Earth on Value of g:

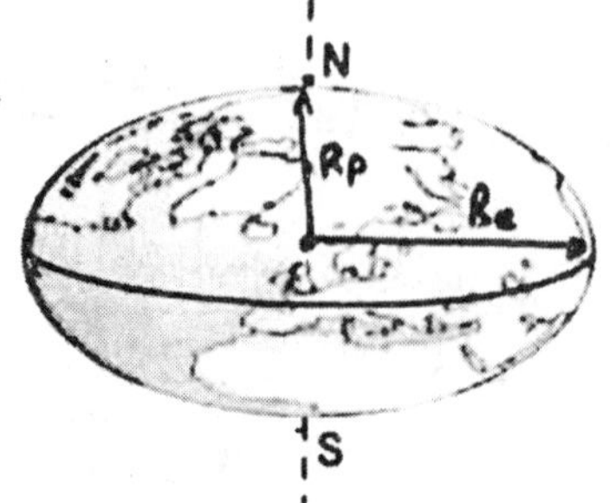

at variation location on Earth Surface

$R_E - R_P \sim 21$ to 24 km.

at diff pos. on earth $g_P \geq g_E$

at various locations we find $g_P - g_E \sim 0.02$ to $0.04\ m/s^2$

NOTE: Due to shape of Earth variation in g is very small and for most of analysis this effect can be ignored.

Scan for Video Explanation

Web Reference at www.physicsgalaxy.com

Module-26: Solved Example-8

Ex : If the radius of earth were to shrink by one percent, its mass remaining the same. What would be new acceleration due to gravity on earth surface.

Soln.:

As we know $g_s = \frac{GM_e}{R_e^2}$

new gravity $g_s' = \frac{GM_e}{(0.99R_e)^2} = \frac{g_s}{(0.99)^2}$

$g_s' = g_s(1-0.01)^{-2} = 1.02\, g_s$

new value of gravity will be increased by 2%. Ans.

Scan for Video Explanation

Web Reference at www.physicsgalaxy.com

Module-27: Solved Example-9

Ex : **At what angular speed should earth rotate so that apparent value of g at equator becomes zero ? What will be the length of the day in this situation [Take $g_s = 9.8\ m/s^2$ and $r_e = 6400$ km]**

Sol^n: due to rot^n of earth the effective gravity at equator

$$g_{eq} = g_s - \omega^2 R_e = 0$$

$$\omega = \sqrt{\frac{g_s}{R_e}} = \sqrt{\frac{9.8}{6400 \times 10^3}}$$

$$= 1.24 \times 10^{-3}\ rad/s. \text{ Ans.}$$

length of the day will be $T = \frac{2\pi}{\omega} = \frac{2 \times 3.14}{1.24 \times 10^{-3}} = 5065$ sec

$\simeq 84.4$ min Ans.

Web Reference at www.physicsgalaxy.com | Scan for Video Explanation

Module-28: Solved Example-10

Ex : **Find the height over the earth surface at which weight of body becomes half of its value of surface.**

Sol^n: at Earth Surface $W = mg_s$

at a height h above $W' = \frac{mg_s}{(1+h/R_e)^2}$

given that $W' = W/2$

$$\frac{mg_s}{(1+h/R_e)^2} = \frac{1}{2} mg_s$$

$$1 + \frac{h}{R_e} = \sqrt{2} \Rightarrow h = R_e(\sqrt{2}-1) \text{ Ans.}$$

Web Reference at www.physicsgalaxy.com | Scan for Video Explanation

Module-29: Solved Example-11

Ex : **If diameter of a planet is four times that of earth. Find the period of a pendulum on the planet, if it is a seconds pendulum on earth. Take mean density of planet equal to that of earth.**

Sol^n: for a seconds pendulum on Earth $T = 2\pi\sqrt{\frac{l}{g_s}} = 2$ sec

on the planet $T' = 2\pi\sqrt{\frac{l}{g_p}} = 2\pi\sqrt{\frac{l}{4g_s}} = \frac{2}{2} = 1$ sec Ans.

on planet surface $g_p = \frac{GM_p}{R_p^2} = \frac{G}{(4R_e)^2} \times \rho \cdot \frac{4}{3}\pi(4R_e)^3$

$= G\rho\left(\frac{4\pi}{3}\right) \cdot 4R_e = 4 \cdot \frac{GM_e}{R_e^2}$

$\rho = \frac{M_e}{\frac{4}{3}\pi R_e^3}$

$g_p = 4g_s$

Scan for Video Explanation

Web Reference at www.physicsgalaxy.com

Module-30: Gravitational Interaction Energy

Gravitational Interaction Energy :

- This is the PE in a SOP due to their grav interaction.
- It is the W/D in assembling the SOP in given configuration from ∞ sep against grav. forces of system.
- As grav forces are always attractive, W/D against these forces in assembling a SOP is always −ve hence grav interaction energy of a system is always −ve as we take zero reference at ∞ separation.

Scan for Video Explanation

Web Reference at www.physicsgalaxy.com

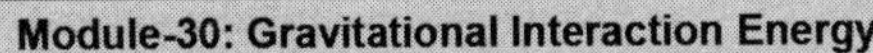

Module-30: Gravitational Interaction Energy

Grav.

Potential Energy of Two point masses:

m_1 ——— r ——— m_2 $\quad F_g = \frac{Gm_1m_2}{x^2}$

m_1 (rest) ——— x ——— dx m_2 $\vec{F}$ → ∞

W/D in bringing m_2 by a dist dx

$$dW = \vec{F}\cdot\vec{dx} = -\frac{Gm_1m_2}{x^2}dx$$

W/D in bringing it from ∞ to r will be

$$W = \int dW = \int_{\infty}^{r} \frac{Gm_1m_2}{x^2}dx = Gm_1m_2\int_{\infty}^{r}\frac{1}{x^2}dx$$

$$= Gm_1m_2\left[-\frac{1}{x}\right]_{\infty}^{r}$$

$$\boxed{W = -\frac{Gm_1m_2}{r} = U_g}$$

Module-31: Gravitational Interaction Energy for a System of Particles

Grav Interaction Energy for a System of Particles:

For a given N mass system - $m_1, m_2 - - - m_N$ separated from each other by distances $r_{12}, r_{13} - - - r_{ij}$. The interaction energy of such a system can be given as -

$$\boxed{U_g = -\frac{1}{2}\sum_{i=1}^{N}\sum_{j=1}^{N}\frac{Gm_im_j}{r_{ij}}}$$

$$\boxed{U_g = -\frac{Gm_1m_2}{r_{12}} - \frac{Gm_1m_3}{r_{13}} - \frac{Gm_2m_3}{r_{23}}}$$

Module-32: Solved Example-12

Ex : **Three particles each of mass m are placed at the corners of an equilateral triangle of side d. Calculate the work done in increasing the sides of triangle from d to 2d.**

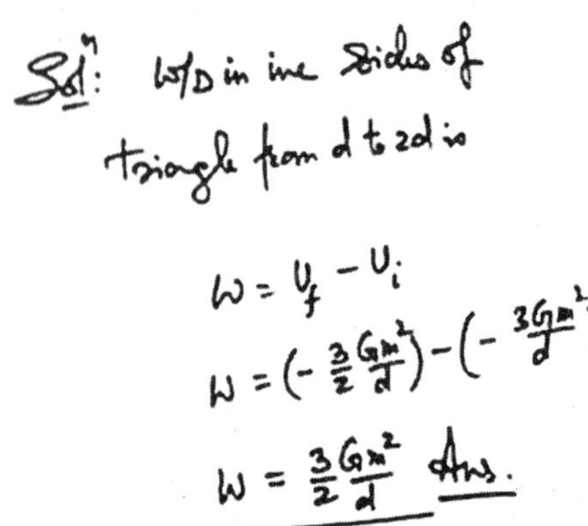

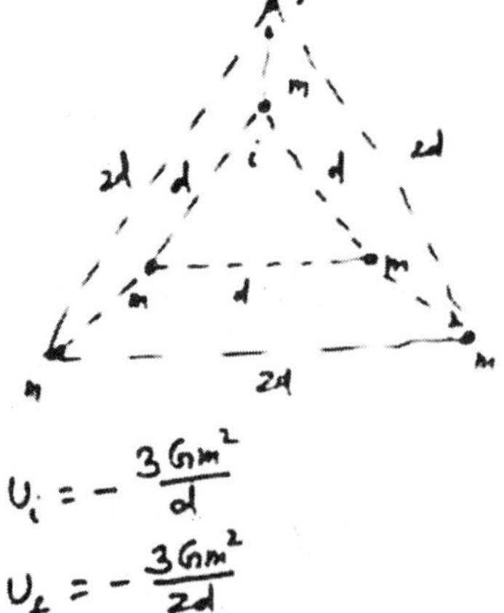

Scan for Video Explanation

Web Reference at www.physicsgalaxy.com

Module-33: Solved Example-13

Ex : **Two particles of masses m_1 and m_2 are initially at rest at infinite separation. When released, find their relative velocity of approach when they are at a separation d.**

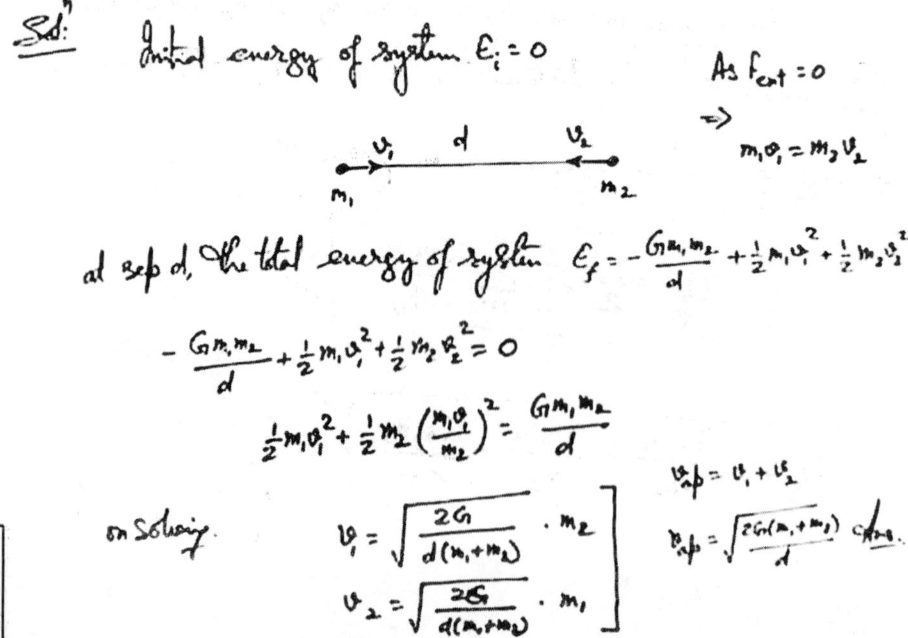

Scan for Video Explanation

Web Reference at www.physicsgalaxy.com

Module-34: Gravitational Potential

Gravitational Potential:

It is defined as grav. interaction energy a unit mass placed at a pt in grav. field.

grav. field.

P . m_0

If interaction energy of mass m_0 at pt P is U_g then grav. potential at pt P is -

$$V_P = \frac{U_g}{m_0} \quad J/kg.$$

At a pt in grav. field grav. potential is defined as the W/D in bringing a unit mass from ∞ to that pt. (at rest)

Web Reference at www.physicsgalaxy.com | **Scan for Video Explanation**

Module-34: Gravitational Potential

If at a pt in grav. field, we know the grav potential say V then on placing a mass m at this pt, the grav interaction energy of this mass with the field can be given as

$$U_g = mV$$

NOTE: In a grav field region, grav. pot^n is a characteristic at each pt in the region.

Web Reference at www.physicsgalaxy.com | **Scan for Video Explanation**

Module-35: Relation in g and V in Gravitational Field

Relation in $\vec{g}$ and V in a gravitational Field:

$$V = -\int_{\infty}^{P} \vec{F_g}\cdot\vec{dx}$$

$$V = -\int_{\infty}^{P} \vec{g}\cdot dx$$

for a unit mass.

$$\vec{F_g} = \vec{g}$$

For a region $\vec{g}$ & V can be related as

$$\vec{g} = -\nabla V = -\text{grad of } V \quad [\text{for Cons. fields}]$$

Scan for Video Explanation

Web Reference at www.physicsgalaxy.com

Module-35: Relation in g and V in Gravitational Field

$$\vec{g} = -\nabla V$$

Where $\nabla \equiv \frac{\partial}{\partial x}\hat{i} + \frac{\partial}{\partial y}\hat{j} + \frac{\partial}{\partial z}\hat{k}$

for unidirection variation in field, we can use

$$\vec{g} = -\frac{dV}{dx}\hat{i}$$

$\vec{g}$ is the −ve of slope of curve of V vs x.

for 3D variation in field, we can use

$$\vec{g} = -\left(\frac{\partial V}{\partial x}\hat{i} + \frac{\partial V}{\partial y}\hat{j} + \frac{\partial V}{\partial z}\hat{k}\right)$$

Scan for Video Explanation

Web Reference at www.physicsgalaxy.com

Module-36: Gravitational Potential due to a Point Mass

Gravitational Potential due to a point mass:

Grav. interaction energy of test mass m_0 in the field of m.

m_0 (test mass) P, r, m

$$U_g = -\frac{Gmm_0}{r}$$

The grav. potential at pt P due to the field of m is

$$\boxed{V = \frac{U_g}{m_0} = -\frac{Gm}{r}} \checkmark$$

Alternatively

$$V_P = -\int_{\infty}^{P} \vec{g}\cdot d\vec{x} = \int_{\infty}^{P} \frac{Gm}{x^2}\,dx = Gm\left[-\frac{1}{x}\right]_{\infty}^{r}$$

$$\boxed{V_P = -\frac{Gm}{r}} \checkmark$$

Web Reference at www.physicsgalaxy.com

Scan for Video Explanation

Module-37: Gravitational Potential due to a Uniform Ring

Gravitational Potential due to a Uniform Ring:

Case-I: V at Centre of Ring.

grav pot^n at C due to dm is

$$dV = -\frac{G\,dm}{R}$$

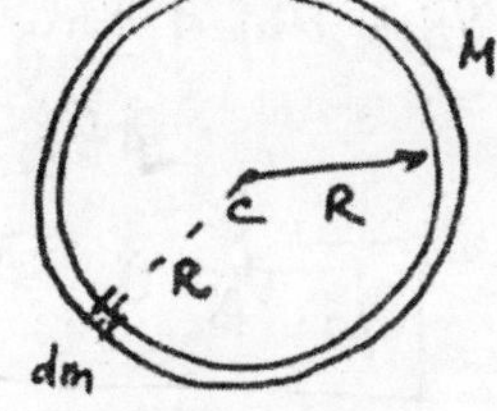

grav pot^n due to Complete ring at C –

$$V_c = \int dV = -\int \frac{G\,dm}{R} = -\frac{G}{R}\int dm$$

$$\boxed{V_c = -\frac{GM}{R}}$$

Web Reference at www.physicsgalaxy.com

Scan for Video Explanation

Module-37: Gravitational Potential due to a Uniform Ring

Case-II: V at an axial pt of ring

Grav pot^n due to dm at pt P is

$$dV = -\frac{G\,dm}{\sqrt{R^2+x^2}}$$

Net pot^n at P due to whole ring is

$$V_P = \int dV = -\int \frac{G\,dm}{\sqrt{R^2+x^2}}$$

$$\boxed{V_P = -\frac{GM}{\sqrt{R^2+x^2}}}$$

Scan for Video Explanation

Web Reference at www.physicsgalaxy.com

Module-38: Work Done in Gravitational Field

\# Work Done in displacement of a body in Gravitational Field:

W/D in disp of body from A to B is –

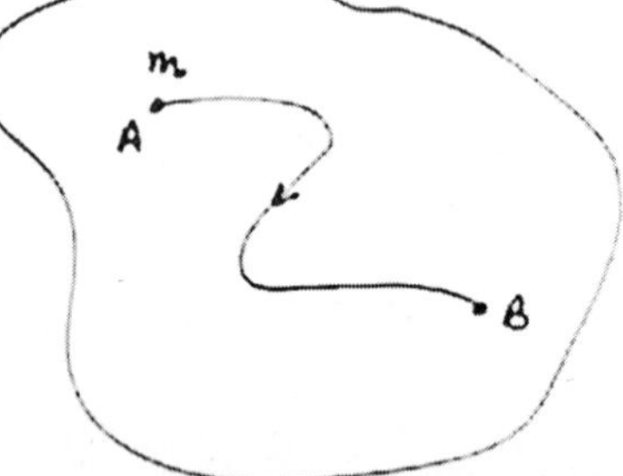

$$\boxed{W = U_B - U_A}$$

$$W = m(V_B - V_A)$$

work = mass × grav. pot^n diff.

If V_A and V_B are grav. potentials at pts A and B

$$U_A = mV_A$$

$$U_B = mV_B$$

$$\boxed{V_B - V_A = \frac{W}{m}}$$ W/D per unit mass.

$$\boxed{V_B - V_A = -\int_A^B \vec{g}\cdot\vec{dx}}$$

Scan for Video Explanation

Web Reference at www.physicsgalaxy.com

Module-39: Gravitational Potential due to a Hollow Sphere

Gravitational Potential due to a Hollow Sphere:

at outer pt $x > R$

$$V_{out} = -\frac{GM}{x}$$

at Surface pt $x = R$

$$V_S = -\frac{GM}{R}$$

at any interior $x < R$

$$V_{in} = -\frac{GM}{R}.$$

$$V_B - V_A = -\int_A^B \vec{g}\cdot d\vec{x} = 0$$

P, M, x, p, x, C, $g_{in} = 0$, R, S

$V_{in} = V_S$

NOTE: In a region if at every pt $g = 0$ then this region can be taken as an equipotential region.

Web Reference at www.physicsgalaxy.com

Scan for Video Explanation

Module-39: Gravitational Potential due to a Hollow Sphere

Variation of gravitational potential due to a hollow sphere:

for $x > R$ $\quad V_{out} = -\frac{GM}{x}$

for $x = R$ $\quad V_S = -\frac{GM}{R}$

for $x < R$ $\quad V_{in} = -\frac{GM}{R}$

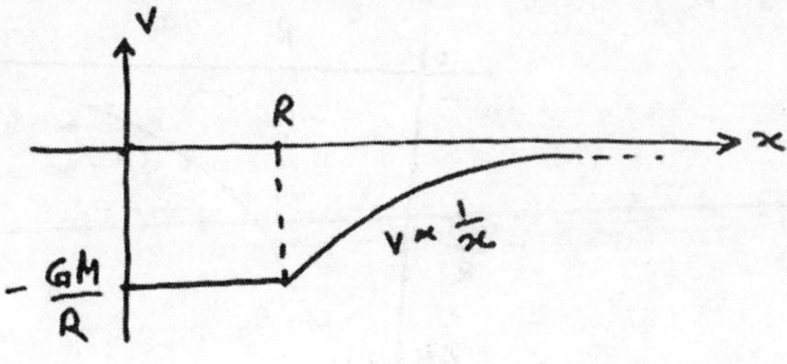

Web Reference at www.physicsgalaxy.com

Scan for Video Explanation

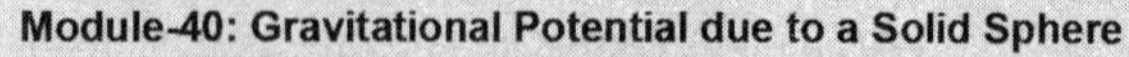

Module-40: Gravitational Potential due to a Solid Sphere

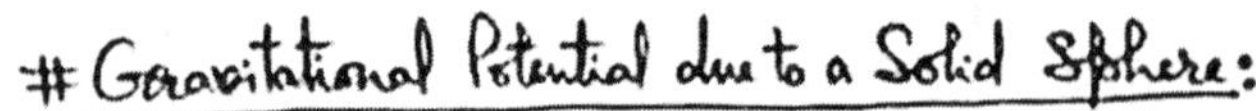

Gravitational Potential due to a Solid Sphere:

for outer pts $x > R$

$$V_{outer} = -\frac{GM}{x}$$

for surface pts $x = R$

$$V_s = -\frac{GM}{R}$$

at inside pts $x < R$

$$V_{in} = -\frac{GM}{2R^3}[3R^2 - x^2]$$

$$V_p = -\int_{\infty}^{x} \vec{g}\cdot\vec{dx}$$

$$= -\left[\int_{\infty}^{R} \vec{g}_{out}\cdot\vec{dx} + \int_{R}^{x} \vec{g}_{in}\cdot\vec{dx}\right]$$

$$= \int_{\infty}^{R} \frac{GM}{x^2}dx + \int_{R}^{x} \frac{GMx}{R^3}\cdot dx$$

$$= -\frac{GM}{R} + \frac{GM}{2R^3}[x^2 - R^2] = -\frac{GM}{2R^3}[3R^2 - x^2]$$

at Centre $x = 0$

$$V_c = -\frac{3}{2}\frac{GM}{R} = \frac{3}{2}V_s$$

Scan for Video Explanation

Web Reference at www.physicsgalaxy.com

Module-40: Gravitational Potential due to a Solid Sphere

Variation of grav. potential due to a Solid Sphere:

$$V_{out} = -\frac{GM}{x}$$

$$V_s = -\frac{GM}{R}$$

$$V_{in} = -\frac{GM}{2R^3}[3R^2 - x^2]$$

$$V_c = -\frac{3}{2}\frac{GM}{R} = \frac{3}{2}V_s$$

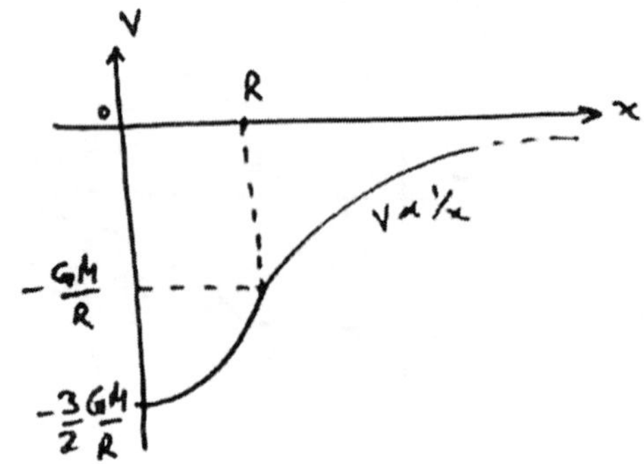

Scan for Video Explanation

Web Reference at www.physicsgalaxy.com

Module-41: Gravitational Potential Energy of a Body on Earth

Gravitational Potential Energy of a Body in Earth's Grav. Field:

Case-I: On Earth Surface.

$$U_g = mV = m\left[-\frac{GM_e}{R_e}\right] = -\frac{GM_e m}{R_e}$$

Case-II: At a height h above the Earth surface

$$U_g = mV = m\left[-\frac{GM_e}{R_e+h}\right] = -\frac{GM_e m}{R_e+h}$$

Case-III: At a depth h from Earth surface inside the earth.

$$U_g = mV = m\left[-\frac{GM_e}{2R_e^3}\left[3R_e^2 - x^2\right]\right]$$

$$U_g = -\frac{GM_e m}{2R_e^3}(3R_e^2 - x^2) \leftarrow x = R_e - h$$

Web Reference at www.physicsgalaxy.com | Scan for Video Explanation

Module-42: Solved Example-14

Ex : **Find workdone in shifting a body of mass m from a height h above the earth surface to a height 2h above the surface.**

Sol^n:

$$W = U_{2h} - U_h$$

When body is at a height h $\quad U_h = -\frac{GM_e m}{R_e+h}$

When body is at a height 2h $\quad U_{2h} = -\frac{GM_e m}{R_e+2h}$

$$W = GM_e m\left[\frac{1}{R_e+h} - \frac{1}{R_e+2h}\right] \quad \text{Ans.}$$

Web Reference at www.physicsgalaxy.com | Scan for Video Explanation

Module-43: Solved Example-15

Ex : Find the gravitational interaction energy of a system consisting of a disc of mass M, radius R and a point mass m situated at a distance x from disc centre on its axis as shown.

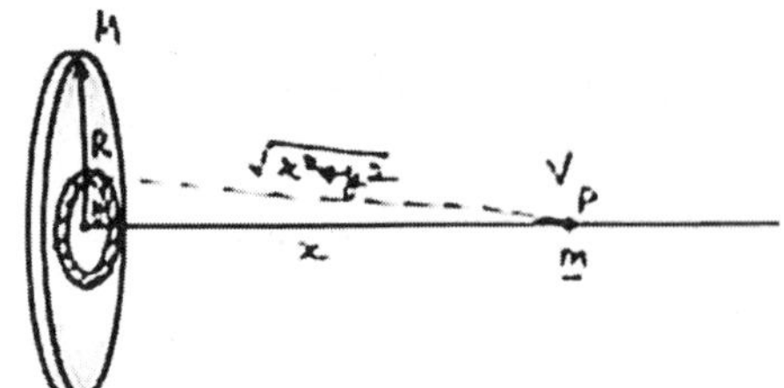

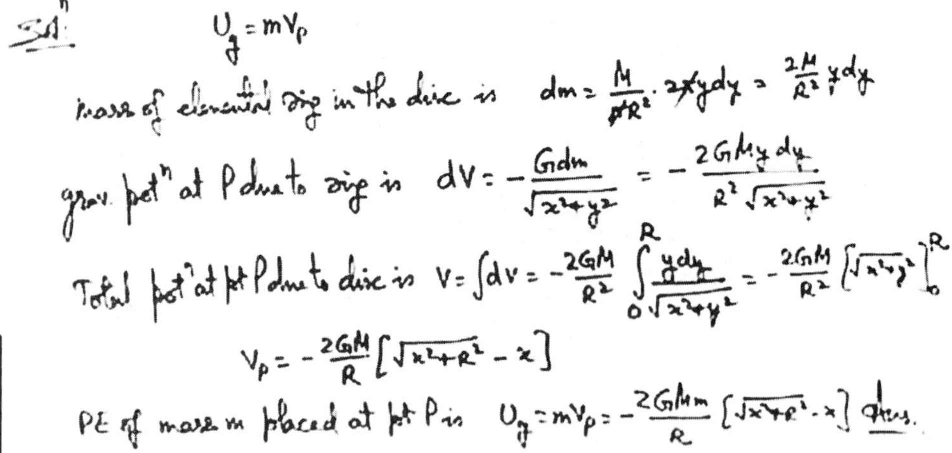

Scan for Video Explanation

Web Reference at www.physicsgalaxy.com

Module-44: Solved Example-16

Ex : Figure shows a fixed solid sphere of mass M and radius R with a narrow smooth tunnel along its diameter. Another particle of mass m is placed at point A at a distance 2R from its centre along the line of tunnel as shown. If the particle is released from rest find its speed when it reaches the centre of sphere.

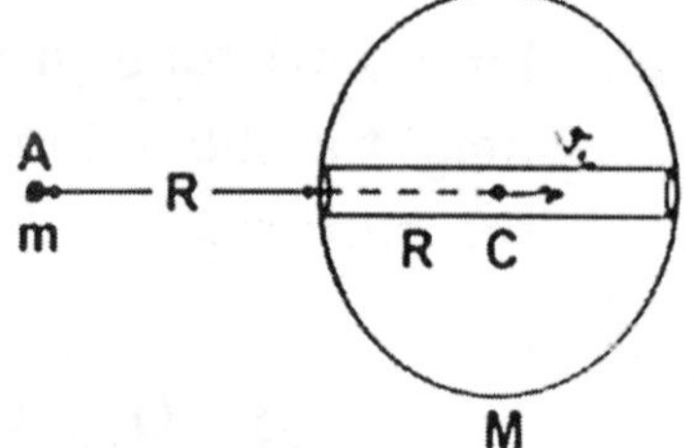

Soln. Potn at A is $V_A = -\frac{GM}{2R}$

Potn at C is $V_C = -\frac{3}{2}\frac{GM}{R}$

using Cons of energy for motion of m from A to C, we have

$$mV_A = mV_C + \frac{1}{2}mv_c^2$$

$$v_c = \sqrt{2(V_A - V_C)} = \sqrt{2\left(-\frac{GM}{R} + \frac{3}{2}\frac{GM}{R}\right)} = \sqrt{\frac{2GM}{R}} \text{ Ans.}$$

Scan for Video Explanation

Web Reference at www.physicsgalaxy.com

Module-45: Solved Example-17

Ex : **On the pole of earth, a body is imparted a velocity v_0 in vertically upward direction. If mass of earth is M_0 and radius R_0, find the maximum height to which body will ascend. Neglect air drag.**

Sol: by energy Cons.

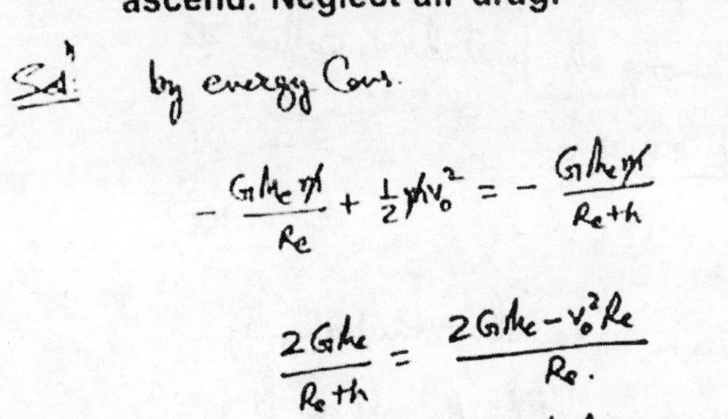

$$-\frac{GM_e m}{R_e} + \frac{1}{2}mv_0^2 = -\frac{GM_e m}{R_e + h}$$

$$\frac{2GM_e}{R_e + h} = \frac{2GM_e - v_0^2 R_e}{R_e}$$

$$R_e + h = \frac{2GM_e R_e}{2GM_e - v_0^2 R_e}$$

$$h = \left(\frac{v_0^2 R_e^2}{v_0^2 R_e - 2GM_e}\right) \text{ Ans.}$$

Web Reference at www.physicsgalaxy.com | Scan for Video Explanation

Module-46: Solved Example-18

Ex : **Find the speed with which a small body of mass m is projected from the centre of a ring of mass M and radius R along its axis so that it will never come back.**

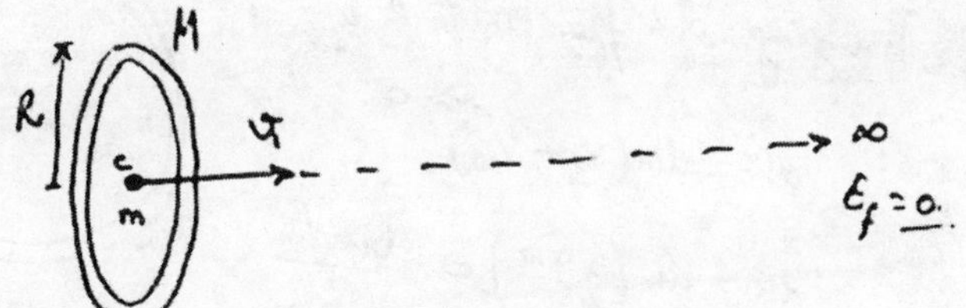

Initial energy of m. $E_i = \frac{1}{2}mv^2 + mV_c$

$$= \frac{1}{2}mv^2 - \frac{GMm}{R} \geq 0$$

$$v \geq \sqrt{\frac{2GM}{R}} \text{ Ans.}$$

Web Reference at www.physicsgalaxy.com | Scan for Video Explanation

Module-47: Gravitational Self Energy of a Body

Gravitational Self Energy of a body:

- PE of a body due to grav. interaction forces inside the body among its particles is called its grav. self energy.

- It is the W/D in assembling the body by bringing all its constituent particles from ∞ to the given shape & size against grav. force between these particles.

Scan for Video Explanation

Web Reference at www.physicsgalaxy.com

Module-48: Gravitational Self Energy of a Uniform Hollow Sphere

Gravitational Self Energy of a Hollow Sphere:

When mass of shell is m and W/D in bringing dm from ∞ to R is

$$dW = dm(V_S - V_\infty)$$

$$dW = dm\left(-\frac{Gm}{R}\right) = -\frac{Gm\,dm}{R}$$

$$W = \int dW = \int_0^M -\frac{Gm\,dm}{R}$$

$$W = -\frac{G}{R}\left[\frac{m^2}{2}\right]_0^M = -\frac{GM^2}{2R}$$

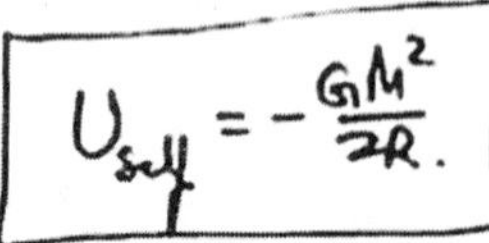

$$U_{self} = -\frac{GM^2}{2R}$$

Scan for Video Explanation

Web Reference at www.physicsgalaxy.com

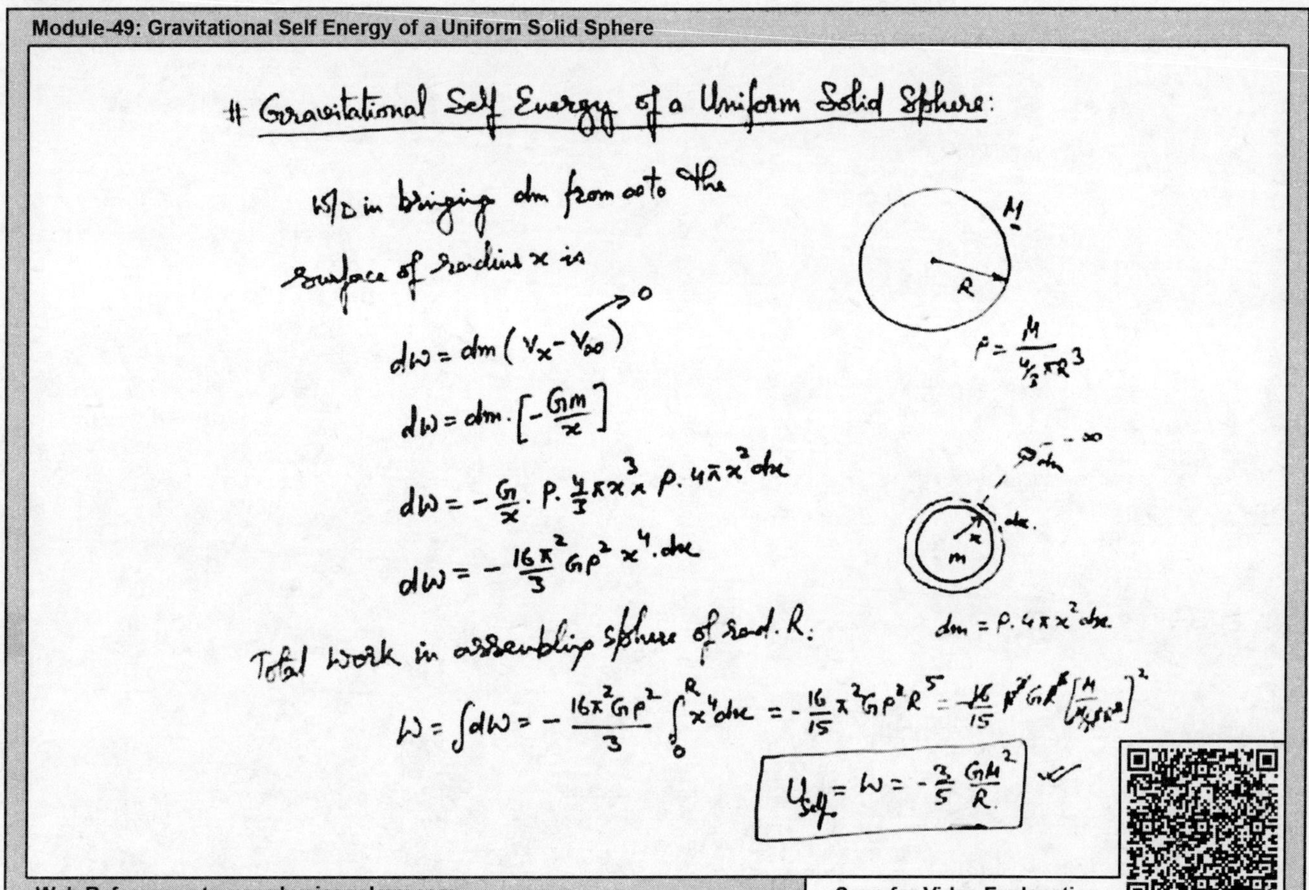
Module-49: Gravitational Self Energy of a Uniform Solid Sphere
Gravitational Self Energy of a Uniform Solid Sphere:
W/D in bringing dm from ∞ to the surface of radius x is
$dW = dm (V_x - V_\infty)$
$dW = dm \cdot \left[-\frac{Gm}{x}\right]$
$dW = -\frac{G}{x} \cdot \rho \cdot \frac{4}{3}\pi x^3 \times \rho \cdot 4\pi x^2 dx$
$dW = -\frac{16\pi^2}{3} G\rho^2 x^4 \cdot dx$
Total work in assembling sphere of rad. R:
$W = \int dW = -\frac{16\pi^2 G\rho^2}{3} \int_0^R x^4 dx = -\frac{16}{15}\pi^2 G\rho^2 R^5 = -\frac{16}{15}\pi^2 G R^5 \left[\frac{M}{\frac{4}{3}\pi R^3}\right]^2$
$U_{self} = W = -\frac{3}{5}\frac{GM^2}{R}$
M
R
$\rho = \frac{M}{\frac{4}{3}\pi R^3}$
dm
∞
dx
x
m
$dm = \rho \cdot 4\pi x^2 dx$
Web Reference at www.physicsgalaxy.com
Scan for Video Explanation

Chapter 18
Satellite Motion

Lecture Notes Modules

Module-1: Introduction to Satellite Motion

Satellite Motion:

for a circular orbit Satellite Motion.

$$\frac{GMm}{r^2} = \frac{mv^2}{r}$$

$$v = \sqrt{\frac{GM}{r}}$$

orbital speed in circular orbit of rad. r.

NOTE: Orbital speed of a satellite does not depend on mass of satellite

Scan for Video Explanation

Web Reference at www.physicsgalaxy.com

Module-1: Introduction to Satellite Motion

Orbital Period of a Satellite in circular orbit:

orbital speed $v = \sqrt{\frac{GM}{r}}$

time period of rev. of satellite

$$T = \frac{2\pi r}{v}$$

$$T = \frac{2\pi r}{\sqrt{GM/r}}$$

$$T = \frac{2\pi}{\sqrt{GM}} r^{3/2} \Rightarrow T \propto r^{3/2}$$

Scan for Video Explanation

Web Reference at www.physicsgalaxy.com

Module-2: Energy of a Satellite in Circular Orbit

Energy of a Satellite in circular orbit:

$$v = \sqrt{\frac{GM_p}{r}}$$

KE of Satellite is

$$K = \frac{1}{2}mv^2 = \frac{1}{2}\left(m\sqrt{\frac{GM_p}{r}}\right)^2$$

$$\boxed{K = \frac{1}{2}\frac{GM_p m}{r}}$$

PE of Satellite $\boxed{P = -\frac{GM_p m}{r}}$

Total energy $E = K + P = \frac{1}{2}\frac{GM_p m}{r} - \frac{GM_p m}{r} = \boxed{-\frac{1}{2}\frac{GM_p m}{r}}$

$$\boxed{|E| = |K| = \frac{1}{2}|P|}$$

Web Reference at www.physicsgalaxy.com | Scan for Video Explanation

Module-3: Solved Example-1

Ex : A satellite is to revolve in an orbit of radius 8000 km around earth. What should be its speed and orbital period. Take R_0 = 6400 km and g_s = 10 m/s^2.

Solⁿ: orbital speed of a Sat $v = \sqrt{\frac{GM_e}{r}} = \sqrt{\frac{g_s R_e^2}{r}}$

$$g_s = \frac{GM_e}{R_e^2} \qquad v = \sqrt{\frac{10 \times (6.4 \times 10^6)^2}{8 \times 10^6}}$$

$$v = 7.1 \times 10^3 \text{ m/s} = 7.1 \text{ km/s}$$

Period of Sat. $T = \frac{2\pi}{\sqrt{GM_e}} \cdot (r)^{3/2}$

$$T = \frac{2\pi}{\sqrt{g_s R_e^2}} \cdot r^{3/2} = \frac{2 \times 3.14}{\sqrt{10 \times (6.4 \times 10^6)^2}} \times (8 \times 10^6)^{3/2}$$

$$= 7021 \text{ sec} \simeq 117 \text{ min} \quad \text{Ans.}$$

Web Reference at www.physicsgalaxy.com | Scan for Video Explanation

Module-4: Solved Example-2

Ex : Two satellites A and B of same mass are orbiting earth at attitudes R and 3R respectively, where R is the radius of earth. Taking their orbits to be circular, calculate ratio of their kinetic energies.

Sol:

KE of a Sat $\underline{K} = \frac{GM_e m_s}{2r}$ $r \to$ rad of orbit

for Sat A & B.

$$\frac{K_A}{K_B} = \frac{R_B}{R_A} = \frac{4R}{2R} = \frac{2}{1} \text{ Ans.}$$

Scan for Video Explanation

Web Reference at www.physicsgalaxy.com

Module-5: Solved Example-3

Ex : A satellite of mass 2×10^3 kg is to be shifted from an orbit of radius $2R_e$ to another orbit of radius $3R_e$ under ideal conditions. Calculate the minimum energy required for this. R_e is radius of earth.

Sol: Initial energy of Sat $E_i = -\frac{GM_e m}{2(2R_e)} = -\frac{GM_e m}{4R_e}$

Final energy of Sat $E_f = -\frac{GM_e m}{2(3R_e)} = -\frac{GM_e m}{6R_e}$

energy reqd to change orbit of Sat -

$$\Delta E = E_f - E_i = \frac{GM_e m}{R_e}\left[\frac{1}{4} - \frac{1}{6}\right] = \frac{GM_e m}{12R_e}$$

$$= \frac{1}{12} m g_s R_e$$

$$g_s = \frac{GM_e}{R_e^2}$$

$$= \frac{1}{12} \times 2\times10^3 \times 10 \times (6.4\times10^6)$$

$$= 1.066 \times 10^{10} \text{ J Ans.}$$

Scan for Video Explanation

Web Reference at www.physicsgalaxy.com

Module-6: Bounded Motion and Escape Velocity

Bounded Motion and Escape Velocity:

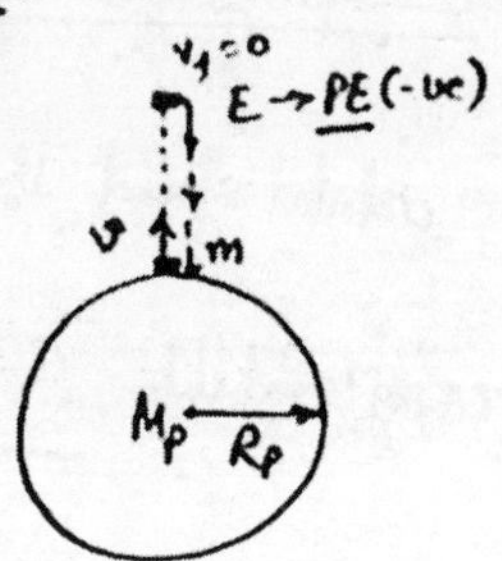

PE of body on surface of planet

$$U = -\frac{GM_pm}{R_p}$$

–ve sign ⇒ Boundness.

if some KE is imparted to body. Then

$$E = \left(\frac{1}{2}mv^2 - \frac{GM_pm}{R_p}\right) < 0$$

If a body is projected such that on surface of planet its TE = 0 ⇒ finally the body will be able to overcome the grav forces of planet & it will escape.

Module-6: Bounded Motion and Escape Velocity

if body is projected at speed v such that

$$\frac{1}{2}mv^2 - \frac{GM_pm}{R_p} = 0$$

$$v = \sqrt{\frac{2GM_p}{R_p}} \leftarrow \text{escape velocity on surface of planet.}$$

for earth (M_e & R_e)

escape vel. $v_e = \sqrt{\frac{2GM_e}{R_e}}$ $\qquad g_s = \frac{GM_e}{R_e^2} = 9.8\,m/s^2$

$$v_s = \sqrt{2g_sR_e} = 11.2\ km/s.$$

NOTE: As planet is taken at rest in this calculation, the escape vel. does not depend on dir of projection.

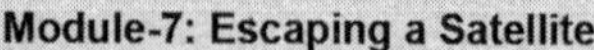

Module-7: Escaping a Satellite

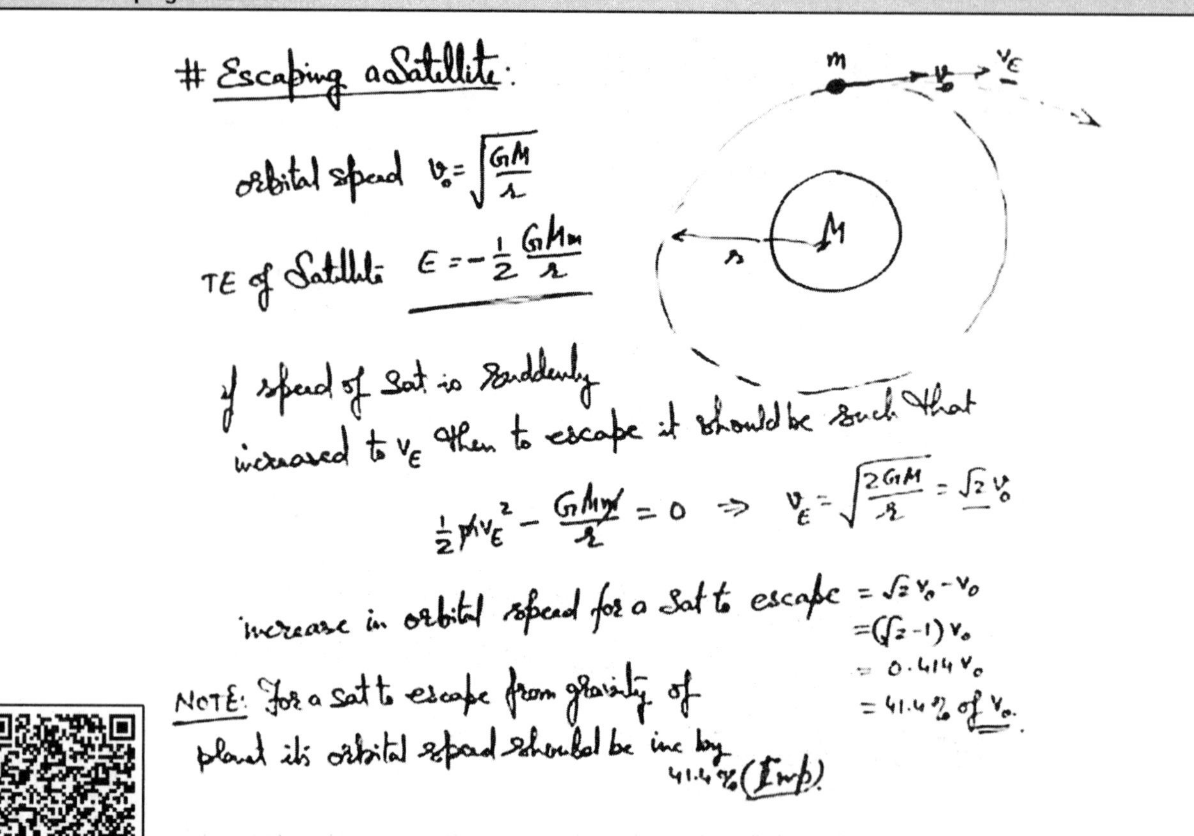

Module-8: Solved Example-4

Ex : **An artificial satellite is moving in a circular orbit around earth with a speed equal to half the escape velocity from earth surface. Find the height of satellite above the earth surface.**

Sol: orbital speed $v = \frac{1}{2}\sqrt{2g_sR_e} = \sqrt{\frac{g_sR_e}{2}}$

if Sat is at a height above earth surface.

$$v_0 = \sqrt{\frac{GM_e}{(R_e+h)}} = \sqrt{\frac{g_sR_e}{2}}$$

$$\sqrt{\frac{GM_e}{(R_e+h)}} = \sqrt{\frac{GM_e}{2R_e}}$$

$$R_e + h = 2R_e$$

$$h = R_e \text{ Ans.}$$

Scan for Video Explanation

Web Reference at www.physicsgalaxy.com

Module-9: Solved Example-5

Ex : A mass of 6×10^{24} kg is to be compressed in a sphere in such a way that the escape velocity from its surface will be 3×10^8 m/s. What should be the radius of such a sphere ?

Sol:
escape vel $v_{esc} = \sqrt{\frac{2GM}{R}}$

$$R = \frac{2GM}{v_{esc}^2}$$

$$R = \frac{2 \times 6.67 \times 10^{-11} \times 6 \times 10^{24}}{(3 \times 10^8)^2}$$

$$= 8.89 \times 10^{-3} \text{ m}$$

$$= 8.89 \text{ mm} \quad \text{Ans.}$$

Web Reference at www.physicsgalaxy.com | Scan for Video Explanation

Module-10: Motion of a Satellite in Elliptical Path

Motion of a Satellite in elliptical path:

orbital speed $v_0 = \sqrt{\frac{GM_e}{x}}$

escape vel $v_e = \sqrt{\frac{2GM_e}{x}}$

If $v_s > \sqrt{\frac{GM_e}{x}}$ but $v_s < \sqrt{\frac{2GM_e}{x}}$

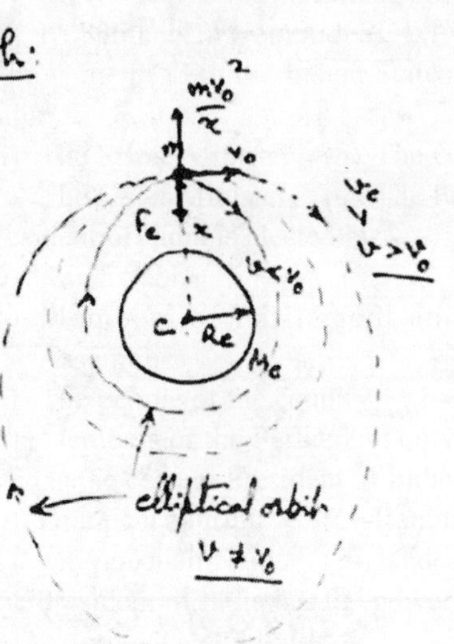

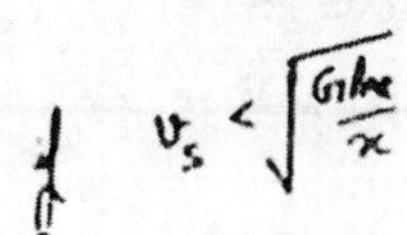

If $v_s < \sqrt{\frac{GM_e}{x}}$

Web Reference at www.physicsgalaxy.com | Scan for Video Explanation

Module-10: Motion of a Satellite in Elliptical Path

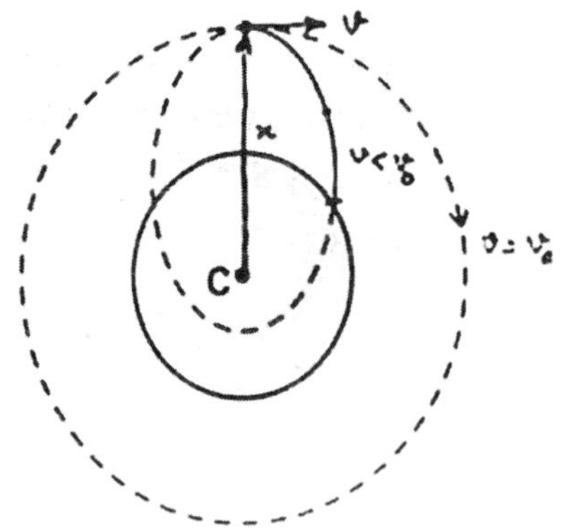

If $v < \sqrt{\frac{GM_e}{x}}$ and having such a value that elliptical trajectory will intersect the earth surface.

In this situation path of body/sat will be an arc of ellipse as shown.

Scan for Video Explanation

Web Reference at www.physicsgalaxy.com

Module-11: Conservation of Angular Momentum in Satellite Motion

Conservation of Angular momentum in Satellite Motion:

In motion of a Sat around a planet, only force on it is gravity directed toward the centre of planet.

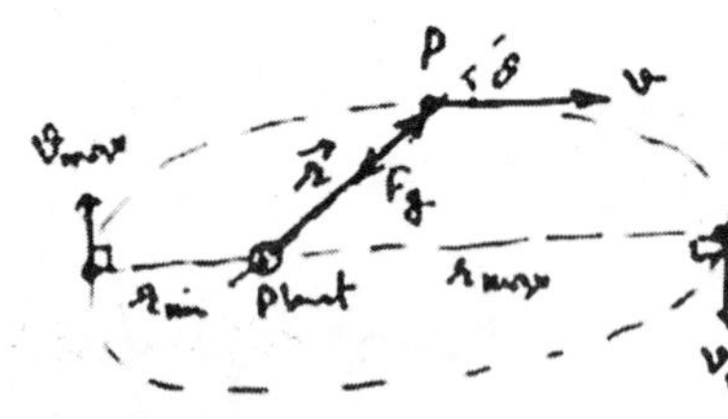

As F_g is passing through centre of planet hence no torque act on Sat w.r.to planet.

⇒ Ang. momentum of Sat w.r.to planet will remain Conserved during its motion

$$L = mvr\sin\theta = \text{Const}$$

$$\left[L = mv_{max}r_{min} = mv_{min}r_{max} = mvr\sin\theta \right]$$

by energy Cons we can write

$$\left[\frac{1}{2}mv_{max}^2 - \frac{GMm}{r_{min}} = \frac{1}{2}mv_{min}^2 - \frac{GMm}{r_{max}} = \frac{1}{2}mv^2 - \frac{GMm}{r} \right]$$

Scan for Video Explanation

Web Reference at www.physicsgalaxy.com

Module-12: Kepler's Laws of Planetary Motion-First Law

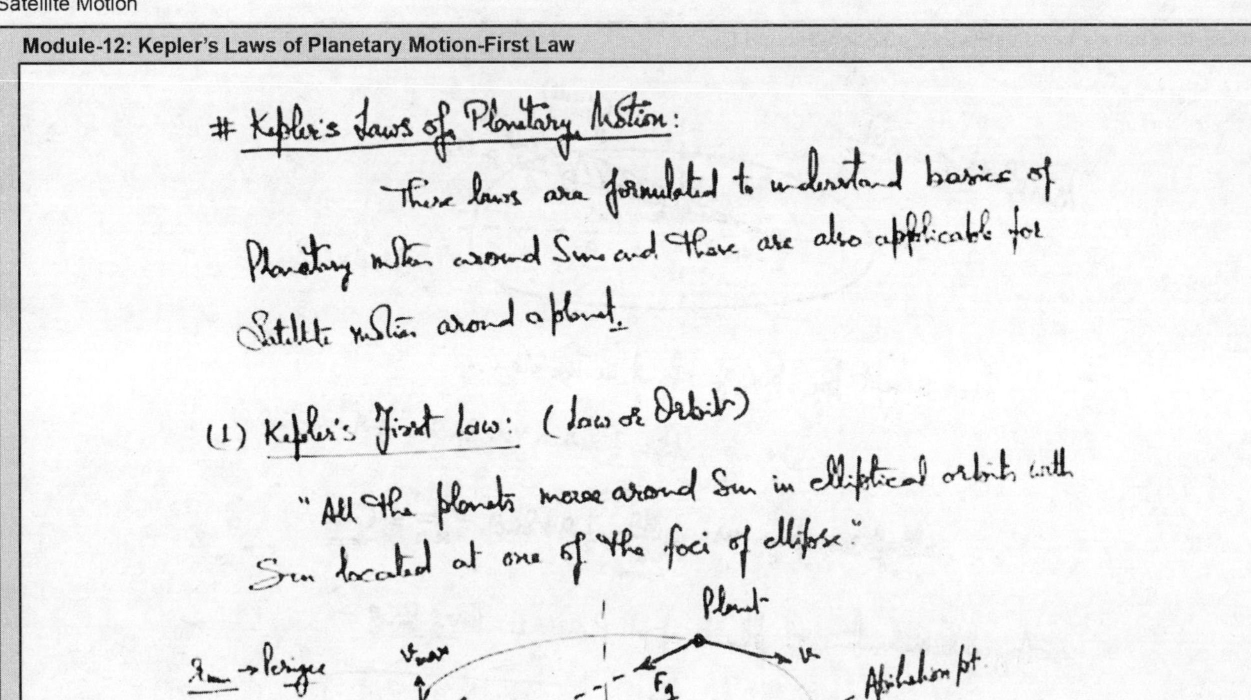

Web Reference at www.physicsgalaxy.com | Scan for Video Explanation

Module-13: Kepler's Laws of Planetary Motion-Second Law

② Kepler's Second Law: (law of Area)

"The line joining the Sun and planet sweeps out equal areas in equal time intervals or the rate of sweeping area by the position vector of planet w.r.to Sun remains Constant."

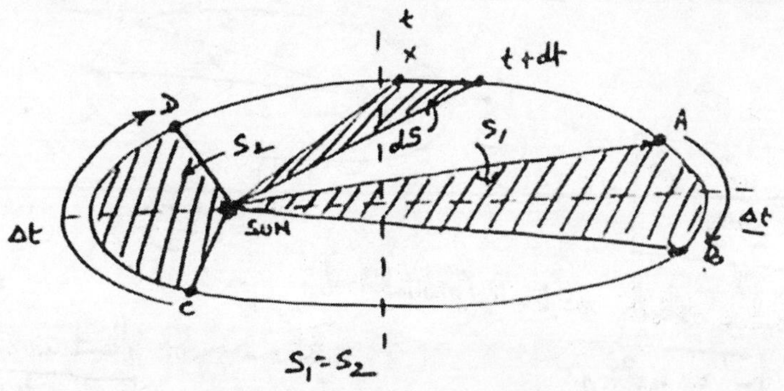

rate of sweeping area by p.v. of planet is $\frac{ds}{dt}$ = Constant.

Web Reference at www.physicsgalaxy.com | Scan for Video Explanation

Module-13: Kepler's Laws of Planetary Motion-Second Law

Area of orbit = πab.

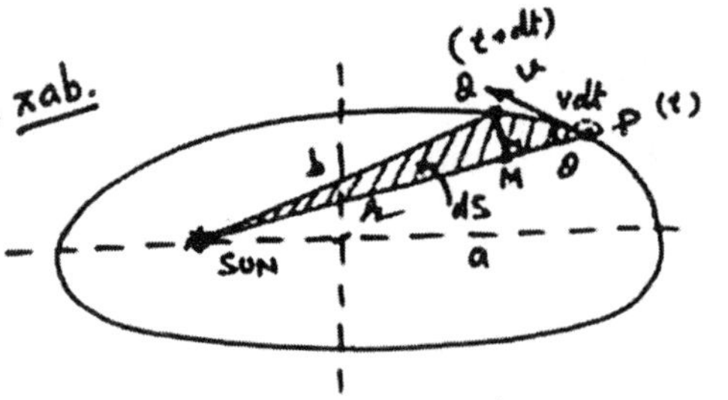

(t+dt) Q v vdt P (t) b r M θ ds SUN a

$QM = v\,dt \sin\theta$

Area swept by p.v of planet in the dt

$$dS = \frac{1}{2} \times r \times v\,dt \sin\theta = \frac{1}{2} r v\,dt \sin\theta$$

rate of sweeping area $\frac{dS}{dt} = \frac{1}{2} r v \sin\theta = \frac{L}{2m} = $ Const.

Angular momentum of planet at pt. P is $L = mvr\sin\theta$

if T is the orbital period of planet $\Rightarrow \boxed{\frac{dS}{dt} = \frac{\pi ab}{T} = \frac{L}{2m}}$

$$L = \frac{2\pi abm}{T} \text{ (Const)}$$

Scan for Video Explanation

Web Reference at www.physicsgalaxy.com

Module-14: Kepler's Laws of Planetary Motion-Third Law

③ Kepler's Third Law: (Law of Period)

"The square of period of rev. of a planet in its orbit is dir proportional to the cube of semi-major axis of the elliptical orbit around sun."

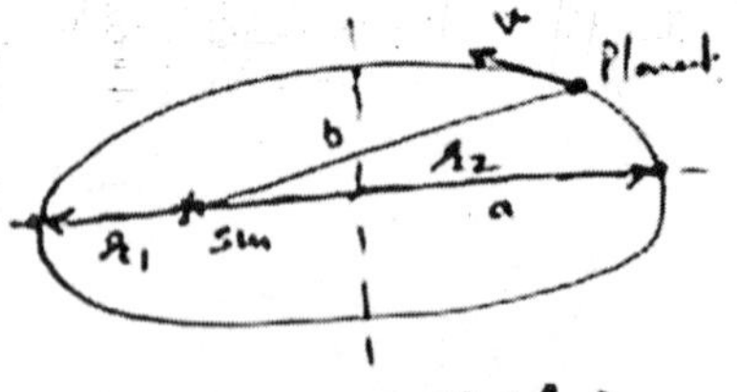

v Planet b r_2 a r_1 Sun

$T^2 \propto a^3$

$$\boxed{T^2 = \frac{4\pi^2}{GM_s} \cdot a^3}$$

$$a = \left(\frac{r_1 + r_2}{2}\right)$$

for circular orbits $a = b = R$ (orbital rad)

$$\boxed{T^2 = \frac{4\pi^2}{GM_s} \cdot R^3}$$

Total energy of planet in elliptical orbit $\boxed{E = -\frac{GM_s m}{2a}}$

Scan for Video Explanation

Web Reference at www.physicsgalaxy.com

Module-15: Projection of Spaceships and Satellites from Earth

Projection of Spaceships and Satellites from Earth:

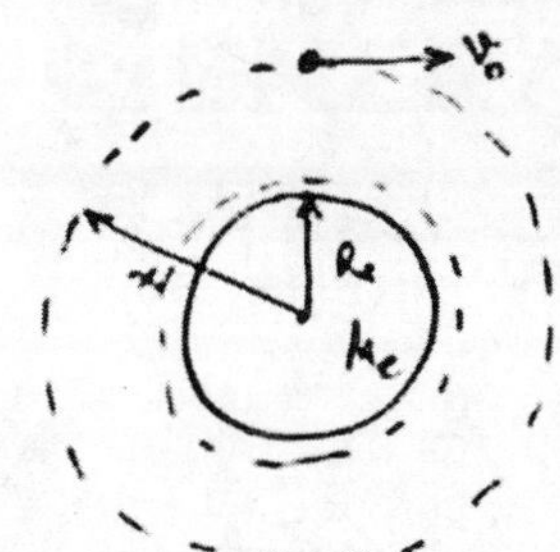

$$v_0 = \sqrt{\frac{GM_e}{x}}$$

if $x \simeq R_e$ [very close to Earth Surface]

$$v_0 = \sqrt{\frac{GM_e}{R_e}} = \sqrt{g_s R_e} \simeq 7.93 \text{ km/sec}$$

first cosmic velocity

The vel reqd to escape from grav attraction of Earth is

$$v_{escape} = \sqrt{2 g_s R_e} \simeq 11.2 \text{ km/s}$$

$$= \sqrt{2}\, v_0$$

Web Reference at www.physicsgalaxy.com

Scan for Video Explanation

Module-15: Projection of Spaceships and Satellites from Earth

Trajectories of Projected bodies:

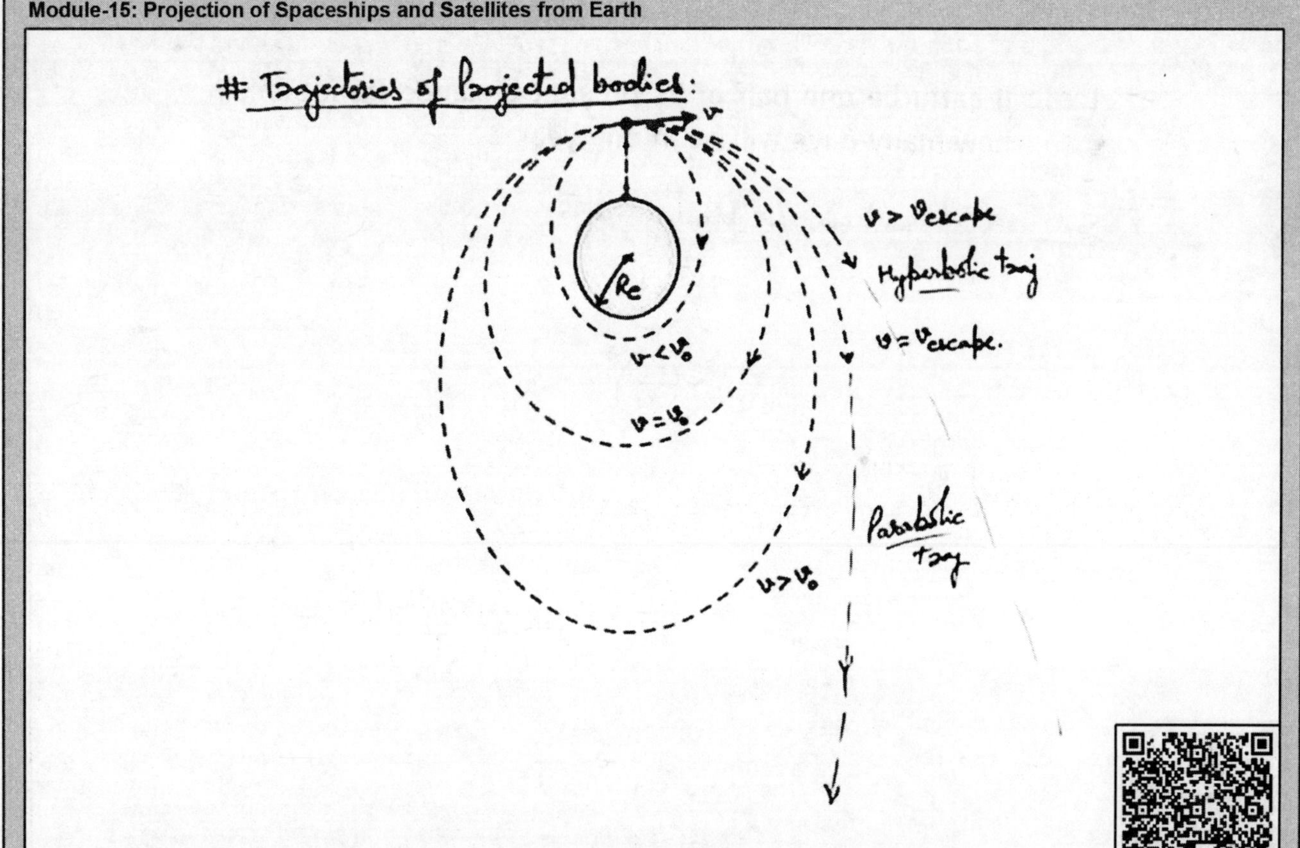

Web Reference at www.physicsgalaxy.com

Scan for Video Explanation

Module-16: Solved Example-6

Ex : The radius of a planet is R_1 and a satellite revolves around it in circular orbit of radius R_2. The period of revolution is T. Find the acceleration due to gravity on the surface of planet.

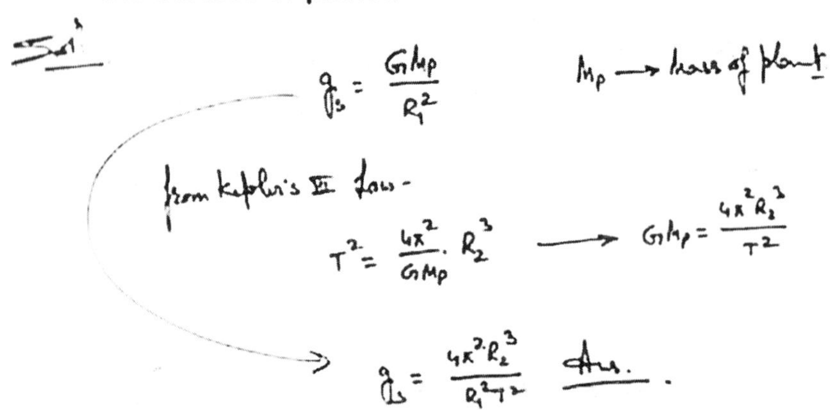

Scan for Video Explanation

Web Reference at www.physicsgalaxy.com

Module-17: Solved Example-7

Ex : If earth be one half of its present distance from sum, how many days will be in one year ?

Sol. As we know for planetary motion

$$T^2 \propto R^3$$

$$\left(\frac{T_1}{T_2}\right)^2 = \left(\frac{R_1}{R_2}\right)^3$$

if $R_2 = R_1/2$

$$T_2 = T_1 \times \left(\frac{R_2}{R_1}\right)^{3/2}$$

$$\Rightarrow \frac{T_1}{2^{3/2}} = \frac{365}{2^{3/2}} = 129 \text{ days} \quad \text{Ans.}$$

Scan for Video Explanation

Web Reference at www.physicsgalaxy.com

Module-18: Solved Example-8

Ex : **A satellite revolves around a planet in an elliptical orbit. Its perigee and apogee are 0.5×10^7 m and 1.5×10^7 m respectively. If the minimum speed of satellite in orbit is 5×10^3 m/s find its maximum speed in orbit.**

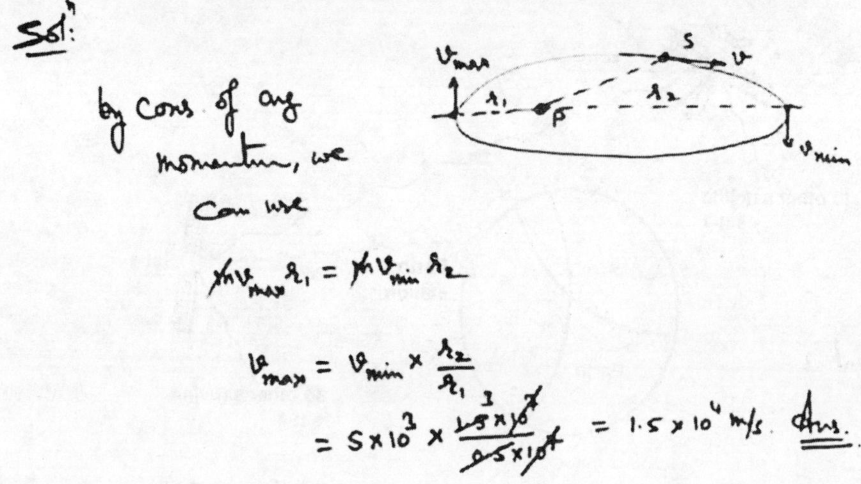

Web Reference at www.physicsgalaxy.com | Scan for Video Explanation

Module-19: Solved Example-9

Ex : **A satellite is revolving around a planet of mass M in an elliptical orbit of semimajor axis a. Show that the orbital speed of the satellite when it is at a distance r from the focus will be given by**

$$v = \sqrt{GM\left[\frac{2}{r} - \frac{1}{a}\right]}$$

Sol:
Total energy of Sat in elliptical motion is

$$E = -\frac{GMm}{2a} = \text{Constant}$$

at a distance r from planet, the energy of Sat -

$$-\frac{GMm}{2a} = -\frac{GMm}{r} + \frac{1}{2}mv^2$$

$$v^2 = GM\left[\frac{2}{r} - \frac{1}{a}\right] \Rightarrow v = \sqrt{GM\left(\frac{2}{r} - \frac{1}{a}\right)}$$

hence proved.

Web Reference at www.physicsgalaxy.com | Scan for Video Explanation

Module-20: Communication Satellites

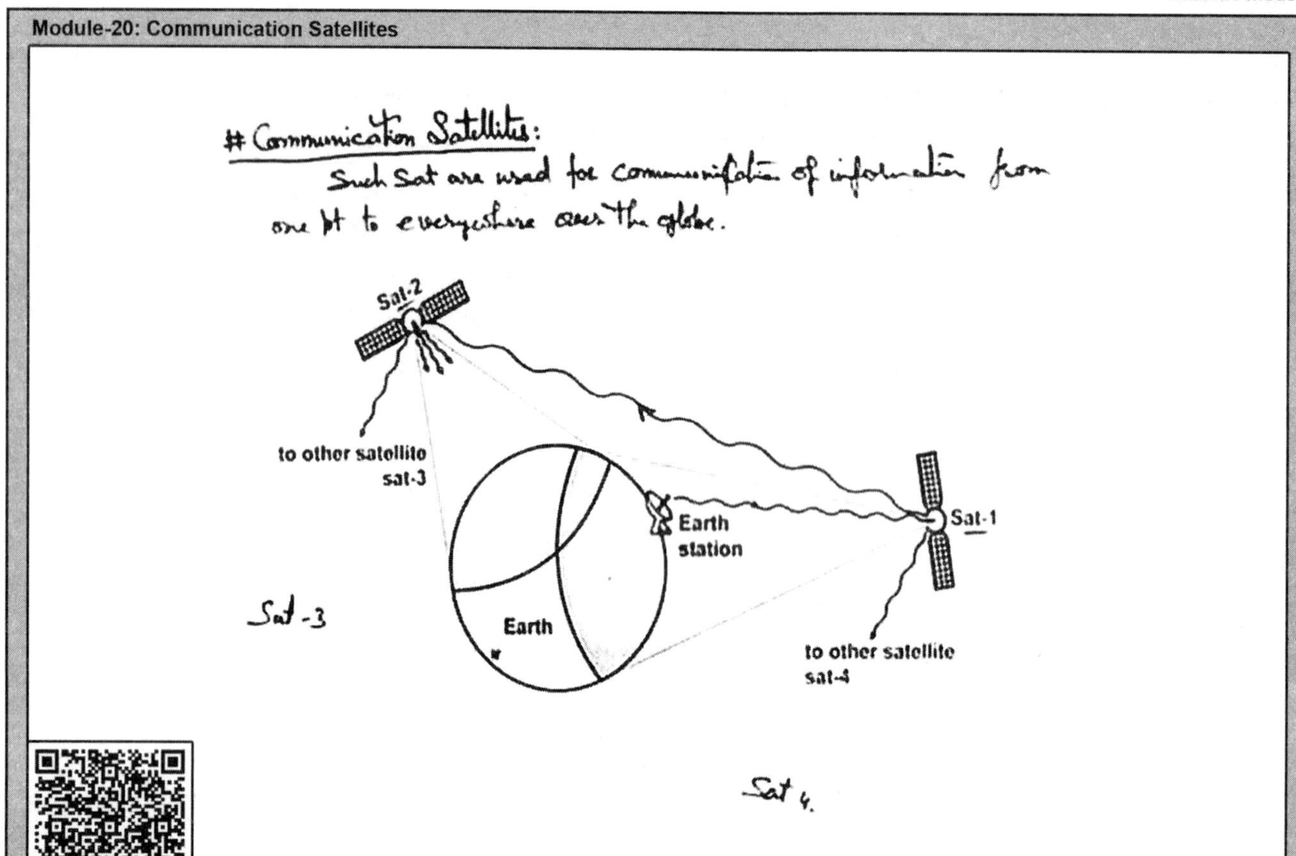

Module-21: Geostationary Satellite

Geostationary Satellite:

Sat which appear stationary as seen from Earth Surface is called a Geostationary Satellite

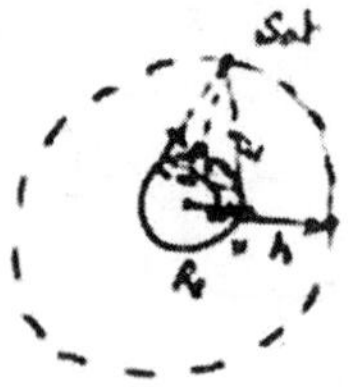

Sat

orbital speed

$$v = \sqrt{\frac{GM_e}{R_e+h}}$$

R_e h

for a G.S. Sat $T = 24$ hrs.

Sat. period. $T = \frac{2\pi}{\sqrt{GM_e}} \cdot (R_e+h)^{3/2}$

$\left(\frac{GM_e}{R_e^2} = g_s\right)$ $T^2 = \frac{4\pi^2}{GM_e}(R_e+h)^3$

$$h = \left(\frac{g_s R_e^2 T^2}{4\pi^2}\right)^{1/3} - R_e$$

$$h \simeq 35950 \simeq 36\times10^3 \text{ km}.$$

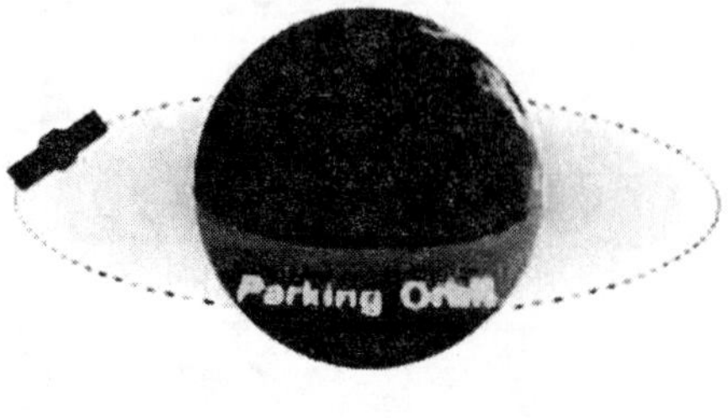

Parking Orbit

Scan for Video Explanation

Web Reference at www.physicsgalaxy.com

Module-21: Geostationary Satellite

NOTE: Parking orbit must be in equatorial plane of Earth.

$\omega_e = \frac{2\pi}{86400}$ rad/sec

G.S. Sat

Parking orbit.

T = 24 hrs.

Web Reference at www.physicsgalaxy.com

Scan for Video Explanation

Module-22: Broadcasting Region of a Satellite

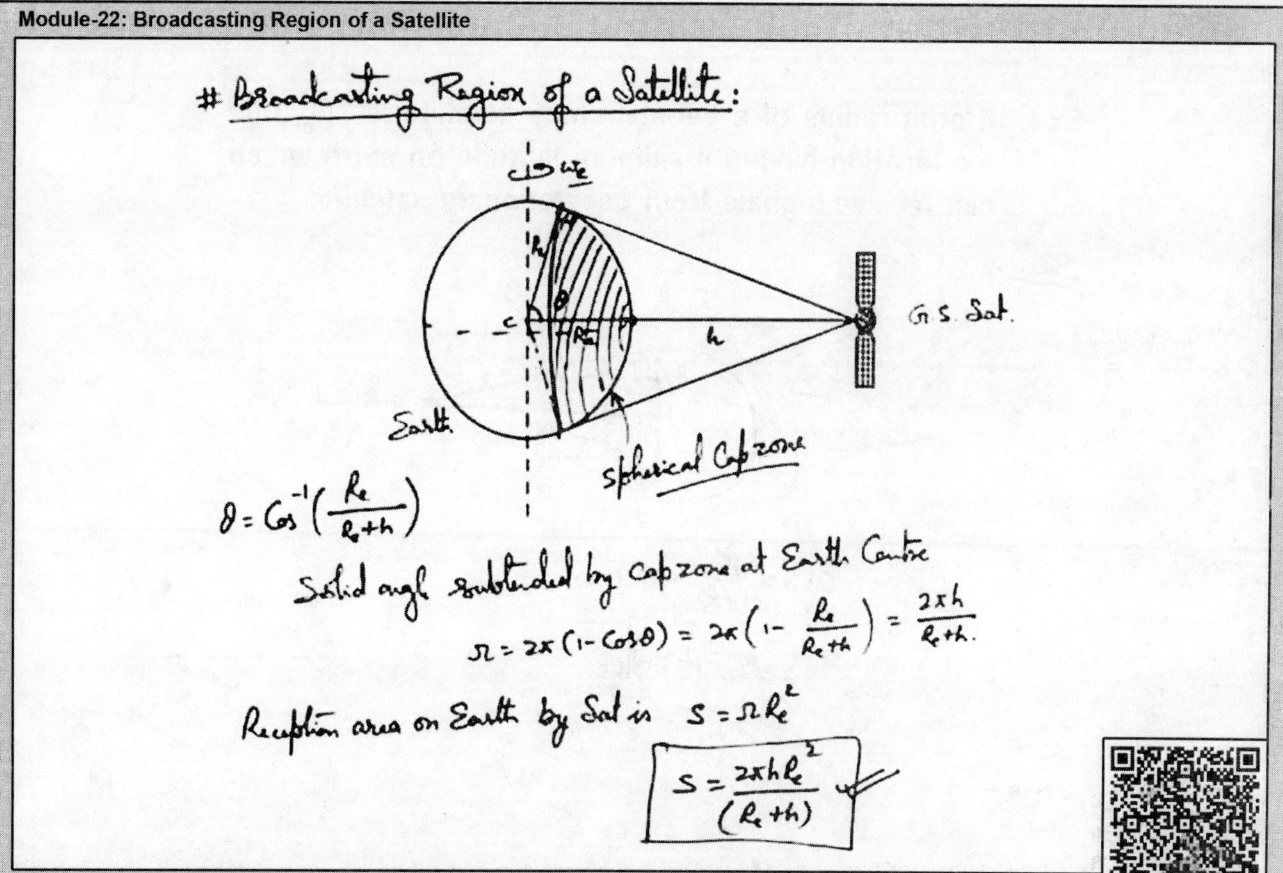

Web Reference at www.physicsgalaxy.com

Scan for Video Explanation

Module-23: Solved Example-10

Ex : If a satellite is revolving around the earth in a circular orbit in a plane containing earth's axis of rotation. If the angular speed of satellite is equal to that of earth, find the time it takes to move from a point above north pole to a point above equator.

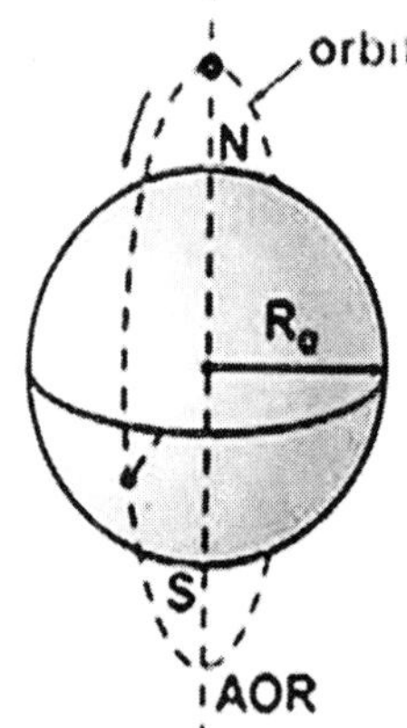

Ang speed of Sat is

$$\omega = \frac{2\pi}{T} = \frac{2\pi}{24} = \frac{\pi}{12} \text{ rad/hr}$$

time taken

$$t = \frac{\theta}{\omega} = \frac{\pi/2}{\pi/12} = 6 \text{ hrs Ans.}$$

Scan for Video Explanation

Web Reference at www.physicsgalaxy.com

Module-24: Solved Example-11

Ex : If orbit radius of a geostationary satellite is $7R_0$, find the location having maximum latitude on earth which can receive signals from geostationary satellite.

Earth

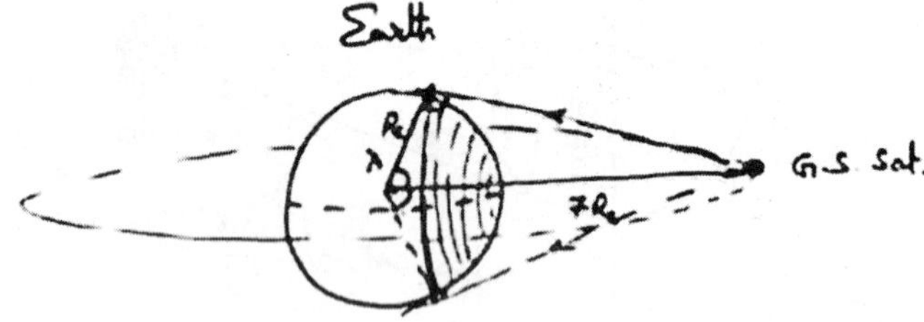

$$\cos\lambda = \frac{R_e}{7R_e}$$

$$\lambda = \cos^{-1}\left(\frac{1}{7}\right) \text{ Ans.}$$

Scan for Video Explanation

Web Reference at www.physicsgalaxy.com

Module-25: Solved Example-12

Ex : A satellite is revolving around the earth in an orbit of radius double that of the parking orbit. Find the time duration between two instants when this satellite is closest to a geostationary satellite.

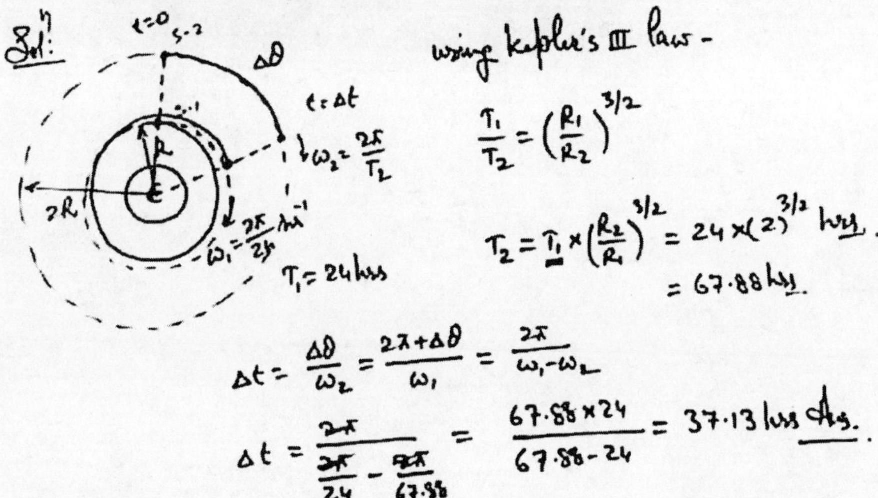

Scan for Video Explanation